# Articles

# PRICE THEORY

## and Applications

### EIGHTH EDITION

## Steven E. Landsburg

**University of Rochester**

SOUTH-WESTERN
CENGAGE Learning™

Australia • Brazil • Japan • Korea • Mexico • Singapore • Spain • United Kingdom • United States

**Price Theory and Applications**
**Eighth Edition**
Steven E. Landsburg

Vice President of Editorial, Business:
Jack W. Calhoun

Publisher: Joe Sabatino

Acquisitions Editor: Steven Scoble

Developmental Editor:
Michael Guendelsberger

Editorial Assistant: Allyn Bissmeyer

Marketing Manager: Betty Jung

Marketing Coordinator: Suellen Ruttkay

Associate Content Project Manager:
Jana Lewis

Media Editor: Deepak Kumar

Frontlist Buyer, Manufacturing:
Sandee Milewski

Senior Marketing Communications
Manager: Sarah Greber

Production Service: Integra Software
Services Pvt. Ltd

Senior Art Director: Michelle Kunkler

Internal Designer: c miller design

Cover Designer: c miller design

Cover Image: © Charles Wysocki, Inc.
Licensed by Mosaic Licensing.

Rights Acquisitions Specialist:
Timothy Sisler

Exam*View*® is a registered trademark of eInstruction Corp. Windows is a registered trademark of the Microsoft Corporation used herein under license. Macintosh and Power Macintosh are registered trademarks of Apple Computer, Inc. used herein under license. © 2008 Cengage Learning. All Rights Reserved. Cengage Learning WebTutor™ is a trademark of Cengage Learning.

Library of Congress Control Number: 2010930410

ISBN-13: 978-0-538-74645-8

ISBN-10: 0-538-74645-9

TEXT ISBN-13: 978-0-538-74518-5

TEXT ISBN-10: 0-538-74518-5

**South-Western Cengage Learning**
5191 Natorp Boulevard
Mason, OH 45040
USA

Cengage Learning products are represented in Canada by Nelson Education, Ltd.

For your course and learning solutions, visit **www.cengage.com**

Purchase any of our products at your local college store or at our preferred online store **www.CengageBrain.com**

Printed in United States of America
1 2 3 4 5 6 7 14 13 12 11 10

**Steven E. Landsburg** is a Professor of Economics at the University of Rochester. His articles have appeared in the *Journal of Political Economy*, the *Journal of Economic Theory,* and many other journals of economics, mathematics, and philosophy. He is the author of six books, including *More Sex Is Safer Sex: The Unconventional Wisdom of Economics* (Free Press/Simon and Schuster 2006) and *The Big Questions: Tackling the Problems of Philosophy with Ideas from Mathematics, Economics and Physics* (Free Press/Simon and Schuster 2009). He writes regularly for *Slate* magazine and has written for *Forbes*, the *New York Times*, the *Washington Post*, and dozens of other publications. He blogs regularly at www.ThebigQuestions.com/blog.

*Dedication:*

To the Red-Headed Snippet

# Brief Contents

# Contents

# Preface

## To the Student

Price theory is a challenging and rewarding subject. The student who masters price theory acquires a powerful tool for understanding a remarkable range of social phenomena. How does a sales tax affect the price of coffee? Why do people trade? What happens to ticket prices when a baseball player gets a raise? How does free agency affect the allocation of baseball players to teams? Why might the revenue of orange growers increase when there is an unexpected frost—and what may we infer about the existence of monopoly power if it does?

Price theory teaches you how to solve similar puzzles. Better yet, it poses new ones. You will learn to be intrigued by phenomena you might previously have considered unremarkable. When rock concerts predictably sell out in advance, why don't the promoters raise prices? Why are bank buildings fancier than supermarkets? Why do ski resorts sell lift tickets on a per-day basis rather than a per-ride basis?

Throughout this book, such questions are used to motivate a careful and rigorous development of microeconomic theory. New concepts are immediately illustrated with entertaining and informative examples, both verbal and numerical. Ideas and techniques are allowed to arise naturally in the discussion, and they are given names (like "marginal value") only after you have discovered their usefulness. You are encouraged to develop a strong economic intuition and then to test your intuition by submitting it to rigorous graphical and verbal analysis.

I think that you will find this book inviting. There are neither mathematical demands nor prerequisites and no lists of axioms to memorize. At the same time, the level of economic rigor and sophistication is quite high. In many cases, I have carried analysis beyond what is found in most other books at this level. There are digressions, examples, and especially problems that will challenge even the most ambitious and talented students.

## Using This Book

This is a book about how the world works. When you finish the first chapter, you will know how to analyze the effects of sales and excise taxes, and you will have discovered the surprising result that a tax on buyers and a tax on sellers have exactly the same effects. When you finish the second chapter, you will understand why oranges, on average, taste better in New York than in Florida. In each succeeding chapter, you will be exposed to new ideas in economics and to their surprising consequences for the world around you.

To learn what price theory is, dig in and begin reading. The next few paragraphs give you a hint of what it's all about.

*Price theory*, or *microeconomics*, is the study of the ways in which individuals and firms make choices, and the ways in which these choices interact with each other. We assume that individuals have certain well-defined preferences and limits to their behavior. For example, you might enjoy eating both cake and ice cream, but the size of your stomach limits your ability to pursue these pleasures; moreover, the amount of cake that you eat affects the amount of ice cream you can eat, and vice versa.

In predicting behavior, we assume that individuals behave *rationally*, which is to say that they make themselves as well-off as possible, as measured by their own preferences, and within the limitations imposed on them. While this assumption (like any assumption in any science) is only an approximation to reality, it is an extraordinarily powerful one, and it leads to many profound and surprising conclusions.

Price theory is made richer by the fact that each individual's choices can affect the opportunities available to others. If you decide to eat all of the cake, your roommate cannot decide to eat some too. An *equilibrium* is an outcome in which each person's behavior is compatible with the restrictions imposed by everybody else's behavior. In many situations, it is possible to say both that there is only one possible equilibrium and that there are good reasons to expect that equilibrium to actually come about. This enables the economist to make predictions about the world.

Thus, price theory is most often concerned with two sorts of questions: those that are **positive** and those that are **normative**. A positive question is a question about what *is* or *will be*, whereas a normative question is a question about what *ought to be*. Positive questions have definite, correct answers (which may or may not be known), whereas the answers to normative questions depend on values.

For example, suppose that a law is proposed that would prohibit any bank from foreclosing on any farmer's mortgage. Some positive questions are: How will this law affect the incomes of bankers? How will it affect the incomes of farmers? What effect will it have on the number of people who decide to become farmers and on the number of people who decide to start banks? Will it indirectly affect the average size of farms or of banks? Will it indirectly affect the price of land? How will it affect the price of food and the well-being of people who are neither farmers nor bankers? and so forth. A normative question is: Is this law, on balance, a good thing?

Economics can, at least in principle, provide answers to the positive questions. Economics by itself can never answer a normative question; in this case your answer to the normative question must depend on how you feel about the relative merits of helping farmers and helping bankers.

Therefore, we will be concerned in this book primarily with positive questions. However, price theory is relevant in the consideration of normative questions as well. This is so in two ways. First, even if you are quite sure of your own values, it is often impossible to decide whether you consider some course of action desirable unless you know its consequences. Your decision about whether to support the antiforeclosure law will depend not only on your feelings about farmers and bankers, but also on what effects you believe the law will have. Thus, it can be important to study positive questions even when the questions of ultimate interest are normative ones.

For another example, suppose that you have decided to start recycling newspapers to help preserve large forests. One of your friends tells you that in fact recycling leads to *smaller* forests because it lowers the demand for trees and induces paper companies to do less planting. Whether or not your friend is correct is a positive question. You might want the answer to that positive question before returning to the normative question: Should I continue to recycle?

The second way in which price theory can assist us in thinking about normative questions is by showing us the consequences of consistently applying a given normative criterion. For example, if your criterion is "I am always for anything that will benefit farmers, provided that it does not drive any bankers out of business," the price theorist might be able to respond, "In that case, you must support such-and-such law, because I can use economic reasoning to show that such-and-such law will indeed benefit farmers without driving any bankers out of business." If such-and-such law does not sound like a good idea to you, you might want to rethink your normative criterion.

In the first seven chapters of this book, you will receive a thorough grounding in the positive aspects of price theory. You will learn how consumers make decisions, how firms make decisions, and how these decisions interact in the competitive marketplace. In Chapter 8, you will examine the desirability of these outcomes from the viewpoints of various normative criteria. Chapter 9 rounds out the discussion of the competitive price system by examining the role of prices as conveyors of information. In Chapters 10 through 14, you will learn about various situations in which the competitive model does not fully apply. These include conditions of monopoly and oligopoly, and circumstances in which the activities of one person or firm affect others involuntarily (e.g., factories create pollution that their neighbors must breathe).

The first 14 chapters complete the discussion of the market for goods, which are supplied by firms and purchased by individuals. In Chapters 15 through 17 you will learn about the other side of the economy: the market for inputs to the production process (such as labor) that are supplied by individuals and purchased by firms. In Chapter 17, you will study the market for the productive input called *capital* and examine the way that individuals allocate goods across time, consuming less on one day so that they can consume more on another.

Chapter 18 concerns a special topic: the role of risk.

Chapter 19 provides an overview of what economics in general, and price theory in particular, is all about. Most of the discussion in that final chapter could have been included here. However, we believe that the discussion will be more meaningful *after* you have seen some examples of price theory in action, rather than before. Therefore, we make the following suggestion: Dip into Chapter 19. Not all of it will make sense at this point, but much of it will. After you have been through a few chapters of the book, dip into Chapter 19 again. Even the parts you understood the first time will be more meaningful now. Later on—say, after you have finished Chapter 7—try it yet again. You will get the most from the final chapter if you read it one last time, thoroughly, at the end of the course.

## Features

This book provides many tools to help you learn. Here are a few hints on how to use them.

### Exhibits

Most of the exhibits have extensive explanatory captions that summarize key points from the discussion in the text.

### Exercises

Exercises are sprinkled throughout the text. They are intended to slow you down and make sure that you understand one paragraph before going on to the next. If you cannot do an exercise quickly and accurately, you have probably missed an important point. In that case, it is wise to pause and reread the preceding few paragraphs. Answers to all of the exercises are provided in Appendix B at the back of the book.

## Dangerous Curves

The dangerous curve symbol appears periodically to warn you against the most common misunderstandings. Passages marked with this symbol describe mistakes that students and theorists often make and explain how to avoid them.

## Marginal Glossary

Each new term is defined in bold in the text and in the margin, where you can easily find it. All of the definitions in the margin glossary are gathered in alphabetical order in the Glossary at the back of the book.

## Chapter Summaries

The summaries at the end of each chapter provide concise descriptions of the main ideas. You will find them useful in organizing your study.

## Author Commentaries

I've written a number of magazine articles that use price theory to illuminate every aspect of human behavior. Many of these can be found on the text Web site at **http://www.cengage.com/economics/landsburg**. Click on the companion site for the text, select a chapter from the drop-down list at the left of the screen, and click on the Author Commentaries link in the left menu. Finally, click the download link to download the commentary. *Slate* articles can also be accessed on this companion site. Additional articles can be found through an archive search on the *Slate* magazine home page at **http://slate.msn.com**. Magazine articles, featuring examples that are relevant to many chapters, are noted on the inside cover of this text. The author regularly blogs at www.TheBigQuestions.com/blog, where you will often find material directly related to what you are learning in this book.

## Review Questions

The Review Questions at the end of each chapter test to see whether you have learned and can repeat the main ideas of the chapter.

## Numerical Exercises

About half of the chapters have Numerical Exercises at the end. By working these, you apply economic theory to data to make precise predictions. For example, at the end of Chapter 7, you are given some information about the costs of producing kites and the demand for kites. Using this and the theory that you have learned, you will be able to deduce the price of kites, the number of kites sold by each firm, and the number of firms in the industry.

## Problem Sets

The extensive Problem Sets at the end of each chapter occupy a wide range of difficulty. Some are quite straightforward. Others are challenging and open-ended and give you the opportunity to think deeply and creatively. Often, problems require additional assumptions that are not explicitly stated. Learning to make additional assumptions is a large part of learning to do economics. In some cases there will be more than one correct answer, depending on what assumptions you made. Thus, in answering problems you should always spell out your reasoning very carefully. This is particularly important in "true or false" problems, where the quality of your explanations will usually matter far more than your conclusion.

About one third of the problems are discussed in Appendix C at the end of the book. These problems are indicated by a shaded box around the problem number. The discussions in Appendix C range from hints to complete answers. In many cases, the answer section lists only conclusions without the reasoning necessary to support them; your instructor will probably require you to provide that reasoning.

If your instructor allows it, you will learn a lot by working on problems together with your classmates. You may find that you and they have different answers to the same problem, and that both you and they are equally sure of your answers. In attempting to convince each other, and in trying to pinpoint the spot at which your thinking diverged, you will be forced to clarify your ideas and you will discover which concepts you need to study further. Now you are ready to begin.

# To the Instructor

One advantage of teaching the same course every semester is that you constantly discover new ways to help students understand and enjoy the subject. I've taught price theory 50 times now, and am eager to share the best of my recent discoveries.

The seventh edition of this book, like the six that preceded it, was well received by both students and instructors. I've therefore continued to preserve the book's basic structure and the many features that have been recognized as highlights—the clarity of the writing, the careful pedagogy (including "Dangerous Curves" signals to warn students of common misunderstandings), the lively examples, and the wide range of exercises and problems.

At the same time, I've continued my practice of rewriting several sections for even greater clarity. These include discussions of Giffen goods in Chapter 4 and a of long run competitive equilibrium (including the break-even condition) in Chapter 7. In Chapter 8, I've added a passage to emphasize that economic inefficiency always entails a missed opportunity to do good, and in Chapter 9 I've added some discussion of the extraordinary series of economic events that began in 2008. The biggest change is in Chapter 13, on externalities, which I've extensively reorganized to emphasize the importance of both Pigovian and Coasian insights.

But I'll repeat here what I said in the previous edition: While I am very pleased with these improvements and innovations, I have not tampered with the fundamental structure and content of the book, which I expect will be as satisfactory to the next generation of students as it was to the previous. The standard topics of intermediate price theory are covered in this edition, and in the previous versions. I have retained all of the book's unique features, of which the following are the most important.

## Use of Social Welfare as a Unifying Concept

Consumers' and producers' surplus are introduced in Chapter 8, immediately following the theory of the competitive. There they are used to analyze the effects of various forms of market interference. Thereafter, most new concepts are related to social welfare and analyzed in this light.

## The Economics of Information

Chapter 9 (Knowledge and Information) surveys the key role of prices in disseminating information and relates this to their key role in equilibrating markets. Section 9.1 emphasizes the price system's remarkable success in this regard while Section 9.3 surveys some of its equally remarkable failures. Section 9.2 studies information in financial markets.

## Treatment of Theory of the Firm

It is often difficult for students to understand the importance of production functions, average cost curves, and the like until after they have been asked to study them for several weeks. To remedy this, Chapter 5 (The Behavior of Firms) provides an overview of how firms make decisions, introducing the general principle of equating marginal costs with marginal benefits and relating this principle back to the consumer theory that the student has just learned.

Having seen the importance of cost curves, students may be more motivated to study their derivation in Chapter 6 (Production and Costs). The material on firms is presented in a manner that gives a lot of flexibility to the instructor. Those who prefer the more traditional approach of starting immediately with production can easily skip Chapter 5 or postpone it until after Chapter 6. Chapter 6 itself has been organized to rigorously separate the short-run theory (in Section 6.1) from the long-run theory (in Section 6.2). Relations between the short and the long run are thoroughly explored in Section 6.3. Instructors who want to defer the more difficult topic of long-run production will find it easy to simply cover Section 6.1 and then move directly on to Chapter 7.

## Extended Analysis of Market Failures, Property Rights, and Rules of Law

This is the material of Chapter 13, which I have found to be very popular with students. The theory of externalities is developed in great detail, using a series of extended examples and illustrated with actual court cases. Section 13.4 (The Law and Economics) analyzes various legal theories from the point of view of economic efficiency.

## Relationships to Macroeconomics

The topic coverage provides a solid preparation for a rigorous course in macroeconomics. In addition, several purely "micro" topics are illustrated with "macro" applications. (None of these applications is central to the book, and all can be skipped easily by instructors who wish to do so.) There are sections on information, intertemporal decision making, labor markets in general equilibrium, and rational expectations. In the chapter on interest rates, there is a purely microeconomic analysis of the effects of federal deficits, including Ricardian Equivalence, the hypotheses necessary for it to hold, and the consequences of relaxing these hypotheses. (This material has been extensively rewritten and simplified for this edition.) The section on rational expectations, in Chapter 18, is presented in the context of a purely micro problem, involving agricultural prices, but it includes a discussion of "why economists make wrong predictions" with a moral that applies to macroeconomics.

## Other Nontraditional Topics

There are extensive sections devoted to topics excluded from many standard intermediate textbooks. Among these are alternative normative criteria, efficient asset markets, contestable markets, antitrust law, mechanisms for eliciting private information about the demand for public goods, human capital (including the external effects of human capital accumulation), the role of increasing returns in economic growth, the Capital Asset Pricing Model, and the pricing of stock options. The book concludes with a chapter on the methods and scope of economic analysis (titled What Is Economics?), with examples drawn from biology, sociology, and history.

# Supplements

The *Instructor's Manual* contains the following features in each chapter: general discussion, teaching suggestions, suggested additional problems, and solutions to all of the end-of-chapter problems in the textbook. The *Manual* can be downloaded by instructors from the text Web site.

The *Test Bank*, prepared by Brett Katzman, Kennesaw State University, Kennesaw, GA, offers true/false questions, multiple-choice questions, and essay questions for each chapter. It has been significantly expanded for this edition.

The *Study Guide*, prepared by William V. Weber, Eastern Illinois University, Charleston, IL, has chapters that correspond to the textbook. Each chapter contains key terms, key ideas, completion exercises, graphical analyses, multiple-choice questions, questions for review, and problems for analysis. Artwork from the text is reprinted in the *Study Guide*, with ample space to take notes during classroom discussion.

*PowerPoint*® slides of exhibits from the text are also available for classroom use, and can be accessed at the text Web site. *PowerPoint* slides incorporating lecture notes and exhibits, also available on the Web site, were prepared by Raymonda Burgman, DePauw University, Greencastle, IN.

## Text Web Site

The text Web site is located at **http://www.cengage.com/economics/landsburg**. On the *Price Theory* Web site are several of the text supplements, teaching resources, learning resources, links to the Author Commentary articles, and additional *Slate* articles. In addition, easy access is provided to the EconNews, EconDebate, EconData, and EconLinks Online features at the South-Western Economics Resource Center.

# Acknowledgments

I first learned economics at the University of Chicago in the 1970s, which means that I learned most of it, directly or indirectly, from Dee McCloskey. Generations of Chicago graduate students were infected by Dee's enthusiasm for economics as a tool for understanding the world, and the members of one generation communicated their exuberance to me. They, and consequently I, learned from Dee that the world is full of puzzles—not the abstract or technical puzzles of formal economic theory, but puzzles like: Could the advent of free public education cause less education to be consumed? We learned to see puzzles everywhere and to delight in their solutions. Later, I had the privilege to know Dee as a friend, a colleague, and the greatest of my teachers. Without Dee, this book would not exist. The exuberance that Dee personifies is endemic at Chicago, and I had the great good fortune to encounter it every day. I absorbed ideas and garnered examples in cafeterias, the library's coffee lounge, and especially in all-night seminars at Jimmy's Woodlawn Tap. Many of those ideas and examples appear in this book, their exact sources long forgotten. To all who contributed, thank you.

Among the many Chicago students who deserve explicit mention are Craig Hakkio, Eric Hirschhorn, and Maury Wolff, who were there from the beginning. John Martin and Russell Roberts taught me much and contributed many valuable suggestions specifically for this book. Ken Judd gave me a theory of executive compensation. Dan Gressell taught me the two ways to get a chicken to lay more eggs.

I received further education, and much encouragement, from the Chicago faculty. I thank Gary Becker, who enticed me to think more seriously about economics; Sherwin Rosen, who had planted the seeds of all this years before; and José Scheinkman, who listened to my ideas even when they were foolish. Above all, Bob Lucas can have no idea of how grateful I have been for his many gracious kindnesses. I remember them all, and value his generosity as I value the inspiration of his intellectual depth, honesty, and rigor.

Since leaving Chicago, my good fortune in colleagues followed me to Iowa and Cornell, and especially to Rochester, where this book was written. There is no faculty member in economics at Rochester who did not contribute to this book in one way or another. Some suggested examples and problems; others helped me learn material that I had thought I understood until I tried to write about it; and many did both. I should name them all, but have space for only a few. William Thomson taught me about mechanisms for revealing the demand for public goods and suggested that they belonged in a book at this level. Walter Oi contributed more entertaining ideas and illustrations than I can remember and told me how Chinese bargemen were paid. Ken McLaughlin dazzled me with insights on pretty much a daily basis. And the late Alan Stockman started teaching me both economics and the joys of economics from the day I met him until the day he died.

I must also mention the contributions of the daily lunch group at the Hillside Restaurant, where no subject is off limits and no opinion too outrageous for consideration. The daily discussions about how society is or should be structured were punctuated by numerous tangential discussions of how various ideas could best be presented in an intermediate textbook. I thank especially Stockman, McLaughlin, Mark Bils, John Boyd, Jim Kahn, Marvin Goodfriend (the first inductee into the Hillside Hall of Fame), and various part-time members.

Harold Winter's extensive written criticism of Chapter 11 led to substantial improvements. His many contributions specifically for this edition are acknowledged above and gratefully acknowledged again here. Wendy Betts gave me the epigram for Section 9.3.

We gratefully acknowledge the contributions of the following reviewers whose comments and suggestions have improved this project:

Ted Amato, *University of North Carolina—Charlotte*

John Antel, *University of Houston*

Charles A. Berry, *University of Cincinnati*

Jay Bloom, *SUNY—New Paltz*

James Bradfield, *Hamilton College*

Victor Brajer, *California State University—Fullerton*

Raymonda Burgman, *DePauw University*

Satyajit Chatterjee, *University of Iowa*

Jennifer Coats, *St. Louis University*

John Conant, *Indiana State University*

John P. Conley, *University of Illinois*

John Conley, *University of Illinois—Urbana*

John Devereux, *University of Miami*

Arthur M. Diamond, *University of Nebraska—Omaha*

John Dodge, *Calvin College*

Richard Eastin, *University of Southern California*

Carl E. Enomoto, *New Mexico State University*

Claire Holton Hammond, *Wake Forest University*

Dean Hiebert, *Illinois State University*

John B. Horowitz, *Ball State University*

Roberto Ifill, *Williams College*

Paul Jonas, *University of New Mexico*

Kenneth Judd, *University of Chicago*

Elizabeth Sawyer Kelly, *University of Wisconsin—Madison*

Edward R. Kittrell, *Northern Illinois University*

Vicky C. Langston, *Austin Peay State University*

Daniel Y. Lee, *Shippensburg University*

Luis Locay, *University of Miami*

Barry Love, *Emory & Henry College*

Chris Brown Mahoney, *University of Minnesota*

Devinder Malhotra, *University of Akron*

Joseph A. Martellaro, *Northern Illinois University*

John Martin, *Baruch College*

Scott Masten, *University of Michigan*

J. Peter Mattila, *Iowa State University*

Sharon Megdal, *Northern Arizona University*

Jack Meyer, *Michigan State University*

Robert J. Michaels, *California State University—Fullerton*

John Miller, *Clarkson University*

David Mills, *University of Virginia*

H. Brian Moehring, *Ball State University*

Robert Molina, *Colorado State University*

John Mullen, *Clarkson University*

Kathryn A. Nantz, *Fairfield University*

Jon P. Nelson, *Penn State University*
Craig M. Newmark, *North Carolina State University*
Margaret Oppenheimer, *De Paul University*
Lydia Ortega, *San Jose State University*
Debashis Pal, *University of Cincinnati*
Michael Peddle, *Holy Cross College*
James Pinto, *Northern Arizona University*
Anil Puri, *California State University—Fullerton*
Libby Rittenberg, *Colorado College*
Russell Roberts, *Washington University—Los Angeles*
Peter Rupert, *SUNY—Buffalo*
Leslie Seplaki, *Rutgers University*
David Sisk, *San Francisco State University*
Hubert Spraberry, *Howard Payne University*
Annette Steinacker, *University of Rochester*
Douglas O. Stewart, *Cleveland State University*
Della Lee Sue, *Marist College*
Vasant Sukhatme, *Macalester College*
Beck Taylor, *Baylor University*
Paul Thistle, *University of Alabama*
Mark Walbert, *Illinois State University*
Paula Worthington, *Northwestern University*
Gregory D. Wozniak, *University of Tulsa*
David Zervos, *University of Rochester*

And special thanks to Jana Lewis, the content project manager without who got pretty much everything right, made it sure it all got done, and, most remarkably of all, put up with me.

*Steven E. Landsburg*

# Supply, Demand, and Equilibrium

Many books begin by telling you, at some length, what price theory is. This book begins by showing you. We'll ask some simple questions, and we'll develop the tools we need to answer them as we go along.

When a frost kills half the Florida orange crop, exactly who ends up with fewer oranges? What happens to the price of beef when the price of chicken falls or when the price of grazing land rises? If car dealerships are taxed, how much of the tax is "passed on" to car buyers—and are car buyers better or worse off than when they are taxed directly?

By the time you've finished this chapter, you'll know how to tackle these questions and many more. In each succeeding chapter, you'll be exposed to new ideas in economics and their surprising consequences for the world around you. To learn what price theory is, dig in and begin reading.

## 1.1 Demand

When the price of a good goes up, people generally consume less (or at least not more) of it. This statement, called the **law of demand,** is usually summarized as

When the price goes up, the quantity demanded goes down.

Economists believe that the law of demand is always (or nearly always) true. We believe this primarily on the basis of observations. In Chapter 4, we'll see that the law of demand follows logically from certain more fundamental assumptions about human behavior, which gives us yet another reason to believe it.

### Demand versus Quantity Demanded

As an example, suppose that the good in question is coffee. The number of cups of coffee that you choose to purchase on a typical day might be given by a table like this:

| Price | Quantity |
|---|---|
| 20¢/cup | 5 cups/day |
| 30¢ | 4 |
| 40¢ | 2 |
| 50¢ | 1 |

**Law of demand**

The observation that when the price of a good goes up, people will buy less of that good.

**Quantity demanded**

The amount of a good that a given individual or group of individuals will choose to consume at a given price.

**Demand**

A family of numbers that lists the quantity demanded corresponding to each possible price.

We say that when the price is 20¢ per cup, your **quantity demanded** is 5 cups per day. When the price is 30¢ per cup, your quantity demanded is 4 cups per day, and so on. Notice that the price is measured *per cup,* and the quantity is measured in *cups per day.* If we had selected different units of measurement, we would have had different entries in the table. For example, if we measured quantity in cups per week, the numbers in the right-hand column would be 35, 28, 14, and 7. To speak meaningfully about demand, we must specify our units and use them consistently.

The information in the table is collectively referred to as your **demand** for coffee. Notice the difference between *demand* and *quantity demanded.* Quantity demanded is a number, and it changes when the price does. Demand is a whole family of numbers, listing the quantities you would demand in a variety of hypothetical situations. (More precisely, demand is a *function* that converts prices to quantities.) The demand table asserts that if the price of coffee were 50¢ per cup, then you would buy 1 cup per day. It does not assert that the price of coffee actually is, or ever has been, or will be, 50¢ per cup.

If the price of coffee rises from 30¢ to 40¢ per cup, then your quantity demanded falls from 4 cups to 2 cups. However, your demand for coffee is unchanged, because the same table is still in effect. It remains true that if the price of coffee were 20¢ per cup, you would be demanding 5 cups per day; if the price of coffee were 30¢ per cup, you would be demanding 4 cups per day; and so on. The sequence of "if statements" is what describes your demand for coffee.

A change in price leads to a change in quantity demanded. A change in price does *not* lead to a change in demand.

## Demand Curves

Unfortunately, when we represent demand by a table, we do not provide a complete picture. Our table does not tell us, for example, how much coffee you will purchase when the price is 22¢ per cup, or 33½¢. Therefore, we usually represent demand by a graph. We plot price on the vertical axis and quantity on the horizontal, always specifying our units.

Exhibit 1.1 provides an example. There, the information in your demand table for coffee has been translated into the black points in the graph. The curve through the points is called your **demand curve** for coffee. It fills in the additional information corresponding to prices that do not appear in the table. If we were to fill in enough rows of the table (and only space prevents us from doing so), then the demand table and the demand curve in Exhibit 1.1 would convey exactly the same information. The demand curve is a picture of your demand for coffee.

**Demand curve**

A graph illustrating demand, with prices on the vertical axis and quantities demanded on the horizontal axis.

Dangerous
Curve

Because demand is a function that converts price (the independent variable) to quantity (the dependent variable), a mathematician would be inclined to plot price on the horizontal axis and quantity on the vertical. In economics, we do exactly the opposite, for good reasons that will be explained in Chapter 7.

Because the demand curve is a picture of demand, every statement that we can make about demand can be "seen" in the curve. For example, consider the law of demand: "When the price goes up, the quantity demanded goes down." This fact is reflected in the downward slope of the demand curve. It is important to remember both of these statements:

| EXHIBIT 1.1 | The Demand Curve |
|---|---|

| Price | Quantity |
|---|---|
| 20¢/cup | 5 cups/day |
| 30¢ | 4 |
| 40¢ | 2 |
| 50¢ | 1 |

The demand table shows how many cups of coffee you would buy per day at each of several prices. The black points in the graph correspond precisely to the information in the table. The curve connecting the points is your demand curve for coffee. It conveys more information than the table because it shows how many cups of coffee you would buy at intermediate prices like 22¢ or 33½¢ per cup. If the table were enlarged to include enough intermediate prices, then the table and the graph would convey exactly the same information.

When the price goes up, the quantity demanded goes down.

and

Demand curves slope downward.

But it is even more important to recognize that these two statements are just two different ways of saying the same thing and to understand *why* they are just two different ways of saying the same thing.

### Example: The Demand for the Mona Lisa

Leonardo DaVinci only painted the Mona Lisa once. But if the original Mona Lisa were available for, say, $1.50, I'd want more than one of them—I think I'd probably hang one in my office, one in my living room, and perhaps one beside my bathroom mirror. So if the price of the Mona Lisa were $1.50, my quantity demanded would be 3. The point with those coordinates is on my Mona Lisa demand curve.

This example is meant to illustrate that points on the demand curve have *nothing to do* with the actual price of the Mona Lisa or the quantity of Mona Lisas that are actually available. My demand curve shows how many Mona Lisas I would *want* at various prices, not how many I *could get*.

## Changes in Demand

If a change in price does not lead to a change in demand, does this mean demand can never change? Absolutely not. Suppose, for example, that your doctor has advised you to cut back on coffee for medical reasons. You might then choose to buy coffee according to a different table, such as this:

| Price | Quantity |
|---|---|
| 20¢/cup | 3 cups/day |
| 30¢ | 2 |
| 40¢ | 1 |
| 50¢ | 0 |

Now your rule for deciding how many cups of coffee to purchase at different prices has changed—and this rule is just what we have called *demand*.

We can also use demand curves to illustrate the difference between a change in quantity demanded and a change in demand. A change in quantity demanded is represented by a movement along the demand curve from one point to another. A change in demand is represented by a shift of the curve itself to a new position.

**Fall in demand**

A decision by demanders to buy a smaller quantity at each given price.

The curve labeled *D* in Exhibit 1.2 is the same as the demand curve in Exhibit 1.1. The curve labeled *D'* illustrates your demand after medical advice to reduce your caffeine intake. Because you now want fewer cups of coffee at any given price, the new demand curve lies to the left of (and consequently below) the old demand curve. We describe this situation as a **fall in demand.**

---

| EXHIBIT **1.2** | **Shifting the Demand Curve** |
|---|---|

TABLE A. Your Original Demand for Coffee

| Price | Quantity |
|---|---|
| 20¢/cup | 5 cups/day |
| 30¢ | 4 |
| 40¢ | 2 |
| 50¢ | 1 |

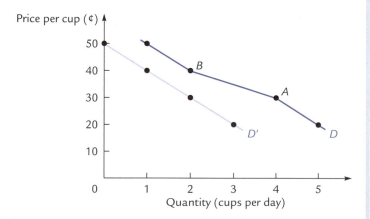

TABLE B. Your New Demand for Coffee after Medical Advice to Cut Back

| Price | Quantity |
|---|---|
| 20¢/cup | 3 cups/day |
| 30¢ | 2 |
| 40¢ | 1 |
| 50¢ | 0 |

Your original demand curve for coffee is the curve labeled *D*. A change in price, say from 30¢ per cup to 40¢ per cup, would cause a movement along the curve from point *A* to point *B*. A change in something other than price, such as a doctor's suggestion that caffeine is bad for your health, can lead to a change in demand, represented by a shift to an entirely new demand curve. In this case the doctor's advice leads to a fall in demand, which is represented by a leftward shift of the curve.

The opposite situation, a **rise in demand,** results in a rightward shift of the demand curve. If you enrolled in a class that required a lot of late-night studying, you might experience a rise in your demand for coffee.

There are many other possible reasons for a shift in demand. If the price of tea were to fall, you might decide to drink more tea and less coffee. The amount of coffee you would choose to buy at any given price would go down. This is an example of a fall in demand. On the other hand, if your aunt gives you a snazzy new coffee maker for your birthday, your demand for coffee might rise.

A change in anything *other* than price can lead to a change in demand.

**Exercise 1.1** If the price of donuts were to fall, what do you think would happen to your demand for coffee? Does a fall in the price of a related good always affect your demand in the same way, or does it depend on what related good we are talking about?

**Exercise 1.2** How might a rise in your income affect your demand for coffee?

## Effect of a Sales Tax

One thing that could change your demand for coffee is the imposition of a **sales tax.**[1] Suppose that a new law requires you to pay a tax of 10¢ per cup of coffee that you buy. What happens to your demand curve?

Before we can begin to think about how a sales tax affects your demand curve, we have to decide what the word *price* means in a world with sales taxes. If a cup of coffee carries a price tag of "50¢ plus tax" and the tax is a nickel, should we say that the price is 50¢ or should we say that the price is 55¢? It doesn't matter which choice we make, but it *does* matter that we make a choice and stick with it. In this book, we will consistently use the word *price* to mean the pretax price, so that the price of that cup of coffee is 50¢. We think of the sales tax as something that you pay *in addition* to the market price. Therefore a new sales tax is a change in something other than the price, and therefore a new sales tax can affect the location of the demand curve.

A sales tax makes buying coffee less desirable; at any given (pretax) price, you now want to buy less coffee than before. Your demand curve shifts to the left and downward. In fact, we can even figure out how far it shifts.

Suppose your demand for coffee in a world without taxes is given by the table in Exhibit 1.1. Let's figure out your demand in a world where coffee is taxed at 10¢ per cup. If the (pretax) price of coffee is 10¢, what will it actually cost you to acquire a cup of coffee? It will cost you 10¢ plus 10¢ tax—a total of 20¢. How many cups of coffee do you choose to buy when they cost you 20¢ apiece? According to the table in Exhibit 1.1, you will buy 5.

**Rise in demand**

A decision by demanders to buy a larger quantity at each given price.

**Sales tax**

In this book, a tax that is paid directly by consumers to the government. Other texts use this phrase in different ways.

Dangerous
Curve

---

[1] In this book we will use the phrase *sales tax* to refer to a tax that is paid to the government by consumers. Some other texts use this phrase in a different way.

Now we can begin to tabulate your demand for coffee in a world with taxes. We know that, with taxes, if the price of coffee is 10¢ per cup, you will choose to buy 5 cups per day. This is the first row of your new demand table:

| Price | Quantity |
|-------|----------|
| 10¢/cup | 5 cups/day |

We can continue in this way. When the price of coffee is 20¢, the actual cost to you will be 30¢. We know from Exhibit 1.1 that you will then choose to buy 4 cups. Thus, we can fill in another row of our table:

| Price | Quantity |
|-------|----------|
| 10¢/cup | 5 cups/day |
| 20¢ | 4 |

If we complete the argument at other prices, we finally arrive at your new demand for coffee, which is shown in Exhibit 1.3. Compare the entries in the two demand tables of that exhibit. Notice that the same quantities appear in each but the corresponding prices are all 10¢ lower in the new demand schedule (Table B). What can we conclude about the demand curves that illustrate these tables? For every point on the original

---

**EXHIBIT 1.3**    **The Effect of a Sales Tax on Demand**

TABLE A. Demand for Coffee without Tax

| Price | Quantity |
|-------|----------|
| 20¢/cup | 5 cups/day |
| 30¢ | 4 |
| 40¢ | 2 |
| 50¢ | 1 |

TABLE B. Demand for Coffee with Sales Tax of 10¢ per Cup

| Price | Quantity |
|-------|----------|
| 10¢/cup | 5 cups/day |
| 20¢ | 4 |
| 30¢ | 2 |
| 40¢ | 1 |

If the price of coffee is 10¢ per cup and there is a sales tax of 10¢, then it will actually cost you 20¢ to acquire a cup of coffee. Table A shows that under these circumstances you would purchase 5 cups per day. This is recorded in the first row of Table B. The other rows in that table are generated in a similar manner.

The rows of Table B contain the same quantities as the rows of Table A, but the corresponding prices are all 10¢ lower. Another way to say this is that each point on the new demand curve lies exactly 10¢ below a corresponding point on the original demand curve. Therefore, the new demand curve lies exactly 10¢ below the original demand curve in vertical distance. The sales tax causes the demand curve to shift downward parallel to itself by the amount of the tax.

demand curve *(D)*, a corresponding point on the new demand curve *(D')* represents the same quantity but a price that is lower by 10¢. This corresponding point lies a vertical distance exactly 10¢ below the original point.

In summary, the sales tax causes each point of the demand curve to shift downward by the vertical distance 10¢. Because each point shifts downward the same distance, we can say that the demand curve shifts downward parallel to itself by the vertical distance 10¢. This gives us a precise prediction of how a sales tax affects demand.

A sales tax causes the demand curve to shift downward parallel to itself by the amount of the tax.

**Exercise 1.3** How would demand be affected by a sales tax of 5¢ per item? How would it be affected by a subsidy under which the government pays 10¢ toward each cup of coffee purchased?

**Exercise 1.4** How would demand be affected by a percentage sales tax—say, a tax equal to 10% of the price paid?

## Market Demand

Until now we have been discussing your demand for coffee or the demand by some individual. We can just as well discuss the demand for coffee by some *group* of individuals. We can speak of the demand by your family, your city, your country, or the entire world. The quantity associated with a given price is the total number of cups per day that the group members would demand.

Of course, because we can speak of a group's *demand* for coffee, we can speak of that group's *demand curve* as well. And, of course, this demand curve slopes downward.

## The Shape of the Demand Curve

We have discussed the meaning of the demand curve's downward slope, but have not yet discussed how steeply the demand curve slopes downward. Your community's demand curve for shoes might look like either panel of Exhibit 1.4. Both of these demand curves slope downward, but one slopes downward far more steeply than the other. If the demand curve looks like panel A, a small change in the price of shoes will lead to a small change in the quantity of shoes demanded. If the demand curve looks like panel B, a small change in the price of shoes will lead to a much larger change in the quantity of shoes demanded.

Often, people want to know the slopes of particular demand curves. If you owned a shoe store, you would be very interested in knowing whether a small price rise would drive away only a few customers or a great many. This is the same thing as asking whether the demand curve for your shoes is very steep or very flat.[2]

---

[2] The simplest measure of a demand curve's steepness is its slope. An alternative measure, more widely used in economics, is its *elasticity*. The *elasticity* is the ratio (percent change in quantity)/(percent change in price) between any two points. In panel A of Exhibit 1.4, where the price rises from $4 to $5 (a 25% increase), the quantity falls from 20 to 18 (a 10% decrease). Thus, the elasticity is –10%/25%, or –4. We will have more to say about elasticity in Chapter 4.

EXHIBIT **1.4**    **The Shape of the Demand Curve**

The two panels depict two possible demand curves for shoes. In panel A a given change in price (say from $4 per pair to $5 per pair) leads to a small change in quantity demanded (from 20 pairs of shoes per week to 18 pairs per week). In panel B the same change in price leads to a large change in quantity demanded (from 20 pairs per week to 8 pairs per week).

**Econometrics**

A family of statistical techniques used by economists.

    To help resolve such questions, economists have developed a variety of statistical techniques known collectively as **econometrics.** These techniques allow us (among other things) to estimate the slopes of various demand curves on the basis of direct observations in the marketplace. In this book we will not study any econometrics, but it is important for you to know that the techniques exist and work tolerably well. In many circumstances economists can estimate the slopes of demand curves with considerable accuracy.

## Example: The Demand for Murder

Many economists have applied the successful techniques of econometrics to the study of demand curves for a variety of interesting "goods" that were previously viewed as outside the realm of economic analysis. Consider, for example, the demand curve for murder.

    Murder is an activity that some people choose to engage in for a variety of reasons. We can view murder as a "good" for these people, and the commission of murder as the act of consuming that good. The price of consuming the good is paid in many forms. One of these forms is the risk of capital punishment.

    This means that we can draw a demand curve for murder, plotting the probability of capital punishment on the vertical axis and the quantity of murders committed on the horizontal axis. We can ask how steep this demand curve is, which is the same thing as asking whether a small increase in the probability of capital punishment will lead to a small or a large decrease in the number of murders committed. In other words, measuring the slope of this demand curve is the same thing as measuring the deterrent effect of capital punishment.

Now, on the one hand, the deterrent effect of capital punishment is something about which there is much discussion and much interest. On the other hand, the slope of a demand curve is something that economists know how to measure.

Over the past 25 years, Professor Isaac Ehrlich has repeatedly measured the slope of the demand curve for murder, using essentially the same techniques that economists use to measure the slope of the demand curves for shoes, coffee, and other consumer goods. His results have been striking. The demand curve for murder appears to be remarkably flat; that is, a small increase in the price of murder leads to a large decrease in the quantity of murders committed. In fact, Ehrlich estimates that over the period 1935–1969 (a period in which executions were more common than they are today, making the statistical tests more reliable), one additional execution in the United States would have prevented, on average, about eight murders per year.[3]

This is a remarkable example of an application of economics to a positive question: "What is the deterrent effect of capital punishment?" It is emphatically *not* an answer to the related normative question: "Is capital punishment a good thing?" It is entirely possible to believe Ehrlich's results and still oppose capital punishment on ethical grounds; in fact, Ehrlich himself opposes capital punishment. However, knowing the answer to the positive question is undoubtedly helpful in thinking about the normative one. The size of the deterrent effect of the death penalty will certainly affect our assessment of its desirability, even though our assessment depends on many other things as well.

## Example: The Demand for Reckless Driving

Reckless driving is another good that people choose to "consume." For this consumption they pay a price, partly by risking death in an accident. When that price is reduced—say, by the installation of safety equipment in cars—we should expect the quantity of reckless driving to increase.

This implies that safety devices like air bags could lead to either an increase or a decrease in the number of driver deaths. With an air bag, an individual accident is less likely to be fatal. But for exactly that reason, people will drive more recklessly and therefore will have more accidents. Whether the number of driver deaths decreases, increases, or remains constant depends on the size of that response; in other words, it depends on whether the demand curve for reckless driving is steep or flat.

When Professors Steven Peterson, George Hoffer, and Edward Millner investigated this question,[4] they found that air bags had almost no effect on the number of driver deaths; in fact, if anything, giving a driver an air bag makes him slightly *more* likely to die in an accident. With the air bag, the driver chooses to engage in enough additional reckless driving to completely offset the safety advantages of the air bag itself.

---

[3] Ehrlich's first pathbreaking study was "The Deterrent Effect of Capital Punishment: A Question of Life and Death," *American Economic Review* 65 (1975), 397–417. His most recent contribution is "Sensitivity Analysis of the Deterrence Hypothesis: Let's Keep Econ in Econometrics" (with Z. Liu), *Journal of Law and Economics* XLII (1999), 455–487.

[4] Steven P. Peterson, George E. Hoffer, and Edward L. Millner, "Are Drivers of Airbag Equipped Cars More Aggressive: A Test of the Peltzman Hypotheses?" *Journal of Law and Economics* 38 (1995), 251–265. Thirty years earlier, Professor Sam Peltzman found similar results for the effects of seat belts, collapsible steering wheels, penetration-resistant windshields, dual braking systems, and padded dashboards. See S. Peltzman, "The Effects of Automobile Safety Regulation," *Journal of Political Economy* 83 (1975), 677–725.

Does that mean drivers don't benefit from air bags? No, it just means they choose to take their benefits in a form other than safety. They get to drive faster, more aggressively, and more recklessly with only a slight increase in their chance of being killed. The real losers are pedestrians and other drivers, who participate in the additional accidents without sharing the safety features of the air bag.

If you find these results difficult to believe, try this experiment. Pick ten friends and read sentence 1 to five of them and sentence 2 to the other five:

1. "If you give a driver an air bag, he'll drive more recklessly."

2. "If you take away a driver's air bag, he'll drive more carefully."

Chances are, the five friends who hear sentence 1 will find it implausible and the five who hear sentence 2 will find it obvious. But the two sentences say exactly the same thing in different words, so your friends' instincts can't all be right. The instinct to disbelieve sentence 1 is an interesting fact about psychology; the fact that the sentence is nevertheless true is an interesting fact about economics.

## The Wide Scope of Economics

The ideas of economics can be applied to every aspect of human behavior. In addition to the demand curves for murder and reckless driving, economists have measured the demand curves for "goods" as diverse as racial discrimination, love, children, religious activity, and cannibalism. Economic theory has yielded startling new insights in political science, sociology, philosophy, and law. The broad applicability of economic reasoning will be a recurring theme in this book.

# 1.2  Supply

**Law of supply**

The observation that when the price of a good goes up, the quantity supplied goes up.

**Quantity supplied**

The amount of a good that suppliers will provide at a given price.

The law of demand states that "when the price goes up, the quantity demanded goes down." The **law of supply** states that "when the price goes up, the quantity supplied goes up." By **quantity supplied** we mean the quantity of some good that a specified individual or group of individuals wants to supply to others per specified unit of time.

The law of supply is not as ironclad as the law of demand. Imagine a manufacturer of bicycles who works 12 hours a day to produce one bicycle that he can sell for $40. If the price of bicycles were to go up to $500, he might choose to work harder and produce more bicycles—but he might choose instead to cut back on production, make one bicycle per week, and spend more time at the beach.[5]

Nevertheless, economists have found that in most circumstances an increase in price leads to an increase in quantity supplied. Throughout this chapter, therefore, we shall assume the validity of the law of supply.

## Supply versus Quantity Supplied

Consider the supply of coffee in your city. It might be given by Table A of Exhibit 1.5. According to the table, if the price is 20¢ per cup, then the individuals who supply

---

[5] However, we will see in Chapter 6 that when the supplier is a profit-maximizing firm, the law of supply must hold.

EXHIBIT **1.5**          **The Supply of Coffee**

| TABLE A. Supply of Coffee to Your City | |
|---|---|
| Price | Quantity |
| 20¢/cup | 100 cups/day |
| 30¢ | 300 |
| 40¢ | 400 |
| 50¢ | 500 |

| TABLE B. Supply of Coffee to Your City Following the Development of Better Farming Methods | |
|---|---|
| Price | Quantity |
| 20¢/cup | 200 cups/day |
| 30¢ | 400 |
| 40¢ | 600 |
| 50¢ | 700 |

Table A shows, for each price, how much coffee would be supplied to your city. The same information is illustrated by the points in the graph. The curve labeled *S* is the corresponding supply curve. It conveys more information than the table by displaying the quantities supplied at intermediate prices. The law of supply is illustrated by the upward slope of the supply curve.

The invention of a cheaper way to produce coffee increases the willingness of suppliers to provide coffee at any given price. The new supply is shown in Table B and is illustrated by the curve *S'*. Although a change in price leads to a movement along the supply curve, a change in something other than price causes the entire curve to shift.

The curve *S'* lies to the right of *S*, indicating that the supply has increased.

coffee to your city will wish to supply a total of 100 cups per day. If the price is 30¢ per cup, then they will wish to supply a total of 300 cups, and so forth. All of these hypothetical statements taken together constitute the **supply** of coffee to your city.

As with demand, a change in price leads to a change in the quantity supplied (which is a single number). Such changes are represented by movements along the supply curve. A change in anything other than price can lead to a change in supply—that is, to a change in the entries in the supply schedule. Such changes are represented by shifts in the supply curve itself.

For example, imagine an innovation in agricultural techniques that allows growers to produce coffee less expensively. This innovation might take the form of a new hybrid coffee plant that produces more beans, or a new idea for organizing harvesting chores so that more beans can be picked in a given amount of time. Such an innovation would make supplying coffee more desirable, and suppliers would supply more at each price than they did before. Table B of Exhibit 1.5 shows what the new supply schedule might look like. The new supply curve is the curve labeled *S'* in Exhibit 1.5.

The shift in supply due to improved agricultural techniques is an example of a **rise in supply.** It is represented by a rightward shift of the supply curve. The opposite situation is a **fall in supply.** If the wages of coffee bean pickers went up, growers would want to provide less coffee at any given price, which is another way of saying that supply would fall. A fall in supply is represented by a leftward shift of the supply curve.

**Supply**

A family of numbers giving the quantities supplied at each possible price.

**Rise in supply**

An increase in the quantities that suppliers will provide at each given price.

**Fall in supply**

A decrease in the quantities that suppliers will provide at each given price.

Dangerous
Curve

In Exhibit 1.5 the new supply curve *S′*, with its higher quantities, lies to the right of the old supply curve *S*. This is because quantity is measured in the horizontal direction, so *higher* translates geometrically into *rightward*. In the vertical direction, *S′* lies below *S*, even though it represents a rise in supply. This is the opposite of what you might at first expect, and you should be on your guard against possible confusion.

**Exercise 1.5** How would the supply of shoes be affected by an increase in the price of leather? How would it be affected by an increase in the price of leather belts?

## Effect of an Excise Tax

**Excise tax**

In this book, a tax that is paid directly by suppliers to the government.

One thing that could lead to a change in supply is the imposition of an **excise tax**—that is, a tax on suppliers of goods.[6] Suppose that a new tax is instituted requiring suppliers to pay 10¢ per cup of coffee sold. Suppose also that in the absence of this tax the supply of coffee in your city is given by Table A of Exhibit 1.6 (which is identical to Table A of Exhibit 1.5). Let us compute the supply of coffee in your city after the tax takes effect.

### EXHIBIT 1.6    Effect of an Excise Tax

| TABLE A. Supply of Coffee without Tax | |
|---|---|
| Price | Quantity |
| 20¢/cup | 100 cups/day |
| 30¢ | 300 |
| 40¢ | 400 |
| 50¢ | 500 |

| TABLE B. Supply of Coffee with Excise Tax of 10¢ per Cup | |
|---|---|
| Price | Quantity |
| 30¢/cup | 100 cups/day |
| 40¢ | 300 |
| 50¢ | 400 |
| 60¢ | 500 |

If the price of coffee is 30¢ per cup and there is an excise tax of 10¢, then a seller of coffee will actually get to keep 20¢ per cup sold. The original supply schedule (Table A) shows that under these circumstances suppliers would provide 100 cups per day. This is recorded in the first row of Table B. The other rows in that table are generated in a similar manner.

The rows of Table B contain the same quantities as the rows of Table A, but the corresponding prices are all 10¢ higher. Thus, each point on the new supply curve *S′* lies exactly 10¢ above a corresponding point on the old supply curve *S*. Therefore, *S′* lies exactly 10¢ above *S* in vertical distance. The excise tax causes the supply curve to shift upward parallel to itself a distance of 10¢.

[6] We shall use the phrase *excise tax* to refer to a tax that is paid to the government by suppliers. As with the phrase *sales tax,* this phrase is not used the same way in all textbooks.

Suppose first that the price of a cup of coffee is 30¢. Then a supplier gets to keep 20¢ for every cup of coffee sold (the supplier collects 30¢ and gives a dime to the tax collector). We want to know what quantity will be supplied under these circumstances. The answer is in Table A of Exhibit 1.6: When suppliers receive 20¢ per cup of coffee sold, they provide 100 cups per day.

Therefore, in a world with an excise tax, a price of 30¢ leads to a quantity supplied of 100 cups per day. This gives us the first row of our supply table for a world with an excise tax:

| Price | Quantity |
|---|---|
| 30¢/cup | 100 cups/day |

The entire new supply schedule is displayed in Table B of Exhibit 1.6.

**Exercise 1.6** Explain how we got the entries in the last three rows of Table B in Exhibit 1.6.

Notice that both of the tables in Exhibit 1.6 list the same quantities, but that the associated prices are 10¢ higher in Table B. This means that the supply curve associated with Table B will lie a vertical distance 10¢ above the supply curve associated with Table A. The graph in Exhibit 1.6 illustrates this relationship.

Notice that the supply curve with the tax (curve $S'$ in the exhibit) is geometrically above and to the left of the old supply curve $S$. This is what we have called a lower supply curve (it is lower because, for example, a price of 30¢ calls forth a quantity supplied of only 100, instead of 300).

We can summarize as follows:

An excise tax causes the supply curve to shift upward parallel to itself (to a new, lower supply curve) by the amount of the tax.

# 1.3 Equilibrium

Demand and supply curves illustrate buyers' and sellers' responses to various hypothetical prices. So far, we've said nothing about how those prices are actually determined or what quantities will actually be available. Demanders cannot purchase more coffee than suppliers are willing to sell them, and suppliers cannot sell more coffee than demanders are willing to buy. In this section we will examine the interaction between suppliers and demanders and the way in which this interaction determines both the prices and the quantities of goods traded in the marketplace.

## The Equilibrium Point

Exhibit 1.7 shows the demand and supply curves for cement in your city. We want to find the point on the graph that describes the price of cement and the quantity of cement that is sold at that price.

The first thing to notice is that there is only one price where the quantity supplied and the quantity demanded are equal. That price is $4.50 per bag, where the quantities supplied and demanded are each equal to 300 bags per week. The corresponding point

EXHIBIT **1.7**          **Equilibrium in the Market for Cement**

The graph shows the supply and demand curves for cement. The equilibrium point, *E*, is located at the intersection of the two curves. The equilibrium price, $4.50 per bag, is the only price at which quantity supplied and quantity demanded are equal.

**Equilibrium point**

The point where the supply and demand curves intersect.

**Satisfied**

Able to behave as one wants to, taking market prices as given.

on the graph is called the **equilibrium point.** The equilibrium point is the point at which the supply and demand curves cross.

To understand the significance of the equilibrium point, we will first imagine what would happen if the market were not at the equilibrium—that is, if the price were something other than $4.50.

Suppose, for example, that the price is $7.50. We see from the demand curve that all demanders taken together want a total of 100 bags of cement each week, while suppliers want to provide 600 bags of cement. The demanders purchase the 100 bags that they want and refuse to buy any more. At least some of the suppliers are not able to sell all of the cement that they want to. Those suppliers are unhappy.

Of course, some demanders may be unhappy too. They may be unhappy because the price of cement is so high. They would prefer a price of $4.50 per bag, and they would prefer even more a price of $0 per bag. But the demanders are perfectly happy in one limited sense: Given the current price of cement, they are buying precisely the quantity that they want to buy. We choose to describe this situation by saying that the demanders are **satisfied.**

In general, a satisfied individual is one who is able to behave as he wants, taking the prices he faces as given. This is so regardless of how he feels about the prices themselves. We take this as a definition. It is the only definition that really makes sense in this context. Nobody is ever completely happy about the prices themselves: Buyers always wish they were lower and sellers always wish they were higher.

So, when the price is $7.50 per bag, the demanders buy 100 bags per week and are satisfied. The suppliers, who want to sell 600 bags per week, sell only 100 bags per week and are unsatisfied. When some suppliers discover that they cannot sell as much cement as they would like at the going price, they lower their prices to attract more demanders.

Suppose that they lower their prices to $6 per bag. Referring again to Exhibit 1.7, we see that demanders want to buy 200 bags of cement per week and suppliers want to sell 400 bags. After 200 bags are sold, the demanders go home satisfied, and some suppliers are still left unsatisfied. They lower their prices further.

We may expect this process to continue as long as the quantity supplied exceeds the quantity demanded. That is, we expect it to continue until the market reaches the equilibrium price of $4.50 per bag.

If the price of cement starts out below $4.50, we can expect the same process to work in reverse. For example, when the price is $1.50, demanders want to buy 500 bags of cement per week, but suppliers want to provide only 100 bags. The suppliers, having provided 100 bags, will go home, leaving some demanders unsatisfied. In order to lure the suppliers back to the marketplace, demanders will offer a higher price for cement. This process will continue until the quantity demanded no longer exceeds the quantity supplied. It will continue until the market reaches the equilibrium price of $4.50 per bag.

The story we have just told gives a reason to expect the market to be in equilibrium. The reason is that if the market were not in equilibrium, buyers and sellers would change their behavior in ways that would cause the market to move toward equilibrium. We still have to ask how realistic our story is. Later in this book we will see that there are some markets for which it is substantially accurate, and other markets for which it may not be accurate at all. For the time being, we will focus on the first type of market. That is, for the remainder of this chapter we will assume that the markets we are studying are always in equilibrium. For a wide range of economic problems, this is a safe and useful assumption to make.

## Changes in the Equilibrium Point

Suppose there is an increase in the cost of feed corn for pigs. What happens to the price and quantity of pork chops?

Here is a *wrong* way to approach this question. First, farmers respond to the cost increase by raising fewer pigs. This means that there are fewer pork chops in the supermarkets, so demanders bid their price up. Next the rise in price induces farmers to raise *more* pigs. This in turn causes the price to be bid back down, whereupon farmers cut back their production again, whereupon....

The problem with this kind of approach is that it never reaches a conclusion. Each step in the analysis is correct, but there are infinitely many steps, and it takes forever to consider them one at a time. Therefore, we need a device that accounts for all of the steps in the argument simultaneously.

Consequently, and perhaps paradoxically, when you want to figure out how a change in circumstances affects price and quantity, you should never begin by thinking about price and quantity. Instead, think about how the change in circumstances affects the demand curve and how it affects the supply curve (these are two separate questions). Embedded in the supply and demand shifts are all of the infinitely many responses and counterresponses that we failed to completely list above. Once you have shifted the curves, you can see what happens to the equilibrium point.

So let's try the same problem again. First, when there is an increase in the cost of feed corn, what happens to the *demand* for pork chops? The answer is nothing;

changes in the cost of feed corn have no effect at all on the number of pork chops that a demander wants to buy at a given price. To convince yourself of this, imagine entering a supermarket where pork chops are on sale for $8 a pound and trying to decide how many pounds you want to buy. In that situation, it is unlikely that you feel compelled to inquire how much it cost to feed the pigs before you can make your decision. That cost is quite irrelevant to you as a demander.

On the other hand, the *supply* of pork chops shifts to the left. Suppliers do care about the cost of feed corn and are willing to produce fewer pork chops at a given price when that cost goes up.

If we plot the demand and supply for pork chops on the same graph, then demand stays fixed while supply shifts to the left, as illustrated in the last panel of Exhibit 1.8. The new equilibrium point lies above and to the left of the old one. Thus the price of pork chops is up, and the quantity is down.

| EXHIBIT **1.8** | **The Effects of Supply and Demand Shifts** |

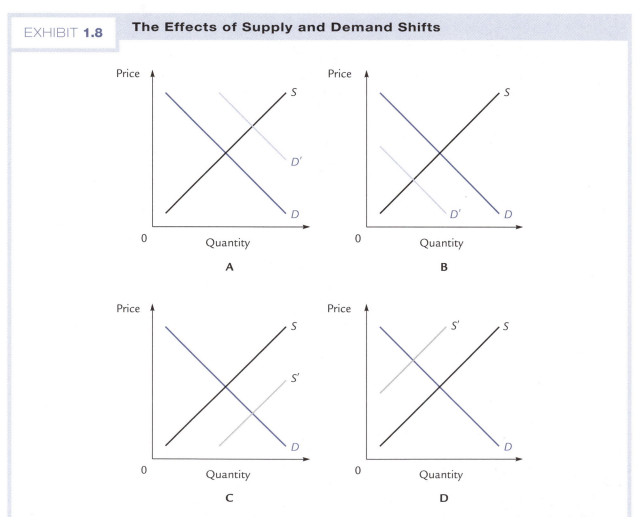

The graphs show the effects of various shifts in demand and supply. For example, in panel A we see that a rise in demand leads to a rise in price and a rise in quantity.

Because the equilibrium price and quantity are determined by the supply and demand curves, anything that affects the curves will affect the equilibrium price and quantity. The panels of Exhibit 1.8 show a variety of ways in which changes in demand or supply can affect the point of equilibrium.

**Exercise 1.7** Taking the panels of Exhibit 1.8 to represent the market for pork chops, which panel shows the effect of a rise in the price of beef? How does a rise in the price of beef affect the equilibrium price and quantity of pork chops?

Keep in mind that *the only way that anything can affect the equilibrium price and quantity is by causing a shift in either the supply curve or the demand curve (or both).* That is why any analysis of a change in equilibrium must begin with the question of how the curves have shifted.

It is important to distinguish causes from effects. For an individual demander or supplier, the price is taken as given and determines the quantity demanded or supplied. For the market as a whole, the demand and supply curves determine both price and quantity simultaneously.

Dangerous
Curve

## Example: The (Non-)Market for Kidneys

In the United States today, there are approximately 50,000 people awaiting kidney transplants. Each year, about 15,000 transplants are performed and about 3,000 people die waiting.

At the same time, hundreds of millions of Americans have spare kidneys (most of us have two, but we can function perfectly well with just one). If just a tiny fraction of those kidneys were made available for transplant, many lives could be saved.

Sometimes people donate their kidneys to relatives, and occasionally (but very rarely) they donate them to strangers. However, current law does not allow an individual to *sell* a kidney.

If kidneys were freely bought and sold, how many would be purchased and at what price? You might think that's impossible to answer, because we've never had an opportunity to observe the supply and demand curves. But economists Gary Becker and Julio Elias have overcome that obstacle.[7]

Donating a kidney means accepting a certain amount of discomfort (usually over a three- to five-week recovery period), about a 1/1000 chance of death during the operation, and a small reduction in quality of life thereafter. But donating a kidney isn't the only thing that entails discomfort and risk; there are plenty of dirty and dangerous jobs (like mining) that are also uncomfortable and risky. We can easily observe the supply of miners (that is, we know, at various wage rates, how many people will volunteer for dangerous duty in mines) and can therefore infer something about the supply of kidneys. If, for a bonus of, say, $10,000, you can get 100 people to volunteer for dangerous mining operations, then for a similar bonus you should be able to get roughly 100 people to volunteer for an equally dangerous kidney donation.

[7] Gary Becker and Julio Elias, Introducing Incentives in the Market for Live and Cadaveric Organ Donations, Working Paper, University of Chicago (2002).

Using such techniques, Professors Gary Becker and Julio Elias estimated the supply of kidneys. They also estimated the demand, and were therefore able to estimate an equilibrium price of approximately $15,000. This will raise the price of a kidney transplant from the current $110,000 to $125,000, but the demand for kidney transplants is presumably quite steep, so the quantity demanded would not change very much from its current value.

## The Nature of Equilibrium: Some Common Mistakes

A standard reference work on the taming and training of parrots reports that "when popular demand for a species exceeds the available supply, prices remain high."[8] A barrage of news reports warns that a frost in Florida could lead to a "shortage" of oranges, with people unable to buy as many as they want. The well-known columnist Michael Kinsley, explaining the market for art, reports in the *New Republic* that "when the price of something goes up, the supply of it increases." Columnist Jack Mabley of the *Chicago Tribune* reports that "General Motors just increased prices another 2.5%" even after a "bad year" and concludes that "if the law of supply and demand were working, GM would reduce prices, not raise them."

Like most people, these writers might benefit from a course in economics. Statements like "demand exceeds supply" make no sense, because demand and supply are not numbers but curves. A glance back at Exhibit 1.7 will remind you that there are always some prices (such as $1.50 in the exhibit) at which the quantity demanded exceeds the quantity supplied, and others (such as $7.50) at which the quantity supplied exceeds the quantity demanded.

What, then, does the parrot expert mean to say? If there is no sense to be made of the statement that "demand exceeds supply," then perhaps he meant to say that "the quantity demanded exceeds the quantity supplied." This would have the advantage of being meaningful (a number *can*, after all, exceed another number) but the disadvantage of being wrong. In equilibrium, the quantities supplied and demanded are equal. This is so regardless of whether the equilibrium price is high, low, or in between.

When the demand curve for parrots shifts rightward (as in panel A of Exhibit 1.8), or when the supply curve shifts leftward (as in panel D), then the price rises to a new equilibrium at which the quantities supplied and demanded again coincide.

Similarly, a frost in the Florida orange groves causes a leftward shift in the supply of oranges and a new, higher equilibrium price at which demanders can purchase all the oranges they want. (They will want fewer than they wanted at the old price.) No shortage need occur.

Michael Kinsley's analysis of the art market is wrong because a change in price causes a change in the quantity supplied, not in the supply. But we can go further and ask what causes the change in price. The answer: The price change itself must be caused by either a change in supply or a change in demand.

Finally, let us examine Jack Mabley's analysis of the rising price of cars. If we interpret Mabley's report of a "bad year" to mean that fewer cars are being sold, then by examining the possibilities in Exhibit 1.8 we can see that either demand has fallen (as in panel B of the exhibit) or supply has fallen (as in panel D). In the first case, the price falls, while in the second it rises. Because Mabley reports that the price has risen, the supply curve must have shifted as in panel D. A simultaneous fall in quantity and rise in

---

[8] E. J. Maluka, *Taming and Training Parrots* (T. F. H. Publications Inc., 1981).

price is nothing so dramatic as a failure of the "law of supply and demand"; it is simply evidence of a leftward shift in supply.

## Effect of a Sales Tax

One thing that we know will influence the demand curve for coffee is the imposition of a sales tax paid by demanders. Let's see how such a tax would affect the equilibrium.

Exhibit 1.9 shows the market for lettuce before and after the imposition of a sales tax of 5¢ per head. The curve labeled $D$ is the original demand curve, and the one labeled $D'$ is the demand curve after the tax is imposed. Recall from our discussion of sales taxes in Section 1.1 that $D'$ lies a vertical distance 5¢ below $D$.

Before the imposition of the tax, the market is in equilibrium at point $E$. When the sales tax is imposed, the downward shift in demand moves the equilibrium to point $F$. How does point $F$ compare with point $E$? The first thing to notice is that it is to the left of point $E$. It corresponds to a smaller quantity than point $E$ does. This gives our first conclusion:

Imposing a sales tax reduces the equilibrium quantity.

What about the equilibrium price? We can see immediately from the diagram that point $F$ is lower than point $E$. In other words, imposing a sales tax causes the equilibrium price to fall. We can even say something about how far the equilibrium price will fall. You should be able to see from the graph in Exhibit 1.9 that the vertical drop from point $E$ to point $F$ is smaller than the vertical distance between the old and the new demand curves. In other words, it is a drop of less than 5¢. (The vertical distance from

| EXHIBIT **1.9** | **The Effects of a Sales Tax in the Lettuce Market** |

The graph shows the market for lettuce before and after the imposition of a sales tax of 5¢ per head. The original demand curve ($D$) intersects the supply curve at $E$, which is the point of equilibrium before the tax. When the tax is instituted, the demand curve moves down vertically a distance 5¢, to $D'$. The new equilibrium point is $F$, and the new equilibrium price for lettuce is $P_F$. However, demanders must pay more than $P_F$ for a head of lettuce—they must pay $P_F$ plus 5¢ tax. Thus, to buy a head of lettuce consumers must pay $P_F$ plus the 5¢ sales tax. To find this amount, begin at $F$ and move up a distance 5¢ to $G$. Because $F$ is on the curve $D'$, $G$ must be on the curve $D$. The price to demanders—that is, the price plus the sales tax—is $P_G$.

point $G$ to point $F$ is 5¢, and the vertical distance from point $E$ to point $F$ is clearly less than this.) In other words:

A sales tax of 5¢ per item causes the equilibrium price to fall by some amount less than 5¢ per item.

The exact amount of the fall in price depends on the exact shapes of the supply and demand curves, but it is always somewhere between 0¢ and 5¢.

---

**Exercise 1.8** Draw some diagrams in which either the demand or the supply curve is either unusually steep or unusually flat. In which cases will a 5¢ sales tax cause the price to drop very little? In which cases will the tax cause the price to drop by nearly 5¢?

---

The price $P_F$ shown in Exhibit 1.9 is the new price of lettuce. However, a consumer wishing to acquire a head of lettuce must pay more than $P_F$. He must pay $P_F$ plus 5¢ tax. To find this amount, we must look for a point 5¢ higher than point $F$. Because point $F$ is on the new demand curve $D'$, a point 5¢ higher than $F$ will be on the old demand curve $D$. (This is because the vertical distance between the demand curves is exactly 5¢.) That point has been labeled $G$ in the exhibit. The full amount that the consumer must pay to get a head of lettuce is the corresponding price $P_G$.

Let us summarize: By shifting the equilibrium from point $E$ to point $F$, a sales tax of 5¢ per head lowers the quantity sold. It lowers the price that sellers collect from the original equilibrium price $P_E$ to $P_F$. It raises the amount that demanders pay from $P_E$ to $P_G$.

**Price to demanders**

Price plus sales tax.

In the exhibit, we have called the new price $P_F$ the *price to suppliers*, because $P_F$ is the only "price" that suppliers care about. We have called the amount $P_G$—the new price plus sales tax—the **price to demanders,** because this is the amount that demanders must pay to get a head of lettuce.

## Effect of an Excise Tax

Now that we have analyzed the effect of a sales tax, let us turn to a different problem: the effect of a 5¢ excise tax. This effect is illustrated in panel B of Exhibit 1.10. The sales tax has disappeared now, so the demand curve has returned to its original position. However, as we discovered in Section 1.2, the 5¢ excise tax will shift the supply curve by a vertical distance 5¢. The new supply curve is labeled $S'$ in panel B. With the excise tax, the new market equilibrium is at point $H$. The quantity traded has fallen, and the price has risen by an amount less than 5¢.

---

**Exercise 1.9** How do we know that the price rise is less than 5¢?

---

In everyday language, we say that the suppliers have "passed on" part of the excise tax to consumers through the rise in the market price of lettuce. This is analogous to the situation brought on by the sales tax: In that case, demanders "passed on" a portion of the tax to producers through the fall in the market price of coffee.

Referring again to panel B of Exhibit 1.10, the market price has risen to $P_H$, and that is the price that demanders pay for a head of lettuce. But a supplier who sells a head of lettuce does not get to keep $P_H$—he can keep only $P_H$ minus the 5¢ that goes to the tax collector. In order to find the amount that the supplier gets to keep, we must drop a vertical distance 5¢ below point $H$. Because point $H$ is on the curve $S'$, this vertical drop will land us on the curve $S$ at the point marked $J$. This gives a **price to suppliers** of $P_J$,

**Price to suppliers**

Price minus excise tax.

below the original equilibrium price that was given by point $E$.

EXHIBIT **1.10**    **A Sales Tax versus an Excise Tax**

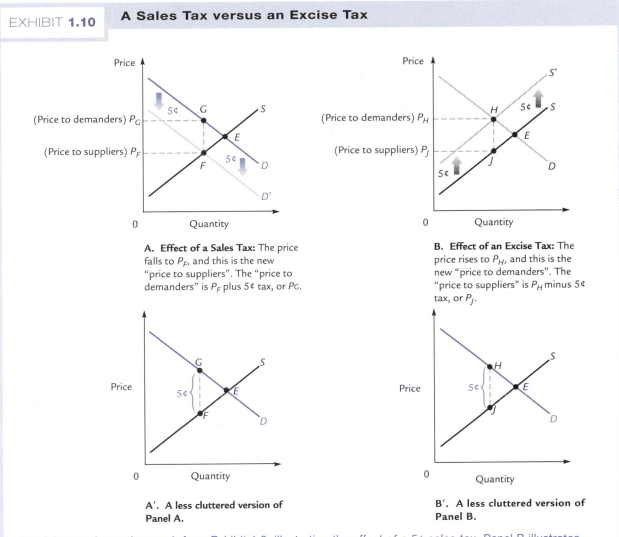

**A. Effect of a Sales Tax:** The price falls to $P_F$, and this is the new "price to suppliers". The "price to demanders" is $P_F$ plus 5¢ tax, or $P_G$.

**B. Effect of an Excise Tax:** The price rises to $P_H$, and this is the new "price to demanders". The "price to suppliers" is $P_H$ minus 5¢ tax, or $P_J$.

**A′. A less cluttered version of Panel A.**

**B′. A less cluttered version of Panel B.**

Panel A reproduces the graph from Exhibit 1.9, illustrating the effect of a 5¢ sales tax. Panel B illustrates the effect of a 5¢ excise tax: The supply curve shifts upward a vertical distance 5¢, leading to a new market equilibrium at point $H$. The corresponding price, $P_H$, is what demanders have to pay; the amount that suppliers get to keep is $P_H$ minus 5¢, which is $P_J$. (Because $H$ is on the curve $S′$, $J$ must be on the curve $S$.)

Panels A′ and B′ are less cluttered versions of panels A and B. In each of these panels, we see two darkened points, one on the original demand curve $D$ and one on the original supply curve $S$, separated by a vertical distance 5¢. There is only one possible location for such a pair of points.

It follows that points $G$ and $F$ in panel A′ (or panel A) are identical with points $H$ and $J$ in panel B′ (or panel B). In other words, the effects of the excise tax are identical to the effects of the sales tax, from the viewpoint of either demanders or suppliers.

## Comparing Two Taxes

Suppose you're a demander of lettuce. Would you rather live in a world with a 5¢ sales tax or a world with a 5¢ excise tax?

If you'd never studied any economics, you might say "I prefer the excise tax, because somebody else has to pay it." But if you've understood Exhibit 1.10, you know that the issue is not that simple. An excise tax *does* affect demanders, by causing the price of lettuce to rise (to $P_H$ in panel B of the exhibit).

So when you're asked which tax you prefer, what you should really seek to do is compare the price $P_G$ in panel A (the price to demanders under a sales tax) with the price $P_H$ in panel B (the price to demanders under an excise tax). If $P_G$ is higher, the sales tax is worse, and if $P_H$ is higher, the excise tax is worse.

Based on what we've said so far, there's no way to decide this question. But with just a bit more analysis, we can discover that in fact $P_G$ and $P_H$ are exactly equal! All we need is three observations:

1.  Point $G$ is on the original demand curve $D$, point $F$ is on the original supply curve $S$, and the vertical distance between them is 5¢. (You can see this in panel A, and you can see it even more clearly in the less cluttered panel A′, which reproduces the relevant parts of panel A.)

2.  Point $H$ is on the original demand curve $D$, point $J$ is on the original supply curve $S$, and the vertical distance between them is 5¢. (You can see this in panel B, and you can see it even more clearly in the less cluttered panel B′, which reproduces the relevant parts of panel B.)

3.  There is only one place to the left of $E$ where the vertical distance between the curves $D$ and $S$ is exactly 5¢. This means that points $G$ and $F$ in panel A′ must occupy exactly the same positions as points $H$ and $J$ in panel B′.

Because points $G$ and $H$ are in exactly the same position, we can conclude that the 5¢ sales tax affects demanders in exactly the same way that the 5¢ excise tax does.

Likewise, because points $F$ and $J$ are in exactly the same position, we can conclude that the 5¢ sales tax affects suppliers in exactly the same way that the 5¢ excise tax does. Neither demanders nor suppliers have any reason to prefer one tax over the other. Economists often summarize this startling conclusion with the slogan:

The economic incidence of a tax is independent of its legal incidence.

In this statement, the **economic incidence** of a tax refers to the distribution of the actual tax burden. The **legal incidence** of the tax is the distribution of the tax burden in legal theory. The sales tax places the legal incidence entirely on demanders, because it is they who are required by law to pay the tax. The excise tax places the legal incidence entirely on suppliers. However, the economic incidence of the sales tax and the economic incidence of the excise tax are the same, because the actual prices paid by suppliers and demanders are the same in both cases.

---

Students sometimes misunderstand the conclusion we have drawn by thinking that the sales tax (or the excise tax) imposes equal burdens on demanders and suppliers. This is not correct. The division of the tax burden depends on the shapes of the supply and demand curves. In Exhibit 1.10, point $F$ might be 4¢ below the original equilibrium ($E$) and point $G$ 1¢ above the original equilibrium; in this case, ⅘ of the tax is being passed on to suppliers and ⅕ is being paid by demanders. With differently shaped curves, the suppliers might be paying ⅕ and the demanders ⅘. What we have argued is that the division of the tax burden will be the same under an excise tax as it is under a sales tax. If suppliers pay ⅘ of the sales tax, they will also pay ⅘ of the excise tax; if they pay ⅕ of the sales tax, they will also pay ⅕ of the excise tax.

---

**Exercise 1.10** Suppose that an excise tax of 2¢ per head of lettuce and a sales tax of 3¢ per head of lettuce were simultaneously imposed. Show that the combined

**Economic incidence**

The division of a tax burden according to who actually pays the tax.

**Legal incidence**

The division of a tax burden according to who is required under the law to pay the tax.

Dangerous
Curve

economic incidence of these taxes will be the same as the economic incidence of either the pure 5¢ sales tax or the pure 5¢ excise tax.

An interesting application involves Social Security taxes. We can view Social Security as a tax on hours worked. "Hours worked" are demanded by firms and supplied by their employees. A Social Security tax that is paid directly by the employees is an excise tax. One that is paid by firms is a sales tax. Whenever Social Security taxes are raised, there is a furor in the legislature about how to divide the legal incidence of the two taxes: Should they be paid entirely by employees, entirely by firms, divided equally, or divided in some other way? The analysis of this section shows that the resolution of this conflict ultimately makes not one bit of difference to anybody.

## Summary

The law of demand says that when the price of a good goes up, the quantity demanded goes down. For any individual or any group of individuals, and for any particular good, such as coffee, we can draw a demand curve. The demand curve shows, for each possible price, how much of the good those individuals or groups will purchase in a specified period of time. Another way to state the law of demand is: Demand curves slope downward.

A change in price leads to a change in quantity demanded, which is the same as a movement along the demand curve. A change in something other than price can lead to a change in demand, which is a shift of the demand curve itself.

One example of a change in something other than price is the imposition of a sales tax, paid directly by consumers to the government. (For purposes of drawing the demand curve, we do not view the tax as a form of price increase. When coffee sells for 50¢ plus 10¢ tax per cup, we say that the price is 50¢, not 60¢.) Consider the effect of a sales tax on coffee. The sales tax makes coffee less desirable at any given (pretax) price and so causes the demand curve to shift downward. In fact, we can calculate that the demand curve will shift downward by a vertical distance equal to the amount of the tax.

The law of supply says that when the price of a good goes up, the quantity supplied goes up. For any individual or any group of individuals, and for any particular good, we can draw a supply curve. The supply curve shows, for each possible price, how much of the good those individuals will provide in a specified period of time. Another way to state the law of supply is: Supply curves slope upward.

A change in price leads to a change in quantity supplied, which is the same as a movement along the supply curve. A change in something other than price can lead to a change in supply, which is a shift of the supply curve itself.

One example of a change in something other than price is the imposition of an excise tax, paid directly by suppliers to the government. Consider the effect of an excise tax on coffee. The excise tax makes providing coffee less desirable at any given price and so causes the supply curve to shift leftward. (The resulting curve is called a lower supply curve, because it has shifted leftward. Geometrically, it lies above and to the left of the original supply curve.) In fact, we can calculate that the supply curve will shift upward by a vertical distance equal to the amount of the tax.

The equilibrium point is the point at which the supply and demand curves intersect. The corresponding equilibrium price is the only price at which the quantity supplied is equal to the quantity demanded. Therefore, it is reasonable to expect that this will be the price prevailing in the market. We make the assumption that this is indeed the case. Later in the book, we will discover that there are many circumstances in which this assumption is well warranted.

Because the point of equilibrium is determined by the supply and demand curves, it can change only if either the supply or the demand curve changes. To see how a change in circumstances affects market prices and quantities, we first decide how it affects the supply and demand curves and then see where the equilibrium point has moved.

As an example, we can examine the effects of a sales tax on coffee. The sales tax causes the demand curve to shift down by the amount of the tax. This leads to a reduction in quantity and a reduction in the market price. The market price is reduced by less than the amount of the tax. To acquire a cup of coffee, a demander must now pay the new market price plus tax; this adds up to a new posttax price to demanders that is higher than the old equilibrium price.

Another example is the effect of an excise tax on coffee. This shifts the supply curve to the left (vertically, it shifts it up by the amount of the tax), leading to a smaller quantity and an increase in the market price. The market price goes up by less than the amount of the tax. When a supplier sells a cup of coffee, he earns the market price minus the amount of the tax; this leaves him with a new posttax price to suppliers that is less than the old equilibrium price.

The sales and excise taxes both reduce quantity, reduce the posttax price to suppliers, and raise the posttax price to demanders. A simple geometric argument shows that the magnitudes of these effects are all the same regardless of whether the tax is legally imposed on demanders or on suppliers. We summarize this by saying that the economic incidence of a tax is independent of its legal incidence. For example, an increase in the Social Security tax will affect both employers and employees in exactly the same way regardless of whether the employers or the employees are required to pay the tax.

# Author Commentary          www.cengage.com/economics/landsburg

The author has written a number of thought-provoking articles relevant to each chapter's topics. These can be found on the text Web site at www.cengage.com/economics/landsburg. Click on the Author Commentary button on the left side of the screen, select your chapter, and then select the articles listed here. Additional articles can be found through an archive search for the name Landsburg on the Slate magazine home page at http://slate.msn.com.

AC1.   Many factors can shift the supply curve. See this article for an example of how home ownership can affect the supply of labor.

AC2.   More political activity will be supplied if politicians receive public financing.

# Review Questions

**R1.** When the price of a good goes up, do we expect to see a change in demand or a change in quantity demanded? Do we expect to see a movement along the demand curve or a shift of the demand curve itself?

**R2.** Give an example of something that might cause a change in the demand for ball-point pens.

**R3.** Which of the following could cause a change in the demand for rice, and which could cause a change in the quantity demanded of rice? (a) A change in the price of wheat. (b) A change in the price of rice.

**R4.** How is the demand curve for cars affected by a $100 sales tax on cars? Explain why the demand curve shifts in this way.

**R5.** How is the supply curve for cars affected by a $100 excise tax on cars? Explain why the supply curve shifts in this way.

**R6.** If the demand for compact discs rises, what happens to the price and quantity of compact discs? Give an example of something that might cause such a rise in demand.

**R7.** If the supply of compact discs rises, what happens to the price and quantity of compact discs? Give an example of something that might cause such a rise in supply.

**R8.** Repeat problems 6 and 7, replacing the word "rises" with the word "falls."

**R9.** Explain what is meant by the phrase, "The economic incidence of a tax is independent of its legal incidence." Explain the geometric argument that leads to this conclusion.

# Numerical Exercises

**N1.** Suppose the demand curve for oranges is given by the equation

$$Q = -200 \bullet P + 1{,}000$$

with quantity ($Q$) measured in oranges per day and price ($P$) measured in dollars per orange. The supply curve is given by

$$Q = 800 \bullet P$$

Compute the equilibrium price and quantity of oranges.

**N2.** Suppose that an excise tax of 50¢ apiece is imposed on oranges. If the original supply and demand curves are as in Exercise N1, what are the equations for the new supply and demand curves? What is the new equilibrium price and quantity of oranges? What is the new posttax price from the supplier's point of view? Illustrate your answer by drawing supply and demand curves.

**N3.** Repeat Exercise N2 for a 50¢ sales tax instead of a 50¢ excise tax.

**N4.** Suppose that an excise tax of 20¢ apiece and a sales tax of 30¢ apiece are imposed simultaneously. Answer again all of the questions in Exercise N2.

# Problem Set

1. **True or False:** If a law were passed requiring all cars sold in the United States to get at least 40 miles per gallon of gasoline, then Americans would surely use less gasoline.

2. **True or False:** The discovery of a new method of birth control that is safer, cheaper, more effective, and easier to use than any other method would reduce the number of unwanted pregnancies.

3. Can you think of some other "goods," such as murder and reckless driving, that are not traded in the traditional economic marketplace but for which people nevertheless have demand curves? For each of these goods, what would it mean for the demand curve to be unusually steep? Unusually flat?

4. Suppose the enrollment at your university unexpectedly declines. **True or False:** Apartment owners in the area will face higher vacancy rates and might raise their rents to compensate.

5. **True or False:** If the demand for lettuce falls, the price will fall, causing the demand to go back up.

6. Nosmo King is an anti-smoking crusader who finds that people who don't recognize him sometimes offer him a cigarette. He always takes the cigarette and throws it away. This happens ten times a year, and Nosmo figures that this way there are ten fewer cigarettes for other people to smoke.

    a. How does Nosmo's policy affect the demand and supply curves for cigarettes?

    b. How does Nosmo's policy affect the equilibrium quantity of cigarettes?

    c. Is Nosmo correct in believing that he reduces the number of cigarettes that other people smoke? Is he correct in believing that he reduces it by ten per year? How do you know?

7. The following item appeared in a major daily newspaper: Does this observation in fact violate the laws of supply and demand?

Though sales are down, prices continue to rise in apparent violation of the law of supply and demand.

8. A socially conscious student has decided to reduce his meat consumption by one pound per week. **True or False:** That way, there will be one more pound of meat each week for somebody else to eat.

9. **True or False:** If we observe that fewer cars are being purchased this year than last year, then we should expect the price of cars to fall.

**10.** In 2003, mad cow disease was first detected in American cattle.

    **a.** What do you expect happened to the demand for American beef?

    **b.** What do you expect happened to the price of American beef?

    **c.** In fact, in the aftermath of the mad cow scare, the price of American beef fell by about 15% and Americans' beef consumption increased. Can you reconcile this observation with the laws of supply and demand? (Hint: The price of beef is determined in a world market, whereas the demand curve is the sum of American demand and foreign demand.)

**11.** The demand and supply for catnip are given by the following tables:

| Demand | | Supply | |
|---|---|---|---|
| Price | Quantity | Price | Quantity |
| $.50/lb | 10 lb | $.50/lb | 4 lb |
| 1.00 | 9 | 1.00 | 5 |
| 1.50 | 8 | 1.50 | 6 |
| 2.00 | 7 | 2.00 | 7 |
| 2.50 | 4 | 2.50 | 10 |
| 3.00 | 3 | 3.00 | 11 |

What quantity is sold in equilibrium, and at what price?

**12.** **a.** Suppose in problem 11 that a sales tax of $2 per pound is imposed on catnip. What is the new market price of catnip? What price do demanders actually pay? What is the new equilibrium quantity?

    **b.** Suppose instead that an excise tax of $2 per pound is imposed on catnip. What is the new market price of catnip? What price do suppliers actually collect? What is the new equilibrium quantity?

    **c.** As a consumer of catnip, would you prefer to live in a world with a sales tax or with an excise tax? How about if you were a supplier of catnip?

**13.** The following diagram shows the supply and demand for cupcakes (with quantity measured in dozens).

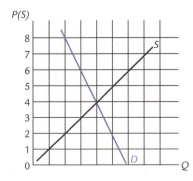

    **a.** Suppose the government imposes a new sales tax of $6 per dozen cupcakes. What will the new price of cupcakes be?

    **b.** Suppose the government imposes a new excise tax of $6 per dozen cupcakes. What will the new price of cupcakes be?

14. In each of the following circumstances, what would happen to the price and the quantity consumed of corn?

   a. The price of fertilizer goes up.

   b. The price of wheat goes up.

   c. An epidemic wipes out half the population.

   d. The wages of industrial workers go up.

15. How would each of the following circumstances affect the price and quantity of beef sold?

   a. The price of chicken falls.

   b. The price of grazing land falls.

   c. There is a report that beef consumption increases longevity.

   d. Average incomes rise.

   e. The price of leather, which is produced from the hides of beef cattle after they are slaughtered, rises.

16. Suppose that the demand curve for lettuce is perfectly vertical. How will an excise tax on lettuce affect the market price?

17. **True or False:** Suppliers' ability to pass on an excise tax to demanders depends on the strength of demand. If the demand curve is very high, a large percentage of the excise tax will be passed on, whereas if demand is very low, suppliers will have to pay most of the tax themselves.

18. At a price of $10,000 apiece, Japanese producers are willing to sell any quantity of compact cars that Americans want to buy. **True or False:** An excise tax on Toyotas sold in the United States would be paid entirely by Americans.

19. Upper Slobbovians smoke 10 million cigarettes per year; so do Lower Slobbovians. To discourage smoking, each country imposes an excise tax of 50¢ per pack. As a result, the price of cigarettes rises by 35¢ per pack in Upper Slobbovia, but by only 15¢ per pack in Lower Slobbovia. **True or False:** The Upper Slobbovian excise tax discourages smoking more effectively (that is, it leads to a bigger decrease in smoking) than the Lower Slobbovian excise tax. *Answer on the assumption that the supply curves for cigarettes are identical in both countries.* Justify your answer.

20. **True or False:** If there are currently 5,000 homeless people in New York City, and if the city builds housing for 1,000 people, then there will be 4,000 homeless people in New York City. (Answer assuming that nobody moves in or out of the city as a result of the new housing project.)

21. Answer the following questions (and fully justify your answers):

   a. If the demand curve for eggs shifts to the right by 100 eggs, in which direction does the price change?

   b. If the supply curve for eggs shifts to the left by 100 eggs, in which direction does the price change?

   c. Which of the two price changes you've just considered is bigger?

22. Suppose an excise tax of 10¢ per apple would cause the price of apples to rise from 20¢ apiece to 23¢ apiece. What would be the effect of a sales tax of 10¢ per apple?

**23.**   Apples currently sell for 20¢ apiece. Label each of the following sentences *certainly true, possibly true*, or *certainly false* and justify your answers.

   **a.**   A 10¢ sales tax would cause the price of apples to fall to 15¢, but a 10¢ excise tax would cause the price of apples to rise to 25¢.

   **b.**   A 10¢ sales tax would cause the price of apples to rise to 25¢, but a 10¢ excise tax would cause the price of apples to fall to 15¢.

   **c.**   A 10¢ sales tax would cause the price of apples to fall to 15¢, and so would a 10¢ excise tax.

   **d.**   A 10¢ sales tax would cause the price of apples to rise to 25¢, and so would a 10¢ excise tax.

   **e.**   A 10¢ sales tax would cause the price of apples to fall to 17¢, and a 10¢ excise tax would cause the price of apples to rise to 27¢.

**24.**   Gasoline currently sells for $3 a gallon. Suppose the government simultaneously institutes a sales tax of 10¢ per gallon and an excise subsidy of 10¢ per gallon. (The "excise subsidy" means that every time you sell a gallon of gasoline, you get a dime from the government.) What is the new price of gasoline? Are demanders helped or hurt by this pair of policies? What about suppliers?

**25.**   The diagram below shows the demand and supply for hamburgers on your college campus.

   **a.**   Suppose your college announces a new plan to improve student life: Any time you buy a hamburger anywhere on campus, you can bring your receipt to the administration building and trade it for a $5 bill. How much does the price of hamburgers change?

   **b.**   Suppose instead that the college announces a different plan: It will pay $5 per hamburger to anyone who sells hamburgers on campus. How much does the price of hamburgers change?

   **c.**   Which plan is better for the students who like to eat hamburgers? Explain your reasoning.

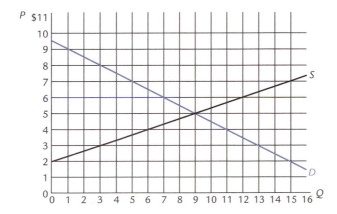

**26.**   Suppose that the government wants to increase Social Security taxes by $1 per hour of work and is undecided between increasing the tax on workers and increasing the tax on employers. According to the last sentence of this chapter, "the resolution of this conflict ultimately makes not one bit of difference to anybody."

a. Explain the meaning of the quoted sentence, in terms that could be understood by a person who had never taken an economics course.

b. Use graphs to explain why the quoted sentence must be true, in terms that could be understood by your fellow students.

27. Eggs currently sell for $10 a dozen. Suppose the government imposes *both* a sales tax of $1 per egg *and* an excise subsidy of $5 per egg ("excise subsidy" means that sellers receive $5 from the government for each egg they sell). Fill in the blanks in this sentence:

"The new price of eggs will be somewhere between _____ and _____."

Justify your answer graphically.

28. It currently costs $500 to install a new shower in your house. A new law requires each new shower to come with digital hot and cold water controls instead of the old-fashioned knobs that everyone uses today. Installing the digital controls costs the manufacturers an extra $200 per shower. Customers value the digital controls at $50 per shower.

a. Illustrate how the demand and supply curves for showers shift as a result of the new law.

b. What happens to the price of a new shower? (Give either the exact new price or a range in which the new price must fall.)

c. Who gains from this new law: Buyers, sellers, both, or neither? Justify your answer.

# Prices, Costs, and the Gains from Trade

Now that we've talked a bit about buying and selling, it's time to pause and ask why people buy and sell things in the first place. Put more succinctly, the question is: Why do people trade?

The answer is twofold. Sometimes people trade because they have different tastes. That ceramic teapot you inherited from your grandmother—the one in the shape of a smiling pig—might seem to you like a piece of junk and to someone else like a charming piece of American folk art. By listing the smiling pig on eBay, you can locate that someone else and make a trade that leaves both of you happier.

We'll have a lot more to say about tastes in Chapters 3 and 4. In this chapter we'll concentrate on the other reason people trade—they have different abilities. No matter how much you like lobster, it makes no sense for you to set your own lobster traps unless you know what you're doing. Better to let someone else set the traps and trade for your lobster.

That much is obvious. But here's a much deeper and far more important point: Even if you are the world's greatest lobster trapper, it *still* might make no sense for you to set your own lobster traps—for the simple reason that you might have something else better to do. Maybe you should be doing your homework, for example—or maybe you're running a profitable business that merits your full attention. In that case, you'll want to trade for your lobster not because of your lobstering abilities but because of your other abilities, whether as a student or as an entrepreneur.

The potential for gains from trade is determined by all of our abilities taken together. The theory of how this all works is called the theory of *comparative advantage,* and it will be the major theme of this chapter. But before proceeding to that theory, we'll take a few pages to solidify some important vocabulary—the vocabulary of *prices* and of *costs.*

## 2.1 Prices

In Chapter 1 we had much to say about prices, on the assumption that everybody knows what prices are. Now it is time for a more precise discussion. In this section we will specify exactly what the word *price* means in microeconomics.

## Absolute versus Relative Prices

Imagine a world without money. In such a world, people would still trade, and it would make perfectly good sense to talk about prices. For example, if you gave your neighbor 2 loaves of bread in exchange for 1 bottle of wine, we would say that the price you paid for the wine was 2 loaves of bread per bottle. At the same time, we would say that your neighbor had purchased 2 loaves of bread at the price of ½ bottle of wine per loaf.

In the real world, we use money to make purchases. Consequently, we usually measure the price of wine in terms of dollars rather than in terms of bread. However, it is still possible to measure the price of wine in terms of bread. If bread sells for $1 per loaf and wine sells for $2 per bottle, it follows that you can exchange 2 loaves of bread for 1 bottle of wine.[1] We can still say that the price of wine is 2 loaves of bread per bottle or that the price of bread is ½ bottle of wine per loaf.

We now have two different meanings for the word *price,* and we must distinguish between them. The number of dollars necessary to purchase a bottle of wine is called the absolute price of the bottle, whereas the number of loaves of bread necessary to purchase a bottle of wine is called the relative price of wine in terms of bread. In general, the absolute price of a good is measured in dollars and the relative price of a good is measured in units of some other good.

Of course, there are many different relative prices of wine. We could measure the relative price of wine in terms of chickens, the relative price of wine in terms of steel, or the relative price of wine in terms of hours of labor.

To illustrate the difference between relative and absolute prices, suppose that the absolute prices of bread and wine in two different years are given by the following table:

|       | 2006      | 2011      |
|-------|-----------|-----------|
| Bread | $1/loaf   | $3/loaf   |
| Wine  | $2/bottle | $6/bottle |

In this example, the absolute price of wine has tripled over a five-year period. However, the relative price of wine in terms of bread has remained fixed at ½ bottle of wine per loaf. This illustrates the important point that changes in absolute prices are not the same thing as changes in relative prices.

In microeconomics, the prices that we study are relative prices. So the price of wine should always be measured in terms of other goods, such as bread. But, we can still use dollars to measure the relative price of wine—provided we assume that the dollar price of bread does not change. We simply must remember that the dollars in which we express the price of wine are really just stand-ins for loaves of bread.

In microeconomics the single word *price* always refers to a relative price.

## Relative Prices When There Are More than Two Goods

If we imagine a world with only two goods, such as bread and wine, the *price of wine* refers to something unambiguous: namely, a certain number of loaves of bread. In the real world, there are many different relative prices for wine: one in terms of bread, one

**Absolute price**

The number of dollars that can be exchanged for a specified quantity of a given good.

**Relative price**

The quantity of some other good that can be exchanged for a specified quantity of a given good.

[1] To do this, you might first have to sell the bread for $2 cash and then use the cash to buy the wine. But the end result is the same as if you had exchanged the bread for the wine directly.

in terms of chickens, and so on. We can also consider the price of wine relative to a basket containing representative quantities of all goods in the economy. Sometimes we will speak of *the* price of wine, in which case we will be referring to the price relative to that representative basket. Often we will measure this relative price in dollars, keeping in mind that the word *dollar* is being used to refer not to a piece of green paper but to a basket of goods.

## Changing Prices

Suppose that in 2010 the absolute price of bread is $1 per loaf, the absolute price of wine is $2 per bottle, and that these are the only two items you consume. Now suppose that because bad weather has damaged the vineyards, you are led to expect that the price of wine will double in 2011. Because we are studying relative prices, this means that in 2011, 1 bottle of wine will trade for 4 loaves of bread rather than for the 2010 price of 2 loaves. The table in Exhibit 2.1 shows only a few of the many different absolute prices at which this could happen.

If in 2011 any of the last four columns of the table describes the prices correctly, then we will be able to say that the price of wine has doubled, just as we predicted it would. All four of these columns fit our prediction equally well. Because microeconomics is concerned only with relative prices, from our point of view there is no real difference between those columns. If you woke up tomorrow morning to discover that all absolute prices (including wages) had doubled (or halved), the world would not really be different in any significant way.

## Relative Price Changes and Inflation

Because relative prices and absolute prices are determined independently of each other, it is always misleading to attribute an absolute price change to a relative price change. It is quite common to hear that there has been inflation (a rise in the level of absolute prices) because of a rise in the price of a particular commodity such as oil, housing, or wine. But we can see from Exhibit 2.1 that a rise in the relative price of wine is equally consistent with either a rise or a fall in the absolute price level.

In fact, when the relative price of wine increases to 4 loaves of bread per bottle, what happens to the relative price of bread? It decreases, from ½ to ¼ bottle of wine per loaf. Any increase in the relative price of wine must be accompanied by a decrease in the relative price of bread.

| EXHIBIT 2.1 | Absolute and Relative Price Changes in a World with Two Goods | | | | |
|---|---|---|---|---|---|

|  | 2010 | 2011(a) | 2011(b) | 2011(c) | 2011(d) |
|---|---|---|---|---|---|
| Bread | $1/loaf | $1/loaf | 50¢/loaf | $5/loaf | 25¢/loaf |
| Wine | $2/bottle | $4/bottle | $2/bottle | $20/bottle | $1/bottle |

The table shows the absolute prices of bread and wine in 2010 and four possibilities for the absolute prices in 2011. In each of the four cases the relative price of a bottle of wine has risen from 2 loaves of bread to 4 loaves of bread. In each case we can correctly assert that "the price of wine has doubled," because in microeconomics the *price* always means the *relative price*.

**Exercise 2.1** Explain why the preceding statement is true.

**Inflation**

An ongoing rise in
the average level of
absolute prices.

**Inflation** is an ongoing rise in the average level of absolute prices. When you hear the commentator on the nightly news program attribute the latest burst of inflation to a rise in the price of gasoline, reflect on what he means. He means that gasoline is now more expensive relative to, say, shoes than it was before. Another way to say the same thing is to state that shoes are now cheaper, relative to gasoline, than they were before. If the rise in the relative price of gasoline causes inflation, why doesn't the fall in the relative price of shoes cause deflation? In fact, relative price changes do not cause absolute price changes—and you now know more than the commentator on the nightly news.

## Some Applications

### The Quality of Oranges

Oranges are grown in Florida and shipped to places like New York. In which state do you suppose that people, on average, eat better oranges?[2]

Most noneconomists guess Florida. But a little understanding of relative prices leads to the surprising conclusion that the answer is New York.

To see why, suppose for simplicity that there are only two kinds of oranges: "good" oranges, which cost $1 in Florida, and "bad" oranges, which cost 50¢ there. When we speak of "bad" oranges, we don't mean to imply that these oranges are entirely undesirable, only that they are not quite so desirable—not so sweet or so juicy—as the "good" ones are.

What, then, is the relative price of a good orange in Florida? The answer is: two bad oranges. The Floridian who chooses to eat a good orange passes up the opportunity to eat two bad ones.

Now let us calculate the relative price of a good orange in New York. The key observation is that it is impossible for a New Yorker to buy just an orange. What he buys, implicitly, is a combination package consisting of an orange and a train ticket to transport that orange to New York. Suppose for illustration that it costs 50¢ to transport an orange to New York. The New Yorker must pay $1.50 for a good orange ($1 for the orange and 50¢ for the transportation) and $1 for a bad orange. The relative price of a good orange in New York is only 1.5 bad oranges. A New Yorker who chooses to eat a good orange passes up the opportunity to eat just 1.5 bad ones.

Who, then, is more likely to select a good orange: the New Yorker facing a relative price of 1.5 bad oranges, or the Floridian facing a relative price of 2 bad oranges? Clearly, the New Yorker, because he faces the lower relative price.

Dangerous
Curve

Of course, the relative price of *oranges* (in terms of, say, apples) is higher in New York than in Florida, and New Yorkers will therefore buy fewer oranges than they would at Florida prices. But once the New Yorker has made the decision to consume an orange, he faces a lower relative price than the Floridian does for choosing a good orange rather than a bad one.

---

[2] The example in this section is adapted from A. Alchian and W. Allen, *Exchange and Production: Theory in Use* (Belmont, CA: Wadsworth, 1969).

Because orange-eating New Yorkers are more likely to choose good oranges than their compatriots in Florida, the average quality of oranges bought in New York is higher than in Florida. Because every orange bought is an orange sold, we can express the same thing by saying that the average quality of oranges sold is higher in New York than in Florida: New York supermarkets carry better oranges, on average, than Florida supermarkets do.

## 2.2 Costs, Efficiency, and Gains from Trade

In the preceding section we discussed the concept of *price*. In this section we will discuss the related concept of *cost*. Once we understand what costs are, we will be able to see how everyone can benefit when activities are carried out at the lowest possible cost. This will provide us with a powerful example of the gains from trade.

### Costs and Efficiency

When you decide to spend an evening at the opera, you must forgo a number of other things. First, you pay a price, say $50, for the ticket. Of course, the money itself is valuable only insofar as you could have used it to buy something else. That "something else"—perhaps ten movie tickets or five pizzas—represents some of the cost of going to the opera.

The ticket price is only part of the cost, because your evening at the opera entails many other sacrifices as well. There is the gasoline that you use to drive to the opera. There is also the time spent actually attending the performance. That time could have been spent doing something else, and the value of that something else is also part of the cost of going to the opera.

In summary, a cost is a forgone opportunity. The cost of engaging in an activity is the totality of all the opportunities that the activity requires you to forgo.

**Cost**
A forgone opportunity.

You may have heard the term *opportunity cost* used to describe such costs as the time sacrificed in attending the opera. This term is quite misleading because it implies that an "opportunity cost" is one of several types of cost. In reality, *every cost is an opportunity cost.* The dollars that you pay for the opera ticket are valuable only insofar as they represent forgone opportunities to purchase other goods. They are of exactly the same nature as the costs represented by your time and your gasoline—forgone opportunities all.

In calculating costs, it is important not to double-count. The time spent at the opera could have been used to go to the movies or to study for an exam, but not both. Therefore, it would not be correct to count both the forgone movie and the forgone studying as costs. The only activities that should be counted as costs are those you would have actually engaged in if you had not gone to the opera.

Dangerous
Curve

How much does it cost your college to maintain a football team? The most obvious costs are those such as coaches' salaries and transportation to games. But other, less obvious costs can be equally important. What, for example, is the cost of using the football stadium? You might think it is zero if the college owns the football stadium, but this overlooks the forgone opportunity to put that land to other uses. If a developer who wants to build a shopping center would be willing to pay $500,000 for the land, then that forgone $500,000 is part of the cost of having a team.

It is sometimes argued that we should pay higher salaries to our elected officials in order to ensure that the most talented and creative individuals run for office. This argument also overlooks an opportunity cost: If a brilliant corporate executive becomes a brilliant U.S. senator, then the nation must make do with one less brilliant corporate executive. It is not obvious that a genius can do more good as 1 of 100 U.S. senators than as the chairman of the board of General Electric. Perhaps we should *lower* senate salaries precisely in order to avoid the cost of attracting talented people into politics!

## Example: The Electrician and the Carpenter

Imagine an electrician and a carpenter, each of whom wants his house rewired and his den paneled. As shown in Table A of Exhibit 2.2, the electrician requires 10 hours to rewire his house and 15 hours to panel his den. The carpenter knows how to do his own rewiring, but because he is less skilled at it than the electrician, it takes him 20 hours instead of 10. And what about paneling? The electrician can panel his den in 15 hours, so you might expect a professional carpenter to be able to do it in a shorter time. But we forgot to tell you that this particular carpenter is a tad on the doltish side, and has some paralysis in his left arm to boot. As a result, paneling his den takes him 18 hours to complete. All of these numbers are summarized in Table A of Exhibit 2.2.

Because the electrician can both rewire and panel faster than the carpenter can, you might think that it is correct to say that he can perform both tasks at a lower cost than the carpenter can. But this is definitely not true. To see why not, we have to remember that costs are defined in terms of forgone opportunities. The electrician needs 10 hours to rewire his house. Alternatively, he could use that same 10 hours to complete $\frac{2}{3}$ of a 15-hour paneling job. That $\frac{2}{3}$ of a paneling job is the cost of his rewiring. Similarly, a paneling job costs him $\frac{3}{2}$ rewirings.

We can do the same kind of calculations for the carpenter. The results are displayed in Table B of Exhibit 2.2.

---

**Exercise 2.2** Explain how we got the entries in the second column of Table B.

---

The electrician can produce a rewiring job more cheaply than the carpenter can because he rewires a house at a cost of $\frac{2}{3}$ of a paneling job, whereas the carpenter rewires at a cost of $\frac{10}{9}$ paneling jobs. We express this by saying that the electrician has a **comparative advantage** at rewiring. This simply means that he can do the job at a lower cost than the carpenter can. Another way to say the same thing is that the electrician is **more efficient** at rewiring than the carpenter is.

It is a bit more surprising, but equally true, that the carpenter is more efficient than the electrician at paneling. This statement may surprise you, since the carpenter takes 18 hours to do a paneling job that the electrician can do in 15 hours. Nevertheless, it is true. The cost to the carpenter of performing a paneling job is only $\frac{9}{10}$ of a rewiring job, whereas the cost to the electrician of performing a paneling job is $\frac{3}{2}$ rewiring jobs. This follows from our definition of cost as a forgone opportunity. The cost of paneling is not the number of hours devoted to the job, but the use to which those hours could have been put. The carpenter is therefore a more efficient paneler than the electrician. He has a comparative advantage at paneling.

**Comparative advantage**

The ability to perform a given task at a lower cost.

**More efficient**

Able to perform a given task at a lower cost; having a comparative advantage.

## EXHIBIT 2.2  The Electrician and the Carpenter

| | Table A | | | Table B | |
| | Electrician | Carpenter | | Electrician | Carpenter |
|---|---|---|---|---|---|
| Rewiring | 10 hours | 20 hours | Rewiring | 2/3 paneling | 10/9 panelings |
| Paneling | 15 hours | 18 hours | Paneling | 3/2 rewirings | 9/10 rewiring |

Table A shows the amount of time needed for the electrician and the carpenter to rewire and to panel. Notice that the electrician can complete either job in less time than the carpenter can. We express this by saying that the electrician has an absolute advantage at each task.

Table B shows the costs of rewiring and paneling jobs performed by each individual. The costs are measured in terms of forgone opportunities; thus the cost of a rewiring job must be measured in terms of paneling jobs and vice versa. All of the information in Table B can be derived from the information in Table A.

Notice that the electrician can rewire at a lower cost than the carpenter, but that the carpenter can panel at a lower cost than the electrician. We express this by saying that the electrician has a comparative advantage at rewiring, whereas the carpenter has a comparative advantage at paneling.

Suppose that each individual wants his house rewired and his den paneled. Table C below shows the total amount of time that each will have to work in order to accomplish both jobs. In the first column we assume that each does all of the work on his own house. For example, the electrician spends 10 hours rewiring and 15 hours paneling, for a total of 25 hours. In the second column, we assume that each specializes in the area of his comparative advantage: The electrician rewires both houses and the carpenter panels both dens.

It is apparent from Table C that trade makes both parties better off. In particular, the electrician can gain from trade with the carpenter, despite his absolute advantages in both areas. This illustrates the general fact that everyone can be made better off whenever each concentrates in his area of comparative advantage and then trades for the goods he wants to have.

| Table C | | |
| | Without Trade | With Trade |
|---|---|---|
| Electrician | 25 hours | 20 hours |
| Carpenter | 38 hours | 36 hours |

Students often make statements like "The electrician is more efficient at rewiring than he is at paneling," or "The electrician has a comparative advantage at rewiring over paneling." Such statements are not only wrong, they are without meaning. The correct statements are "The electrician is more efficient at rewiring than the carpenter is, and less efficient at paneling than the carpenter is," and "The electrician has a comparative advantage over the carpenter at rewiring, whereas the carpenter has a comparative advantage over the electrician at paneling." The comparative in comparative advantage refers to a comparison of two individuals performing the same task and never to a comparison of different tasks performed by the same individual.

Dangerous Curve

## Specialization and the Gains from Trade

We have chosen to define *efficiency* in such a way that the most efficient producer of a good is the one who produces it at the lowest cost, where costs are defined in terms of forgone opportunities. According to this definition, the carpenter is more efficient at paneling than the electrician is. Perhaps this definition strikes you as strange. Why have we chosen it? The answer is that it is the only definition of efficiency that makes the following statement true:

Everyone in society can be made better off if each specializes in the area where he is most efficient, and then trades for the goods he wants to have.

We can illustrate this with the example of the electrician and the carpenter. Suppose that each of these individuals elects to make his own home improvements. Then the electrician spends 10 hours rewiring and 15 hours paneling, for a total of 25 hours. At the same time, the carpenter spends 20hours and 18 hours for a total of 38 hours.

Suppose, on the other hand, that each specializes in his area of comparative advantage and that they trade services. The electrician specializes in rewiring and does both his own house and the carpenter's. These two 10-hour jobs take him 20 hours. In exchange for this, the carpenter panels both dens. These two 18-hour jobs take him 36 hours. All of this is summarized in Table C of Exhibit 2.2.

As you can see, everybody in this society is better off when each exploits his comparative advantage by specializing in the area in which he is the more efficient producer.

When you first looked at Table A in Exhibit 2.2, you might have thought that the electrician could not possibly have anything to gain by trading with the carpenter. You might have thought that this was so because the electrician appeared to be better than the carpenter at everything. Now you know that the carpenter is actually "better" than the electrician at paneling, in the sense that he panels at a lower cost than the electrician does, giving him a comparative advantage. This is the reason that trade can be a profitable activity for both.

An individual's preferences are not sufficient (or even necessarily relevant) for determining what he should produce. The electrician wants both rewiring and paneling, but he is better off when he produces two rewirings than when he produces exactly what he wants. The same is true of groups of individuals. The people of Finland might collectively love grapefruit, but it would not be intelligent for Finland to specialize in domestic grapefruit production. The Finns can have more grapefruit by specializing in the areas of their comparative advantage (in this case, timber and timber products) and then trading for grapefruit and the other commodities they wish to consume.

The benefits of specialization and trade account for most of the material wealth that you see in the world. Wherever you go in the United States, you will find small towns of 500 or 2,000 or 3,000 people. The residents of these towns consume fresh fruit and power tools and air-conditioning and comic books and Hollywood movies and catcher's mitts and artwork. None of the towns produces such a wide variety of goods on its own. Typically, the residents of the town specialize in a few areas of comparative advantage and acquire the goods they want to have by trading with people in other towns who have specialized in other areas. If a town of 2,000 people attempted to produce its own fresh fruit and power tools and Hollywood movies, very little of anything would be accomplished. The difference between the standard of living in that imaginary isolated town and the standards of living actually observed in the United States is due entirely to the principle of comparative advantage. The enormous magnitude of that difference is almost impossible to contemplate.

## Example: Outsourcing

*The New York Times* recently carried an editorial by U.S. Senator Charles Schumer and former Assistant Treasury Secretary Paul Craig Roberts. Schumer and Roberts argued that the principle of comparative advantage is no longer relevant in the modern world and offered two examples.

First, a major New York securities firm plans to replace its team of 800 American software engineers, each earning about $150,000 a year, with an equally competent team in India earning an average of over $20,000. (Hiring foreign professionals to provide services formerly provided by Americans is sometimes called outsourcing.)

Second, the number of radiologists in the United States is expected to decline significantly because M.R.I. data can be sent over the Internet to Asian radiologists capable of diagnosing the problem at a small fraction of the cost.

Schumer and Roberts view these developments as bad. But if Senator Schumer had talked to those of his constituents who purchase software and pay doctors' bills, he might have heard a different viewpoint. Indeed, Senator Schumer appears to be the only U.S. Senator in modern history ever to have complained about a dramatic reduction in medical costs.

If foreign professionals of equal quality work more cheaply than American professionals, it's because the foreign professionals have lower opportunity costs. When a New York securities firm hires Indian software engineers, it releases American engineers to do something more valuable—instead of providing a service that is available elsewhere for $20,000, they can now provide other services. Similarly, ambitious and talented Americans who would otherwise have become radiologists will now find other specialties (both in and out of medicine), providing new services to American consumers.

## Why People Trade

People trade for two reasons, either one of which would be sufficient for trade to take place. They trade because they have different tastes and because they have different abilities.

Imagine a world with only two goods: apples and gasoline. In this imaginary world, each individual receives 5 apples and 5 gallons of gasoline as a gift from heaven once a week. In that world everyone has equal abilities in production—we each "produce" 5 apples and 5 gallons of gasoline per week and can do nothing to increase or decrease that production—but we might still trade with one another because of differences in tastes. If you preferred to stay home every night eating apples while your friend preferred to spend his evenings driving through the countryside, you would have an excellent opportunity for a mutually beneficial exchange.

At the other extreme, imagine a world where everyone has the same preferences regarding apples and gasoline, but some people only know how to grow apples while others only know how to manufacture gasoline. The apple growers will grow apples, the gasoline manufacturers will make gasoline, and then they will trade so that each has a mix of apples and gasoline that is preferable to what the individual could produce for himself.

In each of these imaginary worlds, trade takes place for a different reason. People with identical abilities might trade because of differing tastes, and people with identical tastes might trade because of differing abilities. In a world in which both tastes and abilities differ, people will trade for both reasons.

### It Pays To Be Different

One moral to be drawn from this discussion is that to benefit from trade, *it pays to be different* from everyone else. If you and your neighbor have identical collections of baseball cards, and if you both have all the same favorite players, then you might as well not have a neighbor, at least for the purpose of improving your baseball card collection.

But if either your collection (that is, your *ability* to provide certain baseball cards) or your *taste* is unusual in any way, you and your neighbor should probably talk.

The more different you are, the more you have to gain. If you are the only person in your neighborhood who likes liver, you'll be able to buy it at a very low price and be happy. If you are the only one who hates liver, your neighbors' preferences will leave more prime rib for you. If you are the only person in your neighborhood who hates gardening, you'll be able to hire gardeners at a very low price; if you are the only one who loves it, you can be very happy in the gardening business. These benefits result from differences in tastes; the carpenter and the electrician benefited from differences in abilities. In trading, any difference is an opportunity for mutual gain.

This observation has an important consequence for international trade. All countries benefit from trade, but which countries benefit the most? The answer is: those countries whose citizens are most different from the rest of the world. By and large, these are the small countries. For purely numerical reasons, the average citizen of the United States is not too different from the average North American (counting U.S. and Canadian citizens as North Americans). There are just so many more people south of the U.S.–Canadian border that they dominate the continent-wide average. But the average Canadian may differ substantially, in both tastes and abilities, from the average North American. Because it pays to be different, the Canadians gain more from trade between the two countries.

## Trade Without Differences

The great nineteenth-century economist David Ricardo was the first to recognize the importance of comparative advantage and to analyze its consequences for mutually beneficial trade. Earlier, the great eighteenth-century economist Adam Smith had described another, completely different, way in which trade can benefit all parties.

Sometimes goods can be produced more effectively when they are produced in large quantities. You might be able to bake two dozen cupcakes in less than twice the time that it takes you to produce just one dozen. If you bake alone, you spend an hour producing a dozen cupcakes and another hour making frosting. If you trade with your neighbor, you can spend 1½ hours making two dozen cupcakes while your neighbor spends 1½ hours making a double recipe of frosting. After the appropriate trade, you each have a dozen frosted cupcakes and you have each worked only 1½ hours instead of 2 hours.

This gain from trade is quite different from the others we have discussed in this chapter, because it does not arise from any differences in tastes or abilities. Instead, it is a consequence of the increased productivity that can result when goods are produced in greater quantities. Trade enables each partner to expand the scale of his activities and take advantage of this phenomenon.

## What's Next

Despite the example of the cupcakes, you should not lose sight of our main theme: Trading is beneficial whenever people differ in their abilities or in their tastes. In this chapter we have explored the meaning of *differing abilities* and have made the term more precise through the concept of comparative advantage. We have seen quite explicitly how individuals with different comparative advantages can gain from trade. Our next task is to make a thorough study of tastes and to incorporate them into our study of market behavior. That will be the subject of Chapter 3.

# Summary

In microeconomics, the word *price* is always used to refer to the *relative price* of a good. Thus, the price of a potato is the quantity of some other good or collection of goods that can be exchanged for a potato. The relative price must be distinguished from the *absolute price,* which measures the number of dollars that can be exchanged for a potato. Nevertheless, we often measure relative prices in "dollars." In doing so, we must remember that these dollars are not pieces of green paper but simply a convenient shorthand for referring to collections of other goods in the economy.

The price of a good or of an activity is typically only one component of the cost of acquiring that good or participating in that activity. The full cost of participation is the totality of all alternative opportunities that must be forgone. In calculating this cost, we must be careful to count only those alternatives that we would have actually pursued.

An individual is said to perform a task more efficiently than another if he performs it at a lower cost. An individual is said to have a comparative advantage at a task if he performs it more efficiently than anyone else. In determining who is the most efficient producer of a good, we must keep in mind that all costs are forgone opportunities. Thus, we do not count, for example, time and raw materials, but instead the alternative uses of that time and those raw materials.

Everyone benefits when each person specializes in his area of comparative advantage and then engages in trade. Therefore, an individual's preferences need not enter into his decisions about what to produce.

Differences in ability (in other words, differences in comparative advantage) are one reason for trade. Another reason is differences in taste, which will be examined in Chapter 3.

# Author Commentary    www.cengage.com/economics/landsburg

**AC1.** Read this article for more information on the gains from trade.

# Review Questions

**R1.** Suppose that in 2007 the absolute price of bread is $2 per loaf and the absolute price of wine is $6 per bottle. In 2008, the absolute price of bread is $4 per loaf and the absolute price of wine is $8 per bottle. Has the relative price of bread risen or fallen? What about the relative price of wine?

**R2.** List some of the costs of going to college.

**R3.** Suppose it takes you 2 hours to paint a picture and 8 hours to write a song; it takes your roommate 4 hours to paint a picture and 100 hours to write a song.

Which of the following statements are true, which are false, and which are meaningless:

**a.** You have a comparative advantage over your roommate at painting pictures.

**b.** You have a comparative advantage at painting pictures over writing songs.

**c.** Your roommate has a comparative advantage over you at writing songs.

**d.** If you and your roommate each want to have one original picture to hang on your wall and one original song to call your own, you can both gain from trade.

**e.** It is more efficient for your roommate instead of you to write the songs.

**R4.** Why might a person who loves potatoes and hates squash nevertheless choose to grow squash in his garden?

**R5.** Why do people trade?

# Numerical Exercises

**N1.** Suppose that the amount of time required for the electrician or the carpenter to complete a job of rewiring or paneling is given by the following table:

|  | Rewiring | Paneling |
|---|---|---|
| Electrician | 5 hours | 10 hours |
| Carpenter | 10 hours | 15 hours |

**a.** Compute the costs of performing each of these tasks for each individual.

**b.** Who has the comparative advantage at rewiring? At paneling?

**c.** Suppose that the more efficient rewirer does all of the rewiring and the more efficient paneler does all of the paneling. Does this trade benefit the electrician? Does it benefit the carpenter?

**d.** Suppose that a different trade is worked out whereby the electrician rewires the carpenter's entire house in exchange for the carpenter's doing $3/5$ of the electrician's paneling job. Now how much time does each spend working? Do they each benefit?

*Note:* This problem illustrates the fact that when different parties have different comparative advantages, there is always some trade that will benefit both. However, not *any* trade will benefit both; the trade must take place at an appropriate relative price.

# Problem Set

**1.** In 2010, the absolute price of tea was $12 a pound and the absolute price of a Honda Civic was $16,000. In 2011, the absolute price of tea rose to $15 per pound and the absolute price of a Honda Civic rose to $24,000. Did the relative price of tea in terms of Civics increase or decrease? What about the relative price of Civics in terms of tea?

2. If somebody tells you that all of the relative prices in the economy have increased over the past year, what can you conclude?

3. Suppose that there is a fall in the cost of shipping goods by railroad. What will happen to the difference between the average quality of oranges sold in Florida and the average quality of oranges sold in New York?

4. Where would you expect to find a larger percentage of childless couples: at a cheap movie or at an expensive show? (*Hint:* Childless couples don't have to hire babysitters.)

5. In the 1920s, it was illegal to manufacture or sell whiskey in the United States. Nevertheless, much whiskey was produced and sold, though at higher prices that reflected the cost of evading law enforcement. **True or False:** The average quality of whiskey sold in the United States was probably higher in the 1920s.

6. **True or False:** If Americans can produce both agricultural and industrial products with less effort and fewer raw materials than Mexicans can, then there can be no advantage to the United States in trading with Mexico.

7. Suppose that an acre of land in Iowa can yield either 50 bushels of wheat or 100 bushels of corn, while an acre of land in Oklahoma can yield either 20 bushels of wheat or 30 bushels of corn.
   a. What is the cost of growing 200 bushels of wheat in Iowa? What is the cost of growing 200 bushels of wheat in Oklahoma? Which state has a comparative advantage in growing wheat?
   b. Which state has a comparative advantage in growing corn?
   c. Suppose that the residents of Iowa eat 200 bushels of wheat and 360 bushels of corn, and that the residents of Oklahoma also eat 200 bushels of wheat and 360 bushels of corn. If there is no trade between the states, how many acres must each state devote to agriculture?
   d. In part c, suppose that the states begin to trade, with each specializing in its area of comparative advantage. How many acres of Iowa farmland are freed up for other uses? How many acres of Oklahoma farmland?

8. Dell computers contain hard drives made by other manufacturers. **True or False:** If Dell made its own hard drives, Dell computers would be cheaper.

9. **True or False:** If George types 50 words per minute and Mary types 120, then it certainly makes more sense for Mary to be employed as a secretary than for George to be.

10. **True or False:** A farmer with a lot of children will find it less costly to harvest his crops than a farmer with no children, since he can put his children to work without pay.

11. **True or False:** It would be a good thing if only those students with the most talent for medicine were allowed to become doctors. (Assume that there are enough such students so that we could still have the same number of doctors that we have today.)

12. **True or False:** A small country with widespread starvation would be well advised to concentrate its resources in the production of food rather than in the production of decorative jewelry.

13. **True or False:** A country that is poor in natural resources and has an unskilled population may be unable to trade profitably because it has no comparative advantage at anything.

14. Suppose that the Winkies and the Munchkins are initially identical in terms of their abilities to produce a wide variety of goods, including food and automobiles. One day, the Munchkins discover a new, cheaper way to make automobiles. **True or False:** This puts the Winkies at a comparative disadvantage and therefore makes them worse off.

15. Explain exactly where the following argument goes wrong: The Anderson-Little clothing store buys clothes directly from the manufacturers, whereas Brand X clothing stores buy from middlemen. In each case, there are the same costs of producing, shipping, and marketing the clothes, but with Brand X's system there is also the additional cost of supporting the middlemen. Therefore, clothes will be cheaper at Anderson-Little.

16. **True or False:** If everyone had the same income, substandard housing would disappear.

# The Behavior of Consumers

Here's a test of your prediction skills: A man goes into a restaurant. What does he order?

If your answer is "not enough information," you've passed the test. In fact, you're missing two different kinds of information here. First, you don't know what the man likes to eat. Second, you don't know what's available on the menu. To make a prediction, you'd need to know something about both the man's *preferences* and his *opportunities.*

Here's a harder test: A shopper goes into a grocery store. What does she buy? This is even harder than the man-in-the-restaurant question, because he's choosing one item off a menu, whereas the shopper is choosing an entire *basket* of items. But the same principle applies: To make predictions, you must know something both about preferences (how many lamb chops would the shopper *be willing* to sacrifice in order to have a cherry pie?) and opportunities (how many would the shopper *have to* sacrifice in order to have a cherry pie?). The "opportunities" question breaks down into two subquestions: What are the prices on the items, and how much income does the shopper have?

In Section 3.1, we'll think about preferences, and in Section 3.2 we'll think about opportunities. Once we put all that together, we can start making predictions.

## 3.1 Tastes

The Latin proverb "*De gustibus non est disputandum*" can be translated as "There's no accounting for tastes." Some people like antique wooden furniture; others prefer brass. You are likely to get a variety of answers if you ask different friends whether they would prefer to live in a world without Bach or in a world without clean sheets.

Economists accept the wisdom of the proverb and make no attempt to account for tastes. Why people prefer the things that they do is an interesting topic, but it is not one that we will explore. We take people's tastes as given and see what can be said about them.

### Indifference Curves

Imagine a consumer named Beth who lives in a world with only two goods: eggs and root beer. You might imagine asking Beth which of these two goods she likes better. But although this question sounds sensible at first, it really isn't—for several reasons. First, the answer is likely to depend on the quantities of eggs and root beer being compared. Second, the answer might depend on how many eggs and root beers she's already got in her refrigerator. The question is open to several interpretations: Are we asking which good Beth would least like to do without altogether, or are we asking which she would rather receive for her birthday?

Here is a better question: We can ask Beth whether she'd rather consume a basket of 3 eggs and 5 root beers or a basket with 4 eggs and 2 root beers. In principle, we could discover the answer by taking away all of Beth's possessions and then offering her a choice between the two baskets. A question makes sense when some (possibly imaginary) experiment is capable of revealing the answer.

Of course, there are many possible baskets besides the ones we've described. We can display all of them simultaneously on a graph, as in Exhibit 3.1. Each point on that graph represents a basket containing a certain number of eggs and a certain number of root beers. For example, point *A* represents a basket with 3 eggs and 5 root beers—the first of the 2 baskets we offered to Beth.

---

**Exercise 3.1** Describe the baskets represented by points *B, C,* and *D.* Which represents the second basket of our imaginary experiment?

---

**Goods**

Items of which the consumer would prefer to have more rather than less.

What can we say about Beth's preferences among these baskets? Compare basket *A* to basket *B,* for example. Which would she prefer to own? Basket *B* contains more eggs than basket *A* (4 units instead of 3) and also more root beers (7 instead of 5). *If we assume that eggs and root beer are both* **goods**—items that Beth would prefer to have more of whenever she can—then the choice is unambiguous. Basket *B* is better than basket *A.*

---

EXHIBIT **3.1**    **Basket of Goods**

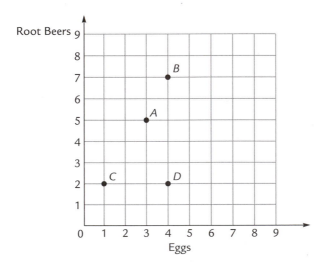

Each point on the graph represents a basket containing a certain number of eggs and a certain number of root beers. For example, point *A* corresponds to 3 eggs and 5 root beers.

**Exercise 3.2** Which is preferable, basket *A* or basket *C*? How do you know?

When it comes to comparing basket *A* with basket *D,* the choice is less clear. Basket *D* has more eggs (4 units versus 3) but less root beer (2 versus 5). Which will Beth prefer? At this point we cannot possibly say. She might like *A* better than *D,* or *D* better than *A.* It is also possible (though not necessary or even likely) that she would happen to like them both equally.

Now consider this question: Where should we look to find the baskets that Beth likes exactly as much as *A*? They can't be to the "northeast" of *A* (like *B*) because the baskets there are all preferred to *A.* They can't be to the "southwest" of *A* (like *C*) because *A* is preferred to all of those baskets. They must all be to either the "northwest" or the "southeast" of *A* (like *D*). This doesn't mean that *D* is necessarily one of them, just that they lie in the same general direction from *A* that *D* does.

If we draw in a few of the baskets that Beth likes just as well as she likes *A,* they might look like the points shown in panel A of Exhibit 3.2. Because each of these baskets is *exactly as good* as *A,* they must all be *exactly as good* as each other. This means that each one must lie either to the northwest or to the southeast of each other one, which accounts for the downward slope that is apparent in the picture.

The baskets shown in panel A of Exhibit 3.2 are only a few of those that Beth likes just as well as *A.* There are many other such baskets as well. The collection of all such

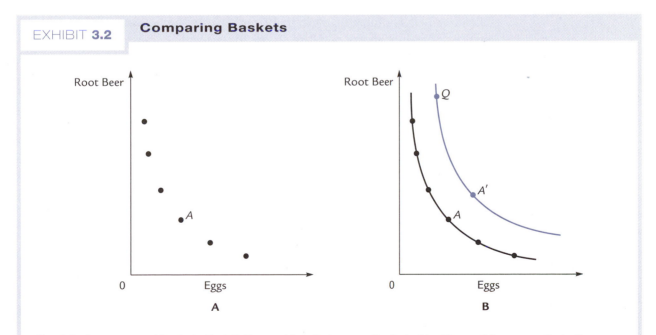

| EXHIBIT **3.2** | **Comparing Baskets** |

Panel A shows several baskets that Beth considers to be equally desirable. None of these can lie to the northeast or southwest of any other one, because if it did, one would be clearly preferable to the other. As a result, they all lie to the northwest and southeast of each other, accounting for the downward slope.

The black indifference curve in panel B includes the points from panel A, as well as all of the other baskets that Beth considers equally as desirable as these. The colored indifference curve shows a different set of baskets, all of which are equally as desirable as each other. Knowledge of Beth's indifference curves allows us to make inferences about her preferences that would otherwise be impossible. For example, we know that Beth likes *Q* and *A′* equally because they are on the same indifference curve and that *A′* is preferable to *A* because it contains more of everything. We may infer that Beth prefers *Q* to *A.*

baskets forms a curve, shown in black in panel B of the exhibit. From our discussion in the preceding paragraph, we know that the curve will be downward sloping. Because Beth is indifferent between any two points on this curve, it is called an indifference curve.

**Indifference curve**

A collection of baskets, all of which the consumer considers equally desirable.

There is nothing special about basket *A*. We could as easily have begun with a different basket, such as *A′* in panel B of Exhibit 3.2. That panel depicts both the indifference curve through *A* (in black) and the indifference curve through *A′* (in color).

The indifference curves do not have to have the same shape, but they do both have to slope downward.

If we know a consumer's indifference curves, we can make inferences that would not be possible otherwise. Try comparing basket *A* to basket *Q* in panel B of Exhibit 3.2. Basket *A* has more eggs than basket *Q*, but basket *Q* has more root beer than basket *A*. Without more information, we cannot say which one Beth will prefer. But the indifference curves provide that additional information. We know that Beth likes *Q* and *A′* equally, because they are on the same indifference curve. We know that she likes *A′* better than she likes *A*, because it is to the northeast of *A* and therefore contains more of everything than *A* does. We may infer that she likes *Q* better than she likes *A*.

In general, a basket is preferable to another precisely when it is on a higher indifference curve, where *higher* means "above and to the right."

## Relationships among Indifference Curves

Of course, Beth has more than two indifference curves. Indeed, we can draw an indifference curve through any point we choose to start with. Because of this, *the indifference curves fill the entire plane.* (More precisely, they fill the entire quadrant of the plane in which both coordinates are positive.)

An important feature of indifference curves is that *indifference curves never cross.* To understand why this must be true, imagine a consumer with two indifference curves that cross, as in Exhibit 3.3.

From the fact that baskets *P* and *Q* are on the same (black) indifference curve, we know that the consumer likes these baskets equally well. From the fact that baskets *R* and *Q* are on the same (brown) indifference curve, we know that he also likes these equally well. Putting these facts together, we conclude that he likes *P* and *R* equally well. But this is impossible, because *R* is to the northeast of *P* and therefore contains more of both goods. In other words, if indifference curves cross, impossible things will happen. We conclude that indifference curves don't cross.

## Marginal Values

We have said that indifference curves slope downward, but we haven't yet said anything about how steep the slope is. In this section, we will interpret the slope of the indifference curve. The first step is to understand how indifference curves can tell us whether certain trades are desirable.

## Desirable and Undesirable Trades

Suppose you have 7 eggs and 2 root beers; this basket is represented by point *C* in Exhibit 3.4. Your friend Jeremy offers to trade you 2 root beers for an egg. If you accept his offer, you'll end up at point *P*. (That is, you'll give Jeremy an egg, leaving you with 6 eggs, and he'll give you 2 root beers, leaving you with 4 root beers. Point *P* illustrates your new basket.)

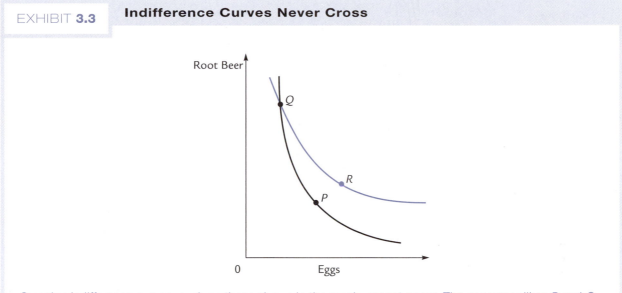

**EXHIBIT 3.3**    **Indifference Curves Never Cross**

Crossing indifference curves, such as those shown in the graph, cannot occur. The consumer likes P and Q equally well because they are both on the same (black) indifference curve. He also likes R and Q equally well because they are both on the same (colored) indifference curve. We may infer that he likes P and R equally well, which we know to be false (in fact, R is preferred to P). Thus, the graph cannot be correct.

Will you accept Jeremy's offer? It depends on your preferences. Suppose, for example, that you have the indifference curve shown in Exhibit 3.4. Then you will *not* accept Jeremy's offer, because—according to your preferences—point P is inferior to point C.

In other words, when Jeremy says, "I'll give you 2 root beers for an egg," you'll say, "No thanks; I'd rather keep the egg." In ordinary language, we'd say that your seventh egg is worth more to you than 2 root beers.

Suppose Jeremy tries again, by offering you 4 root beers for an egg instead of 2 root beers. Now do you accept the trade? If you do, you'll end up at point R, above your original indifference curve. This trade is desirable; it makes you happier; you got more for your egg than you thought it was worth.

**Exercise 3.3** Explain why Jeremy's new offer brings you to point R.

Finally, what if Jeremy had offered you exactly 3 root beers for your seventh egg? This brings you to point Q, which is exactly as desirable as your original point C. That is, trading an egg for 3 root beers makes you neither better nor worse off than you were to begin with. This makes it reasonable to say that your seventh egg is *worth* exactly 3 root beers (to you). We say that (to you) the **marginal value** of an egg is 3 root beers.

In general, the marginal value that you place on good $X$ (in terms of good $Y$) is defined to be the number of $Y$s for which you'd be just willing to trade one $X$.[1] (The adjective *marginal* refers to the fact that you are trading just *one* X.)

Given a consumer's initial basket and the indifference curve through that basket, you can always compute the marginal value of the horizontal good by traveling leftward

**Marginal value of $X$ in terms of $Y$**

The number of $Y$s for which the consumer would be just willing to trade one $X$.

---

[1] In many textbooks, the marginal value is called the *marginal rate of substitution* or *MRS*. Unfortunately, there is quite a bit of confusion associated with this term. The quantity that we've called the marginal value of X in terms of Y is sometimes called the marginal rate of substitution between X and Y, and sometimes called the marginal rate of substitution between Y and X. To avoid this confusion, we will stick with the term *marginal* value.

**EXHIBIT 3.4**    **Marginal Value**

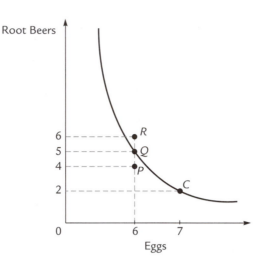

Suppose you start with basket *C*. If someone offers to trade you 2 root beers for an egg, you can move to basket *P*, which is worse; so you'll reject this trade. The minimum price you'd accept for an egg is 3 root beers, moving you to basket *Q*. Thus (to you), the marginal value of an egg is 3 root beers.

1 unit and then seeing how far upward you must travel to reach the indifference curve. In Exhibit 3.4, this means starting at point *C*, traveling leftward 1 egg (from 7 to 6), and then observing that you must travel upward 3 root beers (from 2 to 5); thus—as we have already said—the marginal value of an egg is 3 root beers.

**Exercise 3.4** How can you use the indifference curve of Exhibit 3.4 to illustrate the marginal value of *root beers* in terms of *eggs*?

## Marginal Value as a Slope

Exhibit 3.5 illustrates the indifference curves of two consumers, each starting with basket *C*. We can use these indifference curves to compute the marginal value of an egg to each consumer. For Jack, the marginal value of an egg is 6 root beers; for Jill, the marginal value of an egg is 1 root beer.

**Exercise 3.5** Explain how to compute these marginal values from the graphs in Exhibit 3.5.

Now let's forget about marginal values for a moment and ask a purely geometric question: What is the *slope* of Jack's indifference curve at point *C*? By the slope of a curve we mean the slope of a line tangent to that curve. The tangent line at *C* is well approximated by the illustrated line through *C* and *D*. So we want to compute the slope of that line.

Recalling that the slope of a line is given by the *rise over the run*, we see that in this case the slope is $-6/1 = -6$. The numerator 6 is the vertical distance between points

EXHIBIT **3.5**    **Marginal Value as a Slope**

A: Jack's indifference curve    B: Jill's indifference curve

Jack and Jill each start with basket C. To Jack, the marginal value of an egg is 6 root beers. Thus, trading 1 egg for 6 root beers leaves him on the same indifference curve; in other words, his indifference curve goes through point D and so has slope −6. To Jill, the marginal value of an egg is 1 root beer, so her indifference curve goes through point E and has slope −1. In general, the marginal value of an egg is equal to the absolute value of the slope of the indifference curve.

*C* and *D,* the denominator 1 is the horizontal distance, and there is a minus sign because the curve is downward sloping. The absolute value of this slope is 6 (or, more precisely, 6 root beers per egg). Recall that according to Jack, this is exactly the marginal value of an egg.

Likewise, in panel B the line through *C* and *E* has a slope with absolute value 1, which according to Jill is the marginal value of an egg.

It is no coincidence that these slopes are equal to the corresponding marginal values. In panel A, for example, we compute the marginal value of an egg as the vertical distance from *D* to *C* (that is, 6), while we compute the absolute value of the slope as that same vertical distance divided by the horizontal distance, which is 1. But dividing by 1 leaves the number 6 unchanged.

In general, then, **for a consumer with basket *C,* the marginal value of an egg is equal to the slope of the indifference curve at point *C.*** Consequently, **the steeper the indifference curve, the greater the marginal value of an egg.**

## The Shape of Indifference Curves

A starving person with a refrigerator full of root beer is likely to value an egg more highly (in terms of root beer) than a thirsty person with a refrigerator full of eggs. Because marginal value is reflected by the slopes of indifference curves, we can translate this statement into geometry: As a general rule, we expect indifference curves to be steep near baskets containing few eggs and many root beers and to be shallow near baskets containing many eggs and few root beers.

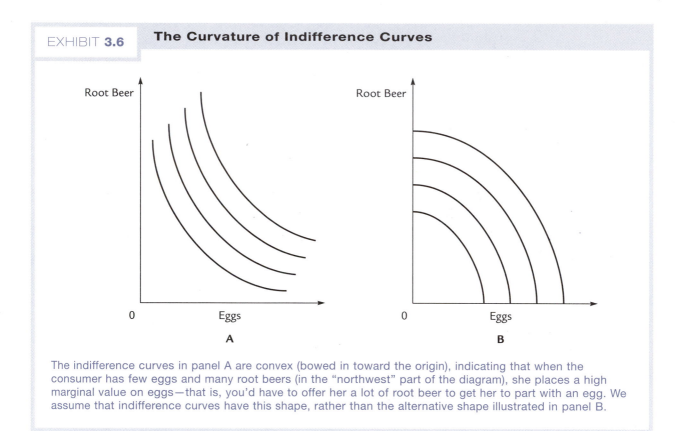

EXHIBIT **3.6**    **The Curvature of Indifference Curves**

A

B

The indifference curves in panel A are convex (bowed in toward the origin), indicating that when the consumer has few eggs and many root beers (in the "northwest" part of the diagram), she places a high marginal value on eggs—that is, you'd have to offer her a lot of root beer to get her to part with an egg. We assume that indifference curves have this shape, rather than the alternative shape illustrated in panel B.

Consider the two sets of indifference curves shown in Exhibit 3.6. Both sets slope downward. The first set slopes steeply in the area where baskets contain few eggs and many root beers (that is, in the "northwest" part of the figure) and shallowly in the area where baskets contain few root beers and many eggs. This consumer conforms to the general rule of the preceding paragraph.

Another consumer might have the indifference curves shown in panel B of Exhibit 3.6. This consumer values eggs highly when she has many eggs and few root beers, but values eggs much less when she has few eggs and many root beers. Such tastes are possible, but they seem unlikely.

Therefore, we will always assume that indifference curves are shaped like those in panel A rather than those in panel B. That is, we assume that indifference curves bow inward toward the origin. This property is expressed by saying that indifference curves are convex. At the end of Section 3.2 we will give another, independent justification for assuming convexity.

**Convex**

Bowed in toward the origin, like the curves in panel A of Exhibit 3.6.

**Exercise 3.6** Under what circumstances do you expect the consumer to value additional root beers highly relative to additional eggs? Combine this answer with your answer to Exercise 3.4 to draw a conclusion about where the indifference curves should be steep and where they should be shallow. Does your conclusion give further support to our assumption that indifference curves are convex, or does it suggest a reason to doubt that assumption?

## More on Indifference Curves

### Properties of Indifference Curves: A Summary

Here are the fundamental facts about a given consumer's indifference curves:

*Indifference curves slope downward, they fill the plane, they never cross, and they are convex.*

A consumer's indifference curves between two goods encode everything that there is to say about the consumer's tastes regarding those goods. A different consumer is likely to have a different family of indifference curves (also satisfying the fundamental facts). This is just another way of saying that tastes may differ across individuals.

---

We have assumed that eggs and root beer are both *goods*—items you'd always prefer to have more of—and we've concluded that indifference curves are downward sloping and convex. A different assumption would lead to different conclusions. End-of-chapter problems 5 and 6 will lead you through the analysis when one or both of the goods is replaced by a *bad*—something you'd prefer to have less of. (In problems 3 and 4, you'll encounter other special circumstances in which the shapes of indifference curves can differ from what is pictured in Exhibit 3.6A.)

---

Dangerous
Curve

### The Composite-Good Convention

In order to draw indifference curve diagrams, we must assume that there are only two goods in the world. This might appear to be a severe limitation, yet in fact it is not. In many applications we will want to concentrate our attention on a single good—say, eggs. In that case we divide the world into two classes of goods, namely, "eggs" and "things that are not eggs," otherwise known as "all other goods." This allows us to draw indifference curves between eggs (on the horizontal axis) and all other goods (on the vertical).

There remains the problem of units. What is a single unit of *all other goods?* The simplest solution to this problem is to measure all other goods in terms of their dollar value.

When we lump together all things that are not eggs and measure it in a single unit like dollars, we say that we are using the composite-good convention.

In the presence of the composite-good convention, the slope of an indifference curve is the marginal value of an egg in terms of other goods, with the other goods measured in dollars. Thus, it is the minimum number of dollars for which the consumer would be willing to trade an egg.

**Composite-good convention**

The lumping together of all goods but one into a single portmanteau good.

# 3.2 The Budget Line and the Consumer's Choice

To predict a consumer's behavior, we need to know two things. First, we need to know the consumer's tastes, which is the same thing as saying that we need to know his indifference curves. Second, we need to know the options available to the consumer. In other words, we need to know his budget.

## The Budget Line

Continue to assume a world with two goods. Instead of calling them eggs and root beers, we're going to start calling them $X$ and $Y$. You may continue to think of them as eggs and root beers if you wish. In order to determine which baskets our consumer can afford, we need to know three things: the price of $X$, the price of $Y$, and the consumer's income.

Rather than make up specific numbers, let's make up names for the three things we need to know:

$$P_X = \text{the price of } X \text{ in dollars}$$
$$P_Y = \text{the price } of \text{ } Y \text{ in dollars}$$
$$I = \text{the consumer's income in dollars}$$

Now let's suppose that the consumer is considering the purchase of a particular basket. Suppose that the basket contains $x$ units of $X$ and $y$ units of $Y$. (Keep in mind that the capital letters $X$ and $Y$ are the *names* of the goods and the small letters $x$ and $y$ are the *quantities*.) How much will it cost the consumer to acquire this basket? The $x$ units of $X$ at a price of $P_X$ dollars apiece will cost $P_X \cdot x$ dollars. The $y$ units of $Y$ at a price of $P_Y$ dollars apiece will cost $P_Y \cdot y$ dollars. The total price of the basket is

$$P_X \cdot x + P_Y \cdot y \text{ dollars}$$

Under what circumstances can the consumer afford to acquire this particular basket? Clearly, he can acquire it only if the price of the basket does not exceed his income. In other words, he can afford the basket precisely if

$$P_X \cdot x + P_Y \cdot y \leq I$$

In fact, we can say a little more. Let's take seriously our assumption that $X$ and $Y$ are the only goods in the world. (In view of the composite-good convention, this assumption is not as outrageous as it seems.) Then the consumer will have to spend his entire income on $X$ and $Y$,[2] and must choose a basket that costs exactly $I$ dollars. The consumer can have the basket in question precisely if

$$P_X \cdot x + P_Y \cdot y = I$$

---

**Dangerous
Curve**

It is important to distinguish the meanings of the various symbols in this equation. $P_X$, $P_Y$, and $I$ are particular, fixed numbers that the consumer faces. The letters x and y are variables that can represent the contents of any basket. As the consumer considers purchasing various baskets, the values of $x$ and $y$ change. For each basket he plugs the relevant values of $x$ and $y$ into the equation, and he asks if the equation is true. Asking "Does this basket make the equation true?" is exactly the same as asking "Can I afford to purchase this basket?"

---

**Budget line**

The set of all baskets that the consumer can afford, given prices and his or her income.

The line described by the equation $P_X \cdot x + P_Y \cdot y = I$ is a picture of all the baskets that the consumer can afford. It is called the consumer's **budget line.**

---

[2] It is possible that the consumer would want to save some income, but in that case we would want to consider savings as another good. If we are using the composite-good convention, we can include savings along with "all other goods."

Another way to write the equation of the budget line (using some simple algebraic manipulations) is

$$y = -\frac{P_X}{P_Y} \cdot x + \frac{I}{P_Y}$$

If you remember that $P_X$, $P_Y$, and $I$ are constants and that $x$ and $y$ are variables, you may recognize this as the equation of a line with slope $-P_X/P_Y$ and $y$-intercept $I/P_Y$. The points on that line are those that satisfy the equation and are therefore those that represent baskets that the consumer can buy. Exhibit 3.7 shows the budget line.

Here is an easy way to remember how to draw the budget line. If you were the consumer and you bought no $X$s at all, how many $Y$s could you afford? Because your income is $I$ and $Y$s sell at a price of $P_Y$ apiece, the answer is $I/P_Y$. This means that the point $(0, I/P_Y)$ must be on the budget line. If you bought no $Y$s at all, how many $X$s could you afford? The answer is $I/P_X$. This means that the point $(I/P_X, 0)$ must be on the budget line. The budget line must be the line connecting the points $(0, I/P_Y)$ and $(I/P_X, 0)$.

What if $P_X$, $P_Y$, and $I$ were all to double simultaneously? This would have no effect on the ratios $I/P_Y$ and $I/P_X$. It follows that a simultaneous doubling of all prices and income would have no effect on the budget line. This accords with our expectation that only relative prices matter.

The geometry of the budget line reflects everything there is to know about the opportunities facing the consumer. For example, the slope of the budget line is $-P_X/P_Y$, and the ratio $P_X/P_Y$ is the relative price of $X$ in terms of $Y$. Therefore, the budget line will be steep when $X$ is expensive relative to $Y$, and it will be shallow when $X$ is inexpensive relative to $Y$.

EXHIBIT 3.7    **The Budget Line**

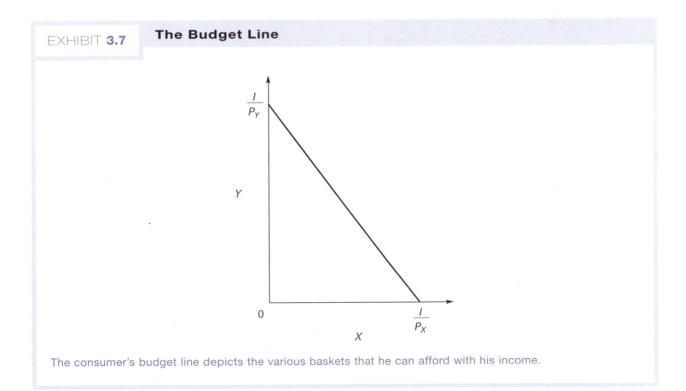

The consumer's budget line depicts the various baskets that he can afford with his income.

## The Consumer's Choice

### The Geometry of the Consumer's Choice

The budget line conveys an entirely different kind of information than the indifference curves do. The indifference curves reflect the consumer's preferences without regard to what he can actually afford to buy. The budget line shows which baskets he can afford to buy (that is, it shows his opportunities) without regard to his preferences. To determine how the consumer will actually behave, we must combine these two kinds of information. To this end, we have drawn the indifference curves and the budget line on the same graph, as in Exhibit 3.8.

We now have enough information to determine which basket this consumer will choose. Look at the baskets pictured. Of these, F is on the highest indifference curve and the one that the consumer would most like to own. (There are also many baskets not pictured that the consumer would like even more than F.) Unfortunately, he can't afford basket F—it's outside the budget line. By contrast, point E is inside the budget line and would fail to exhaust his income; therefore, E is ruled out as well. The baskets that the consumer can acquire are the ones on his budget line. In Exhibit 3.8 these include A, B, O, C, and D.

Of these, he will choose the one on the highest possible indifference curve. It is clear from the picture that this choice is O. In fact, O is not just the best choice among the five baskets we have considered but the best choice of any basket on the budget line. From the picture, the following is clear:

**The Consumer's Optimum**

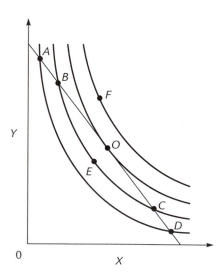

The consumer must choose one of the baskets that is on his budget line, such as A, B, O, C, or D. Of these, he will choose the one that is on the highest indifference curve, namely, O. Thus, the consumer is led to choose the basket at the point where his budget line is tangent to an indifference curve. This point is called the consumer's optimum.

At the consumer's optimum, the relative price of X in terms of Y (given by the slope of the budget line) and the marginal value of X in terms of Y (given by the slope of the tangent line to the indifference curve) are equal. The geometric reason for this is that the budget line is the tangent line to the indifference curve. The economic reason for it is that whenever the relative price is different from the marginal value, the consumer will continue to make exchanges until the two become equal.

The basket the consumer chooses will always be located where his budget line is tangent to one of his indifference curves.

This basket is called the consumer's optimum. Because there is only one such point, the budget line and the indifference curves give sufficient information for us to predict which basket the consumer will choose.

## The Economics of the Consumer's Choice

We can analyze the consumer's problem from a different perspective and still reach the same conclusion about the location of his optimum.

Referring to Exhibit 3.8, suppose that the consumer owns basket A. How much Y would this consumer be willing to trade for an additional unit of X? The answer is given by the marginal value of a unit of X (in terms of Y), which is measured by the absolute value of the slope of his or her indifference curve at A.

How much Y would this consumer actually have to sacrifice in order to acquire an additional unit of X? The answer is given by the relative price of X in terms of Y, which is the ratio $P_X/P_Y$, the absolute value of the slope of his budget line.

Of these two, which is greater, the marginal value or the relative price? At point A the indifference curve is steeper than the budget line. Consequently, the amount of Y that the consumer is *willing* to pay for a unit of X exceeds the amount of Y that he actually *has to* pay for a unit of X. In such a situation, buying a unit of X is an attractive proposition. The consumer will exchange Ys for Xs at the going relative price, ending up with more X and less Y than he started with. This will bring him to a point like B.

Now the same reasoning applies again. At B it is still the case that the marginal value exceeds the relative price. The consumer will want to buy another unit of X, which will move him further down the budget line.

This process will continue until the consumer reaches point O. At that point the price that he is willing to pay for X and the price at which he is able to purchase X have become equal. There is no longer anything to be gained from additional trades.

A similar process occurs if the consumer starts out with basket D. Here the marginal value of X is less than the relative price of X; the consumer values his last unit of X at less than the number of Ys that can be exchanged for it in the marketplace. In this case, he will happily trade away his last unit of X, ending up with more Ys and fewer Xs, at a point like C.

As long as the marginal value of X is less than the relative price of X, the consumer will trade Xs for Ys. This process stops when the marginal value and the relative price become equal, at point O.

Whenever the marginal value of X exceeds the relative price of X, the consumer will want to buy Xs, moving down the budget line. Whenever the marginal value is less than the relative price, the consumer will want to sell Xs, moving up the budget line. The only point at which he can settle is O, where the marginal value and the relative price are exactly equal. Thus, the economic reasoning leads to the same conclusion as the geometric reasoning: Of the points available to the consumer, the optimum occurs where his budget line is tangent to one of his indifference curves.

## Corner Solutions

There is an exception to the rule that the consumer's optimum always occurs at a tangency. This exception is illustrated in Exhibit 3.9. In this case there is no tangency for the consumer to choose.

**Optimum (plural: optima)**

The most preferred of the baskets on the budget line.

| EXHIBIT 3.9 | **A Corner Solution** |

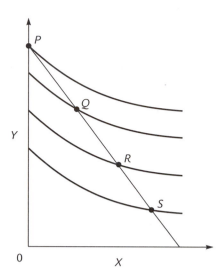

If the consumer's indifference curves look like those pictured, there is no tangency between his budget line and any of his indifference curves. Of all the points on the budget line, the consumer will choose the most desirable, namely, *P*. At any other point on the budget line the marginal value of *X* in terms of *Y* is less than the relative price, so the consumer can sell *X*s for more than they are worth to him and will continue to do so until he has sold all of his *X*s, ending up in the corner at *P*.

To predict the consumer's choice in this situation, we can use simple geometry. We know that the consumer must choose a basket on his budget line. Of all of these baskets, we can see from the picture that the one lying on the highest indifference curve is *P*. Therefore, the consumer chooses basket *P*.

Here is an alternative path to the same conclusion: Suppose the consumer begins with basket *S*. At this point his indifference curve is less steep than his budget line. To this consumer the marginal value of *X* in terms of *Y* is less than the relative price of *X* in terms of *Y*. The last unit of *X* is worth less to him than it will bring in the marketplace. Therefore, he trades *X* for *Y*, moving to a point like *R*. Now the same reasoning applies again, leading the consumer to move first to *Q* and then to *P*. The same reasoning would apply no matter what the original basket was.

**Corner solution**

An optimum occurring on one of the axes when there is no tangency between the budget line and an indifference curve.

The situation depicted in Exhibit 3.9 is called a **corner solution** because the consumer's optimum occurs in a corner of the diagram. As you can see from the picture, he consumes no *X* whatsoever and spends all of his income on *Y*.

## More on the Shape of Indifference Curves

In Section 3.1 we justified the assumption that indifference curves are convex with an appeal to the idea of marginal value. Now we can give an additional reason for making this assumption.

Suppose a consumer has the indifference curves illustrated in Exhibit 3.10. Will this consumer choose to purchase the basket at point *O*? No! He can do better. Points *C* and *D* are both available to him (they are on his budget line), and they are on a higher indifference curve than *O*. And can he do better than *C* and *D*? Yes. Every movement

| EXHIBIT 3.10 | The Consumer's Choice with Nonconvex Indifference Curves |
|---|---|

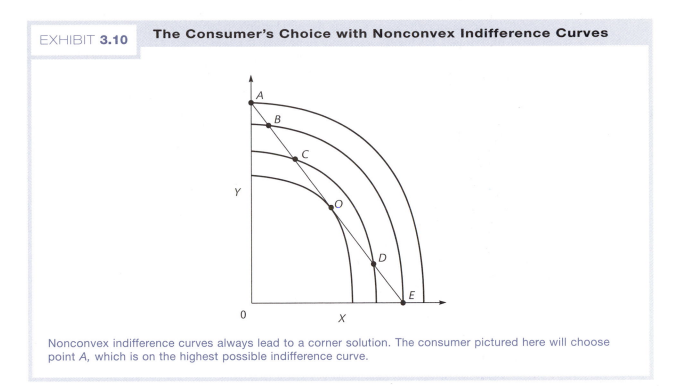

Nonconvex indifference curves always lead to a corner solution. The consumer pictured here will choose point *A*, which is on the highest possible indifference curve.

"outward" along the budget line, away from *O* and toward one of the axes, improves the consumer's welfare. For this reason he will always want to choose a basket on one of the axes—a corner solution. In this case he will choose basket *A*.

**Exercise 3.7** Why does the consumer choose basket *A* rather than basket *E*? How would the budget line have to look for him to choose a point on the *X*-axis rather than the *Y*-axis?

Because this consumer always selects a corner solution, he consumes either zero units of *X* or zero units of *Y*. But goods that consumers choose to purchase none of are not very interesting from the viewpoint of economics. So now we have our additional reason for assuming that indifference curves are convex. They might not be—but in this case one of the goods in question would not be consumed at all, and we would prefer to turn our attention to goods that *are* consumed. Therefore, we usually confine our attention to convex indifference curves.

# 3.3 Applications of Indifference Curves

Now let's put our new tools to use. In this section we'll see several applications of indifference curve analysis.

## Standards of Living

Economic conditions change all the time. Incomes go up and down, and so do prices. How do we tell which changes are good for the consumer and which are bad?

Sometimes it's easy. If your friend Harold's income goes up while prices remain unchanged, his life has certainly improved. If his income stays fixed while all prices rise, he's worse off than before. But what if some prices rise while others fall? Is that good or bad for Harold?

Sometimes there's not enough information to answer that question. Other times there is. Let's take an example: Harold consumes goods $X$ and $Y$. Their prices are $P_X = \$3$ and $P_Y = \$4$. He chooses to buy 4 units of $X$ and 2 of $Y$, exhausting his income of $20. Now the price of $X$ rises to $4 while the price of $Y$ falls to $2, and his income stays fixed at $20. Is Harold better or worse off than before?

To answer, start by drawing Harold's original budget line, marked *Original* in Exhibit 3.11. Given his income of $20 and given $P_X = \$3$, Harold can afford up to $6^2/_3$ $X$s if he buys no $Y$s. Because $P_Y = \$4$, he can afford up to 5 $Y$s if he buys no $X$s. Those calculations determine the two endpoints of his *Original* budget line. We are told that Harold chooses basket $O = (4, 2)$, so there must be an indifference curve tangent to the *Original* budget line at that point, as illustrated in the exhibit.

Now let's draw Harold's *New* budget line, after the prices change to $P_X = \$4$ and $P_Y = \$2$. The endpoints are at $X = 5$ and $Y = 10$, as shown in the exhibit. But knowing the endpoints is not enough to draw the *New* budget line accurately. We also have to think about whether it passes above, below, or through the point $O$.

To settle this question, ask whether Harold can afford basket $O$ at the *New* prices. With $P_X = \$4$ and $P_Y = \$2$, basket $O$ costs $(\$4 \times 4) + (\$2 \times 2) = \$20$, which is exactly Harold's income. So $O$ must be on his *New* budget line, or, to put it another way, his *New* budget line must pass through point $O$. That's how we've drawn it in Exhibit 3.11.

Now let's find Harold's *New* optimum point—the point where his *New* budget line is tangent to an indifference curve. The first thing we can do is rule out point $O$. That's

**Harold's Original and New Budget Lines**

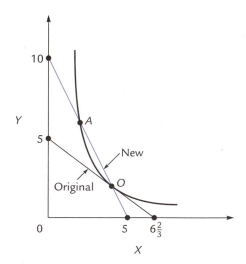

The graph shows Harold's *original* and *new* budget lines. We know that an indifference curve is tangent to the *original* line at the point $O$. We can calculate that the new budget line passes through the point $O$.

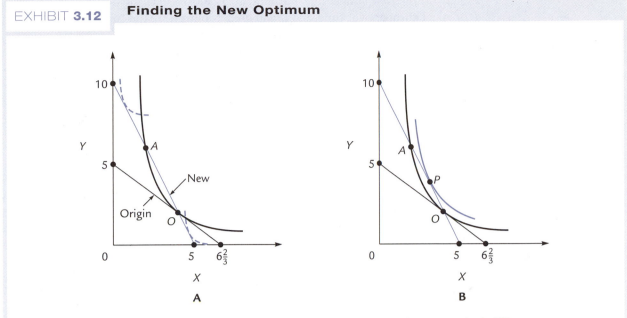

EXHIBIT **3.12**   **Finding the New Optimum**

The dashed indifference curves in panel A cannot be correct, because they cross the indifference curve through O. The only correct way to draw an indifference curve tangent to the *new* budget line is with the tangency between A and O, at a point like P, as in panel B. The new indifference curve is then necessarily higher than the old one, so you are better off at the new optimum.

because *a smooth curve cannot be tangent to two different lines at the same point*—an important fact about geometry that will be useful to keep in mind.

So where is Harold's new optimum? Panel A of Exhibit 3.12 explores some possibilities. The two dashed curves are not possible, because either of them would have to cross the original indifference curve. That means Harold can't have an optimum in the region above and to the left of *A* or in the region below and to the right of *O*. Instead, his new optimum must lie between *A* and *O*, for example, at *P* in panel B. If you look at the panel, you'll see that *P* must lie on a higher indifference curve than *O*. Therefore, the price changes must have made Harold better off.

## Price Indices

To measure how people are affected by price changes, the U.S. Department of Labor, through its Bureau of Labor Statistics, reports estimates of changes in the "cost of living," also called the "price level." Roughly, they do this by tracking the cost of a given basket over time. If the basket gets more expensive, they say that the cost of living has gone up (which suggests that people are worse off); if the basket gets cheaper, they say that the cost of living has gone down (which suggests that people are better off).

The big problem with this procedure is that the answer you get depends on which basket you choose to track. Look again at Exhibit 3.12. Basket *O* costs $20 under the original prices and $20 under the new prices. If you track basket *O*, you'll say the cost of living hasn't changed at all. That's misleading, because, as we've just seen, Harold is definitely happier with the new prices than with the old ones.

If you tracked basket *P*, you'd get a different answer. Basket *P* is outside the *Original* budget line, which means it must cost more than $20 at the original prices. But it is exactly on the *New* budget line, meaning it costs just $20 at the new prices. So basket *P* does get cheaper over time, and if you used it to measure the cost of living you'd say that the cost of living had come down.

The cost of living measurement that you get by tracking the original basket (in this case *O*) is called a Laspeyres price index (pronounced "La-spears"), and it tends to make things look worse than they are. The cost of living measurement that you get by tracking the new basket (in this case *P*) is called a Paasche price index (pronounced "Posh"), and it tends to make things look better than they are. Unfortunately, there is no perfect way to measure changes in the cost of living.

## Differences in Tastes

Germans eat a lot of starch. Italians eat more tomatoes. Greeks use olive oil and the French use hollandaise. Why doesn't everyone eat the same diet?

There are only two possible answers: People in different countries must have either different tastes or different opportunities (or both). Maybe Italians eat tomatoes because they like them better than Germans do—that's a difference in tastes. Or maybe Italians eat tomatoes because tomatoes are cheaper in Italy, or because Italians are too poor to afford a German diet—those are differences in opportunities.

How do we tell which theory is right? There's no question that prices and incomes differ across countries, so there's no question that there are differences in opportunities. The question is whether those differences in opportunities suffice to explain the different choices people make, or whether their tastes must also differ.

Start with a fictional example: Suppose Albert lives in Rome, where tomatoes sell for $2 a pound and potatoes sell for $1 a pound. He earns $10 a day, with which he buys 4 tomatoes and 2 potatoes. Betty lives in Berlin, where tomatoes sell for $3 a pound and potatoes sell for $6 a pound. She earns $45 a day, with which she buys 1 tomato and 7 potatoes. Using these numbers, let's figure out whether Albert and Betty could have identical tastes.

The first step is to plot Albert and Betty's budget lines, which we've done in panel A of Exhibit 3.13. Albert's optimum point (4, 2) is labeled *A,* and Betty's optimum point (1, 7) is labeled *B.*

---

**Exercise 3.8** Make sure the budget lines are drawn correctly.

---

Now let's change the problem slightly. Suppose that instead of buying 1 tomato and 7 potatoes, Betty buys 5 tomatoes and 5 potatoes. Then the picture looks like panel B in Exhibit 3.13. Here we can't tell whether the indifference curves eventually cross, and we can't tell whether Albert and Betty have identical tastes.

---

Dangerous
Curve

To conclude that Albert and Betty have identical tastes, we would have to know that they share all their indifference curves. There are several reasons why we can't draw this conclusion from Exhibit 3.13B. First, we have no idea whether the two pictured indifference curves eventually cross. Second, even if they don't cross, it doesn't follow that Albert and Betty share these indifference curves; it only follows that they *might*. Third, even if Albert and Betty share the two pictured indifference curves, it doesn't follow that they share *all* their indifference curves. So the picture does not contain nearly enough information to answer the question of whether Albert and Betty's tastes are identical.

---

**Laspeyres price index**

A price index based on the basket consumed in the earlier period.

**Paasche price index**

A price index based on the basket consumed in the later period.

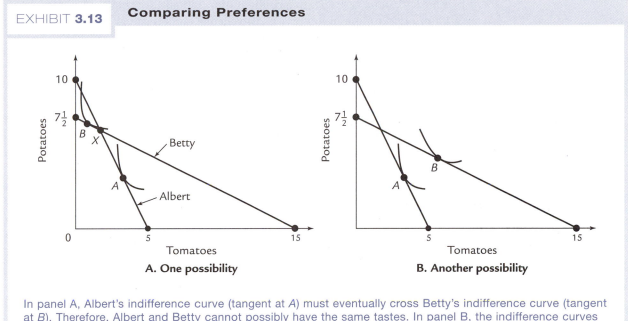

**EXHIBIT 3.13    Comparing Preferences**

**A. One possibility**

**B. Another possibility**

In panel A, Albert's indifference curve (tangent at *A*) must eventually cross Betty's indifference curve (tangent at *B*). Therefore, Albert and Betty cannot possibly have the same tastes. In panel B, the indifference curves might or might not cross and Albert and Betty might or might not have identical tastes.

Now that we've completed our detour into fiction, what about the real world? To seek evidence of taste differences across European countries, we can replace Albert and Betty with "the average German" and "the average Italian," and we can use realistic numbers for the prices of tomatoes and potatoes. Then we can repeat the exercise with Germans and Greeks, or Greeks and Italians, or Poles and Hungarians, and with more than just two goods. If we ever get a picture like panel A of Exhibit 3.13, we've spotted a taste difference.

Harvard Professor Hendrik Houthakker carried out this exercise and found no evidence of any taste differences. In other words, when Professor Houthakker drew his graphs, none looked like panel A of Exhibit 3.13. Instead, every one of his pictures leaves open the possibility that tastes could be either the same or different.

On the one hand, that doesn't prove anything. On the other hand, the more times you look for something and fail to find it, the more you're entitled to suspect it's not really there. Professor Houthakker searched repeatedly for evidence of taste differences and failed to find them. That doesn't prove tastes are remarkably similar across countries, but it is certainly evidence in that direction.

Here's a similar question: Do people's tastes change over time? For example, did the average Englishman in 1950 have different tastes than the average Englishman in 1900? We can use the same techniques: In Exhibit 3.13, replace Albert and Betty with "the average Englishman in the year 1950" and "the average Englishman in the year 1900." Look at not just tomatoes and potatoes but other pairs of goods. A picture like panel A of Exhibit 3.13 would show that tastes had changed over that half-century.

Using 127 different goods in every possible pairing, there are many hundreds of cases where the budget lines cross, raising the possibility of a configuration like panel A of Exhibit 3.13. In no case does that configuration actually occur.[3] In other words, there are a lot of opportunities to observe a taste change and no actual observations. Again, that doesn't prove anything, but it is highly suggestive.

## The Least Bad Tax

Governments raise money in many ways.

First, there are *wage taxes* (also called *payroll taxes*). In the United States, the most important wage tax is the FICA tax that is used to fund the Social Security and Medicare programs. FICA taxes are deducted directly from your paycheck. In most cases, the deduction is about 7.5% of your pay. (Your employer pays a comparable amount.)

Next, there are *income taxes* that tax income from all sources—not just wages, but also income on interest, dividends, and so forth.

Then there are *consumption taxes* that tax the purchases you make. In the United States, most state governments gather large fractions of their income from consumption taxes (more commonly called sales taxes).

Local governments frequently raise funds through *property taxes,* where you pay a percentage of the value of your property, or more frequently, of certain kinds of property such as real estate.

A rarer form of tax is the *head tax* which requires you to pay a certain number of dollars per year, independent of your income or your consumption.

If you've got to be taxed, which is the least painful tax to pay?

Obviously, the answer depends on the size of the taxes. A 1% income tax is better than a $10,000 daily head tax, whereas a $1 daily head tax is better than a 90% income tax.

So to keep the comparison fair, let's assume in each case that you're going to pay exactly, say, $100 a year in taxes. Now which tax is least painful?

A reasonable guess is: If two taxes each cost me $100 a year, then those two taxes are equally painful. This reasonable guess turns out to be wrong, because different taxes lead to different changes in behavior, and some of these changes are less desirable than others.

It's easiest to see this with an extreme example. Which would you prefer—a 0% income tax or a 5,000,000% tax on shoes? Under the 0% income tax, you pay zero. Under the 5,000,000% shoe tax, you also pay zero (because you decide to go barefoot). Either tax costs you the same zero dollars, but the shoe tax is worse because it leaves you with cold feet.

So even when two taxes collect exactly the same amount of revenue, we can't assume they're equally painful. We have to consider their effects on your behavior.

## Wage Taxes versus Head Taxes

For example, when wages are taxed, people might choose to work less and earn fewer wages. To understand the consequences of this choice, we need an indifference curve diagram with "wages earned" on one axis and . . . what on the other? Answer: The alternative to earning wages is having more leisure, so that's what goes on the other axis.

We assume your wage rate is $20 an hour. You can divide your 24-hour day any way you want between leisure and wage-earning. If you take zero hours of leisure (working a full 24 hours) you earn $480 in wages; if you take 24 hours of leisure you earn $0 in wages. These are the endpoints of the budget line labeled *Original* in panel A of Exhibit 3.14. Deciding how many hours to work amounts to choosing a point on this budget line.

---

[3] S. Landsburg, "Taste Change in the United Kingdom," *Journal of Political Economy* 89 (1981): 92–104.

---

EXHIBIT **3.14**     **A Wage Tax versus a Head Tax**

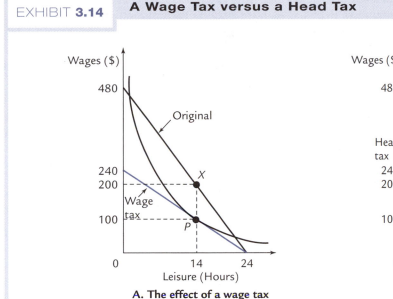

A. The effect of a wage tax

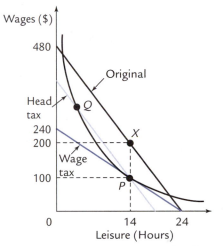

B. A wage tax versus a head tax

You have 24 hours a day to divide between leisure and working at a wage of $20 an hour; this yields the *Original* budget line. When your wages are taxed at 50%, the budget line pivots to the *Wage Tax* line in panel A, and you choose point *P*.

If the wage tax is replaced by a head tax that collects the same number of dollars, the new budget line must be parallel to the *Original* (because it represents a head tax) and must pass through point *P* (because it raises the same number of dollars as the wage tax). This yields the *Head Tax* line in panel B, which enables you to reach a higher indifference curve (with a tangency somewhere between *P* and *Q*). Thus the head tax is preferable to the wage tax.

---

Now suppose you are subject to a wage tax that lowers your after-tax wage from $20 an hour to $10 an hour. Then if you take zero hours of leisure, you earn only $240 in wages. In other words, your budget line pivots inward to the line labeled *Wage Tax* in panel A of Exhibit 3.14.

With the wage tax in effect, you must choose a point on this *Wage Tax* line. Of course you choose the point where an indifference curve is tangent; in the exhibit we have labeled this point *P*. For illustration, we've assumed that *P* has coordinates (14, 100). In other words, you spend 14 hours at leisure and 10 hours at work.

In the absence of a tax, 10 hours of work would have earned you $200, so this wage tax is taking $100 out of your paycheck. To put this another way, if you had worked 10 hours *without* being taxed, you'd have been at point *X*, $100 directly above point *P*.

---

Sometimes students think that *X* must be the optimum on the *Original* budget line. There is no reason to expect this. In the absence of a wage tax, you'd probably work some number of hours other than 10, which is to say that the optimum on the *Original* line is probably somewhere other than *X*. What we're saying here is that if there were no wage tax *and if for some reason you still worked exactly 10 hours,* then you'd be at point *X*.

Dangerous
Curve

---

Now let's compare the wage tax to a head tax. Remember that we want to keep the comparison fair by assuming that each tax collects the same number of dollars. The wage tax collected $100, so we have to compare it to a $100 head tax.

A head tax takes $100 from you no matter how much you work; therefore the entire *Original* budget line is shifted vertically downward (parallel to itself) a distance of $100. Because the *Original* line goes through point *X,* the shifted *Head Tax* line must go through point *P,* exactly $100 below *X,* as shown in panel B of Exhibit 3.14.

With the head tax in effect, you choose a point of tangency on the *Head Tax* line. To avoid crossings, this tangency must lie somewhere between points *P* and *Q.* Notice that any such tangency must lie on a *higher* indifference curve than the one pictured. Therefore:

A head tax is preferable to a wage tax (assuming that both taxes collect the same number of dollars).

What's going on here? How can one tax be preferable to another when they're equally costly? Answer: Suppose you're subject to the wage tax, so your after-tax wage is $10 per hour. Then you choose point *P* in panel A of Exhibit 3.14; at this point the marginal value of your leisure (measured by the slope of your indifference curve) is exactly $10 per hour. Now if the wage tax is suddenly lifted and replaced with a head tax, you have the opportunity to earn $20 for each additional hour of work. Since you value your next hour of leisure at only $10 an hour, you'll be glad to be able to sell it for $20.

## Wage Taxes versus Income Taxes

The difference between a wage tax and an income tax is that while a wage tax discourages work, an income tax discourages both work and saving. (It discourages saving by taxing interest, which is the reward for saving.) To compare the two taxes, then, we need an indifference curve diagram with saving on one of the axes. Alternatively, we can put "future consumption" on one of the axes, because the entire purpose of saving is to enable future consumption.

The alternative to saving is current consumption, so that's what goes on the other axis; you can see the picture in panel A of Exhibit 3.15. Here we suppose that you've just earned $100 in wages. You can spend part of your $100 today and save the rest for tomorrow—say at a 10% interest rate. If you spend everything now, you get $100 worth of current consumption and $0 worth of future consumption; if you save everything, you get $0 worth of current consumption and $110 worth of future consumption. The *Original* budget line shows your menu of choices.

Now consider the effect of a tax on interest only. (We'll return to income taxes shortly, but it's important to understand the effects of interest-only taxes first.) If, say, half your interest earnings are taxed, then you earn an after-tax interest rate of only 5%. You can still spend your entire $100 today, but if you save it all for the future you'll have only $105 to spend. So your budget line pivots as in panel A of Exhibit 3.15.

A tax on interest causes the budget line to pivot.

For comparison, panel B shows the effect of a wage tax, say of 10%. Your after-tax wage is reduced to $90; you can spend the entire $90 today, save it all and spend $99 tomorrow, or do anything in between, as the *Wage Tax* line indicates. Note that the slope of the budget line is unchanged; a wage tax causes this budget line to shift *parallel to itself.*

**EXHIBIT 3.15**    **Taxing Interest, Wages, and Income**

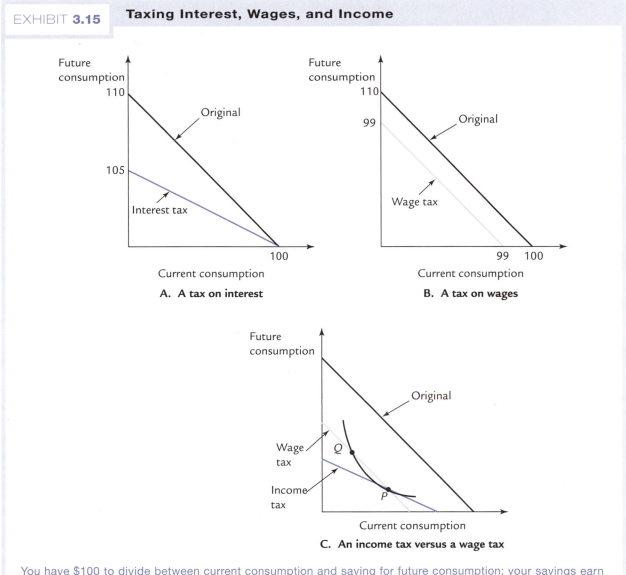

**A. A tax on interest**

**B. A tax on wages**

**C. An income tax versus a wage tax**

You have $100 to divide between current consumption and saving for future consumption; your savings earn a 10% interest rate. This gives you the *Original* budget line.

A tax on interest causes the budget line to pivot (panel A); a tax on wages causes the budget line to shift in parallel to itself (panel B). A tax on income (i.e., on both interest and wages) causes both a pivot and a parallel shift, yielding the *Income Tax* line in panel C.

If the income tax is replaced with a wage tax that collects the same number of dollars, the new *Wage Tax* line is parallel to the *Original* and passes through point *P*. This allows you to reach a higher indifference curve (with a tangency somewhere between *P* and *Q*). Thus the wage tax is preferred to the income tax.

---

In Exhibit 3.14, a wage tax causes the budget line to *pivot,* whereas in Exhibit 3.15, a wage tax causes the budget line to make a *parallel shift.* This is because neither diagram by itself shows the full effect of a wage tax. Ideally, we'd have a four-dimensional diagram with axes for "Current Consumption," "Future Consumption," "Current Leisure," and "Future Leisure." Our paltry two-dimensional diagrams show only pieces of the story. The wage tax causes a pivot in one dimension and a parallel shift in another.

Dangerous
Curve

Panels A and B of Exhibit 3.15 show the effects of an *interest tax* and a *wage tax*. Now what about an *income tax*? An income tax is a tax on both interest *and* wages, so it is represented by both a pivot *and* a shift of the budget line. You can see the *Income Tax* line in panel C. Notice that because of the pivot, it is *not* parallel to the *Original* line.

When you are subject to the income tax, you choose point *P*. Now what if the income tax is replaced by a wage tax that collects the same number of dollars? The *Wage Tax* line must be parallel to the *Original* line (because it represents a wage tax) and must pass through point *P* (because it collects the same number of dollars as the income tax).

Dangerous
Curve

When we're talking about multiple time periods, we have to be careful about what it means for two taxes to collect "the same number of dollars." Given our assumption of a 10% interest rate, we have to count a dollar collected today as equivalent to $1.10 collected tomorrow.

As you can see in panel C, the wage tax allows you to reach a tangency between *P* and *Q*, at a point better than *P*. In other words:

A wage tax is preferable to an income tax (assuming that both taxes collect the same number of dollars).

You should note that Exhibit 3.15C is very similar to Exhibit 3.14B. In each case, the moral is that **a tax that causes the budget line to pivot is worse than a tax that causes a pure parallel shift.**

## Consumption Taxes

Finally, what about a consumption tax? For this, we can look again at Exhibit 3.15B. The picture assumes you have $100, which you can divide between current consumption and saving for future consumption, at a 10% interest rate.

Now suppose you have to pay a sales tax, so that your $100 can only purchase $90 worth of goods. That means you can have up to $90 worth of current consumption. Alternatively, if you save all your money, you'll have $110, which, at the same tax rate, will allow you to buy and consume up to $99 worth of future goods. In other words, your new budget line passes through the points (0, 90) and (99, 0)—*just like the illustrated* Wage Tax *line!* In still other words, the *Consumption Tax* line is *identical* to the *Wage Tax* line.

So a consumption tax and a wage tax (of appropriate sizes) cause your budget line to shift in exactly the same way. Since both taxes yield the same budget line, they must also yield the same optimum—which means there's no reason for you to prefer one over the other.

A wage tax and a consumption tax are interchangeable; there is no reason to prefer one over the other.

## Conclusion

The head tax is best, the wage tax is second best, the consumption tax ties with the wage tax, and the income tax comes in last.

Once again, it's important to remember that all this assumes you're paying the same amount under any of the various tax systems. If you are the average taxpayer, this can be a reasonable assumption; as long as the government sets the tax rate with a target revenue in mind, it will presumably adjust that tax rate to keep total collections fixed.

But not every taxpayer is average. If your income is considerably below average, you might prefer an income tax to a head tax; if your interest income is considerably below average, you might prefer an income tax to a wage tax or a consumption tax.

## Summary

A consumer's behavior depends on his tastes and his opportunities. His tastes are encoded in his indifference curves and his opportunities are encoded in his budget line. By combining this information in a single graph, we can predict the consumer's behavior.

Each consumer has a family of indifference curves. Each curve in the family consists of baskets among which he is indifferent. His indifference curves slope downward, fill the plane, never cross, and are convex. A different consumer will have a different family of indifference curves, also satisfying these properties.

The slope of an indifference curve is equal (in absolute value) to the marginal value of $X$ in terms of $Y$. That is, it is the number of units of $Y$ for which the consumer is just willing to trade one unit of $X$.

As the consumer moves along an indifference curve in the direction of more $X$ and less $Y$, we expect that the marginal value of $X$ will decrease. This accounts for the convexity of indifference curves.

The consumer's budget line depends on his income and the prices of the goods that he buys. Its equation is

$$P_X \cdot x + P_Y \cdot y = I$$

where $P_X$ and $P_Y$ are the prices of $X$ and $Y$ and $I$ is the consumer's income. The slope of the budget line is equal (in absolute value) to the relative price of $X$ in terms of $Y$.

The consumer's optimum occurs where his budget line is tangent to one of his indifference curves. This is the point at which he attains the highest indifference curve that is available to him. At this point the marginal value of $X$ in terms of $Y$ is equal to the relative price of $X$ in terms of $Y$. At any other point either the marginal value would exceed the relative price, in which case the consumer would trade $Y$ for $X$, or the relative price would exceed the marginal value, in which case the consumer would trade $X$ for $Y$. Only at his optimum point is he satisfied not to trade any further.

## Author Commentary                www.cengage.com/economics/landsburg

**AC1.** See these articles for some challenges to the budget line/indifference curve model of consumer choices.

# Review Questions

**R1.** Consider the baskets $A = (3, 4)$, $B = (5, 7)$, $C = (4, 2)$. Without knowing Beth's indifference curves, can you predict which of these baskets she'll like the best? Can you predict which she'll like the least?

**R2.** Explain why indifference curves must slope downward.

**R3.** Explain why two of Beth's indifference curves can never cross.

**R4.** Can one of Beth's indifference curves cross one of Carol's indifference curves? Why or why not?

**R5.** Define the "marginal value of $X$ in terms of $Y$."

**R6.** Suppose Beth owns basket (10, 10) and the slope of her indifference curve at that point is 4. Would Beth be willing to trade her basket for the basket (9, 13)?

**R7.** Write the equation for a consumer's budget line. Which symbols represent constants and which represent variables?

**R8.** Susan has an income of $10. She buys cherries for $2 a pound and grapes for $4 a pound. Write the equation for her budget line and sketch the line. What is its slope?

**R9.** Given the consumer's indifference curves and budget line, how do you find the consumer's optimum point?

**R10.** Suppose the marginal value of $X$ in terms of $Y$ is greater than the relative price of $X$ in terms of $Y$. Is the consumer's basket to the left or to the right of his optimum point? Will he want to buy some $X$ or to sell some $X$? Explain how you know. In which direction will this cause the consumer to move along his budget line?

# Numerical Exercises

**N1.** Every day Fred buys wax lips and candy cigarettes. After deciding how many of each to buy, he multiplies the number of sets of wax lips times the number of packs of candy cigarettes. The higher this number comes out to be, the happier he is. For example, 3 sets of wax lips and 5 packs of candy cigarettes will make him happier than 2 sets of wax lips and 7 packs of candy cigarettes, because 3 × 5 is greater than 2 × 7. Wax lips sell for $2 a pair and candy cigarettes for $1 a pack. Fred has $20 to spend each day.

**a.** Make a table that looks like this:

| Pairs of Wax Lips | Packs of Candy Cigarettes |
|---|---|
| 0 | |
| 1 | |
| 2 | |
| . | |
| . | |
| . | |
| 10 | |

where each row of the chart corresponds to a basket on Fred's budget line. Fill in the second column.

**b.** Draw a graph showing Fred's budget line and marking the baskets described by your table. Draw Fred's indifference curves through these baskets. If he must select among these baskets, which one will Fred choose?

**c.** Add to your table a third column labeled *MV* for the marginal value of wax lips in terms of candy cigarettes. Fill in the *MV* for each basket. (*Hint:* For each basket construct another basket that has one less pair of wax lips but enough more packs of candy cigarettes to be equally desirable. How many packs of candy cigarettes have been added to the basket?) For which basket is the marginal value closest to the relative price of wax lips? Is this consistent with your answer to part (b)?

# Problem Set

1. **True or False:** If the price of wine rises, peoples' tastes will shift away from wine and toward other things.

2. Suppose that you like to own both left and right shoes, but that a right shoe is of no use to you unless you own a matching left one, and vice versa. Draw your indifference curves between left and right shoes.

3. Draw your indifference curves between nickels and dimes, assuming that you are always willing to trade 2 nickels for 1 dime, or vice versa. What is the marginal value of nickels in terms of dimes?

4. Judith loves cats, hates dogs, and is completely indifferent to tropical fish. Draw her indifference curves between (a) cats and dogs, (b) cats and fish, (c) dogs and fish.

5. Suppose that you hate typing and hate filing.

   **a.** Draw a graph with "hours of typing" on the horizontal axis and "hours of filing" on the vertical. Do your indifference curves slope upward or downward? Why?

   **b.** Suppose you currently type for 3 hours a day and file for 5, but you'd be just as happy typing for 2 hours a day and filing for 7. What is the slope of your indifference curve at the point (3, 5)? If you hated typing even more than you do, would you expect the indifference curve to be steeper or shallower?

   **c.** Would you expect the indifference curve to be steeper or shallower at points that represent a lot of typing and very little filing? What does this say about the shape of the indifference curves?

   **d.** Suppose your boss tells you that henceforth, you may divide your 8-hour day any way you wish between these two activities, but the number of hours you spend typing and the number of hours you spend filing must add up to 8. Draw the relevant budget constraint.

   **e.** Given the information in part (b), will you now choose to type more or less than 3 hours a day? Illustrate your new optimum and explain why it is your optimum.

6. Filbert is indifferent between baskets (3, 2) and (4, 1). Lychee is indifferent between baskets (1, 4) and (2, 3). Note that all four baskets lie along a straight line.

**a.** Can you determine whether Filbert and Lychee have identical tastes?

**b.** Suppose that Filbert chooses basket (4, 1) and Lychee chooses basket (1, 4). Can you determine whether Filbert and Lychee pay identical prices for the goods they buy?

**7.** Huey consumes only two goods, X and Y. His indifference curves have the usual shape. He prefers basket (1, 3) to basket (2, 2).

**a.** Is it possible to tell whether Huey prefers (1, 3) to (3, 1)?

**b.** Is it possible to tell whether Huey prefers (3, 1) to (2, 2)?

**8.** Suppose your indifference curves between food and clothing were nonconvex as in Exhibit 3.10. **True or False:** In this case a very small change in price could lead to either no change at all in your consumption of X or to a very large change in your consumption of X.

**9.** Suppose that you consume nothing but beer and pizza. In 2010, your income is $10 per week, beer costs $1 per bottle, pizza costs $1 per slice, and you buy 6 bottles of beer and 4 slices of pizza per week. In 2011, your income rises to $20 per week, the price of beer rises to $2.50 per bottle, and the price of pizza rises to $1.25 per slice.

**a.** In which year are you happier?

**b.** In which year do you eat more pizza? Justify and illustrate your answer with indifference curves.

**10.** In 2010, you buy shoes for $2 a pair and socks for $1 a pair, and your income is $30, with which you buy 12 pairs of shoes and 6 pairs of socks. In 2011, you buy shoes for $1 a pair and socks for $2 a pair, and your income is still $30.

**a.** Draw both years' budget lines. Notice that they cross at the point (10, 10).

**b.** **True or False:** In 2011, you will surely buy more than 10 pairs of shoes.

**c.** **True or False:** In 2011, you will surely buy more than 12 pairs of shoes.

**11.** Your income is $48, which you spend on eggs and wine. Eggs sell for $4 a dozen. Every day you buy 5 dozen eggs. One day the egg salesman offers you a deal: "If you pay $10 a day to join the egg club, you'll be allowed to buy eggs at $2 a dozen." Should you join the club? Justify your answer with indifference curves.

**12.** If the price of eggs were to double from $1 per egg to $2 per egg, Freddy would consume 6 fewer eggs without changing his consumption of other goods. Which would he prefer: The price increase, or losing $6?

**13.** Aubrey buys only apples and peaches. In June, apples sell for $2 each and peaches sell for $1 each. In July, apples sell for $1 each and peaches sell for $2 each. Aubrey's income is $20 in June and $20 in July.

**a.** **True or False:** If Aubrey is equally happy in both months, then she surely eats more apples in July.

**b.** **True or False:** If Aubrey buys exactly eight apples in June, then she is certainly happier in July.

**c.** **True or False:** If Aubrey buys exactly eight apples in June, then she certainly buys more than eight apples in July.

**14.** Cassie shops at Wegman's supermarket, where she spends $20 a week to buy 10 apples and 5 bananas. If she bought the same 10 apples and 5 bananas at Top's supermarket, she'd pay $30. **True or False:** Cassie is wise to continue shopping at Wegman's.

**15.** Gregorian and Boudicca each have incomes of $30 and each shop at Star Market, where apples cost $2 each and bananas cost $1 each. Every day, Gregorian buys 6 apples and 18 bananas, and so does Boudicca. One day a new supermarket (called Acme) opens up. At Acme, apples cost $1 and bananas cost $2. Gregorian prefers to keep shopping at Star Market, but Boudicca switches to Acme.

    **a.** Draw a diagram showing Gregorian's budget lines at Star Market and Acme. Illustrate his indifference curves. Do the same for Boudicca.

    **b.** What is the key difference between the shapes of Gregorian's and Boudicca's indifference curves?

    **c.** **True or False:** At Acme, Boudicca will surely buy more than 10 apples.

    **d.** The president of Star Market Points out that at Acme, Boudicca will no longer be able to afford the basket she's been buying at Star Market. Is this a good reason for Boudicca to reconsider her choice?

**16.** Amelia buys coffee for $1 per cup and tea for 50¢ per cup; every day she drinks 1 cup of coffee and 2 cups of tea. Bernard buys coffee for 50¢ per cup and tea for $1 per cup; every day he drinks 2 cups of coffee and 1 cup of tea. Can you determine whether Amelia and Bernard have identical tastes?

**17.** Chris buys coffee for $1 per cup and tea for 50¢ per cup; every day she drinks 2 cups of coffee and 1 cup of tea. David buys coffee for 50¢ per cup and tea for $1 per cup; every day he drinks 1 cup of coffee and 2 cups of tea. Can you determine whether Chris and David have identical tastes?

**18.** Evelyn buys coffee for $1 per cup and tea for 50¢ per cup; every day she drinks 1 cup of coffee and 2 cups of tea. Frederick buys coffee for 50¢ per cup and tea for $1 per cup; every day he drinks 1 cup of coffee and 1 cup of tea. Can you determine whether Evelyn and Frederick have identical tastes?

**19.** John buys eggs for $2 a dozen and bacon for $5 a pound. Sarah buys eggs for $5 a dozen and bacon for $2 a pound. Can you determine whether John and Sarah have identical tastes?

**20.** In each of the three circumstances (a, b, and c below), determine which of the following conclusions (1, 2, or 3) holds and justify your answer:

    **(1)** John and Mary have identical tastes.

    **(2)** John and Mary have different tastes.

    **(3)** We can't tell whether John and Mary have identical tastes.

    **a.** John and Mary have the same budget line and choose different baskets.

    **b.** John and Mary have the same budget line and choose the same basket.

    **c.** John and Mary have crossing budget lines and choose the same basket.

**21.** John buys shoes for $1 a pair and socks for $1 a pair. His annual income is $20.

    **a.** Draw John's budget line.

    **b.** Now suppose the government institutes two new programs: First, it taxes shoes, so that shoes now cost John $2 a pair. Second, it gives John an annual cash gift of $10. Draw his new budget line.

    **c.** Suppose that with the new programs in place, John chooses to buy 10 pairs of socks and 10 pairs of shoes. Has the pair of government programs made him better off, worse off, or neither?

**22.** **a.** Suppose you have 16 waking hours per day, which you can allocate between leisure and working for a wage of $10 an hour. Draw your budget constraint between "leisure" (measured in hours) and "income" (measured in dollars).

   **b.** Suppose you invent a pill that enables you to get by on four hours of sleep a night, so that you now have 20 waking hours per day. Is it possible that you will now choose to work fewer hours than before?

**23.** The Pullman company has a lot of pull in the town of Pullman. Everybody in town is identical, and they all work for the company, which pays them each $10 a day. Their favorite food is apples, which they get from a mail-order catalog for $1 apiece.

   **a.** Draw the typical resident's budget line between apples and all other goods, with all other goods measured in dollars.

   **b.** Pullman has decided to institute a sales tax of $1 per apple. But to prevent dissatisfied workers from leaving town, Pullman must simultaneously raise wages so that workers are just as happy as before. Draw the typical resident's new budget line, given both the sales tax and the wage increase.

   **c.** Use your graph to illustrate Pullman's new net expense per worker (that is, wages paid minus sales tax collected).

   **d.** Was Pullman wise to institute the tax?

**24.** Suppose that you can work anywhere from 0 to 24 hours per day at a wage of $1 per hour. You are subject to a tax of 50% on all wages over $5 per day (the first $5 per day is untaxed). You elect to work 10 hours per day.

   **a.** Show your budget constraint between labor and wages, and show your optimum point.

   **b.** Suppose that the tax law is changed so that *all* wages are subject to a 25% tax. Do you now work more or less than 10 hours? Does the government collect more or less tax revenue than before?

   **c.** Which do you prefer: the old tax law or the new one?

**25.** Suppose that you have 24 hours per day to allocate between leisure and working at a wage of $1 per hour. Draw your budget line between leisure and dollars. One day the government simultaneously institutes two new programs: a 50% income tax and a plan whereby everybody in the country receives a gift from the government of $6 each year.

   **a.** Draw your new budget line.

   **b.** Suppose that the government chose the level of $6 for the gift because it precisely exhausts the income from the tax. Explain why this means that the average taxpayer must be paying exactly $6 in tax.

   **c.** Assume that you are the average taxpayer, and draw your new optimum. Is it on, above, or below your original budget line?

   **d.** As the average taxpayer, are you working harder or less hard than before the programs went into effect? Are you happier or less happy? How do you know?

**26.** Suppose the government imposes a *temporary* sales tax—one that is in effect for a short time, but will disappear in the future. The government is considering two different tax policies:

   ***A.*** A big excise tax on eggs. This would cause the price of eggs to triple.

   ***B.*** A smaller excise tax on both eggs and wine. This would cause the price of both eggs and wine to double.

**a.** Illustrate your original (no-tax) budget line and your budget line under Policy *A.* Mark your optimum point.

**b.** Suppose that, coincidentally, the government would collect exactly as much money from you under Policy *B* as under Policy *A.* Illustrate your budget line under Policy *B.* How does your graph illustrate the fact that the two policies cost you equal amounts of money?

**c.** Which policy do you prefer? Why?

**27.** Suppose the government imposes a *temporary* sales tax—one that is in effect for a short time, but will disappear in the future. In a diagram relating current consumption to future consumption, how does your budget line shift? Which is preferable: a permanent sales tax or a temporary sales tax (assuming the rates are adjusted so they collect equivalent revenues)?

# Appendix to Chapter 3

## Cardinal Utility

The theory of cardinal utility is an alternative approach to consumer behavior. It has the advantage of sometimes being easier to work with and the disadvantage that it introduces a new quantity—called *utility*—that can never actually be measured. However, it turns out to be the case that *the cardinal utility approach has exactly the same implications as the indifference curve approach.* Thus, the choice between the two is largely a matter of convenience and of taste.

### The Utility Function

In the cardinal utility approach, we assume that the consumer can associate each basket with a number, called the **utility** derived from that basket, that measures how much pleasure or satisfaction he would get from owning that basket. For the basket containing $x$ units of $X$ and $y$ units of $Y$, the utility is often denoted $U(x, y)$. Thus, for example, if we write

$$U(5, 7) = 6$$

**Utility**

A measure of pleasure or satisfaction.

what we mean is that a basket containing 5 $X$s and 7 $Y$s gives the consumer 6 units of utility. The rule for going from baskets to utilities is called the consumer's *utility function.* An example of a utility function is

$$U(x, y) = \sqrt{xy + 1}$$

which would yield the value $U(5, 7) = 6$, as above.

We assume that, given a choice between two baskets, the consumer always chooses the one that yields higher utility. Thus, if the consumer with the preceding utility function were given a choice between basket $A$, with 5 units of $X$ and 7 units of $Y$, and basket $B$, with 6 units of $X$ and 4 units of $Y$, then he would choose basket $A$, because $U(5, 7) = 6$ but $U(6, 4) = 5$.

The assumption that consumers seek to maximize utility enables us to pass from utility functions to indifference curves. The consumer with this utility function is indifferent between the baskets $(6, 4)$, $(8, 3)$, $(12, 2)$, and $(4, 6)$, because they all yield utilities of 5. Thus, all of these baskets must lie on the same indifference curve. More generally, all of the baskets $(x, y)$ that satisfy

$$U(x, y) = 5$$

lie on a single indifference curve, so that the equation of that indifference curve is given by $U(x, y) = 5$. Similarly, there is another indifference curve whose equation is given by $U(x, y) = 6$.

77

If a consumer has the utility function $U(x, y)$, then his indifference curves are the curves with equations $U(x, y) = c$, where c is any constant.

## Marginal Utility

**Marginal utility of X ($MU_x$)**

The amount of additional utility derived from an additional unit of X when the quantity of Y is held constant.

The consumer's **marginal utility of X ($MU_x$)** is defined to be the amount of additional utility he acquires when the amount of X is increased by one unit and the amount of Y is held constant. For example, consider a consumer whose utility function is as given and who consumes 5 units of X and 7 units of Y. His utility is $U(5, 7) = 6$. If we increase his consumption of X by one unit, his utility will be $U(6, 7) \approx 6.557$. Thus, the marginal utility of X for this consumer is about .557.

We define the marginal utility of Y ($MU_Y$) in a similar way. For this consumer, increasing Y by one unit would yield utility $U(5, 8) \approx 6.403$. The marginal utility of Y for this consumer is about .403.

We assume that the marginal utility of X is always positive (more is preferred to less) but that each additional unit of X yields less marginal utility than the previous unit (always holding fixed the consumption of Y). This is known as the principle of *diminishing marginal utility*. For example, we have seen that a consumer who starts with basket (5, 7) has $MU_X \approx .557$. After acquiring a unit of X and moving to basket (6, 7), his marginal utility of X is reduced to $MU_X \approx .514$, as you can verify with your calculator.

## Marginal Utility versus Marginal Value

We can relate the concept of marginal utility to the concept of marginal value. Suppose that we reduce your consumption of X by one unit. This reduces your utility by the amount $MU_X$. Now suppose that we increase your consumption of Y by $\Delta Y$ units. This increases your utility by $MU_Y \bullet \Delta Y$. Finally, suppose that $\Delta Y$ is chosen to leave you just as happy as you were before the changes in your consumption. Then $\Delta Y$ is the marginal value (to you) of X in terms of Y forgone. Because you are equally happy before and after the changes, the loss of utility from consuming less X must equal the gain in utility from consuming more Y; in other words,

$$MU_X = MU_Y \bullet \Delta Y$$

Rearranging terms, we get

$$\frac{MU_X}{MU_Y} \bullet \Delta Y = MV_{XY}$$

where $MV_{XY}$ denotes the marginal value of X in terms of Y.

## The Marginal Utility of Income

Suppose that a consumer facing prices $P_X$ and $P_Y$ finds that his income goes up by a dollar. How much additional utility can he achieve?

First, suppose that he spends the additional dollar entirely on X. Then he can purchase $1/P_X$ units of X, each of which yields an additional $MU_X$ units of utility. By spending an additional dollar on X, the consumer increases his utility by the amount $MU_X \bullet (1/P_X) = MU_X/P_X$. Similarly, by spending an additional dollar on Y, the consumer increases his utility by the amount $MU_Y/P_Y$. We can think of $MU_X/P_X$ and $MU_Y/P_Y$ as the marginal utilities of a dollar spent on X and of a dollar spent on Y.

## The Consumer's Optimum

The consumer allocates his income across $X$ and $Y$ so as to achieve the highest possible level of utility. We will determine the conditions that describe this optimum.

Consider the marginal utility of a dollar spent on $X$, $MU_X/P_X$, and the marginal utility of a dollar spent on $Y$, $MU_Y/P_Y$. We will argue that at the consumer's optimum these two quantities must be equal.

To see why, suppose first that $MU_X/P_X$, is greater than $MU_Y/P_Y$. Then there is a way for the consumer to increase his utility. He can spend one dollar less on $Y$ and use that dollar to buy more of $X$. In doing so, he will sacrifice $MU_Y/P_Y$ units of utility and gain the greater quantity $MU_X/P_X$; thus, he becomes better off. Having increased his consumption of $X$, the consumer finds, due to decreasing marginal utility, that $MU_X$ is reduced; and having decreased his consumption of $Y$, he finds that $MU_Y$ is increased. This brings the quantities $MU_X/P_X$ and $MU_Y/P_Y$ closer together. If $MU_X/P_X$ still exceeds $MU_Y/P_Y$, the consumer will again cut his expenditures on $Y$ and use the freed-up income to buy more of $X$. This continues until $MU_X/P_X$ and $MU_Y/P_Y$ become equal.

The same sort of thing happens if $MU_Y/P_Y$ starts out greater than $MU_X/P_X$. In this case the consumer can increase his utility by spending less on $X$ and more on $Y$, which brings $MU_X/P_X$ and $MU_Y/P_Y$ closer together. Again, the process continues until the two are equal.

Thus, at the consumer's optimum we must have

$$MU_X/P_X = MU_Y/P_Y$$

Rearranging terms, we get

$$MU_X/MU_Y = P_X/P_Y$$

We have encountered this last term before in this appendix; we determined that it is equal to the marginal value of $X$ in terms of $Y$. The term on the right is the relative price of $X$ in terms of $Y$. So our cardinal utility analysis leads us to conclude that the consumer's optimum occurs at that point on his budget line where the marginal value of $X$ in terms of $Y$ is equated to the relative price of $X$ in terms of $Y$—exactly the same conclusion that we reached from the indifference curve analysis in Chapter 3!

# Consumers in the Marketplace

In Chapter 1, we told a simple but powerful story about demand, summarized in a single phrase: *When the price goes up, the quantity demanded goes down.*

In Chapter 3, we told a far more sophisticated story about demand: *When the price goes up, the budget line pivots inward and the consumer moves from one tangency to another.*

Our next task is to understand how these stories fit together. Do they always make the same predictions? If so, why? If not, which should we believe?

This chapter will tackle those questions. We will use the indifference curves and budget lines of Chapter 3 to reach a deeper understanding of the law of demand from Chapter 1.

Along the way, we'll learn a lot about how consumers respond to changing market conditions. It turns out that *income* changes are a little easier to analyze than *price* changes, so we'll start by studying income changes in Section 4.1. In Sections 4.2 and 4.3, we'll turn to the effects of price changes. Finally, in Section 4.4, we'll talk about some numerical measures of all these effects.

## 4.1 Changes in Income

In this section, we consider the effects of a change in income. In order to focus on a single good—call it $X$, which might stand for soft drinks or coffee or eggs—we will use the composite-good convention, lumping together everything except $X$ into a single category called *all other goods*. This allows us to maintain the useful fiction that there are only two goods in the economy: There is $X$, and there is "all other goods," which we label $Y$.

### Changes in Income and Changes in the Budget Line

Let's think about how your budget line moves when your income rises.

Suppose you start with the *Original* budget line in Exhibit 4.1. You can afford any basket on this budget line, including, for example, the illustrated basket $G$.

If your income rises by $5, you can now afford to buy basket $G$ *plus* $5 worth of good $Y$. That is, you can afford point $H$. So point $H$ is on your new budget line.

EXHIBIT **4.1**          **A Rise in Income**

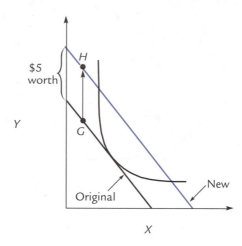

When your income increases by $5, the budget line shifts out parallel to itself. For each point on the original budget line (like G), there is a point on the new budget line (like H) which consists of basket G plus an additional $5 worth of Y.

(If the price of Y is $1 per unit, then the vertical arrow in Exhibit 4.1 has length 5; if the price of Y is $2 per unit, then the vertical arrow has length 2½; if the price of Y is 1¢ per unit, then the vertical arrow has length 500.)

More generally, given *any* point on your old budget line, you can add $5 worth of Y and get a point on your new budget line. So the vertical distance between the two budget lines is always the same "$5 worth." Because this distance is always the same, it follows that the new budget line is parallel to the original.

A change in income causes a parallel shift of the budget line.

**Exercise 4.1** Draw the new budget line that would result from a $5 fall in income.

There is another way to see that a change in income causes a parallel shift of the budget line. Recall from Section 3.2 that the equation of the budget line can be written

$$y = \frac{P_X}{P_Y} \cdot x + \frac{I}{P_Y}$$

so that a change in income (*I*) does not affect the slope ($-P_X/P_Y$). A change in income affects only the *Y*-intercept of the budget line, which is another way of saying that a change in income causes a parallel shift.

## Changes in Income and Changes in the Optimum Point

When your income rises by $5, your budget line shifts out as in Exhibit 4.1. What happens to your optimum point?

In Exhibit 4.2, we suppose that your original optimum point is *A,* where the original budget line (in black) is tangent to the black indifference curve. Now your income

**EXHIBIT 4.2**    **A Rise in Income**

An increase in income causes the budget line to shift outward. If the original tangency is at *A*, then the new tangency cannot be at *O* or *P*, as either possibility would require two indifference curves to cross. (The curves that are shown tangent at these points cannot be indifference curves because they must cross the original black indifference curve.) Instead, the new tangency is at a point like *B*.

rises by $5, causing your budget line to shift out; the new budget line is shown in color. Where can the new tangency be?

The tangency *cannot* be at point *O*. Here's why: If an indifference curve were tangent at *O*, it would be forced to cross the black indifference curve, which cannot happen. (The lightly colored curve shown tangent at *O cannot* be an indifference curve, because it crosses the black indifference curve that is tangent at *A*.) Likewise, the tangency cannot be at point *P*. Instead, the tangency must occur somewhere between points *M* and *N* on the new budget line, at a point like *B*.

## Normal and Inferior Goods

If point *B* is located as in Exhibit 4.2, then a rise in income causes your consumption of *X* to rise. This is because point *B* is to the right of point *A*, so it corresponds to a basket with more *X*.

But alternative pictures are possible. Exhibit 4.3 shows two possibilities. Point *B* could be to the right of *A*, as in the first panel, or point *B* could be to the left of *A*, as in the second panel. In the first case, a rise in income leads you to consume more *X*, and we say that *X* is a **normal good.** In the second case, a rise in income leads you to consume *less X*, and we say that *X* is an **inferior good.**

For example, it is entirely likely that if your income rises, you will consume less Hamburger Helper. That makes Hamburger Helper an inferior good.

**Normal good**

A good that you consume more of when your income rises.

**Inferior good**

A good that you consume less of when your income rises.

The word *inferior* is used differently here than in ordinary English. In ordinary English, *inferior* is a term of comparison; you can't call something inferior without saying what it is inferior to; as a student, you can be inferior to some of your classmates and superior to others. But in economics, a good either is or is not inferior, and inferiority does not have the negative connotations that it has in everyday speech.

Dangerous Curve

EXHIBIT **4.3**          **Normal and Inferior Goods**

Suppose your original tangency is at *A* and your income increases. Then your new tangency *B* could be either to the right of *A* (as in the first panel) or to the left of *A* (as in the second panel). In the first case, a rise in income leads you to consume more *X* and we call *X* a normal good. In the second case, a rise in income leads you to consume less *X* and we call *X* an inferior good.

**Exercise 4.2** In the first panel of Exhibit 4.3, is *Y* an inferior good? What about in the second panel? Where must the tangency *B* be located if *Y* is an inferior good?

## The Engel Curve

**Engel curve**

A curve showing, for fixed prices, the relationship between income and the quantity of a good consumed.

Beth is a consumer who buys eggs and root beer. Her **Engel curve** for eggs is a graph that shows how many eggs she'll consume at each level of income. You can see her Engel curve in the second panel of Exhibit 4.4. When her income is $4, she consumes 3 eggs; when her income is $8, she consumes 6 eggs, and so on.

It turns out that if we know the prices of eggs and root beer, and if we know Beth's indifference curves, then we can *figure out* the coordinates of the points on her Engel curve. For example, suppose we know that the price of an egg is 50¢, the price of a root beer is $1, and Beth's indifference curves are the curves shown in Exhibit 4.4A.

To construct a point on Beth's Engel curve, we follow a five-step process:

1.  Imagine an income for Beth—say, $4.

2.  Draw the corresponding budget line. In this case, given our assumptions about the prices of eggs and root beer, Beth can afford up to 8 eggs (with no root beer) or 4 root beers (with no eggs). Therefore, her budget line is the one labeled "$4 income" in Exhibit 4.4A.

3.  Find the tangency between this budget line and an indifference curve. (We can do this because we've assumed that we *know* Beth's indifference curves.) In this case, the tangency occurs at point A.

4.  Read off the corresponding quantity of eggs—in this case, 3.

5.  Plot the point on the Engel curve, relating the income in step 1 to the quantity in step 4. In this case, we get the point A′ = ($4, 3), illustrated in Exhibit 4.4B.

To get *another* point on Beth's Engel curve, repeat the entire five-step process, beginning with a different income. If you imagine the income $8 in step 1, you'll be led to the quantity 6 in step 4, and you'll plot the point B′ in step 5.

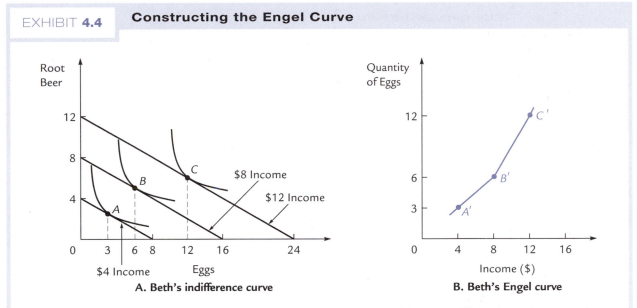

EXHIBIT 4.4    **Constructing the Engel Curve**

**A. Beth's indifference curve**

**B. Beth's Engel curve**

Points *A*, *B*, and *C* in the first panel show Beth's optima at a variety of incomes. (The prices of eggs and root beer are held fixed at 50¢ and $1, respectively.) Points *A′*, *B′*, and *C′* in the second panel record the quantity of eggs that Beth consumes for each of three incomes; these quantities are the horizontal coordinates of points *A*, *B*, and *C*. The curve through *A′*, *B′*, and *C′* is Beth's Engel curve for eggs.

**Exercise 4.3** Explain how to derive the coordinates of point *C′* in Exhibit 4.4B.

The moral of this story is that *the Engel curve contains no information that is not already encoded in the indifference curve diagram.* Once we know the indifference curves, we can generate the Engel curve by a purely mechanical process.

## The Shape of the Engel Curve

The Engel curve in Exhibit 4.4B is upward sloping. In other words, when Beth's income rises, she consumes more eggs. Thus, eggs are a normal good for Beth.

In general, the Engel curve will slope upward for a normal good and downward for an inferior good. If eggs were an inferior good for Beth, then the tangency *B* in Exhibit 4.4A would occur somewhere to the *left* of the tangency *A*—say, with a horizontal coordinate of 2. This would yield the point *B′* = ($8, 2) in Exhibit 4.4B, and the curve through *A′* and *B′* would slope downward.

# 4.2  Changes in Price

We now shift our attention from changes in income to changes in the price of *X*.

## Changes in Price and Changes in the Budget Line

To focus attention on changes in the price of *X*, we assume that your income and the price of *Y* remain fixed. For example, suppose the price of *Y* remains fixed at $3 per unit

## EXHIBIT 4.5    Changes in the Price of *X*

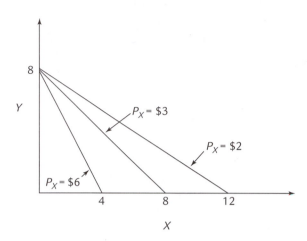

The price of *Y* is fixed at $3 and income is fixed at $24. A rise in the price of *X* causes the budget line to pivot inward around its *Y*-intercept, and a fall in price causes the budget line to pivot outward around its *Y*-intercept.

and your income remains fixed at $24. Exhibit 4.5 shows the budget lines that result when the price of *X* is $2, $3, and $6.

**Exercise 4.4** Verify that the budget lines have been drawn correctly.

There are two important things to notice in Exhibit 4.5. First, a change in the price of *X* has no effect on the *Y*-intercept of the budget line. When you buy zero *X*s, you can always afford exactly 8 *Y*s, regardless of what happens to the price of *X*. Thus:

A change in the price of *X* causes the budget line to pivot around its *Y*-intercept.

The second important thing to notice is the direction in which the budget line pivots. When the price of *X* is low (like $2), the budget line extends out to a high quantity of *X* (in this case, 12); when the price of *X* is high (like $6), the budget line extends out only to a low quantity of *X* (in this case, 4). Thus:

A rise in the price of *X* causes the budget line to pivot inward. A fall in the price of *X* causes the budget line to pivot outward.

## Changes in Price and Changes in the Optimum Point

When the price of *X* rises, your budget line pivots inward, as shown in Exhibit 4.6.

The geometry of Exhibit 4.6 places no restrictions on the location of the new optimum point; it could be anywhere at all on the new budget line. Now we're going to think a little more deeply about the location of that new optimum.

### Giffen and Ordinary Goods

Exhibit 4.7 illustrates two possibilities. In both cases, a rise in the price of *X* causes the optimum point to shift from *A* to *B*. In the first panel, *B* lies to the left of *A*; in the second panel, *B* lies to the right of *A*.

EXHIBIT **4.6**    **A Price Increase**

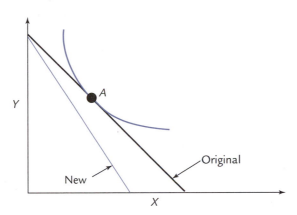

A rise in price causes the budget line to pivot inward. The original optimum is at *A*, and the new optimum could be anywhere at all on the new (brown) budget line.

In the first panel, you can see that when the price of $X$ goes up, the quantity demanded goes down (from $Q_A$ to $Q_B$). That statement should sound familiar; it is the same law of demand that we met in Chapter 1.

In the second panel, you can see that when the price of $X$ goes up, the quantity demanded goes *up*! In this case, $X$ violates the law of demand.

Goods that violate the law of demand (like good $X$ in the second panel of Exhibit 4.7) are called **Giffen goods.** Goods that obey the law of demand (like good $X$ in the first panel of Exhibit 4.7) are called **ordinary goods.**

**Giffen good**

A good that violates the law of demand, so that when the price goes up, the quantity demanded goes up.

Do not confuse the question "Is $X$ Giffen?" with the question "Is $X$ inferior?" To determine whether $X$ is inferior, you must ask what happens when *income* changes, so that the budget line undergoes a parallel shift (as in the two panels of Exhibit 4.3). To determine whether $X$ is Giffen, you must ask what happens when the price of $X$ changes, so that the budget line pivots around its $Y$-intercept, as in the two panels of Exhibit 4.7.

Dangerous Curve

In the panels of Exhibit 4.7, it is not possible to tell by inspection whether $Y$ is a Giffen good. To determine whether $Y$ is Giffen, we have to ask what happens to the consumption of $Y$ when there is a change in the price of $Y$. But the graphs in Exhibit 4.7 illustrate a change in the price of $X$, not a change in the price of $Y$.

Dangerous Curve

**Exercise 4.5** Draw a graph illustrating how the budget line shifts when the price of $Y$ rises. Draw the original optimum. Where is the new optimum located if $Y$ is not a Giffen good? Where is the new optimum located if $Y$ is a Giffen good?

**Ordinary good**

A good that obeys the law of demand: When the price goes up, the quantity demanded goes down.

## A Puzzle: Why Are Giffen Goods so Rare?

Giffen goods are extremely uncommon; in fact, they are so uncommon that the author of your textbook does not know of a single actual instance. That's why the law of demand is called a *law*—it is virtually always obeyed.

**EXHIBIT 4.7    Ordinary Goods and Giffen Goods**

When the price of X goes up, the budget line pivots inward. The optimum moves from point A to point B and the quantity of X that you demand changes from $Q_A$ to $Q_B$. In the first panel, $Q_B$ is less than $Q_A$; in other words "when the price goes up the quantity demanded goes down," as required by the law of demand. In the second panel, $Q_B$ is greater than $Q_A$, so that "when the price goes up the quantity demanded goes *up*," in violation of the law of demand. When the law of demand is violated, X is called a Giffen good.

The theory of indifference curves tells us that there *can* be exceptions to the law of demand—in other words, it is possible to draw a picture like the second panel of Exhibit 4.7. But experience tells us that although such exceptions are possible, they are either extremely rare or completely nonexistent. And therein lies a puzzle. If the theory allows Giffen goods to exist, why don't they?

We will return to this puzzle—and solve it—near the end of Section 4.3.

## The Demand Curve

Let us return our attention to Beth, who buys eggs and root beer. Just as Beth's Engel curve shows the relation between her income and her egg consumption, so her demand curve shows the relation between the price of eggs and her egg consumption.

Dangerous
Curve

The Engel curve plots income on the horizontal axis versus egg consumption on the vertical; the demand curve plots the price of eggs on the vertical axis versus egg consumption on the horizontal.

Like the Engel curve, the demand curve can be derived from the indifference curve diagram. If we know Beth's income, the price of root beer, and her indifference curves, then we can construct her demand curve for eggs.

The process is illustrated in Exhibit 4.8, where we assume that the price of root beer is $3 and Beth's income is $24; thus, the vertical intercept of her budget line is at 8 root beers.

To construct a point on Beth's demand curve, we follow a five-step process:

1. Imagine a price for eggs—say, $2.

2. Draw the corresponding budget line. Given our assumption that Beth's income is $24, she can afford up to 12 eggs (with no root beer). Thus, her budget line has horizontal intercept 12, as illustrated in Exhibit 4.8A.

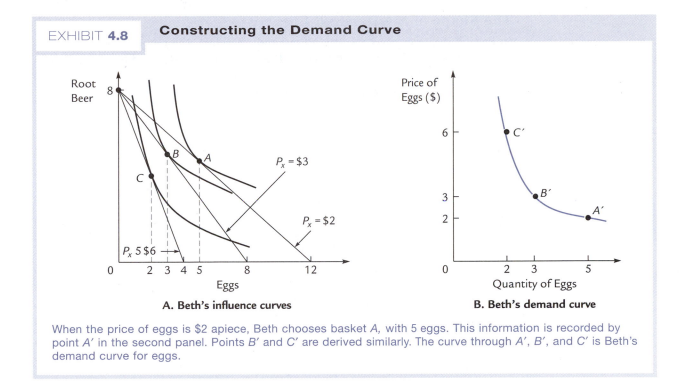

**EXHIBIT 4.8**    **Constructing the Demand Curve**

A. Beth's influence curves

B. Beth's demand curve

When the price of eggs is $2 apiece, Beth chooses basket *A,* with 5 eggs. This information is recorded by point *A′* in the second panel. Points *B′* and *C′* are derived similarly. The curve through *A′*, *B′*, and *C′* is Beth's demand curve for eggs.

**3.** Find the tangency between this budget line and an indifference curve. In this case, the tangency occurs at point *A.*

**4.** Read off the corresponding quantity of eggs—in this case, 5.

**5.** Plot a point on the demand curve relating the price in step 1 to the quantity in step 4. In this case we get the point *A′* in Exhibit 4.8B.

To get *another* point on Beth's demand curve, repeat the entire five-step process, beginning with a different price for eggs. If you imagine the price $3 in step 1, you'll be led to the quantity 3 in step 4, and you'll plot the point *B′* in step 5.

**Exercise 4.6** Explain how to derive the coordinates of point *C′* in Exhibit 4.8B.

As with the Engel curve, we now know that *the demand curve contains no information that is not already encoded in the indifference curve diagram.* Once we know the indifference curves, we can generate the demand curve by a purely mechanical process.

Students sometimes attempt to draw the demand curve and the indifference curves on the same graph. This cannot be done correctly because the two diagrams require different axes (quantities of goods *X* and *Y* for the indifference curves; quantity and price of good *X* for the demand curve).

Other students sometimes think that the labeled points in Exhibit 4.8A illustrate the shape of the demand curve. This is also incorrect. It is true that each point on the demand curve arises from a point in the indifference curve diagram, but translating from one diagram to the other is not simply a matter of copying points. The only way to go from one diagram to the other is via the five-step process just described.

Dangerous
Curve

### The Shape of the Demand Curve

In Exhibit 4.8, eggs obey the law of demand; therefore, the demand curve for eggs slopes down. If eggs were a Giffen good, then the tangency $B$ would be to the *right* of $A$, say, at a quantity of 7. Then the point $B'$ on the demand curve would have horizontal coordinate 7 and the demand curve would slope upward.

# 4.3 Income and Substitution Effects

We have a puzzle to solve: Why, in the real world, do there seem to be essentially no Giffen goods? It would be very satisfying to answer this question by saying that the geometry of indifference curves makes Giffen goods impossible. Unfortunately, that is not the case. Exhibit 4.7 showed that there is no geometric obstruction to the existence of a Giffen good.

So the solution to our puzzle will require an argument that goes beyond geometry. We will start with a purely verbal discussion of two distinct reasons why the law of demand "ought" to hold. After we've understood these effects in words, we will translate our words into geometry and then tie the two approaches together.

## Two Effects of a Price Increase

When the price of a good goes up, we typically expect the quantity demanded to fall. There are two separate, good reasons for this expectation, called the *substitution effect* and the *income effect*.

### The Substitution Effect

Suppose you're in the habit of buying 5 hamburgers a day at $2 apiece. If the price goes up to $3 apiece, you might decide that fifth hamburger is simply not worth the money, and therefore cut back to 4 hamburgers a day. That's the substitution effect of a price increase.

**Substitution effect of a price increase**

A change in consumption due to the fact that you won't buy goods whose marginal value is below the new price.

To put this a little more precisely: We know that each of your five hamburgers must have a marginal value (to you) of at least $2; otherwise you wouldn't have been buying them all along. But their marginal values are not all identical; the second hamburger is worth less than the first, and the third is worth less than the second. So it's entirely possible that the first four hamburgers are worth more than $3 each (to you) and the fifth hamburger is worth less than $3. That's why you still eat some hamburgers, but not as many as before.

So the substitution effect comes down to this: When the price of a good rises, you adjust your consumption downward so as to avoid buying goods whose price is now above their marginal value.

When the price of a good goes up, the substitution effect leads you to consume less of it.

### The Income Effect

Now we will describe the income effect of a price increase.

Suppose the price of hamburgers rises. Then, because you can't spend more than your entire income, you'll have to consume less of *something*. (Another way to say this is that your old basket is outside your new budget line, so you'll have to choose a new basket.) It's then quite likely—though not certain—that hamburgers themselves will be among the goods you cut back on.

We can be more precise about this: The fact that you can no longer afford your original basket is tantamount to a change in *income;* in a very real sense, a price increase makes you *poorer.* When you become poorer, you reduce your consumption of all normal goods, though you increase your consumption of inferior goods.

That's the income effect of a price increase: When the price of hamburgers rises, you are effectively poorer and therefore consume either fewer hamburgers (if hamburgers are a normal good) or more hamburgers (if hamburgers are an inferior good).

When the price of a good goes up, the income effect leads you to consume either less of it (this happens if the good is normal) or more of it (this happens if the good is inferior).

## Isolating the Substitution Effect: An Imaginary Experiment

When the price of candy bars goes up, Albert buys fewer candy bars. At the old (low) price, he might have bought 8, but at the new (high) price, he buys only 3. Question: How much of that reduction is due to the income effect and how much to the substitution effect?

So far, we have no way to tell. As soon as the price rises, Albert feels both effects simultaneously and responds to both of them simultaneously. All we see is the combined response. Of the 5 candy bars he gave up, were 2 due to the income effect and 3 to the substitution effect? Or 3 and 2? Or 1 and 4? Anything is possible.

So let's try a little experiment. Our goal is to *make the income effect go away* so that we can observe the substitution effect in isolation. How can we do this?

Well, why is there an income effect in the first place? It's because Albert, faced with higher prices, feels poorer. How can we make that effect go away? Obviously, by making him feel richer. How can we do that? Obviously, by giving him money.

So let's arrange the following experiment. We raise the price of candy bars. At the same time, we leave a few quarters on the ground for Albert to find. When he pushes his shopping cart down the candy aisle, he gets two surprises at once: The price has risen (which makes him feel poorer) and he's found some money (which makes him feel richer). If we leave him *exactly the right amount* of money, those effects will cancel, and he'll feel just as rich as he felt an hour ago. He'll feel no income effect. Now whatever he does is due to the pure substitution effect. If he puts, say, 5 candy bars in his cart instead of his usual 8, then we can conclude that the substitution effect causes him to give up exactly 3 candy bars.

At this point, we can walk up to Albert, tap him on the shoulder, and say: "Excuse me, but I believe those are my quarters." He returns the money, goes back to feeling poorer, and returns 2 of his 5 candy bars to the shelf, keeping 3. This movement is entirely a result of his feeling poorer, so we're seeing the pure income effect, which we now know is responsible for his giving up exactly 2 candy bars.

## Visualizing the Imaginary Experiment

Exhibit 4.9 illustrates our imaginary experiment. In panel A, Albert enters the grocery store expecting to find candy bars on sale at their traditional price. He therefore expects to have the *Original* budget line, where his tangency is at point *A* and he buys 8 candy bars. But when he arrives at the candy aisle, he sees that the price has risen. This causes his budget line to pivot in to the location of the *New* budget line, where his tangency is at *B*. He therefore buys 3 candy bars. *The reduction from 8 to 3 is due to the income and substitution effects combined.*

**Income effect of a price increase**

A change in consumption due to the fact that you can no longer afford your original basket and are therefore effectively poorer.

That didn't help us distinguish one effect from the other, so we start all over again. This time, we leave some quarters for Albert to find just at the moment when he notices the price increase. The price increase still pivots his budget line in to the *New* location, but then the cash windfall shifts that budget line outward, parallel to itself.

How far out does the budget line shift? That depends on how much cash we give him. How much cash should we give him? Enough to just cancel the income effect. How much is that? Enough to leave him feeling neither richer nor poorer than he was an hour ago. What exactly does that mean? The notion of "feeling richer" is a little vague, but we can interpret it to mean that Albert should be *exactly as happy* as he was an hour ago. In other words, we give him *just enough cash so that he can reach a tangency on his* Original *budget line.*

In panel B of Exhibit 4.9, this means that we give him just enough cash to shift his *New* budget line until it's tangent to his original indifference curve. Think of the *New* line as gradually shifting outward as we leave more and more money for Albert to find; we stop adding to the pile when the budget line just touches the upper indifference curve at a tangency which we label *C*. The resulting budget line is called Albert's *Compensated* budget line, because the additional income exactly compensates for the price increase (in the sense that it leaves him just as happy as he was an hour ago).

**Dangerous Curve**

When they shift the *New* budget line outward, students sometimes try to make it tangent to the upper indifference curve at point *A*. This can't be correct, because the *Original* budget line is already tangent there. Two different lines cannot be tangent to the same curve at the same point.

Having discovered both the price increase *and* the cash, Albert is now on his *Compensated* budget line, where he chooses point *C*, with 5 candy bars. The movement from *A* to *C*—that is, the movement from 8 candy bars to 5—is a pure substitution effect.

Now is when we give Albert the bad news that he doesn't get to keep the cash he found. This shifts his budget line back from the *Compensated* location to the *New* location. He shifts from point *C* to point *B*, or in other words from 5 candy bars to 3. This is the pure income effect.

## Sorting It All Out

In ordinary circumstances, Albert does his shopping without a mad experimenter following in his wake. Therefore, in ordinary circumstances, panel A of Exhibit 4.9 tells the whole story. The price of candy rises, Albert feels two effects at once, and he moves to point *B* because of the two effects combined—as indicated by the horizontal arrow in panel C of the exhibit.

But even though Albert moves directly from *A* to *B*, we can always *imagine* that for a brief moment he received some additional cash, moving him to *C*, and then the additional cash was taken away from him, moving him back to *B* again. The first move is the pure substitution effect and the second move is the pure income effect, as indicated by the other two arrows in panel C.

**Dangerous Curve**

Notice that a price change causes *two* effects whereas a price change accompanied by an offsetting income increase causes *one* effect.

**EXHIBIT 4.9**    **Income and Substitution Effects**

**A. A price increase**

**B. Income compensation**

**C. Schematic**

Albert starts with the *Original* budget line and chooses tangency *A*. If the price of candy bars increases, the budget line pivots in to the *New* location and he chooses tangency *B*. The move from *A* to *B* is caused by the income and substitution effects together, as indicated by the horizontal arrow in panel C.

In panel B, we imagine that Albert's income rises at the same moment that he discovers the candy price increase. This shifts his *New* budget line out parallel to itself. The more his income rises, the further the budget line shifts.

We assume that either by coincidence or through the design of a mad experimenter, Albert's budget line shifts until it *just touches* his original indifference curve, giving him a new tangency at point *C*. The resulting budget line is labeled *Compensated* because the income increase just compensates him for the price increase, leaving him just as happy as he was an hour ago. The movement from *A* to *C* is a pure substitution effect, as indicated by the downward sloping arrow in panel C.

If Albert then loses his newfound income, he returns to the *New* budget line and point *B*; this move from *C* to *B* is a pure income effect.

In reality, Albert is not compensated for price changes, so he moves directly from *A* to *B*. But to separate the substitution and income effects, we can always *imagine* that he moves first to *C* and then to *B*.

**Exercise 4.7** Suppose the price of candy bars were to fall. Draw a diagram analogous to Exhibit 4.9 showing how Albert's consumption changes and separating the change into a substitution effect and an income effect. (*Hint:* When the price of candy bars falls, Albert feels happier than before. To eliminate the income effect, you have to "compensate" him negatively, by taking income away until he is no happier than before.)

## Why Demand Curves Slope Downward

Exhibit 4.10 is a reminder that the shape of the demand curve depends on the configuration of the indifference curves. At the *original* price of candy bars, Albert chooses tangency A and buys 8 candy bars; this is recorded by point A′ on the demand curve. At the higher *new* price of candy bars, Albert chooses tangency B and buys 3 candy bars. This is recorded by point B′ on the demand curve.

Why does the demand curve slope downward? Because point B′ (corresponding to the higher price) is to the *left* of point A′. (That is, higher prices go with lower quantities.) Why is B′ to the left of A′? Because B is left of A on the indifference curve diagram.

So, if you want to know why demand curves slope downward, you've got to ask: Why is B to the left of A? Here's where we can use what we've learned about income and substitution effects.

| EXHIBIT **4.10** | **Why Demand Curves Slope Downward** |
| --- | --- |

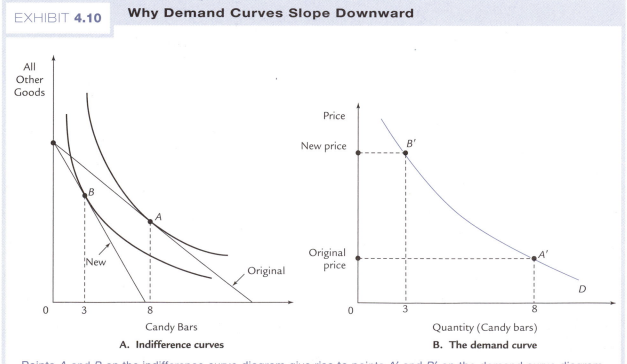

**A. Indifference curves**          **B. The demand curve**

Points A and B on the indifference curve diagram give rise to points A′ and B′ on the demand curve diagram. The demand curve slopes downward because B′ is to the left of A′. In turn, B′ is to the left of A′ because B is to the left of A. So asking "Why do demand curves slope downward?" is the same as asking "Why is B to the left of A?"

The first panel of Exhibit 4.11 reproduces the income and substitution effects that were illustrated in Exhibit 4.9. Remember that when the price of good *X* rises, the substitution effect is the move from *A* to *C* and the income effect is the move from *C* to *B*. Now let's do some geometry.

## Some Geometric Observations

Here are three key observations about the points in Exhibit 4.11:

1. *C* is always to the left of *A*. Here's why: *C* and *A* are on the same indifference curve, but *C* is the tangency with a steeper line, so *C* must be on a steeper part of the curve. Steeper parts of the curve are always to the left. (Notice that this purely geometric observation is equivalent to something we observed earlier: When the price of a good goes up, the substitution effect always leads you to consume less of it.)

2. If *X* is a normal good, then *B* is to the left of *C*. Here's why: The move from *C* to *B* represents a pure change in income (*C* and *B* are tangencies with parallel budget lines). When you move from the *Compensated* line to the *New* line, income falls, so you consume less *X;* that is, you move to the left.

3. If *X* is an inferior good, then *B* is to the right of *C*. In other words, when income falls, you consume *more* of the inferior good *X*.

(In Exhibit 4.11, *B* is drawn to the left of *C,* so in this case *X* is a normal good.)

EXHIBIT **4.11**    **Income and Substitution Effects**

When the price of *X* rises, the consumer moves from *A* to *B*. This move can be broken down into a substitution effect (from *A* to *C*) followed by an income effect (from *C* to *B*). The move from *A* to *C* is always leftward. If *X* is normal, the move from *C* to *B* is also leftward, so the move from *A* to *B* is leftward; therefore, *X* is ordinary. If *X* is inferior, the move from *C* to *B* is rightward. This allows two possibilities: Either *B* is to the left of *A* (this happens when the income effect is small), so that *X* is ordinary, or *B* is to the right of *A* (this happens when the income effect is large), so that *X* is Giffen.

## The Demand Curve for a Normal Good

Suppose that $X$ is a normal good. When the price of $X$ goes up, the consumer in Exhibit 4.11 moves from $A$ to $B$. What is the direction of that move?

We know from the first of our geometric observations that $C$ is to the left of $A$. Because we've assumed that $X$ is normal, we know from the second observation that $B$ is to the left of $C$. Using your best IQ-test skills, what can you conclude about the relative positions of $A$ and $B$?

The answer is revealed in the top row of the right-hand panel in Exhibit 4.11, where you can see that $B$ must be to the left of $A$. In other words, when the price of $X$ goes up, the quantity demanded goes down. In still other words, $X$ is an ordinary (i.e., non-Giffen) good. Because this argument applies whenever $X$ is normal, we can summarize our conclusion as follows:

A normal good cannot be Giffen.

We've just discovered something truly remarkable. To say that a good is normal is to say something about the response to an *income* change. To say that a good is Giffen is to say something about the response to a *price* change. There is no obvious reason why these conditions should have anything to do with one another. But our analysis reveals that they are closely related nevertheless: No normal good can ever be Giffen. The demand curve for a normal good is sure to slope downward.

Although we've phrased the argument in terms of geometry, we can translate it into economics. When the price of $X$ goes up, the substitution effect (from $A$ to $C$) must cause the quantity demanded to fall. At the same time, the income effect (from $C$ to $B$) *also* causes the quantity demanded to fall. These effects reinforce each other, and the quantity demanded certainly falls.

## The Demand Curve for an Inferior Good

Now suppose that $X$ is an inferior good. When the price of $X$ goes up, the consumer in Exhibit 4.11 moves from $A$ to $B$. What is the direction of that move?

We know from the first geometric observation that $C$ is to the left of $A$. Because we've assumed that $X$ is inferior, we know from the second observation that $B$ is to the right of $C$.

Bringing your IQ-test skills to bear on this problem, you'll quickly discover that you can draw no certain conclusion about the relative locations of points $A$ and $B$. There are two possibilities, illustrated in the second and third rows of the right-hand panel in Exhibit 4.11. When the substitution effect is larger than the income effect, $B$ is to the left of $A$ (so that $X$ is ordinary) but when the income effect is larger than the substitution effect, $B$ is to the right of $A$ (so that $X$ is Giffen).

The two panels of Exhibit 4.12 show that each of these possibilities can occur. Therefore:

An inferior good is ordinary if the substitution effect exceeds the income effect, but Giffen if the income effect exceeds the substitution effect.

The economic interpretation is straightforward: When the price of $X$ goes up, the substitution effect (from $A$ to $C$) causes the quantity demanded to fall. At the same time, the income effect (from $C$ to $B$) causes the quantity demanded to *rise* (because $X$ is an inferior good). These effects work in opposite directions, so the quantity demanded of $X$ can fall or rise, depending on which effect is bigger.

EXHIBIT **4.12**      **Income and Substitution Effects for an Inferior Good**

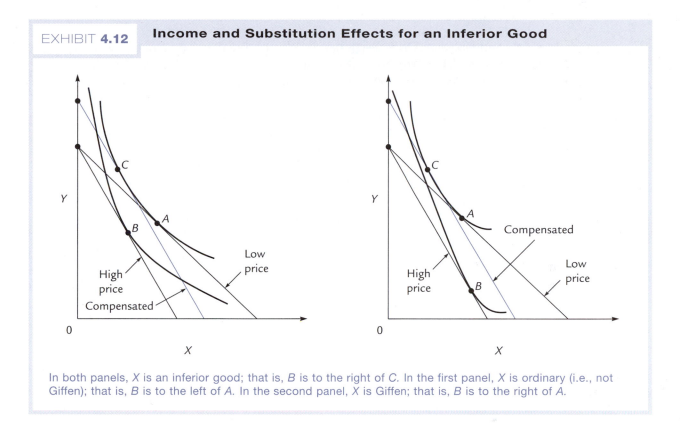

In both panels, X is an inferior good; that is, B is to the right of C. In the first panel, X is ordinary (i.e., not Giffen); that is, B is to the left of A. In the second panel, X is Giffen; that is, B is to the right of A.

## The Size of the Income Effect

Suppose the price of bubble gum rises. Will you feel slightly poorer or a lot poorer? Unless you are a very unusual person—that is, unless you spend a very substantial portion of your income on bubble gum—you will feel only slightly poorer. Therefore, the income effect, which is caused by that sense of being poorer, is likely to be small.

On the other hand, suppose the price of college tuition rises. Depending on who's paying for your education, there's a good chance you'll now feel quite substantially poorer. If tuition expenses account for a substantial fraction of your income, the income effect might be considerable.

In general, the income effect of a price change is large only for goods that account for a large fraction of your expenditure. The laws of arithmetic dictate that there can't be very many such goods (for example, there can be no more than 3 goods that account for at least ⅓ of your expenditure). So large income effects are relatively rare.

## Giffen Goods Revisited

A Giffen good must satisfy two conditions. First, it must be inferior (because a normal good cannot be Giffen). Second, it must account for a substantial fraction of your expenditure (because an inferior good is Giffen only when the income effect exceeds the substitution effect).

Each of these conditions is unusual. Many goods are inferior, but most are not. And only very few goods can account for substantial fractions of your expenditure. Thus, in order to be Giffen, a good must satisfy *two* unusual conditions at once. This explains why Giffen goods are rare.

In fact, one can make an even stronger argument. We've said that a randomly chosen good is likely to be normal. But we can also say that if the randomly chosen good accounts for a large fraction of your expenditure, then it's *particularly* likely to be normal. Here's why: When your income increases, you have to spend the excess on something, and the goods on which you spend relatively little are unlikely to soak up much of that excess. For example, if your income rises by $100 per week, it is unlikely that you'll devote the entire $100 to bubble gum—to do so would require an implausibly large percentage increase in your bubble gum expenditures. Instead, some of the $100 will probably go toward the goods that account for the bulk of your expenditure—which means that those goods are probably normal. So not only do Giffen goods have to satisfy two improbable conditions but one of those improbable conditions causes the other to become even *more* improbable.

Dangerous
Curve

Here's a hypothetical example. Suppose you eat hamburger six days a week and steak on Sunday; suppose also that hamburger is an inferior good. One day the price of hamburger rises. Because you eat so much hamburger, this makes you feel a lot poorer. Because you are now so much poorer, you decide to cut out steak entirely and eat hamburgers seven days a week. When the price of hamburgers goes up, the quantity demanded goes *up*. In this case, hamburgers are a Giffen good.

For this story to work, hamburgers must be inferior *and* you must spend so much on hamburger that the price increase has a major impact on your lifestyle. The moral of Exhibit 4.11 is that this story about hamburgers is essentially the *only* story that could ever produce a Giffen good.

## Example: "Bad" Cigarettes as Giffen Goods

In the real world, big income effects are rare, which is part of why Giffen goods are rare. But in the laboratory, big income effects are easy to create, so the laboratory is where we should look for Giffen goods.

In one experiment,[1] a group of heavy smokers were given incomes of $6 each. They could purchase puffs on either "good" cigarettes (that is, brands they liked a lot) or "bad" cigarettes (brands they liked less). At a price of 25¢ per good puff and 5¢ per bad puff, a typical subject chose 20 puffs of each.

For the duration of the experiment, subjects couldn't buy anything but cigarette puffs. Therefore, both good and bad puffs accounted for substantial fractions of their spending. (One sixth of their spending went to bad cigarettes; by contrast, very few of us spend anywhere close to one sixth of our incomes on any one thing.) All income effects were therefore large. Also, it's reasonable to expect that bad puffs should be an inferior good. This makes the conditions exactly right for bad puffs to be not just inferior, but also Giffen.

And that's exactly what happens. When the price of a bad puff is increased to 12.5¢, our typical subject chooses 24 bad puffs instead of 20. This is exactly what we'd expect based on the logic of the hypothetical hamburger/steak example above. That example remains hypothetical because in the real world, the income effect associated with hamburger is unlikely to be extremely large. Thus, the cigarette experiment confirms our conclusion that Giffen goods arise from large income effects, which reinforces our explanation of why they're rarely observed.

---

[1] R.J. DeGrandpre, Warren Bickel, S. Abu Turab Rizvi, and John Hughes, "Effects of Income on Drug Choice in Humans," *Journal of the Experimental Analysis of Behavior* 59 (1993): 483–500.

# The Compensated Demand Curve

When the price of lettuce rises from $1 to $3, Bugs reduces his consumption from 7 heads of lettuce per day to 1 head of lettuce per day. You can see in the first panel of Exhibit 4.13 that his consumption is reduced from 7 to 3 by the substitution effect and from 3 to 1 by the income effect. Bugs's demand curve, shown in the third panel, records the combined effect by showing that his consumption falls from 7 to 1.

But for some applications, it is useful to keep track of the substitution effect independent of the income effect. (We will meet some of these applications in Chapter 8.) In order to do that, we can draw Bugs's compensated demand curve, which shows that at a price of $3, he would consume 3 heads of lettuce—in the hypothetical circumstance where he feels no income effect.

You can imagine Bugs as the subject of an imaginary experiment, where every time the price of lettuce changes, experimenters adjust his income to keep him on his original indifference curve; we summarize this condition by saying that Bugs is income-compensated for all price changes. The compensated demand curve shows how much lettuce Bugs would consume if he were the subject of that experiment.

Because the substitution effect of a price increase always reduces the quantity demanded, it follows that the compensated demand curve must slope down. In terms of Exhibit 4.13, point C in the first panel is always to the left of point A; therefore, point C′ in the second panel is always to the left of point A′. Again, the conclusion is that the compensated demand curve slopes downward. This is in contrast to the ordinary (uncompensated) demand curve, which slopes upward in the case of a Giffen good.

**Compensated demand curve**

A curve showing, for each price, what the quantity demanded would be if the consumer were income-compensated for all price changes.

The ordinary (uncompensated) demand curve describes the behavior of actual consumers in actual markets. *Whenever we use the unqualified phrase "demand curve," we always mean the ordinary (uncompensated) demand curve.*

Dangerous Curve

---

EXHIBIT **4.13**    **Compensated and Uncompensated Demand Curve**

When the price of lettuce rises from $1 to $3, Bugs reduces his consumption from 7 heads to 1; this is recorded by the ordinary demand curve in the rightmost panel. If he were income-compensated for the price change, he would reduce his consumption from 7 heads to 3; this is recorded by the compensated demand curve in the center panel.

# 4.4 Elasticities

If you owned a clothing store, you'd want to be able to anticipate changes in your customers' buying habits. From the material we have developed so far, you'd be able to draw two general conclusions. First, if their income increases, your customers will probably buy more clothes. Second, if the price of clothing falls, your customers will almost surely buy more clothes.

As the owner of a business who is trying to foresee market conditions, you might find these revelations unsatisfying. Although they predict the *directions* of change, they say nothing about the *magnitude* of change. What you really want to know is: If my customers' incomes increase by a certain amount, by *how much* will they increase their expenditures on clothing? If the price falls by a certain amount, by *how much* will the quantity demanded increase?

Elasticities are numbers that answer these questions. In this section, we will learn what elasticities are and see some sample estimates.

## Income Elasticity of Demand

First we will consider the response to a change in income. This response is depicted by the Engel curve, and one way to measure it is by the *slope* of that curve. We ask: If your income increased by $1, by how many units would you increase your consumption of *X*? That number is the slope of your Engel curve.

Unfortunately, this slope is arbitrary. For one thing, it depends on the units in which *X* is measured. When your income goes up by $1, your yearly coffee consumption might go up by 6 cups, which is the same as 1 pot. If coffee is measured in cups, your Engel curve has slope 6; if coffee is measured in pots, it has slope 1. For another thing, the slope depends on the units in which your income is measured. Your coffee consumption will respond differently if your income increases by one Italian lira instead of one U.S. dollar.

Therefore, we adopt a different measure, one that does not depend on the choice of units. Instead of asking, "If your income increased by *one dollar,* by how many *units* would you increase your consumption of *X*?" we ask, "If your income increased by 1%, by what *percent* would you increase your consumption of *X*?" The answer to this question is a number that does not depend on the choice of units. That number is called the elasticity of your Engel curve, or your **income elasticity of demand.**

**Income elasticity of demand**

The percent change in consumption that results from a 1% increase in income.

If your income *I* changes by an amount $\Delta I$, then the percent change in your income is given by $100 \times \Delta I/I$. If the quantity of *X* that you consume, *Q*, changes by an amount $\Delta Q$, then the percent change in consumption is $100 \times \Delta Q/Q$. The formula for income elasticity is

$$\text{Income elasticity} = \frac{\text{Percent change in quantity}}{\text{Percent change in income}}$$

$$= \frac{100 \cdot \Delta Q/Q}{100 \cdot \Delta I/I}$$

$$= \frac{I \cdot \Delta Q}{Q \cdot \Delta I}$$

Suppose, for example, that your Engel curve for *X* is the one depicted in panel B of Exhibit 4.4. When your income increases from $8 to $12 (a 50% increase), your consumption of *X* increases from 6 to 12 (a 100% increase). In this region, your income elasticity of demand is 100%/50% = 2.

On the other hand, when your income increases from $4 to $8, your consumption of $X$ increases from 3 to 6; a 100% increase in income yields a 100% increase in quantity, so your income elasticity of demand in this region is 1.

---

**Exercise 4.8** What would it mean for your income elasticity of demand for X to be negative?

---

## Applications

Suppose again that you own a clothing store, you foresee an increase in your customers' incomes, and you want to anticipate the change in their clothing expenditures. The critical bit of information is the income elasticity of demand for clothing. In fact, that elasticity has been estimated at about .95.[2] If your customers' incomes increase by 10%, you may expect them to increase their expenditures on clothing by about 9.5%.

Following an increase in income, it usually takes time for people to fully adjust their spending patterns. Thus, we can estimate both a short-run and a long-run income elasticity, reflecting an initial partial response to an income increase and the ultimate full response. We expect the long-run elasticity to exceed the short-run elasticity, and for clothing this is indeed the case. Although the short-run elasticity is .95, the long-run elasticity is 1.17. Following a 10% increase in income, people initially increase expenditures on clothing by 9.5%, but ultimately increase expenditures by 11.7%.

Income elasticities take a wide range of values. The income elasticity of demand for an inferior good is negative. The income elasticity of demand for alcoholic beverages is only about .29. (A 10% increase in income leads to a 2.9% increase in expenditure on alcohol.) The income elasticity of demand for jewelry is about 1, so that expenditure on jewelry increases roughly in proportion with income. The income elasticity of demand for household appliances is 2.72. When income increases 10%, expenditure on appliances increases 27.2%. (The estimates in this paragraph are all short-run elasticities.)

## The Demand for Quality

When people get wealthier, they not only buy *more* goods, they also buy *better* goods. If your income goes up by 10 percent, you might replace your microwave or your stereo with a better microwave or a better stereo.

When economists estimate income elasticities, they usually count a $2,000 stereo system as the equivalent of two $1,000 stereo systems. So when we say that a 10% increase in income yields a 27.2% increase in expenditure on appliances, that might mean a 27.2% increase in the *number* of appliances, or a 27.2% increase in the *quality* of the appliances, or both. (Here we are using price to measure quality, so that by definition a stereo that costs 27.2% more is 27.2% better.)

On average over all goods, economists Mark Bils and Pete Klenow estimate that as people become wealthier, quality grows a little more rapidly than quantity. But the ratio of quality changes to quantity changes is very different for different goods. If you're rich enough to own two microwaves instead of one, they'll cost, on average, about 25% more than your poorer neighbor's single unit. The poor family pays (say) $200 for one microwave; the rich family pays $250 apiece for two (presumably better) microwaves.

---

[2] H. Houthakker and L. Taylor, *Consumer Demand in the United States,* Cambridge: Harvard University Press, 1970. All further elasticity estimates in this chapter are taken from this source.

But if you're rich enough to own two living room tables instead of one, the 25% rule no longer holds; now you'll pay, on average, about 100% more per table. The poor family pays $500 for one living room table while the rich family pays $1,000 apiece for two. A family with twice as many vacuums pays (on average) about 22% more per vacuum; a family with twice as many trucks pays about 140% more per truck.[3]

These numbers suggest that over time, as families on average become richer, the average quality of living room tables should rise faster than the average quality of microwaves, and the average quality of trucks should rise faster than the average quality of vacuums. Of course, it's possible that technological consideration will undercut some of these predictions—we could, in principle, reach a point where it's very hard to make better trucks but still very easy to make better vacuums.

## Price Elasticity of Demand

**Price elasticity of demand**

The percent change in consumption that results from a 1% increase in price.

When the price of salt goes up, people buy less salt. When the price of fresh tomatoes goes up, people buy fewer tomatoes. But the responses are of very different magnitudes. A 10% increase in the price of salt typically leads to about a 1% decrease in the quantity bought. A 10% increase in the price of fresh tomatoes typically leads to about a 46% decrease in the quantity bought.

We express this contrast by saying that the **price elasticity of demand** for tomatoes is 46 times as great as the price elasticity of demand for salt.

More formally, your price elasticity of demand for a good $X$ (also called the elasticity of your demand curve for $X$) is defined by the formula:

$$\text{Price elasticity} = \frac{\text{Percent change in quantity}}{\text{Percent change in price}}$$

$$= \frac{100 \cdot \Delta Q/Q}{100 \cdot \Delta P/P}$$

$$= \frac{P \cdot \Delta Q}{Q \cdot \Delta P}$$

If your demand curve for $X$ slopes downward, then the price elasticity is negative, because an increase (that is, a positive change) in price is associated with a decrease (that is, a negative change) in quantity. For example, suppose that a price of $2 corresponds to a quantity of 5 and a price of $3 corresponds to a quantity of 4. Then a 50% price increase yields a 20% quantity decrease, so the price elasticity of demand is $(-20\%)/50\% = -.4$

Just as we can talk about your personal price elasticity of demand for $X$, so we can talk about the market's price elasticity of demand for $X$. Again, we divide the percent change in quantity by the percent change in price, only now we take our quantities from the market demand curve instead of your personal demand curve.

**Exercise 4.9** Use the formula for price elasticity and the information given at the beginning of this subsection to show that the price elasticities of demand for salt and for fresh tomatoes are −.1 and −4.6.

We say that the demand for a good is highly elastic when the price elasticity of demand for that good has a large absolute value. Thus the demand for tomatoes is

[3] The numbers in this paragraph, and the idea of estimating elasticities for "quality Engel curves," come from M. Bils and P. Klenow, "Quantifying Quality Growth," *American Economic Review,* September 2001.

highly elastic when compared with the demand for salt. We also say that the demand for tomatoes is *more elastic* than the demand for salt.

The next question is: why? Why are tomato buyers so much more price-sensitive than salt buyers? One key factor is the availability of substitutes. If the price of tomatoes goes up, you can substitute any of a dozen other vegetables in your salad. Whenever a good has many substitutes, the demand tends to be highly elastic. That's why the elasticity of demand for Chevrolets is about −4.0 even though the elasticity of demand for cars is around −1.3. There are many good substitutes for a Chevrolet (like a Ford) but not so many good substitutes for a car. Likewise, most soft drinks (like Coke, Diet Coke, or Pepsi) have highly elastic demand curves with elasticities in the range of −3 to −4.

For the same reason, we expect that the demand for Hostess Twinkies is more elastic than the demand for packaged cakes; the demand for packaged cakes is more elastic than the demand for snack foods; and the demand for snack foods is more elastic than the demand for food generally.

---

For a given income and quantity of $X$, high income elasticity is reflected in a relatively steep Engel curve. For a given price and quantity of $X$, high price elasticity is reflected in a relatively flat demand curve. The apparent paradox occurs because the quantity of $X$ is plotted on the vertical axis for an Engel curve and on the horizontal axis for a demand curve.

Dangerous
Curve

---

The price elasticity of demand for electricity is −.13, for water −.20, for jewelry −.41, for shoes −.73, and for tobacco −1.4. If the price of electricity rises by 10%, the quantity demanded falls by 1.3%. If the price of water rises by 10%, the quantity demanded falls by 2%.

---

**Exercise 4.10** If the price of jewelry rises by 10%, by how much does the quantity demanded fall? How about for shoes? For tobacco?

---

## The Relationship between Price Elasticity and Income Elasticity

When the price goes up, the quantity demanded goes down, usually for two reasons: a substitution effect and an income effect. So the price elasticity of demand depends both on the size of the substitution effect and on the size and direction of the income effect.

The income effect is larger for goods that consume a larger fraction of your income. The income effect is also larger for goods with high income elasticities of demand.

The direction of the income effect depends on whether the good is normal or inferior. For normal goods, a larger income effect means a larger price elasticity of demand; for inferior goods the opposite is true.

For example, suppose you go to the movies once a week and spend $10 per movie, while you go to the live theater twice a year and spend $50 each time. Then over the course of a year, you're spending about five times as much on movies as on the theater. This suggests that changes in the price of movies should have larger income effects than changes in the price of live theater performances. So it's a good guess that your price elasticity of demand is higher for the movies.

Similarly, if you eat out at McDonald's 300 nights a year, spending $5 each time for a total of $1,500, and at the 21 Club once a year, spending $200, then your price elasticity of demand for McDonald's hamburgers is probably higher than your price elasticity of demand for dinners at the 21 Club. If the 21 Club raises its prices by 10%, it will lose some fraction of your business, but if McDonald's raises its prices by 10%, it will lose a larger fraction of your business.

## Cross Elasticities

One other circumstance that can affect your demand for X is a change in the price of some other good Y. The cross elasticity of demand for X with respect to Y is a measure of the size of this effect; it is the percent change in consumption of X divided by the percent change in the price of Y.

A change in the price of Y could cause your consumption of X to either rise or fall. In the first case, your cross elasticity of demand is positive, and in the second it is negative. If X is coffee and Y is tea, the cross elasticity is likely to be positive: When the price of tea increases by 1%, your coffee consumption is likely to increase. The percent by which it increases (a positive number) is the cross elasticity of demand. But if X is coffee and Y is cream, a 1% increase in the price of cream is likely to lead to a *decrease* (that is, a *negative* percentage change) in the price of coffee, and so in this case the cross elasticity of demand is negative.

When the cross elasticity of demand for X with respect to Y is positive, we say that X and Y are substitutes. When it is negative, we say that they are complements. Substitutes, as the name indicates, tend to be goods that can be substituted for each other, as in our example of tea and coffee. Other examples might be Coke and Pepsi, or train tickets and airline tickets. Complements tend to be goods that are used together—each complements the other. We have seen the example of coffee and cream. Other pairs of complements might be computers and floppy disks, or textbooks and college courses.

**Cross elasticity of demand**

The percent change in consumption that results from a 1% increase in the price of a related good.

**Substitutes**

Goods for which the cross elasticity of demand is positive.

**Complements**

Goods for which the cross elasticity of demand is negative.

## Example: Is Coke the Same as Pepsi?

Coke is quite a good substitute for Pepsi; we know this because the cross elasticity of demand[4] is a relatively large .34, that is, when the price of Pepsi rises 1%, sales of Coke rise a hefty .34%.

That perhaps is not surprising. What's more surprising is that (regular) Coke is an even better substitute for *Diet* Pepsi; here the cross elasticity of demand is an even larger .45. But Coke is above all a close substitute for Diet Coke where the cross elasticity is an enormous 1.15.

By and large, Coke and Pepsi are good substitutes for most other soft drinks. When the price of Mountain Dew goes up, a lot of people switch to Pepsi (cross elasticity .77). But the reverse is false; when the price of Pepsi goes up, very few people switch to Mountain Dew (cross elasticity only .08).

## Elasticities and Monopoly Power

Does the McDonald's hamburger chain have a monopoly on the products it sells? If consumers think that there is no close substitute for a McDonald's hamburger, then the answer is yes. On the other hand, if consumers think that a Burger King hamburger and a McDonald's hamburger are indistinguishable, then McDonald's faces heavy competition.

When courts are called upon to decide whether a firm has monopoly power, they must ask whether competing firms offer products that are close substitutes in the

---

[4] All the cross elasticities in this section are from Jean-Pierre Dube, "Product Differentiation and Mergers in the Carbonated Soft Drink Industry," *Journal of Economics and Management Strategy* 14 (2005): 879–904.

minds of consumers. But how is the court to tell whether an alternative product is viewed as a close substitute? A solution is to examine the cross elasticity of demand.

Suppose that the cross elasticity of demand between McDonald's and Burger King hamburgers is positive and large. Then the goods are close substitutes and Burger King competes in essentially the same market as McDonald's. The large cross elasticity means that if McDonald's tries to raise its prices, a lot of customers will switch to Burger King, so that McDonald's monopoly power is severely limited. On the other hand, if the cross elasticity is small, McDonald's needs to worry much less about this kind of competition. Large cross elasticities are evidence of competition and small cross elasticities are evidence of monopoly.

Because of the relatively large cross elasticities that are common between soft drinks, regulators have been reluctant to approve mergers between soft drink companies. In recent decades, Coke has been prohibited from acquiring Dr. Pepper, and Pepsi withdrew its interest in acquiring Mountain Dew in anticipation of a negative ruling.

## Summary

Changes in the consumer's opportunities lead to changes in the optimal consumption basket. Changes in opportunities arise from changes in income and changes in prices.

A change in income causes a parallel shift in the budget line. When income rises, consumption of the good $X$ can either rise (in which case $X$ is called a normal good) or fall (in which case $X$ is called an inferior good).

If we fix the prices of goods $X$ and $Y$, we can draw budget lines corresponding to various levels of income. If we also know the consumer's indifference curves, we can find the optimal basket corresponding to each level of income and read off the quantity of $X$ associated with each level of income. We can plot this information on a graph, with income on the horizontal axis and quantity of $X$ on the vertical. The resulting curve is called an Engel curve. The Engel curve slopes upward for a normal good and downward for an inferior good.

A change in the price of $X$ causes the budget line to pivot around its $Y$-intercept—outward for a fall in price and inward for a rise in price. A rise in price can cause the quantity of $X$ demanded to fall (in which case $X$ is called an ordinary good) or rise (in which case $X$ is called a Giffen good).

If we fix the price of $Y$ and the consumer's income, we can draw budget lines corresponding to various prices of $X$. If we also know the consumer's indifference curves, we can find the optimal basket associated with each price of $X$ and read off the quantity of $X$ associated with each price. We can plot this information on a graph, with price on the vertical axis and quantity on the horizontal. The resulting curve is the demand curve for $X$. The demand curve slopes downward if $X$ is not Giffen and upward if $X$ is Giffen.

When the price of $X$ goes up, the consumer changes his consumption of $X$ for two reasons. First, there is the substitution effect: Consumers will not purchase goods whose marginal value is below the price. Second, there is the income effect: Consumers are made effectively poorer when a price goes up. The substitution effect always reduces consumption of $X$. The income effect reduces consumption of $X$ if $X$ is a normal good, but increases consumption of $X$ if $X$ is an inferior good.

For a normal good, the substitution and income effects work in the same direction, ensuring that when the price goes up the quantity demanded goes down. Thus, a normal good cannot be Giffen. For an inferior good, the substitution and income effects work in opposite directions: If the substitution effect is greater, the good is not Giffen, but if the income effect is greater, the good is Giffen.

The compensated demand curve shows, for each price, the quantity of X the consumer would demand if he were income-compensated for every price change. Thus, the compensated demand curve shows only the substitution effect and so must slope downward.

## Author Commentary          www.cengage.com/economics/landsburg

**AC1.** Just as consumers demand *more* goods when their income rises, they also demand *higher quality* goods when their income rises. We can measure that demand for quality by starting with the formula for income elasticity and replacing "percentage change in quantity" with "percentage change in quality."

## Review Questions

**R1.** When income rises, how does the budget line move?

**R2.** What is the definition of an inferior good? What is the definition of a normal good?

**R3.** Suppose the price of X is $3 per unit and the price of Y is $5 per unit. Given the following indifference curve diagram, construct three points on the Engel curve for X.

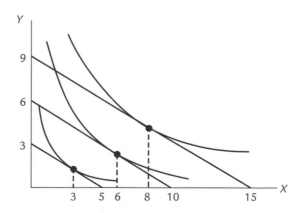

**R4.** When the price of X goes up, how does the budget line move?

**R5.** What is the definition of a Giffen good?

**R6.** Suppose the price of Y is $6 per unit and your income is $24. Given the following indifference curve diagram, construct three points on the demand curve for X.

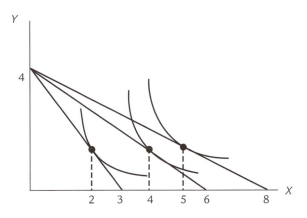

**R7.** Draw a diagram to illustrate the income and substitution effects of a price increase.

**R8.** When the price of a good increases, what is the direction of the substitution effect? Use the geometry of the indifference curves to justify your answer.

**R9.** When the price of a normal good increases, what is the direction of the income effect? When the price of an inferior good increases, what is the direction of the income effect?

**R10.** Are all Giffen goods inferior? Are all inferior goods Giffen? Justify your answer in terms of the directions of the income and substitution effects.

**R11.** What is the difference between a compensated demand curve and an ordinary demand curve?

**R12.** Must the compensated demand curve always slope downward? Why or why not?

**R13.** Give the formulas for the income elasticity of demand and price elasticity of demand.

**R14.** In review question 3, compute the income elasticity of demand for X as income rises from $15 to $30.

**R15.** In review question 6, compute the price elasticity of demand for X as the price rises from $4 to $8.

**R16.** The price elasticity of demand for coffee is about –.25. Suppose that when the price is 50¢ per cup, consumes demand 1,000 cups per day. If the price rises to 60¢ per cup, how many cups will be demanded?

# Numerical Exercises

**N1.** Suppose your indifference curves are all described by equations of the form $x\,y$ = constant, with a different constant for each indifference curve.

  **a.** Show that for any point $P = (x, y)$, the indifference curve through $P$ has slope $-y/x$ at $P$. (This requires calculus. If you don't know enough calculus, you can just pretend you've solved this part and go on to part (b).)

**b.** Suppose that your income is $40, the price of X is $1, and the price of Y is $1. How much X do you buy?

*Hint:* The problem is to find your optimal basket (x, y). First write down an equation that says (x, y) is on the budget line. Next write down an equation that says the slope of the indifference curve at (x, y) is equal to the slope of the budget line at (x, y). (Remember that you have a formula for the slope of the budget line from part (a), and that you can compute the slope of the budget line from the prices of X and Y.) Then solve these two equations simultaneously.

**c.** Suppose your income and the price of Y remain as above, but the price of X rises to $4. Now how much X do you consume? (Use the same hint as in part (b).)

**d.** Based on your answers to parts (b) and (c), draw two points on your demand curve for X.

**e.** After the price of X rises from $1 to $4, suppose that your income rises by just enough to bring you back to your original indifference curve. Now how much X do you buy? (*Hint:* The problem is to find the basket (x, y) where the compensated budget line is tangent to the original indifference curve.) First write down the equation of the original indifference curve (remember that it is of the form xy = constant, and you can figure out the constant because you already know the coordinates of one point on that curve). Next write down an equation that expresses the condition that the slope of the indifference curve must equal the slope of the compensated budget line. Then solve these two equations simultaneously.

**f.** When the price of X rises from $1 to $4, how much of the change in your consumption is due to the substitution effect? How much is due to the income effect?

**N2.** Suppose that your Engel curve for X is given by the equation

$$X = a + bI$$

where $I$ is income and $a$ and $b$ are constants.

**a.** If your income increases from $I$ to $I + \Delta I$, by how much does X increase?

**b.** Write down a formula, in terms of X and $I$, for your income elasticity of demand for X.

**c.** Use the equation $X = a + bI$ to eliminate $I$ from your formula, and write a formula for income elasticity in terms of X alone.

**d.** As your consumption of X increases, what happens to your income elasticity of demand for X?

**e.** If your Engel curve is a line through the origin, what is your income elasticity of demand for X?

**N3.** Suppose that your demand curve for X is given by the equation

$$X = c - dP$$

where $P$ is price and $c$ and $d$ are positive constants.

**a.** Derive a formula for your price elasticity of demand for X, and write your formula in terms of X alone.

**b.** When you consume zero units of X, what is your price elasticity of demand? When the price of X is zero, what is your price elasticity of demand?

**N4.**  Suppose that your demand curve for *X* is given by the equation

$$X = \frac{e}{P}$$

where *P* is price and *e* is a positive constant. Derive a formula for your price elasticity of demand for *X*.

# Problem Set

1. Suppose the only goods you buy are circus tickets and accounting textbooks. One day the price of circus tickets goes up, the price of accounting textbooks goes down, and you notice that you are exactly as happy as you were before the price changes.

   a.  Are you now buying more or fewer circus tickets than before?

   b.  Can you still afford your original market basket?

2. Suppose the only goods you consume are wine and roses. On Tuesday, the price of wine goes up, and at the same time your income increases by just enough so that you are equally as happy as you were on Monday.

   a.  What happens to the quantity of wine that you consume? Illustrate your answer with indifference curves.

   b.  On Tuesday would you still be able to afford the same basket that you were buying on Monday? How do you know?

      On Wednesday there are no new price changes (so the Tuesday prices are still in effect), but your income changes to the point where you can just exactly afford Monday's basket.

   c.  Are you happier on Wednesday or on Monday?

   d.  Is it possible to say with certainty whether you buy more wine on Wednesday than on Monday? If not, on what would your answer depend?

   e.  Is it possible to say with certainty whether you buy more wine on Wednesday than on Tuesday? If not, on what would your answer depend?

3. The only goods you consume are wine and roses. Between Monday and Tuesday, your income falls. Between Tuesday and Wednesday, your income remains at the Tuesday level, but the price of roses falls. On Wednesday, you are exactly as happy as on Monday. **True or False:** If you consume more wine on Wednesday than Tuesday, then wine must be a normal good.

4. For Henry, eggs are inferior but not Giffen. On Henry's indifference curve diagram, illustrate the income and substitution effects when the price of eggs goes up. How does your diagram illustrate that eggs are inferior? How does it illustrate that eggs are not Giffen?

5. In the following diagrams, the black dots represent points where the illustrated lines are tangent to indifference curves.

Figure A

Figure B

Figure C

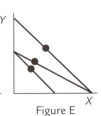
Figure D

Figure E

a. In which figure(s) is *X* a normal good?

b. In which figure(s) is *X* a Giffen good?

c. In which figure(s) is *Y* an inferior good?

d. In which figure(s) is *Y* a Giffen good?

6. Suppose that the only two goods you purchase are *X* and *Y*. One day the price of *X* goes down.

a. Illustrate your old and new budget lines.

b. Illustrate the substitution and income effects on your consumption of *X*.

c. What is the direction of the substitution effect? Why?

d. If *X* is a normal good, what is the direction of the income effect? Why?

e. If *X* is an inferior good, what is the direction of the income effect? Why?

f. **True or False:** If *X* is an inferior good, then a fall in price must lead to a rise in consumption, but if *X* is a normal good, then a fall in price might lead to a fall in consumption. Justify your answer carefully in terms of income and substitution effects.

7. Suppose the only goods you buy are wine and roses.

a. Between Monday and Tuesday, the price of wine goes up (while your income remains fixed). Draw a diagram, with wine on the horizontal axis and roses on the vertical, to illustrate how your budget line moves. Illustrate your optimum points on the two budget lines, labeling Monday's optimum *M* and Tuesday's optimum *T*.

b. On Wednesday, the price of wine returns to its Monday level, but at the same moment your income falls by just enough so that you are just as happy on Wednesday as on Tuesday. Draw Wednesday's optimum point and label it *W*.

In each of parts (c), (d), and (e), determine whether the statement is (1) true always, (2) false always, (3) true if wine is an inferior good, but otherwise false, (4) false if wine is an inferior good, but otherwise true, (5) true if wine is a Giffen good, but otherwise false, or (6) false if wine is a Giffen good but otherwise true.

c. *M* is to the left of *T*.

d. *T* is to the left of *W*.

e. *M* is to the left of *W*.

f. **True or False:** Every Giffen good is an inferior good. Justify your answers by **using the earlier parts of this problem,** *not* by using the argument given in the text.

8. Suppose the only two goods you consume are *X* and *Y*. On Tuesday, the price of *Y* (not *X!*) goes up. On Wednesday, there are no new price changes, but your income rises by just enough so that you can exactly afford Monday's basket.

a. Use a diagram, with *X* on the horizontal axis and *Y* on the vertical, to illustrate your budget lines and optimum points on Monday, Tuesday, and Wednesday. Label the optimum points *M, T,* and *W*.

b. In terms of the locations of points *M, T,* and *W,* what would it mean for *X* to be an inferior good?

c. Is it true that *W* is always to the right of *M*? If so, how do you know? If not, what would your answer depend on?

d.  Call *X* a *Figgen good* if it is true that "when the price of *Y* goes up, the quantity demanded of *X* goes up." In terms of points *M, T,* and *W,* what would it mean for *X* to be a Figgen good?

e.  **True or False:** Every inferior good is a Figgen good.

f.  **True or False:** Every Giffen good is a Figgen good.

9.  The only goods you consume are eggs and wine. Between Monday and Tuesday, your income rises. On Wednesday, the price of eggs goes up. On Wednesday, you are just as happy as you are on Monday. **True or False:** If wine is an inferior good, you certainly buy less wine on Tuesday than on Wednesday. Use your diagram to justify your answer. (*Note:* The price of *eggs* rises, but the question asks you about the quantity of *wine.*)

10. The only goods you consume are eggs and wine. On Tuesday, the price of *wine* increases. On Wednesday, the price of wine returns to its original level, but the price of *eggs* increases. You are equally happy on Tuesday and Wednesday.

a.  Draw a graph showing your budget lines on Monday (before either price changes), Tuesday, and Wednesday, and showing your optimum points. Label them *M, T,* and *W.*

b.  **True or False:** If eggs are a Giffen good, you will certainly consume more eggs on Tuesday than on Monday. Justify your answer by referring to the points on your graph.

11. The following diagram shows your indifference curves for goods *X* and *Y.*

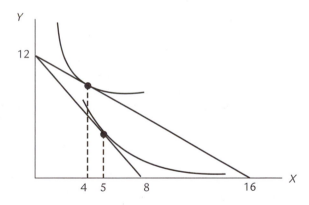

a.  Is *X* an ordinary good or a Giffen good? How do you know?

b.  Is *X* a normal good or an inferior good? How do you know?

c.  Suppose your income is $48 and the price of *Y* is $4 per unit. Give the coordinates of two points on your demand curve for *X.* (The coordinates of a point consist of a *price* and a *quantity.*)

12. Suppose you buy only *X* and *Y,* both of which are normal goods. Suppose also that almost all of your income is spent on *Y.* When the price of *X* goes up, does the quantity of *Y* go up or down?

13. When the price of shoes goes up, Tara goes right on buying just as many shoes as before. **True or False:** Shoes could not possibly be an inferior good for Tara.

14. Tara buys only shoes and socks. When the price of shoes goes up, Tara continues buying exactly the same number of socks as before. **True or False:** Socks could not possibly be an inferior good for Tara.

**15.** Sam consumes only green eggs and ham. Ham is an inferior good for Sam. One day the price of green eggs goes up.

  **a.** Illustrate Sam's old and new optimum points, and show both the substitution and the income effects. How does this graph reflect the fact that ham is an inferior good?

  **b.** **True or False:** When the price of green eggs goes up, Sam certainly buys more ham than before. Justify your answer carefully, by considering the directions of both the substitution and income effects.

**16.** Leopold consumes only kidneys and liver. When the price of kidneys rises, Leopold responds by eating less liver.

  **a.** Can you determine whether liver is an inferior good for Leopold?

  **b.** Can you determine whether liver is a Giffen good for Leopold?

  **c.** *Extra Credit:* what is Leopold's last name?

**17.** Bugs consumes carrots and lettuce, both of which are normal goods. Suppose the price of *carrots* rises.

  **a.** Illustrate the substitution and income effects.

  **b.** Does the substitution effect lead to an increase or a decrease in Bugs's lettuce consumption? Justify your answer. (*Note:* The price of *carrots* changed, but you are asked about the effect on the quantity of *lettuce*.)

  **c.** Does the income effect lead to an increase or a decrease in Bugs's lettuce consumption? Justify your answer.

  **d.** Assume Bugs spends very little of his income on carrots. When the price of carrots rises, do you expect his lettuce consumption to go up or down? Why?

**18.** In January, root beer and orange soda each cost $1 a bottle. Judith's income is $20. She buys 5 root beers and 15 orange sodas. In February, the price of root beer falls to 50¢, the price of orange soda rises to $2, Judith's income remains $20, and she still buys exactly 5 root beers. **True or False:** Root beer is a normal good for Judith.

**19.** In April, Frieda pays $2 apiece for eggs and $1 apiece for sodas. Her income is $40. She buys 18 eggs and 4 sodas. In May, Frieda pays $1 apiece for eggs and $2 apiece for sodas. Her income is $40. She buys 16 eggs and 12 sodas.

  **a.** In which month is Frieda happier?

  **b.** Are eggs a normal or an inferior good for Frieda?

**20.** Herman consumes Munster cheese and no other goods.

  **a.** Munster cheese could not possibly be an inferior good for Herman.

  **b.** Munster cheese could not possibly be a Giffen good for Herman.

**21.** Herman consumes Munster cheese and no other goods.

  **a.** What is the shape of Herman's ordinary (uncompensated) demand curve for Munster cheese?

  **b.** What is the shape of Herman's compensated demand curve for Munster cheese?

  **c.** What is Herman's price elasticity of demand for Munster cheese?

22. Suppose your indifference curves between *X* and *Y* are shaped as in Exhibit 3.10, page 59.

   a.   What is the shape of your ordinary (uncompensated) demand curve for *X*?

   b.   What is the shape of your compensated demand curve for *X*?

   c.   What is your price elasticity of demand for *X*?

23. **True or False:** For a normal good, the compensated demand curve is steeper than the uncompensated demand curve, but for an inferior good the reverse is true.

24. **True or False:** Your compensated and uncompensated demand curves for bubble gum are likely to be very similar to each other, but your compensated and uncompensated demand curves for college tuition might be very different.

25. Suppose the only good you ever consume is Nestle's Crunch bars. What is your income elasticity of demand for Nestle's Crunch bars? What is your price elasticity of demand for Nestle's Crunch bars?

26. A *luxury* is defined to be a good with income elasticity greater than 1. Explain what this means without the technical jargon. Is it possible for all the goods you consume to be luxuries? Why or why not?

27. Which is likely to have a higher elasticity: The demand for gasoline from Gus's gas station or the demand for gasoline generally? Why?

28. In 2003, tolls were raised on seven bridges across the Delaware River, connecting Pennsylvania to New Jersey. In the first two months of the year, bridge traffic fell by 17%, but revenue increased by 123% because of the higher tolls. What is the price elasticity of demand for using these bridges to cross the Delaware River?

29. Suppose that without a seat belt, drivers who travel at 0 mph have a 100% chance of staying alive, while drivers who travel at 100 mph have 0% chance of staying alive. Suppose that with a seat belt, drivers who travel at 0 mph have a 100% chance of staying alive, drivers who travel at 100 mph have a 50% chance of staying alive, and drivers who travel at 200 mph have a 0% chance of staying alive.

   a.   Draw an indifference curve diagram relating safety (measured by chance of staying alive) on the horizontal axis and speed (measured in mph) on the vertical. Draw the budget constraints of a driver with a seat belt and a driver without a seat belt. (You may assume these constraints are straight lines.)

   b.   **True or False:** If speed and safety are both normal goods, then the invention of seat belts will certainly make people drive faster but might or might not save lives. Explain your answer in terms of substitution and income effects.

30. Suppose you have 24 hours per day that you can allocate between leisure and working at a wage of $2 per hour.

   a.   Draw your budget constraint between "leisure hours" on the horizontal axis and "income" on the vertical.

   b.   Draw in your optimum point. Keeping in mind that the number of hours you spend working is equal to 24 minus the number of hours that you spend at leisure, plot a corresponding point on your labor supply curve.

    **c.** Now suppose that the wage rate rises to $3 per hour. Draw your new budget constraint, your new optimum, and a new point on your labor supply curve.

    **d.** On your indifference curve diagram, decompose the effect of the wage increase into a substitution effect and an income effect. What is the direction of the substitution effect? What is the direction of the income effect if leisure is a normal good? What is the direction of the income effect if leisure is an inferior good?

    **e.** **True or False:** If leisure is an inferior good, the labor supply curve must slope upward, but if leisure is a normal good, the labor supply curve could slope either direction.

    **f.** Whose labor supply curve is likely to slope upward more steeply: somebody whose income is derived entirely from wages, or somebody who has a large nonwage income? Why?

**31.** Suppose you have $1,000 today and expect to receive another $1,000 one year from today. Your savings account pays an annual interest rate of 25%, and your bank is willing to lend you money at that same interest rate.

    **a.** Suppose that you save all of your money to spend next year. How much will you be able to spend next year? How much will you be able to spend today?

    **b.** Suppose you borrow $800 and spend $1,800 today. How much will you be able to spend next year?

    **c.** Draw your budget constraint between "spending today" and "spending next year." What is its slope? How does the slope reflect the relative price of spending today in terms of spending next year?

    **d.** How would your budget line shift in each of the following circumstances:

        You find $400 that you'd forgotten was in your desk drawer.

        Your boss informs you that you will receive a $500 bonus next year.

        The interest rate rises to 50%.

    **e.** Under which circumstance would you spend more today: finding a forgotten $400 in a desk drawer or being told that you will receive a $500 bonus next year? Under which circumstance would you spend more next year?

    **f.** Returning to the assumption that you have $1,000 today and expect to receive $1,000 next year, suppose that you choose neither to borrow nor to lend. Illustrate the tangency of your budget line with an indifference curve.

    **g.** In part (f), suppose that the interest rate rises to 50%. Show how your budget line shifts. Do you increase or decrease your current spending? Do you increase or decrease your future spending? Are you better off or worse off than before?

    **h.** In part (g), decompose the change in your consumption into a substitution effect followed by an income effect. Can you determine the direction of the substitution effect? Can you determine the direction of the income effect?

# The Behavior of Firms

Individuals demand goods and services; firms supply them. Just as our study of individual consumers' behavior led us to a deeper understanding of demand, a study of firms' behavior will lead us to a deeper understanding of supply.

All firms are created and owned by individuals. Some, like many corner grocery stores, have one owner, whereas others, like the General Electric Corporation, have many thousands of owners (in this case the General Electric stockholders). In some firms, the owner or owners exert considerable day-to-day control over operations, whereas in others salaried managers serve these functions. With such diversity in the size, nature, and organization of firms, you might wonder how it could be possible to make any statements at all about the behavior of firms in general.

There is, however, one grand generalization about firms that economists have found to be extraordinarily powerful: We assume that firms act to maximize profits. There are reasons to question this assumption. Why should individuals, who are interested in many things other than profits, choose to organize firms that pursue profits single-mindedly? Even if the owners view profit maximization as desirable, does it follow that the managers will behave accordingly? Economists have given much thought to these and related questions.[1] However, most economists also believe that the assumption of profit maximization, while only an approximation to the truth, leads to deep insights into the ways in which goods are supplied.

Therefore, we will use the word **firm** to refer to an entity that produces and supplies goods and that seeks to do so in such a way as to maximize the profits that it earns in any given time period. The goal of profit maximization will enter into every decision that the firm makes. In Section 5.1 we will study a simple problem in which a firm must weigh costs against benefits. This will lead us to the equimarginal principle, which is one of the most fundamental concepts in economics and the key to profit maximization. In Section 5.2 we will see how firms use this principle in deciding how much to produce.

**Firm**

An entity that produces and sells goods, with the goal of maximizing its profits.

---

[1] One of the earliest and most enlightening contributions to this literature is R. H. Coase, "On the Nature of the Firm," *Economica* 4 (1937): 386–405.

# 5.1 Weighing Costs and Benefits

In this section we will examine how firms make decisions by imagining a simple problem that a farmer might face: How many acres of her land should she spray with insecticide? The solution to this problem will reveal one of the key concepts in economics, known as the equimarginal principle. Once this principle has been made explicit, we will see that it applies both to the behavior of firms and to the behavior of individuals.

## A Farmer's Problem

Farmer Vickers's farm is a firm—that is, she operates her farm to maximize profits. She owns 6 acres of land planted with wheat, and her immediate problem is to decide how many acres to spray with insecticide.

By spraying 1 acre, Farmer Vickers can save $6 worth of crops. You might guess that by spraying 2 acres, she saves $12 worth. But a more reasonable guess would be something less than $12. Why? Because the 6 acres are not all identical. Some acres are more fertile than others, and some are closer to standing water and therefore more attractive to insects. When Farmer Vickers sprays just 1 acre, she chooses that acre where spraying yields the greatest benefit. When she sprays 2 acres, she chooses the one where spraying yields the biggest benefit and the one where spraying yields the second biggest benefit. So the gain from spraying 2 acres is probably less than twice the gain from spraying 1 acre.

So a reasonable assumption would be that spraying 1 acre saves $6 worth of crops and spraying 2 acres saves a total of $11 worth of crops. We record these numbers in the "Total Benefit" column of the table in Exhibit 5.1, along with the total benefit of spraying 3, 4, 5, and 6 acres. The same numbers are plotted on the curve labeled "Total benefit" in panel A underneath the chart.

**Marginal benefit**

The additional benefit gained from the last unit of an activity.

The third column of that table, labeled **marginal benefit,** refers to the value of crops saved on the last acre sprayed. For example, spraying 2 acres saves $11 worth of crops and spraying 1 acre saves $6 worth, so the marginal benefit of spraying the second acre is $11 − $6 = $5, which is the second entry in the Marginal Benefit column. Similarly, spraying 4 acres saves $18 worth of crops and spraying 3 acres saves $15 worth, so the marginal benefit of spraying the fourth acre is $18 − $15 = $3, which is the fourth entry in the column. The marginal benefit numbers are plotted on the curve labeled "Marginal benefit" in panel B.

**Exercise 5.1** Verify the other numbers in the third column of the table in Exhibit 5.1. Explain why it is reasonable for these numbers to be decreasing. Explain why the sum of the first 3 (or 4 or 5) entries in the Marginal column is equal to the third (or fourth or fifth) entry in the Total column.

Dangerous
Curve

The marginal benefit is the benefit from spraying one additional acre and is therefore properly measured not in dollars, but in dollars per acre. Therefore, it cannot be plotted on the same graph with total benefit, which is measured in dollars.

## EXHIBIT 5.1 — Maximizing Net Gain

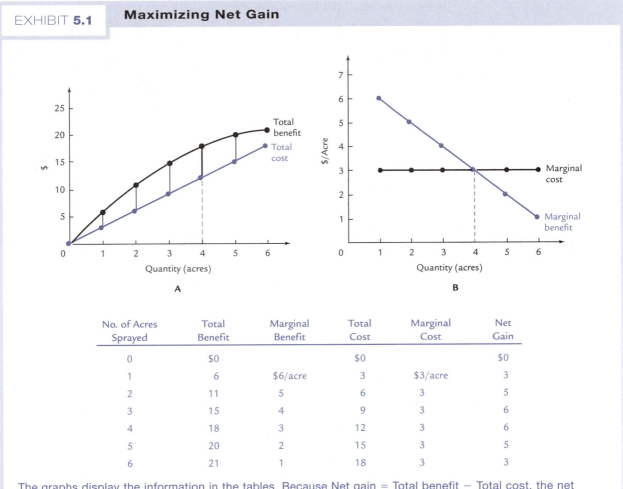

| No. of Acres Sprayed | Total Benefit | Marginal Benefit | Total Cost | Marginal Cost | Net Gain |
|---|---|---|---|---|---|
| 0 | $0 | | $0 | | $0 |
| 1 | 6 | $6/acre | 3 | $3/acre | 3 |
| 2 | 11 | 5 | 6 | 3 | 5 |
| 3 | 15 | 4 | 9 | 3 | 6 |
| 4 | 18 | 3 | 12 | 3 | 6 |
| 5 | 20 | 2 | 15 | 3 | 5 |
| 6 | 21 | 1 | 18 | 3 | 3 |

The graphs display the information in the tables. Because Net gain = Total benefit − Total cost, the net gain is equal to the distance between the Total cost and Total benefit curves in panel A. For example, the heavy vertical line has length $6, representing the net gain of $6 when 4 acres are sprayed. Because the heavy line is the longest of the vertical lines (or, in other words, because $6 is the largest number in the net gain column), the farmer maximizes her net gain by spraying 4 acres. An alternative way to reach the same conclusion (called Method II in the text) is to continue spraying as long as marginal benefit exceeds marginal cost and to stop when they become equal at 4 acres.

We have said that the marginal benefit is the additional benefit from the last acre sprayed. It is important to understand what "last" means. When Farmer Vickers sprays 4 acres, the "last" acre is the one she'd have omitted if she'd been spraying only 3 acres. Once she's hired the crop duster to come in and spray, he might spray the acres in any order that's convenient. The last acre is not the last one the crop duster actually sprays; it's the last one the farmer *decides* to spray.

Dangerous Curve

To decide how many acres farmer Vickers should spray, we need to know not just the benefits but the costs. Let's suppose the farmer can hire a crop duster who charges $3 per acre. In that case, the total cost of spraying 1 acre is $3, the total cost of spraying 2 acres is $6, and so forth. These numbers are recorded in the Total Cost column of Exhibit 5.1 and are plotted on the curve labeled "Total cost" in panel A.

**Marginal cost**

The additional cost associated with the last unit of an activity.

The next column of the table shows the marginal cost associated with each acre sprayed; that is, it shows the additional cost of spraying that last acre. If Farmer Vickers sprays 3 acres, her total cost is $9; if she sprays 4 acres, her total cost is $12. Therefore, the marginal cost of spraying the fourth acre is $12 − $9 = $3. These numbers are plotted on the curve labeled "Marginal cost" in panel B.

The final column in Exhibit 5.1, labeled "Net Gain," is the total value of crops saved minus the total cost of spraying them. For example, if Farmer Vickers sprays 2 acres, her total benefit is $11 and her total cost is $6, so her net gain is $11 − $6 = $5. The net gain numbers are displayed by the vertical bars in the first graph, which indicate the difference between total cost and total benefit. Net gain adds to Farmer Vickers's profits, so net gain is what she wants to maximize. Her problem, remember, is to figure out how many acres to spray. We will give two different methods for solving that problem.

The first and most straightforward method is to look over the net gain column and pick out the biggest number. That number is $6, and it occurs when Farmer Vickers sprays either 3 or 4 acres. Therefore, the solution to her problem is: spray 3 or 4 acres. To remove the ambiguity, let's arbitrarily suppose that whenever she's indifferent between two choices, Farmer Vickers chooses the larger. Thus, the solution to her problem is: spray 4 acres.

---

Dangerous
Curve

Students sometimes get unduly concerned with the question of why we chose 4 acres rather than 3 acres as "the" solution to our problem. Rest assured that the choice is entirely arbitrary; we could as easily have chosen 3 as 4. By sticking to one choice, we will make the subsequent discussion easier to follow:

In any event, either answer—3 or 4—is only an approximation of the truth. Here's why: In real life, Farmer Vickers would have a lot more than six choices. Instead of spraying 2 or 3 or 4 acres, she could spray exactly 3½ acres, or 1.7894 acres, or any other number of acres between 0 and 6. If we allowed all these possibilities, we would find that net gain is actually maximized at some number of acres between 3 and 4, and no arbitrary choice would be necessary. You can view 4 as the "right answer rounded up," which we will treat as exactly equal to the right answer to keep things simple.

---

So that's one way to solve the farmer's problem: Scan the net gain column and pick the biggest number. Let's call that process *Method I*. Now we'll give an alternative method, which we'll call *Method II*.

To use Method II, look only at the Marginal columns in Exhibit 5.1. Start with the row corresponding to 1 acre. Note that the marginal benefit of spraying the first acre ($6) is greater than the marginal cost ($3). Therefore, Farmer Vickers should spray that first acre.

Now move on to the row corresponding to 2 acres. Again, the marginal benefit ($5) exceeds the marginal cost ($3). Therefore, spraying the second acre is also a good idea; it increases net gain by $5 − $3 = $2.

The third acre yields a marginal benefit of $4 for a marginal cost of $3, which is another good deal! This will add $1 to net gain, so Farmer Vickers should spray this acre.

When we get to the fourth acre, we find that the marginal value of the crops saved ($3) is exactly equal to the marginal cost ($3). Therefore, it doesn't matter whether she sprays this acre or not. We've already agreed to eliminate such ambiguities by (arbitrarily) assuming that the farmer moves forward when she is indifferent, so let's suppose she sprays this acre too.

But when it comes to the fifth acre, the marginal benefit ($2) is less than the marginal cost ($3). Spraying this acre would subtract $1 from net gain, so it's a bad idea. Farmer Vickers stops after the fourth acre.

That's Method II: Continue spraying as long as the marginal benefit exceeds the marginal cost, and stop when they become equal. Here's an even briefer summary of Method II: Choose the number of acres that makes the marginal benefit equal to the marginal cost. In terms of the graph in panel B, Method II comes down to choosing the number of acres where the marginal cost and marginal benefit curves cross.

Notice that Methods I and II both yield the same answer: Spray 4 acres. They *must* yield the same answer, because each is a perfectly valid way of maximizing net gain. In view of this, you might wonder why we went to all the trouble of developing Method II when Method I works perfectly well. The answer is that Method II demonstrates the importance of the Marginal columns. It shows that the Marginal information all by itself is enough to guide the farmer's choice. We can say the same thing in a slightly different way: If the Marginal columns don't change, then neither will Farmer Vickers's behavior.

Here's an important application of this last point: Suppose the crop duster changes his pricing policy. He now charges a $4 flat fee for coming out to the farm in addition to the $3 per acre for spraying. ($4 is now the fee for spraying *zero* acres!) Exhibit 5.2 updates Exhibit 5.1 to illustrate the new situation.

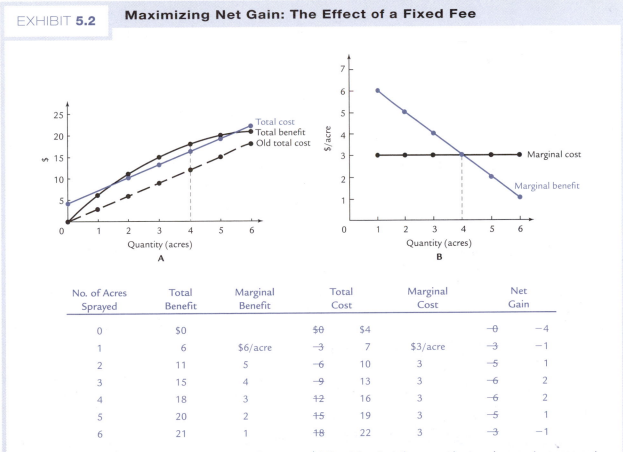

**EXHIBIT 5.2  Maximizing Net Gain: The Effect of a Fixed Fee**

| No. of Acres Sprayed | Total Benefit | Marginal Benefit | Total Cost | | Marginal Cost | Net Gain | |
|---|---|---|---|---|---|---|---|
| 0 | $0 | | $0 | $4 | | −0 | −4 |
| 1 | 6 | $6/acre | −3 | 7 | $3/acre | −3 | −1 |
| 2 | 11 | 5 | −6 | 10 | 3 | −5 | 1 |
| 3 | 15 | 4 | −9 | 13 | 3 | −6 | 2 |
| 4 | 18 | 3 | +2 | 16 | 3 | −6 | 2 |
| 5 | 20 | 2 | +5 | 19 | 3 | −5 | 1 |
| 6 | 21 | 1 | +8 | 22 | 3 | −3 | −1 |

This exhibit modifies Exhibit 5.1 to account for a new $4 fixed fee that the crop duster charges to come out to the farm. The dashed curve in panel A is the old total cost curve from Exhibit 5.1, reproduced here for comparison. The marginal curves remain unchanged. Therefore, the optimal number of acres to spray, which is determined by the intersection of the Marginal cost and Marginal benefit curves, remains unchanged.

Note that although the Total Cost column has changed, with all the numbers increased by $4, the Marginal Cost column is unchanged, as is the Marginal Benefit column. Because the Marginal columns are unchanged, Farmer Vickers's optimum is unchanged: She should spray the number of acres where marginal cost equals marginal benefit, namely, 4 acres. We can confirm this using Method I: Net gain is still maximized when the farmer sprays 4 acres. Graphically, the total cost curve has shifted up parallel to itself a distance of $4, so that the maximum distance between it and the total benefit curve remains at a quantity of 4 acres.

Now here comes the key observation: We could have predicted this result without ever building the table in Exhibit 5.2. All we had to observe was that the change in the crop duster's pricing policy cannot affect either of the Marginal columns in the table and that only these columns are necessary for predicting Farmer Vickers's behavior. Therefore, when the pricing policy changes, her behavior stays unchanged.

It is true that the crop duster's policy is bad news for the farmer: She used to realize a net gain of $6 and now realizes a net gain of only $2. What remains unchanged is the number of acres she sprays: 4 in either case.

**Exercise 5.2** Suppose the crop duster changes his policy again, so that he now charges $5 to come out to the farm plus $3 per acre sprayed. How many acres will Farmer Vickers spray now? Figure out the answer without building a table, and explain how you know your answer is correct. Now build a table and confirm your prediction.

**Exercise 5.3** Suppose the crop duster lowers his price to $1 per acre sprayed. Does this affect anything marginal? Does it affect Farmer Vickers's decision about how many acres to spray?

There is one exception to the rule we've just learned. The rule is: If nothing marginal changes, then Farmer Vickers's behavior won't change. The exception is: If spraying guarantees a negative net gain, then Farmer Vickers won't spray at all. For example, suppose the crop duster changes his policy to $100 to come out to the farm plus $3 per acre sprayed. If you update the numbers in Exhibit 5.2, you'll see that the Marginal columns remain unchanged, but the largest possible net gain is negative. In that case, Farmer Vickers will not continue to spray 4 acres; she'll give up spraying altogether. So a better way to state the rule is: If nothing marginal changes, and as long as Farmer Vickers continues to spray at all, then her behavior won't change.

## The Equimarginal Principle

**Equimarginal principle**

The principle that an activity should be pursued to the point where marginal cost equals marginal benefit.

Farmer Vickers has discovered the **equimarginal principle,** which is the essence of Method II for deciding how many acres to spray:

If an activity is worth pursuing at all, then it should be pursued up to the point where marginal cost equals marginal benefit.

She has also discovered an important consequence of the principle:

If circumstances change in a way that does not affect anything marginal and if an activity remains worth pursuing at all, then the optimal amount of that activity is unchanged.

The equimarginal principle has broad applicability. It applies not only to firms but also to individuals. Indeed, we have already met the equimarginal principle in Chapter 3, where we studied the consumer's optimum. The consumer moves along her budget line, trading $Y$ for $X$ until the relative price of a unit of $X$ (which is the marginal cost of that unit measured in terms of $Y$) is equal to the marginal rate of substitution between $X$ and $Y$ (which is the marginal value of that unit measured in terms of $Y$). Since the benefit to a consumer from owning a unit of $X$ is the same thing as the value to her of that unit, equating marginal cost to marginal value is the same as equating marginal cost to marginal benefit.

## Applying the Principle

Occasionally you will read a newspaper editorial that makes an argument along the following lines: "Our town spends only $100,000 per year to run its police department, and the benefits we get from the police are worth far more than that. Police services are a good deal in our town. We should be expanding the police department, not cutting back on it as Mayor McDonald has proposed." This argument is wrong. The editorial writer has observed (we assume correctly) that the total benefit derived from the police department exceeds the total cost of acquiring those benefits. But this is not relevant to the decision between expanding the department or contracting it. For this decision, only marginal quantities matter.

Reconsider Exhibit 5.1. When Farmer Vickers sprays 4 acres, she gets a good deal: Her gains from spraying exceed her costs by $6. Does it follow that she should expand her spraying program and spray a fifth acre? No, because the *marginal* cost of spraying that fifth acre exceeds the *marginal* gain from doing so. It is true that Farmer Vickers's gains exceeded her costs on each of the first 4 acres she decided to spray. However, if she sprayed a fifth acre, the marginal cost of doing so would exceed the marginal benefit by $1, reducing her total net gain from $6 to $5. Spraying the fifth acre is a bad idea.

Imagine Farmer Jefferson, faced with the same opportunities as Farmer Vickers, who has foolishly decided to spray 5 acres. He is considering cutting back his spraying program. The logic of the editorial would have us say: "Your spraying program is costing you only $20 and the value of the crops it saves is far more than that [$2 more, to be exact]. Your spraying program is a good deal. If anything, you should be expanding it, not cutting back." It is true that Farmer Jefferson's spraying program is a good deal overall, but it is also true that spraying the fifth acre is a bad deal (a $3 marginal cost exceeds a $2 marginal benefit). His spraying program will be an even better deal if that fifth acre is eliminated. Although his total gains exceed his total costs, this is beside the point, because for a decision like this only marginal quantities matter.

# 5.2 Firms in the Marketplace

Armed with our discovery that "only marginal quantities matter," we now set forth to study the behavior of firms in the marketplace.

The Tailor Dress Company produces dresses and sells them in the marketplace. Like all firms in this book, the Tailor Dress Company is interested only in maximizing its profits. The firm's profit in any given period is equal to the revenue it earns from selling dresses minus the cost of producing those dresses. So to understand profit, we have to understand both revenues and costs. We begin with revenues.

## Revenue

The **revenue** that a firm earns in a given time period can be computed by the simple formula:

$$\text{Revenue} = \text{Price} \times \text{Quantity}$$

For the Tailor Dress Company, the *price* is the price at which it sells its dresses, and the *quantity* is the number of dresses it sells in the period under consideration.

The firm can choose either the price or the quantity, but it can't choose both independently. The Tailor Dress Company can decide to sell exactly 9 dresses this week, or it can decide to sell dresses at exactly $100 apiece. But it cannot decide to sell exactly 9 dresses at exactly $100 apiece, because it might not find demanders willing to purchase that many dresses at that price. In other words, Tailor's options are limited by the demand curve for Tailor dresses.

Suppose the demand curve is given by the first two columns of Exhibit 5.3. In the past, when we've exhibited demand curves as charts, we've put price in the left-hand column and quantity in the right-hand column. In this case, we've reversed the order. But you should still read these columns as an ordinary demand curve: If the price is $10 per dress, demanders will buy 1 Tailor dress; if the price is $9 per dress, demanders will buy 2 Tailor dresses, and so forth.

Note that this demand curve is *not* the demand curve for dresses generally; it is the demand curve for *Tailor* dresses. Note also that as with any demand curve, there is a time period agreed on in advance; in this case, let us suppose that the quantities on the demand curve are quantities *per week*.

Using this demand curve, we can see (for example) that if Tailor wants to sell exactly 5 dresses per week, it cannot charge more than $6 per dress. In fact, if Tailor wanted to sell exactly 5 dresses, it should charge *exactly* $6 per dress—that is, the highest price at which demanders will take all 5 dresses.

**Exercise 5.4** If Tailor wants to sell exactly 3 dresses, what price should it charge? If Tailor wants to sell exactly 8 dresses, what price should it charge?

For any given quantity of dresses, Tailor uses the demand curve to find the corresponding price and then computes its **total revenue** by the formula:

$$\text{Revenue} = \text{Price} \times \text{Quantity}$$

The third column of Exhibit 5.3 shows the total revenue corresponding to each quantity, computed according to the formula.

**Exercise 5.5** Verify that the entries in the Total Revenue column are accurate.

The fourth column in Exhibit 5.4 shows the **marginal revenue** associated with each quantity. Marginal revenue is the additional revenue earned from the last item produced and sold. For example, if the firm produces 4 dresses, its total revenue is $28; and if it produces 5 dresses, its total revenue is $30. Thus, the marginal revenue associated with the fifth dress is $2 per dress.

**Exercise 5.6** Verify that the entries in the Marginal Revenue column are accurate.

The total revenue and marginal revenue numbers are plotted in panels A and B of Exhibit 5.3.

## Maximizing Profits at the Tailor Dress Company

EXHIBIT **5.3**

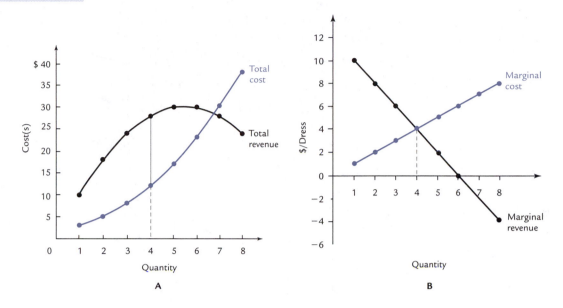

A

B

| Demand Curve | | | | | | |
|---|---|---|---|---|---|---|
| Quantity of Dresses | Price | Total Revenue | Marginal Revenue | Total Cost | Marginal Cost | Profit |
| 0 | | | | $2 | | |
| 1 | $10/dress | $10 | $10/dress | 3 | $1/dress | $7 |
| 2 | 9 | 18 | 8 | 5 | 2 | 13 |
| 3 | 8 | 24 | 6 | 8 | 3 | 16 |
| 4 | 7 | 28 | 4 | 12 | 4 | 16 |
| 5 | 6 | 30 | 2 | 17 | 5 | 13 |
| 6 | 5 | 30 | 0 | 23 | 6 | 7 |
| 7 | 4 | 28 | −2 | 30 | 7 | −2 |
| 8 | 3 | 24 | −4 | 38 | 8 | −14 |

The first two columns show the demand curve for Tailor dresses (these numbers are invented for the sake of the example). For any given quantity of dresses, Tailor reads a price off the demand curve and computes total revenue as price times quantity. The total revenue curve is plotted in panel A.

The marginal revenue from, say, the third dress is equal to the total revenue from producing three dresses ($24) minus the total revenue from producing two dresses ($18). The marginal revenue curve is plotted in panel B. Marginal revenue measures the slope of the total revenue curve.

The Total Cost column shows the total cost of producing various quantities of dresses (these numbers are made up for the sake of the example). Total cost consists of fixed cost (in this case $2) plus variable costs. The fixed cost of $2 is the cost of producing zero dresses. The total cost curve is plotted in panel A.

The marginal cost of producing, say, the third dress is equal to the total cost of producing three dresses ($8) minus the total cost of producing two dresses ($5). The marginal cost curve is plotted in panel B. Marginal cost measures the slope of the total cost curve.

There are two ways for Tailor to choose a profit-maximizing quantity, each of which leads to the same conclusion. Using Method I, Tailor scans the Profit column looking for the largest entry. This is the same as looking for the point of maximum distance between the total cost and total revenue curves in panel A. Using Method II, Tailor scans the Marginal columns and chooses the quantity where marginal cost and marginal revenue are equal. This is the same as looking for the point where the marginal cost and marginal revenue curves cross in panel B. Using either method, Tailor chooses to produce 4 dresses and sell them for $7 apiece.

## EXHIBIT **5.4**     **A Change in Fixed Costs**

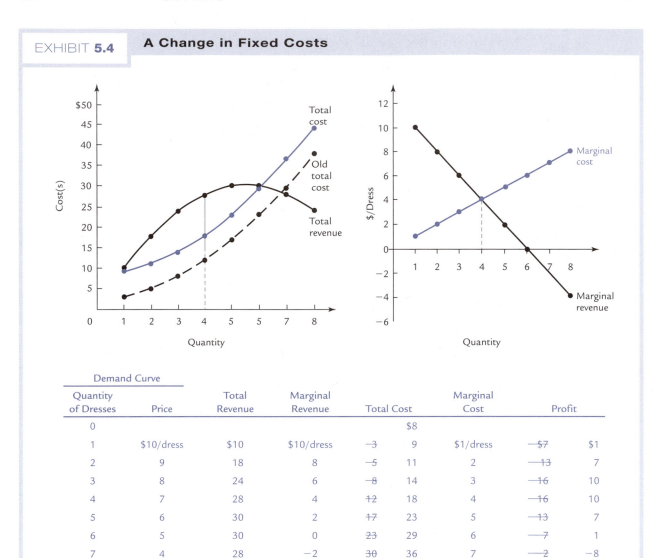

| Demand Curve | | | | | | | |
|---|---|---|---|---|---|---|---|
| Quantity of Dresses | Price | Total Revenue | Marginal Revenue | Total Cost | | Marginal Cost | Profit |
| 0 | | | | | $8 | | |
| 1 | $10/dress | $10 | $10/dress | −3 | 9 | $1/dress | −$7   $1 |
| 2 | 9 | 18 | 8 | −5 | 11 | 2 | −13   7 |
| 3 | 8 | 24 | 6 | −8 | 14 | 3 | −16   10 |
| 4 | 7 | 28 | 4 | 12 | 18 | 4 | −16   10 |
| 5 | 6 | 30 | 2 | 17 | 23 | 5 | −13   7 |
| 6 | 5 | 30 | 0 | 23 | 29 | 6 | −7   1 |
| 7 | 4 | 28 | −2 | 30 | 36 | 7 | −2   −8 |
| 8 | 3 | 24 | −4 | 38 | 44 | 8 | −14   −20 |

When fixed costs rise from $2 a week to $8 a week, all of the total cost numbers rise by $6, so the total cost curve shifts upward, parallel to itself, a vertical distance of $6. The marginal cost numbers are unaffected, so the marginal cost curve does not move. The point of maximum profit (4 dresses at $7 apiece) is unaffected.

Dangerous Curve

Total revenue and marginal revenue must be plotted on different graphs because the vertical axes are measured in different units. Total revenue is measured in dollars, while marginal revenue is measured in dollars per unit. In this example, a "unit" is 1 dress.

### Marginal Revenue as a Slope

In Exhibit 5.3, when Tailor produces 3 dresses, the total revenue is $24, and when Tailor produces 4 dresses, the total revenue is $28. Thus, the points (3, 24) and

(4, 28) appear on the Total revenue curve. The slope of the line joining those points is:

$$\frac{28 - 24}{4 - 3} = \frac{4}{1} = 4$$

which is the marginal revenue for producing the fourth dress.

The line in question is nearly tangent to the Total revenue curve at the point (4, 28). In general, at any given quantity, you can think of marginal cost as the slope of the Total cost curve near that quantity.

Thus, for example, marginal revenue is positive for all quantities between 1 and 6 inclusive, so total revenue slopes upward in that region. Marginal revenue is negative for quantities 7 and 8, and at these quantities, total revenue has a negative (downward) slope.

## Costs

To make a dress, you need a variety of inputs, including fabric, thread, labor, and the use of a sewing machine. The cost of producing a dress is the sum of the costs of the inputs.

Costs come in two varieties. Fixed costs are costs that don't vary with the quantity of output (for a dress company, "output" means "dresses"). An example might be rent on the factory, which costs, say, $2 a week whether the firm produces 1 dress or 100—or even if the firm produces no dresses at all.

The other kind of costs are variable costs, which do vary with the quantity of output. Examples include the cost of fabric (if you make more dresses you need more fabric) and workers' wages (if you make more dresses you need more workers).

Roughly, you can think of fixed costs as the costs of being in business in the first place and variable costs as the costs of actually producing output. Every component of cost is either a fixed cost or a variable cost.

**Fixed costs**

Costs that don't vary with the quantity of output.

**Variable costs**

Costs that vary with the quantity of output.

### Thinking about Variable Costs

At the Tailor Dress Company, the variable cost of making 1 dress is $1; that's what the firm pays for enough fabric and enough workers to make 1 dress.

What is the variable cost of making 2 dresses? Your first guess might be $2. But this is not necessarily the case. The firm has a limited amount of factory space and a limited number of sewing machines. When two workers have to share the machines, they might be less efficient than a single worker who has the machines to himself. So the second dress could cost more to produce than the first.

That's not the only reason the second dress might cost more than the first. If Tailor produces 1 dress, it uses the fabric that's most appropriate for the pattern, hires the worker who is most appropriate for the job, and seats that worker at the most appropriate sewing machine. To produce a second dress, Tailor might have to resort to the second most efficient piece of fabric (maybe an odd-shaped piece that requires more careful cutting), the second most efficient worker, and the second most efficient machine.

Similar phenomena occur in every industry. A farmer growing one acre of wheat uses his most fertile acre; the same farmer growing two acres of wheat must resort to his second most fertile acre. A writer producing one short story uses her best ideas and works at the time of day when she's most efficient; if she wants to produce a second short story, she has to work harder.

So it's plausible to assume that the variable cost of producing 2 dresses is more than $2; let's say it's $3. Then the marginal cost of producing that second dress is:

$$\text{Cost of producing 2 dresses} - \text{Cost of producing 1 dress} = \$3 - \$1 = 2$$

In the fifth column of Exhibit 5.3, we've listed the total cost of producing various quantities of dresses at the Tailor Dress Company. (Like the numbers in the demand curve, these numbers are invented for this example.) We've assumed fixed costs of $2; these fixed costs have to be paid even if there is no output, so $2 is the total cost of producing *zero* dresses. The total cost of producing 1 dress is $3, of which $2 is fixed cost and $1 is variable cost. The total cost of producing 2 dresses is $5, of which $2 is fixed cost and $3 is variable cost.

The corresponding marginal costs are listed in the sixth column.

**Exercise 5.7** Check that all of the marginal cost numbers are accurate.

The total and marginal cost numbers are also plotted in panels A and B of the exhibit.

**Increasing marginal cost**

The condition where each additional unit of an activity is more expensive than the last.

The Tailor Dress company faces the condition of **increasing marginal cost**; in other words, the marginal cost curve in panel B is upward sloping. We've argued already for the plausibility of this assumption, but there are also arguments to be made against it. Perhaps you can construct some. In Chapter 6, we'll make a careful study of how marginal costs arise from the production processes available to the firm, and we'll have much to say about the circumstances in which marginal costs can be expected to increase. Here we'll simply make the assumption of increasing marginal cost.

As with revenue, you can think of marginal cost as the slope of the Total cost curve.

## Maximizing Profit

Let's use Exhibit 5.3 to see how the Tailor Dress Company can maximize its profits. Remember that profit is equal to (total) revenue minus (total) cost. The Profit column on the right side of the chart shows how much profit Tailor can earn for each quantity of dresses it might produce. For example, if Tailor produces 2 dresses, its profit is $18 − $5 = $13.

**Exercise 5.8** Check that the numbers in the Profit column are accurate.

To maximize profits, Tailor must choose the right quantity of dresses. There are two ways to do this. Method I is the direct method: Scan the Profit column and choose the largest number. Graphically, this is equivalent to finding the point where the distance between the total cost and total revenue curves is the largest. This occurs at a quantity of either 3 or 4, where the profit is $16. As in Section 5.1, we arbitrarily assume that when firms are indifferent between two choices, they take a larger of the two. Therefore, Tailor produces 4 dresses and sells them at $7 apiece, $7 being the highest price at which demanders would be willing to buy 4 dresses.

Method II consists of scanning only the Marginal columns. Taking them row by row, Tailor first asks: Is the first dress worth making? The answer is yes, because the marginal revenue earned from selling that dress ($10) exceeds the marginal cost ($1). Next, the company asks if the second dress is worth making. Here again the marginal revenue ($8) exceeds the marginal cost ($2), so the answer is yes. A third dress also makes sense ($6 is greater than $3). When it comes to the fourth dress, marginal revenue and marginal cost are equal (at $4), so it is a matter of indifference whether to produce that fourth dress. We assume Tailor goes ahead and produces it. But when it comes to the fifth dress, the marginal revenue ($2) is less than the marginal cost ($5), so the fifth dress is a mistake. Tailor stops at four.

The short form of Method II is: Find the quantity at which marginal cost equals marginal revenue and produce that quantity. Graphically, this amounts to looking for the point where the Marginal cost and Marginal revenue curves cross.

The validity of Method II is an application of the equimarginal principle. It reveals that:

Any firm produces that quantity at which marginal cost equals marginal revenue.

---

In Exhibit 5.1, the farmer chooses the quantity where marginal cost equals marginal *benefit*. In Exhibit 5.3, the firm chooses the quantity where marginal cost equals marginal *revenue*. The firm is doing the same thing as the farmer, because to a profit-maximizing firm, revenue *is* the benefit that is derived from supplying goods.

---

Dangerous
Curve

## Changes in Fixed Costs

Suppose the rent at the Tailor factory goes up from $2 a week to $8 a week. Exhibit 5.4 shows the consequence. All the numbers in the total cost column are increased by $6. Therefore, the total cost curve is shifted upward a vertical distance of $6. But none of the marginal cost numbers are affected. When the total costs all rise by the same amount, the differences between them are left unchanged.

A change in fixed costs causes the Total cost curve to shift parallel to itself and leaves marginal cost unchanged.

The validity of Method II tells us that if nothing changes in the Marginal columns, the firm's behavior won't change either. In this case, Tailor continues to produce 4 dresses and sell them for $7 each.

You can verify this result by using Method I: Scan the Profit column and you'll find that the largest possible profit—in this case, $10—still occurs at a quantity of 4 dresses.

---

Predict what will happen if the rent goes up to $12 a week. Make a table to verify your prediction.

---

The most important point of this example is that we could have predicted in advance that the rent increase would affect neither price nor quantity, simply on the basis of the observation that the rent increase did not affect anything marginal and the fact that only marginal quantities matter. Therefore, we know that the same result would hold for any change in fixed costs.

A change in fixed costs will not affect the firm's behavior.

There is one exception to this rule: If fixed costs go so high that profits are guaranteed to be negative, the firm will want to go out of business entirely. (In Chapter 7, we'll discuss circumstances in which firms are or are not able to go out of business entirely; the answer depends on the time frame under discussion.)

To illustrate the exception, suppose that Tailor's landlord raises the weekly rent not to $8 but to $108. All of the total cost numbers in Exhibit 5.4 grow by an additional $100, and all of the profit numbers fall by $100. The highest possible profit is −$90, which occurs at a quantity of 4 and a price of $7. If the firm is unable to exit the industry, it will continue to choose that price and that quantity. But it will exit if it can.

## Sunk Costs Are Sunk

Before the rent increase in Exhibit 5.4, Tailor earned a profit of $16. After the rent increase, the profit is reduced to $10. The rent increase leaves Mr. Tailor, the owner, poorer by the amount of $6 per week. You might wonder why Tailor does not attempt to compensate for this loss by changing his price. The answer to this question can be found in Exhibit 5.4: There *is* no price that brings Tailor a profit of more than $10 per week. No change in pricing policy can benefit Mr. Tailor; he can only make himself worse off if he tries.

If this seems counterintuitive, ask yourself the following question: If Tailor could make greater profits by producing some quantity other than 4, or by charging some price other than $7, then why wasn't he already doing so before the rent was increased? If he has been profit-maximizing all along, why would a rent increase cause him to alter his strategy?

If you still aren't convinced, ask yourself these questions: If Tailor had accidentally lost a dollar bill down a sewer, would he change his business practices as a result? If he *did* change his business practices because of this bad luck, wouldn't you wonder whether those practices had been especially well thought out in the first place? Now, is the rent increase any different from losing a dollar bill in a sewer?[2]

Economists sum up the moral of this fable in this slogan:

Sunk costs are sunk.

**Sunk cost**

A cost that can no longer be avoided.

The rent increase is a sunk cost from the moment that the Tailor Dress Company decides to continue producing dresses at all; from that moment it is irretrievable. Once a cost has been sunk, it becomes irrelevant to any future decision making.

However, before you learn too well the lesson that a rent increase does not affect a company's behavior, note one exception: A sufficiently large rent increase might simply drive the firm out of business altogether. Only after the firm is committed to staying in business does the rent become a sunk cost.

Here is another example of the principle that sunk costs are sunk: Suppose the video you've spent $5 to rent turns out to be lousy; you're thinking about turning it off in the middle and watching a TV show instead. How should you decide what to do? Would your decision be any different if you'd gotten the video for free? Would it be any different if the video had cost you $10 instead of $5?

The answer is that the cost of the video is sunk and should therefore be irrelevant to your decision. If you expect the second half of the video to be better than the TV show, you should stick with the video. If you expect the TV show to be better, you should switch to the TV show.

It's true that if you switch to the TV show, you'll lose $5. But it's equally true that if you stick with the video, you'll lose $5. The $5 (or $10, or whatever you paid for the video) is lost no matter what you do; that's exactly what it means to say that this cost is sunk. Once a cost is sunk, it can be a cause for regret, but it should not affect your future behavior.

## Changes in Variable Costs

Of course, variable costs can also change. Suppose, for example, that the price of fabric goes up. In this case, the cost of making a dress will certainly rise. The Tailor

[2] There is one way in which the lost dollar is different from the rent increase. Mr. Tailor might be able to avoid the rent increase by going out of business entirely, but there is no way for him to recover his dollar. However, once Tailor decides to remain in business, either dollar is lost irretrievably.

Dress Company's *total* costs will rise and its *marginal* costs will rise as well. This example is very different from the example of the rent increase, where marginal costs remained fixed.

For a concrete example, suppose it takes a yard of fabric to make a dress, and the cost of fabric goes up by a dollar a yard. That adds $1 to the variable cost of making 1 dress, it adds $2 to the variable cost of making 2 dresses, and so forth. All the numbers in the Total Costs column increase, but they all increase by different amounts. Therefore, the Total cost curve not only rises; it changes shape. You can see the new total cost numbers and the new Total cost curve in Exhibit 5.5.

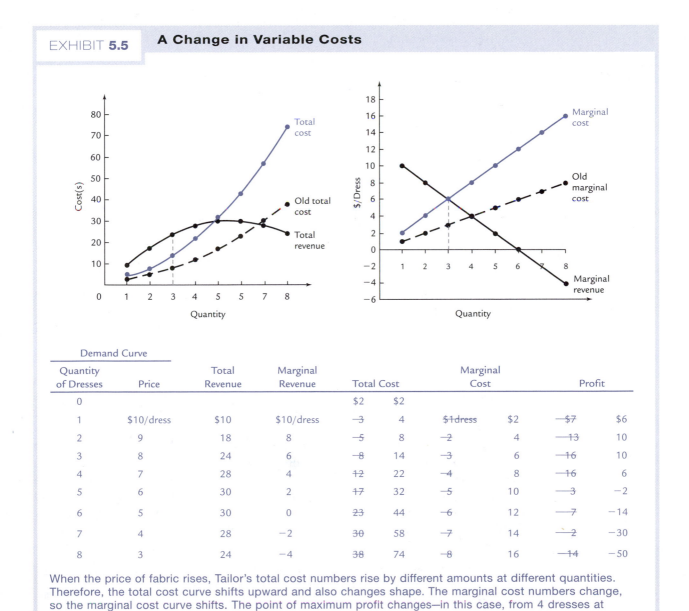

| EXHIBIT **5.5** | **A Change in Variable Costs** |
| --- | --- |

| | Demand Curve | | | | | | | |
| --- | --- | --- | --- | --- | --- | --- | --- | --- |
| Quantity of Dresses | Price | Total Revenue | Marginal Revenue | Total Cost | | Marginal Cost | | Profit | |
| 0 | | | | $2 | $2 | | | | |
| 1 | $10/dress | $10 | $10/dress | ~~3~~ | 4 | ~~$1dress~~ | $2 | ~~$7~~ | $6 |
| 2 | 9 | 18 | 8 | ~~5~~ | 8 | ~~2~~ | 4 | ~~13~~ | 10 |
| 3 | 8 | 24 | 6 | ~~8~~ | 14 | ~~3~~ | 6 | ~~16~~ | 10 |
| 4 | 7 | 28 | 4 | ~~12~~ | 22 | ~~4~~ | 8 | ~~16~~ | 6 |
| 5 | 6 | 30 | 2 | ~~17~~ | 32 | ~~5~~ | 10 | ~~3~~ | −2 |
| 6 | 5 | 30 | 0 | ~~23~~ | 44 | ~~6~~ | 12 | ~~7~~ | −14 |
| 7 | 4 | 28 | −2 | ~~30~~ | 58 | ~~7~~ | 14 | ~~2~~ | −30 |
| 8 | 3 | 24 | −4 | ~~38~~ | 74 | ~~8~~ | 16 | ~~14~~ | −50 |

When the price of fabric rises, Tailor's total cost numbers rise by different amounts at different quantities. Therefore, the total cost curve shifts upward and also changes shape. The marginal cost numbers change, so the marginal cost curve shifts. The point of maximum profit changes—in this case, from 4 dresses at $7 apiece to 3 dresses at $8 apiece.

Because the total cost numbers all increase by different amounts, the differences between them—that is, the marginal cost numbers—also change. The new marginal cost numbers, and the new Marginal cost curve, are also shown in Exhibit 5.5.

A change in variable costs causes the Total cost curve to shift by different amounts at different quantities and affects marginal costs.

Because the Marginal cost curve has shifted, it now crosses the Marginal revenue curve at a different quantity—3 instead of 4. That is the new profit- maximizing quantity (as you can verify by checking the Profit column). Tailor reduces its output from 4 dresses to 3, and consequently the price (which Tailor takes from the demand curve) rises from $7 to $8.

So a change in variable costs does affect the firm's behavior, even though a change in fixed costs does not.

## Changes in the Revenue Schedule

We now understand a great deal about how and when changes in a firm's schedule of costs will affect its economic behavior. However, it is important to realize that this is not the whole story: Changes in the firm's marginal revenue schedule can affect its behavior as well. This is because both marginal revenue and marginal cost are used in the Method II calculations for maximizing profits. Therefore, it is important to understand the circumstances under which a firm's marginal revenue schedule might change.

Referring to Exhibit 5.3, you will see that when we computed marginal revenue, it was determined completely by the demand curve for Tailor dresses. We used the demand curve to determine the right price to charge for any given quantity, then calculated total revenue by multiplying price times quantity, then calculated marginal value revenue from that. What can affect marginal revenue? The answer is: Anything that affects the demand curve.

Our question then becomes: What can affect the demand curve for the Tailor Dress Company? First, anything that affects the demand curve for dresses in general—changes in income, changes in the prices of related goods, and so on. But there are other factors as well. Suppose the Seamstress Dress Company down the street closes up shop for good and its customers have to look elsewhere for dresses. In that case, the demand for Tailor's product will probably rise and so will its marginal revenue curve. It is likely to produce a different number of dresses at a different price.

We can continue this line of inquiry one step further back and ask what might have driven the Seamstress Dress Company out of business. One possibility is a very large increase in rent at the Seamstress building. So we have the remarkable conclusion that although a rise in the Tailor Dress Company's rent will not lead to a change in Tailor's prices, a rise in someone *else's* rent very well *could* have that effect—provided that the "someone else" is a competitor who is driven out of business by the rent increase.

# Summary

We assume that firms act to maximize profits. This implies that they will act in accordance with the equimarginal principle; that is, they will engage in any activity up to the point where marginal cost equals marginal benefit.

When the firm sells goods in the marketplace, it chooses the profit- maximizing quantity. In accordance with the equimarginal principle, this is the quantity at which marginal cost equals marginal revenue. The firm sells this quantity at a price determined by the demand curve for its product.

The total revenue derived from selling a given quantity is given by the formula Revenue = Price × Quantity, where the price is read off the demand curve. Thus, the total revenue curve, and consequently the marginal revenue curve, are determined by the demand curve for the firm's product.

A change in the firm's fixed costs, because it affects nothing marginal, will not affect the quantity or price of the firm's output. There is one exception: A sufficiently large increase in fixed costs will cause the firm to shut down or leave the industry entirely.

A change in marginal costs can lead to a change in the firm's behavior. So can a change in marginal revenue. Any change in the demand curve facing the firm can lead to a change in marginal revenue. For example, a change in the availability of competing products can affect demand and, consequently, marginal revenue and, consequently, the behavior of the firm.

## Author Commentary  www.cengage.com/economics/landsburg

**AC1.** In the simple profit model presented in this chapter, firms produce a given good of a given quality. But in the real world, can firms increase profits by withholding high-quality goods from the market?

## Review Questions

**R1.** Suppose a farmer is deciding how many acres to spray. The crop duster charges $7 per acre. The total benefit of spraying is given by the following chart:

| No. of Acres Sprayed | Total Benefit | Marginal Benefit | Total Cost | Marginal Cost | Net Gain |
|---|---|---|---|---|---|
| 0 | $0 | | | | |
| 1 | 12 | | | | |
| 2 | 22 | | | | |
| 3 | 30 | | | | |
| 4 | 37 | | | | |
| 5 | 42 | | | | |

**a.** Fill in the remaining columns of the chart.

**b.** Use Method I to determine how many acres the farmer should spray.

**c.** Use Method II to determine how many acres the farmer should spray.

**d.** If the crop duster adds a fixed fee of $5 to come out to the farm, how many acres should the farmer spray? Predict the answer without creating a new chart. Then create a new chart to verify your prediction.

**e.** If the crop duster raises his fee to $10 per acre, how many acres should the farmer spray?

**R2.** The chart below shows the demand curve for dog food at Charlie's dog food factory and the total cost of producing various quantities:

| Quantity | Price | Total Revenue | Marginal Revenue | Total Cost | Marginal Cost | Profit |
|----------|-------|---------------|------------------|------------|---------------|--------|
| 1 | $15/lb | | $3 | | | |
| 2 | 13 | | 8 | | | |
| 3 | 11 | | 15 | | | |
| 4 | 9 | | 24 | | | |
| 5 | 7 | | 35 | | | |
| 6 | 5 | | 48 | | | |

**a.** Fill in the rest of the chart.

**b.** How much dog food should Charlie sell, and what price should he charge? Answer first using Method I and then using Method II.

**c.** If Charlie is required to pay a $5 annual license fee to operate his dog food factory, what happens to his total cost numbers? What happens to his marginal cost numbers? What happens to the amount of dog food he sells and the price he charges?

**d.** If Charlie is required to pay an excise tax of $6 per pound of dog food, what happens to his total cost numbers? What happens to his marginal cost numbers? What happens to the amount of dog food he sells and the price he charges?

**R3.** What is the equimarginal principle?

**R4.** What is the formula for profit in terms of revenue and cost? What is the formula for revenue in terms of price and quantity?

**R5.** Which of the following can affect a firm's behavior, and in what way?

**a.** A change in variable costs.

**b.** A change in fixed costs.

**c.** A change in the demand for the firm's product.

**d.** A competitor leaving the industry.

# Numerical Exercises

In the following exercises suppose that $x$ liters of orange juice can be produced for a total cost of $\$x^2$.

**N1.** Write down a formula for the marginal cost of production when $x$ liters of orange juice are produced. Simplify your formula algebraically.

**N2.** Suppose now that orange juice is measured in centiliters (there are 100 centiliters in a liter). Write a formula for the total cost of producing $y$ centiliters of orange juice. (*Hint:* When you produce *y* centiliters, how many liters are you producing? What is the associated cost?)

**N3.** Write a formula for the marginal cost of production when *y* centiliters are produced. Your formula gives the marginal cost in dollars per centiliter. Express the same formula in terms of dollars per liter.

**N4.** On the basis of your answer to Exercise N3, would you be willing to say that the marginal cost when *x* liters are produced is about $2x$ per liter? Why or why not?

**N5.** Now measure orange juice in milliliters (there are 1,000 milliliters in a liter). Write formulas for total cost and marginal cost when orange juice is measured in milliliters. Convert your marginal cost formula from dollars per milliliter to dollars per liter. Are you now more confident of your answer to Exercise N4? What do you think will happen if you measure orange juice in even smaller units?

# Problem Set

**1.** The government has undertaken a highway project that was originally projected to cost $1 billion and provide benefits of $1.5 billion. Unfortunately, the costs have been much higher than anticipated. The government has spent $1.2 billion so far and now expects that it will cost an additional $1.2 billion to finish the project. Should the project be abandoned or completed?

**2.** The ABC company has a problem with vandals, who throw bricks through its windows at random times. The XYZ company has a problem with pilferage: Of everything it produces, about 10% is stolen. **True or False:** Although the vandalism problem will not affect prices at ABC, the pilferage problem might cause XYZ's prices to rise.

**3.** The RH Snippet company has one president and 1000 assembly line workers. Which of the following events would have a bigger impact on the price of RH Snippets and why?

   **a.** The president gets a raise of $1,000,000 a year.

   **b.** A new union contract raises each worker's wages by $1000 a year, but allows the firm to fire as many workers as it wants to.

**4.** There is only one doctor in the town of Erewhon. Every time she treats a patient, she must use a pair of disposable rubber gloves, which costs her $1. She also finds it necessary to keep an X-ray machine in her office, which she rents for $500 a year. The town council has decided to help the doctor meet expenses and is undecided between two plans. Under Plan A, they will provide the doctor with unlimited free rubber gloves; under Plan B they will provide her with a free X-ray machine. Which plan is better for the doctor's *patients* and why?

**5.** In the town of Smallville, there are many dentists but just one eye doctor. Suppose the town institutes a new rule requiring every doctor and every dentist to take an expensive retraining course once a year. Which is more likely to increase: the price of a dental exam or the price of an eye exam?

**6.** Suppose that a new law requires every department store in Springfield to carry $10 million worth of fire insurance. **True or False:** If there is only one department store in Springfield, then none of the insurance costs will be passed on to consumers, but if there are many stores, then some of the costs might be passed on.

7. Suppose that Pat and Sandy's restaurant has just installed fancy new decor costing $10,000. Suppose also that in a distant solar system, there is a planet identical to earth in every way except that at this planet's Pat and Sandy's, the same redecoration cost $20,000. **True or False:** Pat and Sandy's hamburgers will be more expensive in the distant solar system than on earth.

8. Which of the following might affect the price of a hamburger at Waldo's Lunch Counter and why?

   a. The price of meat goes up.

   b. A new restaurant tax of 50¢ per hamburger is imposed.

   c. Waldo's is discovered to be in violation of a safety code, and the violation is one that would be prohibitively expensive to correct. As a result, Waldo is certain to incur a fine of $500 per year from now on.

   d. A new restaurant tax of $500 per year is imposed.

   e. Waldo recalculates and realizes that the redecoration he did last month cost him 15% more than he thought it had.

   f. Word gets around that a lot of Waldo's customers have been having stomach problems lately.

9. Suppose you own a river that many people want to cross by car. You've recently bought a fleet of ferry boats, and you've been charging people to take their cars across the river. It's just occurred to you that if you built a toll bridge, the trip would be faster and people would be willing to pay more per crossing. Unfortunately, if you build the toll bridge, the ferry boats must all be scrapped; they have no alternative uses. Which of the following numbers are relevant to the decision of whether to build the bridge:

   a. The cost of building the bridge.

   b. The revenue you could earn from a bridge.

   c. The cost of the ferry boats.

   d. The revenue you earn from the ferry boats.

10. a. Suppose that a famous Chicago Cubs baseball player threatens to quit unless his salary is doubled, and the management accedes to his demand. **True or False:** The fans will have to pay for this through higher ticket prices.

    b. Now suppose that the Cubs hire a famous and popular player away from the Philadelphia Phillies. Explain what will happen to ticket prices now.

11. A firm faces the following demand and total cost schedules:

| Demand | | Total Cost | |
|---|---|---|---|
| P | Q | Q | TC |
| $20 | 1 | 1 | $2 |
| 18 | 2 | 2 | 6 |
| 16 | 3 | 3 | 11 |
| 14 | 4 | 4 | 18 |
| 12 | 5 | 5 | 26 |

Suppose that the firm is required to produce a whole number of items each month. How much does it produce and at what price? How do you know?

**12.** A firm faces the following demand and total cost schedules, with all quantities listed on a per-month basis. Suppose that it is required to produce a whole number of items each month.

| Demand | | Total Cost | |
|---|---|---|---|
| P | Q | Q | TC |
| $20 | 1 | 1 | $5 |
| 18 | 2 | 2 | 15 |
| 15 | 3 | 3 | 30 |
| 12 | 4 | 4 | 50 |
| 8 | 5 | 5 | 75 |

**a.** How much does the firm produce, and at what price? How do you know?

**b.** Suppose that the firm is subject to an excise tax of $5 per item sold. How much does it produce, and at what price? How do you know?

**c.** Suppose, instead, that the firm is subject to a tax of $20 per month, regardless of how much it produces. How much does it produce, and at what price? How do you know?

**d.** Suppose, instead, that the firm is subject to a tax of $25 per month, regardless of how much it produces. How much does it produce, and at what price? How do you know?

**13.** Fred and Wilma have noticed that prices tend to be higher in stores that are located in high-rent districts. Fred thinks that the high rents cause the high prices, whereas Wilma thinks that the high prices cause the high rents. Under what circumstances is Fred correct? Under what circumstances is Wilma correct?

# Production and Costs

Suppose you want to download more music from the Internet. There are (at least) a couple of ways to do that: You can spend more time downloading, or you can get a faster connection.

If the problem is to download more music *by tonight,* you've got fewer options; a fast connection can take several days to install. In that case, you're just going to have to devote more hours to downloading, and the value of those hours measures the cost (to you) of getting the music files.

But if the problem is to download more music *over the next several months,* then you might want to consider a faster connection. In the long run, you've got more options than in the short run.

Business executives and managers face the same set of issues all the time. Suppose you own a dressmaking factory and you want to ramp up your hourly output. You can do that by having more workers on the premises, or you can do it by investing in more (or better) sewing machines that will make the workers more efficient. In the short run, you've got to go with more workers, because it takes a while to get new machines ordered, delivered, and installed. But in the long run, you'll probably want to go with some combination of more workers *and* more machines.

Your costs depend on two things: How many dresses do you make, and how do you make them? In Chapter 5, we saw that firms choose quantities by equating marginal cost to marginal revenue. But we didn't say very much about where the firm's cost curves come from in the first place. The answer to that question depends on the technology available to the firm. In this chapter we'll see how the firm, taking the available technology as given, chooses a production process, and how that production process determines the firm's costs.

## 6.1 Production and Costs in the Short Run

In the short run, the firm has limited options. A car manufacturer can't build a new factory overnight and a dressmaker has to wait to install new sewing machines. We'll abstract from this situation somewhat by assuming that in the short run, the only way

**Total product (TP)**

The quantity of output produced by the firm in a given amount of time. Total product depends on the quantity of labor the firm hires.

**Short-run production function**

The function that associates to each quantity of labor its total product.

for a dressmaker to produce more dresses is to hire more labor. Our first task is to be more explicit about the relationship between the quantity of labor and the quantity of dresses. Our next task will be to explore that relationship to understand how the firms' cost curves are determined.

## The Total, Marginal, and Average Products of Labor

We'll start with a numerical example, illustrated in Exhibit 6.1.

The first two columns relate the number of workers to the number of dresses the firm can produce in a given period of time (say an hour). The chart shows that 1 worker produces 5 dresses per hour; 2 workers produce 12 dresses, and so on. The number of dresses is called the **total product** (abbreviated **TP**) of labor.

The same information is recorded in the curve displayed underneath the first two columns in the exhibit. That curve is called the firm's **short-run production function.**

The short-run production function slopes upward because each additional worker contributes something to the production process. The number of dresses that each

| EXHIBIT **6.1** | **Total, Marginal, and Average Products** |

| Quantity of Labor | Total Product (*TP*) | Marginal Product of Labor (*MPL*) | Average Product of Labor (*APL*) |
|---|---|---|---|
| 1 worker | 5 dresses | 5 dresses per worker | 5 dresses per worker |
| 2 | 12 | 7 | 6 |
| 3 | 21 | 9 | 7 |
| 4 | 28 | 7 | 7 |
| 5 | 33 | 5 | 6.6 |
| 6 | 36 | 3 | 6 |
| 7 | 37 | 1 | 5.3 |

Total product (*TP*) is the quantity of output (in this case, dresses) that a given number of workers can produce (in a prespecified amount of time). The marginal product of labor (*MPL*) is the additional output due to one additional worker, and the average product of labor is the total product divided by the number of workers. In this example, when there are fewer than 4 workers, the marginal product exceeds the average product, so the average product is rising. When there are more than 4 workers, marginal product is less than average product, so average product is falling.

worker adds is called the **marginal product of labor (MPL)**. In Exhibit 6.1, the sixth worker increases the total product by 3 dresses (from 33 to 36), so that worker's marginal product is 3 dresses. The marginal products of each worker are listed in the third column of the chart and plotted in the right-hand graph.

**Marginal product of labor (MPL)**

The increase in total product due to hiring one additional worker (assuming that capital is held fixed).

**Exercise 6.1** Make sure that all the marginal products have been computed correctly.

The **average product of labor (APL)** is the number of dresses divided by the number of workers. Because the number of dresses is the same thing as the total product, we can write:

$$APL = TP/L$$

where $L$ (which stands for labor) is the total number of workers employed. For example, when 4 workers produce 28 dresses, the average product of labor is 7 dresses per worker. In Exhibit 6.1, the average product of labor is computed in the last column of the chart and graphed in the right-hand graph.

**Average product of labor (APL)**

Total product divided by the number of workers.

**Exercise 6.2** Check that all the average products have been computed correctly.

Total product is measured in *dresses* but marginal and average products are measured in *dresses per worker.* Thus the marginal and average products must be plotted on a separate graph from total product.

Dangerous Curve

The total product and marginal product curves are related: Marginal product gives the *slope* of total product. For example, when the number of workers increases from 5 to 6 (an increase of 1), output increases from 33 to 36 (an increase of 3). The ratio 3/1 is the *slope* of the total product curve near the point (6, 36), and 3 = 3/1 is also the *height* of the marginal value curve at 6.

## The Shape of the Average Product Curve

If 5 bakers can produce 500 cupcakes per day, how many cupcakes per day can 6 bakers produce? If this were an elementary school word problem, the answer would be 600. But in real life the answer might well be different. The sixth baker interacts with the first five bakers in ways that might make them all either more or less productive. For example, his presence might make it easier for all the bakers to specialize—one greases the pans while another mixes the batter and yet another prepares the frosting. In that case 6 bakers might produce *more* than 600 cupcakes. Or, the sixth baker might compete for counter space with the first five and get in their way; in that case, 6 bakers might produce *fewer* than 600 cupcakes.

There are plenty of examples in other industries as well. Two lumberjacks with a two-handed whipsaw can cut down a lot more than twice as many trees as either one could harvest individually, but a hundred lumberjacks might cut down far fewer than a hundred times as many trees, because there just aren't that many trees to cut down. A hundred auto workers are far more productive on average than a single auto worker because they can locate themselves at strategic points along an assembly line, whereas a single worker would have to run all over the factory performing a multitude of tasks. But a thousand auto workers in the same factory might be *less* productive on average, for the simple reason that they crowd the factory and get in each others' way. An army of 10,000 is more than 10,000 times as powerful as an army of one, but even here the advantages of size are limited: The Roman poet Virgil tells us that his army was so crowded that many soldiers had no room to use their weapons.

## The Shape of the Marginal Product Curve

Like the average product curve, and for similar reasons, the marginal product curve has the same general inverted ∪ shape. The second baker contributes more than the first and the third contributes more than the second (so marginal product is increasing), but eventually additional bakers start getting in each others' way and marginal product begins to decrease.

In Exhibit 6.1, marginal product starts decreasing after the third worker comes on board. We say that three workers marks the **point of diminishing marginal returns** for this firm.

**Point of diminishing marginal returns**

The point after which the marginal product curve begins to decrease.

You can see the same phenomenon in Exhibit 6.2, where the curves are smoother and perhaps easier to look at. The point of diminishing marginal returns occurs when the firm has hired $L_0$ workers. After that point, as further workers are added, marginal product continues to fall. Eventually, after $L_1$ workers have been hired, average product begins falling also.

## The Relationship Between the Average and Marginal Product Curves

Suppose your bakery employs 5 bakers to bake 500 cupcakes. The average product of labor is 100 cupcakes per baker.

Now you hire a sixth baker and output goes up to 630 cupcakes. The sixth baker's marginal product is 130 cupcakes, and hiring him raises the average product to 630/6 = 105 cupcakes per baker.

---

**EXHIBIT 6.2**  **The Stages of Production**

When there are fewer than $L_1$ workers, marginal product (*MPL*) exceeds average product (*APL*) and average product is rising. When there are more than $L_1$ workers, marginal product is less than average product and average product is falling. Therefore, average product has the shape of an inverted U and marginal product cuts through average product at the top of the U. The marginal product curve also has an inverted U shape.

The sixth baker raises the average product (from 100 to 105) precisely because his marginal product (130) is above the existing average (100).

Whenever a worker's marginal product is greater than the average product, adding that worker causes average product to rise.

Now suppose you hire a seventh baker and output rises to 700 cupcakes. The seventh bakers' marginal product (70) is below the existing average product of 105, so hiring that baker causes the average product to fall (from 105 to $700/7 = 100$).

Whenever a worker's marginal product is below the average product, adding that worker causes average product to fall.

You can see all this in Exhibit 6.2: Up to the point where $L_1$ workers are hired, each worker's marginal product exceeds the average product (i.e., the marginal product curve lies above the average cost curve). In this region, average cost is rising. After $L_1$ or more workers have been hired, each worker's marginal product is below the average product (i.e., the marginal product curve lies below the average cost curve). In this region, average cost is falling.

It follows that the marginal cost curve must *cross* the average cost curve right at the point where the average cost curve turns around, which is to say right at the top of the inverted U, as you can see in Exhibit 6.2.

## Costs in the Short Run

Remember that firms have both *fixed costs* and *variable costs*. In the example of Exhibit 6.1, we've assumed that in the short run, the only thing the firm can vary is labor. Thus, *in the short run, the only variable cost is the cost of hiring labor.*

---

In a more realistic example, a dressmaker would have other variable costs, including the cost of buying fabric. In this example, we've implicitly assumed that fabric is free. Obviously the assumption is absurd, but fortunately it won't affect the lessons we'll draw from the example.

---

Dangerous Curve

To figure out the firm's variable cost curve, you need to know the total product curve and the **wage rate**. Exhibit 6.3 shows the connection. The first two columns reproduce the total product curve from Exhibit 6.1, and we add the assumption that workers earn a wage rate of $15 per hour. Then, to get the variable cost numbers, we multiply the number of workers by 15. This is done in the fourth column of Exhibit 6.3.

**Wage rate**

The price of hiring labor.

The variable cost curve (shown in the exhibit) relates the number of dresses (*not* the number of workers!) to this variable cost. Thus a quantity of 5 dresses (which can be produced by 1 worker) corresponds to a variable cost of $15; a quantity of 12 dresses (which can be produced by 2 workers) corresponds to a variable cost of $30, and so forth.

---

**Exercise 6.3** Verify that the other points on the variable cost curve have been computed and plotted correctly.

---

To get the firm's total cost curve, we have to know its fixed costs and then add those fixed costs to the variable costs. Typically, the firm's short-run fixed costs are the costs

EXHIBIT **6.3**   **Variable Cost Curve**

| Quantity of Labor | Total Product (*TP*) | Quantity of Output | Variable Cost (*VC*) | Total Cost (*TC*) |
|---|---|---|---|---|
| 1 worker | 5 dresses | 15 | 15 | 65 |
| 2 | 12 | 12 | 30 | 80 |
| 3 | 21 | 21 | 45 | 95 |
| 4 | 28 | 28 | 60 | 110 |
| 5 | 33 | 33 | 75 | 125 |
| 6 | 36 | 36 | 90 | 140 |
| 7 | 37 | 37 | 105 | 155 |

We take as given: the price of capital ($10 per machine), the price of labor ($15 per worker), the quantity of capital (5 machines), and the total product curve (shown on the left half of the exhibit). From this information, we compute points on the variable cost (*VC*) and total cost (*TC*) curves as follows: Given a quantity of output, use the total product curve to find the corresponding number of workers. Multiply by the wage rate ($15 per worker) to get variable cost. Take variable cost and add fixed costs (in this case, 5 machines times $10 per machine, or $50) to get total cost.

**Capital**

Physical assets used as factors of production.

of **capital,** meaning the physical assets, such as machinery and factories, that are used in the production process. Examples of capital include a handyman's van, a secretary's computer, a professor's library, and a cowboy's lariat.

Because we've been talking about a dressmaker, let's assume that the relevant capital consists of sewing machines that can be rented for $10 per hour. Let's also assume the firm has 5 sewing machines. Then the firm's fixed costs are $50 per hour.

Dangerous
Curve

The capital cost of $10 per hour is the same for all firms, regardless of whether they own their own sewing machines. If Connie Daran's dress shop rents machines, Connie pays $10 an hour for them. If Lauren Ralph's dress shop uses its own machines, then Lauren is forgoing the opportunity to rent those machines to Connie, making her opportunity cost $10 per hour per machine.

To get the total cost numbers in Exhibit 6.3, we just take the variable cost numbers and add $50. The resulting total cost curve lies exactly $50 above the variable cost curve.

## Computing Average Costs

The firm's **average variable cost (*AVC*)** is defined by the formula:

$$AVC = VC/Q$$

where $VC$ is variable cost and $Q$ is the quantity of output (the firm's total product). The firm's **average cost (*AC*)** is defined by the formula:

$$AC = TC/Q$$

where $TC$ is total cost. Average cost is sometimes called **average total cost.**

In Exhibit 6.4, we compute $AVC$ and $AC$ for the same firm we studied in Exhibits 6.1 and 6.3. The left half of Exhibit 6.4 reproduces information on total, average, and marginal products from Exhibit 6.1. On the right side, the chart reproduces the Variable Cost and Total Cost columns from Exhibit 6.3. Average variable cost and average cost are computed directly from those columns. For example, at 5 dresses we have:

**Average variable cost (*AVC*)**

Variable cost divided by the quantity of output.

**Average cost, or average total cost (*AC*)**

Total cost divided by the quantity of output.

EXHIBIT **6.4**   **Deriving the Average and Marginal Cost Curves**

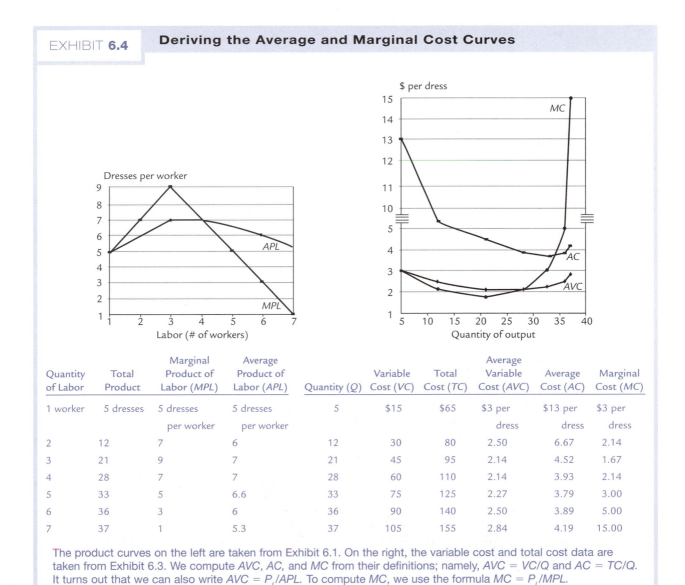

| Quantity of Labor | Total Product | Marginal Product of Labor (*MPL*) | Average Product of Labor (*APL*) | Quantity (*Q*) | Variable Cost (*VC*) | Total Cost (*TC*) | Average Variable Cost (*AVC*) | Average Cost (*AC*) | Marginal Cost (*MC*) |
|---|---|---|---|---|---|---|---|---|---|
| 1 worker | 5 dresses | 5 dresses per worker | 5 dresses per worker | 5 | $15 | $65 | $3 per dress | $13 per dress | $3 per dress |
| 2 | 12 | 7 | 6 | 12 | 30 | 80 | 2.50 | 6.67 | 2.14 |
| 3 | 21 | 9 | 7 | 21 | 45 | 95 | 2.14 | 4.52 | 1.67 |
| 4 | 28 | 7 | 7 | 28 | 60 | 110 | 2.14 | 3.93 | 2.14 |
| 5 | 33 | 5 | 6.6 | 33 | 75 | 125 | 2.27 | 3.79 | 3.00 |
| 6 | 36 | 3 | 6 | 36 | 90 | 140 | 2.50 | 3.89 | 5.00 |
| 7 | 37 | 1 | 5.3 | 37 | 105 | 155 | 2.84 | 4.19 | 15.00 |

The product curves on the left are taken from Exhibit 6.1. On the right, the variable cost and total cost data are taken from Exhibit 6.3. We compute *AVC, AC,* and *MC* from their definitions; namely, $AVC = VC/Q$ and $AC = TC/Q$. It turns out that we can also write $AVC = P_L/APL$. To compute *MC*, we use the formula $MC = P_L/MPL$.

$$AVC = VC/Q = \$15/5 = \$3 \text{ per dress}$$

and

$$AC = TC/Q = \$65/5 = \$13 \text{ per dress.}$$

All of the *AVC* and *AC* numbers are recorded on the curves below the chart.

**Exercise 6.4** In Exhibit 6.4, verify that all the numbers in the *AVC* and *AC* columns have been computed correctly.

When labor is the only variable factor (as we have been assuming), there is another formula for average variable cost. Notice first that if the firm hires $L$ workers, then its variable costs come to $P_L \cdot L$, where $P_L$ is the wage rate of labor. Therefore,

$$AVC = \frac{VC}{Q} = \frac{(P_L \cdot L)}{Q} = \frac{P_L}{(Q/L)} = \frac{P_L}{APL}$$

or, more briefly,

$$AVC = P_L / APL$$

where *APL* 5 *Q/L* is the average product of labor.

**Exercise 6.5** Verify that $AVC = P_L/APL$ in every row of the charts in Exhibit 6.4. (Keep in mind that in this example, $P_L = \$15$.)

## The Marginal Cost Curve

Now we want to construct the firm's marginal cost curve. Recall from Chapter 5 that marginal cost is the additional cost attributable to the last unit of output produced.

Thus, for example, we see in Exhibit 6.4 that the total cost of producing 36 dresses is $140 and the total cost of producing 37 dresses is $155. The difference, $15 per dress, is the marginal cost when 37 dresses are produced. We have recorded the result of that calculation in the Marginal Cost column across from the quantity 37.

But how can we get the other numbers in the Marginal Cost column? For example, how can we compute marginal cost when the firm produces 33 dresses? In principle, we need to take the total cost of producing 33 dresses—which, according to the chart, is $125—and subtract the cost of producing 32 dresses. Unfortunately, that information is missing from our incomplete chart, which lists only the quantities 5, 12, 21, 28, 33, 36, and 37.

But fortunately, there is another way to compute marginal cost. Here's the trick: First, use the total and marginal product curves to determine that when the total product is 33 dresses, the marginal product is 5 additional dresses per additional worker. Second, notice that "5 additional dresses per additional worker" is the same thing as ⅕ additional workers per additional dress." So the marginal cost of producing an additional dress is equal to the cost of hiring ⅕ of a worker. At the assumed going wage rate of $15 per worker, that comes to $3. So we record $3 as the marginal cost of producing 33 units of output.

Dangerous
Curve

You might object that there is no such thing as ⅕ of a worker. But don't forget that everything in our charts is implicitly measured "per hour." That makes it easy to hire ⅕ of a worker—you hire someone to work 12 minutes out of every hour, or one day out of every five.

Similarly, we compute the marginal cost at a quantity of, say, 12: The marginal product of labor is now 7 dresses per worker, so it takes ⅐ of a worker to produce an additional dress. Therefore, the marginal cost is 15 × ⅐, or about $2.14.

This method of calculating marginal costs can be summed up in a simple formula:

$$MC = P_L \times \frac{1}{MPL}$$

or

$$MC = \frac{P_L}{MPL}$$

---

**Exercise 6.6** Check that all of the marginal cost numbers in Exhibit 6.4 have been derived correctly.

---

## The Shapes of the Cost Curves

The right half of Exhibit 6.5 shows the shapes of the cost curves at a typical firm. The left half of the exhibit reproduces the product curves from Exhibit 6.2 for comparison. Here are the key facts about the geometry of the cost curves:

1. The variable cost (*VC*) curve is always increasing, because more output requires more labor and hence higher costs.

2. The total cost (*TC*) curve is determined by the formula *TC* = *FC* + *VC,* where *FC* (fixed cost) is constant. Therefore, it has exactly the same shape as the *VC* curve.

3. The marginal cost (*MC*) curve is ∪-shaped.

4. The average cost (*AC*) and average variable cost (*AVC*) curves are also ∪-shaped.

5. When marginal cost is below average variable cost, average variable cost is falling. In Exhibit 6.5, this refers to the region to the left of $Q_1$. To see why, consider a situation where you've already produced, say, 10 items at an average variable cost of $12 apiece. If the 11th item has a marginal cost below $12 (i.e., if *MC* is below *AVC*), then it will lower the average variable cost below $12 (i.e., average cost falls as the quantity increases from 10 to 11).

6. When marginal cost is above average variable cost, average variable cost is rising. In Exhibit 6.5, this occurs in the region to the right of $Q_1$.

7. Marginal cost crosses average variable cost at the bottom of the average variable cost "∪." This is a geometric consequence of points 5 and 6. When marginal cost is just equal to average variable cost, average variable cost is just changing from falling to rising.

8. The analogs of points 5, 6, and 7 hold when average variable cost is replaced by average cost, and they hold for the same reasons. Thus, when marginal cost is below average cost, average cost is falling; when marginal cost is above average cost, average cost is rising; marginal cost crosses average cost at the bottom of the average cost ∪.

9. The shapes of the cost curves are related to the shapes of the product curves. For example, we have *AVC* = $P_L$/*APL* and *MC* = $P_L$/*MPL*, where $P_L$ (the wage rate of labor) is a constant. These formulas convert the inverted ∪ shapes of *APL* and *MPL* to the ∪ shapes of *AVC* and *MC*.

EXHIBIT **6.5**          **The Geometry of Product Curves and Cost Curves**

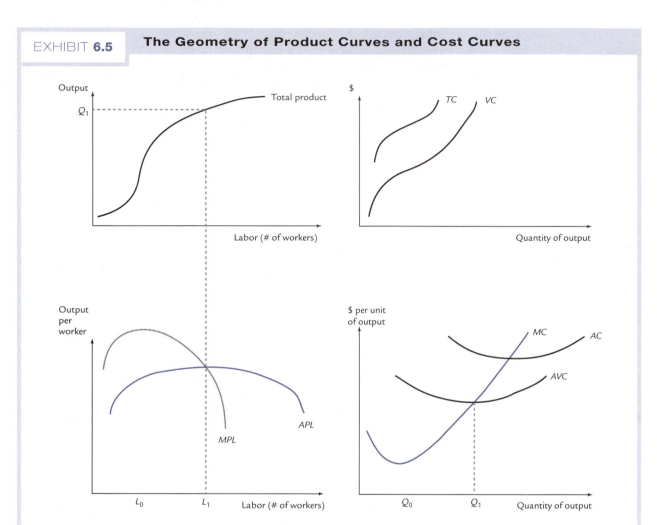

The product curves on the left are reproduced from Exhibit 6.2. Up to this point when there are $L_1$ workers and $Q_1$ units of output, marginal product exceeds average product, average product rises, marginal cost is below average variable cost, and average variable cost falls. Thereafter, marginal product is below average product, average product falls, marginal cost is above average variable cost, and average variable cost rises. Marginal cost cuts through both average variable cost and average cost at the bottom of the respective Us.

Dangerous Curve

In drawing the cost curves, remember that *TC* and *VC* belong on a graph whose vertical axis shows "dollars," while *AVC*, *AC*, and *MC* belong on a graph whose vertical axis shows "dollars per unit of output." Remember, also, that *all* of these curves have an implicit unit of time built into them; thus, when we say that it takes 2 workers to produce 6 units of output, we really mean that it takes 2 workers to produce 6 units of output *in a given, prespecified period of time.*

# 6.2 Production and Costs in the Long Run

Typically, there are many ways to produce a unit of output. What can be done by 3 workers with 5 machines can perhaps also be done by 6 workers with only 1 machine. In the long run, the firm can adjust its employment of both labor and capital so as to achieve the least expensive method of producing a given quantity of output. Our first task will be to develop some geometry to help clarify the firm's considerations.

## Isoquants

Exhibit 6.6 shows the set of all combinations that suffice to produce one unit of a certain good, which we will call $X$, in a given period of time. The vertical axis, labeled $K$, represents capital, and the horizontal axis, labeled $L$, represents labor. ($K$ is traditionally used instead of $C$ for *capital* in order to avoid any possible confusion with *consumption*.) The period of time is implicitly fixed; for example, we might be speaking of producing one unit of $X$ per day. Appropriate units for labor and capital are, for example, "man-hours per day" and "machine-hours per day."

In Exhibit 6.6 every basket of inputs in the shaded part of the graph suffices to produce a unit of $X$. However, points that are off the boundary (like $B$) are **technologically inefficient,** in that there are other baskets of inputs, containing both less capital and less labor, that will also suffice to produce a unit of $X$. (For example,

**Technologically inefficient**

A production process that uses more inputs than necessary to produce a given output.

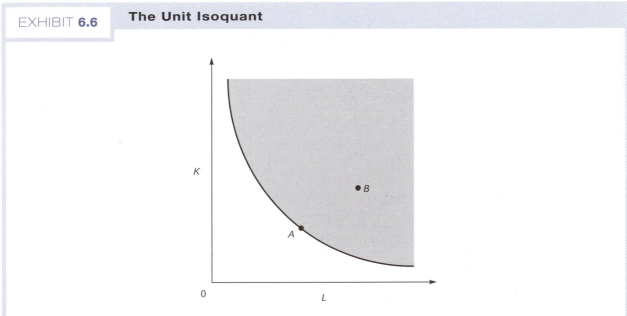

| EXHIBIT 6.6 | **The Unit Isoquant** |

The shaded region represents all of the different baskets of capital and labor that can be used to produce one unit of $X$. Baskets that are off the boundary, like $B$, are technologically inefficient, in that a unit of $X$ can be produced by a different basket (like $A$) containing smaller quantities of both inputs. The technologically efficient baskets for producing a unit of $X$ are those on the unit isoquant, which is the heavy curve that bounds the shaded region.

basket *A* contains smaller quantities of both inputs than basket *B* does.) No firm would want to produce a unit of *X* using a technologically inefficient basket of inputs. Thus, we will ignore these baskets and concentrate on the technologically efficient ones. In Exhibit 6.6 the technologically efficient baskets for producing a unit of *X* are represented by the heavy curve that bounds the shaded region. That curve is called the unit isoquant.

**Unit isoquant**

The set of all technically efficient ways to produce one unit of output.

Why is the unit isoquant shaped as it is? Note first that no point to the northeast of *A* can be on the unit isoquant, because any such point (like *B*) is technologically inefficient. For the same reason, no point to the northeast of *any* point on the unit isoquant can also lie on the unit isoquant. It follows that the points on the isoquant must all be to either the northwest or the southeast of each other. Another way to say this is

The unit isoquant is downward sloping.

### The Marginal Rate of Technical Substitution

Suppose that each day a firm uses the basket of inputs *A* to produce one unit of *X*. One day an employee calls in sick, making it necessary to get by with one less unit of labor. How much additional capital will the firm need in order to maintain the daily output level? The answer is shown in Exhibit 6.7. Reducing labor input by one unit corresponds geometrically to moving one unit to the left; maintaining the output level corresponds geometrically to staying on the isoquant. Taken together, these requirements mandate that the firm move to point *A′*. The vertical distance between *A* and *A′* is the additional capital that must be added to the usual daily ration. That vertical distance has been labeled $\Delta K$ in Exhibit 6.7.

**EXHIBIT 6.7    The Marginal Rate of Technical Substitution**

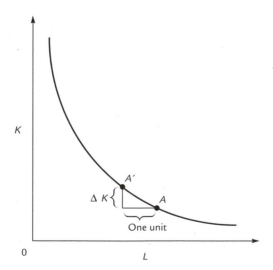

The firm produces one unit of *X* per day using basket *A* of inputs. When labor input is reduced by one unit, capital input must be increased by $\Delta K$ units in order for the firm to remain on the isoquant and maintain its level of output. The number $\Delta K$ is the marginal rate of technical substitution of labor for capital.

For all practical purposes, the distance $\Delta K$ is equal to the slope of the isoquant at the point $A$.[1] The absolute value of this slope is called the **marginal rate of technical substitution of labor for capital** ($MRTS_{LK}$); it is the amount of capital necessary to replace one unit of labor while maintaining a constant level of output.[2]

Suppose that a construction firm produces 1 house per day by employing 100 carpenters and 10 power tools. Then it is reasonable to think that when a carpenter calls in sick, the firm can maintain its level of production through a small increase in power tool usage. On the other hand, if the same firm produces the same 1 house per day by employing 10 carpenters and 100 power tools, we expect it to need a much larger increase in tool usage to compensate for the same absent carpenter. In other words, when much labor and little capital are employed to produce a unit of output, $MRTS_{LK}$ is small, but when little labor and much capital are employed to produce the same unit of output, $MRTS_{LK}$ is large. Geometrically, this means that at points far to the southeast, the isoquant is shallow, while at points far to the northwest, it is steep. That is, the isoquant is convex.

## Marginal Products and the *MRTS*

The marginal products of labor and capital are related to the marginal rate of technical substitution. Suppose labor input is reduced by one unit and capital input is increased by $\Delta K$ units, where $\Delta K$ is just enough to maintain the existing level of output. Then $\Delta K = MRTS_{LK}$.

Consider the two steps in this experiment separately. When one unit of labor is sacrificed, output goes down by the marginal product of labor, *MPL*. When $\Delta K$ units of capital are hired, output goes up by $\Delta K \cdot MPK$, where *MPK* is the marginal product of capital. Because the existing level of output does not change, we must have

$$MPL = \Delta K \cdot MPK = MRTS_{LK} \cdot MPK$$

or

$$MRTS_{LK} = MPL / MPK$$

Thus, the marginal rate of technical substitution is closely related to the marginal products of labor and capital. Keep in mind the conceptual distinction, though: To measure $MRTS_{LK}$, we hold *output* fixed, vary $L$ by one unit, and ask how much $K$ must vary. To measure *MPL*, we hold *capital* ($K$) fixed, vary $L$ by one unit, and ask how much output varies. To measure *MPK*, we hold *labor* ($L$) fixed, vary $K$ by one unit, and ask how much output varies.[3]

---

[1] The line through $A$ and $A'$ is nearly tangent to the isoquant and can be made more nearly tangent by measuring labor in smaller units when it is desirable to do so. Its slope is equal to the rise over the run, which is $-\Delta K/1$, or $-\Delta K$.

[2] Some books call this the *marginal rate of technical substitution of capital for labor;* unfortunately, there is no standard accepted terminology.

[3] The discussion in this section assumed a one-unit change in labor. More generally, if labor had changed by some amount $\Delta L$, the equation would have been

$$\Delta L \cdot MPL = \Delta K \cdot MPK$$

and we would still have reached the conclusion

$$MRTS_{LK} = \frac{\Delta K}{\Delta L} = \frac{MPL}{MPK}$$

---

**Marginal rate of technical substitution of labor for capital ($MRTS_{LK}$)**

The amount of capital that can be substituted for one unit of labor, holding output constant.

---

EXHIBIT **6.8**     **The Production Function**

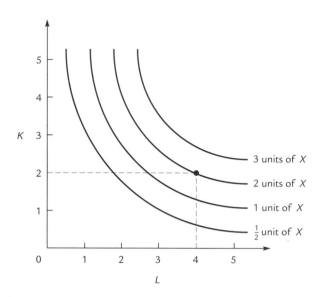

The family of isoquants can be used to determine the maximum level of production that can be attained with any given level of inputs. For example, if the firm uses 4 units of labor and 2 of capital, then it can produce 2 units of output and no more. This rule for calculating the output that can be produced from a given basket of inputs is the firm's production function.

---

## The Production Function

Suppose that the firm wants to produce 2 units of $X$ instead of 1. We can draw an isoquant representing all of the technologically efficient input combinations that the firm can use. This "2-unit" isoquant lies above and to the right of the original "1-unit" isoquant. We can go on to draw isoquants for any given level of output, generating a family of isoquants such as the one shown in Exhibit 6.8.

The important facts about isoquants are these:

Isoquants slope downward, they fill the plane, they never cross, and they are convex.

You should recognize this list of properties; it characterizes families of indifference curves as well.

**Exercise 6.7** Explain why isoquants never cross. Explain why they fill the plane.

Suppose that we want to know how much output the firm can produce with a given basket of inputs. We can use the family of isoquants to answer this question. For example, suppose that we want to know how much the firm can produce using 4 units of labor and 2 units of capital. From Exhibit 6.8 we see that this basket lies on the 2-unit isoquant; thus, the firm can use this basket to produce 2 units of $X$.

The rule for determining how much output can be produced with a given basket of inputs is called the firm's **production function.** If we know the family of isoquants, then we know the production function, and vice versa. Therefore, we can think of the graph in Exhibit 6.8 as providing a picture of the firm's production function.

**Production function**

The rule for determining how much output can be produced with a given basket of inputs.

# Choosing a Production Process

In the long run, no factor of production is fixed, and the firm is free to use any production process. Given a level of output, the corresponding isoquant presents the firm with a menu of ways to produce that output, from which it chooses the option with the lowest cost. We will now develop a geometric device for keeping track of those costs.

## Isocosts and Cost Minimization

Suppose that the firm can hire labor at a going wage rate of $P_L$ and can hire capital at a going rental rate of $P_K$. Suppose also, for the moment, that the firm spends $10 on inputs. Then the firm will be able to purchase $L$ units of labor and $K$ units of capital if and only if $L$ and $K$ satisfy the equation:

$$P_L \cdot L + P_K \cdot K = \$10$$

The collection of pairs $(L, K)$ that satisfy this equation form a straight line with slope, $-(P_L/P_K)$. That line, called the $10 isocost, is shown in Exhibit 6.9. Of the lines shown in the exhibit, the $10 isocost is the one closest to the origin.

If the firm is willing to spend $11 on inputs, then it can hire any combination of labor and capital that satisfies:

$$P_L \cdot L + P_K \cdot K = \$11$$

**Isocost**

The set of all baskets of inputs that can be employed at a given cost.

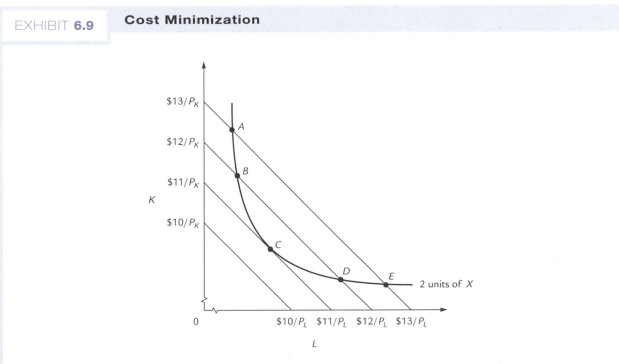

EXHIBIT **6.9**    **Cost Minimization**

The isocost lines display all of the production processes that can be achieved for a given expenditure on inputs. Moving outward from the origin, the straight lines are the $10, $11, $12, and $13 isocosts. In order to produce 2 units of $X$, the firm must select a production process on the 2-unit isoquant. Of these processes, it will choose the one that is least costly, which is to say the one on the lowest isocost, namely, $C$.

The set of available points form another straight line, the $11 isocost, which is also shown in Exhibit 6.9. The exhibit shows the $12 and $13 isocosts as well.

Now suppose that the firm wants to produce 2 units of output. Then it must select a production process that uses a basket of inputs on the 2-unit isoquant, shown in the exhibit. If it selects point *A,* on the $13 isocost, then the cost of production is $13. If it selects point *B,* the cost of production is $12. If it selects point *C,* the cost of production is $11. Of course, the firm wants to minimize its costs, and so it selects the production process corresponding to point *C.* The cost of producing 2 units of output is $11.

Of course, the firm would prefer to spend only $10 to produce its 2 units of output, but this is impossible: No point on the $10 isocost is also on the 2-unit isoquant. The best it can do is to choose point *C.*

In order to minimize the cost of producing a given level of output, the firm always chooses a point of tangency between an isocost and the appropriate isoquant.

## Cost Minimization and the Equimarginal Principle

There is another way to reach the same conclusion. Suppose that the firm considers hiring 1 less unit of labor and replacing it with sufficient capital so that it can continue producing 2 units of output. How much additional capital must it hire? The answer to this question is precisely the number that we have already called the marginal rate of technical substitution, or $MRTS_{LK}$. Recall that $MRTS_{LK}$ is also equal to the absolute value of the slope of the isoquant.

What are the marginal costs and benefits of such a decision? The marginal benefit is a saving of $P_L$ when the firm hires 1 less unit of labor. The marginal cost arises from hiring $MRTS_{LK}$ additional units of capital at $P_K$ each; the bill comes to $MRTS_{LK} \cdot P_K$.

The equimarginal principle tells us that the firm should seek to equate marginal cost with marginal benefit. That is, it should seek to set

$$MSTS_{LK} \cdot P_K = P_L$$

or

$$MRTS_{LK} = \frac{P_L}{P_K}$$

The left side of this equation is the absolute value of the slope of the isoquant, and the right side is the absolute value of the slope of the isocost. So the equation tells us that the firm should seek a point where the slopes of the isoquant and the isocost are equal, that is, a point of tangency.

To understand this better, let us think about what the firm can do if it is *not* at a point of tangency. What if the firm makes the mistake of operating at point *A* in Exhibit 6.9? Here the isoquant is steeper than the isocost; that is,

$$MRTS_{LK} > \frac{P_L}{P_K}$$

If the firm hires 1 more unit of labor and $MRTS_{LK}$ fewer units of capital, it can stay on the isoquant, decrease its capital costs by $MRTS_{LK} \cdot P_K$, and increase its labor costs by $P_L$. Because the last displayed inequality can be rewritten $MRTS_{LK} \cdot P_K > P_L$, this is a wise move for the firm to make. It shifts to the right and down along the isoquant to a point like *B.* Here, $MRTS_{LK}$ still exceeds $P_L/P_K$ and the process is repeated; the firm keeps moving southeast along the isoquant until it reaches point $C$, where $MRTS_{LK}$ and $P_L/P_K$ are equal.

**Exercise 6.8** Explain the adjustment process if the firm starts at a point like $E$.

## Output Maximization

We will describe one more way to see that the firm always chooses to operate at a tangency. Exhibit 6.9 illustrates the problem of a firm that has chosen its level of output (in this case, 2 units) and seeks the least expensive way to produce it. Exhibit 6.10 illustrates the problem of a firm that has instead chosen its expenditure on inputs and is now deciding how much to produce.

If the chosen expenditure is $E$, then the firm must choose a production process on the $E$ isocost, shown in Exhibit 6.10. How much does the firm want to produce? Surely, the most that it possibly can, which is to say that it wants to be on the highest available isoquant. In the figure, it is clear that this occurs at point $H$, the point of tangency.

In summary, there are two ways of looking at the firm's problem, but both lead to the same conclusion. Whether the firm wants to minimize the cost of producing a given output (as in Exhibit 6.9), or to maximize its output for a given expenditure (as in Exhibit 6.10), it is led to the same conclusion: Produce at a point where an isocost is tangent to an isoquant.

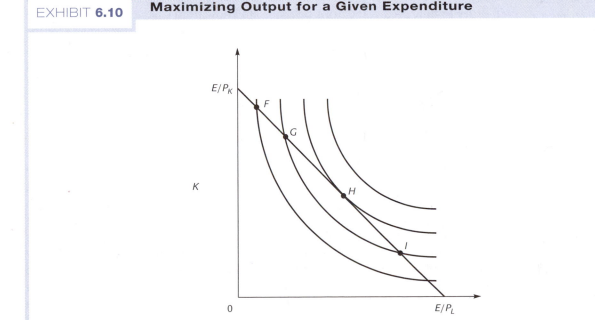

| EXHIBIT **6.10** | **Maximizing Output for a Given Expenditure** |

If the firm spends the amount $E$ to hire inputs, it can choose any production process along the isocost line, such as $F$, $G$, $H$, or $I$. Of these, it will choose the one that yields the greatest output, which is the point of tangency $H$.

## The Expansion Path

All this should have a familiar ring to it; it is reminiscent of the way consumers choose bundles of output goods to purchase. However, the analogy is less close than it first appears. There is one critical difference between the consumer (who seeks a tangency between his budget line and an indifference curve) and the firm (which seeks a tangency between an isocost and an isoquant).

The difference is this: A consumer has a *given* income to divide among consumption goods, whereas a firm can *choose* its level of expenditure on inputs. Put another way, a consumer is constrained to only one budget line, whereas a firm has a whole *family* of isocosts (one for each level of expenditure) from which it can choose.

Unlike an individual, a firm has no budget constraint. The reason is that individuals pursue consumption, whereas firms pursue profits. As a result, the firm can "afford" to spend any amount on inputs that is appropriate to its goal. Even when there is a limited amount of cash on hand, a profit- maximizing firm can borrow against its future profits to achieve whatever is the optimal level of expenditure and output.[4] The same borrowing opportunities are not available to an individual who decides he wants to visit Hawaii.

In terms of our graphs, the consequence of all this is that we must consider the entire family of isocost lines available to the firm. They are parallel, because they all have the same slope, $-(P_L/P_K)$, but those reflecting higher levels of expenditure are farther out than others.[5] This is shown in Exhibit 6.11.

The tangencies between isocosts and isoquants lie along a curve called the firm's expansion path. We know that the firm chooses one of these tangencies. However, we have not yet said anything that allows us to determine *which* tangency the firm selects. In order to fully predict the firm's behavior, we know from Chapter 5 that we need to take account of the marginal revenue curve, which is derived from the demand for the firm's output. Because this information does not appear in the expansion path diagram, it is not surprising that we cannot use the diagram to predict the firm's behavior, at least with respect to its output decision. We will not return to this question until Chapter 7.

**Expansion path**

The set of tangencies between isoquants and isocosts.

## The Long-Run Cost Curves

To derive a firm's long-run cost curves, we need to know its production function (i.e., the isoquants) and the input prices $P_L$ and $P_K$ (which determine the isocosts). By way of example, we will assume that the isoquants are as shown in Exhibit 6.11 and that the input prices are $P_K = \$10$, $P_L = \$15$. Given this information, we can plot the isocosts as in Exhibit 6.11 and draw in the expansion path by connecting the tangencies. All of this has been done in the exhibit.

Suppose the firm plans to produce 33 units of output per day. It selects a tangency on the 33 unit isoquant, which you can see from the exhibit occurs at the point where $K = 6$ and $L = 4$. Therefore, the firm hires 6 units of capital and 4 of labor for a total cost of $(6 \times \$10) 1 (4 \times \$15) = \$120$. This is the firm's long-run total cost of producing 33 units.

**Long-run total cost**

The cost of producing a given amount of output when the firm is able to operate on its expansion path.

[4] In practice, there might actually be limitations on the firm's ability to borrow that are not accounted for by our simple model. However, the standard assumption in elementary treatments of the theory of the firm is that all of the firm's profits from production are available for the purchase of inputs, even before production takes place. Economists are aware that firms can face borrowing constraints and have intensely studied the consequences of those constraints, but this is a more advanced topic.

[5] We are assuming that $P_L$ and $P_K$ are not affected by the actions of the firm. This assumption would fail only if the firm in question hired a significant proportion of either all the labor or all the capital in the economy.

## EXHIBIT 6.11 Deriving Long-Run Total Cost

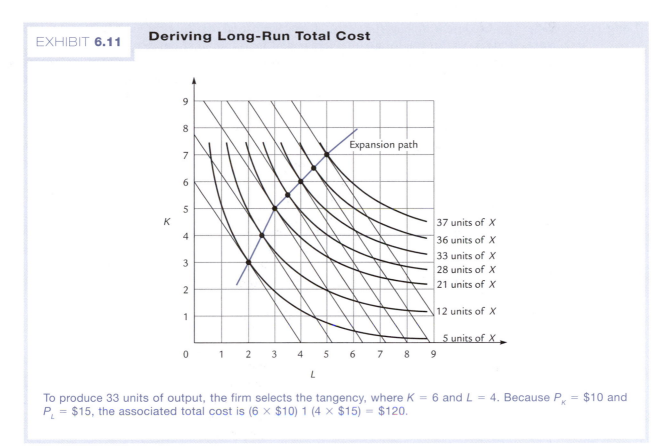

To produce 33 units of output, the firm selects the tangency, where $K = 6$ and $L = 4$. Because $P_K = \$10$ and $P_L = \$15$, the associated total cost is $(6 \times \$10)\ 1\ (4 \times \$15) = \$120$.

Similarly, if the firm wants to produce 21 units of output, then it uses 5 units of capital and 3 of labor for a total cost of $(5 \times \$10)\ 1\ (3 \times \$15) = \$95$.

These points can be plotted on a long-run total cost curve with output on the horizontal axis and total cost on the vertical. There is a point at (33, $120) and another at (21, $95).

---

We have discovered that *if* the firm wants to produce 33 units a day, the best way to do that is with 6 units of capital and 4 units of labor. We have *not* said that there's any reason the firm should want to produce exactly 33 units a day.

The logic goes as follows: For each possible quantity of output (e.g., 33 units a day), we figure out the cost-minimizing way to produce the output. Only *after* we have computed the cost for each quantity will we have enough information to begin thinking about what quantity the firm should actually produce.

Dangerous
Curve

---

**Exercise 6.9** What is the total cost of producing 37 units of output? 5 units of output? 12 units of output?

## Long-Run Average and Marginal Costs

In Exhibit 6.4, we constructed the (short-run) average and marginal cost curves from our knowledge of the (short-run) total cost curve. We can follow exactly the same

**Long-run average cost**

Long-run total cost divided by quantity.

**Long-run marginal cost**

That part of long-run total cost attributable to the last unit produced.

procedure with long-run costs. The long-run total cost curve of Exhibit 6.12, panel A, gives rise to the long-run average and marginal cost curves shown in panel B. **Long-run average cost** is given by the formula $LRTC/Q$ and **long-run marginal cost** is the increment to long-run total cost attributable to the last unit of output produced. At a quantity of 33 units, we have $LRAC = TC/Q = \$120/(33\text{ units}) = \$3.63$ per unit. At a quantity of 37 units, we have $LRMC = \$145 - \$132.50$ per unit $= \$12.50$ per unit. (All of the numbers here are taken from the table in Exhibit 6.12.)

If we want to compute the long-run marginal cost at a quantity of 28 units, we must subtract from $107.50 the long-run total cost of producing 27 units, a number that is not shown in the table. However, you could in principle determine this number from Exhibit 6.11, if the 27-unit isoquant were drawn in.

Comparing the long-run Exhibit 6.12 with the short-run Exhibit 6.4, you will find that there is one fewer curve in Exhibit 6.11: In the long run, the average variable cost

## EXHIBIT 6.12    Long-Run Total, Marginal, and Average Costs

| Quantity of Output | Factors Employed | | Cost of Factors | | Total Cost |
|---|---|---|---|---|---|
| | K | L | K | L | |
| 5 | 3 | 2 | $30 | $30 | $60 |
| 12 | 4 | 2.5 | 40 | 37.50 | 77.50 |
| 21 | 5 | 3 | 50 | 45 | 95 |
| 28 | 5.5 | 3.5 | 55 | 52.50 | 107.50 |
| 33 | 6 | 4 | 60 | 60 | 120 |
| 36 | 6.5 | 4.5 | 65 | 67.50 | 132.50 |
| 37 | 7 | 5 | 70 | 75 | 145 |

These cost curves are all derived from the graph in Exhibit 6.11. The table illustrates computations like the one in the caption to Exhibit 6.11. These computations yield points on the total cost curve. Points on the average cost curve are computed by dividing total cost by quantity: When 33 units are produced, the average cost is $120/33 = $3.63. Points on the marginal cost curve are computed by taking differences in total cost: When 37 items are produced, the marginal cost is $145 − $132.50 = $12.50. To compute the marginal cost when 28 items are produced, we must start with $107.50 and subtract the total cost of producing 27 items. The latter number does not appear in the table, but could be computed from the graph in Exhibit 6.11.

curve has disappeared. This is because all costs are variable in the long run; therefore, in the long run there is no distinction between average cost and average variable cost.

## Returns to Scale and the Shape of the Long-Run Cost Curves

Our goal is to determine the shape of the firm's long-run marginal and average cost curves. Because these curves are derived from the long-run total cost curve, which is in turn derived from the production function, it behooves us to start by thinking a little harder about the production function itself.

Here is an important question about the production function: When all input quantities are increased by 1%, does output go up by (1) more than 1%, (2) exactly 1%, or (3) less than 1%? Depending on the answer to this question, we say that the production function exhibits (1) **increasing returns to scale,** (2) **constant returns to scale,** or (3) **decreasing returns to scale.**

---

Students often confuse the concepts of diminishing marginal returns, on the one hand, and decreasing returns to scale, on the other. The two concepts are entirely different, and they are entirely different in each of two ways. The most important difference is that diminishing marginal returns is a short-run concept that describes the effect on output of increasing *one* input while holding other inputs fixed. Decreasing returns to scale is a long-run concept that describes the effect on output of increasing *all* inputs in the same proportion. The other difference is that the concept of diminishing marginal returns deals with marginal quantities, whereas the concept of decreasing returns to scale deals with total and average quantities. When we ask about diminishing marginal returns, we ask, "Will the next unit of this input yield more or less output *at the margin* than the last unit did?" When we ask about decreasing returns to scale, we ask, "Will a 1% increase in all inputs yield more or less than a 1% increase in *total* output?"

---

For given input prices, diminishing marginal returns are reflected by an increasing short-run marginal cost curve. Decreasing returns to scale, as we shall soon see, are reflected by an increasing long-run average cost curve.

### Increasing Returns to Scale

Increasing returns to scale are likely to result when there are gains from specialization or when there are organizational advantages to size. Two men with two machines might be able to produce more than twice as much as one man with one machine, if each can occasionally use a helping hand from the other. At low levels of output, firms often experience increasing returns to scale.

### Constant and Decreasing Returns to Scale

At higher levels of output, the gains from specialization and organization having been exhausted, firms tend to produce under conditions of constant or even decreasing returns to scale. Which of the two, constant or decreasing returns, is more likely? A good case can be made for constant returns. When a firm doubles all of its inputs, it can, if it chooses, simply set up a second plant, identical to the original one, and have each plant produce at the original level, yielding twice the original output. This strategy

**Increasing returns to scale**

A condition where increasing all input levels by the same proportion leads to a more than proportionate increase in output.

**Constant returns to scale**

A condition where increasing all input levels by the same proportion leads to a proportionate increase in output.

Dangerous
Curve

**Decreasing returns to scale**

A condition where increasing all input levels by the same proportion leads to a less than proportionate increase in output.

generates constant returns to scale and suggests that the firm should never have to settle for decreasing returns. This argument is often summed up in the slogan "What a firm can do once, it can do twice."

Students sometimes object to this argument for constant returns. They argue that doubling the number of workers and the number of machines can lead to congestion in the factory and consequently to less than a doubling of output. This objection overlooks the fact that factory space is itself a productive input. When we measure returns to scale, we assume that *all* inputs are increased in the same proportion. In particular, we must double the space in the factory as well as the numbers of workers and machines.

A related objection is that when the scale of an operation is doubled, the owners can no longer keep as watchful an eye on the entire enterprise as they could previously. But if we view the owners' supervisory talents as a productive input, this objection breaks down as well. Any measurement of returns to scale must involve the imaginary experiment of increasing these talents in the same proportion as all other productive inputs.

As long as *all* productive inputs are truly variable, the argument for constant returns is a convincing one. However, if there are some inputs (such as managerial skills or the owner's cleverness as an entrepreneur) that are truly *fixed even in the long run,* then there may be decreasing returns to scale with respect to changes in all of the variable inputs. As a result, most economists are comfortable with the assumption that firms experience decreasing returns to scale at sufficiently high levels of output.

Dangerous
Curve

We assumed at the outset that in the long run every input is variable. When we now admit the possibility that some inputs may not be variable in the long run, we are admitting that our original model might not be a fully adequate description of reality.

## Returns to Scale and the Average Cost Curve

Under conditions of increasing returns to scale, the firm's long-run average cost curve is decreasing. This is because a 1% increase in output can be accomplished with less than a 1% increase in all inputs. It follows that an increase in output leads to a fall in the average cost of production.[6]

Under conditions of decreasing returns to scale, the firm's long-run average cost curve is increasing.

**Exercise 6.10** Justify the assertion of the preceding paragraph.

Under conditions of constant returns to scale, the firm's long-run average cost curve is flat. This is the situation where "What a firm can do once it can do twice." If the firm wants to double its output, it does so by doubling all of its inputs. The average cost per unit of output never changes.

If we assume that a firm experiences increasing returns to scale at low levels of output and decreasing returns thereafter, the firm's long-run average cost curve is

---

[6] This argument assumes that the firm can hire all of the inputs that it wants to at a going market price. Without this assumption, the long-run average cost curve could be increasing even in the presence of increasing returns to scale. The same caveat applies to all of our arguments in this subsection.

U-shaped, as in panel B of Exhibit 6.12. Only at one level of output (the quantity at which long-run average cost is minimized) does the firm face constant returns to scale.

When long-run marginal cost is below long-run average cost, long-run average cost is decreasing; and when long-run marginal cost is above long-run average cost, long-run average cost is increasing. Consequently, when long-run average cost is U-shaped, it is cut by long-run marginal cost at the bottom of the U. This is true in the long run for the same reason that it is true in the short run.

In general, the upward-sloping part of the firm's long-run marginal cost curve will be much more elastic than the upward-sloping part of its short-run marginal cost curve. Marginal cost rises much more quickly when the firm is constrained not to vary certain inputs (in the short run) than when it can vary all inputs to minimize costs for each level of output (in the long run).

# 6.3 Relations Between the Short Run and the Long Run

In Section 6.1, we studied the firm's short-run production function and cost curves; in Section 6.2, we studied the firm's long-run production function and cost curves. Our remaining task is to relate the two points of view.

## From Isoquants to Short-Run Total Cost

Consider a firm that rents capital at a rate of $P_K = \$10$ and hires labor at a rate of $P_L = \$15$. The firm's production function is illustrated in Exhibit 6.13. Its capital is fixed in the short run at 5 units (thus, if a "unit" is a machine, the firm has the use of 5 machines; if a "unit" is 100 square feet of office space, the firm has the use of 500 square feet).

In the short run, the firm can only choose input baskets that contain exactly 5 units of capital, which is to say that it can only choose baskets that are located on the blackened horizontal line. To produce 5 units of output, it must select a basket that is both on this line and on the 5-unit isoquant; that is, it must select the point with 5 units of capital and 1 unit of labor. The firm's total cost is then $5 \times \$10 = \$50$ for capital plus $1 \times \$15 = \$15$ for labor, or $65. (Of this $65, the $50 spent on capital is a fixed cost and the $15 spent on labor is a variable cost.) This calculation is recorded in the first row of the table, under the columns headed "Short Run."

Similarly, if the firm wants to produce 12 units of output, it must select a point on both the blackened horizontal line and the 12-unit isoquant; that is, it must use 5 units of capital and 2 units of labor. Its total cost is $80, as recorded in the second row of the table.

From the numbers in the Short Run half of the table, we can discover the firm's total product and total cost curves. The first column shows quantities of output, and the third shows the quantity of labor needed to produce that output. The information here is identical to the information in the first two columns of the table in Exhibit 6.1. The moral is this: If you know the isoquants and the fixed quantity of capital, you can derive the (short-run) total product curve.

If, in addition, you know the factor prices, then you can also derive the short-run variable cost and total cost curves, as we showed in Exhibits 6.2 and 6.3. The same computations are shown again in Exhibit 6.13, under the Short Run columns showing

| EXHIBIT **6.13** | **Short-Run and Long-Run Total Cost Curves** |

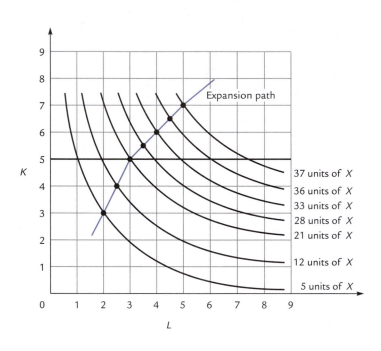

|  | Short Run |  |  |  |  | Long Run |  |  |  |  |
|---|---|---|---|---|---|---|---|---|---|---|
|  | Factors Employed |  | Cost of Factors |  |  | Factors Employed |  | Cost of Factors |  |  |
| Quantity of Output | K | L | K | L | Total Cost | K | L | K | L | Total Cost |
| 5 | 5 | 1 | $50 | $15 | $65 | 3 | 2 | $30 | $30 | $60 |
| 12 | 5 | 2 | 50 | 30 | 80 | 4 | 2.5 | 40 | 37.50 | 77.50 |
| 21 | 5 | 3 | 50 | 45 | 95 | 5 | 3 | 50 | 45 | 95 |
| 28 | 5 | 4 | 50 | 60 | 110 | 5.5 | 3.5 | 55 | 52.50 | 107.50 |
| 33 | 5 | 5 | 50 | 75 | 125 | 6 | 4 | 60 | 60 | 120 |
| 36 | 5 | 6 | 50 | 90 | 140 | 6.5 | 4.5 | 65 | 67.50 | 132.50 |
| 37 | 5 | 7 | 50 | 105 | 155 | 7 | 5 | 70 | 75 | 145 |

(Continues)

the cost of labor and total cost. The resulting short-run total cost curve, labeled *SRTC* in the second panel of Exhibit 6.13, is identical to the one shown in Exhibit 6.3.[7]

## From Isoquants to Long-Run Total Cost

Exhibits 6.11 and 6.12 already illustrated the derivation of long-run total cost from isoquants and factor prices. These computations are repeated in the "Long Run" columns

---

[7] In Section 6.1 we wrote *TC* for short-run total cost. We are now writing *SRTC* to distinguish the short-run total cost curve from the long-run total cost curve.

| EXHIBIT 6.13 | Short-Run and Long-Run Total Cost Curves (Continued) |

With $P_K$ = $10 and $P_L$ = $15, the isoquant diagram gives rise to the table. Points from the table are plotted on the graph. The short-run total cost (*SRTC*) curve is drawn on the assumption that capital employment is fixed at 5 units. It is the same curve that was constructed in Exhibit 6.3. Because the firm always chooses the least expensive production process in the long run, long-run total cost is never greater than short-run total cost. If the firm happens to want to produce exactly 21 units of output, then its desired long-run capital employment is equal to its existing capital employment of 5 units. In this fortunate circumstance, the firm can produce at the lowest possible cost even in the short run. For any other level of output, short-run total cost exceeds long-run total cost.

of the table in Exhibit 6.13, and the resulting *LRTC* curve is redrawn in the second panel of that exhibit.

## Short-Run Total Cost versus Long-Run Total Cost

To produce 12 units of output, the firm in Exhibit 6.13 selects the least expensive production process in the long run. Its costs total $77.50. In the short run, the firm is forced to use a more expensive process, and so its costs are higher, totaling $80. This illustrates something important:

Short-run total cost is always at least as great as long-run total cost.

The reason is simple. In the long run, the firm produces at the lowest possible cost. The short-run cost has no chance of being less than the lowest possible! Geometrically, this means that *SRTC* never dips below *LRTC*. You can see that this is true in Exhibit 6.13.

We can say even more. There is exactly one quantity of output for which the short-run and long-run total costs are equal. In Exhibit 6.13, that quantity is 21. This is the quantity at which the firm's long-run desired capital employment (in this case, 5 units) happens to precisely equal the fixed amount of capital it has available. You can see in the exhibit that the *SRTC* and *LRTC* curves touch at a quantity of 21.

## A Multitude of Short Runs

All of the *short-run* numbers in Exhibit 6.13 are derived on the assumption that the firm's capital is fixed at 5 units. What if capital is fixed at 4 units instead? Now what is the short-run total cost of producing 5 units of output? In order to achieve the 5-unit isoquant with 4 units of capital, the firm must employ 1.5 units of labor. The short-run total cost is (4 × \$10) 1 (1.5 × \$15) = \$62.50. To produce 12 units of output, the firm must employ 2.5 units of labor, and the short-run total cost is \$77.50.

---

**Exercise 6.11** With 4 units of capital, what is the *SRTC* when quantity is 28? When it is 33? When it is 36?

---

Plotting these points, we can construct a new short-run total cost curve, different from the one we constructed before. The new *SRTC* curve again touches the *LRTC* curve at exactly one point, this time at a quantity of 12.

For every quantity of capital, there is a corresponding *SRTC* curve, touching the *LRTC* curve at exactly one point. The geometry is illustrated in Exhibit 6.14.

---

| EXHIBIT **6.14** | **Many Short-Run Total Cost Curves** |
| --- | --- |

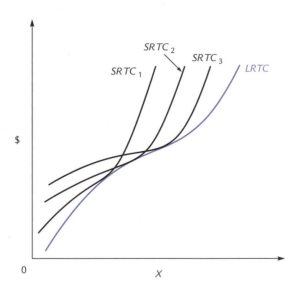

When we draw a short-run total cost curve, we assume a fixed level of capital employment. If we assume a different fixed level of capital employment, we get a different short-run total cost curve. The graph shows the short-run total cost curves that result from various assumptions.

Each total cost curve touches the long-run total cost curve in one place, at that level of output for which the fixed capital stock happens to be optimal. In that case, the firm's long-run and short-run choices of production process coincide. The long-run total cost curve is the lower boundary of the region in which the various short-run total cost curves lie.

## Short-Run Average Cost versus Long-Run Average Cost

Instead of plotting total cost curves, we can plot average cost curves. There is a different short-run average cost curve for each quantity of capital. You can think of capital as a measure of "plant size," so that the short-run average cost curves in Exhibit 6.15 describe the situation for a small, a medium-size, and a large plant. If the firm wants to produce quantity $Q_1$, average cost is minimized by the small plant represented by the curve $SRAC_1$. If the firm is required to operate with the medium-size plant represented by curve $SRAC_2$, its average cost is higher; if it operates with the large plant represented by $SRAC_3$, its average cost is even higher yet. In the long run, if $Q_1$ is the desired output, the firm chooses the small plant to minimize its average cost. Consequently, at $Q_1$ units, the long-run average cost is the same as the small plant's short-run average cost. That is why the $SRAC_1$ and $LRAC$ curves touch at $Q_1$.

If the firm wants to produce $Q_3$ units, it achieves the lowest average cost with the large plant, a somewhat higher average cost with the medium-size plant, and an even higher average cost with the small plant. In the long run, it chooses the large plant, so $LRAC$ is the same as $SRAC_3$ for $Q_3$ units of output.

**Exercise 6.12** Suppose that the firm wants to produce $Q_2$ units of output. Which plant size is best? Which is second best? Which plant size will it choose in the long run? How is this fact reflected in the graph?

---

**EXHIBIT 6.15**    **Many Short-Run Average Cost Curves**

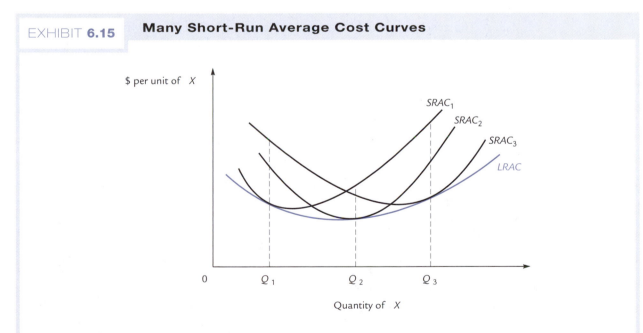

The curves $SRAC_1$, $SRAC_2$, and $SRAC_3$ show short-run average cost for a small, a medium-size, and a large plant. To produce $Q_1$ units, the firm finds that the small plant minimizes average cost, and so chooses that size plant in the long run. Thus, $LRAC = SRAC_1$ when quantity is $Q_1$. If only three plant sizes are available, the $LRAC$ curve consists of the black portions of the $SRAC$ curves shown. If a continuous range of plant sizes is available, there are many other $SRAC$ curves, and the $LRAC$ curve is the color curve shown.

If the firm has only three possible plant sizes, then its long-run average cost curve consists of the black parts of the three short-run average cost curves. (For any quantity, the firm selects the optimal plant size and so achieves a point on one of the three SRACs.) In most of this chapter, we have assumed instead that the firm has a continuous range of plant sizes (i.e., it can choose any quantity of capital it desires). In this case, there are many other SRAC curves besides those pictured, and LRAC is the color curve in the graph. Each point on LRAC is then a point of tangency with some SRAC curve.

## Summary

The role of the firm is to convert inputs into outputs. The cost of producing a given level of output depends on the technology available to the firm (which determines the quantities of inputs the firm will need) and the prices of the inputs.

In the short run, the firm is committed to employing some inputs in fixed amounts. In the long run, it is free to vary its employment of every input, always producing at the lowest possible cost.

For illustrative purposes, we consider a firm that employs labor and capital, with capital fixed in the short run. The options available to the firm are then illustrated by its total product (TP) curve, also called its *short-run production function.* From the TP curve, we can derive the marginal product of labor (MPL) curve by computing the additional output derived from each additional unit of labor: The value of MPL is the slope of TP.

The average product of labor (APL) is defined to be TP/L, where L is the amount of labor employed. At low levels of output (the first stage of production), each additional worker increases the productivity of his colleagues. Therefore, marginal product exceeds average product and average product is rising. At higher levels of output (the second stage of production), each additional worker reduces the productivity of his colleagues. Therefore, marginal product is below average product and average product is falling. The average product curve has the shape of an inverted U, with the marginal product curve cutting through it at the highest point.

For a given level of output, the firm faces a fixed cost (FC), which is the cost of renting capital, and a variable cost (VC, which is the cost of hiring labor. FC can be computed as $P_K \cdot K$, where $P_K$ is the price of capital and $K$ is the firm's (fixed) capital usage. VC can be computed as $P_L \cdot L$, where $P_L$ is the wage rate of labor and L is the quantity of labor needed to produce the desired output; the value of L that corresponds to a given quantity of output can be found by examining the TP curve.

The firm's total cost (TC) is the sum of FC and VC. Its average cost (AC) is TC/Q, where Q is the quantity of its output. Its average variable cost (AVC) is VC/Q. Its marginal cost is the increment to total cost attributable to the last unit of output.

Typically, the average, average variable, and marginal cost curves are ∪-shaped. MC cuts through both AC and AVC at their minimum points.

In the long run, the firm's technology is embodied in its production function, which is illustrated by the isoquant diagram. The slope of an isoquant is equal to the marginal rate of technical substitution between labor and capital. We expect $MRTS_{LK}$ to decrease as we move down and to the right along the isoquant, with the result that isoquants are convex.

In the long run, the firm minimizes costs for a given level of output, which leads it to choose a point of tangency between an isocost and an isoquant. Alternatively, we can think of the firm as maximizing output for a given expenditure on inputs; this reasoning also leads to the conclusion that the firm operates at a tangency. The set of all such tangencies forms the firm's expansion path.

To compute the long-run total cost for $Q$ units of output, find the tangency of the $Q$-unit isoquant with an isocost, and compute the price of the corresponding input basket.

Long-run average and marginal costs can be computed from long-run total cost.

The long-run average cost curve is downward sloping, flat, or upward sloping, depending on whether the firm experiences increasing, constant, or decreasing returns to scale. We expect increasing returns (decreasing average cost) at low levels of output because of the advantages of specialization. At higher levels of output, there will be constant returns to scale unless some factor is fixed even in the long run; however, this case is very common because of limits on things like the skills and supervisory ability of the entrepreneur. Therefore, we often draw the long-run average cost curve increasing at high levels of output, making the entire curve ∪-shaped. (That is, we assume decreasing returns to scale at high levels of output.) Long-run marginal cost cuts through long-run average cost at the bottom of the ∪.

The same isoquant diagram that is used to derive long-run total cost can be used to derive short-run total product and total cost curves as well. Each possible plant size for the firm results in a different short-run total cost curve and consequently a different short-run average cost curve. The short-run cost curves never dip below the long-run cost curves. The short-run total cost curve associated with a given plant size touches the long-run total cost curve only at that quantity for which the plant size is optimal; the same is true for average cost curves.

## Author Commentary          www.cengage.com/economics/landsburg

**AC1.** The efficient design of biological organisms has much in common with the efficient choice of a production process.

## Review Questions

**R1.** What are the first and second stages of production?

**R2.** What is the shape of the *APL* curve? Why?

**R3.** Where does the *MPL* curve cross the *APL* curve? Why?

**R4.** What is the relationship between the *MPL* curve and the total product curve?

**R5.** Explain how to derive the firm's *VC* and *TC* curves from its *TP* curve.

**R6.** Explain how to derive the firm's *AC, AVC,* and *MC* curves.

**R7.** What geometric relationships hold among *AC, AVC,* and *MC*? Why?

**R8.** Define the marginal rate of technical substitution.

**R9.** What is the relationship between the marginal products of the factors of production and the marginal rate of technical substitution?

**R10.** What are the geometric properties of isoquants? Why do we expect these properties to hold?

**R11.** Explain why firms want to operate at a tangency between an isoquant and an isocost.

**R12.** Explain how to derive a firm's long-run total cost curve from its isoquant diagram and knowledge of the factor prices.

**R13.** What are increasing, constant, and decreasing returns to scale? How are they related to the shape of the long-run average cost curve?

**R14.** Explain how to derive the firm's (short-run) total product and total cost curves from the isoquant diagram. How would these curves be affected by a change in the rental rate on capital? How would they be affected by a change in the wage rate of labor?

**R15.** What is the relationship between the firm's long-run and short-run total cost curves?

# Numerical Exercises

**N1.** A firm discovers that when it uses $K$ units of capital and $L$ units of labor, it is able to produce $\sqrt{KL}$ units of output.

    **a.** Draw the isoquants corresponding to 1, 2, 3, and 4 units of output.

    **b.** Suppose that the firm produces 10 units of output using 20 units of capital and 5 units of labor. Compute the $MRTS_{LK}$. Compute the $MPL$. Compute the $MPK$.

    **c.** On the basis of your answers to part (b), is the equation $MRTS_{LK} = MPL/MPK$ approximately true? (It would become closer to being true if we measured inputs in smaller units.)

    **d.** Suppose that capital and labor can each be hired at $1 per unit and that the firm uses 20 units of capital in the short run. What is the short-run total cost to produce 10 units of output?

    **e.** Continue to assume that capital and labor can each be hired at $1 per unit. Show that in the long run, if the firm produces 10 units of output, it will employ 10 units of capital and 10 units of labor. (*Hint:* Remember that in the long run the firm chooses to set $MPK/P_K = MPL/P_L$.) What is the long-run total cost to produce 10 units of output?

    **f.** Does this production function exhibit constant, increasing, or decreasing returns to scale?

**N2.** Repeat problem N1, replacing the function $\sqrt{KL}$ with the function $K^{1/3}L^{2/3}$.

# Problem Set

1.  Suppose that you hire workers to address and stamp envelopes. Each worker earns $5 per hour and produces 50 addressed, stamped envelopes per hour. You have unlimited free office space and can therefore add as many workers as you want to with no fall-off in productivity. You have no expenses other than paying workers. Draw the total product, marginal product, average product, total cost, average cost, average variable cost, and marginal cost curves.

2.  Suppose in the preceding problem that you rent a stamping machine with unlimited capacity, for $10 per hour. This makes it possible for workers to increase their output to 100 addressed, stamped envelopes per hour. Draw the new total product, marginal product, average product, total cost, average cost, average variable cost, and marginal cost curves.

3.  In the situation of problems 1 and 2, suppose that you have a choice between renting the machine or not renting it. For what levels of output will you choose to rent the machine? For what levels of output will you choose not to? Suppose that in the long run you can decide whether or not to rent the machine. Draw your long-run total and average cost curves.

4.  Suppose that your factory faces a total product curve that contains the following points:

    | Quantity of Labor | Total Product |
    | --- | --- |
    | 6 | 1 |
    | 10 | 2 |
    | 13 | 3 |
    | 15 | 4 |
    | 18 | 5 |
    | 23 | 6 |
    | 30 | 7 |
    | 40 | 8 |

    If labor costs $2 per unit, and you have fixed costs of $30, construct tables showing your variable cost, total cost, average cost, and average variable cost curves.

5.  Suppose that in the short run, capital is fixed and labor is variable. **True or False:** If the price of capital goes up, the firm's (short-run) average cost, average variable cost, and marginal cost curves will remain unaffected.

6.  Suppose that in the short run, capital is fixed and labor is variable. **True or False:** If the price of labor goes up, the firm's (short-run) average cost, average variable cost, and marginal cost curves will all shift upward.

7.  **True or False:** A wise entrepreneur will minimize costs for a given output rather than maximize output for a given cost.

8.  Suppose that a firm is operating at a point off its expansion path, where

$$MRTS_{LK} > \frac{P_L}{P_K}$$

Explain how this firm could increase its output without changing its total expenditure on inputs. Use this to give an additional argument for why a firm operating off its expansion path would want to move toward its expansion path.

9. Widgets are produced using thingamabobs and doohickeys. For some reason, a certain firm always produces exactly three widgets per day. **True or False:** If the price of thingamabobs increases, then in the long run the firm is certain to switch to a production process that uses fewer thingamabobs and more doohickeys.

10. A firm faces the following total product curves depending on how much capital it employs:

| K = 1 Unit | | K = 2 Units | | K = 3 Units | |
|---|---|---|---|---|---|
| Quantity of Labor | Total Product | Quantity of Labor | Total Product | Quantity of Labor | Total Product |
| 1 | 100 | 1 | 123 | 1 | 139 |
| 2 | 152 | 2 | 187 | 2 | 193 |
| 3 | 193 | 3 | 237 | 3 | 263 |
| 4 | 215 | 4 | 263 | 4 | 319 |
| 5 | 233 | 5 | 286 | 5 | 366 |
| 6 | 249 | 6 | 306 | 6 | 407 |
| 7 | 263 | 7 | 323 | 7 | 410 |

a. Suppose that the firm currently employs 1 unit of capital and 3 of labor. Compute $MRTS_{LK}$. Compute $MPL$. Compute $MPK$.

b. Suppose that the firm currently employs 2 units of capital. The price of capital is $4 per unit and the price of labor is $10 per unit. What is the short-run total cost of producing 263 units of output? What is the long-run total cost of producing 263 units of output?

c. Suppose that the price of capital increases to $20 per unit and the price of labor falls to $5 per unit. Now what is the long-run total cost of producing 263 units of output?

d. Beginning with 1 unit of capital and 2 units of labor, does this production function exhibit increasing, constant, or decreasing returns to scale? Which way does the long-run average cost curve slope?

11. Terry's Typing Service produces manuscripts. The only way to produce a manuscript is for 1 secretary to use 1 typewriter for 1 day. Two secretaries with 1 typewriter or 1 secretary with 2 typewriters can still produce only 1 manuscript per day.

a. Draw Terry's 1-unit isoquant.

b. Assuming that Terry's technology exhibits constant returns to scale, draw several more isoquants.

c. Assuming that Terry rents typewriters for $4 apiece per day and pays secretaries $6 apiece per day, draw some of Terry's isocosts. Draw the expansion path.

d. Terry has signed a contract to rent exactly 5 typewriters. Illustrate the following, using tables, graphs, or both: the total product and marginal product of labor; the short-run total cost, variable cost, average cost, average variable cost, and marginal cost; the long-run total cost, long-run average cost, and long-run marginal cost.

**12.** The desert town of Dry Gulch buys its water from LowTech Inc. LowTech hires residents to walk to the nearest oasis and carry back buckets of water. Thus, the inputs to the production of water are workers and buckets. The walk to the oasis and back takes one full day. Each worker can carry either 1 or 2 buckets of water but no more.

**a.** Draw some of LowTech's isoquants. With buckets renting for $1 a day and workers earning $2 per day, draw some of LowTech's isocosts. Draw the expansion path.

**b.** LowTech owns 5 buckets. It could rent these out to another firm at $1 per day, or it could rent additional buckets for $1 per day, but neither transaction could be arranged without some delay. Illustrate the following, using tables, graphs, or both: the total product and marginal product of labor; the short-run total cost, variable cost, average cost, average variable cost, and marginal cost; the long-run total cost, long-run average cost, and long-run marginal cost.

# Competition

A real organization called the Brotherhood for the Respect, Elevation, and Advancement of Dishwashers encourages restaurant patrons to leave tips not just for the waiters and waitresses but also for the kitchen staff who bus tables and wash dishes. What will happen if this organization achieves its goals?

In the short run, life will be better for dishwashers. They'll collect tips, and they'll probably decide to work additional hours to collect even more tips. But in the long run, people in other occupations—car wash attendants, grocery baggers, and others—will attempt to get on the gravy train. Restaurant kitchens will be flooded with job applicants, and the wages of dishwashers will be bid down. In fact, wages are likely to be bid down by the full amount of the tips—if tips amount to, say, $2 an hour, then wages fall from $8 an hour to $6 an hour. It turns out that respect, elevation, and advancement don't show up in take-home pay.

Later in this chapter, we'll do a full analysis of the market for dishwashers and the effect of tipping. We'll discover the reason why wages are bid down by the full amount of the tips, and we'll learn something surprising about who *does* benefit from tipping. The key to the analysis is a recognition that dishwashing constitutes a *competitive industry*, and this chapter will give us the tools for analyzing competitive industries in general.

## 7.1 The Competitive Firm

A firm is called **perfectly competitive** (or sometimes just **competitive** for short) if it can sell any quantity it wants to at the going market price. The standard example is a farm. If wheat is selling for a going market price of $5 a bushel, then Farmer Vickers can sell 10 bushels or 1,000 bushels or any other quantity she chooses at that price.

Microsoft is a good example of a firm that is *not* perfectly competitive. That's because Microsoft has already served all the customers willing to pay the current price for its Windows operating system. Unlike Farmer Vickers, if Microsoft wants to sell more of its product, it must lower the price.

Ordinarily, firms are competitive when they serve a small part of the market. As long as you're small, you can greatly increase your output and still find customers at

**Perfectly competitive firm**

One that can sell any quantity it wants to at some going market price.

the going price. By contrast, firms with large market shares typically must lower their prices to attract more customers.

Another way to say all this is that a competitive firm faces a *horizontal* demand curve for its product, whereas a noncompetitive firm faces a *downward-sloping* demand curve for its product. For example, if the going price of wheat is $5 per bushel, then the demand curve for Farmer Vickers's wheat is horizontal at the $5 price. That's because she can sell any quantity she wants to at that price, so the demand curve must associate every possible quantity with the going price of $5.

Of course, the demand curve for *wheat* is still downward sloping; it is just the demand for *Farmer Vickers's* wheat that is horizontal. To see how this can be, look at the two demand curves depicted in Exhibit 7.1. Notice in particular the units on the quantity axis. When Farmer Vickers increases output from 1 bushel to 10 bushels, she is moving a long distance to the right on her quantity axis. At the same time, she has moved the wheat industry a practically infinitesimal distance to the right—say, from 10,000,000 bushels to 10,000,009 bushels. This tiny change in the industry's output requires essentially no change in price.

Farmer Vickers's horizontal demand curve results from her being a very small part of a very large industry in which all of the products produced are interchangeable and buyers can quite easily buy from another producer if Farmer Vickers tries to raise her price. All of these conditions tend to lead to perfect competition, but perfect competition can happen even without them. The only requirement for a firm to be called perfectly competitive is that the demand curve for its product be horizontal (for whatever reason).

EXHIBIT **7.1**    **The Demand Curve for Wheat**

A. Demand for wheat

B. Demand for Farmer Vickers's wheat

Panel A shows the downward-sloping demand curve for wheat. Panel B shows the horizontal demand curve for Farmer Vickers's wheat. If the price of all wheat goes up from $P_0$ to $P_1$, consumers will buy less wheat. If the price of just Farmer Vickers's wheat goes up from the market price of $P_0$ to $P_1$, consumers will buy none of it at all; they will shop elsewhere.

## Revenue

Suppose you're a bicycle manufacturer, selling bicycles at a going price of $50 apiece. If you sell one bicycle, your total revenue is $50; if you sell two, your total revenue is $100, and so forth. Regardless of how many bicycles you sell, your *marginal* revenue from selling an additional bicycle is always exactly $50, as illustrated in Exhibit 7.2.

In general, for any competitive firm we have the equations

$$\text{Total Revenue} = \text{Price} \times \text{Quantity}$$
$$\text{Marginal Revenue} = \text{Price}$$

As you can see in the second panel of Exhibit 7.2:

The competitive firm's marginal revenue curve is flat at the level of the going market price.

In other words, the firm's marginal revenue curve coincides with the demand curve for the firm's product, which is also flat at the going market price.

| EXHIBIT **7.2** | **Total and Marginal Revenue at the Competitive Firm** |

| Quantity | Total Revenue | Marginal Revenue |
|----------|---------------|------------------|
| 1 | $5 | $50/item |
| 2 | 10 | 50 |
| 3 | 15 | 50 |
| 4 | 20 | 50 |

A firm sells bicycles at a going price of $50 apiece. The firm's total revenue is given by the equation $TR = \$50 \times Q$. The firm's marginal revenue curve is flat at the going price of $50, hence identical to the demand curve for the firm's bicycles.

## The Firm's Supply Decision

Continuing to assume you're a bicycle maker, how do you decide how many bicycles to make? We answered this in Chapter 5: You keep making bicycles until marginal revenue equals marginal cost.

If your firm is competitive, we've just learned that marginal revenue is always equal to the going market price. So:

A competitive firm, if it produces anything at all, produces a quantity where

Price = Marginal Cost

Suppose, for example, that the going price of a bicycle is $50 and that your marginal cost curve is the simple upward sloping curve shown in Exhibit 7.3. Then you'll want to produce exactly 4 bicycles because 4 is the quantity where marginal cost = $50. Notice that this makes perfect sense: The first bicycle costs you only $20 to produce and you can sell it for $50; of course you'll produce it. Similarly for the second, third, and fourth (you just break even on the fourth one). But it would be silly to produce a fifth bicycle, because you'd have to spend $60 to make a bicycle you could sell for only $50.

| EXHIBIT **7.3** | **The Optimum of the Competitive Firm** |
| --- | --- |

| Quantity | Marginal Cost | Marginal Revenue |
| --- | --- | --- |
| 1 | $20/bicycle | $50/bicycle |
| 2 | 30 | 50 |
| 3 | 40 | 50 |
| 4 | 50 | 50 |
| 5 | 60 | 50 |
| 6 | 70 | 50 |

If bicycles sell for $50 apiece, a competitive firm will produce bicycles up to the point where marginal cost = $50. In this example, the firm produces 4 bicycles. But if the price rises from $50 to $70, the firm produces 6 bicycles.

What will you do if the market price of bicycles rises to $70? First, of course, you'll rejoice. Then you'll rethink how many bicycles you want to make. Now you *are* willing to produce that fifth bicycle—and a sixth one as well.

## The Competitive Firm's Supply Curve

Now let's construct your supply curve. We've said that at a price of $50, you'd want to supply 4 bicycles. And we've said that at a price of $70, you'd want to supply exactly 6 bicycles. That gives us two points on your supply curve:

| Price | Quantity |
| --- | --- |
| $50 | 4 |
| $70 | 6 |

We've plotted these points (among others) in the second panel of Exhibit 7.4.

The left panel of Exhibit 7.4 shows the firm's marginal cost curve (which we take as given); the right panel shows the supply curve (which we are trying to derive). To get a

| EXHIBIT **7.4** | **Marginal Cost and Supply** |
| --- | --- |

| Marginal Cost Curve | | Supply Curve | |
| --- | --- | --- | --- |
| Quantity | Marginal Cost | Price | Quantity |
| 1 | $20/bicycle | $20/bicycle | 1 |
| 2 | 30 | 30 | 2 |
| 3 | 40 | 40 | 3 |
| 4 | 50 | 50 | 4 |
| 5 | 60 | 60 | 5 |
| 6 | 70 | 70 | 6 |

When the price is $50, the firm faces demand curve *d*; *d* is also the marginal revenue curve. To maximize profit, the firm produces 4 bicycles (where *MC* = *MR*). Thus, $50 goes with a quantity of 4 on the supply curve. Similarly, $60 goes with 5 and $70 goes with 6. After we plot their points in the right-hand panel, we see that the supply curve looks exactly like the marginal cost curve.

new point on the supply curve, imagine a new price—say $60. Draw the corresponding flat demand curve (*d′* in the Exhibit) and read off the quantity where the price of $60 is equal to the firm's marginal cost. In this case, that quantity is 5. Therefore, we can plot the point ($60, 5) in the right-hand panel.

Proceeding in this way, we discover that each point on the supply curve in the right-hand panel is identical to a point on the marginal cost curve in the left-hand panel; in other words:

For a competitive firm with an upward sloping marginal cost curve, the supply curve and the marginal cost curve look exactly the same.

---

Although the supply and marginal cost curves in Exhibit 7.4 are identical as curves, their interpretations are quite different. To use the marginal cost curve, you "input" a quantity on the horizontal axis and read off the corresponding marginal cost on the vertical. To use the supply curve, you "input" a price on the vertical axis and read off the corresponding quantity on the horizontal. The way to make this distinction mathematically precise is to say that marginal cost (*MC*) and supply (*S*) are inverse functions. In Exhibit 7.4, we have:

$$MC \text{ (5 bicycles)} = \$60 \text{ per bicycle}$$

and

$$S \text{ (\$60 per bicycle)} = 5 \text{ bicycles}$$

Dangerous
Curve

Notice that the marginal cost function *MC* is plotted just as it would be in a math class—with the input variable on the horizontal axis and the output variable on the vertical. By contrast, the supply function is plotted with the input on the vertical and the output on the horizontal—a reversal of the usual "math class" rules.

Another thing you might recall from math class is that the graph of an inverse function is the *mirror image* of the graph of the original function. Therefore you might expect the supply curve to be a mirror image of the marginal cost curve. But the graph of the supply curve is mirror imaged a *second* time because of the reversal of the axes. Thus, the supply curve is a *double* mirror image of the marginal cost curve—once because it is an inverse function and once because the axes are reversed. Of course, a double mirror image looks exactly like the original; that's why the supply curve looks exactly like the marginal cost curve. And in fact that's *why* we reverse the axes on the supply curve—so that we only have to draw one curve instead of two.

---

## The Short Run Versus the Long Run

In Chapter 6, we learned that firms face different marginal cost curves in the short run and the long run. Which marginal cost curve should we use when we construct the firm's supply curve? It depends on whether we want to study the firm's supply responses in the short run or in the long run. When the price of bicycles rises from $50 apiece to $70 apiece, bicycle manufacturers respond in the short run by hiring more workers and producing more bicycles. They respond in the long run by hiring more workers *and* expanding their factories *and* buying more machinery and producing even *more* bicycles. Thus the firm has two different supply curves: One illustrates the short-run response to a price change and the other illustrates the long-run response. If you want to construct the short-run supply curve, use the short-run marginal cost curve; if you want to construct the long-run supply curve, use the long-run marginal cost curve.

### U-shaped Marginal Cost Curves

In Exhibit 7.4, the firm has an upward sloping marginal cost curve. But we saw in Chapter 6 that many marginal cost curves are actually cup-shaped (shown as U-shaped). How does this affect the analysis?

Exhibit 7.5 shows the U-shaped marginal cost curve of a competitive firm facing a market price of $50. We know that such a firm, if it produces at all, produces a quantity at which marginal cost and the market price are equal. We can see from the graph that there are two quantities at which this occurs: $Q_1$ and $Q_2$. Which does the firm choose?

Suppose that it produces $Q_1$ items. Then the firm can produce an additional item at a marginal cost below the market price. (That is, if the firm goes a little past quantity $Q_1$, the marginal cost of production is below $50.) It follows that the firm can do better by producing another item. It continues producing as long as price exceeds marginal cost, and then stops; that is, it produces $Q_2$ items.

A competitive firm, if it produces at all, will always choose a quantity where price equals marginal cost *and* the marginal cost curve is upward sloping. Only the upward-sloping part of the marginal cost curve is relevant to the firm's supply decisions.

## Shutdowns

In Exhibits 7.3, 7.4, and 7.5, we asked how many bicycles the firm wants to produce. In asking that question, we implicitly assumed that the firm does want to produce bicycles. Now let's question that assumption. *Does* the firm want to produce bicycles?

EXHIBIT **7.5**    **The Supply Decision with a U-Shaped Marginal Cost Curve**

At a market price of $50 the firm produces $Q_2$ items (assuming it produces at all). It takes losses on the first $Q_1$ of these, all of which are produced at a marginal cost of more than $50, and it earns positive profits on the others. If those positive profits fail to outweigh the losses on the first $Q_1$ items, the firm will shut down.

**Shutdown**

A firm's decision to stop
producing output. Firms
that shut down continue
to incur fixed costs.

**Exit**

A firm's decision to leave
the industry entirely.
Firms that exit no longer
incur any costs.

The answer, of course, depends on the alternative. In the short run, the alternative to producing bicycles might be to continue paying rent on an idle factory. In the long run, the alternative is to terminate your lease and get out of the bicycle business altogether.

We distinguish between a shutdown, which means that the firm stops producing bicycles but still has to pay fixed costs such as rent on the factory, and an exit, which means that the firm leaves the industry entirely. We make the following key assumption:

In the short run, firms can shut down but can't exit. In the long run, firms can exit.

Here we will investigate the firm's shutdown decision. In Section 7.4, we will investigate the firm's exit decision.

## The Shutdown Decision

If you run a bicycle firm, then in the short run you have to decide whether to operate or to shut down.

If you operate, you'll earn a profit equal to $TR - TC$, where $TR$ stands for total revenue and $TC$ stands for total cost. If this profit is positive, you'll certainly want to continue operating. If it's negative, you'll have to ask which is worse: the negative profit you're earning now, or the negative profit you'd earn by shutting down.

In other words, you must compare your profit from operating, $TR - TC$, with your profit from shutting down, which is $-FC$, where $FC$ stands for fixed costs.

Operating beats shutting down if:

$$TR - TC > -FC$$

Substituting the identity $TC = FC - VC$, this condition becomes:

$$TR - FC - VC > -FC$$

or:

$$TR > VC$$

The latter inequality should make good intuitive sense. Fixed costs don't appear in this inequality because they are irrelevant to the shutdown decision; they are irrelevant to the shutdown decision because you've got to pay them whether you shut down or not. By contrast, variable costs are highly relevant to the shutdown decision, because the whole point of shutting down is to avoid paying variable costs. Staying in operation is a good idea precisely if the firm can earn sufficient revenue to cover these costs, in other words, if $TR > VC$.

Remembering now that $TR = P \cdot Q$ (where $P$ is price and $Q$ is quantity), we can rewrite our inequality as:

$$P \cdot Q > VC$$

Then if we divide each side by $Q$, the inequality becomes:

$$P > AVC$$

where $AVC$ is average variable cost.

In other words, the firm continues to operate in the short run if, at the profit-maximizing quantity, the price of output exceeds the average variable cost.

## The Competitive Firm's Short-Run Supply Curve

In Exhibit 7.4, we studied a firm with an upward-sloping marginal cost curve and concluded that the firm's supply and marginal cost curves are identical.

Now that we're studying firms with ∪-shaped marginal cost curves, we have to modify that discussion slightly. That's because we've just learned that when the price falls below average variable cost, the firm shuts down and produces nothing at all.

Exhibit 7.6 shows the cost curves of a typical competitive bicycle manufacturer. If the price of bicycles falls below $P_0$, the firm cannot cover its variable costs and shuts down, producing no bicycles. As long as the price is above $P_0$, the firm will want to produce bicycles and will supply quantities taken from the marginal cost curve just as in Exhibit 7.4. Therefore the firm's supply curve is equal not to the entire marginal cost curve, but just to that part of the marginal cost curve that lies above the price $P_0$. That is, the supply curve is the boldfaced portion of the marginal cost curve shown in the exhibit.

The competitive firm's short-run supply curve is identical to that part of the short-run marginal cost curve that lies above the average variable cost curve.

## Why Supply Curves Slope Up

When the competitive firm's marginal cost curve is ∪-shaped, its supply curve consists of that part of the marginal cost curve that lies above average variable cost. Because the marginal cost curve cuts the average variable cost curve from below, the entire supply curve is upward sloping.

To the question "Why do supply curves slope up?" we can answer "Because average and marginal cost curves are ∪-shaped." This is correct, but it raises another question: "Why are the cost curves ∪-shaped?" The answer, as we saw in Chapter 6, is that this is a consequence of diminishing marginal returns to the variable factors of production. The technological fact of diminishing marginal returns suffices to account for the upward-sloping supply curves of competitive firms.

**EXHIBIT 7.6**    **The Competitive Firm's Short-Run Supply Curve**

As long as the price exceeds $P_0$, the firm's supply curve coincides with its marginal cost curve. At prices below $P_0$, the firm produces nothing. Therefore, the firm's supply curve is equal to the boldfaced portion of the marginal cost curve.

## The Elasticity of Supply

**Elasticity of supply**

The percent change in quantity supplied resulting from a 1% increase in price.

We can compute the **elasticity of supply** at a firm using the same formula that we use to compute the elasticity of demand:

$$\text{Elasticity} = \frac{\text{Percentage change in quantity}}{\text{Percentage change in price}}$$

$$= \frac{100 \cdot \Delta Q/Q}{100 \cdot \Delta P/P}$$

$$= \frac{P \cdot \Delta Q}{Q \cdot \Delta P}$$

The elasticity of supply is positive because an increase in price brings forth an increase in the quantity supplied. Given two supply curves through the same point, the flatter one has the higher elasticity.

# 7.2 The Competitive Industry in the Short Run

In Section 7.1 we studied the short-run behavior of a single competitive firm. In this section, we will study the short-run behavior of a **competitive industry**; that is, an industry in which all firms are competitive.

**Competitive industry**

An industry in which all firms are competitive.

## Defining the Short Run

We take the *short run* to be a period of time in which no firm can enter or exit the industry, so that the number of firms cannot change. By contrast, the *long run* is a period in which any firm that wants to can enter or leave the industry.

How long is the long run and how short is the short run? It depends. In the sidewalk flower vending industry, the short run is very short indeed (at least if there is no waiting time for a vendor's license). The time that it takes to acquire some flowers and walk down to the corner, or for an existing vendor to sell out his stock and go home, is already the long run. By contrast, if Barnes and Noble booksellers were to cease operations, it would face a lengthy process of selling off its inventory and negotiating ends to its store leases. For that matter, when the online pet-supply store pets.com went out of business in the year 2000, it had little inventory to dispose of, but its exit was nevertheless delayed while it sought a buyer for the rights to its popular sock puppet mascot. The long run does not arrive until this exiting process is complete.

Dangerous Curve

As we've already mentioned (in Section 7.1), it is important not to confuse an *exit* with a *shutdown*. As soon as Barnes and Noble stops selling books, it has shut down, but as long as it remains in possession of valuable capital, it has still not left the industry. When a firm shuts down, it stops producing but continues to incur fixed costs (in Barnes and Noble's case, the opportunity cost of not yet having sold its inventory). An exit implies that the firm has divested itself of all its fixed costs and thereby severed all of its ties with the industry. Shutdowns are a short-run phenomenon; exits are long-run.

# The Competitive Industry's Short-Run Supply Curve

In the short run, entry and exit are not possible, so the number of firms in the industry is fixed. Given the short-run supply curves of the individual firms, we simply add them to construct the short-run supply curve for the entire industry. At a given price, we ask what quantities each of the firms will provide; then we add these numbers to get the quantity supplied by the industry.

Because different firms have different cost curves, different firms have different shutdown prices. Therefore, the number of firms in operation tends to be small at low prices and large at high prices. As a result, the industry supply curve tends to be more elastic than the supply curves of the individual firms. This can be seen in Exhibit 7.7. Here firms A, B, and C have the individual supply curves shown. At price $P_1$, only firm A produces, so the quantity supplied by the industry is the same as the quantity supplied by firm A. At the higher price $P_2$, firm B produces as well, and the industry supplies the sum of firm A's output and firm B's output. (In fact, firm A produces 2½ units and firm B produces 4½, for an industry total of 7.) At prices high enough for firm C to produce, industry output is correspondingly greater.

---

**Exercise 7.1** At price $P_3$, how much does each firm produce? How much does the industry produce?

---

The industry supply curve in Exhibit 7.7 jumps rightward each time it passes a firm's shutdown price. In an industry with many firms, the effect of this is to greatly flatten the industry supply curve relative to those of the individual firms.

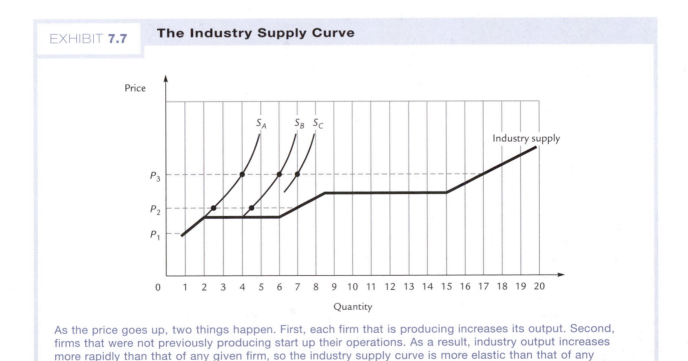

| EXHIBIT 7.7 | **The Industry Supply Curve** |

As the price goes up, two things happen. First, each firm that is producing increases its output. Second, firms that were not previously producing start up their operations. As a result, industry output increases more rapidly than that of any given firm, so the industry supply curve is more elastic than that of any given firm.

## Supply, Demand, and Equilibrium

In Chapter 5 we learned that any supplier, if it produces at all, chooses to operate where marginal cost is equal to marginal revenue. In Section 7.1, we learned that for a competitive producer the marginal revenue curve is the same as the demand curve, and, in the region where it produces at all, the marginal cost curve is the same as the supply curve. Therefore, we can just as well say that a competitive supplier chooses to operate at the point where supply is equal to demand.

In an industry in which all of the firms are competitive, each firm operates where supply equals demand, and so the industry-wide supply (which is the sum of the individual firms' supplies) must equal the industry-wide demand (which is the sum of the demands from the individual firms). In other words, such an industry will be at equilibrium, simply as a consequence of optimizing behavior on the part of individuals and firms.

In Chapter 1 we gave some "plausibility arguments" for the notion that in many industries prices and quantities would be determined by the intersection of supply and demand. Now we have a much stronger reason to believe the same thing. If an industry is competitive, profit-maximizing firms will be led to the equilibrium outcome—as if by an invisible hand.

## Competitive Equilibrium

Exhibit 7.8 illustrates the relationship between the competitive industry and the competitive firm. The industry faces a downward-sloping demand curve for its product.

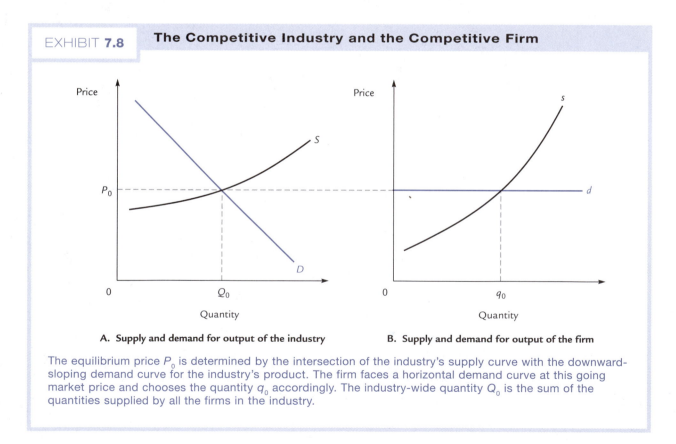

**EXHIBIT 7.8**       **The Competitive Industry and the Competitive Firm**

**A. Supply and demand for output of the industry**       **B. Supply and demand for output of the firm**

The equilibrium price $P_0$ is determined by the intersection of the industry's supply curve with the downward-sloping demand curve for the industry's product. The firm faces a horizontal demand curve at this going market price and chooses the quantity $q_0$ accordingly. The industry-wide quantity $Q_0$ is the sum of the quantities supplied by all the firms in the industry.

The price $P_0$ is determined by industry-wide equilibrium, and this same price $P_0$ is what appears to the individual firm as the "going market price," at which it faces a flat demand curve. The firm then produces the quantity $q_0$, at which its supply curve $S$ (that is, its marginal cost curve) crosses the horizontal line at $P_0$.

## Changes in Fixed Costs

Now we can investigate the effect of a change in costs. Suppose, first, that there is a rise in fixed costs, such as a general increase in the cost of large machinery or a new licensing fee for the industry. What happens to an individual firm's supply curve? Nothing, because marginal cost is unchanged. What about the industry's supply curve? It remains unchanged also, because industry supply is the sum of the individual firms' supplies and these remain fixed. Thus, no curves shift in Exhibit 7.8, so both price and quantity remain unchanged.

This analysis is correct and complete in the short run. However, we will see in Sections 7.5 and 7.6 that in the long run there is more to be said. The reason for this is that in the long run any increase in costs can drive firms from the industry; their exit can then affect prices and quantities.

Dangerous
Curve

## Changes in Variable Costs

Next consider a rise in variable costs, such as a rise in the price of raw materials or the imposition of an excise tax. Here's what happens:

First, the firm's supply curve shifts leftward. Here's why: When variable costs rise, marginal costs rise; therefore, the firm's marginal cost curve shifts vertically upward. But the firm's supply and marginal cost curves coincide, so we can equally well say that the firm's supply curve shifts vertically upward, and that's the same thing as shifting to the left.

Second, the industry supply curve shifts leftward. That's because the industry supply is the sum of the individual firms' supplies. At any given price, each firm supplies less than before, so the industry in total supplies less than before.

Third, the supply shift causes the equilibrium price to rise from $P_0$ to $P_2$ in the first panel of Exhibit 7.9. Therefore, the demand curve facing the firm rises from $d$ to $d'$ in the second panel.

The firm's output changes from $q_0$ to $q_2$. In Exhibit 7.9, $q_2$ is to the left of $q_0$, but if the curves had been drawn a little differently, $q_2$ could equally well have been to the right of $q_0$. Thus the firm's output could go either up or down.

Note, however, that the *industry's* output unambiguously falls (from $Q_0$ to $Q_2$ in the first panel). Thus the *average* firm's output must fall, even though not every firm's output must fall.

**Exercise 7.2** Draw graphs illustrating the effect of a fall in variable costs.

## Changes in Demand

Exhibit 7.10 illustrates the effect of an increase in the demand for the industry's product. The new market equilibrium price of $P_3$ is taken as given by the firm, which increases its output to $q_3$.

## EXHIBIT 7.9    A Rise in Variable Costs

**A. Supply and demand for output of the industry**   **B. Supply and demand for output of the firm**

A rise in variable costs causes the firm's supply curve to shift left from $s$ to $s'$ in panel B. The industry supply curve shifts left from $S$ to $S'$ in panel A, both because each firm's supply curve does and because some firms may shut down. The new market price is $P_2$. The firm operates at the intersection of $s'$ with its new horizontal demand curve at $P_2$. Depending on how the curves are drawn, the firm could end up producing either more or less than it did before the rise in costs. (That is, $q_2$ could be either to the left or to the right of $q_0$.)

## EXHIBIT 7.10    A Change in Demand

**A. Supply and demand for output of the industry**   **B. Supply and demand for output of the firm**

An increase in the demand for the industry's output raises the equilibrium price to $P_3$ and the firm's output to $q_3$.

**Exercise 7.3** Draw graphs illustrating the effect of a fall in demand for the industry's product.

## The Industry's Costs

In the short run the competitive industry consists of a fixed number of firms. These firms collectively produce some quantity of output. The total cost of producing that output is the sum of the total costs of all the individual firms.

Suppose that you were appointed the czar of U.S. agriculture and given the power to tell each farmer how much to produce. You would like to maintain the production of wheat at its current level of 1 million bushels per year, but you would like to do this in such a way as to minimize the total costs of the industry. How would you go about this?

The equimarginal principle points the way to the answer. Suppose that the marginal cost of growing wheat is $5 per bushel at Farmer Black's farm and $3 per bushel at Farmer White's. Then here is something clever you can do: Order Black to produce one less bushel and White to produce one more. In that way, the industry's total cost is reduced by $2, and the level of output is maintained. You should continue to do this until the marginal costs of production are just equal at both farms.

Indeed, as long as any two farms have differing marginal costs, you can use this trick to reduce total costs. Total costs are not minimized until marginal cost is the same at every farm.

Now, the miracle: In competitive equilibrium, every farmer chooses to produce a quantity at which price equals marginal cost. Because all farmers face the same market price, it follows that all farmers have the same marginal cost. From this we have the following result:

In competitive equilibrium, the industry automatically produces at the lowest possible total cost.

Students sometimes think that this result follows from firms' attempts to minimize their costs. But no firm has any interest in the costs of the industry as a whole. The minimization of industry-wide costs is a feature of competitive equilibrium that is not sought by any individual firm.

Dangerous
Curve

What is the marginal cost to the industry of producing a unit of output? You might think that this question is unanswerable, because the industry consists of many firms, each with its own marginal cost curve. How are we to decide which firm to think of as producing the "last" unit of output in the industry?

The answer to the last question is that it doesn't matter. We have just seen that in competitive equilibrium, the cost of producing the last unit of output is the same at every firm. That cost is the industry's marginal cost of production.

At each point along its supply curve, the competitive industry produces a quantity that equates price with marginal cost. Therefore, the industry's supply curve is identical to the industry's marginal cost curve, just as each individual firm's supply curve can be identified with its own marginal cost curve.

# 7.3 The Competitive Firm in the Long Run

There are two differences between the short run and the long run:

First, some costs that are fixed in the short run become variable in the long run. It takes time for a restaurant to add grills to the kitchen; therefore, the cost of the grills is fixed in the short run but variable in the long run.

Second, and more importantly, firms can enter or exit from the industry in the long run.

In this section we will see how these factors determine the firm's long-run supply curve.

## Long-Run Marginal Cost and Supply

In the long run, just as in the short run, a competitive firm wants to operate where Price = Marginal Cost; the only difference is that in the long run we must interpret "marginal cost" to mean *long-run* marginal cost.

Thus at any given price, the firm chooses to supply a quantity that can be read off its long-run marginal cost curve. In other words:

*As long as the firm remains in the industry, its long-run supply curve is identical with its long-run marginal cost curve.*

### Comparing Short-Run and Long-Run Supply Responses

A restaurant produces hamburgers using inputs that include ground beef, short-order cooks, and kitchen grills. How does this restaurant respond to a rise in the price of hamburgers? In the short run, it can increase quantity by purchasing more beef and hiring more cooks. The resulting quantity of hamburgers is recorded on the short-run supply curve.

In the long run, however, the restaurant might decide to expand its operation by purchasing more grills. Typically, this means that quantity increases by more in the long run than it does in the short run. In other words, the long-run supply curve is more elastic than the short-run supply curve.

Exhibit 7.11 shows the picture. The restaurant has sold hamburgers at a going price of $P_0$ for a long time and has thus adjusted the number of grills so as to produce $Q_0$ hamburgers at the lowest possible cost. The quantity $Q_0$ can be read from the long-run supply curve. Because the kitchen hardware is all in place, $Q_0$ is the quantity read from the short-run supply curve as well.

Now suppose that the price rises to $P_1$. In the short run, with the number of grills fixed, quantity rises to $Q_1$, which we can read off the short-run supply curve. In the long run, after the facilities are expanded, quantity rises further, to $Q_1'$. With its expanded kitchen equipment, the firm has a new short-run marginal cost curve and hence a new short-run supply curve, called $S'$ in the exhibit. Notice that $S'$ must go through the new supply point at $(P_1, Q_1')$.

## Profit and the Exit Decision

These are two differences between the long run and the short run. First, as we've seen, the firm's long run and short run supply curves can be different. The second difference concerns the firm's decision whether to supply anything at all. In the short run firms

## EXHIBIT 7.11 Long-Run and Short-Run Supply Responses

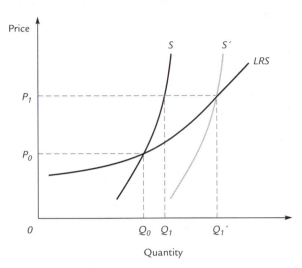

In long-run equilibrium at $P_0$, the firm is on both its long-run and short-run supply curves. A change in price, to $P_1$, has the immediate effect of causing the firm to move along its short-run supply curve $S$ to the quantity $Q_1$. In the long run, the firm can vary its plant capacity (for example, a hamburger stand can install more grills) and move along its long-run supply curve, $LRS$, to $Q_1'$. With the new plant capacity, the firm has a new short-run supply curve $S'$. In the new equilibrium at price $P_1$ and quantity $Q_1'$, the firm is again on both its long-run and short-run supply curves.

can *shut down* (without leaving the industry) but in the long run firms can *exit*. To understand long-run supply, we must understand the exit decision.

Firms leave the industry when their profits are too low to justify sticking around. So to understand the exit decision, we have to make sure we understand profit.

Profit is just revenue minus cost. But it's important to remember that to an economist (though not, perhaps, to an accountant), *cost* includes all forgone opportunities.

For example: Suppose you run a newspaper business, buying 100 newspapers a day for 15¢ each and reselling them for a quarter. Your accountant will calculate your revenue to be $25 and your costs to be $15, leaving a $10 profit.

That's your **accounting profit.** But to calculate your **economic profit,** we've got to subtract the accounting profit you *could have* earned by pursuing your next best opportunity. If instead of delivering newspapers, you could have earned a $7 accounting profit selling lemonade, then your economic profit is $10 − $7 = $3.

Or, if you could have earned a $12 accounting profit selling lemonade, then your economic profit in the newspaper business is $10 − $12, or *minus* $2.

When noneconomists use the word *profit*, they usually mean accounting *profit*. But in an economics course or a book about economics, profit means economic profit.

You'll want to leave the newspaper business if selling lemonade (or some other activity) is more attractive than selling newspapers, and this happens exactly when your economic profit is negative. You'd be well advised to leave that business and sell lemonade instead. Therefore;

Firms want to exit the industry when their economic profits are negative.

**Accounting profit**

Total revenue minus those costs that an accountant would consider.

**Economic profit**

Total revenue minus all costs, including the opportunity cost of being in another industry.

Now imagine a world with 1,000 identical newspaper sellers, all earning negative economic profit. You might think that eventually they'll all leave the industry. But that's not necessarily true. As firms leave, the price of newspapers will rise—leading to higher profits for the remaining firms.

So negative economic profits lead to exit, which leads (eventually) to zero economic profit for the remaining firms.

Why are firms willing to stick around and earn zero profit? Because "zero economic profit" is not the same as "zero accounting profits." Zero economic profit simply means that you're doing no better—but also no worse—than you could do in some other business.

## The Algebra of the Exit Decision

Firms want to exit when their economic profits are negative. Profit, of course, is total revenue ($TR$) minus total cost ($TC$) (where total cost includes the forgone opportunity to be in some other industry!). Total revenue, in turn, is price times quantity, or $P \times Q$. So firms want to exit when $P \times Q - TC$ is negative.

Sometimes it's easier to think about the firm's profit *per item*, which we get by taking $P \times Q - TC$ and dividing by the quantity produced. Because $TC/Q = AC$, this gives the expression

$$P - AC$$

and once again, firms want to exit when this quantity is negative, which happens when

$$P < AC$$

In other words:

When price is below average cost, firms want to leave the industry.

This should make perfect sense. If you sell your widgets at a price that is below the average cost of producing them, you're in the wrong business.

## The Firm's Long-Run Supply Curve

In the long run, as in the short run, firms maximize profit by choosing the quantity where price equals marginal cost. Of course, in the long run, "marginal cost" means "long-run marginal cost." Therefore, as long as a firm wants to be in business at all, its long-run supply curve coincides with the upward sloping part of its long-run marginal cost curve.

And when does the firm *not* want to be in business? Answer: when profits are negative; that is, when price is below average cost. So those prices are excluded from the long-run supply curve.

Exhibit 7.12 shows the long-run marginal and average cost curves at Sam's House of Widgets. If widgets sell for a going price of $5, the best Sam can do is sell 2 widgets (the quantity where price equals marginal cost). Here the *average* cost of production exceeds $5, so Sam's profit is negative and he wants to get out. Therefore, $5 corresponds to no point at all on Sam's long-run supply curve.

But at a price of, say, $11, Sam will produce 6 widgets and earn a positive profit (because at a quantity of 6, average cost is below $11). Therefore, the point with price = $11 and quantity = 6 is on his supply curve.

In general, the points on Sam's supply curve are those that lie above his average cost curve, which is to say they are the boldfaced points in Exhibit 7.12.

EXHIBIT 7.12 **The Firm's Long-Run Supply Curve**

At any given price, Sam's House of Widgets sells the quantity where price equals marginal cost. Therefore, as long as Sam wants to be in business at all, his (long-run) supply curve coincides with his (long-run) marginal cost curve.

But at sufficiently low prices (like $5), Sam prefers to exit the industry. Therefore, the point corresponding to $5 is excluded from the supply curve. The supply curve is the boldfaced portion of the marginal cost curve—the part that lies above average cost.

The firm's long-run supply curve is the part of its long-run marginal cost curve that lies above its average cost curve.

Note the twin distinctions between the short run and the long run. In the short run, the firm *shuts down* (without leaving the industry) if price falls below *average variable cost*. In the long run, the firm *exits* if price falls below *average cost*.

Dangerous
Curve

## 7.4 The Competitive Industry in the Long Run

Before we study the competitive industry in the long run, let's briefly recall what we know about the competitive industry in the short run. The key picture is Exhibit 7.8, relating industry-wide supply and demand (in the left panel) to firm-specific supply and demand (in the right). By manipulating the four curves in that picture, we can solve a variety of problems (as in, for example, Exhibits 7.9 and 7.10).

Our goal is to construct a similar picture for the long run. Once again we will have four curves. There is an industry-wide demand curve, which slopes downward and reflects consumers' preferences. There is a firm-specific demand curve, which is flat at the going market price. There is a firm-specific supply curve, which slopes upward and coincides with the firm's marginal cost curve.

Actually, as we saw in Exhibit 7.12, the firm's supply curve coincides with only a *part* of its marginal cost curve, but it will do no harm for us to ignore that subtlety for now.

Dangerous
Curve

Dangerous
Curve

Because the firm might have different marginal cost curves in the short run and the long run (see Exhibit 7.11), it might have different supply curves in the long run and the short run. But the *theory* of the supply curve—that is, the fact that it coincides with the marginal cost curve—is the same in either case.

That accounts for three of our four curves. Next, we need to describe the industry-wide supply curve. That will take a little more work.

## The Long-Run Supply Curve

In the short run, we got the industry-wide supply curve by adding the supply curves of individual firms (see Exhibit 7.7). In the long run, that procedure won't work, because firms can enter and exit in the long run. If we were adding the individual firms' supply curves, which firms would we count? Those currently in the industry? Those that might be poised to enter? Those that might enter someday?

Rather than tackle that question, we proceed a different way: We construct the long-run industry supply curve from scratch, exactly as we would construct *any* supply or demand curve from scratch, namely, one point at a time. We hypothesize a price, figure out the corresponding quantity, and plot a point. Then we hypothesize another price and repeat the process.

First we need to know what the suppliers' cost curves look like. Exhibit 7.13 shows the cost curves of a typical barber, both graphically (in panel A) and numerically (in the chart directly below). *We will assume for now that all barbers have the same cost curves*; we express this assumption by saying that barbershops form a **constant-cost industry**. In Section 7.5, we will relax this assumption.

**Constant-cost industry**

An industry in which all firms have identical costs.

Now we are ready to begin constructing the supply curve. First, we hypothesize a price—say $5 per haircut. How would Floyd the Barber respond to this price? As long as he's in business, Floyd maximizes profit by choosing the quantity where price equals marginal cost. You can see in the graph (or the chart) in Exhibit 7.13 that this occurs at quantity 2.

If this were a short-run problem, we'd be done. But because it's a long-run problem, we need to think about whether Floyd wants to go on barbering. That means we have to think about his profits.

First, Floyd's total revenue, when he sells 2 haircuts at $5 each, is $10. His total cost, which you can read off the chart in Exhibit 7.13, is $15. So his profit is $10 − $15 = −$5, a negative number. So Floyd wants to leave the industry, and in the long run, that's exactly what he'll do.

And so will every other barber, because we've assumed that all barbers are exactly like Floyd (or at least have exactly the same cost curves). Conclusion: When the price of a haircut is $5, there is no such thing as a barber.

Dangerous
Curve

If the price of a haircut were $5, it is not in fact true that all barbers would leave the industry. What would happen is this: Some barbers would leave, and as they left, the price of haircuts would get bid up. Eventually, the price would get bid up high enough to convince some barbers to stay in business.

However, and this is a key point, *none of that is relevant to the construction of the supply curve.* A point on the supply curve answers a hypothetical question: *If* the price of haircuts were $5 (and if it were stuck at $5 and unable to change), *then* what would happen? Answer: There would be no barbers. So on the supply curve, a price of $5 goes with: nothing at all.

## EXHIBIT 7.13    Constructing the Long-Run Supply Curve

**A. Cost curves for a typical barber**

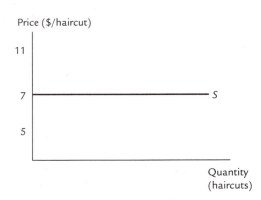

**B. Long-run industry-wide supply**

| Quantity | Total Cost (TC) | Marginal Cost (MC) | Average Cost (AC) |
|---|---|---|---|
| 1 | $10 | $2/haircut | $10/haircut |
| 2 | 15 | 5 | 7.50 |
| 3 | 21 | 6 | 7.00 |
| 4 | 28 | 7 | 7.00 |
| 5 | 37 | 9 | 4.00 |
| 6 | 48 | 11 | 8.00 |

Panel A shows the cost curves of a typical barber, which we take as given. In panel B, we construct the long-run industry supply curve, one point at a time.

If the going price of haircuts is $5, each barber provides 2 haircuts, earning a profit of $10 – $15 = –$5. Therefore each barber exits and the haircut industry disappears.

If the going price of haircuts is $11, then each barber provides 6 haircuts and earns a positive profit of $66 – $48 = $18. Now every firm in the world becomes a barbershop; the quantity of haircuts provided is equal to 6 per firm times an unlimited number of firms. The corresponding quantity is completely off the chart.

If the going price of haircuts is $7, then each barber provides 4 haircuts and breaks even. The total quantity supplied is 4 haircuts per barber times any number of barbers; in other words, it is anything. So a price of $7 goes with every quantity.

Let's try again. We hypothesize another price—say $11 this time—and we see what happens. Now Floyd chooses the quantity where marginal cost is $11—that is, the quantity 6. His total revenue is $6 \times \$11 = \$66$ and his total cost is $48 (read from the chart in Exhibit 7.13). His profit is $18.

Remember that this is an *economic* profit. It means that Floyd can earn more as a barber than in any other industry. And therefore so can anyone else. (Here we are still making the strong assumption that everyone has the same cost curves Floyd does; we'll relax this assumption in later sections.) In other words, *every firm in the Universe wants to convert itself to a barbershop*, and in the long run, they all do.

Okay, now how many haircuts are provided? Answer: 6 per firm, times the number of firms, and the number of firms is essentially infinite. Therefore, an essentially infinite number of haircuts is supplied. The price of $11 goes with the quantity "infinity"—or at least with a number so large it's way off our graph. There's no way to plot this point.

Dangerous
Curve

In reality, when barbershops earn positive profits, firms enter, driving down the price of haircuts until the positive profits are bid away and the flow of entry stops. But once again, this has *no relevance* to the supply curve. The supply curve asks "What would happen *if* the price of a haircut were stuck at $11?" And the answer is: In that purely hypothetical situation, all of the world's resources would be devoted to barbering.

We have now tried twice to construct points on our industry supply curve. Let's try once more. We'll hypothesize that haircuts sell for $7. Floyd chooses the quantity 4 (where price equals marginal cost) and earns a total revenue of $4 \times \$7 = \$28$. His total cost (read from the chart in Exhibit 7.13) is also $28. His (economic) profit is zero.

Does Floyd stick with barbering or does he convert his shop into its next best alternative—say a lemonade stand? Answer: He might do either. Both activities are equally profitable (that's what it means for economic profit to be zero), so there's no reason for him to prefer one to another.

And likewise for other firms. Which will be barbershops and which will be lemonade stands, or gas stations, or whatever is next-best for them? We have absolutely no basis for prediction. So—how many barbershops will there be? Maybe none. Maybe one. Maybe ten, or a hundred, or a thousand, or ten thousand. Anything is possible.

And how many haircuts will be provided? Well, 4 per barbershop, times the number of barbershops, which could be anything. In other words, it could be 0, or 4, or 40, or 400, or 4,000, or 40,000, or anything at all. So on the long-run supply curve, *every quantity* is associated with a price of $7. We've plotted this in panel B of Exhibit 7.13, where you can see that:

In a constant-cost industry, the long-run industry supply curve is flat.

## The Break-Even Price

In Exhibit 7.13, barbers who must sell haircuts at $5 earn negative profits; therefore, they exit the industry. Barbers who must sell haircuts at $11 earn positive profits, so at this price every firm in the Universe becomes a barbershop. Barbers who sell haircuts at $7 just **break even**; that is, they earn zero economic profit. Therefore, the supply curve is flat at $7, and $7 is called the break-even price in this industry.

**Break-even price**

The price at which a seller earns zero profit.

We calculated the break-even price by trial and error, but there's also a faster way: The break-even price occurs at the point where the marginal and average cost curves cross. At this price, barbers choose to supply a quantity where price and average cost are equal, so they earn zero profit. (This was essentially the point of Exhibit 7.12.)

We've gone through the trial and error process here because the author of your textbook believes it goes a long way toward clarifying the issues and the meaning of the supply curve. But the fast way to find the break-even price is to look for the intersection of the marginal and average cost curves.

## The Break-Even Price and the Supply Curve

Now that we've defined the break-even price, we can restate everything we've learned in a sentence:

In a constant-cost industry, the long-run industry supply curve is flat at the level of the break-even price.

## Changes in the Break-Even Price

What could cause the break-even price to change? The answer is: any change in costs (whether it's a change in variable costs or in total costs). If you can just break even selling haircuts for $7 apiece on Monday, and if your costs go up on Tuesday, then you can no longer break even selling haircuts for $7 on Tuesday. When costs rise, the break-even price must rise also.

This is important to remember, because the long-run supply curve is flat *at the break-even price* and therefore shifts every time the break-even price changes. So:

Any increase in costs will cause the long-run industry supply curve to shift upward. Any decrease in costs will cause the long-run industry supply curve to shift downward.

Notice that this is very different from what happens in the short run. In the short run, only variable costs matter. In the long run, fixed costs matter too.

Dangerous
Curve

Take an example: Suppose you run a bubble gum company. Every day, you sell 100 sticks of bubble gum for $1 a piece, and you just break even; $1 is your break-even price. Now you are suddenly required to pay an excise tax of 20¢ per stick of bubble gum. What happens to your break-even price? Answer: You would need to charge an extra 20¢ per stick of gum to cover the cost of the tax. Your break-even price is now $1.20.

That doesn't mean demanders would pay $1.20; it means only that $1.20 is what you would have to charge to break even. Whether you *can* break even is a separate question.

Dangerous
Curve

Or take another example: You sell 100 sticks of bubble gum for $1 apiece and you just break even; once again your break-even price is $1. Now you are subjected to an annual license fee of $20. What is your new break-even price? Answer: To break even, you'd have to charge enough to cover your additional $20 in costs. That comes to approximately an extra 20¢ per stick of gum, making your new break-even price approximately $1.20.

Why *approximately*? Because at a price of $1.20, you'd presumably choose to supply some quantity of gum other than 100. But as long as your quantity stays *close* to 100, your new break-even price is somewhere around $1.20.

**Exercise 7.4** In the example of Exhibit 7.13, suppose every barber must pay an annual license fee of $18. What is the new break-even price?

## Equilibrium

The relationship between the competitive industry and the competitive firm is the same in the long run as in the short run: The market price is determined by the intersection of the industry-wide supply and demand curves, and the firm faces a flat demand curve at the going market price. You can see the picture in Exhibit 7.14.

### The Zero-Profit Condition

As you can see in Exhibit 7.14, the long-run equilibrium price is always equal to the break-even price (because that's the level at which the industry supply curve is flat). If

## EXHIBIT 7.14    Long-Run Competitive Equilibrium

The industry-wide equilibrium occurs at the break-even price. Firms face a demand curve that is flat at that price.

the break-even price for barbershops is $7 per haircut, then the equilibrium price of a haircut will be $7, regardless of where the demand curve lies. Thus, in the long-run equilibrium, all barbers earn exactly zero profit.

It's clear why this must be so. If the price of haircuts were below $7, barbers would earn negative profits and begin leaving the industry. As they left, the price of haircuts would rise, and continue rising until the price reached $7 and there was no reason for further exit. On the other hand, if the price of haircuts were above $7, profits would be positive, firms would enter, and the price of haircuts would fall, driving the price back down to $7.

In a constant-cost industry, in long-run equilibrium, all firms earn zero economic profit.

Remember, though, that entry and exit take time. In the real world, a firm cannot instantly convert itself from a clothing store to a barbershop. If the demand for haircuts rises, barbers might earn positive profits for quite awhile until enough firms enter the industry to drive profits back down to zero. During that time, the industry is not in long-run equilibrium.

Many economists argue that long-run zero-profit equilibrium is almost never reached, because demand curves and cost curves shift so often that the entry and exit process never settles down. Although this is arguably true in many industries, the zero-profit condition remains a useful approximation to the truth.

### Cost Minimization

The zero-profit condition has an interesting side effect: A firm earning zero profit must be operating at the point where its marginal and average cost curves cross. But we saw way back in Exhibit 6.5 that the marginal and average cost curves cross at the *bottom* of the average cost curve. Therefore:

In long-run equilibrium in a constant-cost industry, every firm produces at the lowest possible average cost.

No firm *sets out* to minimize average cost. Firms seek only to maximize profit. In Exhibit 7.13, if haircuts were selling for $11 each, Floyd the Barber would cheerfully provide 6 haircuts a day at an average cost of $8, which is well above the minimum of 7. Only when profit is zero—that is, when the price of haircuts falls back to $7—does Floyd move to the bottom of his average cost curve.

Dangerous
Curve

## Changes in Equilibrium

The analysis of long-run equilibrium differs from the analysis of short-run equilibrium in two important ways. First, the industry-wide supply curve is flat. Second, the industry-wide supply curve moves in response to any change in costs, whether fixed or variable.

Here are some examples.

### Changes in Fixed Costs

Suppose new legislation requires every barbershop to pay a daily license fee. What happens in the long run?

Exhibit 7.15 shows the answer. The firm's marginal cost curve is unaffected, but the break-even price rises. (Go back to Exercise 7.2 if you need to be reminded of why.) Thus, the industry supply curve shifts vertically upward to the level of the new break-even price. Each firm produces more haircuts than before; the industry as a whole now produces fewer.

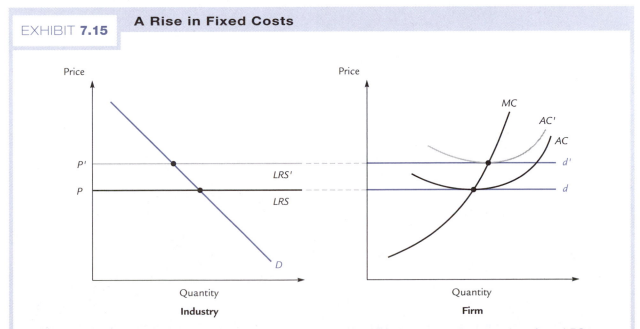

**EXHIBIT 7.15**    **A Rise in Fixed Costs**

If fixed costs rise, the break-even price rises also, so the long-run industry supply curve rises from *LRS* to *LRS'*. Quantity increases at each individual firm and decreases in the industry. The firm's average cost curve rises from *AC* to *AC'*, indicating that profit is zero in the new equilibrium.

If each barber cuts more hair, how can the total number of haircuts go down? The answer is that in the long run, the number of barbers must fall. In the short run, such an outcome would be impossible.

There is no way to predict which individual barbers will exit. All we know is that *some* barbers will exit, and exit continues until the price is bid up to its new break-even level. The right half of Exhibit 7.15 shows the situation at one of those barbershops that happens to remain.

**Dangerous Curve**

In Chapter 6, we argued that in the long run, firms have no fixed costs because they can vary their employment of any factor of production. As long as the firm's costs consist entirely of payments to factors, it is correct to say that the firm has no long-run fixed costs. However, the license fee we've just considered is in a separate category from those payments to factors. It does not vary with output and is therefore a fixed cost even in the long run.

It is important to distinguish a fixed cost from a sunk cost. Although the license fee is a fixed cost for any firm that decides to remain in the industry, it is not yet a sunk cost at the point when the entry/exit decision is being made. Thus, it is relevant to the decision. A cost that is truly sunk, in the sense that it cannot be avoided even by leaving the industry, will not affect anything.

## Changes in Variable Costs

An increase in variable costs has two effects: First, the firm's marginal cost curve shifts upward. Second, the break-even price increases, so the industry supply curve shifts upward. Exhibit 7.16 shows the consequences. The quantity supplied by individual firms might either increase or decrease, while the quantity supplied by the industry must decrease.

There's one special case where we can say more: Suppose that marginal cost shifts upward by the same amount at every quantity (so that the marginal cost curve shifts upward

## EXHIBIT 7.16    A Rise in Variable Costs

If variable costs rise, the firm's marginal cost curve rises from *MC* to *MC'*. The break-even price rises, so the long-run industry supply curve rises from *LRS* to *LRS'*. The industry quantity falls; the firm quantity can either fall or rise. The average cost curve shifts from *AC* to *AC'*, and the firm earns zero profit at the new equilibrium.

parallel to itself). Then the break-even price rises by that same amount (as does the average cost curve). Consequently, the new equilibrium quantity at the firm is unchanged.

## Changes in Demand

Suppose the demand for haircuts increases. At the top of Exhibit 7.17, you can see the long-run consequence. Industry-wide demand shifts rightward. The market price remains unchanged, so nothing changes in the "firm" part of the picture. Individual

### EXHIBIT 7.17    A Rise in Demand

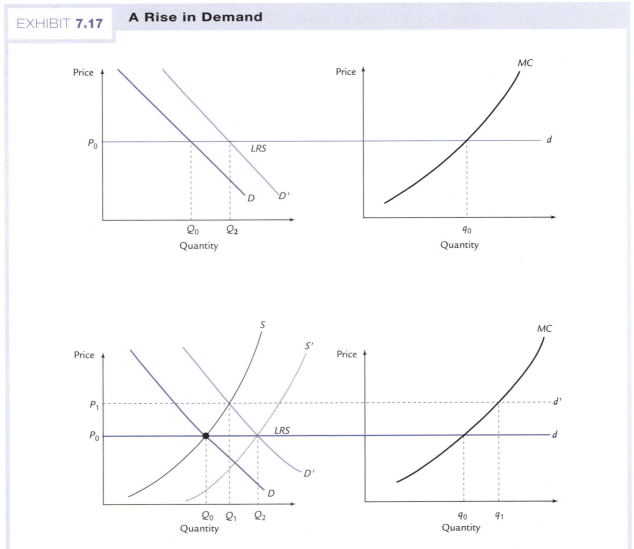

The top of this exhibit shows the long-run effect of an increase in demand for the product of a constant-cost industry. The industry demand curve shifts from $D$ to $D'$. There is no change in price and hence no change in the "firm" part of the picture. Firms produce exactly as before, but the industry quantity increases. The bottom of the exhibit contrasts the short-run and long-run responses. The industry is initially in both short-run and long-run equilibrium at price $P_0$. When demand shifts from $D$ to $D'$, the price is bid up to $P_1$. Firms increase their output from $q_0$ to $q_1$, and the industry output rises to $Q_1$. Now firms earn positive profits, so in the long run there is entry. Entry continues until the price is bid back down to $P_0$. At this point, firms return to producing quantity $q_0$, and the industry produces quantity $Q_2$. Entry causes the short-run supply curve to shift rightward to $S'$. The short-run supply curve shifts in the long run, not in the short run.

barbershops continue producing just as before, but the industry-wide quantity of haircuts increases, because of entry.

It is instructive to compare the long run with the short run. At the bottom of Exhibit 7.17 you can see this comparison. The industry is initially in both short-run and long-run equilibrium at the price $P_0$ and quantity $Q_0$. The increase in demand initially leads to a movement along the short-run supply curve $S$ to the higher price $P_1$. Firms now provide $q_1$ haircuts apiece, for an industry-wide total of $Q_1$. The higher price leads to positive profits and attracts entry in the long run. Thereupon the price is bid back down to $P_0$ and the industry-wide quantity rises further to $Q_2$, although individual firms return to the original quantity $q_0$.

Dangerous
Curve

In Exhibit 7.17, entry causes the short-run industry supply curve to shift rightward from $S$ to $S'$. This shift takes place only in the long run; in the short run, there is no entry, so the short-run supply curve does not shift.

Notice that entry does *not* cause a shift in the *long-run* supply curve, because the consequences of entry are already *built in* to that curve. But the short-run supply curve ignores the effects of entry, and so it must shift to a new location after entry takes place.

## Application: The Government as a Supplier

Suppose your city's government decides there is not enough housing available and decides to do something about it by building and operating a new apartment complex. Will this policy succeed in increasing the quantity of housing?

In the short run, yes. The new apartment complex causes the short-run housing supply curve to shift to the right. In Exhibit 7.18, you can see that the equilibrium price of housing falls from $P_0$ to $P_1$ and the quantity increases from $Q_0$ to $Q_1$.

But the long-run supply curve does not shift. That's because the long-run supply curve is determined by the break-even price. For example, if it costs landlords $400 a month to provide an apartment, then the long-run supply curve is flat at $400 a month.

---

**EXHIBIT 7.18**     **The Government as a Supplier**

When the government builds an apartment complex, the short-run housing supply curve shifts rightward, but the long-run housing supply curve remains fixed. Thus, the quantity of housing increases from $Q_0$ to $Q_1$ in the short run, but returns to $Q_0$ in the long run.

It follows that in the long run, the price of housing must return to $P_0$ and the quantity must return to $Q_0$. That is, in the long run, the number of privately owned apartments withdrawn from the market must just equal the number of new apartments built by the government. (Otherwise, the price would remain below $P_0$ and landlords would earn negative profits, prompting further exit.) Thus, in the long run, the government's new apartment complex adds exactly nothing to the supply of housing.

## Some Lessons Learned

Ask a non-economist why the price of cheddar cheese is, say, $5 a pound, and you're likely to get an answer like "that's what the market will bear," which suggests that prices are explained by demand. But in fact, in competitive industries in the long run, prices are determined primarily by supply. We've just seen that—at least in certain ideal circumstances—the long-run supply curve is flat. Therefore, the supply curve alone determines price. Demand has nothing to do with it. (More precisely, a shift in demand has no effect on price, as we've seen in Exhibit 7.17.)

Another lesson is that changes in costs don't benefit suppliers in the long run, because in the long run profits are always zero. Therefore, when costs fall, all of the benefits are ultimately transferred to consumers. You might think that, if it became cheaper to feed cows, for example, dairy farmers would benefit. In the long run they won't, because the price of dairy products falls until profits return to zero. The winners are the consumers of milk and cheese.

What's true of cost reductions is also true of subsidies. A government subsidy to, say, corner grocery stores would not, in the long run, benefit the owners of grocery stores; because of the long-run flat supply curve, the full benefit of the subsidy would be transferred to consumers. And conversely, a tax on grocery stores (or on milk or cheese) would, in the long run, fall entirely on consumers.

One additional lesson to take from our analysis is that you'll never get rich by imitating the successes of others. If those successes were easy to imitate, everybody would imitate them and they'd garner no rewards. If you want to get rich, you have to break out of the model (which assumes all firms are identical) by identifying needs nobody else has identified, or by finding solutions nobody else has thought of, or by finding genuinely new ways to make people understand that your solutions are worth adopting.

# 7.5 Relaxing the Assumptions

When you travel by car, the other drivers on the road are both a blessing and a curse. On the one hand, they compete with you for resources: They take up space on the road, and they bid up the price of gasoline. On the other hand, those other drivers are a large part of the reason why it was worth someone's while to pave the road, and worth someone else's while to set up gas stations and roadside rest stops.

Likewise, if you start, say, a printing business, competing firms are both a blessing and a curse. On the one hand, they might bid up the price of ink. On the other hand, they might entice inkmakers into existence.

Our analysis so far has ignored these effects. We've assumed that all firms are identical, so that the break-even price is the same at every firm. In this section, we will see what happens when we relax these assumptions.

## The Break-Even Price

The cornerstone of our theory is that in long-run equilibrium, firms must earn zero profit and therefore must sell their output at the break-even price. For such a theory to make sense, there must be a single break-even price that applies to all firms and that does not change as a result of entry and exit. In other words, we need to assume:

Assumption 1: All firms are identical; that is, all firms have identical cost curves.

Assumption 2: Those cost curves do not change as the industry expands or contracts.

Assumption 1 is probably true for sidewalk flower vendors and false for breeders of world-class orchids. There are a lot of people who can run sidewalk flower stands about equally well; thus, all of them have the same cost curves. But only very few people have the delicate skills to breed orchids efficiently. Those with fewer skills will find it substantially more costly to produce a given quantity of orchids. (If ½ of your flowers die before you can bring them to market, that adds substantially to the average cost of producing a marketable orchid.)

In general, Assumption 1 will be true in industries that do not require unusual skills, and false in industries where unusual skills are required. Hamburger stands satisfy Assumption 1; gourmet restaurants do not.

Assumption 2 is also probably true for sidewalk flower vendors. If you're selling flowers, there's no reason why the arrival of new competitors should affect your costs. (New arrivals can affect your *profits* by competing for customers, but that's not the same thing as affecting your costs.) However, Assumption 2 is probably false for farmers. Here's why: An influx of new farmers bids up the rental price of *land*, and the rental price of land is one of the costs of farming.

The key difference is this: Sidewalk flower vendors cannot significantly bid up the wholesale price of flowers, because sidewalk flower vendors, taken as a whole, do not use a significant fraction of the world's flowers. Farmers, by contrast, *can* bid up the price of land, because farmers, taken as a whole, *do* use a significant fraction of the world's arable land.

Dangerous
Curve

When you think about flower vendors, be sure to distinguish between the retail price of sidewalk flowers (the price at which the vendors *sell* their wares) and the wholesale price of flowers (the price at which vendors *buy* their wares). To affect costs, competitors must affect the wholesale price of flowers.

Dangerous
Curve

Here's an exception: Suppose that instead of buying their flowers from reputable dealers, the flower vendors pick their flowers from a small public park. Then the arrival of new competitors will make it harder to find flowers in the park, which increases the cost of acquiring flowers. In this case, sidewalk flower vending does not satisfy Assumption 2.

In general, Assumption 2 will be true in industries that are not large enough to affect the price of any input (where inputs are things like wholesale flowers or arable land), and false in industries that are large enough to affect the price of some input. Here the phrase "large enough" must be interpreted relative to the size of the market for the input in question. For example, the jewelry industry is large enough to affect the price of diamonds, because a substantial fraction of the world's diamonds are used in jewelry. By contrast, hamburger stands use a lot of meat, but probably not enough to affect its price: Only a small fraction of the world's meat is used to make fast food hamburgers. Thus, hamburger stands, like sidewalk flower vendors, are likely to satisfy Assumptions 1 and 2.

## The Significance of the Assumptions

Assumptions 1 and 2 make it possible to talk unambiguously about *the* break-even price. Without Assumption 1, different firms would have different cost curves and therefore different break-even prices. Without Assumption 2, a given firm's cost curves—and hence its break-even price—would change as other firms entered or left the industry. But given both assumptions, all firms have the same break-even price and that break-even price is unaffected by entry or exit; it is *the* break-even price for the industry.

Even though we have stressed that there is just one break-even price for the industry, that break-even price can change if cost curves change for some reason other than entry or exit—such as an increase in the cost of some raw material, or a new annual license fee that every firm in the industry must pay.

Dangerous
Curve

# Constant-Cost Industries

An industry is called a constant-cost industry if it satisfies Assumptions 1 and 2. Constant-cost industries are the industries to which the analysis of Section 7.4 applies. In the remainder of this section, we will examine some alternative types of competitive industry.

In Section 7.4, we said that an industry is **constant-cost** if all firms have the same cost curves. Here we are calling an industry constant-cost if all firms have the same cost curves *and* those cost curves are unaffected by entry and exit. In fact, the analysis of Section 7.4 used both assumptions, though we didn't state them explicitly.

**Constant-cost industry**

A competitive industry in which all firms have identical cost curves, and those cost curves do not change as the industry expands or contracts.

Dangerous
Curve

# Increasing-Cost Industries

An increasing-cost industry is a competitive industry where the break-even price for new entrants increases as the industry expands.

There are two reasons why an industry might be increasing-cost. First, some firms might have higher break-even prices because they are less efficient. Second, an expansion of the industry might bid up the price of some factor of production and thereby raise the break-even price for everyone—as when an expansion of the farming industry bids up the price of land (this is the *factor-price effect*, which we also encountered in the short run). In either case, we shall see that the long-run industry supply curve slopes upward.

**Increasing-cost industry**

A competitive industry where the break-even price for new entrants increases as the industry expands.

## Less-Efficient Firms

Suppose that Floyd the barber can break even selling haircuts at $7 apiece. His less-efficient cousin Lloyd has to charge $9 per haircut to break even. In this case, Assumption 1 is violated.

When the market price of haircuts is $7, Floyd cuts hair but Lloyd does something else. If the price rises to $9, Lloyd enters the barbering industry. Between them, Floyd and Lloyd cut more hair than Floyd alone. Thus, a higher price of haircuts leads to a greater quantity of haircuts supplied. In other words, the long-run supply curve slopes upward.

## The Factor-Price Effect

Suppose instead that Floyd and Lloyd are equally efficient. Either one can break even selling haircuts at $7 apiece.

But suppose also that if Floyd and Lloyd *both* become barbers, they bid up the price of razors—because two barbers demand more razors than one barber. This adds to their costs and makes it impossible for them to continue breaking even at $7. Thus, as long as haircuts sell for $7, only one barber can survive. If the price of haircuts rises to $9, it becomes possible for Floyd and Lloyd to break even simultaneously. In this case, Assumption 2 is violated.

Once again, a higher price of haircuts leads to more haircuts being supplied. Once again, the long-run supply curve slopes upward.

Dangerous
Curve

This example is entirely unrealistic, because in reality barbers cannot bid up the price of razors. That's because the entire world population of barbers accounts for only a small fraction of the world's demand for sharpened steel. We've used this example only for easy contrast with earlier examples.

The moral of both Floyd/Lloyd examples is this:

In an increasing-cost industry, the long-run supply curve slopes upward.

## An Intermediate Case: A Few Super-Efficient Firms

One case of interest is that in which a few firms are especially efficient and a great number of other firms are essentially identical. In this case, a few efficient firms will be willing to enter the industry even when the price is low, yielding a small but nonzero quantity supplied. When the price rises high enough for the "ordinary" firms to break even, any quantity can be supplied. Thus, the long-run supply curve slopes upward for a short while and then becomes flat, as in Exhibit 7.19. In such an industry, when there is sufficient demand for equilibrium to occur on the flat part of the supply curve, it is usually harmless to assume (for simplicity) that the entire supply curve is flat.

## Example: The Motel Industry

In the motel industry, there might well be a few super-efficient firms, but there are also a vast number of essentially interchangeable motels with (it is reasonable to assume) pretty much the same cost curves. Therefore, to a reasonable approximation, Assumption 1 is satisfied. What about Assumption 2?

Assumption 2 is violated if there is a factor-price effect—in other words, if the price of some input changes when the motel industry expands or contracts. Should we expect to see such a violation?

One of the major inputs into the motel industry is land. Motels take up space, and that space has to be paid for. (Of course, it doesn't matter whether the motel owns the land it sits on or rents it from a landlord. Rent paid to the landlord is a cost; rent forgone by using your own land is equally a cost.)

**EXHIBIT 7.19**    **Long-Run Supply with a Few Efficient Firms**

Suppose there are a few exceptionally efficient firms and a great number of identical "ordinary" firms. At low prices, only the efficient firms enter and the quantity supplied is small. At the break-even price of the ordinary firms (*P*), the supply curve becomes flat.

So: Does the expansion (or contraction) of the motel industry change the price of land?

It depends. If we're talking about the industry consisting of motels in, say, downtown Dayton, Ohio, probably not. Most of downtown Dayton is populated by shopping malls, office buildings, and parking lots. Motels use a very small fraction of the land, so even a substantial expansion of the motel industry won't have a noticeable effect on land prices. New motels can enter without changing the break-even price (say $70 per motel room per night). These motels form a constant-cost industry.

But if we're talking about the industry consisting of motels clustered around a particular highway exit, the story is very different. It's not uncommon for half the land near a highway exit to be populated by motels. Expand the motel industry and the rental price of land goes up. When a new motel enters the market, existing motels might find that they can no longer break even selling rooms for $70 a night; maybe the new break-even price is $80 instead. Assumption 2 is violated, the industry is increasing-cost, and the long-run supply curve slopes upward.

## Decreasing-Cost Industries

In 2001, the average laptop computer sold for $1,640; in 2004 it sold for $1,250 and by 2005 the price was down to $1,000—though by then you could get a perfectly usable machine, complete with the latest wireless technology, for as little as $650.

The reason, according to an article in the *Wall Street Journal*,[1] was increasing demand. For years, laptops were used pretty much exclusively by businesspeople, a relatively small market that prevented manufacturers from achieving economies of scale. Now that most college students have laptops, the market has expanded, laptops are produced more efficiently, and prices have fallen.

[1] Gary McWilliams, "Laptop Prices Hit New Lows," *Wall Street Journal*, August 31, 2005.

**Decreasing-cost industry**

A competitive industry where the break-even price for new entrants falls as the industry expands.

The computer industry is an example of a decreasing-cost industry where costs (and therefore break-even prices) fall as the industry expands. At one time, manufacturers like Dell and Gateway produced many of their own internal components. Nowadays, components (like disk drives) tend to be supplied by specialists, freeing up Dell and Gateway to concentrate on the things they do best. But a drive manufacturer can survive only when the industry is big enough to support it, so the growth of the industry drives down break-even prices. Thus, on the industry supply curve, a greater quantity is associated with a lower price; that is:

In a decreasing-cost industry, the long-run supply curve slopes downward.

At the end of Chapter 2, we briefly discussed the gains from trade that are due simply to the scale of operations, as opposed to those that are due to comparative advantage. Decreasing-cost industries provide examples of such gains. Suppose that each of two isolated countries has a small computer industry, insufficient to support a specialized drive manufacturer. If these two countries begin to trade with each other, the combined market for computers might suffice to bring a drive manufacturer into the market. By concentrating on the production of drives in large quantities, the drive manufacturer can produce at a lower average cost than any of the computer manufacturers can, thereby reducing the average cost of a laptop computer. Residents of both countries can benefit from the savings.

## Equilibrium

The analysis of long-run equilibrium in the increasing-cost and decreasing-cost cases is just as in the constant-cost case; the only thing that differs is the shape of the long-run industry supply curve. Several examples are provided in Exhibit 7.20 and Exhibit 7.21.

# 7.6 Applications

## Removing a Rent Control

In the town of Llareggub, apartments rent for $400 per month. The town passes a law setting a maximum rent of $200 a month. Some years later, the law is repealed. Nothing changes in the interim. Does the rent on apartments return all the way up to its old level of $400 per month?

To analyze this problem, look at Exhibit 7.22. The market is initially in both short-run and long-run equilibrium at a price of $400 and a quantity of $Q_0$. When the price is artificially lowered to $200, landlords' short-run response is to provide fewer apartments. The new quantity can be read off the short-run supply curve $S$ at a price of $200. (This quantity is not marked on the graph.) In the long run, as landlords seize additional opportunities to convert apartments to commercial or other uses, or just decide not to keep some existing apartments in adequate repair, the quantity falls still further, to $Q_1$, which is read off the long-run supply curve at a price of $200.

EXHIBIT **7.20**    **An Increase in Costs in an Increasing-Cost Industry**

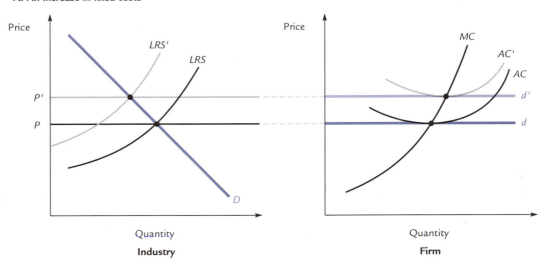

**A. An increase in fixed costs**

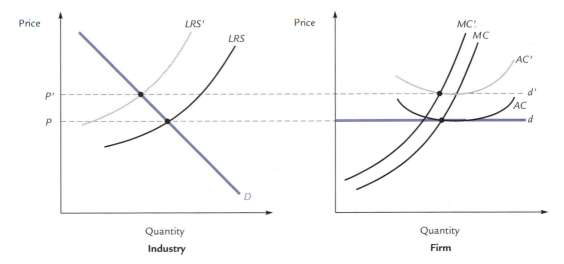

**B. An increase in variable costs**

The top panels show an increase in fixed costs and the bottom panels show an increase in marginal costs. In both cases, the break-even price increases, so the long-run industry supply curve shifts. The firm's marginal cost curve shifts only in the second of the two examples. In both examples, the price rises and the industry supplies a smaller quantity. In the first example, the firm's quantity surely increases; in the second, the firm's quantity could increase or decrease.

EXHIBIT **7.21**    **A Change in Demand**

Increasing-cost industry

Decreasing-cost industry

When demand increases, price rises in an increasing-cost industry, but it falls in a decreasing-cost industry. In both cases, the industry-wide quantity increases.

EXHIBIT **7.22**    **Removing a Rent Control**

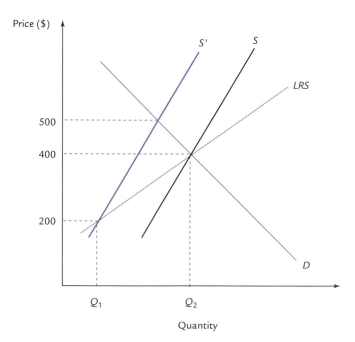

The market is initially in both short-run and long-run equilibrium at a price of $400. A maximum legal rent of $200 is imposed. Eventually, quantity falls to $Q_1$ and the short-run supply curve falls from $S$ to $S'$.

When the rent control is removed, the market moves to a new short-run equilibrium at a price of $500, *above* the original uncontrolled price. Eventually, it returns to the long-run equilibrium.

With the stock of apartments reduced, there is a new short-run supply curve $S'$. When the rent control is lifted, the new equilibrium is at \$500 and a quantity somewhere between $Q_0$ and $Q_1$. Thus, the answer to the question "Does the rent return all the way up to \$400?" is no; actually, it goes *above* \$400.

At \$500, landlords earn positive profits and slowly they reconvert commercial buildings to use as apartments. Eventually, the market does return to the old long-run equilibrium at a price of \$400 and a quantity of $Q_0$. The reason for this is quite simple: Neither the demand curve nor the long-run supply curve has shifted, so the equilibrium can't change.

## A Tax on Motel Rooms

Suppose your town imposes a \$5-per-night sales tax on motel rooms. Who pays the tax?

In the short run, the number of motel rooms is nearly fixed so the supply curve is nearly vertical. (It is not completely vertical because, for example, a motel owner might be able to provide more clean rooms per night by hiring a larger maintenance staff.) Therefore, the tax is paid almost entirely by suppliers (i.e., motel owners) as you can see in panel A of Exhibit 7.23, where the price falls from $P$ to $P'$, almost the full amount of the tax.

In the long run, the answer depends on exactly which motel industry we're talking about. We saw on page 203 that downtown motels are likely to form a constant-cost industry and motels near a highway exit are likely to form an increasing-cost industry. So for downtown motels, the long-run supply curve is flat, the price of a room is unaffected by the tax, and therefore the tax is paid entirely by demanders. You can see this

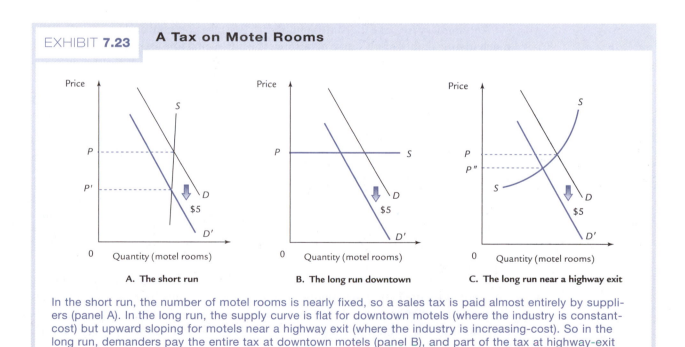

EXHIBIT **7.23**    **A Tax on Motel Rooms**

A. The short run          B. The long run downtown          C. The long run near a highway exit

In the short run, the number of motel rooms is nearly fixed, so a sales tax is paid almost entirely by suppliers (panel A). In the long run, the supply curve is flat for downtown motels (where the industry is constant-cost) but upward sloping for motels near a highway exit (where the industry is increasing-cost). So in the long run, demanders pay the entire tax at downtown motels (panel B), and part of the tax at highway-exit motels (panel C).

in Exhibit 7.23B. For highway-exit motels, the relevant picture is Exhibit 7.23C, where in the long run, the tax is split between suppliers and demanders.

---

**Exercise 7.5** Illustrate the short-run and long-run effects of a government program that subsidizes motel visits.

---

## Tipping the Busboy

Let us return to the Brotherhood for the Respect, Elevation, and Advancement of Dishwashers (bread), mentioned in the introduction to this chapter. The organization's purpose is to encourage people to give tips to busboys. Who will benefit if they succeed in establishing this custom?

A partial answer is: not busboys. The talents required of a busboy are reasonably widespread in society. A grocery bagger or a parking lot attendant can easily decide to become a busboy. Because there are no (or very few) individuals with special "busboy skills," busboys' services are provided at a constant cost.

It follows that the total compensation of busboys cannot change. If tips increase, wages must decrease by the same amount. The increase in tips causes positive profits; the positive profits cause grocery baggers to become busboys; the entry of the grocery baggers causes wages to fall; and the whole process continues until grocery bagging and busing tables are again equally attractive.

---

Dangerous Curve

Students sometimes argue that as grocery baggers leave their own industry to become busboys, the wage of baggers will rise. This would be true if bagging were the only other unskilled occupation. But because the new busboys come from many other industries, the number coming from any one other industry is negligibly small.

---

Another way to make the same point is this: Because potential busboys are all pretty much identical, the supply curve of busboys is a horizontal line at the entry price determined by the condition that busing be just as attractive as bagging. If the supply curve for a good is horizontal, then changes in demand cannot change its price.

If busboys don't gain, who does? Tipping reduces the costs of restaurant owners, who now pay lower wages. Suppose that customers leave a tip of size $T$ at each meal. Then busboys' wages are reduced by $T$ per meal served, which lowers the industry's supply curve by the amount $T$. The short-run effect is illustrated in panel A of Exhibit 7.24. The fall in costs leads to a fall in the price of restaurant meals, to $P_1$. Who benefits? The restaurateurs and, ironically, the customers themselves.[2]

In the long run, there are two possibilities to consider, both of which are shown in Exhibit 7.24. In each case, the long-run supply curve falls by $T$. If the restaurant industry has constant costs, as in panel B, then the price of a meal drops by exactly $T$, the full amount of the tip. Although the customers would like to tip the busboys, the entire value of their tips is returned to them in the form of lower meal prices!

The other possibility is that there are increasing costs in the restaurant industry. This would be the case, for example, if the potential entrants have varying aptitudes for restaurant management. That case is shown in panel C. Here the price of restaurant meals drops, but not by the full amount of the tips. The tips are split between the

---

[2] There may be an additional effect as restaurateurs decide to hire a larger number of busboys at the lower wage. This effect is irrelevant to anything we are considering in this example.

**EXHIBIT 7.24**

**Tipping the Busboy**

A. The short run

B. The long run if all restaurateurs are identical

C. The long run if restaurateurs have varying abilities

Suppose that people decide to start tipping busboys. Because busing services are provided at constant cost (there are many essentially identical busboys), the total compensation of busboys cannot change. Therefore, wages are reduced by the amount of the tip, $T$. The marginal cost of serving meals falls by this amount.

In the short run (panel A), price falls, but by less than $T$. Part of the tip is returned to the customer through the lower price, and the rest goes to the restaurant owner.

In the long run, if all restaurateurs are identical (panel B), entry bids profits back down to zero only when the price of meals falls by the full amount $T$. We can see this geometrically: The horizontal supply curve falls by $T$, and the price falls by this full amount.

If not all restaurateurs are identical, then entry by less-efficient firms can drive profits to zero even though the price is reduced by less than the full amount of the tip. This is shown in panel C, where the upward-sloping long-run supply curve drops by the amount $T$, but the price of meals falls by something less, which we label $U$. Those restaurateurs who were in the industry originally gain $T - U$ per meal served (their marginal costs fall by $T$ but their price falls by $U$, so they gain the difference), while customers get back $U$ in the form of a lower price. The tip is split between the restaurateur and the customer; the busboy gets nothing.

restaurateurs and their customers, with the customers getting back more in the long run than they do in the short run.

Our analysis assumes that BREAD is successful in making diners feel good about tipping the busboy. An alternative assumption is that BREAD makes diners feel guilty about not tipping the busboy. In that case, the tip is essentially a tax on diners, and the demand for restaurant meals falls by the amount of the tip.

Dangerous Curve

# 7.7 Using the Competitive Model

Exhibits 7.9 and 7.10 illustrate changes in short-run competitive equilibrium; Exhibits 7.15, 7.16, and 7.17 illustrate changes in long-run competitive equilibrium for a constant-cost industry; and Exhibits 7.20 and 7.21 illustrate changes in long-run competitive equilibrium for other sorts of industries. Problems 4, 10, 11, and 12 at the end of the chapter call for you to provide a large number of similar analyses. Here we will list the most important principles to keep in mind when you work problems of this type.

As in the exhibits, you should begin by drawing supply and demand curves for both the industry and the firm. The industry supply curve is always upward sloping in the short run. In the long run, it can be either flat (if the industry is constant-cost) or upward sloping (if the industry is increasing-cost). There is also the possibility of a downward-sloping long-run industry supply curve, but we will not discuss that case here. The firm's demand curve should be drawn flat at the price determined by industry-wide equilibrium.

To analyze a change in equilibrium, you must decide how the curves shift. Usually this means thinking about each curve separately. Here are the fundamental principles to keep in mind.

*Shifts in the Firm's Supply Curve*   The firm's supply curve coincides with its marginal cost curve. Therefore, only a change in marginal costs can affect it. A cost is marginal only if it varies with output. In the short run, marginal costs include labor and raw materials. In the long run, they also include those items of capital equipment that can be varied in the long run. For example, if a restaurant decides to serve more hamburgers, it will use more meat and more waiters in the short run and will expand its kitchen facilities in the long run. Therefore, a change in the price of meat or the wages of waiters causes the firm's supply curve to shift in both the short-run analysis and the long-run analysis, whereas a change in the price of kitchen facilities causes the supply curve to shift only in the long-run analysis. Some costs (e.g., annual license fees) do not vary with output even in the long run and so do not shift the firm's supply curve even in the long run (unless they cause the firm to exit altogether).

*Shifts in the Short-Run Industry Supply Curve*   In the short run, the industry supply curve is the sum of the individual firm's supply curves. Therefore, it shifts only if there is a change in supply at the individual firms.

*Shifts in the Long-Run Industry Supply Curve*   The long-run industry supply curve shifts in response to any change in profitability—unless the change in profitability is due to a change in the price of output, in which case it is reflected by a movement *along*, rather than *of*, the long-run supply curve. However, remember that sunk costs are sunk, so only future costs are relevant. Costs that have been paid and are irretrievable do not affect future profits; therefore, they do not affect entry and exit decisions, and therefore they do not affect the industry supply curve.

*The Individual Firm's Exit Decision: The Constant-Cost Case*   In a constant-cost industry, every firm is completely indifferent about whether to remain in the industry. Thus, anything that reduces profits at just one firm must drive that firm from the industry. For example, suppose that newsstands constitute a constant-cost industry and a single newsstand owner is notified of a rent increase. The owner will certainly leave the industry. On the other hand, if *all* newsstand owners are notified of rent increases, then the industry supply curve shifts, some firms exit, the industry-wide price of newspapers rises until zero profits are restored, and any *particular* newsstand might very well remain in business. There is no way to predict which firms exit under these circumstances.

Note again that sunk costs are sunk. A fire at an individual newsstand is not like a rent increase. The costs of the fire are sunk (even if the firm exits, it continues to bear the costs via a reduction in the resale value of its merchandise); the rent increase can be avoided by exit and is therefore not sunk. The fire, therefore, has no effect, while the rent increase drives the firm from the industry.

In an increasing-cost industry, some firms might be particularly efficient and therefore prefer this industry over any of the alternatives. Such a firm might decide to remain in the industry even following an individual rent increase.

*Demand Curves*  After shifting the firm's and the industry's supply curves, and after deciding whether the firm remains in the industry, determine whether there is any shift in the industry demand curve. Then if there has been a shift in industry equilibrium (due to shifts in either industry supply, industry demand, or both), draw the new firm demand curve as horizontal at the new industry equilibrium price.

*Exceptions*  The rules listed here will serve you well most of the time. As you work the problems at the end of the chapter, you will find a few exceptions due to unusual circumstances. As always, each problem needs to be considered individually.

# Summary

A perfectly competitive firm is one that faces a horizontal demand curve for its product; that is, it can sell any quantity it wants to at the going market price. The total revenue curve for such a firm is a straight line through the origin, and the marginal revenue curve is a horizontal line at the going market price. Thus, the marginal revenue curve is identical to the demand curve.

Like any producer, competitive or not, the competitive firm produces, if it produces at all, where marginal cost equals marginal revenue. Because marginal revenue equals price for a competitive firm, we can say that such a firm produces, if it produces at all, where marginal cost equals price. To see what the firm will produce in the short run, we use its short-run marginal cost curve; and to see what it will produce in the long run, we use its long-run marginal cost curve.

In the short run, the firm operates only if its revenue exceeds its variable costs. This is the same as saying that the firm operates only if the market price exceeds its average variable cost. Thus, the firm's short-run supply curve is that portion of its marginal cost curve that lies above average variable cost.

A competitive industry is one in which all firms are competitive.

To derive the short-run industry supply curve, we assume a fixed number of firms and add their quantities supplied at each price.

The competitive industry operates at the point where supply and demand are equal, because each individual firm maximizes profits at this point. In competitive equilibrium, the total cost of producing any quantity of output is minimized. This is because each firm has the same marginal cost (equal to the market price).

In the long run, the firm operates where price is equal to long-run marginal cost, provided that it earns positive profits. If profits are negative (which happens when price falls below average cost) the firm leaves the industry. Therefore, the firm's long-run supply curve is that part of its long-run marginal cost curve that lies above its long-run average cost curve.

To study long-run equilibrium, we must account for the possibility of entry and exit. Entry and exit are driven by profit. If all firms are identical, then all firms must earn zero profit in long-run equilibrium.

In the simplest analysis, we assume that all firms share a single break-even price, and that the break-even price is unaffected by entry and exit. In that case, the break-even price is the only price that can prevail in long-run equilibrium; therefore, the long-run supply curve is flat at the break-even price.

A second possibility is that the industry is increasing-cost, which means that the break-even price for new entrants increases as the industry expands. This could happen either because new entrants are less efficient than existing firms or because new entrants bid up the price of inputs, causing everyone's costs to increase. In this case, the industry supply curve slopes upward.

A third possibility is that the industry is decreasing-cost, which means that the break-even price for new entrants falls as the industry expands. For example, when the industry reaches a certain size, specialized sub-industries can be formed. In this case, there is a downward-sloping long-run supply curve.

## Author Commentary        www.cengage.com/economics/landsburg

**AC1.**   In a perfectly competitive market, there is a single going market price that everyone takes as given. In many markets, prices are determined by bargaining and through auctions—for example, eBay. Read this article for a discussion of eBay bidding strategy.

## Review Questions

**R1.**   Which of the following are true for all firms? Which are true for competitive firms only? Which are false for all firms?

   **a.**   The firm faces a flat demand for its product.

   **b.**   The firm faces a flat marginal revenue curve.

   **c.**   The firm seeks to operate where marginal revenue equals marginal cost.

   **d.**   The firm seeks to operate where price equals marginal cost.

**R2.**   If a competitive firm *fails* to maximize profits, which of the following statements are true and which are false?

   **a.**   Price equals marginal cost.

   **b.**   Price equals marginal revenue.

   **c.**   Marginal cost equals marginal revenue.

**R3.**   What is the difference between a shutdown and an exit?

**R4.**   **True or False:** A firm shuts down whenever its profits are negative.

**R5.**   Suppose a competitive widget firm has an upward-sloping marginal cost curve, and that the marginal cost of producing 6 items is $12 per widget. Explain carefully why the point with coordinates ($12, 6 widgets) must be on the firm's supply curve.

**R6.**   What determines the short-run industry-wide supply curve in a competitive industry?

**R7.** In short-run competitive equilibrium, what happens to output at an individual firm following an industry-wide rise in fixed costs?

**R8.** In short-run competitive equilibrium, what happens to output at an individual firm following an industry-wide rise in variable costs?

**R9.** In short-run competitive equilibrium, what happens to output at an individual firm following an industry-wide rise in demand?

**R10.** What is the difference between accounting profit and economic profit?

**R11.** Assuming that all firms are identical, explain why all firms must earn zero profit in long-run equilibrium.

**R12.** Explain why the long-run industry supply curve must be flat in a constant-cost industry.

**R13.** In long-run competitive equilibrium, what happens to output at an individual firm following an industry-wide rise in fixed costs? (Assume a constant-cost industry if necessary.)

**R14.** In long-run competitive equilibrium, what happens to output at an individual firm following an industry-wide rise in variable costs? (Assume a constant-cost industry if necessary.)

**R15.** In long-run competitive equilibrium, what happens to output at an individual firm following an industry-wide rise in demand? (Assume a constant-cost industry if necessary.)

**R16.** What are the two key assumptions in the definition of a constant-cost industry?

**R17.** What is the shape of the long-run industry supply curve in an increasing-cost industry? Why?

**R18.** What is the shape of the long-run industry supply curve in a decreasing-cost industry? Why?

# Numerical Exercises

**N1.** Every firm in the widget industry has fixed costs of $6 and faces the following marginal cost curve:

| Quantity | Marginal Cost |
| --- | --- |
| 1 | $2 |
| 2 | 4 |
| 3 | 6 |
| 4 | 8 |
| 5 | 10 |

**a.** Suppose the price of widgets is $10. How many widgets does each firm produce? How much profit does the firm earn? Is the industry in long-run equilibrium? How do you know?

**b.** In the long run, will there be entry or exit from this industry? What will be the price of widgets in the long run? How many widgets will each firm produce?

**N2.** Moose-nose pies are produced by a constant-cost industry where all firms are identical and each firm has fixed costs of $15. The following chart shows the industry-wide demand curve and the marginal cost curve of a typical firm:

| Industry-Wide Demand | | Firm's Marginal Cost Curve | |
| --- | --- | --- | --- |
| Price | Quantity | Quantity | Marginal Cost |
| $5 | 750 | 1 | $5 |
| 10 | 600 | 2 | 10 |
| 15 | 450 | 3 | 15 |
| 20 | 300 | 4 | 20 |
| 25 | 150 | 5 | 25 |

Suppose the industry is in long-run equilibrium.

**a.** What is the price of moose-nose pies?

**b.** What is the number of firms in the industry?

**c.** On the industry-wide short-run supply curve, what quantity corresponds to a price of $10?

**N3.** Widgets are produced by a constant-cost industry. The following chart shows the industry-wide demand curve and the marginal cost curve of each firm.

| Demand | | Firm's Marginal Cost Curve | |
| --- | --- | --- | --- |
| Price | Quantity | Quantity | Marginal Cost |
| $5 | 1500 | 1 | $5 |
| 10 | 1200 | 2 | 10 |
| 15 | 900 | 3 | 15 |
| 20 | 600 | 4 | 20 |
| 25 | 300 | 5 | 25 |

There are currently 600 firms in the industry. Each firm has fixed costs of $30.

**a.** What is the price of widget today?

**b.** What is the profit of a widget firm today?

**c.** In the long run, what is the price of a widget?

**d.** In the long run, how many firms exit the industry?

**N4.** Widgets are provided by a competitive constant-cost industry where each firm has fixed costs of $30. The following chart shows the industry-wide demand curve and the marginal cost curve of a typical firm.

| Industry-Wide Demand | | Firm's Marginal Cost Curve | |
| --- | --- | --- | --- |
| Price | Quantity | Quantity | Marginal Cost |
| $5 | 1500 | 1 | $5 |
| 10 | 1200 | 2 | 10 |
| 15 | 900 | 3 | 15 |
| 20 | 600 | 4 | 20 |
| 25 | 300 | 5 | 25 |
| 30 | 200 | 6 | 30 |
| 35 | 140 | 7 | 35 |
| 40 | 50 | 8 | 40 |

**a.** What is the price of a widget?

**b.** How many firms are in the industry?

For the remaining four parts of this problem, suppose the government imposes an excise tax of $15 per widget.

**c.** In the short run, what is the new price of widgets?

**d.** In the short run, how many firms leave the industry?

**e.** In the long run, what is the new price of widgets?

**f.** In the long run, how many firms leave the industry?

**N5.** In the widget industry, each firm has fixed costs of $10 and faces the following marginal cost curve:

| Quantity | Marginal Cost |
|---|---|
| 1 | $2 per widget |
| 2 | 4 |
| 3 | 5 |
| 4 | 7 |
| 5 | 11 |
| 6 | 13 |

The industry-wide demand curve is given by the following chart:

| Price | Quantity |
|---|---|
| $2 | 60 per widget |
| 4 | 48 |
| 5 | 36 |
| 7 | 24 |
| 11 | 12 |
| 13 | 0 |

Assume the industry is in long-run equilibrium.

**a.** What is the price of a widget?

**b.** What quantity is produced by each firm?

**c.** How many firms are in the industry?

Now suppose that the demand curve shifts outward as follows:

| Price | Quantity |
|---|---|
| $2 | 96 per widget |
| 4 | 84 |
| 5 | 72 |
| 7 | 60 |
| 11 | 48 |
| 13 | 36 |

**d.** In the short run, what is the new price of widgets, and how many does each firm produce?

**e.** In the long run, what is the new price of widgets and how many does each firm produce? How many firms will enter or leave the industry?

**N6.** In the gadget industry, each firm must have one gadget press, regardless of how many gadgets it produces. The cost of a gadget press is the only fixed cost that firms face in this industry. Entry by gadget firms can bid up the cost of gadget presses. The following charts show (1) the demand for gadgets; (2) the marginal cost of producing gadgets at each individual firm; and (3) the cost of a gadget press as a function of the number of firms in the industry:

| Price | Quantity Demanded |
|---|---|
| 1 | 800 |
| 2 | 700 |
| 3 | 600 |
| 4 | 500 |
| 5 | 400 |
| 6 | 300 |

| Quantity | Marginal Cost |
|---|---|
| 1 | $1 |
| 2 | 2 |
| 3 | 3 |
| 4 | 4 |
| 5 | 5 |
| 6 | 6 |

| Number of Firms | Cost of Gadget Press |
|---|---|
| 0–75 | $6 |
| 76–150 | 10 |
| 151–225 | 15 |
| 226–300 | 18 |
| >300 | 21 |

What is the long-run equilibrium price of gadgets? (*Hint:* Start by figuring out, for each price, the number of firms and the profits at each firm.)

**N7.** Kites are manufactured by identical firms. Each firm's long-run average and marginal costs of production are given by:

$$AC = Q + \frac{100}{Q} \text{ and } MC = 2Q$$

where $Q$ is the number of kites produced.

**a.** In long-run equilibrium, how many kites will each firm produce? Describe the long-run supply curve for kites.

**b.** Suppose that the demand for kites is given by the formula:

$$Q = 8,000 - 50P$$

where $Q$ is the quantity demanded and $P$ is the price. How many kites will be sold? How many firms will there be in the kite industry?

**c.** Suppose that the demand for kites unexpectedly goes up to:

$$Q = 9,000 - 50P$$

In the short run, it is impossible to manufacture any more kites than those already in existence. What will the price of kites be? How much profit will each kitemaker earn?

**d.** In the long run, what will the price of kites be? How many new firms will enter the kite-making industry? How much profit will they earn?

**N8.** Suppose that a law is passed requiring each kite maker to have one fire extinguisher on the premises. (These are the same kite makers we met in the preceding exercise.) The supply curve of fire extinguishers to kitemakers is

$$Q = P$$

For example, at a price of $3, 3 fire extinguishers would be provided. Suppose that the kite industry reaches a new long-run equilibrium.

**a.** Let $F$ be the number of firms in the kite industry. Explain why each now has long-run cost curves given by

$$AC = Q + \frac{100}{Q} + \frac{F}{Q} \text{ and } MC = 2Q$$

**b.** How many kites will each firm produce? (You will have to express your answer in terms of $F$.) How many kites will the entire industry produce? (Again, you will have to express your answer in terms of $F$.) What will the price of kites be?

**c.** If the price of kites is $P$, what is the number of firms $F$? How many kites will the industry produce in terms of $P$? Write a formula for the long-run industry supply curve.

**d.** Suppose, as in Exercise N6, that the demand for kites is

$$Q = 8,000 - 50P$$

What will be the price of kites? How many kites will be produced? By how many firms?

How much profit does each firm earn?

# Problem Set

**1.** Gus the cab driver rents a cab and pays for gas. In each of the following circumstances, describe the short-run effect on the price and quantity of rides Gus offers.

**a.** The price of gas falls.

**b.** The rental price of cabs falls.

**c.** Word gets out that Gus is a really lousy driver.

**d.** A new bus company opens up.

**e.** Gus gets the bill for the new upholstery he installed in his back seat last month and discovers it's 15% more than he expected.

**f.** The wages of factory workers go up, though this ends up having no effect on the demand for cab rides.

**g.** A huge fire destroys half the cabs in town, not including Gus's.

h.  The city imposes a $1 excise tax on cab rides, but exempts Gus from the tax because he is a good friend of the mayor.

i.  The city imposes a $100 annual license fee on cab drivers, but gives Gus a free license because he is a good friend of the mayor.

j.  The city starts a new free taxi service, which offers free rides to 500 customers per day.

k.  The city offers to subsidize gas purchases for every cab driver except Gus because he is a special enemy of the mayor.

l.  The city announces that it will start fining cab drivers who play loud music; Gus (unlike most cab drivers) loves loud music, so he has to pay a lot of fines.

m.  A customer who was almost killed by Gus's recklessness agrees to accept a large payment in exchange for keeping quiet about the incident.

2.  **True or False:** If a firm in a competitive industry discovers a cheaper way to produce output, it might lower its price in order to steal its competitors' customers.

3.  **True or False:** When price equals marginal cost, profit equals zero.

4.  **True or False:** In the short run, any firm earning a negative profit will shut down.

5.  In the Woody Allen film Radio Days, a character who has never been successful in business decides to start a career engraving gold jewelry. He argues that this should be especially lucrative, because the engraver gets to keep the gold dust from other people's jewelry. Comment.

6.  Books with many mathematical formulas are generally more expensive than similar books written entirely in prose. **True or False**: Because typesetting is not part of the marginal cost of producing a book, the cost of typesetting mathematical formulas cannot explain this price difference.

7.  **True or False:** In a competitive constant-cost industry, an excise tax is partly passed on to demanders in the short run but completely passed on to demanders in the long run.

8.  If New York City provides better shelters for the homeless, then in the long run homeless New Yorkers will be better off.

9.  The town of Whoville has 100 identical consumers and 50 identical car washes. Each consumer has an income of $24. The diagram and chart below show the

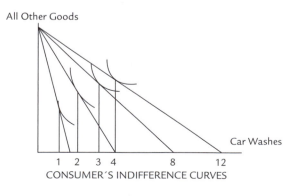

CONSUMER'S INDIFFERENCE CURVES

| Quantity | MC |
|---|---|
| 1 | $3 |
| 2 | 4 |
| 3 | 5 |
| 4 | 6 |
| 5 | 7 |
| 6 | 8 |
| 7 | 9 |
| 8 | 10 |

FIRM'S MARGINAL COSTS

indifference curves of a typical consumer and the marginal cost curve of a typical car wash.

    **a.** What is the price of a car wash today?

    **b.** Suppose that in the long run there is no entry or exit from the car wash industry. What can you conclude about the fixed costs at an individual car wash?

**10.** Redo all the parts of Problem 1, describing the long-run effects instead of the short-run effects. Assume that cab driving is a constant-cost industry.

**11.** Redo all the parts of Problem 1, describing the long-run effects instead of the short-run effects. Assume that cab driving is an increasing-cost industry.

**12.** Redo all the parts of Problem 1, describing the long-run effects instead of the short-run effects. Assume that cab driving is a decreasing-cost industry.

**13.** Suppose the government institutes a new sales tax on shoes, which are provided by a competitive constant-cost industry.

    **a.** Does the price of shoes change by more in the short run or in the long run?

    **b.** Does the industry-wide quantity change by more in the short run or in the long run?

    **c.** Does the quantity provided by each shoemaker change by more in the short run or in the long run?

    **d.** Do the profits of shoemakers change by more in the short run or in the long run?

**14.** Suppose that shoes are provided by a competitive constant-cost industry. Suppose the government starts requiring each shoemaker to pay an annual license fee.

    **a.** Does the price of shoes change by more in the short run or in the long run?

    **b.** Does the industry-wide quantity change by more in the short run or in the long run?

    **c.** Does the quantity provided by each shoemaker change by more in the short run or in the long run?

    **d.** Do the profits of shoemakers change by more in the short run or in the long run?

**15.** Suppose there is a fall in the demand for shoes, which are provided by a competitive constant-cost industry.

    **a.** Does the price of shoes change by more in the short run or in the long run?

    **b.** Does the industry-wide quantity change by more in the short run or in the long run?

    **c.** Does the quantity provided by each individual shoemaker change by more in the short run or in the long run?

    **d.** Do the profits of shoemakers change by more in the short run or in the long run?

**16.** Widgets are provided by a constant-cost industry. Each firm employs one executive and a variable number of workers. Consider the following two scenarios:

    **Scenario A.** Executive salaries rise, causing the price of a widget to rise by $5 in the long run.

    **Scenario B.** Workers' salaries rise, causing the price of a widget to rise by $5 in the long run.

Of the two scenarios, which leads to a larger quantity of *widgets per firm* in the long run?

17. Suppose the government imposes an excise tax of $10 per pair of shoes, but simultaneously launches a program of giving a gift of $10,000 per year to each shoestore.

   a. In the short run, what happens to the price of shoes, the number of shoes sold in total, and the number of shoes at any particular shoestore?

   b. Suppose that by coincidence, the long-run effect of the two programs combined is to return the price of shoes right back to its original level. In the long run, what happens to the number of shoes sold in total, the number sold at any given store, and the number of stores in the industry?

18. Suppose health clinics form a competitive constant-cost industry. One day, the government unexpectedly opens a new clinic, which treats 800 patients a day for free.

   a. In the short run, what happens to the number of patients served by private clinics? Does it rise or fall? By more or less than 800 per day?

   b. In the long run, what happens to the number of patients served by private clinics? Does it rise or fall? By more or less than 800 per day?

19. The widget industry is a constant-cost industry, so that all firms are identical. The following chart shows the industry-wide demand curve and the marginal cost curve of a typical firm:

| Industry-Wide Demand | | Firm's Marginal Cost Curve | |
|---|---|---|---|
| Price | Quantity | Quantity | Marginal Cost |
| $2 | 500 | 1 | $2 |
| 3 | 400 | 2 | 3 |
| 5 | 300 | 3 | 5 |
| 6 | 200 | 4 | 6 |
| 8 | 100 | 5 | 8 |
| 9 | 50 | 6 | 9 |
| 12 | 25 | 7 | 12 |
| 15 | 10 | 8 | 15 |

The industry is in long-run equilibrium and there are a hundred firms.

   a. What are the fixed costs at each firm?

   b. What is the price of a widget?

20. In Problem 19, suppose that the city imposes a license fee of $11 per firm.

   a. In the short run, what is the new price of a widget?

   b. In the long run, what is the new price of a widget?

   c. In the long run, how many firms leave the industry?

21. In problem 19, suppose the city imposes a sales tax of $6 per widget.

   a. In the short run, what is the new price of a widget?

   b. In the long run, what is the new price of a widget?

   c. In the long run, how many firms leave the industry?

**22.**    In Problem 19, suppose the city imposes an excise subsidy of $3 per widget. (That is, widget manufacturers receive $3 from the government for each widget they produce.)

    **a.**    In the short run, what is the new price of a widget?

    **b.**    In the long run, what is the new price of a widget?

    **c.**    In the long run, how many firms enter the industry?

**23.**    In Problem 19, suppose that the demand for widgets doubles (so that, for example, on the new demand curve, prices of $2, $3, and $5 go with quantities of 1,000, 800, and 600).

    **a.**    In the short run, what is the new price of a widget?

    **b.**    In the long run, what is the new price of a widget?

**24.**    Widgets are made only in America. They are provided by a constant-cost industry, which is in long-run equilibrium. The following charts show the American demand curve for widgets, the foreign demand curve for widgets, and the marginal cost curve of a typical American widget firm.

| American Demand | | Foreign Demand | | Firm's Marginal Cost Curve | |
|---|---|---|---|---|---|
| Price | Quantity | Price | Quantity | Quantity | Marginal Cost |
| $3 | 200 | $3 | 150 | 1 | $2 |
| 5 | 160 | 5 | 140 | 2 | 5 |
| 7 | 75 | 7 | 120 | 3 | 7 |
| 9 | 60 | 9 | 100 | 4 | 9 |
| 11 | 45 | 11 | 90 | 5 | 11 |
| 13 | 30 | 13 | 80 | 6 | 13 |
| 15 | 15 | 15 | 70 | 7 | 15 |
| 17 | 10 | 17 | 60 | 8 | 17 |

Initially, American firms are not allowed to sell to foreigners. (Thus, the foreign demand curve is irrelevant.) In the United States, the industry is in long-run equilibrium and widgets sell for $7 apiece. Now the government decides to issue 10 export licenses; a firm with an export license can sell as many widgets to foreigners as it wants to. The export licenses are sold at auction to the highest bidders.

    **a.**    What is the price of an American widget sold on the foreign market?

    **b.**    What is the price of an export license?

    **c.**    In the short run, what is the new price of a widget sold in America? Be sure to justify your answer.

    **d.**    In the long run, what is the new price of a widget sold in America?

    (*Hint*: A firm that can sell as much as it wants to foreigners at a high price will not choose to sell anything at all to Americans at a low price.)

**25.**    **True or False:** In the long run, profit-maximizing firms seek to minimize their average cost.

**26.**    Suppose the wholesale price of gasoline falls by 50¢ a gallon. Does the retail price fall by more than 50¢, by 50¢, or by less than 50¢?

a. Answer assuming that gas stations constitute a competitive constant-cost industry.

b. Answer assuming that gas stations constitute a competitive increasing-cost industry.

27. Upper, Middle, and Lower Slobbovia are distant countries that do not trade with each other or the rest of the world. In Upper Slobbovia, kites are provided by a competitive constant-cost industry. In Middle Slobbovia, kites are provided by a competitive increasing-cost industry. In Lower Slobbovia, kites are provided by a single monopolist. All three countries have just imposed a new tax on kite producers of $1,000 per firm per year. Rank the three countries in terms of what fraction of this tax is passed on to consumers in the long run. Justify your answer carefully.

28. **True or False:** An excise tax on the product of a decreasing-cost industry would raise the price by more than the amount of the tax.

29. Suppose the demand for seafood increases one year and then unexpectedly returns to its former level the following year. **True or False**: As soon as the demand returns to its former level, price and quantity will return to their former levels too.

# Welfare Economics and the Gains from Trade

Should some people be taxed to pay for other people's health care and education? If so, how much? Should the government subsidize purchases of home insulation? Should foreign goods be taxed to protect American workers and manufacturers?

Should governments pass laws to lower the prices of some goods and raise the prices of others? How do we know which policies are best for the economy?

The answer is that there is no answer, because there is no such thing as what's "best for the economy." Every policy you can imagine is good for some people and bad for others.

How then can you know which policies to support? Perhaps you're guided partly by self-interest. Or perhaps you prefer to balance your self-interest against what you think is fair and just for your fellow citizens.

But when a tax or a subsidy or a new law benefits some of those fellow citizens at the expense of others, how can you decide whether that policy is on net good or bad? What you need is a *normative criterion*—a way of balancing the benefits that accrue to some people against the costs that are imposed on others.

Economic theory can't tell you what your normative criterion should be. It can, however, suggest some candidates for normative criteria and help you understand what it would mean to adopt one criterion or another. In this chapter, we'll make a particularly detailed analysis of one candidate, called the *efficiency criterion.*

But before we can talk about weighing benefits against costs, we need a way of *measuring* benefits and costs. We'll start by measuring the gains from trade. When a consumer purchases a dozen eggs from a farmer, each is better off (or at least not worse off)—otherwise no trade would have occurred in the first place. The question we will address is: How *much* better off are they?

Once we know how to measure the gains from trade, we can ask how these gains are affected by various changes in market conditions. Such changes include taxes, price controls, subsidies, quotas, rationing, and so forth. We will be able to see who gains and who loses from such policies and to evaluate the size of these gains and losses.

Finally, we will learn one of the most remarkable facts in economics: In a competitive equilibrium, the sum of all the gains to all the market participants is as large as possible. This fact, called the *invisible hand theorem,* suggests one normative standard by which market outcomes can be judged. In the appendix to the chapter, we will compare this normative standard with a variety of alternatives.

# 8.1 Measuring the Gains from Trade

When a consumer buys eggs from a farmer, each one gains from the trade. Our first task is to measure the extent of these gains.

## Consumers' and Producers' Surplus

First we consider the gains to the consumer. We begin by developing a geometric measure of the value that the consumer places on his purchases.

### Marginal Value and Demand

Suppose you're so hungry that you're willing to pay up to $15 for an egg. Does it follow that you'd be willing to pay up to $30 for 2 eggs? Probably not. Once you've eaten your first egg, you might be willing to pay only $10 for a second, or, in other words, $25 total for 2 eggs.

**Marginal value**

The maximum amount a consumer would be willing to pay to acquire one additional item.

In this case we say that (to you) the marginal value of the first egg is $15 and the marginal value of the second is $10. The total value (again to you) of 1 egg is $15 and the total value of 2 eggs is $25.

In general, we expect the marginal value of your second egg to be less than the marginal value of your first, and the marginal value of your third egg to be even lower. Why? Because when you have only 1 egg, you put it to the most valuable use you can think of. Depending on your tastes, that might mean frying it for breakfast. When you have a second egg, you put it to the second most valuable use you can think of—maybe by making egg salad for lunch. Even if you combine your 2 eggs to make an omelet, it's reasonable to think that the second half of that omelet is worth less to you than the first half.

**Total value**

The maximum amount a consumer would be willing to pay to acquire a given quantity of items.

As you acquire more eggs, their marginal value continues to fall. Consider a consumer whose marginal values are given by Table A in Exhibit 8.1. If the market price is $7 per egg, how many eggs does this consumer buy? He certainly buys a first egg: He values it at $15 and can get it for $7. He also buys a second egg, which he values at $13 and can also get for $7. Likewise, he buys a third egg. The fourth egg, which he values at $7 and can buy for $7, is a matter of indifference; we will assume that the consumer buys this egg as well. The fifth egg would be a bad buy for our consumer; it provides only $5 worth of additional value and costs $7 to acquire. He buys 4 eggs.

---

**Exercise 8.1** Add to Table A in Exhibit 8.1 a "Net Gain" column displaying the difference between total value and total cost. Verify that the consumer is best off when he buys 4 eggs.

---

**Exercise 8.2** How many eggs does the consumer buy when the market price is $5 per egg? Explain why.

---

There is nothing new in this reasoning; it is just an application of the equimarginal principle. The consumer buys eggs as long as the marginal value of an egg exceeds its price and stops when the two become equal. In other words, he chooses that quantity at which price equals marginal value. In Table B of Exhibit 8.1 we record the number of eggs the consumer will purchase at each price. Table B is the consumer's demand

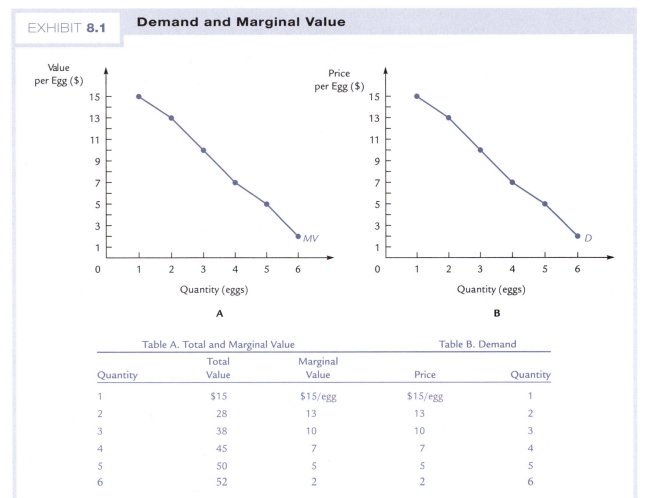

**EXHIBIT 8.1**    **Demand and Marginal Value**

|  | Table A. Total and Marginal Value | | Table B. Demand | |
|---|---|---|---|---|
| Quantity | Total Value | Marginal Value | Price | Quantity |
| 1 | $15 | $15/egg | $15/egg | 1 |
| 2 | 28 | 13 | 13 | 2 |
| 3 | 38 | 10 | 10 | 3 |
| 4 | 45 | 7 | 7 | 4 |
| 5 | 50 | 5 | 5 | 5 |
| 6 | 52 | 2 | 2 | 6 |

At a given market price the consumer will choose a quantity that equates price with marginal value. As a result, his demand curve for eggs is identical with his marginal value curve.

schedule, and the corresponding graph is a picture of his demand curve for eggs.[1] (Compare this reasoning with the derivation of Farmer Vickers's supply curve in Exhibit 7.4.)

The graphs in Exhibit 8.1 display both the consumer's marginal value curve and his demand curve for eggs. The curves are identical, although they differ conceptually. To read the marginal value curve, take a given quantity and read the corresponding marginal value off the vertical axis. To read the demand curve, take a given price and read the corresponding quantity off the horizontal axis.

Again, what we have learned is not new. The marginal value of an egg, measured in dollars, is the same thing as the consumer's marginal rate of substitution between

---

[1] More precisely, the graph is a picture of his *compensated* demand curve. When we talk about "willingness to pay" for an additional egg, we are asking what number of dollars the consumer could sacrifice for that egg and remain equally happy. The points on the marginal value curve all represent points on the same indifference curve for the consumer.

    All of the demand curves in this chapter are really compensated demand curves. However, the compensated and uncompensated demand curves coincide when income effects are small, so measurements using the ordinary (uncompensated) demand curve are good approximations for most purposes.

eggs and dollars: It is the number of dollars for which he would be just willing to trade an egg. In an indifference curve diagram between eggs and dollars, the marginal value is the slope of an indifference curve and the price is the slope of the budget line. We saw in Section 3.2 that the consumer's optimum occurs at a point where the marginal value is equal to the price and that this is the source of the consumer's demand curve.

## Total Value as an Area

Suppose the consumer of Exhibit 8.1 acquires 4 eggs. We would like to depict geometrically their total value. We begin by depicting the $15 in value represented by the first egg. This $15 is the area of rectangle 1 in panel A of Exhibit 8.2. The height of the rectangle is 15, and the width of the rectangle (which stretches from a quantity of 0 to a quantity of 1) is 1. Thus, the area is $15 \times 1 = 15$. The $13 in value that the consumer receives from the second egg is represented by rectangle 2 in the same graph. The height of this rectangle is 13 and its width is 1, so its area is $13 \times 1 = 13$.

The area of rectangle 3 is the marginal value of the third egg, and the area of rectangle 4 is the marginal value of the fourth egg. The total value of the 4 eggs is the sum of the 4 marginal values, or the total area of the 4 rectangles. That is, the total value is $(15 + 13 + 10 + 7) = $45$.

Actually, what we have done is only approximately correct. That is because the marginal value table in Exhibit 8.1 omits some information. It does not show the value of 11/2 eggs or 31/4 eggs, for example.[2] In order to consider such quantities, we might make our measurements not in *eggs,* but in *quarter-eggs.* If we do so, the quantity of quarter-eggs bought is 16, and the four rectangles of panel A of Exhibit 8.2 are replaced by the 16 rectangles of panel B, each one-quarter as wide as the original ones. Refining things even further, we could measure quantities in hundredth-eggs, making 400 rectangles. As our fundamental units get smaller, our approximation to the total value of 4 eggs gets better. The total value of the consumer's 4 eggs is exactly equal to the shaded area in panel C.

The total value of the consumer's purchases is equal to the area under the demand curve out to the quantity demanded.[3]

Dangerous
Curve

The total value of 4 eggs is completely independent of their market price. Imagine offering the consumer a choice of living in two worlds, both identical except for the fact that in one world he has no eggs and in the other he has 4 eggs. Ask him what is the most he would be willing to pay to live in the second world rather than the first. His answer to that question is the total value that he places on 4 eggs.

---

[2] You might think it is impossible to buy just one-quarter of an egg, but this is not so. Remember that every demand curve has a unit of time implicitly associated with it. If our demand curves are *per week,* then the way to buy exactly one-quarter of an egg per week is to buy one every four weeks.

[3] If you have had a course in calculus, you might be interested to know that we have just "proven" the fundamental theorem of calculus! Think of total value as a function (where quantity is the variable). The marginal value is the addition to total value when quantity is increased by one small unit. In other words, marginal value is the derivative of total value. The area under the marginal value curve out to a given quantity is the integral of marginal value from zero out to that quantity. We have argued that this integral is equal to the total value associated with that quantity. In other words, integrating the derivative brings you back to the original function.

Perhaps you knew the fundamental theorem of calculus but always accepted it as a mysterious fact of nature. If so, thinking about the economics of total and marginal values should give you some real insight into why the fundamental theorem is true.

EXHIBIT **8.2**    **Total Value**

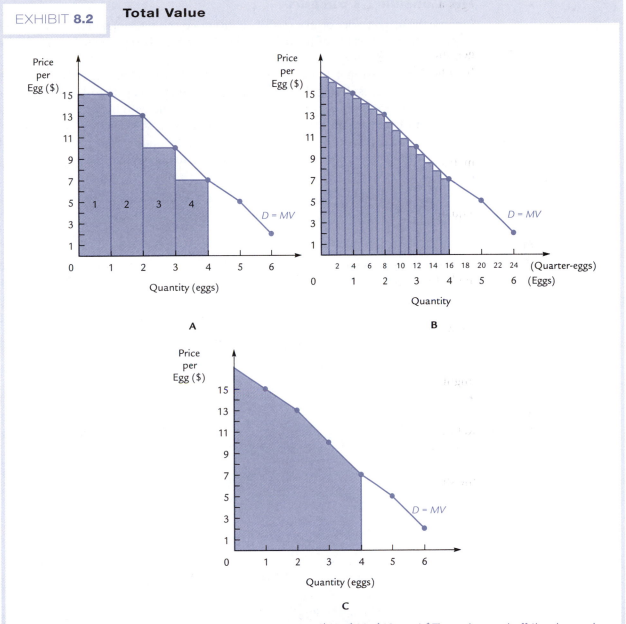

A

B

C

When the consumer buys 4 eggs, their marginal values ($15, $13, $10, and $7) can be read off the demand curve. Their values are represented by the areas of rectangles 1 through 4 in panel A. Therefore, their total value is the sum of the areas of the rectangles, or $45.

We can get a more accurate estimate of total value if we measure eggs in smaller units. Panel B shows the calculation of total value when we measure by the quarter-egg instead of by the whole egg. As we take smaller and smaller units, we approach the shaded area in panel C, which is the exact measure of total value when the consumer buys 4 eggs.

## The Consumer's Surplus

Suppose the market price of an egg is $7. At this price, the consumer of Exhibit 8.1 buys 4 eggs, with a total value of (approximately) $45, which is represented by the entire shaded area in Exhibit 8.3.[4]

When the consumer buys those eggs, his total expenditure is only 4 × $7 = $28—a bargain, considering that he'd have been willing to pay up to $45. That $28 is represented in Exhibit 8.3 by area *B*, which is a rectangle with height 7 and width 4. The extent of the bargain is measured by the difference $45 − $28 = $17, which is area *A*. We call that area the consumer's surplus in the market for eggs. It is the total value (to him) of the eggs he buys, minus what he actually pays for them. In summary, we have:

**Consumer's surplus**

The consumer's gain from trade; the amount by which the value of his purchases exceeds what he actually pays for them.

| Total Value | = | A + B | = | $45 |
|---|---|---|---|---|
| Expenditure | = | B | = | $28 |
| Consumer's Surplus | = | A | = | $17 |

This consumer would be willing to pay up to $17 for a ticket to enter a grocery store where he can buy eggs. If the store lets him in for free, it's as if the consumer has received a gift (i.e., a free admission ticket) that he valued at $17. You can think of the consumer's surplus as the value of that gift. Geometrically, we have seen that

The consumer's surplus is the area under the demand curve down to the price paid and out to the quantity demanded.

**EXHIBIT 8.3    The Consumer's Surplus**

In order to acquire 4 eggs, the consumer would be willing to pay up to the entire shaded area, *A* + *B*. At a price of $7 per egg, his actual expenditure for 4 eggs is $28, which is area *B*. The difference, area *A*, is his consumer's surplus.

---

[4] $45 is the area of the four rectangles in Exhibit 8.2A, which is approximately the same as the shaded regions in Exhibits 8.2C and 8.3. The approximation is good enough that from now on, we will say that the area of the shaded region is $45.

WELFARE ECONOMICS AND THE GAINS FROM TRADE

Dangerous
Curve

Notice that the consumer's surplus is measured in units of *dollars*. In general, horizontal distances represent *quantities,* vertical distances represent *prices* (in units of, for example, dollars per egg), and areas represent numbers of *dollars.*

## The Producer's Surplus

The consumer is not the only party to a transaction and not the only one to gain from it. We can also calculate the *producer's* gains from trade. Imagine a producer with the marginal cost curve shown in Exhibit 8.4. Suppose that this producer supplies 4 eggs to the marketplace. What is the cost of supplying these 4 eggs? It is the sum of the marginal cost of supplying the first egg ($1), the marginal cost of the second ($3), the marginal cost of the third ($5), and the marginal cost of the fourth ($7). These numbers are represented by the 4 rectangles in panel A of Exhibit 8.4. Their heights are 1, 3, 5, and 7, and they each have width 1.

As with the consumer's total value, we must realize that the rectangles of panel A provide only an approximation, because we are making the faulty assumption that eggs can be produced only in whole-number quantities. A more accurate picture would include very thin rectangles, and the sum of their areas would be the area labeled *D* in the second panel. This is the cost of providing 4 eggs.[5] Area *D* is approximately equal to $ (1 + 3 + 5 + 7) = $16.

**EXHIBIT 8.4** **The Producer's Surplus**

If the producer supplies 4 eggs, his cost is the sum of the 4 marginal costs, which are represented by the rectangles in panel A. If we measure eggs in very small units, we find that an exact measure of his cost is area *D* in panel B. At a market price of $7, revenue is $7 × 4 = $28, which is the area of rectangle *C* + *D*. Thus, the producer's surplus is area *C*.

---

[5] By adding up the producer's marginal costs, we are excluding any fixed costs that the producer might have. This is because we are considering only how the producer is affected by trade, whereas the producer would incur the fixed costs even without trading. This makes the fixed costs irrelevant to the discussion.

Next we depict the producer's total revenue. This is easy: He sells 4 eggs at $7 apiece, so his revenue is $4 \times \$7 = \$28$, which is the area of the rectangle $C + D$ in Exhibit 8.4.

Now we can compute the producer's gains from trade: Total revenues are $C + D$ and production costs are $D$. The difference, area $C$, is called the **producer's surplus** and represents the gains to the producer as a result of his participation in the marketplace. In this example, we have

| Total Revenue | = | $C + D$ | = | $28 |
|---|---|---|---|---|
| − Production Costs | = | $D$ | = | $16 |
| Producer's Surplus | = | $C$ | = | $12 |

This producer would be willing to pay up to $12 for a license to sell eggs. If no license is required, it's as if the producer has received a gift (i.e., a free license) that he valued at $12. You can think of the producer's surplus as the value of that gift.

If the producer is competitive, his marginal cost curve can be identified with his supply curve. Therefore:

The producer's surplus is the area above the supply curve up to the price received and out to the quantity supplied.

For a noncompetitive producer, we would want to change *supply curve* to *marginal cost curve* in the preceding sentence, but for a competitive producer these are the same thing.

## Social Gain

In panel A of Exhibit 8.5 we have drawn both the supply and the demand curve on the same graph. The consumer's surplus is taken from Exhibit 8.3 and the producer's surplus is taken from Exhibit 8.4.

The consumer's and producer's surpluses depicted in Exhibit 8.5 provide a measure of the gains to both parties. Their sum is called the **social gain,** or **welfare gain,** due to the existence of the market. Students sometimes want to know where these gains are coming from: If the consumer and the producer have both gained, then who has lost? The answer is *nobody.* The process of trade creates welfare gains, which simply did not exist before the trading took place. The fact that the world as a whole can be made better off should not strike you as surprising: Imagine the total value of all the goods in the world 100 years ago and compare it with the value of what you see around you today. In a very real sense the difference can be thought of as the sum of all the little triangles of surplus that have been created by consumers and producers over the passage of time.

There is another way to measure the welfare gains created by the marketplace. Rather than separately computing a consumer's surplus and a producer's surplus, we can calculate the total welfare gain created by each egg. This is shown in panel B of Exhibit 8.5. The first rectangle represents the difference between the marginal value of the first egg and the marginal cost of producing it, which is precisely the welfare gain due to that egg. The height of the rectangle is $15 - 1 = 14$, and its width is 1, giving an area of 14. The second rectangle has a height of $13 - 3 = 10$ and a width of 1, giving an area of 10, which is the welfare gain from the second egg. The welfare gain due to the exchange of 4 eggs is the sum of the 4 rectangles (the fourth "rectangle" has height zero!). As usual, our focus on whole numbers has forced us to approximate: The total welfare gain is actually the entire shaded area between the supply and demand curves out to the equilibrium point.

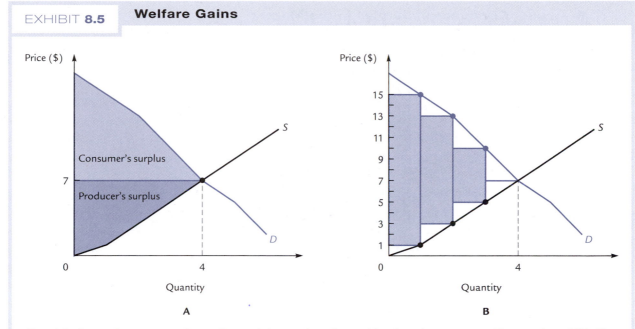

**EXHIBIT 8.5**    **Welfare Gains**

Panel A shows the consumer's surplus and the producer's surplus when 4 eggs are sold at a price of $7. The sum of these areas is the total welfare gain. The second panel shows another way to calculate the welfare gain. The first egg creates a gain equal to the area of the first rectangle, the second creates a gain equal to the area of the second rectangle, and so on. When units are taken to be small, the sum of these areas is the shaded region, which is the sum of the consumer's and producer's surpluses.

Notice that the total welfare gain (shown in panel B) is the sum of the consumer's and producer's surpluses (shown in panel A). This is as it should be: All of the gains have to go somewhere, and there are only the consumer and the producer to collect them.

## Social Gains and Markets

Next we want to consider markets with more than one consumer and with more than one producer. It turns out that consumers' and producers' surpluses can again be computed in exactly the same way.

Imagine a world with three consumers: Larry, Moe, and Curly. Exhibit 8.6 displays each man's marginal value schedule for eggs. In this world, when the price is $15, Larry buys 1 egg and Moe and Curly each buy 0 eggs. The total quantity demanded is 1. At a price of $13, Larry and Moe buy 1 each and Curly buys 0; the quantity demanded is 2. At a price of $11, Larry buys 1, Moe buys 2, and Curly buys 0 for a total of 3, and so on. The resulting demand curve is also shown in Exhibit 8.6.

The rectangles below the demand curve represent the marginal values of the eggs that are bought. Each rectangle is labeled with the name of the man who consumes the corresponding egg: The first egg sold is bought by Larry, the second and third by Moe, the fourth by Larry, the fifth and sixth by Curly.

Now suppose that the price of eggs is $7. How many eggs are sold, and what is their total value? Larry buys 2 (the first and fourth), Moe buys 2 (the second and third), and Curly buys 1 (the fifth). The values of these eggs are given by the areas of the

EXHIBIT **8.6**          **Consumers' Surplus in the Market**

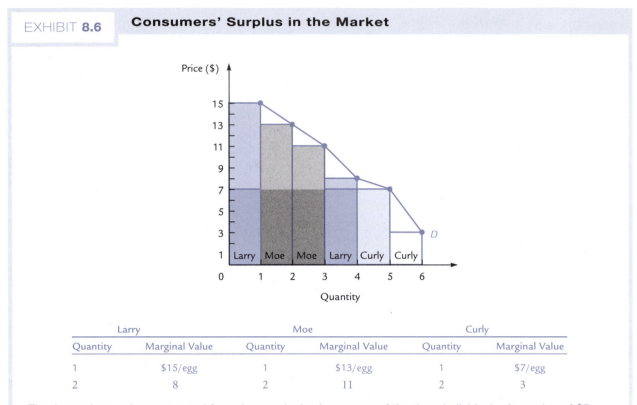

| Larry | | Moe | | Curly | |
|---|---|---|---|---|---|
| Quantity | Marginal Value | Quantity | Marginal Value | Quantity | Marginal Value |
| 1 | $15/egg | 1 | $13/egg | 1 | $7/egg |
| 2 | 8 | 2 | 11 | 2 | 3 |

The demand curve is constructed from the marginal value curves of the three individuals. At a price of $7, Larry buys 2 eggs that he values at $15 and $8, Moe buys 2 that he values at $13 and $11, and Curly buys 1 that he values at $7. These marginal values are represented by the first 5 rectangles under the demand curve, each labeled with the appropriate consumer's name. The total value of the 5 eggs to the consumers is the sum of the areas of the first 5 rectangles. The cost to the consumers is the darker area. The consumers' surplus is what remains; it is the area under the demand curve down to the price paid and out to the quantity purchased.

corresponding rectangles, and the total value to the consumers is the sum of the 5 areas, which are shaded in Exhibit 8.6. From this must be subtracted the total amount that the consumers pay for the 5 eggs, which is represented by the darker, lower portions of the rectangles. The remaining portion, above the $7 price line, is the consumers' surplus. The consumers' surplus is composed of many rectangles, and each consumer receives some of these rectangles as his share of the welfare gain. But, just as before, the total consumers' surplus is represented by the area under the demand curve down to the price paid and out to the quantity demanded.

An analogous statement holds for producers' surplus. Suppose that three different firms have the marginal cost schedules shown in Exhibit 8.7. The total supply curve is given by the graph. The colored rectangles corresponding to individual eggs are labeled with the names of the firms that produce them. Producers' surplus is given by total revenue (the entire shaded region) *minus* the sum of the areas of these rectangles, out to the quantity produced. That is, the producers' surplus is the gray part of the shaded region in the exhibit. This surplus is divided up among the producers, but the total of all the producers' surplus is still given by the area above the supply curve up to the price received and out to the quantity supplied.

| EXHIBIT 8.7 | Producers' Surplus in the Market |
|---|---|

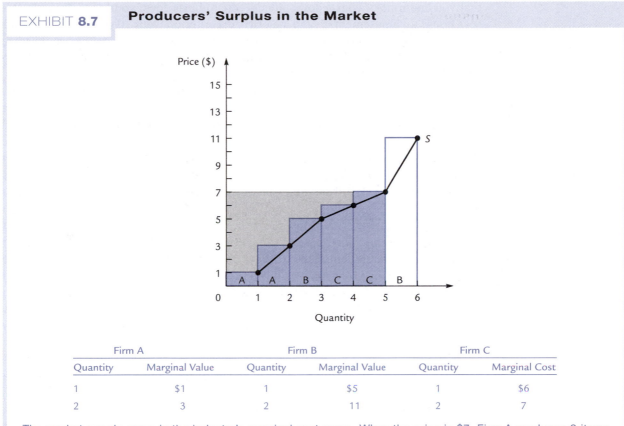

| Firm A | | Firm B | | Firm C | |
|---|---|---|---|---|---|
| Quantity | Marginal Value | Quantity | Marginal Value | Quantity | Marginal Cost |
| 1 | $1 | 1 | $5 | 1 | $6 |
| 2 | 3 | 2 | 11 | 2 | 7 |

The market supply curve is the industry's marginal cost curve. When the price is $7, Firm A produces 2 items at marginal costs of $1 and $3, Firm B produces 1 at a marginal cost of $5, and Firm C produces 2 at marginal costs of $6 and $7. These costs are represented by the colored rectangles below the supply curve. The revenue earned by producers is the entire shaded region. The gray portion of that region above the supply curve is the producers' surplus.

## 8.2 The Efficiency Criterion

Suppose the government decides to impose a sales tax on coffee and give away the tax revenue (say, as welfare payments or Social Security payments). Is that a good or a bad policy?

Both coffee drinkers and coffee sellers will tend to oppose this policy, because a sales tax simultaneously raises the price to demanders and lowers the price to suppliers. On the other hand, the citizens who are slated to receive the tax revenue will tend to favor the policy. How should we weigh the interests of one group against those of another?

A **normative criterion** is a general method for making this sort of decision. One example of a normative criterion is *majority rule:* Every citizen gets one vote to cast for or against the tax, and we bow to the will of the majority. In this case, the tax will probably be defeated if the coffee buyers and coffee sellers outnumber the tax recipients, and the tax will probably pass if the tax recipients outnumber the buyers and sellers.

One problem with the majority rule criterion is that it allows the slight preference of a majority to overrule the strong preference of a minority. For example, suppose

**Normative criterion**

A general method for choosing among alternative social policies.

that you and nine of your fellow students vote to burn down your economics professor's house for amusement. By the majority rule criterion, your 10 votes in favor of this activity outweigh the professor's 1 vote against. Nevertheless, most people would agree that burning down the house is a bad thing to do. So there is apparently something wrong with unrestricted majority rule.

An alternative to majority rule is the efficiency criterion. According to the efficiency criterion, everyone is permitted to cast a number of votes proportional to his stake in the outcome, where your stake in the outcome is measured by how much you'd be willing to pay to get your way. So, for example, if 10 students each think it would be worth $10 to watch the professor's house go up in flames, while the professor thinks it would be worth $1,000 to prevent that outcome, then each of the students gets 10 votes and the professor gets 1,000 votes. The house burning is defeated by a vote of 1,000 to 100.

**Efficiency criterion**

A normative criterion according to which your votes are weighted according to your willingness to pay for your preferred outcome.

Is that the right outcome? Most people seem to think so, for several reasons. Here's one of those reasons: The house burning essentially takes $1,000 from the professor in order to give the students $100 worth of enjoyment. But as long as you're willing to take $1,000 from the professor, wouldn't it make more sense to take it in cash, hand out $100 to the students (making them just as happy as the house burning would), and then have $900 left over to do more good? You could, for example, give even more money to the students, give some back to the professor, or give it all to someone else, or any combination of those things.

The house burning is *inefficient* in the sense that it takes $1,000 worth of house, converts it into $100 worth of pleasure, and effectively throws $900 away. The efficiency criterion says precisely that this kind of inefficiency is a bad thing.

One advantage of the efficiency criterion is that when it is applied consistently, you'll have the most influence on the issues you care about the most. In the appendix to this chapter, we will consider several alternatives to the efficiency criterion. In this section, we will explore the consequences of accepting the efficiency criterion and applying it to evaluate public policies. This will enable us to judge various policies—such as the sales tax on coffee—to be either "good" or "bad" *as judged by the efficiency criterion*. Of course, it does not follow that those policies are necessarily either good or bad in a larger sense. The efficiency criterion is one possible method of choosing among policies, and it is a method that you might come either to approve or disapprove.

To help you decide whether you like the efficiency criterion, it will be useful to see what it recommends in a variety of specific circumstances. That's what we'll do in this section.

## Consumers' Surplus and the Efficiency Criterion

Suppose that we are deciding whether it should be legal to produce, sell, and buy eggs. Among the parties who will be interested in the outcome of this debate are the people who like to eat eggs for breakfast. They'll want to vote for legal egg sales. How many votes should we give them?

The answer, according to the efficiency criterion, is that they should receive votes in proportion to their willingness to pay for the right to buy eggs. That willingness to pay is measured by the consumers' surplus. For example, consider the consumer depicted back in Exhibit 8.3; this consumer receives a number of votes proportional to area *A*.

If we want to know how many votes should be allocated to *all* egg consumers (as opposed to the *single* egg consumer of Exhibit 8.3), we can use the market demand curve to measure the total consumers' surplus. For example, suppose the area under the market demand curve, out to the quantity of eggs consumed and down to the market price of eggs, is equal to $10,000. Then we know that egg consumers *as a group* should receive 10,000 pro-egg votes. (In other words, each consumer receives a number of votes proportional to his individual consumer's surplus, and we know that the sum of all these numbers is 10,000.)

Likewise, we can use the producers' surplus to compute the number of pro-egg votes cast by egg producers. If there are any anti-egg votes (say, from people who hate living next door to chicken farms), their number is a bit harder to calculate in practice. But in principle, the farmer's neighbors get a number of votes proportional to what they would be willing to pay to make the chickens go away. (The easiest case is the case where there are no unhappy neighbors; then there might be *zero* votes in favor of banning egg production.)

## The Effect of a Sales Tax

Now let's return to the issue of a sales tax on coffee and evaluate that policy according to the efficiency criterion.

Panel A of Exhibit 8.8 shows the supply and demand for coffee. Panel B shows the same market after a 5¢-per-cup sales tax is placed on consumers. As we know from Chapter 1, this has the effect of lowering the demand curve vertically a distance of 5¢.

Before the sales tax is imposed, the consumers' and producers' surpluses are as shown in panel A. The sum of these is the total welfare gained by all members of society, and we will refer to it as the *social gain*. In terms of the areas in panel B, we have:

| | | |
|---|---|---|
| Consumers' Surplus | = | $A + B + C + D + E$ |
| Producers' Surplus | = | $F + G + H + I$ |
| Social Gain | = | $A + B + C + D + E + F + G + H + I$ |

Once the sales tax is imposed, we need to recompute the consumers' and producers' surpluses. The consumers' surplus is the area below the demand curve down to the price paid and out to the quantity demanded. The question now arises: Which demand curve? The answer is: The original demand curve, because this is the curve that reflects the consumers' true marginal values. Which price? The price paid by demanders: $P_d$. Which quantity? The quantity that is bought when the tax is in effect: $Q'$. The consumers' surplus is area $A + B$.

In other words, the sales tax causes the consumers' surplus to fall by the amount $C + D + E$. Thus, consumers would collectively be willing to pay up to $C + D + E$ to prevent the tax, and we will eventually allow them to cast $C + D + E$ votes against it.

What about producers' surplus? We need to look at the area above the supply curve up to the price received and out to the quantity supplied. The relevant price to suppliers is $P_s$, and the relevant quantity is the quantity being sold in the presence of the sales tax: $Q'$. The producers' surplus is $I$. The tax costs producers $F + G + H$, so we will allow them to cast $F + G + H$ votes against the tax.

We can now make the following tabulation:

| | Before Sales Tax | After Sales Tax |
|---|---|---|
| Consumers' Surplus | $A + B + C + D + E$ | $A + B$ |
| Producers' Surplus | $F + G + H + I$ | $I$ |
| Social Gain | $A + B + C + D + E$ $+ F + G + H + I$ | ? |

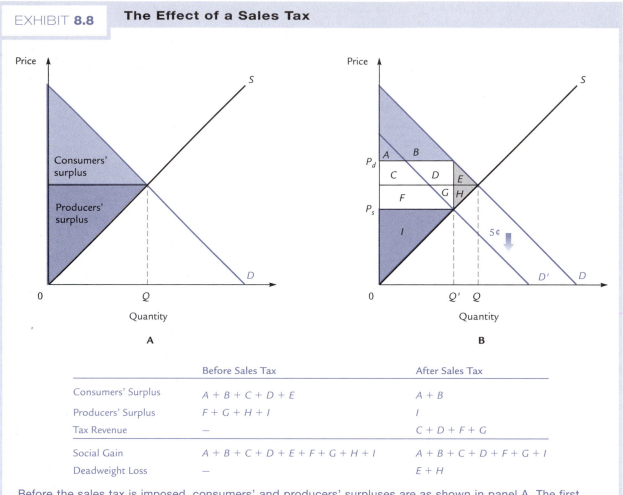

**EXHIBIT 8.8    The Effect of a Sales Tax**

|                     | Before Sales Tax                        | After Sales Tax                     |
|---------------------|-----------------------------------------|-------------------------------------|
| Consumers' Surplus  | $A + B + C + D + E$                      | $A + B$                             |
| Producers' Surplus  | $F + G + H + I$                          | $I$                                 |
| Tax Revenue         | —                                       | $C + D + F + G$                     |
| Social Gain         | $A + B + C + D + E + F + G + H + I$      | $A + B + C + D + F + G + I$         |
| Deadweight Loss     | —                                       | $E + H$                             |

Before the sales tax is imposed, consumers' and producers' surpluses are as shown in panel A. The first column of the chart shows these surpluses in terms of the labels in panel B. The second column shows the gains to consumers and producers after the imposition of the sales tax and includes a row for the gains to the recipients of the tax revenue. The total social gain after the tax is less than the social gain before the tax. The difference between the two is area $E + H$, the deadweight loss.

What about the social gain after the sales tax is imposed? Can't we find it by simply adding the consumers' and producers' surpluses? The answer is no, because there is now an additional component to consider. We must ask what becomes of the tax revenue that is collected by the government. The simplest assumption is that it is given to somebody (perhaps as a welfare or Social Security payment). Alternatively, it might be spent to purchase goods and services that are then given to somebody. In some form or another, some individual (or group of individuals) ultimately collects the tax revenue, and that individual is part of society. The revenue that the recipients collect is welfare gained.

How much tax revenue is there? The answer: It is equal to the tax per cup (5¢) times the number of cups sold ($Q'$). Because the vertical distance between the two demand curves is 5¢, the amount of this revenue is equal to the area of the rectangle $C + D + F + G$ (height = 5¢, width = $Q'$). The recipients of the tax revenue gain $C + D + F + G$

as a result of the tax, and so will be allowed to cast $C + D + F + G$ votes in its favor. The final version of our table is this:

|  | Before Sales Tax | After Sales Tax |
|---|---|---|
| Consumers' Surplus | $A + B + C + D + E$ | $A + B$ |
| Producers' Surplus | $F + G + H + I$ | $I$ |
| Tax Revenue | — | $C + D + F + G$ |
| Social Gain | $A + B + C + D + E$ $+ F + G + H + I$ | $A + B + C + D + F$ $+ G + I$ |

The social gain entry is obtained by adding the entries in the preceding three rows. Even after the tax revenue is taken into account, the total gain to society is still less after the tax than it was before. The reduction in total gain is called the deadweight loss due to the tax. In this example, the deadweight loss is equal to the area $E + H$. Other terms for the deadweight loss are *social loss, welfare loss,* and *efficiency loss.*

Let's tabulate the votes for and against this tax. Consumers cast $C + D + E$ votes against; producers cast $F + G + H$ votes against, and the recipients of tax revenue cast $C + D + F + G$ votes in favor. The tax is defeated by a margin of $E + H$ votes, so, according to the efficiency criterion, the tax is a bad thing.

It is no coincidence that the margin of defeat ($E + H$) is equal to the deadweight loss. The efficiency criterion always recommends the policy that creates the greatest social gain. If an alternative policy creates a smaller social gain, the difference is equal to the deadweight loss from that policy *and* to the margin by which that policy loses in the election prescribed by the efficiency criterion.

**Deadweight loss**

A reduction in social gain.

---

In doing the computations, we have considered three separate groups: consumers, producers, and the recipients of tax revenue. Some individuals might belong to two or even all three of these groups. A seller of coffee might also be a drinker of coffee; a drinker of coffee might be one of the group of people to whom the government gives the tax proceeds. Such an individual receives shares of more than one of the areas in the graph. Someone who both supplies and demands coffee will get a piece of the producers' surplus in his role as a producer and a piece of the consumers' surplus in his role as a consumer. Nevertheless, we keep track of the consumers' and producers' surpluses separately.

---

Dangerous
Curve

## The Hidden and Nonhidden Assumptions

Our rejection of the sales tax is based on several hidden assumptions. First, we assumed that in the absence of the sales tax, the market price would be determined by the intersection of supply and demand. (We used this assumption when we computed the consumers' and producers' surpluses in the "no tax" column.) Although that assumption holds in competitive markets, we will see in Chapter 10 that it need *not* hold when there are firms with monopoly power.

Second, we assumed that the government simply gives away the tax revenue, as opposed to using it for some purpose that is even more valuable. We used this assumption when we entered the value of tax revenue at $C + D + F + G$. That's the amount of revenue *collected,* and it's certainly still the value of the revenue if it's simply given away. But if, for example, $C + D + F + G = \$100$, and if the government uses that $100 to construct a post office that has a value of $300 (measured by people's willingness to pay for the post office), then our calculation of social gain in the "after sales tax" column is off by $200. In Chapter 14, we will discuss the circumstances in which governments might be able to spend money more efficiently than individuals can.

Third, we assumed that the production and consumption of coffee does not affect anyone but the producers and consumers. But suppose that coffee producers use heavy machinery that keeps their neighbors awake at night or that coffee drinkers use styrofoam cups that they throw by the roadside when they're done. Then there should be additional rows in our chart to reflect the concerns of sleep-deprived neighbors and Sunday motorists who prefer not to confront other people's litter. By omitting these rows, we assumed that there are no significant concerns of this kind. In Chapter 13, we will discuss how to incorporate such concerns in the analysis.

In addition to these hidden assumptions, we have made the nonhidden assumption that the efficiency criterion is an appropriate way to judge a policy. If any one of these assumptions is violated, we might need to reconsider the desirability of the sales tax on coffee.

## Understanding Deadweight Loss

Exhibit 8.9 presents another view of the deadweight loss. The prices and quantities are the same as in panel B of Exhibit 8.8. At the original equilibrium quantity $Q$, the social gain is the sum of all the rectangles. At $Q'$, which is the quantity with the tax, the social gain consists of only the color rectangles. The next cup of coffee after $Q'$ would increase welfare if it were produced, because the marginal value it provides (read off the demand curve) exceeds the marginal cost of producing it (read off the supply curve). However, that cup is not produced and an opportunity to add to welfare is lost.

**Deadweight Loss**

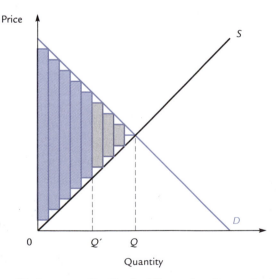

If the market operates at the equilibrium quantity $Q$, all of the rectangles are included in the social gain. If for any reason the market operates at the quantity $Q'$ (e.g., because of a tax), then only the color rectangles are included. The units of output that could create the gray rectangles are never produced, and those rectangles of gain are never created. The gray rectangles, representing gains that could have been created but weren't, constitute the deadweight loss.

The deadweight loss calculated in Exhibit 8.9 is the same as the deadweight loss calculated in Exhibit 8.8, where it corresponds to the area $E + H$.

If we think of the social gain as a pie divided among various groups, then a tax has two effects: It changes the way the pie is distributed, and it simultaneously changes the size of the entire pie. Thus, in Exhibit 8.8, the pie originally consists of all the lettered areas. The tax reduces the consumers' and producers' pieces. On the other hand, the recipients of the tax revenue, who get nothing in the absence of the tax, now receive a piece of the pie. After adding up everyone's pieces, we find that the total pie has shrunk; the losses to the losers exceed the gains to the winners. The shrinkage in the pie is the deadweight loss.

Dangerous Curve

The deadweight loss is *not* due in any way to the costs of collecting the tax. We have been assuming that these costs are negligible. If, in fact, it is necessary to hire tax collectors, to provide them with office space, and to buy them computers, or if it is costly for citizens to compute their taxes or to deliver them to the government, these are additional losses that are not included in our computation of the deadweight loss.

**Exercise 8.3** In Exhibit 8.8 how much does each group of losers lose? How much does each group of winners win? Is the excess of losses over gains equal to the deadweight loss?

A moral of this story is that "taxes are bad"—though not in the sense you might think. You might think that taxes are bad because paying them makes you poorer. True, but collecting them makes somebody else richer. In Exhibit 8.8 the areas $C + D + F + G$ that are paid in taxes do end up in somebody's pocket. Whether this is a good thing or a bad thing depends on whose pocket you care about most. The aspect of the tax that is unambiguously "bad" is the deadweight loss. This is a loss to consumers and producers that is not offset by a gain to anybody.

**Exercise 8.4** Work out the effects of an *excise* tax of 5¢ per cup of coffee. (*Hint:* We already know that an excise tax has exactly the same effects as a sales tax, so you will know your answer is right if it gives exactly the same results as in Exhibit 8.8.)

Whenever a policy creates a deadweight loss, it is possible to imagine an alternative policy that would be better for everybody. Exhibit 8.10 revisits the effect of a 5¢ sales tax. The tax costs consumers the amount $C + D + E$, costs producers the amount $F + G + H$, and delivers $C + D + F + G$ to the tax recipients.

Suppose that *instead* of the 5¢ sales tax, we adopt the following plan: One night, without warning, the tax collector breaks into the homes of the consumers and steals a total of $C + D + E$ dollars from their dresser drawers; then he breaks into the homes of the producers and steals a total of $F + G + H$. As far as the consumers and producers are concerned, this is neither better nor worse than being taxed. The tax collector then gives $C + D + F + G$ dollars to the tax recipients—the same amount they'd have received in tax revenue. The tax collector now has $E + H$ dollars left over to do some additional good with. The collector can return part of it to the consumers and producers, give part of it to the tax recipients, give part of it to charity, keep part of it, or do any combination of these things. If he wants to, he can give *everyone* a small sliver of that $E + H$ and make *everyone* better off.

By eliminating the deadweight loss of $E + H$ dollars, the tax collector can do exactly an additional $E + H$ dollars worth of good. This isn't too surprising: When there's more surplus to go around, we can always find a way to increase everyone's share. Or in other words: When the pie is bigger, you can always give everyone a bigger piece.

## EXHIBIT 8.10  Eliminating Deadweight Loss

|  | No Tax | With Sales Tax |
|---|---|---|
| Consumers' Surplus | $A + B + C + D + E$ | $A + B$ |
| Producer's Surplus | $F + G + H + I$ | $I$ |
| Tax Revenue | — | $C + D + F + G$ |
| Social Gain | $A + B + C + D + E + F$ $+ G + H + I$ | $A + B + C + D$ $+ F + G + I$ |
| Deadweight Loss | — | $E + H$ |

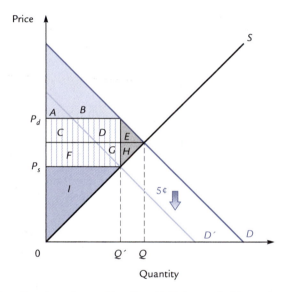

The sales tax costs consumers $C + D + E$ and producers $F + G + H$. If, instead of imposing a sales tax, the collector simply steals these amounts from the consumers and the producers, he can give $C + D + F + G$ to the tax recipients (just as they'd receive under the sales tax) and still have $E + H$ left over to do some additional good.

Dangerous
Curve

An important feature of our alternative policy is that it is totally unexpected and nobody can do anything to avoid it. If people know in advance, for example, that the tax collector will be stealing from all producers of coffee, the producers will react to this as they would to a tax and produce less. Their exact reaction will depend on the collector's exact policy: If he steals more from those who produce more, he is effectively imposing an excise tax, which causes each firm to reduce its quantity. If he steals equally from all producers, the main effect will be to drive some producers out of the industry altogether.

When people anticipate the collector's actions, they will take steps to avoid them. These steps will include producing and consuming less coffee, and this will create a deadweight loss. The only way to avoid a deadweight loss is for the market to produce the equilibrium quantity of coffee, and this happens only if nobody is given a chance to alter his or her behavior in order to reduce the tax burden.

As with the tax policy, we are ignoring any costs involved with implementing the alternative policy (such as the collector's expenditure on burglar tools or the value of his time). Any such costs would lessen the social gain.

Dangerous
Curve

It would be enormously impractical to subject consumers and producers to random unexpected thefts. That's one reason we still have taxes, despite the deadweight loss. When a tax creates a reasonably small deadweight loss, we might be willing to live with it; when another tax creates a much larger deadweight loss, we might be more inclined to think hard about alternatives.

Dangerous
Curve

## Other Normative Criteria

The simplest of all normative criteria is the Pareto criterion, according to which one policy is "better" than another when it is preferred unanimously. In Exhibit 8.10, this means that the alternative policy is better than the sales tax, because everyone—consumers, producers, *and* recipients of tax revenue—agrees on this assessment. But according to the Pareto criterion, there is no way to decide between the "no tax" policy in the first column and the "sales tax" policy in the second column. Consumers and producers prefer the first, while tax recipients prefer the second. There is no unanimity; therefore, the Pareto criterion remains silent.

**Pareto criterion**

A normative criterion according to which one policy is better than another when it is preferred unanimously.

The great advantage of the Pareto criterion is that its recommendations, when it makes them, are extremely noncontroversial. Who can disagree with the outcome of a unanimous election? The offsetting disadvantage is that the Pareto criterion usually makes no recommendation at all, because unanimity is rarely found.

One modification of the Pareto criterion is the potential Pareto criterion, according to which any proposal that *could* be unanimously defeated should be rejected—even if the proposal that defeats it is not really in the running. For example, suppose in Exhibit 8.10 that we are asked to choose between the "no tax" proposal in the first column and the "sales tax" proposal in the second. According to the potential Pareto criterion, we should reject the sales tax because it loses unanimously to the alternative proposal in the third column—and that's enough to disqualify it, even if the alternative policy is not under serious consideration.

**Potential Pareto criterion**

A normative criterion according to which any proposal that can be unanimously defeated—even by a candidate not under consideration—should be rejected.

In all of our examples, the potential Pareto criterion and the efficiency criterion will make identical recommendations. It's easy to see why if you return to the pie analogy: The efficiency criterion says that we should always try to make the total "pie" of social gain as big as possible. The potential Pareto criterion says that if there's a way to make everyone's piece of pie bigger, you're not doing things right. But to say that everyone's piece could be made bigger is the same thing as saying that the pie could be made bigger—so whatever the potential Pareto criterion rejects, the efficiency criterion will reject as well.

Many economists regard the potential Pareto criterion and the efficiency criterion as good rough guides to policy choices, though few would defend them as the sole basis on which to make such decisions. Regardless of your feelings on this issue, calculations of social gains and deadweight losses can still be useful in understanding the consequences of various alternatives. If a policy causes a large deadweight loss, it is at least worth considering whether there is some good way to revise the policy so that the loss can be made smaller.

# 8.3 Examples and Applications

The machinery of consumers' and producers' surpluses is widely applicable, as the following sequence of examples will illustrate. All of them use just one basic procedure, which is summarized in Exhibit 8.11.

## Subsidies

Suppose that the government institutes a new program whereby buyers of home insulation receive a rebate of $50 for every unit of insulation they purchase. This has the effect of shifting the demand curve upward a vertical distance $50, from $D$ to $D'$ in Exhibit 8.12.

With the subsidy, the quantity sold is $Q'$, at a market price of $P_s$. This is the price suppliers receive for insulation. However, consumers actually pay less, because they receive a payment of $50 from the government, so that the consumer's actual cost is $P_s - \$50 = P_d$.

To calculate consumers' and producers' surpluses before the subsidy, we use the equilibrium price and quantity. This is shown in the first column of the table in Exhibit 8.12.

After the subsidy, consumers purchase quantity $Q'$ at a price to them of $P_d$. Their consumers' surplus is the area under the *original* demand curve $D$ out to this quantity and down to this price. We use the original demand curve because it is this curve that represents the true marginal value of insulation to consumers. The intrinsic value of home insulation is not changed by the subsidy. Therefore, the consumers' surplus is the area $A + C + F + G$, as recorded in the second column of the table.

To calculate producers' surplus, we use the quantity $Q'$ and the producers' price $P_s$. This yields the area $C + D + F + H$, which is also recorded in the table.

We are still not finished. The subsidy being paid to consumers must come from somewhere, presumably from tax revenues. This represents a cost to taxpayers equal to the number of units of insulation sold times $50 per unit. Geometrically, this is

---

**EXHIBIT 8.11    Calculating the Consumers' and Producers' Surpluses**

You will often be asked to calculate the effects of governmental policies on consumers' and producers' surpluses. Here are some rules to help you:

1. Begin by drawing a supply and demand diagram showing equilibrium both before and after the policy is imposed. Draw horizontal and vertical lines from the interesting points in your diagram to the axes. After a while you will get a feel for which lines to draw and which to omit. It never hurts to draw more than you need.
2. Before you proceed, label every area that is even possibly relevant.
3. When calculating consumers' surplus, use only the demand curve and prices and quantities that are relevant to the consumer. When calculating producers' surplus, use only the supply curve and prices and quantities relevant to the producer.
4. Remember that the demand and supply curves are relevant only because they are equal to the marginal value and marginal cost curves. If for some reason the demand curve should separate from the marginal value curve, continue to use the marginal value for calculating consumers' surplus. Do likewise if the supply curve should separate from the marginal cost curve.
5. Check your work with a picture like Exhibit 8.9: Calculate the social gain directly by drawing rectangles of "welfare gains" for each item actually produced and by summing the areas of these rectangles. The sum should equal the total of the gains to all of the individuals involved.

| EXHIBIT 8.12 | The Effect of a Subsidy |

| | Before Subsidy | After Subsidy |
|---|---|---|
| Consumers' Surplus | $A + C$ | $A + C + F + G$ |
| Producer's Surplus | $F + H$ | $C + D + F + H$ |
| Cost to Taxpayers | — | $-(C + D + E + F + G)$ |
| Social Gain | $A + C + F + H$ | $A + C + F + H - E$ |
| Deadweight Loss | — | $E$ |

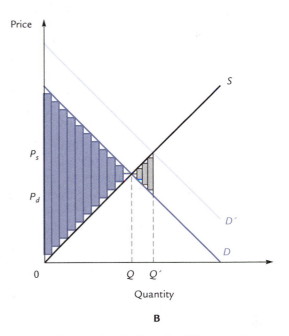

A                                                    B

The table shows the gains to consumers and producers before and after the institution of a $50-per-unit government subsidy to home insulation. With the subsidy in effect, there is a cost to taxpayers that must be *subtracted* when we calculate the social gain. We find that the social gain with the subsidy is lower by $E$ than the social gain without the subsidy. $E$ is the deadweight loss.

To check our work, we can consider the social gain created by each individual unit of insulation, shown in panel B. Each unit up to the equilibrium quantity $Q$ creates a rectangle of social gain. After $Q$ units have been produced, we enter a region where marginal cost exceeds marginal value. Each unit produced in this region creates a social *loss* equal to the excess of marginal cost over marginal value; these losses are represented by the gray rectangles, which stop at the quantity $Q'$ that is actually produced. The social gain is equal to the sum of the colored rectangles minus the sum of the gray ones. Because the social gain without the subsidy is just the sum of the colored rectangles, the gray rectangles represent the deadweight loss.

represented by the rectangle $C + D + E + F + G$. This cost is a *loss* to the taxpayers and so must be *subtracted* in the computation of social gain. The deadweight loss of $E$ is the difference between social gain before and after the subsidy.

According to the efficiency criterion, the subsidy should be rejected: It gathers $F + G$ votes in favor from consumers and $C + D$ votes in favor from producers, but

$C + D + E + F + G$ votes opposed from taxpayers. Thus, it loses by a margin of $E$, which (noncoincidentally) is the deadweight loss.

**Exercise 8.5** Verify the calculation of social gain in Exhibit 8.12.

Dangerous
Curve

Students often want to know how areas $C$ and $F$ can be part of both the consumers' surplus and the producers' surplus. The answer is that surplus is not an area at all—the area is just a *measure* of surplus. The fact that you have 12 yards of carpet and your friend has 12 yards of carpet does not mean that you both own the same "yards," only that each of you owns carpeting that can be measured by the same yardstick. The areas of surplus are yardsticks with which we measure different individuals' gains from trade.

Panel B in Exhibit 8.12 provides a way to check our work. The colored rectangles to the left of equilibrium represent gains to social welfare just as in Exhibit 8.9. In this case, however, *more* than the equilibrium quantity is produced. Consider the first item produced after equilibrium. The marginal value of this item to consumers (read off the original demand curve) is *less* than the marginal cost of producing it. The difference between the two is the area of the first gray rectangle. This area therefore represents a net welfare *loss* to society. Similarly, the next item produced represents a welfare loss in the amount of the area of the second gray rectangle, and so on out to the quantity $Q'$. The total welfare loss is the sum of these rectangles, which is equal to the area $E$ in panel $A$. Therefore, area $E$ should be the deadweight loss, and the calculation in the table is confirmed.

An alternative way to calculate the consumers' surplus is shown in Exhibit 8.13. For most purposes, it suffices to use either the method of Exhibit 8.12 or that of Exhibit 8.13. Because both always lead to the same answers, you need to master only one of them. However, there will be a few occasions later on in this book where you will find it much easier to use the alternative method of Exhibit 8.13.

## Price Ceilings

**Price ceiling**

A maximum price at which a product can be legally sold.

**Effective price ceiling**

A price ceiling set below the equilibrium price.

A **price ceiling** is a legally mandated maximum price at which a good may be sold. The effect of a price ceiling depends on its level. If the legal maximum is above the equilibrium price that prevails anyway, then the price ceiling has no effect (a law forbidding any piece of bubble gum to sell for more than $2,000 will not change anyone's behavior). An **effective price ceiling** is one set below the equilibrium price, like the price $P_0$ in Exhibit 8.14.

At the price $P_0$, producers want to sell the quantity $Q_s$ and consumers want to buy the quantity $Q_d$. What quantity actually gets traded? The answer is $Q_s$, because as soon as $Q_s$ units are sold, the sellers pack up and go home. When buyers and sellers disagree about quantity, the group wanting to trade fewer items always wins, because trading stops as soon as either party loses interest.

Another, and very real, possibility must be considered: Because buyers are frustrated, they will be willing to offer prices higher than $P_0$, and sellers may accept these prices in violation of the law. For purposes of our simple analysis, we will assume that the law is perfectly enforced and this does not occur. We will also assume that the

EXHIBIT **8.13**    **Another Way to Do It**

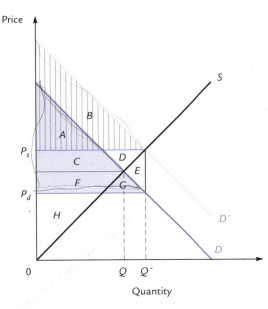

The method that we have been using to calculate social gain is adequate for most problems. However, there is an alternate method that may occasionally be more convenient.

We illustrate with the "subsidy" example from Exhibit 8.12. The graph here is identical to panel A in that exhibit. There are two ways of viewing a $50 rebate for home insulation. The first way, which we adopted in Exhibit 8.12, is to say that the rebate does not alter the value of home insulation. Consumers benefit from the subsidy by being able to buy insulation at a lower price. This is why we use the *old* demand curve (the true marginal value curve) and the price paid by consumers ($P_d$) as boundaries for the area of consumer surplus. This gives the shaded area $A + C + F + G$.

An alternative and *equally valid* point of view is to say that a subsidy is like a $50 bill taped to each unit of insulation. This raises the marginal value of the insulation by $50. However, we now have to view the insulation as being purchased at the market price $P_s$. If we said that the insulation has increased in value *and* that the consumer is paying less than market price for his insulation, we would be wrongly double-counting the $50 rebate.

From the alternative point of view, the consumer surplus is the area under the *new* demand curve down to the *market* price $P_s$ and out to the quantity $Q'$. That is, the striped area $A + B$.

If both points of view are equally valid, how can they give different answers? The answer is: They don't. In fact, area $A + B$ is equal to area $A + C + F + G$. They have to be equal, because each represents the consumers' surplus calculated correctly, and there can be only one consumers' surplus. If you find that argument unconvincing, try proving directly that the two areas are equal. This is an exercise in high school geometry if you assume all curves are straight lines; it is an exercise in calculus otherwise.

enforcement is costless (otherwise, the cost of enforcement would have to be subtracted from social gain).[6]

The quantity sold is $Q_s$. What price do consumers pay? You may think the answer is obviously $P_0$, but this is incorrect. At a price of $P_0$, consumers want to buy more goods than are available. Therefore, *they compete with each other* to acquire the limited supply.

[6] Here is an interesting puzzle. Why is it that in "victimless crimes" like prostitution and the sale of drugs, both parties are held criminally liable, whereas in the equally "victimless" crime of violating a price control, only the seller faces legal consequences? For an interesting discussion of this puzzle, see J. Lott and R. Roberts, "Why Comply: One-Sided Enforcement of Price Controls and Victimless Crime Laws," *Journal of Legal Studies* 18 (1989).

EXHIBIT **8.14**     **A Price Ceiling**

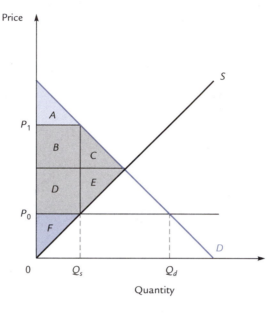

| | Before Ceiling | After Ceiling |
|---|---|---|
| Consumers' Surplus | $A + B + C$ | $A$ |
| Producers' Surplus | $D + E + F$ | $F$ |
| Social Gain | $A + B + C + D + E + F$ | $A + F$ |
| Deadweight Loss | — | $B + C + D + E$ |

At a maximum legal price of $P_0$, demanders want to buy more than suppliers want to sell. Therefore, they compete against each other for the available supply, by waiting in line, advertising, and so forth. This increases the actual price to consumers. The full price to consumers must be bid all the way up to $P_1$ because at any lower price the quantity demanded still exceeds the quantity supplied, leading to increases in the lengths of waiting lines.

The deadweight loss comes about for two reasons. First, there is the reduction in quantity from equilibrium to $Q_s$. This loss is the area $C + E$. Second, there is the value of the consumers' time spent waiting in line. This is equal to $P_1 - P_0$ times the quantity of items purchased, which is the rectangle $B + D$.

Depending on the nature of the good, this may take the form of standing in line, searching from store to store, advertising, or any of a number of other possibilities. All of these activities are costly, in time, gasoline, energy, and other currency, and these costs must be added to the "price" that consumers actually pay for the item.

How high does the price go? It must go to exactly $P_1$ in Exhibit 8.14. At any lower price the quantity demanded still exceeds $Q_s$, and consumers intensify their efforts. Only when the "price" reaches $P_1$ does the market equilibrate.

Of course, even though $P_1$ is the price paid by consumers, the price received by suppliers is still $P_0$. Therefore, we use $P_1$ to calculate consumers' surplus and $P_0$ to calculate producers' surplus. In each case, the appropriate quantity is $Q_s$, the quantity actually traded. The computations are shown in Exhibit 8.14.

**Exercise 8.6** Verify the correctness of the table in Exhibit 8.14.

The deadweight loss calculated in Exhibit 8.14 comes about for two reasons. First, there is the reduction in quantity from $Q$ to $Q_s$, which leads to a social loss of $C + E$, just as in the case of a tax. However, now there is another sort of loss as well. The value of the time people spend waiting in lines is equal to the value of the time-per-unit-purchased $(P_1 - P_0)$ times the quantity of units purchased $(Q_s)$, which is the rectangle $B + D$. Taken together, these effects account for the entire deadweight loss.

Notice that from a social point of view there is a great difference between a *price control* that drives the demanders' price up to $P_1$ and a *tax* that drives the demanders' price up to $P_1$. Because the revenue from a tax is wealth transferred from one individual to another, it is neither a gain nor a loss to society as a whole. But the value of the time spent waiting in lines is wealth lost and never recovered by anyone.

Some of the deadweight loss can be avoided if there is a class of people whose time is relatively inexpensive. Those people will offer their services as "searchers" or "line-standers" and consumers will pay them up to $P_1 - P_0$ per item for their services. The income to the line-standers, minus the value of their time, is a gain that offsets part of the lost area $B + D$.

Of course, some consumers whose time has low value might stand in line to make their own purchases. We view these consumers as having purchased line-standing services from themselves at the going price of $P_1 - P_0$. Such a consumer earns part of area $A$ as a consumer and part of area $B + D$ as a line-stander.

Dangerous Curve

The reduction in deadweight loss through the use of line-standers doesn't work if too many people have low time values. In that case, all of those people attempt to become line-standers and the lines get longer, so that the value of the time each one spends waiting gets bid back up to $P_1 - P_0$.

Dangerous Curve

## Tariffs

Suppose that Americans buy all of their cameras from Japanese companies. It is proposed that a tariff of $10 per camera be imposed on all such imports and that the proceeds be distributed to Americans chosen at random. What areas must we measure to see whether the tariff makes Americans as a whole better off?

Exhibit 8.15 shows the market for cameras, with both the original and post-tariff supply curves. The table shows the gains to Americans before and after the tariff. These gains are calculated using the pretariff price and quantity of $P_0$ and $Q_0$ and the posttariff price and quantity of $P_1$ and $Q_1$. Notice that we do not include the producers' surplus, because this is earned by the Japanese companies and the question asks only about the welfare of Americans. If we had been asked about the welfare of the entire world, we would have included producers' surplus in our calculations.

**Exercise 8.7** Calculate the social gains to the entire world before and after the tariff is imposed.

EXHIBIT **8.15**     **A Tax on Imported Cameras**

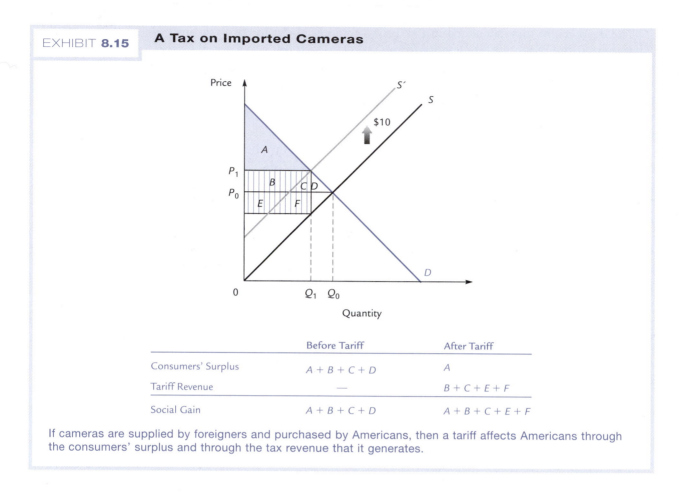

|  | Before Tariff | After Tariff |
|---|---|---|
| Consumers' Surplus | $A + B + C + D$ | $A$ |
| Tariff Revenue | — | $B + C + E + F$ |
| Social Gain | $A + B + C + D$ | $A + B + C + E + F$ |

If cameras are supplied by foreigners and purchased by Americans, then a tariff affects Americans through the consumers' surplus and through the tax revenue that it generates.

Now we return to the question: What areas must we measure? The answer is evidently that one must compare area $D$ with area $E + F$. If $E + F$ is bigger, the tariff improves the welfare of Americans; otherwise it reduces their welfare.

In practice, these areas can be estimated if the supply and demand curves can be estimated, and, as we remarked in Chapter 1, there are econometric methods available for this. Therefore, an economist can contribute meaningfully to a debate about tariffs by computing the relevant areas and reporting which policy is better—*provided* that the goal is to maximize Americans' welfare.

It is often a reasonable assumption that a country faces flat supply curves for imported items. The reason for this is that Japanese firms sell cameras in many foreign countries, and the United States is only a small part of their market. Thus, changes in quantity that appear big (from our point of view) may in fact correspond only to very small movements along the Japanese supply curves and hence to small changes in price. Exhibit 8.16 shows the analysis of a tariff when the supply curve is flat. In this case, you can see that the tariff always reduces Americans' welfare.

## Tariffs and Domestic Industries

A more interesting example involves tariffs on a product that is produced both domestically and abroad. Suppose that Americans buy cars from Japan subject to a flat Japanese supply curve at a price $P_0$, and that domestic car manufacturers have

**EXHIBIT 8.16** **A Tariff on Imported Cameras That Are Elastically Supplied**

| | Before Tariff | After Tariff |
|---|---|---|
| Consumers' Surplus | $A + B + C$ | $A$ |
| Tariff Revenue | — | $B$ |
| Social Gain | $A + B + C$ | $A + B$ |
| Deadweight Loss | — | $C$ |

If the United States is a small part of the market to which the Japanese sell cameras, then Americans will face a flat supply curve. In this case, a tariff always reduces the welfare of Americans.

the upward-sloping supply curve shown in panel A of Exhibit 8.17. Assuming that all cars are identical, no consumer will be willing to pay more than $P_0$ for a domestic car, because the consumer can always buy an import instead. Therefore, all cars sell at a price of $P_0$. At this price, domestic manufacturers produce $Q_0$ cars and domestic consumers buy $Q_1$. The difference, $Q_1 - Q_0$, is the number of imports. Table A in Exhibit 8.17 shows the consumers' and producers' surpluses.

Now suppose that we impose a tariff of $500 on each imported car. This raises the foreign supply curve $500 to a level of $P_0 + \$500$. The price of cars goes up to $P_0 + \$500$, the quantity supplied domestically goes up to $Q_0'$ (in panel B of Exhibit 8.17), and the quantity demanded falls to $Q_1'$. The quantity imported falls to $Q_1 - Q_0'$.

In Exhibit 8.17 Table B shows the consumers' and producers' surpluses both before and after the tariff. (The "before" column, of course, simply repeats the calculation from Table A.) What about revenue from the tariff? The number of imported cars is $Q_1' - Q_0'$, and the tariff is $500 on each of these. Thus, the tariff revenue (which ends up in American pockets) is $(Q_1' - Q_0') \times \$500$, and this is the area of rectangle $I$. This is recorded in Table B, along with a comparison of social gains.

We can see that even when there is a domestic industry that benefits from the tariff, and even though the tariff revenue is a gain to the country, tariffs still cause a deadweight loss (we say that they are *inefficient*) because consumers lose more than all other groups gain.

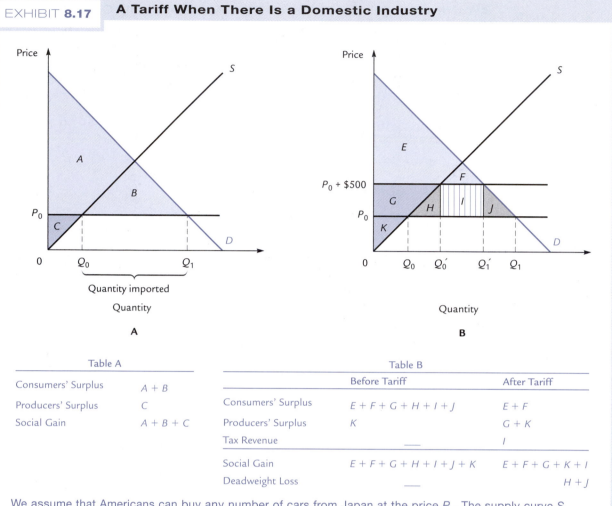

**EXHIBIT 8.17    A Tariff When There Is a Domestic Industry**

**A**

**B**

|  | Table A |
|---|---|
| Consumers' Surplus | $A + B$ |
| Producers' Surplus | $C$ |
| Social Gain | $A + B + C$ |

**Table B**

|  | Before Tariff | After Tariff |
|---|---|---|
| Consumers' Surplus | $E + F + G + H + I + J$ | $E + F$ |
| Producers' Surplus | $K$ | $G + K$ |
| Tax Revenue | — | $I$ |
| Social Gain | $E + F + G + H + I + J + K$ | $E + F + G + K + I$ |
| Deadweight Loss | — | $H + J$ |

We assume that Americans can buy any number of cars from Japan at the price $P_0$. The supply curve $S$ shows how many cars American manufacturers will provide at each price. At the price $P_0$, American producers supply $Q_0$ cars and American consumers purchase $Q_1$ cars. The difference, $Q_1 - Q_0$, is the number of cars imported. Table A shows the gains to Americans.

In panel B we see the effect of a $500 tariff on imported cars. The price of a foreign car rises to $P_0 + \$500$, and the number of imports falls to $Q_1' - Q_0'$. Table B compares gains before and after the tariff. Note that the first column of Table B is identical to Table A except that it uses the labels from panel B rather than panel A. The tariff revenue is computed by observing that the area of rectangle $I$ is $(Q_1' - Q_0') \times \$500$.

**Exercise 8.8** Suppose that the government wants to benefit domestic auto producers and the recipients of tax revenue at the expense of car buyers. Devise an efficient (though perhaps impractical) way of doing this that makes everybody happier than a tariff does.

## Robbery

From the point of view of economic efficiency (i.e., the maximization of the total gains to all members of society), a loss to one group that is exactly offset by a gain to another group is a "wash." To one who is interested only in maximizing social gain, such a transfer is neither a good thing nor a bad thing. How, then, should such a one feel about *robbery?*

Many people think that robbery constitutes a social loss equal to the value of what is stolen. Their reasoning is simple but faulty: They notice the loss to the victim without noticing the offsetting gain to the robber. A more sophisticated answer would be that robbery is a matter of indifference, because stolen goods do not disappear from society; they only change ownership.

However, this more sophisticated answer is also wrong. There *is* a social cost to robbery. It is the opportunity cost of the robber's time and energy. The robber who steals your bicycle could, perhaps, with the same expenditure of energy, be building a bicycle of his own. If he did, society would have two bicycles; when he steals yours instead, society has only one. The option to steal costs society a bicycle.

This shows that robbery is socially costly; we still have to ask: *How* costly? To answer this, it is reasonable to treat robbery as a competitive industry: Robbers continue to rob until the marginal cost (in time, energy, and so on) of committing an additional crime is equal to the marginal revenue (in loot). The cost is what interests us, the loot is observable, and we know that the two are equal. So, at the margin, we can reckon the cost of a robbery as approximately equal to the value of what is stolen.

This tells us that the amount stolen is a correct measure of the cost of the last robbery committed. In Exhibit 8.18 we calculate the total social cost of all robberies. Suppose that a robber can expect to earn $R each time he commits a robbery. Then robbers steal until the marginal cost of stealing is equal to $R; that is, they commit Q robberies. The amount stolen is $R \times Q$, the area $A + B$. However, the robbers' total costs are given by the area under the supply curve, $A$. This cost to the robbers is society's cost as well. Therefore, the total social cost of all robberies ($A$) is less than the value of what is taken ($A + B$).

---

This analysis ignores the very real possibility that people will take costly steps to protect themselves from robbery—installing burglar alarms, deadbolt locks, and the like. These additional costs are also due to the existence of robbery and must be added to area $A$ in order to calculate the full social cost of robberies.

Dangerous Curve

---

The more general lesson of this example is that effort expended in nonproductive activity is social loss. Accountants devising new methods of tax avoidance, lawyers in litigation, lobbyists seeking laws to transfer wealth to their clients, and all of the resources that they employ (secretaries, file clerks, photocopy machines, telephone services, and so on) are often unproductive from a social point of view. Whatever they win for their clients is a loss for their adversaries. In the absence of this activity, all of these resources could be employed elsewhere, making society richer.

On the other hand, some of this seemingly unproductive activity serves hidden and valuable purposes. Suppose that a law is passed requiring that all owners of apple orchards donate $5,000 each to the president's brother. The owners of apple orchards might hire a lobbyist to assist them in having this law overturned. If the effort is successful, apple growers win only what the president's brother loses, and so at one level of analysis the lobbyist's time contributes nothing to the welfare of society. On the other hand, if all orange growers were made very nervous by this law and planned to burn down their orange trees as a precaution against their being next, then the lobbyist saves a lot of valuable orange trees through his efforts. Insofar as redistributing income affects the incentives to engage in productive activities, it can indirectly affect society's welfare.

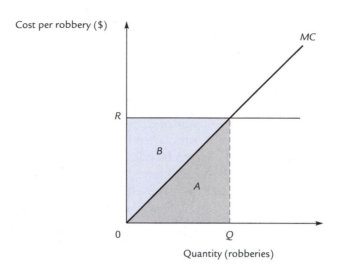

EXHIBIT **8.18**    **The Social Cost of Robbery**

| Producers' Surplus (Earned by Robber) | B |
|---|---|
| Loss to Victim | A + B |
| Social Loss | A |

We suppose that a robber can expect to earn $R for each robbery he commits. Then robberies will take place until the robbers' marginal cost (the opportunity cost of their time, energy, and so on) equals $R. The number of robberies committed is Q, and robbers earn a producers' surplus of B. However, victims lose the amount stolen, which is A + B. There is a net social loss of A. If society pursues economic efficiency, A is the maximum amount it would be willing to spend to prevent all robberies.

## Theories of Value

We have defined value in terms of consumers' willingness to pay, and we have discovered that the price of an item is equal to its marginal value. Other theories of value have arisen in the history of economics, only to be abandoned when careful analysis revealed them as erroneous. Because such errors are still common in much discussion by noneconomists, it is worth examining them to see why they should be avoided.

### The Diamond–Water Paradox

Many classical economists were puzzled by the so-called diamond–water paradox. How can it be that water, which is essential for life and therefore as "valuable" a thing as can be imagined, is so inexpensive relative to diamonds, which are used primarily for decoration and the production of nonessential goods? If price reflects value, shouldn't a gallon of water be worth innumerable diamonds?

The paradox is resolved when you realize that price reflects not *total* value, but *marginal* value. Exhibit 8.19 depicts the demand curves for water and for diamonds, together with their market prices and the corresponding consumer's surpluses. The marginal value of your first gallon of water is indeed much higher than the marginal value of your first diamond, and this is reflected by the heights of the demand curves

EXHIBIT **8.19**    **The Diamond–Water Paradox Resolved**

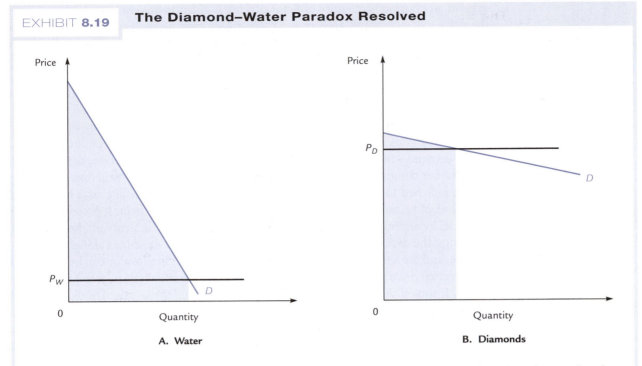

A. Water

B. Diamonds

If you had no water and no diamonds, you would be willing to pay far more for a first bucket of water than for a first diamond. Therefore, your marginal value (= demand) curve for water starts out much higher than your marginal value curve for diamonds. At the market prices $P_W$ and $P_D$, you consume $Q_W$ buckets of water and $Q_D$ diamonds, so that the marginal value of a bucket of water ($P_W$) is much less than the marginal value of a diamond ($P_D$).

It is true that the total value of all your water (the shaded area in panel A) is greater than the total value of all your diamonds (the shaded area in panel B). The graphs show that this is perfectly consistent with a low marginal value for water and a high marginal value for diamonds. The price, which is equal to the marginal value, should not be expected to reflect the total value.

at low quantities. But this has nothing to do with the *price* of water; the price is equal to the marginal value of the last bucket consumed, and this may be very low if you consume many gallons.

Notice that the total value (the colored area) in the market for water is much higher than in the market for diamonds: If you lost all of your water and all of your diamonds, you would be willing to pay more to retrieve the water than to retrieve the diamonds. In consequence, the consumers' surplus is much higher in the market for water than in the market for diamonds. Exhibit 8.19 shows that there is nothing paradoxical about a low price and a large consumers' surplus existing simultaneously.

## The Labor Theory of Value

The **labor theory of value** is an error that deceived such diverse economists as Adam Smith and Karl Marx. In its simplest form it says that the price of an item is determined by the amount of labor used in its production.[7] In this form it is clearly false: You can

**Labor theory of value**

The assertion that the value of an object is determined by the amount of labor involved in its production.

---

[7] Of course, this is a simpler form than economists have ever believed; typical versions restrict attention to "socially necessary" labor and include the labor of previous generations who built machines used in current production.

expend an enormous quantity of labor digging a gigantic hole in your backyard, and the price that hole commands in the marketplace may be far less than the price of a short story produced by a good writer in an afternoon, sitting at a word processor in an air-conditioned house sipping lemonade.[8]

For a theory so evidently false, the labor theory of value (even in this simple form) is remarkably pervasive. You will hear it argued that doctors "ought to" earn high salaries because of all the effort involved in earning their medical degrees, or that people in occupation A "ought to" earn as much as people in occupation B because they work equally hard. Such arguments ignore the fact that value is determined not by the cost of inputs, but by demand—the consumer's willingness to pay for the good or service being offered.

Another common belief that embodies the labor theory fallacy is that a meaning can be attached to the "book value" of a firm. A firm's "book value" is a measure of what it would cost to produce the actual physical assets of the firm. It is computed, for example, by adding up the cost of the bricks used to build the firm's plants and office buildings, the desks and chairs in the executive offices, the machines along the assembly line, and the letterhead stationery in the cabinets. This book value can be compared to the actual price at which one could acquire the entire firm (say, by purchasing all its stock). It sometimes happens that a firm can be acquired for less than book value, and it is widely believed that this represents a bargain.

Not so. The fact that a factory is built from $1 million worth of bricks does not make that factory worth $1 million, any more than your application of $1 million worth of labor would make a hole in your backyard worth $1 million. If your labor is devoted to the production of something that nobody wants, or if the bricks are glued together to form a factory that produces nothing useful, this will be reflected in the price. What we have here is a *brick theory of value,* different perhaps from the labor theory of value, but perfectly analogous and just as false.

A final example illustrates both the diamond–water and the labor theory paradoxes. It is sometimes argued that something must be wrong with society's values when a baseball player (for example) earns a seven-figure salary for playing a game that (1) he enjoys anyway and (2) produces little social value compared with something like teaching elementary school, which is far less lucrative. The first point is the labor theory of value again. It errs by assuming that how hard the baseball player works determines the value of what he produces. The second point uses the erroneous reasoning that underlies the diamond–water paradox. It may very well be that teachers (like water) produce far more total social value than star baseball players. But it can be simultaneously true that *one additional teacher* produces less social value than one additional star baseball player. This can be the case, for example, if there are many teachers and few star baseball players. We should not expect the price of a teacher or a baseball player to tell us anything about the total value to society of the two professions.

## 8.4 General Equilibrium and the Invisible Hand

Based on the examples in Section 8.3, you might have begun to suspect that any deviation from competitive equilibrium leads to a reduction in social gain. In this section, we will see that this is, in fact, the case.

---

[8] It *is* true, of course, that in a competitive market, price equals marginal cost (and a competitive producer will not choose to dig a hole in his backyard for sale in the marketplace). But marginal cost is not labor cost. Some labor costs may be sunk (and therefore irrelevant), and many relevant costs have nothing to do with labor. The relevant costs, as always, are the opportunity costs—the writer could be writing a movie script instead.

## The Fundamental Theorem of Welfare Economics

Exhibit 8.20 shows the competitive market for potatoes. We can ask two questions about this market ostensibly as different as questions can be:

1.  What is the quantity of potatoes actually produced and sold?

2.  Suppose you were a benevolent dictator, concerned only with maximizing the total welfare gains to all of society. What quantity of potatoes would you *order* produced and sold?

Note well the dissimilarity between these questions. One is a question about what *is;* the other is a question about what *ought* to be.

We know the answers to each of these questions. They are:

1.  The quantity of potatoes produced and sold is at $Q_0$, where supply equals demand. We have seen that individual suppliers and demanders, seeking to maximize their own profits and their own happiness, choose to operate at this point.

2.  To maximize social gains, you would continue ordering potatoes to be produced as long as their marginal value exceeds the marginal cost of producing them. You would stop when marginal cost equals marginal value, that is, at $Q_0$.

The choice of $Q_0$ yields a social gain of $A + B$ in Exhibit 8.20. A despot who made the mistake of ordering only $Q_1$ potatoes produced would limit social gain to area $A$. If the same benevolent dictator made the mistake of ordering $Q_2$, area $C$ would be subtracted from the social gain, because it is made up of rectangles whose areas represent an excess of marginal cost over marginal value.

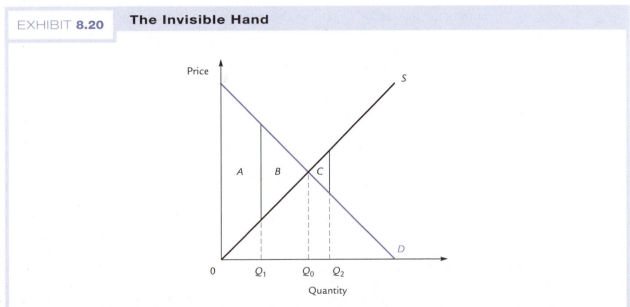

| EXHIBIT **8.20** | **The Invisible Hand** |

Under competition, the quantity produced is $Q_0$, where supply equals demand. A benevolent dictator who wanted to maximize social gain would employ the equimarginal principle and order potatoes to be produced to a quantity where marginal cost equals marginal value. This also occurs at quantity $Q_0$.

If the dictator ordered $Q_1$ potatoes produced, social gain would be area $A$; if he ordered $Q_2$, social gain would be $A + B - C$. The maximum social gain, at $Q_0$, is $A + B$.

It is astounding that the two questions have identical answers. The coincidence results from the prior coincidences of the supply curve with the marginal cost curve, and of the demand curve with the marginal value curve.

It is not only astounding that the two answers are identical but it is fortunate. It means that people living in a competitive world achieve the maximum possible social gain without any need of a benevolent despot. The market alone achieves an outcome that is economically efficient. To say the same thing in different words, competitive equilibrium is Pareto-optimal.

The eighteenth-century economist Adam Smith was so struck by this observation that he described it with one of the world's most enduring metaphors. Of the individual participant in the marketplace, he said: "He intends only his own gain, and he is … led by an invisible hand to promote an end which was no part of his intention."[9]

Noneconomists frequently misunderstand what Smith meant by the *invisible hand*. Some think it is a metaphor for an ideology or a philosophical point of view; the notion has even been described as a theological one! In fact, the *invisible hand* expresses what is at bottom a mathematical truth. The point of equilibrium (where competitive suppliers operate "intending only their own gain") is also the point of maximum social gain (an end that is no part of any individual participant's intention).

## The Idea of a General Equilibrium

The preceding analysis is striking, but it is incomplete. By participating in the potato market, people change conditions in other markets as well. When he grows more or fewer potatoes, a farmer consequently grows less or more of something else. The amount of labor that he hires changes. When a consumer changes his potato consumption, he probably also changes his consumption of rice, and of butter. At one further remove, any change in the potato market affects the potato farmer's income, which affects his purchases of shoes, which affects the market for leather, which affects the market for something else, ad infinitum. If we really want to understand the welfare consequences of competitive equilibrium in the potato industry, we need to consider its effects in all of these other markets as well. Could it be that by maximizing welfare gains in one market, we are imposing a net welfare *loss* in the totality of all other markets?

It was not until the 1950s, nearly 200 years after Adam Smith, that economists developed the mathematical tools necessary to deal fully with this complicated question. In that decade, economists such as Kenneth Arrow, Gerard Debreu, and Lionel McKenzie devised techniques that make it possible to study all the markets in the economy at one time. In this they were advancing a subject called general equilibrium analysis, first invented by the nineteenth-century economist Lèon Walras. One of the great and powerful results of general equilibrium theory is that even in view of the effects of all markets on all other markets, competitive equilibrium is still Pareto-optimal. This discovery is usually called the *first fundamental theorem of welfare economics*, or the *invisible hand theorem*.

**General equilibrium analysis**

A way of modeling the economy so as to take account of all markets at once and of all the interactions among them.

The invisible hand theorem says, in essence, that in competitive markets, people who selfishly pursue their own interests end up achieving an outcome that is socially desirable. Outside of competitive markets, such good fortune is not to be expected. The governor of Colorado recently told of walking down a suburban street where each homeowner was out blowing leaves onto his neighbor's lawn. Each homeowner acted

[9] From Book 4 of Smith's monumental work *The Wealth of Nations*, first published in 1776.

selfishly, and the outcome was highly undesirable. If the homeowners had all agreed to spend the afternoon watching football, they would have enjoyed themselves more and had the same number of leaves on their lawns at the end of the day. Because the decision to blow leaves takes place outside of the market system, there is no reason to expect it to yield outcomes that are in any sense desirable. In Chapters 10 through 14 we will see many more such examples. The fact that the invisible hand theorem fails so easily in so many contexts makes it utterly remarkable that it succeeds in the particular context of competitive markets.

The Pareto optimality of competitive equilibrium is a deep and wondrous fact about the price system. No analogous statement is true in the absence of competition or in the absence of prices. The invisible hand theorem is a remarkable truth.

## An Edgeworth Box Economy

The invisible hand theorem is true in very complex economies with many participants and many markets, but we will illustrate it (and the basic ideas of general equilibrium analysis) only in the simplest possible case. Assume a world with two people (Aline and Bob) and two goods (food and clothing). We will simplify further by assuming that there is no production in this world; Aline and Bob can only trade the goods that already exist. These assumptions will enable us to present a complete general equilibrium model and to illustrate the invisible hand theorem.

Because there is no production in this world, there is only a fixed, unchangeable amount of food and clothing. In panel A of Exhibit 8.21 we draw a box that has a width equal to the amount of food in existence, and a height equal to the amount of clothing. Such a box is called an Edgeworth box.[10] Using the lower left-hand corner as the origin, we draw Aline's indifference curves between food and clothing. We also mark one point of special interest: It is Aline's endowment point, O, representing the basket of food and clothing that she owns at the beginning of the story.

In panel B we do a strange thing: We turn the entire page upside down, and we draw Bob's (black) indifference curves in the same box. For him, the food axis is the line that Aline views as the top of the box, and the clothing axis is the line that Aline views as the right side of the box.

To plot Bob's endowment point, remember that the width of the box is equal to the sum of Bob's and Aline's food endowments and that the height is equal to the sum of their clothing endowments. A moment's reflection should convince you that Bob's endowment point (measured along *his* axes) is the same as Aline's endowment point (measured along *her* axes).

Panel C shows a piece of panel B: All but two indifference curves have been eliminated. We have retained only those indifference curves (one of Aline's and one of Bob's) that pass through the endowment point.

Now suppose that Bob and Aline discuss the possibility of trade. Aline vetoes any trade that moves her into region *A, C,* or *E,* because these all represent moves to lower indifference curves from her point of view. Similarly, Bob vetoes any trade that moves him into region *A, B,* or *E.* (Hold the book upside down for help in seeing this!) However, a movement anywhere inside region *D* benefits both Aline and Bob. For this reason, region *D* is called the region of mutual advantage, and Aline and Bob can arrange a trade that moves them into this area.

**Edgeworth box**

A certain diagrammatic representation of an economy with two individuals, two goods, and no production.

**Endowment point**

The point representing the initial holdings of an individual in an Edgeworth box.

**Region of mutual advantage**

The set of points that are considered at least as good as the initial endowment.

---

[10] The Edgeworth box is named after the nineteenth-century British economist F. Y. Edgeworth.

# EXHIBIT 8.21    Trade in an Edgeworth Box Economy

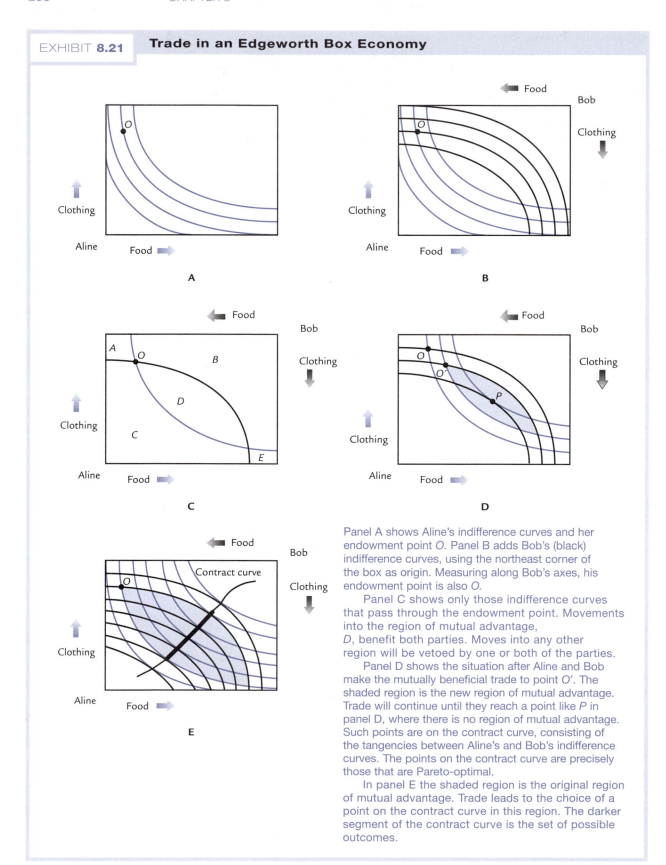

Panel A shows Aline's indifference curves and her endowment point *O*. Panel B adds Bob's (black) indifference curves, using the northeast corner of the box as origin. Measuring along Bob's axes, his endowment point is also *O*.

Panel C shows only those indifference curves that pass through the endowment point. Movements into the region of mutual advantage, *D*, benefit both parties. Moves into any other region will be vetoed by one or both of the parties.

Panel D shows the situation after Aline and Bob make the mutually beneficial trade to point *O'*. The shaded region is the new region of mutual advantage. Trade will continue until they reach a point like *P* in panel D, where there is no region of mutual advantage. Such points are on the contract curve, consisting of the tangencies between Aline's and Bob's indifference curves. The points on the contract curve are precisely those that are Pareto-optimal.

In panel E the shaded region is the original region of mutual advantage. Trade leads to the choice of a point on the contract curve in this region. The darker segment of the contract curve is the set of possible outcomes.

After moving to a new point, $O'$, inside the region of mutual advantage, Aline and Bob face a new, smaller region of mutual advantage, as shown in panel D. They will move to a new point in this new region and will continue this process until no region of mutual advantage remains. This occurs precisely when they reach a point where their indifference curves are tangent to each other, such as the point $P$ in panel D.

A point of tangency between Aline's and Bob's indifference curves is a point from which no further mutually beneficial trade is possible. In other words, such a point is Pareto-optimal; from that point no change can improve both parties' welfare. The collection of all Pareto-optimal points forms a curve, which is called the contract curve and is illustrated in panel E.

We do not know in advance exactly what point Aline and Bob will reach through the trading process. We know only that it will be somewhere within the original region of mutual advantage, and that it will be on the contract curve. The set of possible outcomes is the darker segment of the contract curve shown in panel E.

## Competitive Equilibrium in the Edgeworth Box

Our analysis has revealed an infinite variety of possible outcomes for the bargaining process. Next we ask what can happen if Aline and Bob play according to a far more restrictive set of rules. Instead of letting them bargain in whatever way they choose, we require them to bargain through the mechanism of a price system.

The new rules of the game work this way: Aline and Bob decide on a relative price for food and clothing. At this price, each decides how much of each commodity he or she would like to buy or sell. If their desires are compatible (i.e., if Aline wants to buy just as much food as Bob wants to sell), they carry out the transaction. If their desires are not compatible, they decide on a new relative price and try again. This process continues until they find a relative price that "clears the market" in the sense that quantities demanded equal quantities supplied.

Why would Aline and Bob ever agree to such a strange and restricted set of rules? They wouldn't, because two people can bargain far more effectively without introducing the artifice of market-clearing prices. But our interest in Aline and Bob is not personal; we are concerned with them only because we are interested in the workings of much larger markets, and such markets *do* operate through a price mechanism. So we shall force Aline and Bob to behave the way people in large markets behave, hoping that their responses will teach us something about those large markets.

Suggesting a relative price is equivalent to suggesting a slope for Aline's budget line. Once we know this slope, we know her entire budget line. This is because her budget line must pass through her endowment point, in view of the fact that she can always achieve this point by refusing to trade. Bob's budget line (viewed from his upside-down perspective) is the same as Aline's. In panel A of Exhibit 8.22 a relative price has been suggested that leads Aline to choose point $X$ and Bob to choose point $Y$. The total quantity of food demanded is more than exists in the world; the total quantity of clothing demanded fails to exhaust the available supply. The market has not cleared and a new relative price must be tried. In view of the outcome at the current price, it seems sensible to raise the relative price of food. That is, we try a steeper budget line, as in panel B. This time Aline and Bob both choose the same point $Z$ and the market clears.

The mutually acceptable point $Z$ in panel B is called a competitive equilibrium for this economy. It requires finding a budget line that goes through the original endowment point and leads to the same optimum point for Aline that it does for Bob.

**Contract curve**

The set of Pareto-optimal points.

**Competitive equilibrium**

A point that everyone will choose to trade to, for some appropriate market prices.

**EXHIBIT 8.22**   **Competitive Equilibrium in an Edgeworth Box Economy**

In panel A a relative price has been suggested that leads to the budget line pictured. (This is Aline's budget line from her perspective and Bob's budget line from his.) Aline chooses point *X* and Bob chooses point *Y*. But these points are not the same; the quantities that Aline wants to buy and sell are not the same quantities that Bob wants to sell and buy.

In panel B a different relative price has been suggested. At this price Aline's desires are compatible with Bob's. Point *Z* is a competitive equilibrium.

It is not immediately obvious that a competitive equilibrium should even exist, but it turns out to be possible to prove this.[11]

### The Invisible Hand in the Edgeworth Box

At the competitive equilibrium *Z* of Exhibit 8.22, Aline's indifference curve is tangent to the budget line, and Bob's indifference curve is tangent to the same budget line. It follows that Aline's and Bob's indifference curves are tangent to each other. This, in turn, means that the competitive equilibrium is a point on the contract curve—that is, it is Pareto-optimal.

This reasoning shows that in an Edgeworth box economy, any competitive equilibrium is Pareto-optimal. That is, the invisible hand theorem is true.

We began this section by noticing that competitive equilibrium is Pareto-optimal in the context of a single market. We have just seen that the same is true in the context of an entire economy (albeit an extraordinarily simple economy in which no production takes place). The same is also true in far more complex models involving many markets and incorporating production, though this requires advanced mathematics to prove.

### General Equilibrium with Production

In the Edgeworth box economy there is no production. Next we will study general equilibrium in an economy where production is possible.

---

[11] In fact, *you* can prove it, if you have had a course in calculus. Define the *aggregate excess demand* for food as the sum of the quantities demanded by Bob and Aline, *minus* the world supply of food. At a price of zero, draw the budget line and compute the aggregate excess demand. Do the same at an infinite price. Now use the intermediate value theorem to complete the proof.

## Robinson Crusoe

Robinson Crusoe lives alone on an island where the only foods he can produce are tomatoes and fish. He grows the tomatoes and catches the fish. Because each activity takes time, he can have more of one only by accepting less of the other.

Exhibit 8.23 shows the various combinations of tomatoes and fish that Robinson could produce in a week. If he grows no tomatoes, he can catch 15 fish. If he catches no fish, he can grow 18 tomatoes. The curve displaying all of his options is called Robinson's **production possibility curve.**

If Robinson starts at point *E* in the diagram and gives up a single tomato, he can catch $\Delta F$ additional fish. We can think of $\Delta F$ as the relative price of tomatoes in terms of fish. $\Delta F$ is also the slope of the production possibility curve at *E*. Therefore, the slope of the production possibility curve is equal to the relative price of tomatoes in terms of fish.

At point *E*, Robinson grows a lot of tomatoes. Because of diminishing marginal returns to farming on a fixed quantity of land, it takes a lot of effort to grow one more tomato. By giving up his last tomato, Robinson frees up a lot of time and catches a large number ($\Delta F$) of fish. By contrast, if Robinson started out at a point near the northwest corner of the production possibility curve, the marginal tomato would require less effort.

Giving it up would only free a small amount of time; moreover, diminishing marginal returns to fishing render that time relatively unproductive. (Notice that Robinson is already catching a lot of fish.) In consequence, the price of a tomato in terms of fish is very low near the northwest corner, just as it is very high near the southeast corner. Remembering that price equals slope, this tells us that

The production possibility curve bows outward from the origin.

**Production possibility curve**

The curve displaying all baskets that can be produced.

---

EXHIBIT **8.23**    **The Production Possibility Curve**

The curve shows the various combinations of tomatoes and fish that Robinson can produce. Its slope shows how many fish he can have in exchange for one tomato and can therefore be thought of as the relative price of tomatoes. At point *E* that relative price is the distance $\Delta F$. Robinson chooses a point of tangency with an indifference curve; that is, he chooses point *B*.

To complete the analysis, we must bring Robinson's indifference curves into the picture. Robinson chooses his favorite point on his production possibility curve, which is the tangency B. At this point, Robinson equates the relative price of tomatoes (the slope of the production possibility curve) with the marginal rate of substitution between tomatoes and fish (the slope of the indifference curve).

## The Open Economy

Now suppose that Robinson establishes contact with the natives of a large nearby island. His own island is transformed into an open economy, one that can trade with outsiders at prices determined in world markets. The going price of a tomato on this other island is P fish dinners.

Robinson now faces two separate choices. First, how should he allocate his time between farming and fishing? Second, how should he allocate his consumption between tomatoes and fish?

We know how to answer the second question. Robinson chooses the tangency between his budget line and an indifference curve. What is his budget line? It is a line with absolute slope P (P being the relative price of tomatoes) and passing through the point representing Robinson's production. Why must it pass through that point? Because Robinson can always consume at that point by simply not trading with his neighbors. Since that point is available to him, it must be on his budget line.

Panel A of Exhibit 8.24 shows several lines with absolute slope P. If Robinson produces either basket A or basket E, his budget line is the lightest of these. If he produces B or D, his budget line is the middle one. If he produces C, the dark line is his budget line. It is best to have a budget line as far from the origin as possible, so C is Robinson's best choice. That is,

Production occurs at the point where the production possibility curve is tangent to a line of slope P. The line of tangency becomes the budget line.

Panel B of Exhibit 8.24 shows Robinson's consumption choice. Having produced basket C, he has the budget line shown; along this budget line he selects basket X. Notice that X is superior to the basket B that Robinson would consume in the absence of trade. Robinson gains from trade with his neighbors. We can go on to ask: How much does he gain?

To answer this question, we must compare two different prices. One is the autarkic relative price that would prevail on Robinson's island if there were no trade. With no trade, Robinson would choose point B in Exhibit 8.25 and would have the budget line shown in color. The slope of that line is the autarkic relative price of tomatoes.

The second interesting price is the world relative price at which Robinson can trade with his neighbors. Suppose first that the world relative price happens by chance to equal the autarkic relative price. In that case, Robinson's budget line must be tangent to the production possibility curve and parallel to the colored line; that is, his budget line is the colored line itself. He produces at the point B and consumes at the point B. But this is exactly the same point that Robinson chose in Exhibit 8.23, when there was no opportunity to trade. In other words,

If the autarkic and world relative prices are equal, then there is no gain from trade.

Suppose, alternatively, that the world relative price is given by the slope of the black line in Exhibit 8.25. Then Robinson produces at C and consumes at X, which makes him happier than if he were to consume at B. In this case, he gains from trade.

**Open economy**

An economy that trades with outsiders at prices determined in world markets.

**Autarkic relative price**

The relative price that would prevail if there were no trade with foreigners.

**World relative price**

The relative price that prevails in the presence of trade with foreigners.

EXHIBIT **8.24** | **Production and Consumption with Foreign Trade**

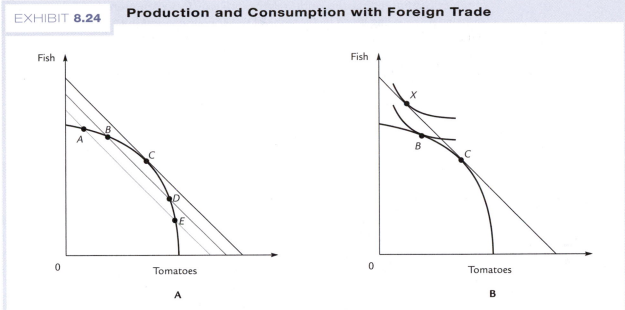

When Robinson can trade with his neighbors at a relative price of *P* fish per tomato, he faces a budget line of absolute slope *P*. All of the lines in panel A have that slope. By choosing a basket to produce, Robinson can choose his budget line from among the lines pictured. If he produces basket *A* or basket *E*, he has the light budget line; if he produces basket *B* or basket *D*, he has the middle budget line; if he produces basket *C*, he has the dark budget line. The dark budget line is the best one to have, so Robinson produces basket *C*. He then trades along the budget line to his optimal basket *X*, shown in panel B. Without trade, Robinson would choose basket *B*. Since basket *X* is preferred to basket *B*, Robinson gains from trade.

EXHIBIT **8.25** | **Autarkic versus World Relative Prices**

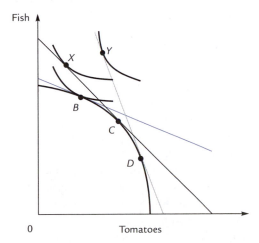

The slope of the brown line represents the autarkic relative price on Robinson's island. If the world relative price is the same as the autarkic relative price, then Robinson both produces and consumes basket *B*, just as he would with no opportunity to trade.

   If, instead, the world relative price is given by the slope of the black line, then Robinson produces basket *C* and consumes basket *X*, which is an improvement over basket *B*. If the world relative price goes up to the slope of the gray line, then Robinson produces basket *D* and consumes basket *Y*, which is a further improvement.

Next, suppose that the world relative price differs even more from the autarkic relative price, being given by the slope of the gray line in Exhibit 8.25. Then Robinson produces *D* and consumes *Y*, which is better even than *X*.

The more the world relative price differs from the autarkic relative price, the more Robinson gains from trade.

**Exercise 8.9** The black and gray lines in Exhibit 8.25 represent world relative prices that are greater than the autarkic relative price. Draw some budget lines that result when world relative prices are *less* than the autarkic relative price. Check that it remains true that the gains from trade are greater when the world relative price is further from the autarkic relative price.

What determines the world relative price? The answer is: supply and demand by everyone in the world, including Robinson. Thus, the world price is a sort of average of the autarkic relative prices on all of the various islands in Robinson's trading group. If Robinson's supply and demand constitute a large percentage of the world's supply and demand, then his own autarkic relative price counts quite heavily in this average, bringing the world relative price closer to the autarkic one. This, in turn, reduces Robinson's gains from trade.

If, on the other hand, Robinson is an insignificant player in the world market, then there is a greater chance that the world relative price differs substantially from his autarkic one. In this case, Robinson's gains from trade are greater.

All of this serves to illustrate a point we made back in Chapter 2: To gain from trade, it pays to be different from the world. Small countries are more likely to be different from the world than large countries are. Therefore, small countries have more to gain from international trade than large ones do. For many goods, world relative prices do not differ significantly from U.S. relative prices, so the United States has relatively little to gain from trade in these goods. But New Zealand, for example, where the autarkic relative price of wool is quite low, benefits greatly from being able to trade its wool for other goods at the comparatively high world relative price.

## The World Economy

We have seen how Robinson Crusoe reacts to world prices, and we have asserted that these world prices are determined by supply and demand. To complete the picture of the world economy, we have only to understand exactly how the world supply and demand curves are determined.

To derive a point on the supply curve for tomatoes, we imagine a price and ask what quantity Robinson supplies. Referring again to Exhibit 8.25, suppose that the colored budget line has absolute slope *P*. Then Robinson produces basket *B*, and the quantity of tomatoes he supplies is the horizontal coordinate of this point (whether he supplies them to himself or to someone else is not relevant here). The price *P* corresponds to this quantity on the supply curve.

To get another point on the supply curve, suppose the black budget line has absolute slope *P′*. At this price, Robinson produces at point *C*, and the corresponding quantity of tomatoes is paired with price *P′* on his supply curve.

A similar procedure generates points on Robinson's demand curve. When the price is *P*, he has the colored budget line and demands a quantity of tomatoes given by the horizontal coordinate of point *B*. When the price is *P′*, he has the black budget line and demands a quantity given by the horizontal coordinate of point *X*.

In this way, we can generate Robinson's supply and demand curves for tomatoes. We can do the same for all his trading partners. We get world supply and demand curves by adding the individual supply and demand curves, and these determine a world equilibrium price.

## Summary

Consumers and producers both gain from trade. Consumers' and producers' surpluses are measures of the extent of their gains.

When the consumer buys a good X, the total value of his purchase is given by the area under his demand curve out to the quantity. This area is the most that he would be willing to pay in exchange for that quantity of X. After we subtract the total cost to the consumer, we are left with the area under his demand curve down to the price paid and out to the quantity consumed. This area is his consumer's surplus. It is the amount that the consumer would be willing to pay in exchange for being allowed to purchase good X.

The producer's surplus is the excess of the producer's revenues over his costs. It is measured by the area above the supply curve up to the price received and out to the quantity supplied.

When there is more than one consumer or more than one producer, the total surplus to all consumers is given by the area under the market demand curve down to the price paid and out to the quantity demanded. The total surplus to all producers is given by the area above the market supply curve up to the price received and out to the quantity sold.

Policies such as taxes or price controls can change prices and quantities and consequently change the consumers' and producers' surpluses. They also sometimes generate tax revenue (which is a gain to somebody) or impose a cost on taxpayers (which is a loss). Social gain is the sum of consumers' and producers' surpluses, plus any other gains, minus any losses. If a policy reduces social gain below what it might have been, the amount of the reduction is known as a deadweight loss.

Whenever there is deadweight loss, it is possible to devise an alternative policy that is Pareto-preferred (i.e., preferred by everybody) to the current policy. A policy is said to be Pareto-optimal, or efficient, if no other policy is Pareto-preferred.

The efficiency criterion is a normative criterion asserting that we should prefer policies that maximize social gain, or, equivalently, minimize deadweight loss. Few (if any) would argue that the efficiency criterion should be the sole guide to policy, but many economists consider it reasonable to use it as a rough guideline. When a policy creates large deadweight losses, there may be a Pareto-preferred policy that is actually possible to implement.

The invisible hand theorem states that competitive equilibrium is Pareto-optimal. That is, in a competitive market where each individual seeks only his own personal gains, it turns out to be the case that social gains are maximized. This is true in individual markets and remains true when the entire economy is taken into account. The Edgeworth box presents an example of a complete economy that can be used to illustrate the workings of the invisible hand.

It is also possible to study general equilibrium in economies with production. The opportunity to trade with outsiders confers benefits on the members of such an economy. The more world prices differ from autarkic relative prices, the greater those benefits tend to be.

# Author Commentary          www.cengage.com/economics/landsburg

**AC1.**  Read about the conflict between the Pareto criterion and individual freedom. Also read about how good voting systems are hard to find, both in politics and in sports.

# Review Questions

**R1.**  Explain why a consumer's demand curve is identical to his marginal value curve.

**R2.**  What geometric areas represent the value of the goods that a consumer purchases and the cost of producing those goods? What geometric area represents the social gain from the goods' production, and why?

**R3.**  What geometric areas represent the consumers' and producers' surpluses, and why?

**R4.**  Analyze the effect on social welfare of a sales tax.

**R5.**  Analyze the effect on social welfare of a subsidy.

**R6.**  Analyze the effect on social welfare of a price ceiling.

**R7.**  Analyze the effect on social welfare of a tariff, assuming that the country imposing the tariff constitutes a small part of the entire market. First answer assuming that the good in question is available only from abroad, then repeat your answer assuming that there is a domestic industry.

**R8.**  "The fact that secretaries are paid less than corporate executives shows that society values secretarial services less than it values the work of executives." Comment.

**R9.**  State the invisible hand theorem. Illustrate its meaning using supply and demand curves.

**R10.**  Explain the difference between the allocation of resources and the distribution of income. With which is the efficiency criterion concerned?

**R11.**  Using an Edgeworth box, illustrate the region of mutual advantage and the contract curve. Explain why trade will always lead to a point that is both in the region and on the curve.

**R12.**  Using an Edgeworth box, illustrate the competitive equilibrium. Explain how you know that the competitive equilibrium is on the contract curve. How does this illustrate the invisible hand theorem?

**R13.**  Show how Robinson Crusoe chooses his consumption point when he is unable to trade. Show how he chooses his production and consumption points when trade becomes an option.

# Problem Set

1.  **True or False:** If consumers buy 1,000 heads of lettuce per week, and if the price of lettuce falls by 10¢ per head, then the consumer's surplus will increase by $100.

2.  Suppose that your demand curves for gadgets and widgets are both straight lines but your demand curve for gadgets is much more elastic than your demand curve for widgets. Each is selling at a market price of $10, and at that price you choose to buy exactly 30 gadgets and 30 widgets.

    a.  From which transaction do you gain more surplus?
    b.  If forced at gunpoint to buy either an extra gadget or an extra widget, which would you buy?
    c.  Illustrate the change in your consumer's surplus as a result of the forced transaction of part (b).

3.  Adam and Eve consume only apples. Of the following allocations of apples, which are preferred to which others according to (a) the Pareto criterion, and (b) the efficiency criterion?

    a.  Adam has 12 apples and Eve has 0 apples.
    b.  Adam has 9 apples and Eve has 3 apples.
    c.  Adam has 6 apples and Eve has 6 apples.
    d.  Adam has 0 apples and Eve has 12 apples.
    e.  Adam has 5 apples and Eve has 5 apples.

4.  **True or False:** Cheap foreign goods hurt American producers and are therefore bad according to the efficiency criterion.

5.  **True or False:** If there is a fixed amount of land in Wyoming, then a sales tax on Wyoming land will have no effect on social welfare.

6.  Home insulation is currently subsidized. Draw a graph (as in Exhibit 8.12) that shows the gains and losses to all relevant groups. Explain how you could, in principle, make *everyone* happier by eliminating the subsidy and instead transferring income from some people to others. Be explicit about exactly who you'd take income from, how much you would take, and how you would distribute it.

7.  The demand and supply curves for gasoline are the same in Upper Slobbovia as in Lower Slobbovia. However, in Upper Slobbovia everybody's time is worth just $1 per hour, while in Lower Slobbovia everybody's time is worth $10 per hour. **True or False:** If both countries impose a price ceiling on gasoline, the value of time wasted in waiting lines will be higher in Lower Slobbovia than in Upper Slobbovia.

8.  In the preceding problem, suppose that there is also a country of Middle Slobbovia, where the value of various people's time ranges between $1 and $10. If Middle Slobbovia imposes a price ceiling on gasoline, how will the value of time wasted in waiting lines compare to the time wasted in Upper and Lower Slobbovia?

9.  Suppose the equilibrium price of potatoes is $5 per pound, but the government imposes a price ceiling of $2 per pound, creating a deadweight loss. **True or False:** If the government imposes an *excise tax* of $1 per pound of potatoes (while continuing to maintain the price ceiling), then the deadweight loss will get even larger.

**10.** Suppose the equilibrium price of potatoes is $5 per pound, but the government imposes a price ceiling of $2 per pound, creating a deadweight loss. **True or False:** If the government imposes a *sales tax* of $1 per pound of potatoes (while continuing to maintain the price ceiling), then the deadweight loss will get even larger.

**11.** Suppose there is a federal excise tax on gasoline of 4.3¢ per gallon. A United States senator has proposed eliminating this tax, but requiring oil companies to pass all of the savings on to the consumer (by maintaining a new price at the pump that is 4.3¢ lower than the current price). Show the deadweight loss under the current tax and under the senator's plan. Can you tell which is bigger?

**12.** **True or False:** A price ceiling on wheat would cause the price of bread to fall.

**13.** In equilibrium, 500 pounds of potatoes are sold each week. However, the government prints up and randomly distributes 250 non-reusable ration tickets each week, and requires that buyers present one ration ticket for each pound of potatoes they buy. Therefore consumers can purchase only 250 pounds of potatoes per week. Ration tickets can be freely bought and sold. Draw a graph illustrating the market for potatoes, and on your graph indicate:

**a.** The price of a pound of potatoes.

**b.** The price of a ration ticket.

**c.** The consumer and producer surplus in the potato market.

**d.** The value of the ration tickets to the citizens who are randomly chosen to receive them.

**e.** The deadweight loss.

**14.** The American supply and demand curves for potatoes cross at $5 a pound, but potatoes are available in any quantity from abroad at $2 a pound. Each week, American sellers produce 500 pounds of potatoes and American buyers purchase a total of 1,200 pounds. Suppose the government prints and randomly distributes 250 non-reusable ration tickets each week, and requires that buyers present one ration ticket for each pound of *imported* potatoes that they buy. (You don't need a ration ticket to buy an American potato.) Ration tickets can be freely bought and sold. Draw a graph illustrating the market for potatoes, and on your graph indicate the price Americans now pay for potatoes, the price of a ration ticket, the gains and losses to all relevant groups, and the deadweight loss.

**15.** Widgets are produced by a competitive industry and sold for $5 apiece. The government requires each widget firm to have a license, and charges the highest license fee firms are willing to pay. If the government were to impose an excise tax of $3 per widget, how much would the license fee have to change? (Illustrate your answer as an area on a graph). Would total government revenue (i.e., excise tax revenue plus revenue from license fees) rise or fall as a result of the excise tax?

**16.** In equilibrium, 2,000 pounds of potatoes are sold each month. A new law requires sellers to buy permits before they can sell potatoes. One permit allows you to sell one pound, and permits can't be reused. The government creates only 1,000 permits and sells them to the highest bidders. Use a graph to show the new price of potatoes, the price of a permit, the gains and losses to all relevant groups, and the deadweight loss.

**17.** Toys are produced by a competitive industry. Santa Claus gives away one million free toys each year. Illustrate Santa's effect on a) the price of toys, b) the consumer surplus, c) the producer surplus earned by commercial toy manufacturers, and d) social gain. (Don't worry about gains or losses to Santa.) (*Hint:* Remember that the toys Santa distributes are free.)

**18.** Suppose the government sets an effective price *floor* (i.e., a price above equilibrium) in the market for oranges and agrees to buy all oranges that go unsold at that price. The oranges purchased by the government are discarded. Illustrate the number of oranges purchased by the government. Illustrate the gains and losses to all relevant groups of Americans and the deadweight loss.

**19.** The American demand and supply curves for oranges cross at a price of $8, but all Americans are free to buy or sell oranges on the world market at a price of $5. One day, the U.S. government announces that it will pay $6 apiece for American oranges and will buy as many oranges as Americans want to sell at that price. The government then takes these oranges and resells them on the world market at $5 apiece. Illustrate the gains and losses to all relevant groups of Americans, and illustrate the deadweight loss.

**20.** In the tariff example of Exhibit 8.17, divide the two triangles of deadweight loss into individual rectangles of loss, as in Exhibit 8.9. Give an intuitive explanation of the loss that each of those rectangles represents.

**21.** Suppose the U.S. supply and demand curves for automobiles cross at a price of $15,000 but (identical) automobiles can be purchased from abroad for $10,000. Now suppose the government imposes a $2,000 excise tax on every car produced in the United States (regardless of whether the car is sold in the United States or abroad).

    **a.** What price must Americans pay for cars before the tax is imposed? What price must Americans pay for cars after the tax is imposed? (*Hint:* Americans can always buy cars on the world market and so will never pay more than the world price for a car.) What prices do U.S. producers receive for their cars before and after the tax is imposed?

    **b.** Before and after the tax is imposed, calculate the gains to all relevant groups of Americans. What is the deadweight loss due to the tax?

**22.** The equilibrium price of an apple is 25¢. The government sets a price ceiling of 15¢ per apple, and requires sellers to provide as many apples as buyers want to buy at that price. Draw a graph to illustrate the price ceiling and answer the following questions in terms of areas on your graph:

    **a.** What areas would you measure to determine whether sellers continue selling apples in the short run? (To answer this, you can assume that all sellers are identical.)

    **b.** If sellers continue selling apples, what area represents the deadweight loss and why?

    **c.** If sellers don't continue selling apples, what area represents the deadweight loss and why?

**23.** Suppose the U.S. supply and demand curves for automobiles cross at a price of $15,000 but (identical) automobiles can be purchased from abroad for $10,000. Now suppose the government imposes a $2,000 sales tax on every American who buys a car (regardless of whether the car is produced domestically or abroad).

    **a.** What price must Americans pay for cars before the tax is imposed? What price must Americans pay for cars after the tax is imposed? (*Hint:* American suppliers can always sell cars abroad for $10,000 and so will never sell cars for less.) What prices do U.S. producers receive for their cars before and after the tax is imposed?

**b.** Before and after the tax is imposed, calculate the gains to all relevant groups of Americans. What is the deadweight loss due to the tax?

**24.** Suppose the U.S. supply and demand curves for automobiles cross at a price of $15,000 but (identical) automobiles can be purchased from abroad for $10,000. Now suppose the government offers a subsidy of $2,000 to each American who buys an imported car. Buyers of domestic cars receive no subsidy.

**a.** What price do Americans pay for domestic cars before the subsidy is offered? What is the most an American will pay for a domestic car after the subsidy is offered?

**b.** Given your answer to part (a), and given that anyone can buy or sell cars abroad at the world price of $10,000, how many cars will U.S. producers want to sell in the United States?

**c.** Before and after the subsidy is offered, calculate the gains to all relevant groups of Americans. What is the deadweight loss due to the subsidy?

**d.** How does your answer change if U.S. producers are prohibited from selling cars abroad?

**25.** Suppose the U.S. supply and demand curves for automobiles cross at a price of $15,000 but (identical) automobiles can be purchased from abroad for $10,000. Now suppose the government offers U.S. producers a $2,000 subsidy for every car they produce (regardless of whether the car is sold in the United States or abroad).

**a.** What prices must Americans pay for cars before and after the subsidy is offered? What prices do U.S. producers feel they are receiving before and after the subsidy is offered?

**b.** Before and after the subsidy is offered, calculate the gains to all relevant groups of Americans. What is the deadweight loss due to the subsidy?

**26.** Suppose the U.S. supply and demand curves for automobiles cross at a price of $15,000 and that (identical) automobiles can be purchased from abroad for $10,000. Now suppose the government offers a $2,000 subsidy to every American who buys a car (regardless of whether the car is foreign or domestic).

**a.** At what prices do U.S. producers sell their cars before and after the subsidy is offered? What prices do U.S. consumers feel like they are paying before and after the subsidy is offered?

**b.** Before and after the subsidy is offered, calculate the gains to all relevant groups of Americans. What is the deadweight loss due to the subsidy?

**27.** The American supply and demand curves for cars cross at $15,000. Foreigners will sell us any number of cars at the world price of $10,000. Now the government announces two new taxes: a sales tax of $1,000 on each American car, and a sales tax (i.e., a tariff) of $3,000 on each foreign car. Illustrate the gains and/or losses to all relevant groups of Americans as a result of the combined tax program, and illustrate the deadweight loss.

**28.** There is currently a sales tax on all cars, foreign and domestic. In order to help the American car industry, the government is thinking of eliminating the sales tax.

Plan A is to eliminate the tax for domestic cars only; Plan B is to eliminate the tax for both domestic and foreign cars.

**a.** Which plan is better for domestic car makers?

**b.** **True or False:** Plan B, combined with an appropriate redistribution of income, can make *everybody* happier than Plan A. If your answer is true, explicitly describe the appropriate redistribution of income. If your answer is false, explain carefully why no such redistribution is possible.

**29.** The American supply and demand curves for bananas cross at $5. Foreigners will buy as many bananas as Americans want to sell at $10. The government subsidizes exports by giving sellers $2 for each banana they sell abroad. Bananas cannot be imported into the United States.

**a.** Illustrate the deadweight loss from the subsidy.

**b.** Devise a program that *everyone*—buyers, sellers, and the recipients of the revenue—prefers to the subsidy.

**30.** The American supply and demand curves for widgets are illustrated at the top of the next page. Foreign widget makers will sell any quantity of widgets to Americans at a price of $2 apiece.

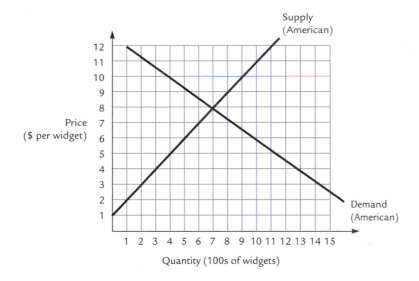

Suppose the government distributes 500 ration coupons, which can be freely bought and sold. To buy a foreign-made widget, you must present a ration coupon. (An American widget requires no coupon.) What is the price of a ration coupon? (Your answer should be a number.)

**31.** Suppose that the government successfully maintains a price $P_0$ for wheat that is above the equilibrium price. At this price, consumers want to purchase $Q_d$ bushels of wheat and farmers want to produce $Q_s$. The way that the government maintains the price $P_0$ is by offering farmers a cash reward for limiting their production.

**a.** By how much must farmers agree to cut back production in order for the program to be successful?

**b.** Show on a graph the minimum payment that the government must make to farmers in order for them to agree to the deal.

**c.** Assuming that the government makes this minimum payment, use your graph to show the gains and losses to consumers, producers, and taxpayers from this arrangement. Calculate the deadweight loss.

**32.** The American demand and supply curves for labor cross at a wage rate of $25 per hour. However, American firms can hire as many foreign workers as they want to at a wage of $15 per hour. (Assume that foreign workers are exactly as productive as American workers.) A new law requires American firms to pay $25 an hour to Americans and to hire every American who wants to work at that wage. Firms may still hire any number of foreigners at $15 per hour.

**a.** Before the law is enacted, what wage do American workers earn? Illustrate the consumers' and producers' surpluses earned by American workers and American firms.

**b.** After the law is enacted, illustrate the number of Americans hired and the number of foreigners hired, the consumers' and producers' surpluses earned by American workers and American firms, and the deadweight loss.

**33.** Widgets are produced by a constant-cost industry. Suppose the government decides to institute an annual subsidy of $8,000 per year to every firm that produces widgets.

**a.** Explain why, in the long run, each firm's producer surplus must fall by $8,000.

**b.** Suppose the subsidy causes the price of widgets to fall by $1. With the subsidy in place, does each firm produce more than, fewer than, or exactly 8,000 widgets a year?

**c.** Suppose the government replaces the per-firm subsidy with a per-widget subsidy of $1 per widget produced. In the long run, is this change good or bad for consumers? Is it good or bad for producers? (*Hint:* Remember the zero-profit condition!) Is it good or bad for taxpayers? Is it good or bad according to the efficiency criterion?

**34.** **True or False:** If all thieves are identical, then the social cost of robbery is equal to the value of the stolen goods.

**35.** Popeye and Wimpy trade only with each other. Popeye has 8 hamburgers and 2 cans of spinach, and Wimpy has 2 hamburgers and 8 cans of spinach. Their indifference, somewhat unusually, are all straight lines, Popeye's being much steeper than Wimpy's:

**Popeye's indifference curves**

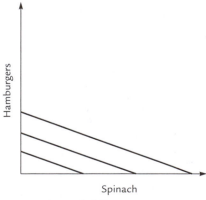

**Wimpy's indifference curves**

In an Edgeworth box, show the initial endowment, the region of mutual advantage, the contract curve, and the competitive equilibrium.

36. Robinson Crusoe lives alone on an island, producing nuts and berries and trading with people on other islands. If his production possibility curve is a straight line, what can you conclude about the quantities of nuts and berries he will produce?

37. Robinson Crusoe lives alone on an island, producing nuts and berries and trading with people on other islands. **True or False:** If nuts are an inferior good for Robinson, then his supply curve for nuts must be upward sloping.

# Appendix to Chapter 8

## Normative Criteria

Suppose that by ordering the execution of one innocent man you could save the lives of five others, equally innocent. Should you do it?

**Consequentialist moral theories** assert that the correctness of an act depends only on its consequences. A simple consequentialist position might be that one lost life is less bad than five lost lives, so the execution should proceed.

Other views are possible. You might argue that if the one man to be executed is happy and fulfilled, while the other five lead barely tolerable lives, then it would be better to spare the one and sacrifice the five. This position is still consequentialist, because it judges an action by its consequences: The sacrifice of one happy life versus the sacrifice of five unhappy lives.

There are also moral theories that are not consequentialist. Some are based on natural rights. One could argue that a man has a natural right to live and that there can be no justification for depriving him of this right, regardless of the consequences. There can be no execution, even if it would save a hundred innocent lives.

In the heated public debate about abortion, both sides have tended to make arguments that go beyond consequentialism. One side defends a "right to choose," while the other defends a "right to life." A strictly consequentialist view would discard any discussion of "rights" and judge the desirability of legalized abortion strictly on the basis of its implications for human happiness. This is not enough to settle the issue; one must still face extraordinarily difficult questions about how to trade off different people's happiness and potential happiness. Consequentialism, like natural rights doctrine, accommodates many precepts and conclusions.

The efficiency criterion is an example of a consequentialist normative theory. Which kind of world is better: One with 10 people, each earning $50,000 per year, or one with 10 people, of whom 3 earn $30,000 and 7 earn $100,000? According to a strict application of the efficiency criterion, the second world is better, because total income is $790,000 instead of $500,000. The world with more wealth is the better world.

There are many other possible viewpoints, some consequentialist and some not. One might argue that certain people are more deserving of high income than others, and so there is no way to choose between the two income distributions without knowing more about the characteristics of the people involved. Such a position introduces criteria other than the ultimate consequences for human happiness, and so can be characterized as nonconsequentialist.

Judging the desirability of outcomes requires a normative theory. Economics can help us understand the implications of various theories, and perhaps help us choose among them. For the most part, economic analysis tends to focus on the various

**Consequentialist moral theories**

Moral theories that assert that the correctness of an act can be judged by its consequences.

consequentialist theories. This is not because natural rights doctrines are uninteresting; it just seems to be the case that (so far) economics has less to say about them.

## Some Normative Criteria

Here are a few of the normative criteria that economists have thought about.

### Majority Rule

According to this simple criterion, the better of two outcomes is the one that most people prefer.

A number of objections can be raised. One is that majority rule does not provide a coherent basis for choosing among *three* or more possible outcomes. Sharon, Lois, and Bram plan to order a pizza with one topping. Their preferences are shown in the following table:

|               | Sharon    | Lois      | Bram      |
|---------------|-----------|-----------|-----------|
| First Choice  | Peppers   | Anchovies | Onions    |
| Second Choice | Anchovies | Onions    | Peppers   |
| Third Choice  | Onions    | Peppers   | Anchovies |

A majority (Sharon and Bram) prefers peppers to anchovies, a different majority (Sharon and Lois) prefers anchovies to onions, and a third (Lois and Bram) prefers onions to peppers. No matter what topping is chosen, there is some majority that prefers a different one.

A more fundamental objection to majority rule is that it forces us to accept outcomes that almost all people agree are undesirable. If 60% of the people vote to torture and maim the other 40% for their own amusement, a true believer in majority rule is forced to admit the legitimacy of their decision.

A less flamboyant example is a proposed tax policy that would have the effect of increasing 51% of all household incomes by $1 per year while decreasing 49% of all household incomes by $10,000 per year. The majority supports the proposal. Do you think it should be implemented?

### The Kaldor–Hicks Potential Compensation Criterion

The British economists Nicholas Kaldor and Sir John Hicks suggest a normative criterion under which a change is a good thing if it would be possible in principle for the winners to compensate the losers for their losses and still remain winners.

If a policy increases Jack's income by $10, reduces Jill's by $5, and has no other effects, should it be implemented? According to Kaldor–Hicks, the answer is yes, because Jack could in principle reimburse Jill for her loss and still come out ahead. On the other hand, a policy that increases Jack's income by $10 while reducing Jill's by $15 is a bad thing, because there is no way for Jack to reimburse Jill out of his winnings.

In applications like this, the Kaldor–Hicks criterion and the efficiency criterion amount to the same thing. When Jack gains $10 and Jill loses $5, social gains increase by $5, so the policy is a good one. When Jack gains $10 and Jill loses $15, there is a deadweight loss of $5, so the policy is bad.

However, there are potential subtleties that we did not address when we discussed the efficiency criterion in Section 8.1. Suppose that Jack has a stamp collection that he values very highly. Aside from his stamp collection, he owns nothing of great value and in fact barely gets enough to eat. Nevertheless, he would be unwilling to sell his stamp collection for anything less than $100,000. On the other hand, if the collection were taken from him, he would be willing to pay only $100 to get it back; any higher payment would mean starvation.

Jill values Jack's stamp collection at $50,000, regardless of who currently owns it. Should the collection be taken from Jack and given to Jill? If so, she would gain $50,000 in surplus, which is not enough to compensate Jack for his $100,000 loss. The Kaldor–Hicks criterion opposes such a move.

On the other hand, suppose that the stamp collection has already found its way into Jill's hands. If it is restored to Jack, he gains something that he values at $100, not enough to compensate Jill for her $50,000 loss. Kaldor–Hicks opposes this move also.

Thus, we get the somewhat paradoxical result that Jack gets to keep his stamp collection, unless it accidentally finds its way into Jill's hands, in which case Jack is not allowed to get it back.

Such paradoxes did not arise when we applied the efficiency criterion in Section 8.1. Why not? When we experimented with changing government policies, making some people better off and others worse off, we implicitly assumed that there were no resulting income effects on demand. If there are income effects, they cause the demand curve to shift at the moment when the policy is implemented. (In the present example, Jack's demand for stamps shifts dramatically depending on whether he already owns them or not.) This makes welfare analysis ambiguous: Should we calculate surplus using the old demand curve or the new one?

However, when the changes being contemplated do not affect large fractions of people's income, the Kaldor–Hicks criterion becomes unambiguous and equivalent to the efficiency criterion we have already studied.

## The Veil of Ignorance

Let us repeat an earlier question. Is it better for everyone to earn $50,000 or for 70% of us to earn $100,000 while the rest earn $30,000?

The philosopher John Rawls has popularized a way to think about such problems.[1] Imagine two planets: On Planet X everyone earns $50,000; on Planet Y 70% earn $100,000 and the rest earn $30,000. On which planet would you rather be born? Your honest answer reveals which income distribution is morally preferable.

When you choose where to be born, it is important that you not know who you will be. If you knew that you'd be rich on Planet Y, you would presumably choose Y; if you knew you'd be poor on Y you would presumably choose X. But Rawls insists that we imagine making the decision from behind a *veil of ignorance,* deprived of any knowledge of whose life we will live.

A potential problem with the "veil of ignorance" criterion is that there might be honest disagreements about which is the better world. But Rawls contends that such disagreements arise because of different circumstances in our present lives. If we take seriously the presumption of the veil, that we have not yet lived and are all equally likely to live one life as another, then the reasons for disagreement will vanish and we will achieve unanimity. The unanimous decision is the right decision.

Suppose that a potential change in policy would enrich one billionaire by $10,000 while costing eight impoverished people $1,000 each. The efficiency criterion

---

[1] See J. Rawls, *A Theory of Justice* (Harvard University Press, 1971). A similar idea had appeared in J. C. Harsanyi; "Cardinal Utility in Welfare Economics and the Theory of Risk Taking," *Journal of Political Economy* 61 (1953): 434–435.

pronounces such a policy a good one. Rawls's criterion probably would not. If you did not yet know whether you were going to be the billionaire or one of the impoverished, it seems likely that you would oppose this policy, on a variety of grounds. First, $10,000 is unlikely to make much difference in a billionaire's life, while a loss of $1,000 can be devastating if you are very poor. Second, it is 8 times more likely that you will be poor than rich. Rawls would argue that behind the veil of ignorance, the vote against this policy would be unanimous. Therefore, the policy is bad.

The veil of ignorance can be used to justify various forms of social insurance, in which income is redistributed from the more to the less fortunate. Some misfortunes do not usually strike until late in life, and we can buy insurance against them at our leisure. But other misfortunes are evident from birth, making insurance impossible. You can't insure against being born into poverty, or with below-average intelligence. There is a plausible case that behind the veil, we *would* insure ourselves, by agreeing that those born into the best circumstances will transfer income to those born into the worst. Because everyone behind the veil would want this agreement, it is a good thing and should be enforced.

## The Maximin Criterion

The maximin criterion says that we should always prefer that outcome which maximizes the welfare of the worst-off member of society. Taken to the extreme, this means that a world in which everyone is a millionaire, except for one man who has only $200, is not as good as a world in which everyone has only $300 except for one man who has $201.

Perhaps nobody would want to apply the maximin criterion in a circumstance quite so extreme as this. But John Rawls believes that for the most part, souls living behind the veil of ignorance would want the maximin criterion to be applied. This is because people abhor risk and worry about the prospect of being born unlucky. Therefore, while still behind the veil, their primary concern is to improve the lot of the least fortunate members of society.

According to Rawls, then, the maximin criterion is not really a new criterion at all, but instead prescribes essentially the same outcomes that the veil of ignorance criterion prescribes.[2]

## The Ideal Participant Criterion

This is a slight variant on the veil of ignorance criterion, developed by Professor Tyler Cowen for the purpose of thinking about the problem of population but applicable more generally. (We will briefly address the population problem later in this appendix.) According to this criterion, we should imagine living many lives in succession, one each in the circumstances of every person on earth. The right outcomes are the ones we would choose before setting out on this long journey.

In comparing the ideal participant criterion with the more standard veil of ignorance criterion, you might want to consider two critical questions. First, in what

[2] A complete statement of Rawls's position would have to incorporate at least two additional subtleties. First, Rawls believes that from behind the veil, people's first priority would be to design social institutions that guarantee individual liberty. Having narrowed down to this set of institutions, they would then choose among them according to the maximin criterion. Second, Rawls does not want to apply the maximin criterion to particular details of the income distribution or human interactions. He wants to apply it instead to the design of social institutions. Thus, a Rawlsian might focus not on designing the ideal income distribution but rather on designing an ideal tax structure, from which the income distribution would arise. Rawls seeks that tax structure, among all of those that are consistent with individual liberty, which maximizes benefits to the least well-off members of society.

circumstances would these criteria lead to the same choices and in what circumstances would they disagree? Second, is there some more fundamental moral principle from which we can deduce a preference for one of the two criteria over the other? So far, economists have not found much to say about either of these issues.

## Utilitarianism

**Utilitarianism,** a creation of the philosopher Jeremy Bentham, asserts that it is meaningful to measure each person's *utility,* or happiness, by a number. This makes it possible to make meaningful comparisons across people: If your utility is 4 and mine is 3, then you are happier than I am. (By contrast, many modern economists deny that any precise meaning can be attached to the statement "Person X is happier than Person Y.")[3]

Starting from the assertion that utilities are meaningful, utilitarians argue that the best outcome is the one that maximizes the sum of everybody's utilities. By this criterion, it is often better to augment the income of a poor man than a rich man, because an extra dollar contributes more to the poor man's utility than to the rich man's. This conclusion need not follow, however. One can imagine that the poor man has for some reason a much lower *capacity for happiness* than the rich man has, so that additional income contributes little to his enjoyment of life.

A generalized form of utilitarianism proposes that we assign a *weight* to each person and maximize the *weighted* sum of their utilities. If Jack has weight 2 and Jill has weight 3, then we choose the outcome that maximizes twice Jack's utility plus 3 times Jill's. The source of the weights themselves is left open, or is determined by any of various auxiliary theories.[4]

Under quite general circumstances, it is possible to prove that utilitarianism, with any choice of weights, always leads to a Pareto-optimal outcome and that utilitarian criteria are the only criteria that always lead to Pareto-optimal outcomes. This is so even if we drop the assumption that it is meaningful to compare different people's utilities.

## Fairness

Economists have attempted to formalize the notion of fairness in a variety of ways, usually in the context of allocating fixed supplies of more than one good. In a world with 6 apples and 6 oranges, it seems absurd to insist that Jack and Jill each end up with 3 of each fruit; after all Jack might have a strong preference for apples and Jill for oranges. On the other hand, it seems quite unfair for either Jack or Jill to have all of the food while the other one starves. What precisely distinguishes those allocations that we think are equitable?

A widely studied criterion is that allocations should be envy-free, which means that no person would prefer somebody else's basket of goods to his own. Any allocation of apples and oranges is envy-free if neither Jack nor Jill would want to trade places with the other, given the choice.

### Utilitarianism

The belief that utility, or happiness, can be meaningfully measured and that it is desirable to maximize the sum of everyone's utility.

### Envy-free allocation

An outcome in which nobody would prefer to trade baskets with anybody else.

---

[3] Utilitarians are not the only ones who believe that they can compare different people's happiness. In order to apply the maximin criterion, for example, it is necessary to make sense of the notion of the "least well-off" member of society.

[4] The primary proponents of utilitarianism among economists were H. Sidgwick and F. Y. Edgeworth (the same Edgeworth of the Edgeworth box). For a very interesting attempt to reconstruct the weights that Sidgwick and Edgeworth had in mind, see M. Yaari, 'Rawls, Edgeworth, Shapley, Nash: Theories of Distributive Justice Re-examined,' *Journal of Economic Theory* 24 (1981): 1–39.

In an Edgeworth box economy, it is possible to show that if each trading partner starts with equal shares of everything (3 apples and 3 oranges each), then any competitive equilibrium is envy-free. This is an important result, because we already know that any competitive equilibrium is efficient as well; that is, it satisfies the efficiency criterion. This implies that in such an economy, it is always possible to achieve an outcome that is simultaneously efficient and envy-free, satisfying two criteria at once.

## Optimal Population

What is the right number of people?[5] If large populations imply crowding and unpleasantness, then how much is too much? Would it be better if there were only 10 people, each deliriously happy, or if there were 1 billion people, each slightly less happy? Where should we draw the line?

It should first be noted that the implied premise is at least debatable. A 10% increase in the current world population would change a lot of things, some for the better and some for the worse. The new arrivals would consume resources (which is bad for the rest of us) and produce output (which is good for the rest of us); it is unclear whether we'd be better or worse off on balance.

Still, it is probable that beyond some point—though it might be very far beyond the point we're at now—increases in population will make life less pleasant for everyone. At what point does the population become 'too big'? The population problem tends to confound the usual normative criteria, which are designed to address the problem of allocating resources among a fixed number of people.

We could adopt the utilitarian prescription, attempting to maximize total utility. A world of 1 billion reasonably happy people is better than a world with 100 extremely happy people, because total utility is higher in the first of these worlds. But the same criterion dictates that a world of 10 trillion people, each leading a barely tolerable existence, can be superior to the world of 1 billion who are reasonably happy. To some economists, this conclusion is self-evidently absurd. Professor Derek Parfit has endowed it with a proper name: He calls it the Repugnant Conclusion.[6] To Parfit and others, any moral theory that entails the Repugnant Conclusion must be rejected. There are others, though, who think that the repugnance of the Repugnant Conclusion is far from evident.

An alternative is to maximize average (as opposed to total) utility. In practice, people are probably happier on average when the population is reasonably large (so that there is greater efficiency in production, a wider range of consumer goods, and a better chance of finding love). Therefore, a world of 1 billion might lead to higher average utility than a world of 100, even though a grossly overcrowded world of 1 trillion is worse than either. An objection to the average utility criterion is that it always implies that the world would be a better place if everyone with below-average utility were removed.

Alternatively, we can step behind the veil of ignorance and ask how many of us should be born. The trade-off is this: If the population is too large, the world is an unpleasant place, but if it is too small, most of us never get a chance to live. The conceptual problem here is to decide exactly how many souls there are behind the veil. Is there one for every person who *might* be born? Is that an infinite number? If so, then

[5] This entire section owes much to Tyler Cowen's paper "Normative Population Theory," *Social Choice and Welfare* 6 (1989): 33–43.

[6] D. Parfit, *Reasons and Persons* (Oxford University Press, 1984).

each has effectively zero chance of being among the finitely many lucky ones who do get born, rendering each indifferent to what the world is like. If instead there is a large, finite number of souls behind the veil, what determines that large, finite number?

Tyler Cowen has raised an additional objection to the veil of ignorance criterion. He asks a form of the following question: Suppose that you were offered a bet, whereby there is a 1% chance that 100 duplicate copies of earth will be created and a 99% chance that all human life will disappear. Would you take the bet? Behind the veil you would, because it actually increases the chance of your birth without changing the average quality of human life. Yet, Cowen argues, the bet is obviously a bad one.[7] Because the veil criterion leads us to choose a bad bet, it must be a bad criterion.

Cowen has argued that the Ideal Participant Criterion is the ideal criterion for considering problems of population. You can read his arguments in the paper cited in the footnote at the beginning of this section. But the issue is very far from settled. In a world where we can't agree on what the speed limit should be, a consensus on population size will probably be a long time coming.

## Author Commentary            www.cengage.com/economics/landsburg

**AC1 A-1.**    Good voting systems are hard to find, both in politics and in sports.

**AC1 A-2.**    If we take the veil of ignorance seriously, what does it dictate? For some back-of-the-envelope calculations, read this article.

**AC1 A-3.**    Read about one point of view on various normative criteria applied to tax policy.

**AC1 A-4.**    What does utilitarianism say about the case for environmental conservation?

**AC1 A-5.**    For more on optimal population, see this article.

**AC1 A-6.**    This is an article on optimal population.

---

[7] It should perhaps be mentioned that what is obvious to Cowen is not obvious to everyone, among them the author of your textbook.

# Knowledge and Information

Every night the 1.5 million residents of Manhattan Island go to bed confident that when they awake, they will be able to purchase food, clothing, gasoline, and dozens of other items that are sent to New York City from thousands of miles away. How can Iowa farmers and Texas oil producers know what products to ship to Manhattan and in what quantities? Because each individual supplier makes an independent decision about how much to send, why do residents of the city not find all the stores nearly empty on some days or full to overflowing on others? When New Yorkers want more pork, how do the suppliers of feed corn know to increase production so that the hog farmers can raise more hogs? How is this activity coordinated with the activities of the butchers and truck drivers and refrigerator repairmen who are the hog farmers' partners in the production of pork chops? How *can* it be coordinated, when all of these producers are unknown to each other?[1]

In this chapter, we will see how prices serve to convey information so that complex social activities can be organized and implemented. This will extend our understanding of the social role of prices that was developed in Chapter 8. There we saw how the price system acts to allocate resources efficiently by ensuring that appropriate quantities will be produced. Here we will focus on how prices contribute to the efficient production and distribution of those quantities by embodying vast amounts of knowledge not available to any individual. The two effects work together—hand in invisible hand—to lead to social outcomes that take account of producers' costs and consumers' preferences in ways that no individual planner could hope to accomplish.

## 9.1 The Informational Content of Prices

### Prices and Information

The prestigious journal *Science* once carried an article titled "Limits to Exploitation of Nonrenewable Resources." It contained this passage:

---

[1] Such questions were raised by the nineteenth-century French economist Frederic Bastiat in his book *Economic Sophisms* (1873).

*To society...the profit from mining (including oil and gas extraction) can be defined either as an energy surplus, as from the exploitation of fossil and nuclear fuel deposits, or as a work saving, as in the lessened expenditure of human energy and time when steel is used in place of wood in tools and structures.*[2]

Presumably, the "energy surplus" associated with, say, a coal deposit refers to the difference between the energy that can be extracted from the coal deposit on the one hand, and the energy required to excavate it on the other.

By this accounting, a society's choice of energy sources becomes a matter of simple arithmetic. Suppose, for simplicity, that it is necessary to choose between two projects: mining coal (which is located in the eastern half of the United States) and drilling for oil (which is located in the West). Coal mining yields sufficient fuel to provide 1,000 British thermal units[3] of energy per month, but the mining process itself consumes 500 BTUs in the same time period. Oil drilling yields 800 BTUs per month but consumes 200 BTUs. Because the "social profit" from oil (600 BTUs per month) exceeds that from coal (500 BTUs), society should choose to drill for oil.

Alas, the world is not so simple. A subsequent issue of the same journal carried a letter from Harvard economist Robert Dorfman, who elucidated the fallacy. Suppose that the land in the West is the only land suitable for growing hops. A society that drills for oil will then be a society without beer. Then perhaps it is best to mine coal instead. Or perhaps not—the eastern land might be the best place to raise cattle. On the other hand, the West might be where everyone wants to live, because of its better climate and greater scenic beauty. (See Exhibit 9.1.) What should society do?

A rational choice involves weighing the importance of the alternative uses of land in the different regions of the country. Essentially, there are two ways to do this. One is to empanel a blue-ribbon commission, peopled by experts in mining, agriculture, ranching, housing, and other fields, and to empower this commission to collect evidence about public desires and technological constraints. The panel would inquire into how the eastern land might be made suitable for the growing of hops, and at what cost. It would ask whether there is a way to make beer without hops, or whether beer can be adequately imported, or whether there is some other beverage that might easily take the place of beer. Having settled these questions, it would move on to analogous questions about housing. At some point the commission would issue a report, making the best recommendation it could on the basis of the information it had been able to acquire.

An alternative is to observe the *price* of land in each region. The price of a parcel of land is equal (under competition) to the marginal cost of providing that parcel. Because a cost is nothing but a forgone opportunity, the price is a measure of the value of the land in the most valuable of its alternative uses.

When we observe that an acre of land in the West sells for $1,000 and that an acre in the East sells for $800, we know that someone values the western land at $1,000 per acre and that no one values the eastern land at more than $800 per acre. The price alone does not reveal the most valuable use of the western land, but it does reveal how much the land is worth in that use.[4]

Which method is more informative? The commission's report, which may fill three bound volumes and represent two years' work, can be worse than useless if the panelists fail to take account of even one important fact. Not knowing about a new breed of

---

[2] E. Cook, "Limits to Exploitation of Nonrenewable Resources," *Science* 191 (1976): 677–682.
[3] British thermal units, or BTUs, are the basic units in which energy is measured.
[4] There are exceptions to this rule, as we shall see in Chapter 13.

## EXHIBIT 9.1  Information and Prices

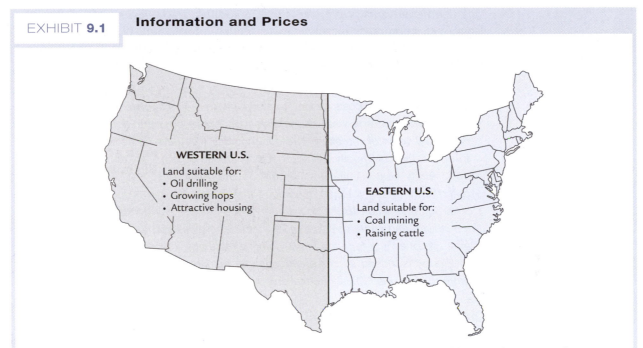

**WESTERN U.S.**
Land suitable for:
• Oil drilling
• Growing hops
• Attractive housing

**EASTERN U.S.**
Land suitable for:
• Coal mining
• Raising cattle

Even if we know that oil drilling produces more energy than coal mining, we still do not have enough information to choose between the two projects. If we drill for oil, we must do without beer and attractive housing, while if we mine coal we must do without beef. The desirability of either alternative depends on the availability of substitutes for beer, western housing, and beef. A blue-ribbon commission can make a disastrously wrong decision if it is missing just one fact. For example, if the commission is unaware of a new breed of cattle that thrives in the West, it might rule out coal mining in the mistaken belief that eastern land is the only source of beef.

However, prices convey the relevant information. The existence of the new breed of cattle drives up the price of western land and drives down the price of eastern land. Although the prices do not reveal the existence of the new breed of cattle, they do reveal that *something* has raised the value of western land and lowered the value of eastern land. This is precisely the kind of information that is needed to choose between the two energy sources.

cattle that thrives in the West, it recommends that the East be reserved for the vital role of producing beef, and that the West be exploited for energy—sacrificing both beer and good living and unnecessarily impoverishing society.

Had the commissioners observed the high price of land in the West, they would have known that something was afoot—in this case, the owners of the new breed of cattle bidding up the price of land. Although observers of the price might know less about ranching than the commissioners do, they will know more about how to extract energy efficiently.

Prices convey information. They reflect the information available to all members of society (in this case, the small number who know about the new cattle reveal the relevant part of their knowledge through the price of land). The commissioners, no matter how wise and how benevolent, can never gather more than a fraction of the information that may be relevant to their decision—but *all* of that information is reflected in the price.

Prices have at least two other advantages over expert panels. One is that observing prices is free. Expert panels consume resources—lots of resources, if they do their jobs well.

The other advantage of prices is that in addition to conveying information, they also provide appropriate incentives to act on that information. When a price tells you (by being high) that western land is valuable to someone, you will not choose to use it yourself unless it is even more valuable to you.

Here is Dorfman again:

*Clearly, then, social costs cannot be measured in…simple physical units. The only adequate measure is what economists call "social opportunity costs," meaning the social value of the alternative commodities that have to be forgone in order to obtain the commodity being produced. Under certain idealized conditions this opportunity cost is measured by the dollars-and-cents cost of producing the commodity. Under realistic conditions the dollars-and-cents production cost is a fair approximation to the social cost. Under almost any conceivable conditions the dollars-and-cents cost is a much better approximation to social cost than the amounts of energy expended or any other simple physical measure.*

*Energy is indeed a scarce and valuable resource; but…there is a good deal more to life…than British thermal units.*[5]

## The Problem of the Social Planner

Try the following experiment: Ask your friends to name the two ways to get a chicken to lay more eggs. Few will know. The two ways to get a chicken to lay more eggs are to feed it more or to provide it with more heat from blowers that are usually powered by natural gas.[6] In chicken farming natural gas and chicken feed are close substitutes.

Imagine a chicken farm next door to a steel mill. In a typical week each consumes 100 cubic feet of natural gas. The steel mill has no economical alternative production process, and it would have to curtail its operation significantly if natural gas became unavailable. The chicken farmer, at an additional cost of a few cents per day, could switch off the blowers and use more chicken feed.

One day it transpires that only 100 cubic feet of natural gas per week will be available in the future. A benevolent economic planner, seeking only to benefit society, must decide how to allocate this natural gas. Perhaps he observes that the steel mill and the chicken farmer have historically used natural gas in equal quantities, and on this basis he decides that their "needs" for natural gas are roughly equal. He assigns 50 cubic feet per week to the steel mill and 50 cubic feet to the chickens.

As a result, there is a substantial cutback in steel output, to society's detriment. If all 100 cubic feet had been assigned to the steel mill, production would have continued about as before, with the chicken farmer having slightly higher costs and perhaps cutting egg production by a small amount.

Why does the benevolent planner not recognize his mistake? Because he—like the friends you were invited to poll on this question, and almost everybody else except for chicken farmers and the readers of this book—has never remotely suspected that chicken feed can be substituted for natural gas. Why doesn't the chicken farmer tell him? If he did, he would lose his natural gas allocation and his costs would go up—only slightly, to be sure, but the incentive is still to keep mum.

An alternative social arrangement is to abolish the planner and to allocate the gas via the price system. Now when natural gas becomes more scarce, the price gets bid up.

---

[5] From *Science,* letter to editor by R. Dorfman, 1976.
[6] Chickens use calories from feed to produce both eggs and body warmth. A chicken in a heated henhouse can divert more calories to egg production.

This has two effects on the chicken farmer: He acquires the information that the available natural gas is more valuable to someone else than it is to him, and he acquires an incentive to react accordingly. He puts in an order for some chicken feed.[7]

## The Use of Knowledge in Society

In 1945, Friedrich A. Hayek (later a Nobel Prize winner) addressed the American Economic Association on the occasion of his retirement as its president. The title of his address was "The Use of Knowledge in Society." In it he called attention to the social role of prices as carriers of information, allowing the specialized knowledge of each individual to be fully incorporated in decisions concerning resource allocation. He contrasted this knowledge with so-called scientific knowledge and found it unjustly underrated by comparison:

> A little reflection will show that there is beyond question a body of very important but unorganized knowledge which cannot possibly be called scientific in the sense of knowledge of general rules: the knowledge of the particular circumstances of time and place. It is with respect to this that practically every individual has some advantage over all others in that he possesses unique information of which beneficial use might be made, but of which use can be made only if the decisions depending on it are left to him or are made with his active cooperation. We need to remember only how much we have to learn in any occupation after our theoretical training, how big a part of our working life we spend learning particular jobs, and how valuable an asset in all walks of life is knowledge of people, of local conditions, and special circumstances. To know of and put to use a machine not fully employed, or somebody's skill which could be better utilized, or to be aware of a surplus stock which can be drawn upon during an interruption of supplies, is socially quite as useful as the knowledge of better alternative techniques. [Emphasis added.][8]

The special knowledge of the chicken farmer is a sort of knowledge of the particular circumstances of time and place. But Hayek is referring here to knowledge even much more specialized (and inaccessible to the planner) than that: the knowledge of the foreman that a leak in a certain machine can be plugged with chewing gum, the knowledge of a manager that one of the file clerks has a knack for plumbing repairs, the knowledge of a shipper that a particular tramp steamer is half-full. No planner can have access to this knowledge:

> The sort of knowledge with which I have been concerned is knowledge of the kind which by its nature cannot enter into statistics and therefore cannot be conveyed to any central authority in statistical form. The statistics which such a central authority would have to use would have to be arrived at precisely by abstracting from minor differences between the things, by lumping together, as resources of one kind, items which differ as regards location, quality, and other particulars, in a way which may be very significant for the specific decision.[9]

---

[7] Economist, financial planner, and chicken expert Dan Gressel reports that when natural gas prices were controlled in the 1970s, chicken farmers routinely consumed large and socially inefficient quantities of natural gas. When the controls were lifted and prices rose, farmers switched to chicken feed.

[8] F. A. Hayek, "The Use of Knowledge in Society," *American Economic Review* 35 (September 1945): 519–530.

[9] Ibid.

Suppose that you and your friends discover a new science fiction writer whose works you all rush out to buy. It may not occur to you that this requires more linseed plants to be grown in Asia, but it does, because the oil from those plants is used to make the ink to print the books that the stores now want to restock. The Asian linseed farmer is no more aware of the change in your reading habits than you are of your need for his services, but he nevertheless responds by increasing his output. Your increased demand for books causes a rise in the price of linseed and informs the farmer that someone, somewhere, wants more linseed for some reason.

A competing economics textbook begins its first chapter by observing that "the rest of us people" (together with nature) "dominate your life and prevent you from having all you want."[10] However, the authors warn:

> Do not suppose that if we were less greedy, more would be within your grasp. For greed impels us to produce more, not only for ourselves, but, miraculously, more for you too...

What the authors have in mind is that other people's greed enables you to offer them incentives to act as you want. It is because the carpenter is "greedy" that you can hire him to build your house.[11] In fact, we can say more. Although greedy neighbors are more likely than apathetic neighbors to respond to your desires, you might imagine that the best possibility is a third one that the authors did not consider: What if the rest of the world were neither greedy nor apathetic, but actively altruistic, attempting to cater to all of your wishes? Although such a world would have obvious advantages, it would also have a less obvious disadvantage: In the absence of a price system, you would be severely limited in your ability to communicate your desires. The farmer in Asia, wanting only to make your life more pleasant, has no criterion by which to choose between producing more linseed or more of some other crop. You have no way of informing him because you don't realize that a yen for science fiction creates a need for more linseed oil—or, if you do realize this, then you don't realize that you also need more glycerin, to make the glue with which the books are bound.

Your need for the selfishness of others stems not just from the fact that it motivates them to respond to your desires—altruism on their part would serve that purpose even better. It also stems from your need to *communicate* those desires. Students—and others who have not previously encountered the idea—generally find it quite surprising that a major role of prices in society is to fulfill this need.

## The Costs of Misallocation

We now want to explicitly relate the "informational" aspect of prices to the "equilibrating" aspect that has been stressed in previous chapters. Exhibit 9.2 displays the marginal value curves of three consumers in the market for eggs and the corresponding market demand curve. (The graph and tables are identical to those of Exhibit 8.6.)

The rectangles represent marginal values associated with individual eggs, each labeled with the name of the man who buys the corresponding egg and receives the corresponding value. When the market price is $7 per egg, 5 are sold and the top parts of the shaded rectangles constitute the consumer's surplus.

---

[10] A. Alchian and W. Allen, *Exchange and Production: Theory in Use* (Belmont, CA: Wadsworth, 1969).

[11] Adam Smith put this very well. In *The Wealth of Nations,* he said, "It is not from the benevolence of the butcher, the brewer, or the baker that we expect our dinner, but from their regard to their own interest. We address ourselves not to their humanity but to their self-love."

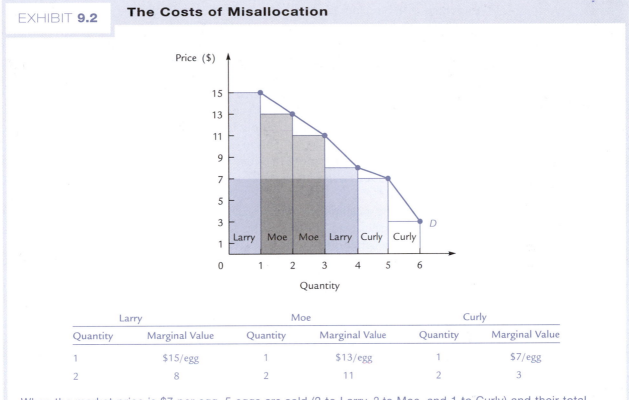

**EXHIBIT 9.2**

## The Costs of Misallocation

| Larry | | Moe | | Curly | |
|---|---|---|---|---|---|
| Quantity | Marginal Value | Quantity | Marginal Value | Quantity | Marginal Value |
| 1 | $15/egg | 1 | $13/egg | 1 | $7/egg |
| 2 | 8 | 2 | 11 | 2 | 3 |

When the market price is $7 per egg, 5 eggs are sold (2 to Larry, 2 to Moe, and 1 to Curly) and their total value (the sum of the shaded rectangles) is $54. If the same 5 eggs were distributed by a mechanism other than the market, the total value might be less. For example, if a social planner gave 2 eggs to Larry, 1 to Moe, and 2 to Curly, the total value would be only $46. In this case, therefore, the usual measures of social gain would overstate the true social gain by $8.

---

**Exercise 9.1** Assume a flat supply (5 marginal cost) curve at $7 and calculate the total value of the eggs produced, the total cost of producing them, and the social gain. (Assume that eggs can be consumed only in "whole-number" quantities for this calculation.)

---

Now let us reintroduce our benevolent social planner. Although the price system has been abolished he has managed through painstaking research to discover the demand and supply curves for eggs. Plotting both of these on the same graph, he discovers that equilibrium occurs at a quantity of 5. Wishing to maximize social gain and realizing that this is accomplished at equilibrium, he orders 5 eggs to be produced and distributed to consumers.

It appears that the social planner has succeeded in duplicating the workings of a competitive market, but this need not be true and, in fact, is not likely to be. Suppose that the planner orders the 5 eggs to be distributed as follows: 2 to Larry, 1 to Moe, and 2 to Curly. The marginal values of these eggs are equal to the areas of the first, second, fourth, fifth, and sixth rectangles in Exhibit 9.2. In comparison with competition, Moe has lost his second egg (worth $11 to him), and Curly has gained a second egg (worth only $3 to him). There is a net social loss of $8.

**Exercise 9.2** Calculate the total value and total cost of the 5 eggs distributed by the planner. Compare these with your answer to Exercise 9.1.

In attempting to justify his actions, the social planner might look at the graph in Exhibit 9.2 and argue: "It is clear from this graph that social gain is maximized at a quantity of 5. That is the quantity I ordered produced. Therefore, social gain is maximized." But in actuality the social gain is a sum of 5 rectangles. We compute it by looking at the area under the demand curve out to a quantity of 5, implicitly assuming that it is the sum of the *first* 5 rectangles. This in turn assumes that the 5 eggs are distributed where they will be valued the most. In a competitive market this assumption is justified (Curly simply won't buy a second egg at $7, whereas Moe will). In the absence of a price system, it is not.

What must the social planner do to really maximize welfare? He must give Curly's second egg to Moe instead. (Of course, by doing this, he increases welfare and so can make both parties better off.)

**Exercise 9.3** Describe explicitly how the social planner can make both Curly and Moe better off.

Now we return to the problem that is the theme of this chapter. How is the planner to *know* that Moe values a second egg more than Curly does? This information is available only to Moe and Curly. Its inaccessibility to the social planner renders him powerless to make improvements.

We can summarize as follows:

When allocation decisions are not made on the basis of price, the traditional measures of social gain (via areas) overstate the actual gains to society. Equivalently, the traditional measures of deadweight loss underestimate the losses.

**Exercise 9.4** Suppose that the supply curve for eggs is as given in Exhibit 9.3 (which is identical to the curve in Exhibit 8.7). A social planner orders 5 eggs to be produced, 1 by Firm A and 2 each by Firms B and C. What is the extent of the social loss due to the social planner's failure to perceive that A is the low-cost producer?

## Example: A Military Draft

Society, through its armed forces, demands military services that are supplied by young people between the ages of 18 and 26. Suppose that the armed forces are able to set a maximum price (below equilibrium) that they will pay for military services, and suppose that they can *compel* young people to supply the quantity of military services that is demanded at that price ($Q_d$ in Exhibit 9.4). The "*Draft*" column of the table in Exhibit 9.4 shows the distribution of gains; the "Volunteer Army" column shows the gains in equilibrium for comparison.[12]

Exhibit 9.5 elaborates on the reason why the producers' surplus is $F - C - D - E$ in the presence of a draft. Panel A of Exhibit 9.5 reproduces the relevant part of the graph

[12] By drawing one graph, we are implicitly assuming that all young people would make equally good soldiers. To dispense with this assumption, we could draw several graphs, each showing the demand for soldiers of a different level of quality. None of our conclusions would be substantially altered.

| EXHIBIT **9.3** | **Planning versus Market** |
|---|---|

|  | Firm A |  | Firm B |  | Firm C |
|---|---|---|---|---|---|
| Quantity | Marginal Cost | Quantity | Marginal Cost | Quantity | Marginal Cost |
| 1 | $1 | 1 | $5 | 1 | $6 |
| 2 | 3 | 2 | 11 | 2 | 7 |

At a market price of $7, 5 eggs are produced in the least costly way possible. If a social planner orders 5 eggs to be produced and fails to realize that the low-cost producer is Firm A, then the total cost of production will be higher than necessary.

in Exhibit 9.4. Revenue to producers (i.e., the wages paid to soldiers) is given by price times quantity, that is, the rectangle $X + Z$. The sum of the marginal costs to producers is the sum of the rectangles in panel B, which is the same as area $Y + Z$ in panel A. The difference is $(X + Z) - (Y + Z) \times X - Y$, which is the same as $F - C - D - E$ in Exhibit 9.4.

**Exercise 9.5** Verify the deadweight loss in Exhibit 9.4 by calculating social gain directly (i.e., using rectangles representing marginal value minus marginal cost, without breaking things down into consumers' and producers' surpluses).

Now consider an alternative policy. Suppose that at the same controlled price $P$, the armed forces can compel services only from that number of young people who would have enlisted voluntarily at the equilibrium price. In Exhibit 9.4, the number of soldiers is $Q_0$ and the social gains are computed in the "Limited Draft" column of the table. Notice that the measured deadweight loss becomes *zero*.

**Exercise 9.6** Verify all of the entries in the "Limited Draft" column of the table. Recompute the deadweight loss by a different method and make sure the answers coincide.

Notice that, compared with the volunteer army, the new "limited" version of the draft transfers the amount $B + C$ from young people to the other members of society.

## EXHIBIT 9.4    A Military Draft

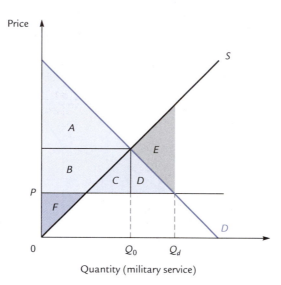

|  | Volunteer Army | Draft | Limited Draft |
|---|---|---|---|
| Consumers' Surplus | $A$ | $A + B + C + D$ | $A + B + C$ |
| Producers' Surplus | $B + F$ | $F - C - D - E$ | $F - C$ |
| Social Gain | $A + B + F$ | $A + B + F - E$ | $A + B + F$ |
| Deadweight Loss | — | $E$ | — |

Military services are supplied by young people and demanded by society through the armed forces. The first column shows the gains at equilibrium, with a volunteer army. We assume that the wage rate is set at $P$, so that more young people are demanded than will volunteer. If the army can draft as many young people as it wants to at the price $P$, it will choose the quantity $Q_d$, and social gains will be as depicted in the second column. If, on the other hand, the army is permitted to hire only $Q_0$ young people, social gains will be as in the third column, seemingly eliminating the deadweight loss. This leads to the apparent conclusion that the limited draft is as efficient as the volunteer army. As explained in the text, however, this conclusion is misleading.

**Exercise 9.7** Give an economic interpretation of the area $B + C$ in Exhibit 9.4.

Now we are closing in on the main point: Even though the computed deadweight loss is zero, the limited draft is still inferior to the volunteer army from the point of view of economic efficiency. There are social costs associated with the draft that are not captured in our representation of deadweight loss.

Consider the calculation of producers' surplus, which is illustrated anew in Exhibit 9.6. We begin with the total revenue of soldiers and subtract from it the sum of the shaded rectangles. These rectangles are the costs of joining the army for the $Q_0$ young people who would volunteer at the equilibrium price. But it is unlikely that these are the same young people who are drafted. Instead of drafting the young people represented by rectangles *a, b,* and *c,* the authorities may draft those represented by rectangles *d, e,* and f. The true producers' surplus is reduced by the area $(d + e + f) - (a + b + c)$. The measured producers' surplus—and consequently the measured deadweight loss—is too optimistic.

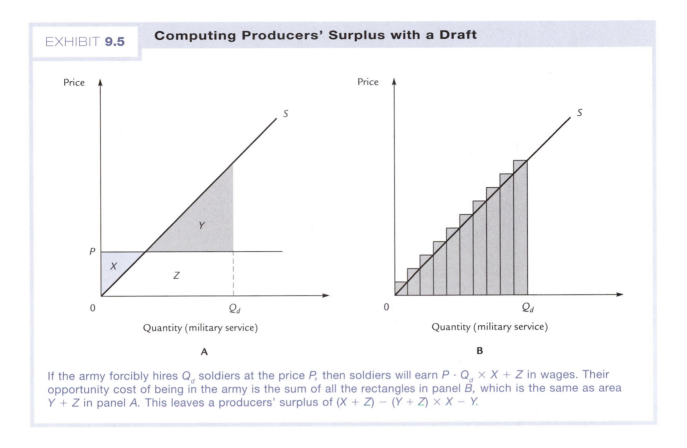

**EXHIBIT 9.5**

**Computing Producers' Surplus with a Draft**

If the army forcibly hires $Q_d$ soldiers at the price $P$, then soldiers will earn $P \cdot Q_d \times X + Z$ in wages. Their opportunity cost of being in the army is the sum of all the rectangles in panel $B$, which is the same as area $Y + Z$ in panel $A$. This leaves a producers' surplus of $(X + Z) - (Y + Z) \times X - Y$.

In concrete terms, what this means is that the Selective Service Board will draft young people who are potentially brilliant brain surgeons, inventors, and economists—young people with high opportunity costs of entering the service—and will leave undrafted some young people with much lower opportunity costs. The social loss is avoided under a voluntary system, in which precisely those with the lowest costs will volunteer.

What if the authorities choose to draft only the low-cost young people? Here, of course, the problem of knowledge becomes insurmountable. Information about individual opportunity costs, available for free under a voluntary system, is available only at high cost and with great uncertainty in the absence of prices. The Selective Service authorities can pass out questionnaires—but who will freely reveal that his costs are low? They can observe people's behavior—but who can observe the difference between two starving novelists in garrets, one with a brilliant vision that needs only careful nurturing to become great literature, the other barren of ideas, frustrated, and ready to quit?

It is often argued that the draft is better for society than a volunteer army because it is less costly. This argument is wrong.[13] The cost of maintaining an army is the sum of the opportunity costs of its soldiers and is independent of the wages paid to those soldiers. Higher wages mean less wealth for taxpayers and more for soldiers, but no more or less for society, to which taxpayers and soldiers equally belong. There are two ways

---

[13] Of course, there are many other arguments for and against the draft, but their validity does not concern us here.

EXHIBIT **9.6**          **Underestimating Deadweight Loss**

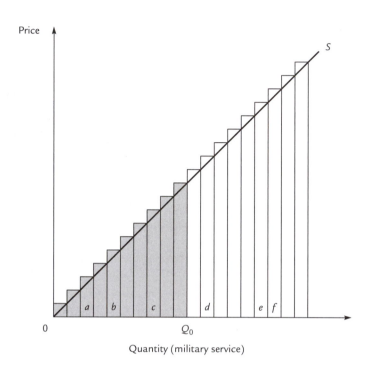

$Q_0$ is the number of young people who would join a volunteer army. Each of these young people has an opportunity cost of joining that is represented by one of the shaded rectangles. When we compute producers' surplus, we take the total revenue earned by young people and subtract this shaded area.

Under a limited draft, the same number of young people enter the army. However, those who are drafted are not identical to those who would have volunteered. Suppose that the draft board selects the young people represented by rectangles *d, e,* and *f* instead of rectangles *a, b,* and *c*. In that case, social welfare is reduced by the area $(d + e + f) - (a + b + c)$, even though this reduction is ignored in the usual welfare computations. Hence, the measured deadweight loss is overly optimistic.

in which an army can be unnecessarily costly: It can be the wrong size or it can consist of the wrong people. Exhibits 9.4 and 9.6 illustrate these two mistakes.

## The Social Role of Rent

**Rent**

Payments to a factor of production in excess of the minimum payments necessary to call it into existence. In other words, the producer's surplus earned by the factor.

An issue of great importance in the history of economic thought has been the social function of the rent on land. The nineteenth-century English economist Henry George argued in his book *Progress and Poverty* that because the quantity of land is fixed, the payment of rent to landlords serves no economic purpose. Increased demand for land (which, he argued, is an inevitable consequence of population growth) bids up prices, but, unlike in other markets, this increased price calls forth no additional output. Landlords are enriched to no social end.

This analysis, applied to a more general notion of "rent," was a recurrent theme in the writings of Fabian socialism.[14] The **rent** earned by a factor of production is the

---

[14] The Fabian Society was a major contributor to British political discourse in the early part of the twentieth century. Its most prominent spokesmen were the economists Sidney Webb and George Bernard Shaw.

excess of payments received by that factor over the minimum payments necessary to call it into existence. When Jennifer Lopez earns $20 million a picture for starring in movies that she would be willing to star in for $100,000, the difference, $19.9 million, is rent. In other words, rent is producers' surplus. The lowest annual income that would induce J. Lo to become a movie star is equal to the area under her supply curve out to the quantity of movies she appears in each year. Her revenue is a rectangle representing the quantity of movies times the wage per movie. The difference is producers' surplus, or rent.

Exhibit 9.7 shows the markets for land and for Jennifer Lopez. We adopt, for the sake of argument, George's assertion that the supply curve for land is vertical.[15] In this case, all of the revenue collected by landlords is rent (the shaded area in panel A of Exhibit 9.7). J. Lo's supply curve becomes essentially vertical above a certain price; there is a limit to the number of movies that a person can make in a year. As a result, her revenue (area $A + B$ in panel B) consists almost entirely of rent (the shaded area $A$). In general:

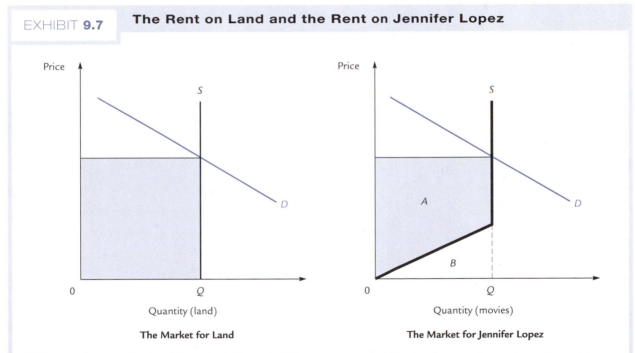

**EXHIBIT 9.7**   **The Rent on Land and the Rent on Jennifer Lopez**

**The Market for Land**

**The Market for Jennifer Lopez**

If the supply curve for land is vertical, then all of the revenue earned by landowners is producers' surplus, or rent (the shaded area in panel A). If the supply curve for Jennifer Lopez's services becomes vertical at a quantity where the demand price is still very high, then almost all of her income is rent (the shaded area $A$ in panel B). Rent can be interpreted as the amount by which a factor's income exceeds what is necessary to call it into existence. Because the land would exist even if its owners earned no income, all of their income is rent. Because J. Lo earns $A + B$ for making $Q$ movies, but would be willing to make $Q$ movies if she were paid $B$ to do so, her rent is $A$.

---

[15] In fact, this is probably false in any reasonable sense. The relevant market for a given purpose is not land, but "agricultural land" or "land suitable for building," and the like. Such things *can* be created: Irrigation converted the Negev Desert to productive farmland, for example.

When a factor is in fixed (or nearly fixed) supply, the revenue it earns will consist entirely (or almost entirely) of rent.

The Fabians argued that there would be no social cost associated with the appropriation of rents by the government. Suppose that landlords were not permitted to collect rent, but were told by the government to allow designated individuals to use their land at a price of zero. Suppose that J. Lo, who now makes two movies per year, were given a government salary equal to area *B* in panel B of Exhibit 9.7 and ordered to continue making two movies per year. Such confiscation of rents (the Fabians argued) would not affect social welfare.

**Exercise 9.8** Compute consumers' and producers' surpluses in the markets for land and for Jennifer Lopez's services, both before and after the confiscation of rents. Verify that there is no deadweight loss.

The fly in the Fabian ointment is that land is not equally valuable in all uses, and Jennifer Lopez is not equally valuable in all movies. Exhibit 9.8 shows the sort of error that can arise in the allocation of land. When landlords earn rents, they let their land to the people who will pay the most for it: those represented by the shaded rectangles. If land is not allocated to precisely those people, there is a diminution in social welfare. If land is not allocated by price, there is no way to identify those people.

 **The Social Role of Rent**

With the supply of land fixed at 4 acres, landlords let those acres to those who value them the most. The total value of the land to its users is the sum of the 4 shaded rectangles. If all rent were confiscated, the 4 acres of land would still exist, which led some thinkers to believe that no social harm would be done. But in fact the confiscation of rents leaves landlords with no incentive to seek out the users represented by the 4 shaded rectangles. Land will be used for less valuable projects, represented by the unshaded rectangles, and social welfare will be diminished.

Similarly, it matters not only that Jennifer Lopez makes two movies per year; it matters *which* movies she makes. Those movie producers who will pay her the highest salary are those who value her talents most highly; that is, those who think that her presence will most enhance people's desire to see their movies. If she works on projects where her talents contribute less, efficiency is lost. Notice that even if J. Lo is given the freedom to choose her acting assignments, and even in the event that she is entirely altruistic and wants to work only where she is most valuable, she is unlikely to *know* where she is most valuable if the studios cannot bid for her services.

The Fabian literature contains much interesting economic argument, some of it correct, and the tracts by Shaw are both readable and highly entertaining. His *Intelligent Woman's Guide to Socialism and Capitalism* is a rare phenomenon: economic writing by a master of English prose. It is a fertile source of propositions on which you can test out the analytic skills you have been developing in this course. It's also fun to read.

# 9.2 Asymmetric Information

*Everybody bet lots of money on the eggplant, thinking that if a vegetable challenges a live animal with four legs to a race, then it must be that the vegetable knows something.*

—D. Pinkwater, Borgel

Although the price system routinely accomplishes miracles in the dissemination of information, it also sometimes fails to deliver all that one could hope for. When information is distributed asymmetrically, so that some types of knowledge are more readily available to one group than to another, market outcomes can fail to be Pareto-optimal. Other times, Pareto-optimal outcomes are achieved, but in unexpected ways. In this section, we present a potpourri of examples in which asymmetric information can produce surprising outcomes.

## Signaling: Should Colleges Be Outlawed?

Going to college will probably increase your income. Perhaps you will also pick up some useful skills along the way. But even if colleges taught nothing of practical value, and even if employers were fully aware of this deficiency, a college education could still be a path to higher wages.

To see why, let us make the cynical assumption that everything you are taught in school is completely useless. However, the ability to graduate requires a certain level of intelligence and ambition. If employers have no other way to distinguish one high school graduate from another, they will prefer to hire the ones who have gone on to success in college. And that alone can make college a good investment for a bright student.

In this case, going to college is an example of what economists call a *signal*. This means that on the one hand, it produces nothing of any value (such as actual skills or knowledge), but on the other hand its owner reaps rewards because of the information that it telegraphs to others (in this case, it signals employers about your basic abilities).

Signals are socially costly. In our example, the resources spent on college don't increase anyone's productivity and hence constitute pure social waste. Whenever there is social waste, there is room for an improvement that could benefit everybody.

Suppose that we closed all the colleges and simply asked each high school graduate whether she *would* have gone to college given the opportunity; suppose also that everybody answered honestly. Employers would have exactly the same information for sorting job candidates that they have today, and bright students would save four years and many thousands of dollars. They could, of course, share part of this windfall with those of their high school friends who never were college material, as a reward for their honesty, making *every* high school graduate better off.

Unfortunately, that social improvement is impossible to achieve as long as colleges are allowed to exist. If we relied strictly on voluntary announcements, then each dull student would have an incentive to misrepresent herself as bright. Employers would have no way to distinguish bright students from dull ones, and the genuinely bright students would return to college in order to signal their truthfulness.

However, we could still increase social welfare by outlawing colleges completely. Employers would no longer be able to distinguish bright students from dull ones and would treat each student equally, paying them more than if they were known to be dull and less than if they were known to be bright; the gains to one group would balance the losses to the other. And the bright students' losses might be more than compensated by their savings in tuition costs. Thus, both groups of students can gain. Finally, employers end up with the same pool of employees as before and pay them the same salary on average. Therefore, employers neither lose nor gain, and social welfare is unambiguously increased.

---

Dangerous
Curve

This discussion implicitly assumes that although bright students are more productive than dull ones, they both perform essentially the same tasks. In fact, employers might prefer to reserve certain tasks for the best and brightest and other tasks for the rest of us. If the signal is abolished, this becomes impossible, so productivity falls and the abolition imposes real social costs. Those costs might or might not outweigh the benefit of removing the costly signal.

---

So far we have assumed that bright students can survive college and dull students can't. But the same conclusions hold even with a less radical assumption. Suppose instead that any student can survive college, but it is in some way less costly for bright students to survive than for dull ones. For example, bright students need to spend less time studying than dull students, or they have less need to hire tutors for exams and ghostwriters for term papers, or they pay less extra tuition making up courses that they have failed. Then even if we continue to assume that colleges teach nothing of value, the bright students might still choose to go to college.

To see why, suppose that employers are willing to pay more to bright students than to dull ones—enough so that it is worth $10,000 to convince an employer that you are bright. Suppose that it costs a bright student $7,000 to get through college and a dull student $15,000. Then bright students will find the college signal worthwhile, dull students will find that it is not worthwhile, only bright students will go to college, and employers will continue to reward college graduates because the college graduates really *will* be smarter than their non-college-trained contemporaries.

Once again, the college education is pure social waste. If dull students were willing to voluntarily identify themselves, then bright students would still get the better jobs and save themselves $7,000 each. This $7,000 could be shared to make *everybody* better off. Once again, though, this agreement cannot be maintained because dull students would misrepresent themselves. Only an absolute ban on colleges could have a chance of yielding an actual improvement.

## Dressing for Success

Signaling behavior is a widespread social phenomenon. "Dressing for success" is a signal. Surely the clothes you wear do not make you a more productive manager, but your ability to choose clothes that are both tasteful and fashionable without being too ordinary is a meaningful signal of your ability to interpret social norms and to be creative within acceptable limits. These are skills that are extremely valuable in business, and it can be rational to invest in displaying them just as it can be rational to invest in an unproductive education that displays your intellect.

Here again it is genuinely rational for the signaler to invest in sending the signal and for the observer to be guided by it. Nevertheless, as with college, everyone could benefit if the signal were abolished. We might all be better off if wearing clothes to job interviews were against the law.

## Signaling in the Animal Kingdom

The male birds of many species—peacocks and birds of paradise most prominently—have tails that appear to be too long for their own good. Besides requiring nutrients that could be put to other productive uses, the tails are cumbersome and actually impede locomotion. They make the birds more vulnerable to predators.

How could such a characteristic survive the pressures of natural selection? A simple theory is that the tails are part of a signaling equilibrium. Suppose that the healthiest males can bear the burdens of a long tail more cheaply than weaker males can. Suppose also that females have a natural preference for healthy males. (Such a preference would be naturally selected for, because healthy males tend to produce healthy offspring, so a female with this preference has a greater chance of eventually becoming a grandmother.) Then it can be to the reproductive advantage of every male to signal his health with a long tail, even if the tail itself is a burden in everyday life. Females choose the males with the longest tails, and tails get longer over time until the marginal cost of additional growth outweighs the marginal advantage in terms of attracting females.

Such a signaling equilibrium is suboptimal. If all the males agreed to cut their tails in half, the females would still be able to identify the longest tails and would make exactly the same choices as they do now. No valuable information would be lost, and the costs of excessive tail growth would be partly eliminated. Unfortunately for the birds, such an agreement must fall apart. Each individual male would try to cheat by letting his tail grow, and the original signaling equilibrium would soon be restored.

## The Supply of Jokes

Why do people tell jokes? Frequently, it is to entertain their friends. But there are other reasons. According to an article in *The Wall Street Journal,*

> Jokes still play an important role in the discourse of financial markets, where the sober business of making money is lubricated by fast, topical jokes. "If you're going to be perceived as a great salesman, proving you have information first is really important," says a trader at a small securities firm. "If someone calls you up and starts a joke, and you can finish it, you have the edge. It proves you're plugged in."

If all salesmen could be induced to honestly reveal how "plugged in" they are, they wouldn't have to spend time learning jokes. That would be a welfare improvement. But because there is no mechanism to induce those honest revelations, jokes survive as a signal of general knowledgeability.

# Adverse Selection and the Market for Lemons

The seller of a used car typically knows more about its quality than potential buyers do. Professor George Akerlof has demonstrated that under such circumstances, it can be impossible for high-quality cars ever to be sold.[16]

Suppose that there are two equally common types of used cars: "good" cars and "lemons." Potential sellers value the good cars at $100 and potential buyers value them at $120. Potential sellers value the lemons at $50 and potential buyers value them at $60. If there were perfect information, there would be separate markets for the two kinds of cars, and all of them would sell.

---

**Exercise 9.9** What is the possible range of prices at which a good car could sell? What about a lemon?

---

Suppose for the moment that neither buyers nor sellers can distinguish between a good car and a lemon. Each seller figures that if her car is good, it's worth $100 to her and if not, it's worth $50; taking account of both possibilities, she values the car at $75. Each buyer does a similar calculation, figuring that the car is equally likely to be worth either $120 or $60 and valuing it at $90. All of the cars sell at some price between $75 and $90.

But now suppose instead that the sellers actually know the quality of the cars. We shall see that this simple assumption has drastic consequences.

What can the price of a used car be? Suppose first that it is over $100. At that price, all sellers put their cars up for sale. Buyers, who cannot tell one car from another, value a used car at only $90 and will not pay the asking price. So the quantity supplied (namely, all the cars) exceeds the quantity demanded (namely, zero). There can be no equilibrium price above $100.

Now suppose that the price is above $60 but below $100. In this range, sellers are willing to part with their lemons (which they value at $50), but not their good cars (which they value at $100). Only lemons come on the market. Buyers, realizing this, are willing to pay only $60 (the value that they place on a lemon). Once again the quantity demanded is zero, so we still haven't found an equilibrium.

Suppose a price below $50. At this price, buyers want to buy, but no sellers want to sell. That leaves only one possibility: The market price must be above $50 but below $60. At such a price, sellers supply only lemons and buyers are willing to buy them. But no good car ever changes hands.

If all sellers were truthful about the quality of their cars, social welfare could be improved, because the good cars would find their way into the hands of the buyers, who value them more than the sellers do. Unfortunately, such truthfulness cannot be maintained, because if there is any market at all for good cars, each lemon owner will want to deceptively sell her car in that market to command a higher price.

## Adverse Selection and Insurance Markets

In the lemons market, one group of traders (in this case the sellers) knows more than the other group (the buyers), and each uses the extra information to decide whether to participate in the market. In equilibrium, the "high-quality" participants are driven out altogether.

---

[16] G. Akerlof, "The Market for Lemons: Qualitative Uncertainty and the Market Mechanism," *Quarterly Journal of Economics* 84 (1970): 484–500.

This **adverse selection** problem arises in several contexts and is particularly acute in the market for insurance.

**Adverse selection**

The problem that arises when people know more about their own risk characteristics than others do.

If your insurance company knows you have a 10% chance of getting sick next year, it will sell you $10 worth of insurance for $1. If the company knows your less healthy neighbor has a 90% chance of getting sick, it will sell him the same $10 worth of insurance for $9. But what if the company can't tell which of you is the healthy one? You might think they'd charge you each a compromise price, like $5. But as long as *you* know you're unlikely to get sick, you might not be willing to pay that much. The result? Healthy people like you choose to stay uninsured; sickly people like your neighbor get their insurance for $5, and the insurance company goes broke.

Obviously, that's not sustainable in equilibrium. Instead, at least as long as the insurance company can offer only one kind of policy, it charges $9, insures sickly people like your neighbor, and leaves healthy people like you uninsured.

But there's an alternative. The company can offer a choice: $1 worth of insurance for a dime (a fair price for you), or $10 worth of insurance for $9 (a fair price for your neighbor). At those prices, you'll buy the cheap policy, but your sickly neighbor—who expects to be making a lot of insurance claims—wants the expensive one. By allowing people to buy only *small* amounts of insurance at the 10% rate, the company can keep both kinds of customer.

That's still imperfect. What you would really like—and what the insurance company would be perfectly willing to sell you if it could—is $10 worth of insurance for $1. But the company dares not offer that policy, lest your neighbor buy one and bankrupt them.

The real social optimum is for sickly people to identify themselves so the insurance company can set rates separately for each customer. But of course sickly people have no incentive to do that. As in the lemons market, the social optimum is not an equilibrium.

## The Financial Crisis of 2008

Beginning in 2008, the world suffered from a shattering financial crisis: It became very difficult for borrowers to find willing lenders, and therefore much economic activity ground to a halt.

The simplest economic models seem to predict that such crises are impossible. If borrowers want more loans than lenders are willing to provide, we'd expect the price of loans (that is, the interest rate) to rise until the quantities supplied and demanded became equal.

Why didn't this happen in 2008? Economists don't completely understand what went wrong, but many believe that adverse selection had a lot to do with it.

The problems seem to have begun in the market for home mortgages. Suppose you borrow money to buy a house from, say, the First Bank of Springfield. You agree to make monthly payments, and the bank's right to collect those payments is called a mortgage. If the First Bank needs to raise some money in a hurry, it might sell your mortgage to the Second Bank of Springfield. The First Bank collects some money upfront, and the Second Bank acquires the right to collect your monthly payments. Selling mortgages is one way the First Bank raises money to lend to other customers.

In 2008, housing prices fell dramatically, leading many homeowners to default on their mortgages—essentially, people were no longer willing to make large monthly payments for houses that were no longer worth very much. As a result, mortgages became less valuable and their prices fell.

That by itself is not enough to cause a crisis. As long as everyone's aware that a particular mortgage comes with, say, a 30% chance of default, then the price of that mortgage should fall by about 30%—but mortgages should continue to be traded.

But now add one more element to the story: Suppose some mortgages are riskier than others, and suppose also that *the First Bank has better information than the Second Bank about which mortgages are riskiest.* In that case, the First Bank will try to pass off its "lemons" to the Second Bank; and the Second Bank, foreseeing this, will be unwilling to trade.

The market stops functioning for exactly the same reason that a used car market might stop functioning. If there are good mortgages worth $100 and bad mortgages (that is, mortgages with a high default probability) worth $50, and if everyone knows which are which, then the good mortgages will sell for $100 and the bad ones will sell for $50. That's not a problem. If *nobody* knows which are which, then you might expect all mortgages to sell for about $75—again no problem. But in a world where only the First Bank can tell the good mortgages from the bad ones, a $75 price won't work. At that price, the First Bank offers only the bad mortgages, and the Second Bank, realizing what the First Bank is up to, refuses to buy them. As a result, the First Bank has difficulty raising funds that it needs to continue serving its customers.

Many, but not all, economists believe that this sort of adverse selection played a major role in the events of 2008 and their aftermath. The dissenters have argued, among other things, that there's no reason the First Bank should have any better information than the Second Bank about default probabilities. After all, these economists argue, the First Bank probably acquired most of its mortgages from the Third Bank, which acquired them from the Fourth Bank. If the First Bank has never dealt directly with the homeowners, then it might well be just as uncertain as anyone else about which homeowners are most likely to keep up their payments.

So did adverse selection contribute significantly to the crisis of 2008 or didn't it? It's a sure bet that economists will be working hard on this question for many years to come.

## Moral Hazard

People who are insured take more risks than people who aren't. Insurance companies, recognizing this, adjust their rates accordingly.

Suppose that there is a 1 in 10 chance that your uninsured house will burn next year. After you buy insurance, you become lax about checking for frayed electrical wires and take up smoking in bed. Consequently, the chance of a fire rises from 1 in 10 to 1 in 5.

Which probability is reflected in your insurance rate? The answer is the one that is relevant for insured homeowners, namely, 1 in 5. $10 worth of fire insurance will sell for $2, not $1.

If you could promise to buy insurance and still remain as careful as ever, the company would be able to reduce your premium to $1. Unfortunately, because it can't watch you every minute of the day, the company has no way to know whether you are keeping your promise. This leaves you with no incentive to keep it, which the insurance company realizes. The bottom line is that your standard of care goes down and your insurance premium goes up.

**Moral hazard**

The incentive for an individual to take more risks when insured.

The problem here is called a moral hazard. Moral hazards arise when an insured driver is more reckless than an uninsured one, when a homeowner fails to install a security system because she is insured against break-ins, and when a person with health insurance takes more risks on the ski slopes than she otherwise would. If you live in a rented apartment, your rent is probably higher because of moral hazard: Your landlord cannot be certain that you won't scratch the floors or write on the walls and wants to be compensated for her risk.

Moral hazard occurs whenever you behave differently because you're insured. Sometimes "behaving differently" means taking more risks; other times it means demanding better remedies. One study[17] found that patients are far more likely to buy expensive brand-name medicines when an insurance company is footing the bill, but to switch to cheaper generics when they're covering the costs themselves.

If the moral hazard were eliminated, insurance rates would fall and everyone could benefit. And in fact, there are some remedies available. Insurance companies can refuse to insure you unless you agree to modify your behavior.

Some homeowner's policies are offered only to those with burglar alarms, and some health insurance is offered only to nonsmokers. However, these remedies are effective only insofar as the company can observe its customers' behavior.

There is another class of remedies in which the insurance company, even though it cannot require good behavior, creates incentives to elicit it. Your fire insurance company cannot require you to install a fire extinguisher, but it can offer to sell you a fire extinguisher at a subsidized price that you are likely to accept.[18] Your health insurance company can make it easier for you to stay healthy by sending you free newsletters about the advantages of diet and exercise.

There is another kind of moral hazard that arises from the insurance company's inability to verify that you have a valid claim. When you report that your insured diamond ring has been stolen, the company might well wonder whether you are telling the truth. Because the company has to be compensated for such risks, theft insurance rates are higher than they would otherwise be.

In cases where the legitimacy of a claim is completely unverifiable, insurance markets might disappear completely. An unexpected fire and an unexpected urge to visit Hawaii can be equally devastating financially, but you can insure against one and not the other. The ashes of your house are easily observable; the depths of your psyche are not.

---

*Students sometimes find it hard to tell the difference between adverse selection and moral hazard. In the adverse selection problem, one group of people starts out at higher risk than the other. In the moral hazard problem, people incur additional risks as a result of being insured.*

Dangerous Curve

---

## Principal–Agent Problems

When you've hired somebody to fix your roof, it is difficult to be sure how good a job he's doing. You can offer to pay extra for more careful work, but you can never be certain that you're getting what you've paid for.

When an employer cannot fully monitor his employees' work efforts, we say that there is a **principal–agent problem.** The word *principal* refers to the employer, the word *agent* refers to the employee, and the word *problem* refers to the fact that an opportunity for social gain is being lost. If the employer could be sure of getting what he pays for, he could offer a higher wage for better work, to the benefit of both employer and employee.

**Principal–agent problem**

The inability of the principal to verify the behavior of the agent.

---

[17] Douglas Lundin, Moral Hazard in Physician Prescription Behavior, *Journal of Health Economics* 19 (2000): 639–662.

[18] This doesn't necessarily work without some further restrictions, because it would enable you to buy insurance, go into the fire extinguisher business, and bankrupt the insurance company by buying all your inventory from them.

In December 1990, the *New York Times* reported the plight of Harriette Ternipsede, a ticket agent at TWA. The airline uses sophisticated computer methods to monitor her performance, and supervisors are alerted instantly if she so much as stands up to stretch her muscles. Mrs. Ternipsede and other workers are taking legal action in an attempt to prevent TWA from keeping such close tabs on them.

It might seem obvious to you that employees would be better off without their supervisors breathing over their shoulders at every moment. But strict supervision does not just allow the employer to observe low productivity; it allows him to observe high productivity too. This in turn enables him to reward high productivity so as to elicit more of it. On the other hand, if monitoring is impossible, employees (except for those with extraordinary motivation) put forth the minimum effort and employers pay accordingly.

Short of perfect monitoring, the market provides a variety of partial solutions to the principal–agent problem. The economists Paul Yakoboski and Kenneth McLaughlin have stressed the importance of productive fringe benefits.[19] Suppose you hold a job in which having a $1,000 home computer would increase your productivity by $2,000. In a world of perfect monitoring, you buy the computer and your wages increase by more than enough to compensate you. In a world with no monitoring, your employer is unaware of the productivity increase and does not reward you, so you never buy the computer. In the real world we live in, your employer might buy you a computer as part of your fringe benefit package, offering himself some assurance that it will be put to good use.

Another way to improve employees' performance is to offer them a share of the firm's profits. Unfortunately, the resulting incentives are still far from optimal. An employee who is entitled to 1% of the profits must increase his output by $100 to reap a $1 reward. If the necessary effort costs him $5, he won't undertake it, and an opportunity to increase social welfare by $95 ($100 in extra profits minus $5 in extra costs) is sacrificed.

There is, however, an extreme version of profit sharing, which *does* work perfectly, at least in principle. It requires paying each employee 100% of the firm's profits. Under such a plan, the worker who saves the firm $100 earns $100 for himself. If he can accomplish this at a personal cost of less than $100, he will be entirely self-motivated to do so. There is never any need for the employer to provide additional incentives.

The problem that has probably occurred to you is that the owners of a firm with 8 employees might be reluctant to pay out 800% of their profits in wages. The solution is that each worker pays, up front, a large flat fee in exchange for his job, so that his net compensation is reasonable. Once he starts working, the flat fee becomes a sunk cost and does not affect his incentive to perform.

Why, then, does this scheme strike us as outrageous? Probably because profits depend on a lot of random events, not just on worker performance. An unexpected change in market conditions can cause a large corporation's profits to fluctuate by tens of millions of dollars. It would be a rare worker who was either able or willing to accept that kind of fluctuation in his yearly income. In the absence of large random fluctuations, the 100% profit-sharing plan might work.

## Efficiency Wages

Another solution to the principal–agent problem is to punish severely those employees who get caught shirking. Although most shirkers never get caught, the possibility of a

---

[19] P. Yakoboski, "Productive Fringe Benefits: Theory and Evidence," Ph.D. Dissertation, University of Rochester, 1990; also P. Yakoboski and K. McLaughlin, "The Economics of Productive Fringe Benefits," 1990.

sufficiently severe punishment still serves as a strong incentive to perform. Workers respond to the incentive, become more productive, and earn higher salaries.

An impediment to this solution is that there are limits to the employer's ability to punish. Usually the most severe punishment available is termination. If the worker can just move on to an identical job at another firm, this is no punishment at all. To overcome this impediment, the employer might offer an efficiency wage; that is, a wage higher than the market equilibrium. This makes the job a particularly desirable one that workers will be reluctant to risk losing.

Now you might think that if *every* employer offers an efficiency wage, then losing your job and having to move on is still no punishment. But this is not correct. The reason is that when employers offer higher wages, they demand less labor. Thus, efficiency wages lead to unemployment. The wage is set higher than the market equilibrium and the quantity of labor demanded is less than the quantity supplied. This in turn means that the worker who loses his job risks not finding another one.

Efficiency wages lead to higher productivity by employed workers who are scared of losing their jobs but also to unemployment of other potentially productive workers. Many economists believe that efficiency wages should play a significant role in macroeconomic models of unemployment.

**Efficiency wage**

A wage higher than market equilibrium, which employers pay in order to make workers want to keep their jobs.

## Executive Compensation

The principal–agent problem is a major factor in the relationship between shareholders and corporate executives. Shareholders want executives to pursue aggressive, creative, and intelligent strategies to maximize corporate income. Because it is impossible to monitor all of the executives' behavior, it is hard for shareholders to reward good decisions and punish bad ones. If General Motors has an opportunity to build a new electric car that would revolutionize the industry, and if the chief executive officer (CEO) of General Motors passes up the opportunity out of foolishness or sloth, stockholders might never become aware of his mistake. On the other hand, if he builds the car and it fails in the marketplace, stockholders are left to wonder whether an intelligent risk happened to turn out badly or whether further market research should have revealed the paucity of demand before it was too late. When the CEO spends $10 million to upgrade the executive air fleet, stockholders can never be certain whether the decision was motivated by the best interests of the firm or the personal comfort of the chairman.

Therefore, we should expect to see executive compensation schemes that reward executives for good performance and punish them for the opposite. The way to do this is to create a close link between the firm's profits and the CEO's wealth. Typically, this is accomplished in two ways: First, the CEO gets an annual bonus that depends on the firm's performance; a typical bonus might be zero in a bad year and twice the CEO's annual salary in a very good year. Second, the CEO is either given or required to purchase a large quantity of the company's stock or take stock options. Typically, a stock option issued in the year 2001 might give the CEO the right to buy shares of stock 10 years down the line, in 2011, at the 2001 price. This gives the CEO an incentive to take immediate actions that will raise the share price 10 years in the future.

Salaries and bonuses are typically not very sensitive to firm performance; this might be because they are set by boards of directors who owe their positions to the CEO. Thus, most of the CEO's performance incentives come from stock ownership and stock options, both of which have become dramatically more important over the past 15 years. As a result, CEOs do reap substantial rewards and punishments. According to

**Stock option**

The right to buy a share of stock at some future date at a price specified in advance.

Professors Brian Hall and Jeffrey Liebman,[20] a CEO who raises his firm's performance from the 30th to the 70th percentile (that is, from a bit below average to a bit above average) can expect to see his compensation rise from $1 million to $5 million.

We have focused on the problem of motivating executives to expend effort and avoid waste. Another source of conflict between executives and shareholders involves their attitude toward risk. The typical shareholder has only a small percentage of his wealth invested in any single corporation. Consequently, he is prepared to have the corporation take on considerable risk in return for the prospect of considerable gains. Even if the corporation goes bankrupt, the shareholder's lifestyle is unlikely to be greatly affected.[21] The executive, by contrast, can have a large personal stake in the corporation's success. Consequently, CEOs are likely to be far more cautious than stockholders prefer.

In fact, the two principal–agent problems call for diametrically opposite solutions! If you're afraid your CEO is not working hard enough, you want him to hold more stock in the company so his efforts will be better rewarded. But if you're afraid your CEO is too cautious, you want him to hold *less* stock in the company so he'll be willing to take more risks. Attempts to solve one problem make the other problem worse.

There are other ways to limit a CEO's downside risk. One is to assure him that he is unlikely to be fired even if some of his decisions turn out badly—and in fact, it appears that as few as 4% of CEOs lose their jobs because of poor performance. Another is to assure him that even if things do turn out so badly that he gets fired, he will still receive a substantial severance payment. Such payments are sometimes called *golden parachutes.* Many people cannot understand why corporations pay tens of millions of dollars to former officials who have been fired for poor performance. An answer is that without the implied assurance of those settlements, the successors to those officials would exercise great caution in their decisions, contrary to the interests of the stockholders.

Shielding executives from risk improves their willingness to take chances but damages their incentives to perform responsibly. Is there an alternative way to elicit more risk taking, without such detrimental side effects? Possibly. In general, people with high incomes are more willing to risk large losses. Essentially, this is because a smaller percentage of their income is at risk.[22] Therefore, a simple solution might be to make certain that corporate executives are wealthy. Stockholders can accomplish this easily by paying high salaries. This could partially explain why CEO salaries are as high as they are. When the president of General Motors must decide whether to introduce a new model line, stockholders do not want him unduly influenced by concern about making his next month's mortgage payment.

## A Theory of Unemployment

For many decades before the 1970s, economists observed a correlation between the rate of inflation and the level of employment. When inflation (the rate of increase in absolute prices) was higher than usual, employment tended to be high also. In periods of low inflation, employment was low. More recently, this relationship has broken down. Many explanations have been offered for these phenomena, although there is no consensus among economists as to which come closest to the truth. Here we will present

---

[20] B. Hall and J. Liebman, "Are CEO's Paid Like Bureaucrats?", National Bureau of Economic Research, 2000.
[21] We will give a more rigorous treatment of attitudes toward risk—and will return to this example—in Chapter 17.
[22] Chapter 18 elaborates on this point also.

one possible explanation, of particular interest because it focuses on the informational content of prices. The version we will present is a caricature; a fully articulated model is more appropriate for a course in macroeconomics. In its general outlines, however, the theory we will present has been a highly influential one and has occupied a central role in macroeconomic thinking for the last 20 years.[23]

We know from Chapter 2 that only relative prices are relevant to the determination of equilibrium. If all prices (including wages) were to double tomorrow, markets could remain in equilibrium without any quantity adjustments. If it were known that such a doubling occurred every Wednesday, nothing of any real economic significance would be affected.[24]

Now imagine an unemployed worker. He is unemployed not because there are no jobs available to him but because the only available jobs pay wages lower than he is willing to accept. The highest wage offer he has received has been $8,000 a year, but he is not willing to work for less than $10,000.

One night, while our worker is sleeping, all prices and all wages double. He is awakened the next morning by a telephone call from an employer who says, "I am now prepared to offer you an annual salary of $16,000." Of course, $16,000 today will buy only what $8,000 bought yesterday, so the worker, if he is fully informed, will not accept the position.

But what if he is *not* fully informed? What if he went to sleep unaware of the changes that were to take place in the middle of the night, and, having just been awakened by a telephone call, is still unaware of them? In that case, he will accept the job, convinced that he will be earning far more than his minimum requirement of $10,000.

Now, after a day on the job, our hero is likely to stop at the supermarket to indulge the temptations of his new economic status. When he sees the prices on the items, he will recognize himself to be the victim of a cruel hoax and begin the mental task of composing a letter of resignation.

This story suggests a reason why an increase in inflation could lead to an increase in employment. It also suggests that the effect is ephemeral. More important, it implies that employment is affected only by *unexpected* inflation. When inflation becomes the norm (as it did in the 1970s), workers can no longer be "fooled" by high absolute wages.

Another important implication is that the increase in employment resulting from an unexpected inflation is not socially beneficial—it is a consequence of deceiving people into working more than they would choose to if they were fully aware of their economic environment.

The fundamental role of inflation in this model is to dilute the informational content of prices. A rise in the nominal wage rate for plumbers may indicate either an increase in demand for plumbers' services or a rise in the general price level. If plumbers know the inflation rate, they can make the distinction. An increased demand for plumbers will lead to a higher relative price for their time and call forth more plumbing services—an example of prices transmitting the necessary information to the appropriate parties. If plumbers are uncertain of the inflation rate, they will be uncertain of the real value of their wages and may provide the "wrong" amount of service from a social point of view. If they underestimate the rate of inflation, they will provide too much plumbing; if they overestimate, they will provide too little.

---

[23] The broad outlines of this theory were sketched around 1968 by Milton Friedman and Edmund Phelps (working independently). The first careful development was by Robert E. Lucas, Jr., in "Expectations and the Neutrality of Money," *Journal of Economic Theory* 4 (1974): 103–124.

[24] There is one important exception to this statement. Briefly, a rise in absolute prices reduces the purchasing power of money, so an expected rise in absolute prices makes it more desirable to hold nonmonetary assets, such as real estate. The increase in demand for these "inflation-proof" assets has real effects. For the current discussion, those effects are irrelevant.

---

**Exercise 9.10** Explain in detail why a plumber who has overestimated the rate of inflation will provide less plumbing service as a result.

---

Macroeconomists have devoted considerable effort to understanding the ways in which uncertainty about inflation introduces "static" into the price signals that people use to make economic decisions. Much research is devoted to the methods that people use to disentangle valuable information from this static and to the consequences of the necessary imperfections in these methods. An underlying theme is that society is best served by the accurate dissemination of knowledge and that prices are the most effective known tool for accomplishing this task.

# 9.3 Financial Markets

Hayek's 1945 article was prescient. Since that time the vision of prices as carriers of information has become ubiquitous in economics. This is especially true in the study of markets for financial securities, such as stock exchanges. Financial markets are extraordinarily efficient processors and disseminators of information. Their informational role affects our understanding of issues ranging from the social allocation of resources to individual investment strategy.

## Efficient Markets for Financial Securities

**Efficient market**

A market in which prices fully reflect all available information.

An efficient market is one in which prices fully reflect all available information. Here we shall be interested in the markets for financial securities, such as the shares of corporate stock that are traded on stock exchanges. The owner of a share of stock owns a fraction of the corporation and participates fully in its profits and losses.

Efficient securities markets serve an important social function, because they allow firms to make appropriate decisions regarding the allocation of resources (how much to produce, how much to invest in future growth, and so on) and assure investors that the prices they are paying for assets are meaningful indications of those assets' actual value. However, many noneconomists believe that asset markets in general and the stock market in particular are inefficient.

## Technical Analysis

The most extreme believers in inefficient markets are the so-called *chartists,* or *technical analysts.* They argue that a careful study of the past prices of a given stock conveys useful information about future prices.

It is easy to see why this analysis cannot be correct if markets are efficient. Suppose that the past behavior of the stock of XYZ Corporation exhibits a pattern that indicates a probable price rise in the near future. That probable price rise is an important feature of XYZ stock, making it more valuable to hold. In an efficient market that higher value will already be reflected in the *current* price. (It is also easy to see the mechanism by which this would occur: Smart investors, observing the pattern, expect a price rise tomorrow and rush out to buy the stock today. This bids up *today*'s price.) If the market is perfectly efficient, the chartist cannot expect to profit, because any stock that can be identified as a "good buy" will be expensive—and therefore *not* such a good buy!

There is overwhelming evidence against the chartists.[25] Hundreds of careful statistical studies indicate that knowledge of past price changes contributes nothing to the prediction of future price changes. All of the information contained in the past history of the stock is already embedded in a single number—the current price.

## Analysis of Market Conditions

Some dissenters from the efficient-markets hypothesis are less extreme. While admitting the unprofitability of technical analysis, they claim that a more general analysis of market conditions (still making use only of publicly available information) can provide important clues to the savvy investor. This proposition is harder to test than the claims of the chartists, and the empirical evidence is correspondingly less definitive. Nevertheless, the overwhelming majority of researchers in the field, basing their conclusions on decades of empirical work, reject this claim as well. The theoretical basis for this rejection is the same as that for rejecting chartism: Any publicly available information indicating that a stock will soon go up (or down) will cause an immediate shift in demand and an immediate price adjustment, leaving no opportunity for profit.

There is still room for argument over the meaning of the word *immediate*. How quickly do prices adjust to new information? If the adjustment process takes sufficiently long, an observant investor may have time to cash in. To put the question another way: Prices reflect all available information in the long run, but how long is the long run? Recent evidence supports the hypothesis that the long run is shorter than 30 seconds—that is, all information entering the marketplace is fully incorporated into prices within 30 seconds of its arrival.[26] Hardly comforting news to the investor who analyzes patterns at leisure over a cup of coffee and the daily business page.

## Asset Markets and the Royal Head-Flipper

Does this mean that no technical analyst will ever succeed in the stock market? Of course not; some will do well, for the same reasons that some people do well at the roulette wheel. If there are enough such analysts (and there are), a few will even win consistently, by the simple laws of probability. All of these will attribute their success to their singular talents. To them we dedicate a bit of economic folklore: The Fable of the Royal Head-Flipper.

In a faraway land with 64 million inhabitants, the king wished to appoint a royal head-flipper. Calling all of his subjects before him, he gave each one a coin and ordered all to flip. Thirty-two million came up heads and 32 million came up tails. Those who flipped tails were obviously no good at flipping heads and were eliminated from the competition. The remaining 32 million flipped again. When 16 million failed, they too were sent home. On the 25th trial, only 2 remained. They each flipped, and one prevailed. He was appointed the royal head-flipper by the king, who congratulated him with a toast: "Here's to the royal head-flipper, whose prowess has enabled him to flip heads 26 times in a row. According to the royal statistician, the odds against such a feat occurring by chance are a staggering 64 million to 1!"

---

[25] See E. Fama, "Efficient Capital Markets: A Review of Theory and Empirical Work," *Journal of Finance* 25 (May 1970): 383–417, for an overview.

[26] See L. J. Feinstone, "Minute by Minute: Efficiency, Normality and Randomness in Intra-Daily Asset Prices," *Journal of Applied Econometrics* 2 (1987): 193–214.

## Stock Market Crashes

In October 2008, the value of stocks traded in U.S. markets fell by about 20% in a single week; worldwide, other markets faced similar declines. Dramatic as it was, the crash of 2008 was hardly a once-in-a-lifetime event. Just 21 years earlier, in October 1987, U.S. stocks fell by over 28%. And even more recently, in the spring of 2000, technology-based stocks (as measured by the NASDAQ composite index) fell by about 40% over a few months; a year later, they had fallen almost 60%.

The theory of efficient markets suggests that even such remarkable price drops must be responses to new information about firms' expected future profitability. In 2000, for example, the government was aggressively pursuing antitrust action against Microsoft, raising expectations that other firms would soon come under similar scrutiny. In 2008, the crash followed a sudden drop in house prices that led many homeowners to default on their mortgages, wreaking havoc among banks and other financial firms, as we've discussed on page 301–302.

Why were house prices so high to begin with? It's widely believed that in the years leading up to 2008, the housing market was driven by self-fulfilling expectations: Everyone expected prices to keep rising, so everyone wanted to buy, so prices kept rising. The resulting speculative bubble eventually burst (as all speculative bubbles must), resulting in a sharp decline in prices.

**Speculative bubble**

A situation in which expectations of rising prices cause prices to rise.

Might stock prices themselves be subject to speculative bubbles, and could this help to explain the crashes of 1987, 2000, and 2008? Nobody knows for sure. But Professor Sanford Grossman of the University of Pennsylvania has laid out a plausible scenario, based on two related assumptions. First, he assumes there are a large number of investors who are determined not to let their wealth fall below a predetermined level. When a downturn in the market brings them close to that level, they become extremely sensitive to negative fluctuations. Even a slight downward movement in prices can cause many such investors to sell simultaneously.

Grossman's second assumption is that some traders are better informed than others about real financial conditions. When prices begin to fall, poorly informed traders (and even well-informed traders who aren't sure that they are well-informed) cannot be sure whether the downturn is due to some genuine bad news that other traders have discovered. The possibility that bad news is in the process of spreading leads them (rationally) to sell immediately. This in turn exacerbates the downturn. The same process in reverse can magnify upturns as well. The net effect is to substantially increase the volatility of stock prices, particularly in the short run. Grossman argues that such a theory is necessary, because observed short-run price volatility appears to be greater than can be accounted for by traditional theory.

The two phenomena Grossman describes can be mutually reinforcing. A small downturn causes a group of investors to protect their assets by selling stocks; a second group worries that the first group knows something bad, leading them to sell also. This in turn causes the first group to sell more, and so forth.

Following a stock market crash, there's always quite a bit of public discussion about how to prevent future crashes. But it's not at all clear that crashes are bad, or that preventing them is desirable. If a fall in stock prices is a response to genuine bad news about future corporate productivity, then it is almost surely a good thing. The signal it sends to investors is: "Stop diverting so many resources to enterprises that are about to become less productive." On this interpretation, the markets don't cause the bad news; they merely publicize the bad news while there's still time to limit the damage. If that's correct, then taking steps to prevent future crashes is like taking steps to prevent messengers from alerting you that your troops need reinforcements.

# Summary

The price of an item reflects the value of that item to some potential user. It also provides an incentive for others to act on that information. If the item is valuable elsewhere, the high price will tell potential users to search for substitutes.

Prices allow complex economies to be coordinated in ways that take account of vast amounts of knowledge. This knowledge includes what Hayek called the "particular circumstances of time and place." Each individual producer and consumer has access to special information that is not available to anyone else, and prices lead him to use this information in deciding how to allocate resources. A social planner without access to all of this information will allocate resources less efficiently.

The conventional measures of social welfare that were introduced in Chapter 8 make the implicit assumption that all goods are produced by the low-cost producers and distributed to the consumers who value them the most. In the absence of a price system, this assumption may be unjustified, in which case the usual measures of social welfare are overly optimistic.

When the informational content of prices is diluted, as by an inflation that makes it difficult for people to distinguish absolute from relative price changes, resources are allocated less efficiently. This provides one possible explanation of why the level of employment will change in response to an unexpected inflation but not to an expected one.

When information is distributed asymmetrically, surprising and sometimes inefficient outcomes can result. Examples include signaling equilibria, adverse selection, moral hazard, and principal–agent problems.

# Author Commentary          www.cengage.com/economics/landsburg

**AC1.** There is a principal–agent problem when corporate officers engage in hiring practices that are detrimental to stockholders.

**AC2.** News stories and scientific theories are more likely to get published when they're surprising and more likely to be surprising when they're wrong. So, unlike financial markets, markets for news can systematically lead to *inefficient* outcomes where stories that get published are more likely to be wrong than right.

**AC3.** For more on the informational content of college grades, read this article.

**AC4.** Just as stockholders depend on executives, voters depend on politicians— and similar principal–agent problems arise for both.

# Review Questions

**R1.** A social planner equipped with knowledge of all market supply and demand curves would still lack much of the knowledge necessary to duplicate the functioning of the price system. Give some examples of the knowledge that would be lacking. How is this knowledge taken into account when prices are used to allocate resources?

**R2.** Explain why a rise in soldiers' wages does not increase the cost of maintaining an army.

**R3.** What is the social role of rent? If all rents were confiscated, would there be a consequent loss of efficiency? Why or why not?

**R4.** What is an efficient market?

**R5.** "If it is well known that IBM will soon release a new and highly desirable product, then it is a good idea to buy IBM stock." Explain why this statement is wrong.

**R6.** What is a signaling equilibrium? In what sense is it inefficient?

**R7.** What is adverse selection? What is inefficient about the equilibria that result from adverse selection?

**R8.** What is moral hazard? What are some of the ways in which an insurance company can attempt to reduce moral hazard?

**R9.** Give some examples of principal–agent problems.

**R10.** Explain why stockholders might want their CEO to own more stock. Now explain why stockholders might want their CEO to own *less* stock.

# Problem Set

**1.** A race of timid elves passes the time by sneaking out at night, locating machinery that is in disrepair, and fixing it while people are sleeping. The human beneficiaries of this largesse are, of course, surprised and delighted when they discover the elves' handiwork the following morning. **True or False:** If the elves were to start charging for their services, humans would certainly be made worse off.

**2.** A chemical company is considering locating a plant on the outskirts of a certain town. Although the town welcomes the benefits that this plant will bring, some residents have expressed concern about the possibility of an accident involving toxic chemicals. The city council has met to discuss the matter. Although none of the council has any background in chemistry or engineering, many have strong opinions (some pro and some con) about whether a building permit should be issued. One councilor, who has remained neutral throughout, suggests that the permit be issued if and only if the chemical company can demonstrate the ability (either through its own assets or an adequate insurance policy) to reimburse the townspeople for any damage caused by its factory. Explain the councilor's reasoning. Explain why this policy might be expected to lead to a socially optimal decision.

**3.** In 1993, the Mississippi River flooded, causing widespread devastation and leaving midwesterners desperate to acquire basic necessities such as food and ice (for food storage). Profiteers soon emerged, selling ice for as much as $50 per pound. Editorialists and politicians decried this price-gouging and called for an end to it.

    **a.** Suppose that the authorities had effectively prohibited price-gouging. What would have been the effect on the amount of ice brought into the affected area?

**b.** Suppose that the authorities had effectively prohibited price-gouging and somehow managed to ensure that their action had no effect on the quantity of ice in the area. What would have been the effect on social welfare?

**c.** Suppose that a pure altruist in the affected area had come into possession of a small amount of ice. Explain why he might have charged $50 a pound for it, even if he was completely unconcerned with his own welfare.

**d.** Do you think that it would have been a good idea to prohibit price-gouging?

**4.** **True or False:** In a large corporation it is usually better for the central management to make decisions rather than divisional managers, because the central management has access to a wider range of information.

**5.** Aramis, Porthos, and Athos have the following marginal value schedules for swords:

| Number of Swords | Marginal Values | | |
| --- | --- | --- | --- |
| | Aramis | Porthos | Athos |
| 1 | $15 | $9 | $13 |
| 2 | 11 | 5 | 7 |
| 3 | 0 | 3 | 2 |
| 4 | 0 | 1 | 0 |

Aramis, Porthos, and Athos are the only buyers of swords in the community, and swords are produced at a constant marginal cost of $7 per sword.

**a.** If the industry is competitive, how many swords will be produced and at what price will they be sold? Justify your answer.

**b.** Suppose that a social planner orders 5 swords to be produced, with 4 distributed to Porthos and 1 to Athos. What is the social loss in this situation (compared with competitive equilibrium)? Justify your answer.

**6.** Evaluate the following methods of providing an army. Rank them in order of preference from the point of view of (a) young people, (b) consumers of military service, and (c) economic efficiency. Assume that the army will be of the same size in all cases.

**a.** A volunteer army, financed by a tax on all citizens.

**b.** A draft, with soldiers paid a wage of zero.

**c.** A volunteer army, financed by a tax on young people.

**d.** A draft, with soldiers paid a wage of zero but with the proviso that draftees may hire other young people to take their place.

**7.** Suppose that the supply curve for land is perfectly vertical.

**a.** **True or False:** Although the Fabians were wrong to argue that a 100% tax on land rents entails no social loss, it would be *right* to argue that a 99% tax on land rents entails no social loss.

**b.** Would your answer change if it requires some effort for landlords to locate the highest bidder for their land?

**8.** Suppose the equilibrium price of haircuts is $2 per haircut. A new law sets the price at $5 per haircut and requires certain demanders to buy as many haircuts as suppliers want to sell at that price.

**a.** Illustrate the smallest possible deadweight loss from this program, and justify your answer.

**b.** Explain why the actual deadweight loss is almost surely greater than what you calculated in part (a).

9. The University of Rochester has a fixed number of parking spaces for students on campus. They are currently sold at a price that clears the market. It has been proposed that the price should be lowered and a lottery held to determine who may park on campus. Each winner of the lottery would receive a ticket entitling him to purchase a parking space, and these tickets could be freely bought and sold. The number of winners would be equal to the number of parking spaces.

**a.** Graph the supply and demand for parking spaces. Show on your graph the price of a ticket. Show the consumers' surplus (earned by parkers), the producers' surplus (earned by the university), and the total value of the tickets to the winners of the lottery. Who gains, who loses, and who is unaffected if this plan is adopted?

**b.** The nearby University of Retsehcor is identical to the University of Rochester in every way except two. First, nobody at Retsehcor has proposed a lottery plan as at Rochester. Second, someone at Retsehcor has proposed that the university hold a lottery and give cash gifts to randomly chosen students. (An alternative proposal is to simply randomize tuition.) Compare the effects of the Retsehcor plan with those of the Rochester plan.

**c.** An alternative proposal at the University of Rochester would institute the lottery without allowing the resale of tickets. The university would carefully monitor compliance, expelling any lottery winner who allowed his parking spot to be used by anybody else. How would this revision affect welfare if the enforcement mechanism were successful? If it were unsuccessful?

10. Pizza is provided by a competitive industry. Suppose that in a burst of generosity, the producers of pizza decided to continue producing the same quantity as always, but to give their pizzas away for free.

**a.** Use a graph to show the change in consumer and producer surpluses.

**b.** Is it possible that (despite what your graph shows) this burst of generosity could make consumers as a group worse off? Why or why not?

11. Santa Claus always gives away exactly 1,000,000 toys per year, at a price of zero. It costs him nothing to produce these toys. There is also a market where toys can be purchased from commercial toy manufacturers.

**a.** Use a graph to show how the existence of Santa Claus affects the supply of toys, the price of toys, the number of toys that consumers acquire, and the number of toys that are provided by commercial manufacturers.

**b.** Use your graph to show how Santa affects the consumer surplus in the toy market and the producer surplus earned by commercial toy manufacturers. (Don't forget that the toys Santa gives away are free.)

**c.** According to your graph, how much does Santa add to social welfare? Explain why this answer may overestimate the true social value of Santa Claus. (*Hint:* How does Santa decide who gets the toys?)

12. No coffee is produced in the United States. Americans can buy as much coffee as they want from foreign producers at a price of $10 per pound. At this price, they buy 1,000 pounds per week. The U.S. government has decided to make coffee available to all U.S. citizens at a price of $3 per pound. It gets the coffee by purchasing it from foreigners.

a. Show the gains and losses to all relevant groups of Americans as a result of this program. Compute the deadweight loss.

b. **True or False:** The deadweight loss in this problem is entirely attributable to the fact that Americans consume an inefficiently large quantity of coffee.

c. Suppose that the government modifies the program. It will continue to sell coffee at $3, but will provide only 1,000 pounds per week, choosing randomly those citizens who are permitted to buy them. Recompute the deadweight loss by the methods of Chapter 8, and show that it is now zero.

d. What important social costs does the analysis of part (c) overlook?

13. In equilibrium, 500 widgets are sold at $40 apiece. Suppose a new law prohibits the sale of widgets but requires certain firms to produce a total of 600 widgets and give them away for free. The recipients of the widgets are allowed to resell them.

a. Use a graph to illustrate the new price of widgets.

b. Assuming the widgets are produced as cheaply as possible, illustrate the gains and/or losses to consumers, producers, and the people who get the free widgets. Illustrate the deadweight loss.

c. Explain why the "as cheaply as possible" assumption is overly optimistic, and how it biases your computation of the deadweight loss.

14. Suppose that a bright student can get through college for a cost of $A, a dull student can get through college for a cost of $B, and that it is worth $C to convince an employer that you are bright. Suppose also that nothing of value is learned in college. In which of the following circumstances would bright students go to college?

a. $C > B > A$

b. $B > C > A$

c. $B > A > C$

15. Ten people with different incomes have applied for membership in an exclusive club. One of the club's criteria in deciding whom to accept is to favor those applicants whose incomes are high relative to other applicants'. Each applicant knows his own income and can reveal it voluntarily by submitting his income tax returns. Also, everyone happens to know that there is exactly one applicant whose income is $10,000, one whose income is $20,000, and so forth up to $100,000. How many applicants reveal their incomes?

16. a. What are some of the consequences of prohibiting insurance companies from charging higher rates to people who are in high-risk groups for AIDS?

b. What are some of the consequences of prohibiting insurance companies from requiring AIDS tests as a precondition for coverage?

17. The government is considering a law that would require all sellers of used cars to provide independent certification of their quality. Make an argument in defense of such a law, from the viewpoint of promoting social welfare.

18. Many insurance companies sell group policies that cover all of the employees at a particular firm, or all of the members of a particular organization. How could this policy help to overcome the problem of adverse selection?

19.    If all used cars were required to come with warranties, we might solve an adverse selection problem while creating a moral hazard problem to take its place. Explain.

20.    Many insurance companies sell auto insurance that includes a "deductible" of $250 or $500. If you have an accident, your insurance covers all of your costs *minus* the amount of the deductible. The amount that they pay on a typical claim is far more than the amount of the deductible. **True or False:** If the deductible were eliminated, the percent increase in claim payments would be small. Therefore, because insurance companies must earn zero profits, the percent increase in premiums would be small as well.

# Monopoly

Is Microsoft a monopoly? Let's start by asking what the word means. Etymology suggests (and popular usage affirms) that a "monopoly" is a *single seller,* the only firm in its industry. Well then, is Microsoft a *single seller?* Obviously, Microsoft is the only firm that sells Windows. Equally obviously, Microsoft is *not* the only firm that sells operating systems. So whether Microsoft is a single seller depends on how narrowly you define the market.

Is Coca-Cola a single seller? It's the only firm that sells Coke but it's not the only firm that sells cola drinks. You might answer the "single seller" question one way if you think that Coke and Pepsi are basically identical, and quite another way if you're convinced you can always tell the difference.

We would prefer to avoid having to make such difficult judgments, so we'll use a different definition. We'll say that a firm has **monopoly power** (or **market power**) if it faces a downward-sloping demand curve for its product; in other words, a firm has monopoly power if it is not perfectly competitive. We will use the word *monopoly* informally to refer to any firm with market power. Single sellers are therefore a good example to keep in mind, but not the only examples.

By that definition, Microsoft is surely a monopoly; the demand curve for Windows slopes downward. In other words, if Microsoft wants to increase the sales of Windows, it has to lower the price. Everyone who's willing to buy Windows at the current price has already bought it. Your neighborhood convenience store probably also has some degree of monopoly power: to draw more customers, it must lower its prices. This contrasts with the competitive wheat farmer who can triple his output and still sell it all at the going market price.

How do monopolies behave, and is monopoly power ever a good thing? Those are the questions we will address in this chapter. We'll learn how monopolists set prices and quantities, and we'll study the welfare consequences of those choices. In the second section, we'll study the sources of monopoly power, which will lead to a deeper welfare analysis. Finally, in the third section, we will learn about a variety of profitable pricing strategies that are available to a monopolist but not viable under perfect competition.

**Market power or monopoly power**

The ability of a firm to affect market prices through its actions. A firm has monopoly power if and only if it faces a downward-sloping demand curve.

# 10.1 Price and Output under Monopoly

In this section, we will learn how a monopolist chooses price and quantity and will examine the welfare consequences of these choices.

## Monopoly Pricing

The Tailor Dress Company, which we first met in Exhibit 5.3, is a monopolist. The demand curve for its product, displayed in Exhibit 10.1, is downward sloping. The exhibit also displays Tailor's marginal revenue curve (which can be computed from the demand curve) and its marginal cost curve.

| EXHIBIT **10.1** | **Monopoly Price and Output** |
| --- | --- |

| Demand Curve | | | | | |
| --- | --- | --- | --- | --- | --- |
| Quantity of dresses | Price | Total Revenue | Marginal Revenue | Total Cost | Marginal Cost |
| 0 | | | | | |
| 1 | $10/dress | $10 | $10/dress | 3 | $1/dress |
| 2 | 9 | 18 | 8 | 5 | 2 |
| 3 | 8 | 24 | 6 | 8 | 3 |
| 4 | 7 | 28 | 4 | 12 | 4 |
| 5 | 6 | 30 | 2 | 17 | 5 |
| 6 | 5 | 30 | 0 | 23 | 6 |
| 7 | 4 | 28 | −2 | 30 | 7 |
| 8 | 3 | 24 | −4 | 38 | 8 |

The Tailor Dress Company produces 4 dresses (the quantity at which marginal cost equals marginal revenue) and sells them at a price of $7 apiece. The price is read off the demand curve at a quantity of 4.

Like any firm, Tailor operates at the point where marginal cost equals marginal revenue; that is, it produces 4 dresses. Tailor charges the highest price at which demanders will purchase those dresses; reading from the demand curve at a quantity of 4, we find that price to be $7.

## The Monopolist's Marginal Revenue Curve

In Exhibit 10.1 the marginal revenue curve lies everywhere below the demand curve. To understand why, let's compute the marginal revenue when the Tailor Dress Company produces 3 dresses. Suppose the company has already produced 2 dresses, which can be sold for $9 each, yielding a total revenue of $18. When it makes a third dress, two things happen. First, because the price of dresses is now $8, and because Tailor is making 1 more dress, total revenue goes up by $8. Second, the first 2 dresses, which could have been sold for $9 each, can now be sold for only $8 each, reducing total revenue by $2. The marginal revenue derived from the third dress is $8 − $2 = $6. The marginal revenue is less than the demand price of $8.

In general, there are two components to a monopolist's marginal revenue: There is the *price* at which he can sell an additional item (an increment to revenue), and the *price reduction* on earlier items that will now have to be sold at a lower price in order to induce demanders to accept the new quantity (a decrement). Combined, these yield a marginal revenue that is less than the demand price.[1]

---

**Exercise 10.1** Compute the two components of marginal revenue at a quantity of 4. Do they add up to the number in the table in Exhibit 10.1?

---

Notice that a competitive producer faces only the first component of marginal revenue. Because he can sell any quantity at the market price, he does not need to reduce this price when he increases his output. This is why marginal revenue is equal to (demand) price for a competitive producer, although it is always less than that for a monopolist.

## Elasticity and Marginal Revenue

Suppose you're a monopolist and you want to sell one more item. How much do you have to lower your price?

The answer depends on the demand curve you're facing. In particular, it depends on the elasticity of that demand curve, which is a concept we met back in Chapter 4. Remember that the elasticity of the demand curve (also called the price elasticity of demand) is denoted by $\eta$ and given by the formula:

$$\eta = \frac{P \cdot \Delta Q}{Q \cdot \Delta P}$$

where $\Delta Q$ and $\Delta P$ are the changes in quantity and price. Another way to write this is:

$$\Delta P = \frac{P \cdot \Delta Q}{Q \cdot \eta}$$

---

[1] If you have had calculus, you may recognize this as an application of the product rule for differentiation. Because Total revenue = Price × Quantity, we can write

$$MR = \frac{dTR}{dQ} = P + Q\,\frac{dP}{dQ}$$

The term $dP/dQ$, being calculated along the downward-sloping demand curve, is negative.

In this case, we've asked a question about what you have to do to sell just *one more item*; in other words, we're thinking about the case where $\Delta Q = 1$. So our formula simplifies to:

$$\Delta P = \frac{P}{Q \cdot \eta}$$

This is the formula that tells you how much your price must change to move that additional item off your shelf. Note that $\Delta P$ should be negative: To sell an extra item, you have to *lower* your price, not *raise* it! And the right-hand side of the formula confirms that $\Delta P$ is indeed negative, just as it should be, because $P$ and $Q$ are both positive but $\eta$ is negative. We can also write the absolute value of $\Delta P$ as:

$$|\Delta P| = \frac{P}{Q \cdot |\eta|}$$

Let's think a little more about the consequences of selling an additional item. We've just seen how much your *price* must change; now let's figure out how much your *revenue* changes.

Your revenue changes for two reasons. First, you're selling another item at the price $P$. That adds $P$ to your revenue. Second, your price falls by the amount $|\Delta P|$, and this affects all the items you're selling, so your revenue falls by $|\Delta P| \cdot Q$. The net effect is that your revenue changes by the amount:

$$P - |\Delta P| \cdot Q$$

Plugging in our formula for $|\Delta P|$, we can rewrite this as:

$$P - \frac{P}{Q \cdot |\eta|} \cdot Q = P - P \cdot \frac{1}{|\eta|} = P \cdot \left(1 - \frac{1}{|\eta|}\right)$$

That's how much your revenue changes when your quantity increases by 1. In other words, that's your marginal revenue. To summarize, for a monopolist we have:

$$MR = P \cdot \left(1 - \frac{1}{|\eta|}\right)$$

To gain some further insight into this formula, let's recall what we already know about marginal revenue. If you take another look at Exhibit 10.1, you'll see that $MR$ is sometimes positive (in this case, for quantities less than 6) and sometimes negative (in this case, for quantities greater than 6). You'll also see that *at the monopoly quantity* (which in this case is 4), $MR$ is positive. That's because at the monopoly quantity, $MR = MC$, and $MC$ is always positive.

Now the formula tells us that in order for $MR$ to be positive, we must have $|\eta| > 1$. And we've just agreed that at the monopoly quantity, $MR$ is positive. So we can conclude that at the monopoly quantity, $|\eta| > 1$.

When $|\eta| > 1$ we say that *the demand curve is elastic,* and when $|\eta| < 1$ we say that *the demand curve is inelastic.* So our conclusion can be reworded:

A monopolist always operates on the elastic portion of the demand curve.

## Measuring Monopoly Power

In competition, price equals marginal cost. Under monopoly, price can exceed marginal cost; the difference is sometimes called the firm's *markup*. In other words, the markup is given by the formula $P - MC$. Sometimes we express the markup as a fraction of the price; the resulting measure

$$P - \frac{MC}{P}$$

is called the firm's **Lerner Index.** For a competitive firm, the Lerner Index is zero. For a monopolist, it should be positive.

We have already shown that $MR = P\left(1 - \frac{1}{|\eta|}\right)$, and theory tells us that firms

operate where $MC = MR$. So in the formula for the Lerner Index, we can replace $MC$

with $P\left(1\left(\frac{1}{|\eta|}\right)\right)$ to get

$$\text{Lerner Index} = \frac{P - MC}{P} = \frac{P - P\left(1 - \frac{1}{|\eta|}\right)}{P} = \frac{1}{|\eta|}$$

**Lerner Index**

The excess of price over marginal cost, expressed as a fraction of the price.

In other words, the markup (as a fraction of the price) is equal to one over the elasticity of demand; therefore, the less elastic the demand curve, the higher the markup.

Regulatory agencies use the Lerner Index as a measure of monopoly power. In the rubber industry, the index is a quite small .049; in the retail gasoline industry, it is .100; in the soft drink industry it is .600 (.640 for Coca-Cola and .560 for Pepsi-Cola). In other words, Coca-Cola sells for about 64% more than the marginal cost of production, while Pepsi-Cola sells for about 56% more than the cost of production. Perhaps surprisingly, the Lerner Index in the electric power industry fluctuates around .05, which means that electricity is pretty close to competitively priced.

## The Price of Gasoline, The Price of Oranges, and Monopoly Power

Back in 1999, Middle Eastern oil producers nearly tripled the price of crude oil. You might think this was bad for American oil companies who buy crude oil and then convert it to gasoline. But by the summer of the year 2000, gas prices had risen so much that oil company profits were actually higher than in previous years.

Around the same time, a frost in Florida destroyed a substantial portion of the orange crop. You might think this was bad for growers who had spent an entire year raising those crops. But the price of oranges rose so much that growers ended up having an unusually profitable year.

Why were oil companies and orange growers able to prosper in the face of apparent disaster? Many news reporters and politicians have said that it's because they were exploiting monopoly power. But economic analysis reveals that exactly the opposite is true: Rising costs can lead to rising profits only in the *absence* of monopoly power. The fact that the gas companies and orange growers did so well in difficult times is proof that they are *not* acting as monopolists.

Here's why: A monopolized industry does not have to wait for a disaster before raising prices. A monopolized oil industry would *already* have raised its prices to the point where additional price increases were no longer profitable. Likewise for the orange growers.

Here's the same argument in more precise terms: A monopolist operates at the point where marginal revenue equals marginal cost. But marginal cost is never negative, so marginal revenue is never negative. Thus a monopolist always operates at a point where *higher quantities mean more revenue.*

Saying exactly the same thing in reverse, *lower quantities mean less revenue.* So if a monopolist raises his price—thereby lowering his quantity—his revenue must fall. If you see the opposite—a rise in price accompanied by a rise in revenue—you must not be looking at a monopolist.

We can say exactly the same thing in the language of elasticities: We've seen that a monopolist always operates on the elastic part of the demand curve. But because the oil and orange industries were able to raise prices with little reduction in quantity, they must have been on the inelastic parts of their demand curves; they cannot have been controlled by monopolists.

## Greedy Recording Studios or Greedy Artists?

The famous recording artist Ellenell has a contract that gives him 20% of all revenue from his recordings. The studio that issues those recordings charges $15 for an Ellenell CD. But Ellenell has denounced his own studio for excessive greed and says he'd like to see the price come down to $10, even though it would cost him money.

That story is fiction, but it's often repeated in fact: Musicians frequently criticize recording studios for overpricing their music out of "greed." Does that mean that musicians care more about their fans than producers do?

Not necessarily. Because the fact is that under standard recording contracts, *any* musician—even one motivated entirely by personal greed—would want to see the price of CDs reduced.

Here's why: Remember that profit is maximized when marginal revenue equals marginal cost. For the record company, the marginal cost of producing another CD is equal to the cost of burning, packaging, and shipping that CD—say about $1. Therefore, the record company chooses a quantity and a price where marginal revenue equals $1 per disk.

For the artist, who receives a percentage royalty (let's say 20%) from each disk sold, that means that marginal revenue is 20¢ per disk. But for the artist, who is not involved with production and shipping, the marginal *cost* per disk is zero. That means that from the artist's point of view, marginal revenue exceeds marginal cost, so profits are not being maximized. To maximize profits, quantity must be increased (and hence price must be decreased) until marginal revenue equals zero.

Thus a purely profit-maximizing entertainer will always lobby the producer to lower the price of CDs. Of course, if the entertainer can mask his self-interested motivation as a concern for the welfare of his fans, he might very well be tempted to do that.

## The Monopolist Has No Supply Curve

Where is the monopolist's supply curve? Points on the supply curve answer questions such as: "How much would you produce at a going market price of $1?" and "How much would you produce at a going market price of $2?" and so on. These are questions that a monopolist is never asked, because he never faces a going market price. The price is a consequence of the monopolist's actions, rather than a datum to which he must react. Therefore, a monopolist has no supply curve; a supply curve presumes the existence of a going market price.

# Welfare

Suppose the shoe industry is dominated by a monopoly supplier of the "single seller" breed. Suppose also that a competitive shoe industry would produce with the same (industrywide) marginal cost curve as the monopolist's. Exhibit 10.2 shows the quantities produced by the monopolist ($Q_M$) and the competitive industry ($Q_C$) and the prices that they charge. The table shows consumers' and producers' surpluses in each case.

**Exercise 10.2** Verify the entries in the table in Exhibit 10.2.

From Exhibit 10.2 it is clear that consumers' surplus is reduced by the existence of the monopoly. It is less obvious, but nonetheless true, that producers' surplus is increased. The monopoly producer's surplus exceeds the competitive producers' sur-

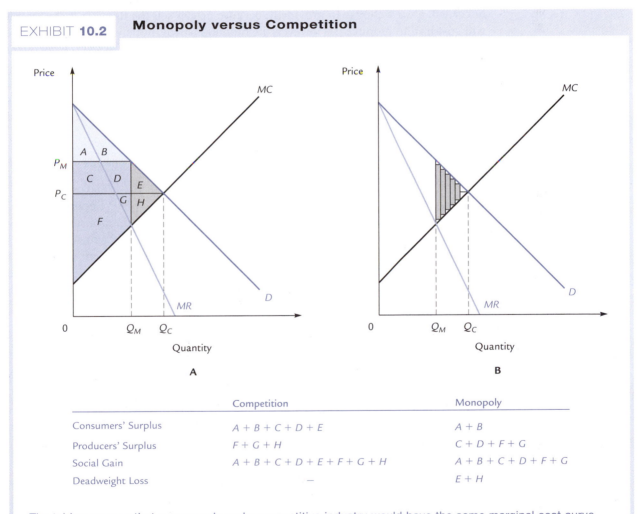

**EXHIBIT 10.2** — **Monopoly versus Competition**

|  | Competition | Monopoly |
| --- | --- | --- |
| Consumers' Surplus | $A + B + C + D + E$ | $A + B$ |
| Producers' Surplus | $F + G + H$ | $C + D + F + G$ |
| Social Gain | $A + B + C + D + E + F + G + H$ | $A + B + C + D + F + G$ |
| Deadweight Loss | — | $E + H$ |

The table assumes that a monopoly and a competitive industry would have the same marginal cost curve. The competitive industry produces the equilibrium quantity $Q_C$, and the monopolist produces its profit-maximizing quantity $Q_M$. Because marginal value still exceeds marginal cost at $Q_M$, it would be efficient for additional units to be produced. The social gains from additional units after $Q_M$ are represented by the rectangles in panel B. Because the monopolist does not produce those units, those social gains are sacrificed, giving a deadweight loss of $E + H$.

plus by the amount $C + D - H$, and your first thought might be that it would be necessary to measure areas in order to determine whether this is positive or negative. Recall, however, that the monopolist is choosing the strategy that will benefit him the most. Because the monopolist could choose the competitive output $Q_C$ but prefers the smaller output $Q_M$ instead, we infer that the producer's surplus is higher at $Q_M$ than at $Q_C$. In other words, $C + D + F + G > F + G + H$.

Exhibit 10.2 also shows a social welfare loss of $E + H$ due to the existence of the monopoly. This is the amount by which the consumers' losses exceed the producer's gains. It is easy to see the reason for this welfare loss: When output is at $Q_M$, marginal value still exceeds marginal cost. It is socially beneficial to produce another pair of shoes, creating the first rectangle of social gain shown in panel B of the exhibit. From the viewpoint of efficiency, additional pairs of shoes should be produced, as they would be under competition.

When an item's marginal value exceeds its marginal cost, the competitive producer will always choose to provide it, because he can sell the item for more than it will cost him to produce it. However, the monopolist will not always make the same choice. The monopolist must reason as follows: "It is true that I can sell the next item for more than it will cost me to produce it. But it is also true that producing this item will reduce the price at which I can sell all of the items I've already decided to produce. I have to weigh both of these considerations before deciding to proceed." The second consideration is, of course, irrelevant to the competitor, whose actions do not affect the market price.

## Monopoly and Public Policy

What can be done to reduce the efficiency loss due to monopoly? Because the inefficiency results from a reduction in output caused by the monopolist's pursuit of high profits, some might argue that the government should tax away the monopolist's ill-gotten gains, say, by imposing an excise tax. However, this "solution" only reduces efficiency still further. The original problem is that production is less than it should be from a social viewpoint, and the effect of an excise tax is to lower production still further. The tax increases the deadweight loss.

**Exercise 10.3** Draw the monopolist's demand, marginal revenue, and marginal cost curves both before and after the imposition of an excise tax on his output. Label the areas of deadweight loss both before and after the tax.

### Subsidies

The preceding observation suggests that the real solution might be to give the monopolist a *subsidy* per unit of output.

Exhibit 10.3 shows the effect of an "ideal" subsidy, that is, one of exactly the right size to induce the monopolist to supply the competitive quantity $Q_C$. We know that this quantity maximizes social gain, so the deadweight loss is reduced to zero.

To see how the gains and losses are distributed over society, notice that the ideally subsidized monopolist produces the same quantity at the same price as does a competitive market. Therefore, the consumers' surplus is the same in either case. The monopolist earns both the competitive producers' surplus and the revenue from the subsidy; the latter, of course, comes from the taxpayers.

| EXHIBIT 10.3 | A Subsidized Monopolist |
|---|---|

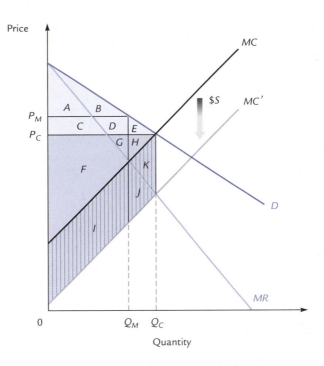

|  | Competition | Unsubsidized Monopoly | Subsidized Monopoly |
|---|---|---|---|
| Consumers' Surplus | $A + B + C + D + E$ | $A + B$ | $A + B + C + D + E$ |
| Producers' Surplus | $F + G + H$ | $C + D + F + G$ | $F + G + H + I + J + K$ |
| Cost to Taxpayers | — | — | $I + J + K$ |
| Social Gain | $A + B + C + D + E + F$ | $A + B + C + D + F + G$ | $A + B + C + D + E$ |
|  | $+ G + H$ |  | $+ F + G + H$ |

An unsubsidized monopolist produces the quantity $Q_M$. The subsidy of $\$S$ per unit of output, which lowers the marginal cost curve to $MC'$, is chosen to be of just the right size so that the monopolist will now produce the competitive quantity $Q_C$. Because the competitive quantity maximizes social gain, the deadweight loss is eliminated. The table confirms that social gain is the same as it would be under competition.

We can see this distribution in Exhibit 10.3. In the presence of the $\$S$-per-unit subsidy, the monopolist chooses the quantity $Q_C$ and the price $P_C$. Therefore, the consumers' surplus is $A + B + C + D + E$, just as in competition. To compute the producers' surplus by our usual methods, we would have to draw a horizontal line at the "price received by suppliers," a distance $\$S$ above the price charged in the marketplace. This would clutter the diagram beyond all redemption, so we resort to an alternative method, which was introduced in Exhibit 8.13. According to this method, we calculate using the price charged in the marketplace and the new, lower marginal cost curve. This gives a producers' surplus of $F + G + H + I + J + K$. By elementary geometry, the cost to taxpayers, $\$S \times Q_C$, is represented by the area of the trapezoid $I + J + K$. These calculations are shown in the third column of the table in Exhibit 10.3. The social gain is just what it would be under competition, so the deadweight loss is zero, as we have already argued that it must be.

Of course, this analysis assumes an "ideal" subsidy, which in turn assumes that policymakers are able to discern both the competitive equilibrium quantity and the size of the subsidy needed to call forth that quantity from the monopolist. A more reasonable expectation is that the subsidy will either be too small or too large. If it is too small, it is still certain to be welfare-improving, but perhaps by less than we might hope. If it is too large, it will encourage overproduction. Depending on the size of the subsidy, this could be either less or more detrimental than the underproduction it was designed to replace.

**Exercise 10.4** Draw diagrams depicting the effects of subsidies that are smaller or larger than the optimal one. Indicate the areas of deadweight loss in each. Compare these areas with the areas of deadweight loss from an unsubsidized monopoly.

## Price Ceilings

From an efficiency standpoint, it is desirable to subsidize a monopolist, although the size of the optimal subsidy may be difficult to determine. From a political viewpoint, it can be difficult to generate support for subsidies to a monopolist who is already perceived as wealthier than he "deserves" to be. There is, however, another approach to the "problem" of monopoly.

Consider a price ceiling imposed on a monopolist at the level of the competitive price. This is shown in panel A of Exhibit 10.4. If the price ceiling is perfectly enforced, the monopolist effectively faces a flat demand curve at the price $P_C$ out to the quantity $Q_C$. This is because no demander can ever offer a price higher than $P_C$, so that portion of the demand curve that lies above $P_C$ becomes irrelevant to the monopolist's calculations. The new demand curve is as shown in panel B of Exhibit 10.4; it is flat out to

**EXHIBIT 10.4    A Price Ceiling**

If a monopolist is required by law to charge no more than the competitive price $P_C$, then it effectively faces the demand and marginal revenue curves shown in panels B and C. It produces at the point $Q_C$, where marginal cost and marginal revenue are equal.

$Q_C$ and becomes identical with the old demand curve thereafter. The new marginal revenue curve is shown in panel C of the exhibit: In the region where demand is flat at $P_C$, we always have marginal revenue equal to $P_C$ (just as in the competitive case). In the region of downward-sloping demand, the original marginal revenue curve is still in effect; thus, the new marginal revenue curve jumps downward at the quantity $Q_C$.

The monopolist produces the quantity where its new marginal revenue curve meets its marginal cost curve, that is, the competitive quantity $Q_C$ (refer to panel A to see this). Consumers' surplus and producers' surplus are what they would be under competition, and there is no deadweight loss.

**Exercise 10.5** Give the reasons for the assertions made in the preceding paragraph. In a competitive market, price controls cause social loss due to time spent waiting in line and so on, yet no such social loss takes place in the market pictured in Exhibit 10.4. Why not?

Unfortunately, finding the optimal price ceiling may be no easier for the policymaker than finding the right level of subsidy. In the absence of a competitive market, it is difficult to determine what the competitive price would be. It is therefore possible to set the price ceiling either too high or too low. If it is set too high, its effect will be diminished. Deadweight loss will be reduced but not eliminated altogether. If it is set too low, there will be deadweight loss due to underproduction. If it is set very low, the deadweight loss can be greater than with an unregulated monopoly.

**Exercise 10.6** Draw diagrams depicting price ceilings that are higher or lower than the optimal one. Show the areas of deadweight loss and compare them with the deadweight losses in the absence of a price control.

## Rate-of-Return Regulation

In practice, many monopolists (such as public utility companies) are required to set prices in such a way that they will earn no more than a "normal" rate of return on their capital investment. That is, they must earn no more than they could by investing the same amount of capital in some other industry; they are required to earn zero economic profits.

It is sometimes argued that this policy is desirable because the goal is to make monopolists behave more like competitors, and competitors earn zero profits in long-run equilibrium. The problem with this argument is that it is not the zero-profits aspect of competition that one wishes to reproduce; it is the efficiency aspect. Although efficiency and zero profits are compatible under competition, they are very unlikely to be compatible under monopoly.

Exhibit 10.5 shows two possible configurations of demand, marginal revenue, marginal cost, and average cost curves. In each case the monopolist earns zero profits when it produces the quantity $Q_Z$ and sells at the price $P_Z$. At this point, price exactly covers average cost. However, in each case the efficient level of output is $Q_C$, where a competitive industry would produce. In panel A, a monopolist that is required to earn zero profits will produce too much from the viewpoint of efficiency. In panel B, the monopolist will produce too little.

There are additional problems with regulation requiring the monopolist to earn zero profits. One is that such regulation provides the monopolist with no incentive to

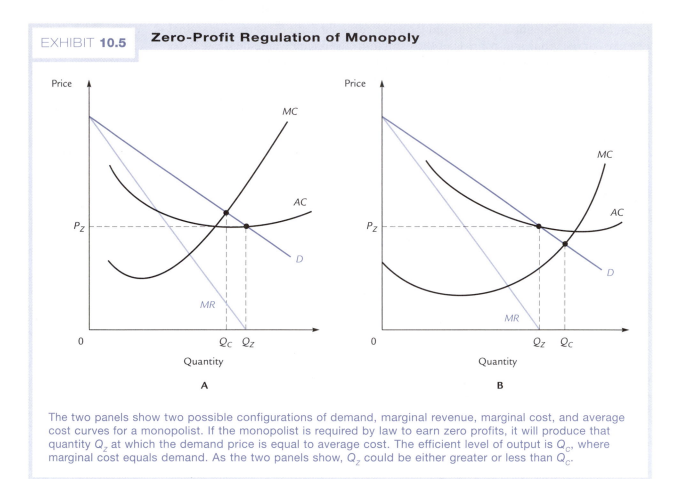

**EXHIBIT 10.5** | **Zero-Profit Regulation of Monopoly**

The two panels show two possible configurations of demand, marginal revenue, marginal cost, and average cost curves for a monopolist. If the monopolist is required by law to earn zero profits, it will produce that quantity $Q_z$ at which the demand price is equal to average cost. The efficient level of output is $Q_C$, where marginal cost equals demand. As the two panels show, $Q_z$ could be either greater or less than $Q_C$.

seek more efficient methods of production. If a new technology would lower the average cost and if the result of this is that the monopolist must lower its price accordingly, then there is no reason for it to adopt the new technology.

# 10.2 Sources of Monopoly Power

We turn now to the question of why monopolies arise in the first place. The answers will make it necessary to modify some of our welfare analysis.

## Natural Monopoly

Suppose you want to produce a new word processing program. Your fixed costs (the costs of developing the software) are likely to be quite high, but your marginal costs (the costs of copying the software onto disks) will be extremely low. In fact, if the software is distributed over the Internet, your marginal cost might be essentially zero.

In a competitive market, word processing software would sell at marginal cost—that is, it would be almost free. But at that price, all firms earn negative profits, so nobody is willing to enter the industry. Therefore, a competitive market for word processors cannot survive.

By contrast, a monopolist can sell software for substantially more than its marginal cost. Microsoft Word sells for many times the cost of producing an additional copy. Therefore, Microsoft can earn enough to cover its fixed costs and is willing to remain in business.

Notice that Microsoft's average cost curve is decreasing. To see why, consider an extreme example: Suppose it costs $1,000 to write the software, and suppose it costs exactly zero to run off a copy. Then if Microsoft sells 1 copy, its average cost is $1,000 per copy; if it sells 2 copies, its average cost is $500 per copy; if it sells 3 copies, its average cost is $333.33 per copy, and so on.

Whenever a firm's average cost curve is decreasing at the point where it crosses market demand, we say that there is a condition of **natural monopoly.** This condition is illustrated in Exhibit 10.6. We have just seen that Microsoft is an example of a natural monopoly. We shall now see that, more generally, under conditions of natural monopoly, a competitive industry cannot survive.

If the firm in Exhibit 10.6 were forced to set prices and quantities as if the industry were competitive, it would produce the quantity $Q_C$ at the price $P_C$. However, at this point average cost is greater than the price $P_C$, so the firm earns negative profits. If firms are forced to price competitively, none will remain in the industry.

**Natural monopoly**

An industry in which each firm's average cost curve is decreasing at the point where it crosses market demand.

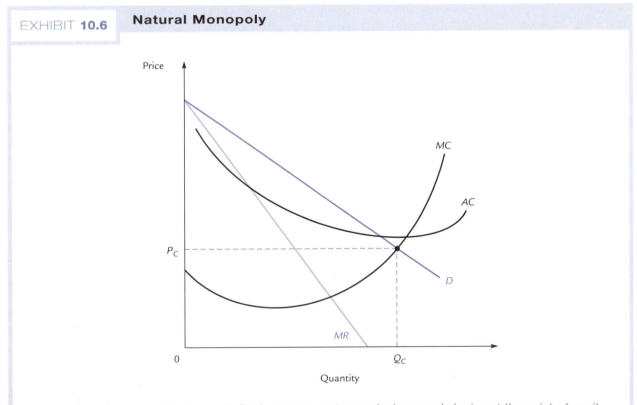

**EXHIBIT 10.6**   **Natural Monopoly**

A natural monopoly occurs when each firm's average cost curve is downward sloping at the point where it crosses industry demand. Because marginal cost crosses average cost at the bottom of the U, marginal cost must cross demand at a point where price is below average cost. Thus, if the firm priced competitively, it would earn negative profits.

In fact, if the industry were competitive, the situation would be even worse than we have just described, because the industry supply curve, being the sum of all of the firms' supply curves, would lie to the right of the marginal cost curve shown in the exhibit. Therefore, the equilibrium price would be even lower than $P_C$.

It follows that at the competitive price, no firm can cover its costs. A monopoly producer, however, may be able to enter the industry and prosper. The industry can survive only if it is monopolized.

## The Welfare Economics of Natural Monopoly

In Exhibit 10.2, we compared the social gain under monopoly with the social gain that would be available if the industry were perfectly competitive. Now we've seen that in the case of a natural monopolist, the comparison is misleading, because if the industry were perfectly competitive, it could never survive. So the first observation is that, realistically, the monopoly outcome might be the best we can hope for.

But not always. There can still be competition, even when the competition is not perfect. You might have noticed that Microsoft, despite having achieved considerable monopoly power, was never the world's only producer of computer software, or even the world's only producer of word processors. What social purpose is served by such competition?

If other firms produce exact clones of Microsoft Word, there's a lot of social waste: Each firm duplicates Microsoft's development costs without doing anything to reduce the (already very low) marginal cost of producing copies. Still, this activity might have some offsetting social benefits, by putting downward pressure on the prices of word processors. As long as the price remains high enough for firms to survive, any price reduction leads to more sales and a higher social gain.

But that's not the only effect of competition in the market for word processors. The fact is that other firms *don't* produce exact clones of Microsoft Word; instead, they're always trying to produce something better—and Microsoft is always trying to stay ahead of them. There might always be monopoly power in the software industry, but firms still compete to capture that monopoly power for themselves—and they do so by upgrading the quality of their products; in other words, they *innovate*.

What is the social value of all the innovation? It's a mixed bag. On the one hand, consumers benefit from better products. On the other hand, a lot of resources get devoted to adding small bells and whistles, and those resources might have been better employed elsewhere.

Take an extreme example: Suppose that by investing $50 million, you could create a word processor just slightly better than those that are currently available. The reward to that effort is enormous, because you'll capture a very large fraction of the market. But the benefit to consumers might be very much less than $50 million, because your product is only slightly better than its competitors. In that case, you will surely invest the $50 million, even though the gains to consumers are minimal—say, $10 million. Thus your innovation creates a net social loss of $40 million.

## Patents

Patents are another source of monopoly power with ambiguous welfare consequences. A patent confers a legally protected monopoly for 17 years after the development of a new invention. In the absence of this monopoly, the invention could be copied by others and produced competitively. On the other hand, if there were no patents, the incentive to invent would be much reduced and many inventions might not come into being in the first place. In deciding on the optimal length of a patent, it is necessary to weigh the losses from monopoly production against the gains from promoting inventive activity.

Keep in mind, though, that there is an optimal quantity of inventive activity, and that it is socially undesirable to grant incentives for people to be inventive past the point where the marginal benefits of inventions exceed the marginal gains from inventors' alternative employment. Another factor often ignored is that patents divert creative individuals *away* from making socially valuable innovations that are not patentable. The inventors of the Macintosh computer received many valuable patents; the inventor of the supermarket received none. If the length of patent protection is increased, society will have more inventions like the Macintosh and fewer like the supermarket; it is very hard to judge the optimal mix.

With all of these uncertainties in mind, you should be somewhat skeptical of attempts to estimate the optimal life of a patent, but such attempts have been made.[2] Although the results necessarily depend on a number of ad hoc assumptions, they tend to suggest that the existing 17-year limit is a reasonable one.

## The History of Photography: Patents in the Public Domain

Patents are good because they encourage innovation; patents are bad because they confer monopoly power. Is there a way to get the good without the bad?

Perhaps. When Louis Daguerre invented photography in the eighteenth century, the French government granted him a patent—and then purchased the patent from him and placed it in the public domain. That way Daguerre was rewarded for his invention, but photography still became widely available at a competitive price.

Harvard Professor Michael Kremer has proposed that the same idea could be implemented on a much wider scale. Inventors could be granted patents just as they are today, but the government could make a practice of purchasing each new patent and placing it in the public domain.

The problem is to determine how much the government should pay for a patent. The glib answer is: They should pay what it's worth. But how can they discover what it's worth?

Kremer's idea is to auction off the patent and then have the government step in at the last minute and purchase the patent for an amount equal to the winning bid. This works as long as auction bidders bid sensibly. But what is their incentive to bid sensibly if they never actually get to buy the patent?

Here, then, is Kremer's modified suggestion: Auction off each patent. At the end of the auction, flip a coin. If the coin comes up heads, the government steps in to buy the patent; if not, then the winning bidder gets it. The fact that the coin might come up tails keeps bidders honest; at the same time, half of all patents end up in the public domain, which is better than none.

Of course, there's no need to use a fair coin. A coin that comes up heads 90% of the time might do just as well. All that's necessary is for bidders to feel that there's enough chance of winning that they'll do their research and their bidding with appropriate care.

---

[2] One of the most famous attempts is by William Nordhaus, *Invention, Growth and Welfare* (Cambridge, MA: MIT Press, 1969).

## Resource Monopolies

Monopolies occasionally result when a single firm gains control of a productive input that is necessary to the industry. The most commonly cited example is Alcoa (Aluminum Company of America), which completely dominated the market for aluminum in the first 40 years of the twentieth century. Alcoa initially established its monopoly position by acquiring critical patents, but it was able to maintain its position long after the patents expired largely by virtue of owning essentially all of the sources of bauxite (the ore from which aluminum is derived) in the United States.

## Economies of Scope

**Economies of scope**

Efficiencies resulting from producing multiple products at a single firm.

The Sony Corporation produces televisions, DVD players, videocassette recorders, digital cameras, MP3 players, computers, video game consoles, and more. These products use overlapping technologies and, in many cases, some of the same components. Often multiple products can be produced in the same factory using the same equipment. These economies of scope allow Sony to produce more efficiently than smaller and more specialized firms, and helps to explain Sony's substantial market shares. More generally, whenever it's cheaper to produce several products in a single factory, we expect to see large multiproduct firms, which might, because of their size, enjoy substantial monopoly power.

## Legal Barriers to Entry

In many industries, legal barriers to entry constitute a source of monopoly power. We will have more to say on this topic in Section 11.3. Here we will give one brief example. In many states travelers on limited-access highways can visit restaurants and gas stations at "oasis stops" without having to leave the highway. The number of oases is determined by an agency of the state government, which also decides which restaurants will be granted the rights to do business there. Because entry is restricted, these rights confer considerable monopoly power. (In many states the restaurants are subject to price controls, but they still appear to price higher than competitively.) There is a great deal of competition among restaurants to acquire these rights, much of which takes the form of lobbying appropriate government officials and applying other forms of political pressure. This lobbying process itself can consume valuable resources (lobbyists' time, for example) without producing offsetting social gains. The concomitant losses should be *added* to the welfare cost of monopoly, which is therefore underestimated by the methods of Section 10.1.

---

**Exercise 10.7** Explain why it would be socially more efficient to legalize bribery of state officials who decide on the placement of roadside restaurants.

---

Some economists have used the observation of Exercise 10.7 to explain the preponderance of lawyers as members of state and federal legislative bodies. The reason is that it is easier to bribe a lawyer than (for example) a medical doctor. This is not because of any moral superiority on the part of physicians; it is a purely technological phenomenon. Many of the firms that seek favors from legislators have considerable need for legal services, and they can contrive to hire those services from favored lawyer–legislators at inflated fees. A number of U.S. congressmen from widely scattered parts of the country are associated with previously undistinguished law firms whose business has thrived since one of the partners went to Washington. A small-town medical practice would find it far more difficult to plausibly collect million-dollar fees for services rendered to large corporations thousands of miles away.

# 10.3 Price Discrimination

The analysis of monopoly pricing in Section 10.1 assumes that the monopolist will sell all of his output at a single price. In this section, we will see that, unlike a competitor, a monopolist can benefit by charging different prices for identical items.

### Example: Monopoly in the Pie Market

Exhibit 10.7 shows the market for Mrs. Lovett's pies. Mrs. Lovett faces a downward-sloping demand curve, so she acts as a monopolist. That is, she produces the quantity $Q_0$ where marginal cost equals marginal revenue and charges $10 per pie, read off the demand curve.

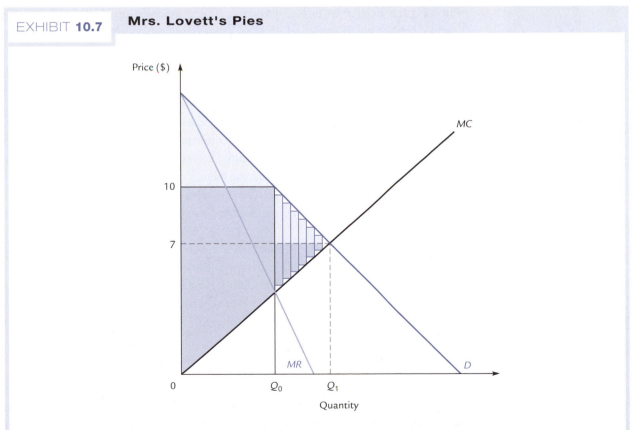

**EXHIBIT 10.7**   **Mrs. Lovett's Pies**

Mrs. Lovett, as a monopolist, produces $Q_0$ pies and sells them at a price of $10. Once she has done so, she can still sell additional pies at prices that exceed her marginal cost. For example, at the competitive price of $7, she could sell an additional $Q_1 - Q_0$ pies, creating additional social gains represented by the rectangles. The upper portions of the rectangles represent additions to consumers' surplus, and the lower portions represent additions to Mrs. Lovett's producer's surplus.

Mrs. Lovett could sell additional pies if she charged any price less than $10. For example, some customers may approach Mrs. Lovett and offer to buy additional pies at the competitive price of $7. Because this price exceeds Mrs. Lovett's marginal cost, both she and her customers would benefit from such a transaction. That is to say, both the producer's and consumers' surpluses will be increased. Each additional pie beyond $Q_0$ creates a rectangle of social gain, as in the exhibit. Mrs. Lovett earns the lower portions of these rectangles as additional producer's surplus. Her customers gain the upper portions.

Although the transaction would benefit everyone, it still might not take place. Why not? Because Mrs. Lovett will be willing to market additional pies at the lower price of $7 only on the condition that her customers continue to buy $Q_0$ high-priced pies. Ideally, Mrs. Lovett would like to market some pies at $10 and other identical pies at $7, and then post a sign in her shop reading: "Please buy as many $10 pies as you are willing to before purchasing any $7 pies." Realistically, she fears that her customers will not cooperate. This fear leads her to produce only $Q_0$ pies at a single monopoly price of $10.

Conceivably, Mrs. Lovett could attempt some approximation to the scheme she has just rejected. If she believes that the typical customer is willing to buy two pies at $10 each, she can sell pies at "$10 each, 3 for $27." This effectively enables her to sell each customer a third pie for $7 without cutting into the sales of $10 pies.

But this plan, too, has its flaws. First, some of her customers might in fact have been willing to pay $10 for a third pie. A more important (and perhaps fatal) flaw is this: Some customers may buy a third pie for $7, then resell the pie for $9 to somebody else who would have been willing to buy it from Mrs. Lovett for $10. In effect, she makes it possible for her own customers to go into competition with her! We will return to these problems later in this section.

**Price discrimination**

Charging different prices for identical items.

The act of charging different prices for identical items is known as **price discrimination.** Any monopolist faces the temptation to price discriminate, because he produces where marginal value exceeds marginal cost. Consequently, he can always sell additional items at a price higher than the marginal cost of producing them.

A competitive producer, by contrast, faces no temptation to price discriminate. This is because he can sell any quantity he wants to at the going market price, so there is never any reason for him to sell for less.

In order to price discriminate successfully, a monopolist must be able to prevent the low-priced units from being resold, undercutting his own higher-priced sales. This is easier in some industries than in others. Utility companies offer quantity discounts, for example, because technological barriers prevent a customer from buying lots of cheap electricity and reselling it to his friends at a profit.

## First-Degree Price Discrimination

Returning to Mrs. Lovett, we find that there is yet another pricing policy with even greater potential to increase her revenue. Exhibit 10.8 shows again the market for Mrs. Lovett's pies; the curves are exactly as in Exhibit 10.7. The rectangles represent the marginal values that her customers place on pies. Each rectangle is labeled with the initial of the corresponding customer. Flicka has the highest marginal value, valuing her first pie at $14. Ricka values her first pie at $13, Dicka values her first pie at $12, Flicka values her second pie at $11, and so on. If Mrs. Lovett knows all this, she

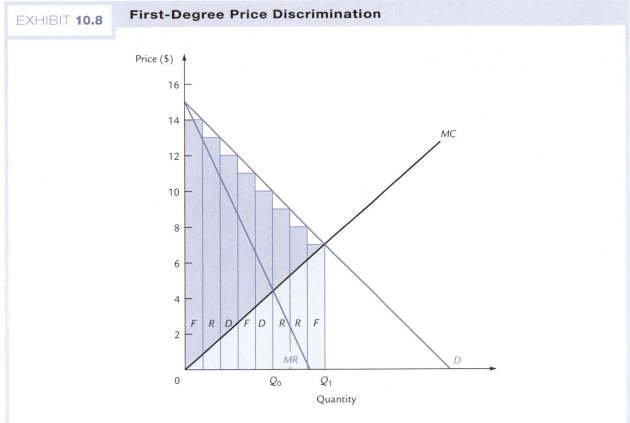

**EXHIBIT 10.8** **First-Degree Price Discrimination**

The rectangles show the marginal values of pies to Mrs. Lovett's customers, with each labeled by the initial of the corresponding customer. If she charges each customer the maximum amount that she is willing to pay for a pie, Flicka will have to pay $14 for her first pie, Ricka will pay $13 for her first pie, and so on. Because each customer pays her marginal value for each pie, there is no customers' surplus. All of the surplus is earned by Mrs. Lovett, who gains the entire shaded area.

can price her pies as follows: To Flicka the first pie is $14 and the second is $11. To Ricka the first pie is $13. To Dicka ... and so on.

This scheme allows Mrs. Lovett to capture all of the social gains for herself. Each customer pays the maximum amount she would be willing to pay for each pie, so that she earns no surplus, while Mrs. Lovett gains the shaded areas shown in the exhibit. Mrs. Lovett will sell pies as long as she can collect prices higher than her marginal cost, so she will produce the competitive quantity $Q_1$. Therefore, there is no deadweight loss.

This scheme is called **first-degree price discrimination,** to distinguish it from the **second-degree price discrimination** that Mrs. Lovett practiced when she offered quantity discounts. In second-degree price discrimination each customer is offered the same set of prices, although the price may depend on the quantity purchased. In first-degree price discrimination each individual customer is charged the highest price he is willing to pay for each item.

Either form of price discrimination leads to an increase in output and an increase in welfare. Second-degree price discrimination benefits both the producer and the consumers. First-degree price discrimination benefits the producer in two ways. First, it allows him to appropriate the consumers' surplus. Second, it allows him to produce out to the competitive quantity, creating additional welfare gains, all of which go to the producer.

**First-degree price discrimination**

Charging each customer the most that he would be willing to pay for each item that he buys.

**Second-degree price discrimination**

Charging the same customer different prices for identical items.

## Third-Degree Price Discrimination

**Third-degree price discrimination**

Charging different prices in different markets.

The third and most common form of price discrimination is called **third-degree price discrimination.** This occurs when a seller faces two (or more) identifiably different groups of buyers having different (downward-sloping) demand curves. Such a seller can increase profits by setting different prices for the two groups, provided resales can be prevented.

### Example: Two Markets for Pies

Consider again Mrs. Lovett, who has discovered a second market for her pies. A grocery store in a large city 200 miles away is willing to buy as many pies as Mrs. Lovett wants to sell at a price of $7 each.[3]

What quantity of pies will Mrs. Lovett provide to her local customers? The ordinary monopoly quantity is $Q_0$ in Exhibit 10.9. At this quantity, her marginal revenue is $5 per pie. But Mrs. Lovett can always sell pies to the big-city grocery store at a marginal revenue of $7 per pie. Given this, it pays to sell fewer pies locally and more in the big city. Mrs. Lovett will keep transferring pies from the local market to the big-city market as long as the local marginal revenue is less than $7. This will reduce the local quantity to $Q_2$ in Exhibit 10.9.

In general:

Any producer selling in two different markets will choose quantities so that his marginal revenue is the same in each market.

The reason for this is that if marginal revenue in Market 1 were higher than marginal revenue in Market 2, the producer could increase his profits by selling one more item in Market 1 and one less in Market 2.

Because Mrs. Lovett sells only $Q_2$ pies at home, she is able to command a price of $11 for them. Then she will turn to the big-city market and will sell pies there as long as her marginal revenue ($7 per pie) exceeds her marginal cost. That is, she will produce $Q_1$ pies altogether, selling $Q_2$ of them at home for $11 each and $Q_1 - Q_2$ of them in the big city for $7 each.

The table in Exhibit 10.9 shows social gains in three situations: Mrs. Lovett as a competitor, Mrs. Lovett as an ordinary monopolist, and Mrs. Lovett as a price-discriminating monopolist.

If Mrs. Lovett sold only in the local market, the deadweight loss would be $I + M$. When she can sell in both markets and price discriminate, the deadweight loss is $E + H + I$. $E + H$ can be either greater or less than $M$; therefore, Mrs. Lovett's price discrimination can be either beneficial or detrimental to welfare. On the other hand, it certainly hurts the local consumers.

Of course, like all price discriminators, Mrs. Lovett has to worry about resale. One of her neighbors may get the idea to drive to the city, buy a truckload of pies at $7 apiece, bring them back, and sell them locally for $10.50. Before long, Mrs. Lovett may find that she is no longer a monopolist in her hometown.

---

[3] By coincidence, $7 is also the competitive price in Mrs. Lovett's own hometown. Such remarkable coincidences are not to be expected. We make the assumption for purposes of this example, and only because it helps to keep the graph readable. None of the ideas that we will stress depend on this assumption.

## EXHIBIT 10.9  Third-Degree Price Discrimination with Monopoly in One Market and Competition in Another

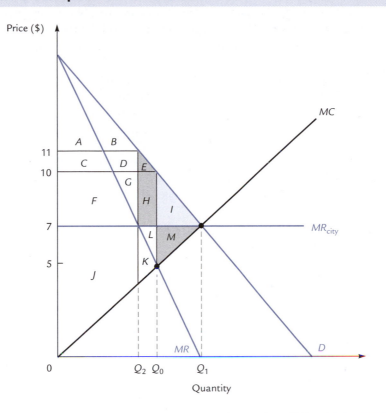

| | Competition | Ordinary Monopoly | Price-Discriminating Monopoly |
|---|---|---|---|
| Consumers' Surplus | $A + B + C + D + E + F$ $+ G + H + I$ | $A + B + C + D + E$ | $A + B$ |
| Producers' Surplus (Local) | $J + K + L + M$ | $F + G + H + J + K + L$ | $C + D + F + G + J$ |
| Producer's Surplus (City) | — | — | $K + L + M$ |
| Social Gain | $A + B + C + D + E + F$ $+ G + H + I + J + K$ $+ L + M$ | $A + B + C + D + E + F$ $+ G + H + J + K + L$ | $A + B + C + D + F + G$ $+ J + K + L + M$ |
| Deadweight Loss | — | $I + M$ | $E + H + I$ |

The demand and marginal revenue curves are from Mrs. Lovett's hometown market. In the distant city she can sell all of the pies she wants to at the competitive price of $7. In that case, she will sell only $Q_2$ pies at home, as opposed to the ordinary monopoly quantity $Q_0$. The reason is that she can always earn $7 marginal revenue by selling pies in the city, so that she will not sell pies at home when her marginal revenue there falls below $7. When she sells $Q_2$ pies at home, she sets a price of $11, higher than the ordinary monopoly price of $10. The table shows what social gains would be if the pie industry were competitive, if Mrs. Lovett were an ordinary monopolist, and if Mrs. Lovett were able to sell pies in both markets at different prices. In each case, the consumers' surplus comes entirely from the local market. There is no consumers' surplus in the city market, because the demand curve there for Mrs. Lovett's pies is flat.

## A Monopolist in Two Markets

If Mrs. Lovett sells pies both in her hometown and in the big city, then she is a monopolist in one market and a competitor in another. Sometimes a producer is a monopolist in two markets. His behavior will be essentially the same as Mrs. Lovett's. Benjamin Barker is a barber who cuts the hair of both adults and children. Adults have one demand curve and children have another.

Benjamin wants to decide how many haircuts to sell to adults and how many to sell to children. We will call these quantities $Q_A$ and $Q_C$. Then Benjamin wants to choose $Q_A$ and $Q_C$ so that his marginal revenue in the adults' market, his marginal revenue in the children's market, and the marginal cost to him of producing $Q_A + Q_C$ haircuts are all equal.

---

**Exercise 10.8** Explain why Benjamin wants all three of these numbers to be equal. If any two were not equal, how could he alter his behavior to make himself better off? How would this change in his behavior tend to equalize the three quantities?

---

Exhibit 10.10 shows a graphic method for determining how many haircuts Benjamin will sell to each group. The $MR_A$ and $MR_C$ curves are the marginal revenue curves that he faces in the adults' and children's markets. The $MR$ curve is obtained by summing $MR_A$ and $MR_C$ horizontally. That is, for any price, read the corresponding quantities off $MR_A$ and $MR_C$; then add these to get the corresponding quantity on $MR$.

Benjamin can equalize his marginal cost and both marginal revenues by choosing the quantity where his marginal cost curve $MC$ crosses the $MR$ curve. In the exhibit this means that he produces a total of $Q_A + Q_C$ haircuts, so that his marginal cost is $5 per haircut. He sells $Q_A$ of these haircuts to adults and $Q_C$ to children, so that his marginal revenue is $5 per haircut in each market.

| EXHIBIT 10.10 | **Third-Degree Price Discrimination by a Monopolist in Two Markets** |
|---|---|

Benjamin Barker sells haircuts to adults and children. The two groups have different marginal revenue curves, labeled $MR_A$ and $MR_C$ in panel A. The heavier curve, $MR$, is obtained by horizontally summing the curves $MR_A$ and $MR_C$. Benjamin produces the quantity $Q_A + Q_C$ where $MC$ crosses $MR$, selling $Q_A$ haircuts to adults and $Q_C$ to children. He chooses the corresponding prices off the adults' and children's demand curves, which are shown in panel B.

Once Benjamin has chosen the quantities $Q_A$ and $Q_C$, he reads prices off the adults' and children's demand curves, just like any good monopolist. These prices, $P_A$ and $P_C$, are shown in panel B of Exhibit 10.10.

## Elasticities and Price Discrimination

There is an interesting relationship between the prices $P_A$ and $P_C$ in Exhibit 10.10. Write $\eta_A$ for the elasticity of the adults' demand curve at $P_A$ and $\eta_C$ for the elasticity of the children's demand curve at $P_C$. Because the marginal revenue is $5 in each market, the equation that relates price to marginal revenue says that:

$$P_A\left[1 - \left(\frac{1}{|\eta_A|}\right)\right] = \$5 \text{ and } P_C\left[1 - \left(\frac{1}{|\eta_C|}\right)\right] = \$5$$

It follows that:

$$P_A\left[1 - \left(\frac{1}{|\eta_A|}\right)\right] = P_C\left[1 - \left(\frac{1}{|\eta_C|}\right)\right]$$

From this equation we can see that:

$$if \; |\eta_C| > |\eta_A|, \text{ then } P_C < P_A$$

whereas:

$$if \; |\eta_C| < |\eta_A|, \text{ then } P_C > P_A$$

In other words:

The group with the more elastic demand is charged the lower price.

In more everyday language, elasticity of demand is described as "price sensitivity." So what we've really learned is that:

A price-discriminating monopolist offers the lowest prices to the most price-sensitive customers.

Movie theaters that offer discounts to students and senior citizens are engaging in third-degree price discrimination. So are railroads that sell special "youth passes." In each case, a lower price is offered to these customers, who are more sensitive to price. A possible reason for this price sensitivity is that students and senior citizens have either below-average incomes or low values of time. In either case, they will be more likely than others to shop around for alternatives when prices go up. This makes it desirable to price discriminate in their favor.

## Price Discrimination and Welfare

When a monopolist moves from setting a single price to practicing third-degree price discrimination, his total output might go either up or down. Social welfare can also go either up or down. It is often quite difficult to predict the direction of the change in social welfare. However, under a variety of conditions, it is possible to prove that *if* total output falls, *then* social welfare must fall also. The proof is not easy.[4]

---

[4] See R. Schmalensee, "Output and Welfare Implications of Monopolistic Third-Degree Price Discrimination," *American Economic Review* 71 (1981):242–247; H. Varian, "Price Discrimination and Social Welfare," *American Economic Review* 75 (1985):870–875; and M. Schwartz, "Third-Degree Price Discrimination and Output: Generalizing a Welfare Result," *American Economic Review* 80 (1990): 1259–1263.

## Conditions for Price Discrimination

We can now summarize the conditions necessary to make price discrimination profitable. First, the seller must have some degree of monopoly power. (Thus, wheat farmers never offer senior citizen discounts.) Second, resales must be controllable. Therefore, price discrimination is most often observed in markets for goods that have to be consumed immediately upon purchase, such as education. (Does your college charge different tuitions to different students by offering scholarship aid to some and not to others?) Each of these two conditions applies to any form of price discrimination. Finally, in the case of third-degree price discrimination, some mechanism must be found for offering lower prices to precisely those demanders who are more sensitive to price. (Are those students who get scholarships by and large the ones who would be most likely to go elsewhere—or to not attend college at all—if they had to pay full tuition?)[5]

## Examples of Price Discrimination

One day recently, Dell Computer listed an ultralight laptop for $2,307 on its Web page for sales to small businesses. On the Web page for sales to health care companies, the same machine was listed at $2,228 and on the page for sales to state and local governments the price was $2,072.[6]

If your college library wants to subscribe to the *Proceedings of the National Academy of Sciences* (a prestigious scholarly journal), it will have to pay anywhere from $650 per year to $6,600 per year, depending on the size of your college.

Discount coupons for supermarket shopping constitute a mechanism for offering a lower price to appropriate consumers. The shoppers who find it worth their while to clip these coupons are those with a relatively low value of time (e.g., because their wages are low); by and large, these are the customers with a greater propensity for comparison shopping. The supermarket's ideal pricing policy is, "lower prices to those who would otherwise shop elsewhere." A practical approximation to this ideal is, "lower prices to those with enough free time to clip coupons."

It is important to notice that there would be no point to coupons if everyone redeemed them; in this case the store could just lower its prices and have the same effect. Similarly, there would be no point to coupons if only a random set of customers redeemed them. The point of coupons is that they offer lower prices to precisely those customers who are most sensitive to price.

Manufacturers' rebates (e.g., buy a coffeemaker and get a coupon that can be redeemed for $5) work much the same way. They are redeemed by precisely the shoppers who are willing to devote some extra time and energy to recovering a few dollars. These are the same shoppers who are most likely to compare prices at many stores or to decide to do without a coffeemaker altogether.

Promotions that require customers to save game cards, scratch off designated areas to reveal numbers, and the like serve the same purpose. These promotions may appeal primarily to families with children, who can be enlisted to paste, scratch, tear, and cut. It is reasonable to think that those with children are those most likely to be watching pennies in their food budgets.

---

[5] A few years back, MIT sent a letter to parents announcing that it was raising both tuition and the amount of scholarship aid that it would provide. How would the parents have reacted if MIT had announced that it was going to exercise monopoly power more fully through an increase in price discrimination?

[6] These numbers appeared in a *Wall Street Journal* article by G. McWilliams.

Students sometimes reason that if grocery stores engage in price discrimination, for which monopoly power is a prerequisite, then grocery stores must be monopolies, so we should never use the competitive model when we study them. But, in fact, we use different models to describe different phenomena. Consider a simple analogy from physics: If we want to describe the interactions of several moving balls on a billiard table, it is often safe to assume there is no friction, because friction does not play an important role in the phenomenon under study. But if we want to explain why the balls roll instead of slide, friction suddenly becomes important and we switch to a description that takes account of it. Similarly, when we want to study the determination of prices and quantities in the grocery industry, the assumption of competition may be close enough to truth to yield deep and important insights. When we switch to studying a phenomenon like price discrimination, monopoly power acquires central importance and must be explicitly included in the description.

Dangerous
Curve

When you order a pizza and get "free delivery," you are being charged less for a pizza than somebody who picks one up at the take-out counter. (When you take out, you pay for both the pizza and for gasoline, making the effective price of the pizza higher.) People ordering pizzas by telephone have more elastic demand because they can easily hang up the phone and order a pizza elsewhere. Whenever a producer offers "free extras" that only some customers take, you should ask how the extras have been designed to appeal to the more elastic demanders.

Why, for example, do coffee shops in downtown office buildings typically offer free cup lids? Such a coffee shop has two classes of customers: those who work in the building and those who pass by the building on their way to work elsewhere. With regard to the first group, the shop has some monopoly power (people would rather not go outside for coffee). With regard to the second, it is nearly in perfect competition (people walking by can always stop somewhere else for coffee). Therefore, they would like to offer a "free extra"—such as a cup lid—that is taken primarily by those who are walking by.[7]

Many hotels offer rooms at two different prices. Often the only difference between a $50 room and a $60 room is $10. If you call ahead for a reservation, you will get a $50 room. If you walk in at 11 P.M. looking tired, the $50 rooms will all be filled.

Airlines charge less for travelers who are staying over a Saturday night. These are the nonbusiness travelers who are likely to find another mode of transportation, or choose not to travel, when prices are high.

Many jewelry stores will give you a discount on a new watch if you trade in your old watch. The watches they receive as trade-ins are immediately discarded. People who already have watches are effectively charged less than those who don't. Can you see why the first group has the more elastic demand?

Many furniture stores offer "free delivery." If a delivery ordinarily costs $25 and all customers take advantage of the free delivery, then the price of furniture increases by $25 and the "free delivery" has no real effect. What, then, is the point of free delivery? A more sophisticated analysis must recognize that if only some customers accept the free delivery, then it can be a form of price discrimination. Professor Robert Michaels of the California State University at Fullerton points out that "free delivery is not free for many buyers." You have to wait at home for the delivery truck and are often not told when to expect it; if you and the driver miss each other, you have to wait a long time for

---

[7] This example, invented by Robert Topel of the University of Chicago, is intended to be frivolous. An alternative (and perhaps more plausible) explanation is that cup lids are priced at marginal cost, and the best practical approximation to a marginal cost of .001¢ is zero.

your delivery to be rescheduled. Customers with a low enough opportunity cost to wait at home for a weekday delivery also have a low opportunity cost of shopping and hence more elastic demand for furniture from a particular store. Free delivery (and hence an effectively lower price) is offered to the more elastic demanders.

In each of these examples you should give thought to the question of how resales are controlled. Firms have been known to get very creative about this. Many years ago the Rohm and Haas chemical company produced a compound called methyl methacrylate that was used both in dentistry and industrial production. There were few good substitutes for this compound in dentistry, but there were many in industry. As a result, dentists were charged a much higher price than industrial users; as a further result, industrial users bought cheap and sold to dentists. The marketing directors at Rohm and Haas considered many strategies to combat this activity, one of which was to add arsenic to the compound before selling it in the industrial market. This plan was never implemented, but a closely related one was: They started a *rumor* that they had added the arsenic. This had the desired effect.

## Versioning

**Versioning**

Offering an inferior product to facilitate price discrimination.

**Versioning** occurs when a company offers an inferior version of its product, not because it's less costly to produce but because it facilitates price discrimination.

In the 1990s, IBM offered two products—the Laser Printer and the Laser Printer E. The two products were identical except that the Laser Printer E contained an extra chip that caused it to print more slowly. This enabled IBM to price discriminate by charging a high price for the Laser Printer and a lower price for the Laser Printer E.

In the nineteenth century, railroads offered third-class seats in carriages without roofs. The writer Jules Dupuit explained why:

> It is not because of the few thousand francs which would have to be spent to put a roof over the third-class carriage. What the company is trying to do is to prevent the passengers who can pay the second-class fare from traveling third class. It hits the poor not because it wants to hurt them, but to frighten the rich.

Book publishers offer both hardcover and softcover editions of their books. Contrary to what you might expect, the paperbacks are cheaper *not* because they're cheaper to produce (in fact the costs of production for a hardback and a paperback are surprisingly similar) but because publishers want to charge more to those readers who are willing to pay for a hardcover.

It's worth stressing that for the hardcover/paperback scheme to work, hardbacks must have special appeal to the least price-sensitive customers. Why might that be the case? Arguably, the least price-sensitive customers are precisely those who are most likely to fall in love with their books and hence to want books that will last for several decades.

## Example: Priceline.Com

Airlines price discriminate through services like Priceline.Com, which allows you to "name your own price" for airline tickets. Priceline's customers can specify their dates of travels, but not the times. To use Priceline's service, you must agree that if your bid is accepted, you will be willing to fly at any time of morning, noon, or night.

That's a form of price discrimination—travelers who go through Priceline pay lower prices than those who book through the airlines or through traditional travel agents. Why do the airlines want to target discounts to Priceline users? By and large, travelers who can be flexible about their departure times can also be flexible about whether to fly at all. If you don't care when you fly, it's pretty clear you're not trying to get to an urgent business meeting—so you might be willing to kill a day taking the train, or to cancel your trip altogether.

That's why Priceline works—it targets discounts to the most price-sensitive customers. You might imagine that Priceline would be even more successful if it allowed you to specify preferred travel times, and promised to book you at those times if possible. Unfortunately, that scheme would draw travelers to Priceline who might otherwise be willing to pay full fare—and the airlines would prefer not to offer discounts unnecessarily. Successful price discrimination requires—as much as possible—confining the discounts to the customers who are unwilling to pay full price.

In the year 2000, Priceline tried to set up a subsidiary that would allow you to "name your own price for gasoline." Anyone who has taken an economics course could have told them not to bother. Gasoline is sold in competitive markets, and price discrimination is a viable strategy only where there is some monopoly power. Predictably, Priceline's gasoline project failed almost immediately.

## Counterexamples

Price discrimination is evidence of monopoly power, and students confronted with so many examples sometimes infer that monopoly power is ubiquitous. It is important, then, to realize that many practices having the appearance of price discrimination are, in fact, something quite different. Price discrimination occurs when the same product is sold at two different prices. Often, a careful examination will reveal that two apparently identical products are actually quite different.

Many restaurants offer a lower price at the salad bar to those who order an entrée. This has the appearance of price discrimination, but an alternative explanation is that people who order entrées tend to take less food at the salad bar. This would explain a lower price on the basis of a lower cost to the restaurant. Ice cream shops usually charge less for a second scoop than for a first. Is this second-degree price discrimination? Neither the preparation of the cone, nor the opening of the freezer, nor the ringing of the cash register has to be repeated for the second scoop of ice cream. Such factors make serving the second scoop genuinely cheaper for the ice cream shop and provide an alternative explanation.

In fact, almost everything that appears to be price discrimination admits at least one alternative explanation. Alternative theories are available even for the most widely accepted examples, some of which we have used in this book. Earlier we offered grocery store coupons as an example of price discrimination. A different hypothesis is that coupon-clippers have low values of time and hence can arrange to do their shopping when the store is not crowded. Nonclippers arrive at 5 P.M. on their way home from work, when the store is crowded, adding to general congestion and the lengths of the checkout lines. The nonclippers are therefore genuinely more expensive to serve, and so pay higher prices.

An objection to this new theory is that if grocery stores really want to charge less at certain times of the day, they can just announce discount prices for those who shop at those times. There is no need to introduce the artifice of coupons. A counter to the objection is that time-of-day discounts can be a logistical nightmare: What do you do with the customer who complains that he would have checked out at 2:59 rather than 3:01 if only he had gotten competent service at the meat counter?

In general, economists who are disinclined to believe in substantial monopoly power will welcome this kind of analysis. Those who believe that monopoly power is a significant economic force will be more comfortable with a diagnosis of price discrimination. But in analyzing any particular market, it pays to put prejudice aside and weigh the inherent plausibility of competing theories.

## Price Discrimination at the Dry Cleaners?

Many dry cleaners charge more to clean and press a woman's shirt than a man's, even when the shirts are made of the same material. Is this price discrimination?

To believe it's price discrimination, you have to believe that dry cleaners have some monopoly power; otherwise price discrimination could not survive. Suppose, for example, that because of price discrimination, the going price for a man's shirt is $3 and the going price for a woman's shirt is $5. Then under competition, no dry cleaner accepts any men's business at all; they all declare themselves to be specialists in women's clothing. That bids down the price of women's shirts and bids up the price of men's— and this continues until the two prices are equal.

Only under monopoly can price discrimination survive: A monopolist might exhaust the market of women who are willing to pay $5 and then move on to men who are willing to pay $3. To believe that dry cleaners price discriminate, you must believe that dry cleaners are monopolists.

But are they? There are six virtually identical dry cleaners within walking distance of your textbook author's house. How can they have monopoly power?

One answer is that there might be a lot of brand loyalty. If customers are very reluctant to switch from one dry cleaner to another, then each cleaner has some monopoly power and price discrimination is possible.

But another possibility is that dry cleaners really are competitive, in which case the price differential for men's and women's clothes cannot be an instance of price discrimination; instead it must reflect a real difference in costs. And in fact there's a good candidate for what that difference is. It's more expensive to press a woman's shirt than a man's for two reasons. First, men's shirts come in standard shapes and can be pressed by machine; women's shirts are more varied and often have to be pressed by hand. Second, men's shirts, unlike women's, are usually worn under jackets, so the pressing doesn't have to be as perfect.

## Price Discrimination and the Internet

Andrew Odlyzko, of the Digital Technology Center at the University of Minnesota, has argued that the Internet presents unprecedented opportunities for price discrimination. A traditional bookseller doesn't know very much about your reading habits, but Amazon.Com, if you are a repeat customer, knows quite a bit. In principle, Amazon could use that information to set different prices for different consumers.

There is widespread public discomfort about the "privacy violations" that occur when companies like Amazon keep track of individual buying habits. In a provocative article,[8] Odlyzko argues that much of this discomfort can be traced to consumer resistance to price discrimination. Whether or not you find his article convincing, you'll almost surely find it an entertaining source of anecdotes about price discrimination, several of which have found their way into this chapter.

---

[8] "Privacy, Economics and Price Discrimination on the Internet," A. M. Odlyzko. ICEC2003: Fifth International Conference on Electronic Commerce, N. Sadeh, ed., ACM, 2003, pp. 355–366.

## Two-Part Tariffs

Disneyland amusement park has substantial monopoly power. How should Disneyland wield that power? Should it charge a low admission price, to draw lots of visitors who will pay monopoly prices for the rides and other attractions? Or should it charge low prices for the rides, to draw lots of visitors who will pay a monopoly price to get in?

Polaroid is the only maker of Polaroid cameras and Polaroid film. Should the company charge a low price for the cameras to increase the demand for high-priced film? Or should it charge a low price for film to increase the demand for high-priced cameras?

Some monopolists—like Disneyland and Polaroid—get to charge their customers twice. There's an initial fee (for admission to the park or the Polaroid camera) and then ongoing charges for the purchase of goods or services (like ride tickets or Polaroid film).

In both examples, the initial fee itself buys you nothing except the right to make future purchases. For the most part, the only reason to enter Disneyland is so you can spend more money after you get inside. And surely the only reason to buy a Polaroid camera is so you can start buying and using film.

There are more examples. Some private dining clubs charge yearly membership fees that entitle the member to buy meals. Banks charge annual fees for credit cards that allow you to borrow money at interest. Neither the membership nor the credit card is of any value until you start using it.[9]

When a firm charges a fee for the right to buy its products, we say that it has set a **two-part tariff.** Most of the time, the word *tariff* refers to a tax on imported goods, but the phrase *two-part tariff* is an exception to the rule. Here the word *tariff* simply means "price."

**Two-part tariff**

An entry fee that allows you to purchase goods or services.

## Setting the Entry Fee

Let's figure out the optimal strategy for a two-part tariff monopolist. Exhibit 10.11 shows the demand, marginal revenue, and marginal cost curves for a firm such as Disneyland or Polaroid. The quantity on the horizontal axis is the quantity of the good that customers purchase *after* they've paid the entry fee; in the case of Disneyland it is the quantity of rides, while in the case of Polaroid it is the quantity of film.

First let's see what happens if the firm charges the monopoly price $P_M$ in Exhibit 10.11. The first observation is that the firm earns $C + D + F + G$ in producer's surplus on the sale of the ride tickets, film, or whatever else it is selling. Now how much will the firm charge consumers for the right to buy those products? The answer, of course, is that it will charge the maximum amount consumers are willing to pay—and that amount is measured by the consumer's surplus, in this case $A + B$. So if the firm charges the price $P_M$ for its products, it will earn $C + D + F + G$ in producer's surplus on the sales and an additional $A + B$ in admission fees. The total is $A + B + C + D + F + G$. Notice that consumers are left with no surplus at all.

Now let's see what happens if the firm charges the competitive price $P_C$. Producer's surplus on product sales is reduced to $F + G + H$. But admission fees can be raised $A + B + C + D + E$, giving the firm a total of $A + B + C + D + E + F + G + H$. This

---

[9] With the credit card, as with Disneyland, our assumptions are only approximations to the truth: In reality, some people want to enter Disneyland just to enjoy the atmosphere, and some people want credit cards just for convenience, paying off their full balances each month to avoid all interest charges. But if there are few enough of those unusual people, our analysis will be close to correct.

**EXHIBIT 10.11**    **Pricing Strategy with a Two-Part Tariff**

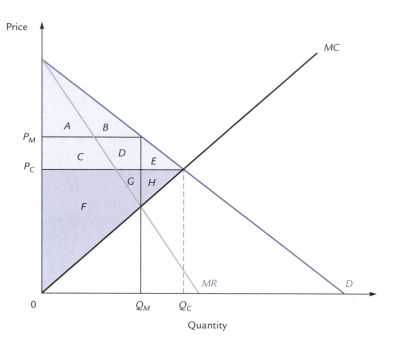

If the firm sells the monopoly quantity $Q_M$ at the monopoly price $P_M$, it will earn a producer's surplus of $C + D + F + G$ and will be able to charge the consumer $A + B$ as an entry fee. But if it sells the competitive quantity $Q_C$ at the lower price $P_C$, it will earn the smaller producer's surplus $F + G + H$ while collecting the larger entry fee $A + B + C + D + E$. Under the second strategy, the firm's net earnings are increased by $E + H$.

is more than it earns at the monopoly price $P_M$. Once again, consumers are left with no surplus at all. All of the social gain goes to the firm.

So the firm does best by charging a competitive price for its goods. That way, it is therefore not surprising that the firm does best by charging a competitive price—as long as it is collecting all the social gain, it will want that social gain to be as large as possible, and that's accomplished by competitive pricing.

## Differences among Customers

Let's be clear on what it means to charge the full consumer's surplus as an admission fee. Here's an example. Suppose in Exhibit 10.11, that area $A + B + C + D + E$ is equal to $1,000, and the firm has 100 identical customers. Then each of the 100 customers earns a consumer's surplus of $10, so the right admission fee is $10 per customer.

But what if the customers are not identical? Suppose, for example, that one of them earns a consumer's surplus of $901, while the others earn $1 each. Then area $A + B + C + D + E$ will still equal $1,000, but if the monopolist tries to capture this area by charging an admission fee of $10, it will drive away 99% of its customers!

The problem here is that while the *average* customer earns a consumer's surplus of $10, it's not true that every customer is average, except in the case where every customer is identical. As long as all (or most) of the customers are *nearly* identical, they will all (or almost all) earn consumer's surpluses of *about* $10, so an admission fee of just a bit under $10 will retain all (or most) of the customers and allow the monopolist to earn nearly $1,000 in admission fees. But when the differences among customers are dramatic, the monopolist cannot capture the bulk of the consumers' surplus in this way. In this case, our conclusion—that the monopolist should price his product competitively—no longer holds.

## Two-Part Tariffs and Price Discrimination

When there are significant differences among customers, a monopolist will look for opportunities to price discriminate. For a two-part tariff monopolist, there's a clear strategy for price discrimination: By charging a low entry fee and a high price for the product, the monopolist effectively charges lower prices to the lightest users, and there is a good chance that the lightest users are precisely the ones who will walk away in the absence of a discount.

At Disneyland, for example, those patrons who come only to ride the roller coaster are very different from those who feel a compulsion to go on every ride. Disneyland might reasonably expect that those in the former group will go and find a *different* roller coaster unless they get a discount, while those in the latter group are unlikely to find many good substitutes for Disneyland. Thus, the goal is to target discounts to the roller-coaster-only crowd. This goal is accomplished through a low admission price coupled with a high price for ride tickets; roller-coaster riders buy only one ticket while their more compulsive neighbors buy dozens.

Similarly, if Polaroid charges a low price for cameras and a high price for film, it is effectively charging more to those who take a lot of pictures. The *real* goal is to charge more to those who are willing to pay the most; but by and large, those who are willing to pay the most might be precisely the ones who take the most pictures.

## The Bottom Line

A two-part tariff monopolist with identical customers will want to capture as much surplus as possible by setting a low (competitive) price for the product and a high admission fee. A two-part tariff monopolist with very different customers will want to price discriminate by setting a low admission fee and a high price for the product.

The typical firm faces a base of customers who are neither identical nor dramatically different, and therefore will want to compromise between the two strategies; firms with more diverse groups of customers will shade more toward the high admission fee.

Sometimes a firm has to experiment for a while in order to learn how different its customers are. Disneyland has gone through a series of different pricing policies, ranging from free admission and high-priced rides to free rides and high-priced admission.

## Popcorn at the Movie Theater

Suppose you own a movie theater, where you have some monopoly power and you make money both at the box office and the popcorn stand. Should you charge a high price for admission and a low price for popcorn, or vice versa?

If your customers are all identical, Exhibit 10.11 provides the answer, interpreting the "price" and "quantity" in that exhibit as the price and quantity of popcorn. By pricing popcorn competitively, you earn a total of $A + B + C + D + E + F + G + H$ in producer's surplus at the popcorn stand plus admission fees at the box office. If you priced the popcorn at the higher price $P_M$, you would earn only $A + B + C + D + F + G$. Thus, you should price the popcorn competitively.

People who have not studied economics usually get this wrong. They reason that once customers have entered the theater, the theater owner might as well take advantage of his monopoly power at the popcorn stand. That argument overlooks the fact that higher prices at the popcorn stand must mean either lower prices at the box office or fewer people going to the movies.

What if the customers are very different? Then you might think that you can apply the same reasoning we used for Disneyland and Polaroid cameras to conclude that popcorn should be priced high and the admission fee should be low in order to price discriminate. But that's not quite right. The case of the movie theater is not exactly like the case of the Polaroid camera, and here's why: A Polaroid camera is valuable *only* because it allows you to buy film, but it's not true that admission to the movie theater is valuable only because it allows you to buy popcorn. Consumers earn surplus just by entering the premises and being allowed to see the movie. A theater owner will want to try to capture some of that surplus. The best way to do so is not apparent from Exhibit 10.11, which shows only the surplus earned at the popcorn stand and not the surplus earned from seeing the movie.

The problem is to charge a high overall price to those who are willing to pay that price and a low overall price to those who would otherwise go to a ball game or stay home and watch TV. *If* the people who especially love going to the movies are the same people who buy a lot of popcorn, then the right strategy is to price discriminate with a high price at the popcorn stand. But if the people who especially love going to the movies are the same people who buy relatively *little* popcorn, then the right strategy can be to price discriminate in their favor with a *low* price at the popcorn stand—even with a price below marginal cost. You will be invited to work out the details of the analysis in Problem 27 at the end of this chapter.

## Summary

A firm has monopoly power when it faces a downward-sloping demand curve for its product. Such a firm also faces a downward-sloping marginal revenue curve that lies everywhere below the demand curve. Like any producer, the monopoly firm chooses the quantity where marginal cost equals marginal revenue, and then charges the price that corresponds to that quantity on the demand curve.

Because marginal revenue lies below demand, the monopolist chooses a quantity at which marginal cost is less than the consumer's marginal value. Thus, it underproduces from the point of view of social welfare. Various public policies can address this problem. If the monopolist is given a subsidy per unit of output, it will increase production. If a price ceiling is set at the competitive price, the monopolist will essentially face a flat marginal revenue curve and behave like a competitor.

Monopolies arise for various reasons. An industry where each firm's average cost curve is decreasing at the point where it crosses market demand is known as a natural monopoly. If price were set equal to marginal cost in such an industry, profits would be negative and no firms would enter. A monopoly producer, however, may be able to survive because he can charge a price that is higher than marginal cost.

One common source of natural monopoly is the combination of high fixed costs and low marginal costs. However, this is not the only source. Other sources of monopoly power include patents, the control of resources, and barriers to entry erected by the government.

Sometimes a monopolist can increase its profits by charging different prices for identical items. This practice is known as price discrimination. In first-degree price discrimination, each consumer is charged the maximum he would be willing to pay for each item. If successful, this allows the monopolist to collect all of the social gain for himself, and it provides an incentive to produce the competitive quantity. In practice, perfect first-degree price discrimination is almost never possible, but it can sometimes be approximated.

In second-degree price discrimination, each customer is offered the same set of prices, but prices vary with the items purchased. Quantity discounts can be an example of second-degree price discrimination. However, quantity discounts are not always price discrimination. They can result instead from genuine cost savings to the seller when larger quantities are exchanged.

The most common type of price discrimination is third-degree price discrimination, in which two identifiably different groups of customers are charged different prices. In this case, the lower price will go to the group with the more elastic demand curve. Senior citizen discounts at movie theaters are an example.

For price discrimination to be profitable, the firm must have monopoly power, must be able to find a device that discriminates in favor of the appropriate group, and must be able to prevent resales.

Another pricing policy available to some monopolists is a two-part tariff, where the customer is charged a one-time fee for the right to buy goods from the monopolist. If the monopolist prices at marginal cost and sets an entry fee equal to the consumer surplus, he can maximize social gain and capture all of this gain for himself. However, if different consumers have different demand curves, this strategy requires knowing each consumer's demand curve and setting his entry fee accordingly. In practice, this is usually not possible. Therefore, the monopolist's pricing problem is a difficult one. Pricing at marginal cost creates more gain for him to capture through entry fees. On the other hand, in some cases (like Polaroid film), pricing above marginal cost offers the opportunity to price discriminate. Choosing the right strategy is a complicated matter, involving both the characteristics of the product and the characteristics of the demanders.

## Author Commentary          www.cengage.com/economics/landsburg

**AC1.**  Read this article for another view of the patent system.

**AC2.**  For more examples of price discrimination, read this article.

## Review Questions

**R1.**  Explain why a monopolist's marginal revenue curve lies below the demand curve. Explain why this leads the monopolist to produce an inefficient quantity.

**R2.**  If a monopolist were operating on the inelastic part of the demand curve, what could the monopolist do to increase profits?

**R3.**  A frost in Florida kills half the orange crop, and the price of oranges rises by so much that orange growers' revenue is actually higher than in a normal year. **True or False:** This indicates that Florida orange growers have some monopoly power.

**R4.**  Draw a graph to show what happens when a monopolist is offered an optimal subsidy.

**R5.**  Draw a graph to show what happens when a monopolist is subjected to an optimal price ceiling.

**R6.**  List a few sources of monopoly power.

**R7.**   What is a natural monopoly? In the presence of natural monopoly, how must the welfare analysis of monopoly pricing be modified?

**R8.**   Describe the three types of price discrimination. Give examples of each.

**R9.**   **True or False:** Only a competitor would offer discounts to selected customers, because a monopolist can always require his customers to pay full price.

**R10.**  Why might a monopolist who can charge an entry fee choose to price his product at marginal cost? Under what conditions is this a wise strategy?

# Numerical Exercises

**N1.**   Suppose that a monopolist faces the demand curve:

$$Q = a - bP$$

where $a$ and $b$ are constants. Show that his marginal revenue curve is given approximately by the equation:

$$MR = a - \frac{2Q}{b}$$

(This approximation becomes exact when very small units are chosen.)

**N2.**   Suppose that a monopolist sells in two markets with demand curves:

$$Q_A = 100 - 10P_A$$
$$Q_B = 8 - 2P_B$$

**a.**   Show that for any given quantity, demand is more elastic in market A than in market B.

**b.**   Suppose that the monopolist produces at zero marginal cost. How much does he supply in each market, and what prices does he charge? (*Hint:* Use the formula for marginal revenue from the preceding problem.)

**c.**   Suppose that the monopolist's marginal cost curve is given by:

$$MC = Q/21$$

How much does he supply in each market, and what prices does he charge?

**d.**   Reconcile your answers to parts (a), (b), and (c) with the statement in the text that the group with more elastic demand is always charged the lower price.

**e.**   Suppose that the monopolist's marginal cost curve is given by

$$MC = Q/3$$

What will the monopolist do?

**N3.**   A monopoly barber sells haircuts to adults for $30 and to children for $10. Let $\eta_A$ represent adults' elasticity of demand for haircuts and let $\eta_C$ represent children's elasticity of demand.

**a.**   Explain why $|\eta_A|$ and $|\eta_C|$ must both be greater than 1.

**b.**   Find a formula for $\eta_A$ in terms of $\eta_C$.

**c.**   What is the largest possible value for $|\eta_A|$?

# Problem Set

**1.** Rework problem 1 from Chapter 7, on the assumption that Gus is the only cab driver in town.

**2.** **True or False:** Unlike competitors monopolists have the option of earning higher profits by raising their prices.

**3.** A monopolistic firm produces widgets at a constant marginal cost of $10 apiece. One day it discovers a new production process that would lower its marginal cost by $1 per widget. Use a graph to show how much its producer's surplus will increase if it adopts the new production process.

**4.** For a good supplied by a monopolist, how does a sales tax of $1 per item affect the marginal revenue curve?

**5.** **True or False:** If they could, the customers of an ordinary (non-price-discriminating, non-admission-charging) monopolist would get together and bribe the monopolist to charge lower prices. Justify your answer by discussing how much the customers would be willing to offer and how much the monopolist would be willing to accept.

**6.** We know that for a competitively supplied good the economic incidence of a tax is independent of the legal incidence; that is, a sales tax and an excise tax of equal magnitudes have exactly the same effects. Is the same thing true for a good supplied by a monopolist?

**7.** **True or False:** An excise tax on a monopolist that causes quantity to fall by one unit is just as detrimental to social welfare as an excise tax on a competitive industry that causes quantity to fall by one unit.

**8.** **True or False:** If the supply of land is fixed, then it can be equally efficient for land to be supplied by a monopolist or by competitors.

**9.** Fuzzy dice are produced only by Americans and consumed only by non-Americans. Can an excise tax on fuzzy dice improve the welfare of Americans? If so, use a graph to illustrate the optimal size of the excise tax. If not, use a graph to show why any excise tax must create a deadweight loss for Americans.

**10.** The following table shows the total cost of producing various quantities of shoehorns and the total value of those shoehorns to consumers. What are the price and quantity produced if the shoehorn industry is competitive? What are they if it is monopolized? What is the extent of the social loss due to the existence of the monopoly? (The answers to all of these questions should be numbers. Assume that only a whole number of shoehorns can be produced.)

| Q | TC | TV | Q | TC | TV |
|---|-----|-----|---|-----|-----|
| 1 | $2 | $10 | 5 | $15 | $37 |
| 2 | 4 | 19 | 6 | 19 | 41 |
| 3 | 7 | 26 | 7 | 24 | 43 |
| 4 | 11 | 32 | 8 | 29 | 44 |

**11.** The following diagram shows the (industrywide) demand for widgets and the associated marginal revenue curve. When the industry is monopolized, the marginal cost curve is $MC_M$. When the industry is competitive, the industry's marginal cost curve is $MC_C$. Suppose the industry is currently monopolized and you are a judge with the power to break up the monopoly into several competing firms. In order to exercise that power in accordance with the efficiency criterion, which four of the labeled areas would you want to measure? (You are allowed to measure any four areas but no more.) How would you use that information to guide your decision?

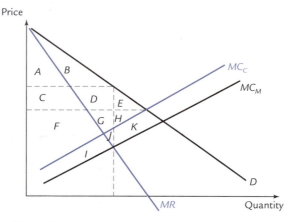

12. **True or False:** To make a natural monopolist behave more efficiently, subsidies will work better than price controls.

13. **True or False:** If a natural monopolist is required to earn zero profits, it will produce less than is optimal, but if any other kind of monopolist is required to earn zero profits, it will produce more than is optimal.

14. **True or False:** A regulated monopoly is more likely to engage in discriminatory hiring practices than is an unregulated monopoly.

15. Bad Ideas Inc. is the world's only manufacturer of disposable sweaters. After a sweater is made, Bad Ideas can attach buttons on the right, making it suitable for men, or on the left, making it suitable for women. No man will wear a woman's sweater and no woman will wear a man's sweater. Bad Ideas faces the following demand and marginal cost schedules for its sweaters:

| Quantity | Men's Demand Price | Women's Demand Price | Marginal Cost |
|---|---|---|---|
| 1 | $10 | $24 | $1 |
| 2 | 9 | 16 | 1.5 |
| 3 | 8 | 12 | 2 |
| 4 | 7 | 9.50 | 2.5 |
| 5 | 6 | 4 | 3 |
| 6 | 5 | 0 | 3.5 |
| 7 | 4 | 0 | 4 |
| 8 | 3 | 0 | 4.5 |

How many sweaters does it produce? How many does it sell to men, and at what price? How many does it sell to women, and at what price?

16. **True or False:** Heavy competition among firms for a limited number of customers leads to such devices as discounts for students and senior citizens.

17. Many hotels allow children to stay in their parents' rooms for free. Why?

18. Some Canadian restaurants (especially in tourist areas) will accept U.S. currency at a more favorable exchange rate than the banks will give. Why?

19. In many cities, when three people share a taxicab to exactly the same address, the fare depends on whether the three were traveling together at the time they hailed the cab. Riders who know each other are charged less than those who don't. Why?

20. The Taos Pueblo is an ancient American Indian community in New Mexico that admits tourists. The admission fee is $5 per car plus $5 per camera.

    a. Give an explanation of this pricing strategy that is based on price discrimination.

    b. Give an explanation of this pricing strategy that is not based on price discrimination.

    c. Which of your explanations do you believe? Why? What further evidence would help you to decide between your two theories?

21. Many cable television services will allow you to purchase viewing rights to several channels but will not allow you to purchase viewing rights to just one. Why might this be a profit-maximizing strategy for them? What determines the fee for the full cable service?

22. The Fredonia Gas and Electric Company is required by law to distribute all its profits to the citizens of Fredonia. **True or False:** The average Fredonian won't mind paying a monopoly price for electricity, because the monopoly profits are all returned to the citizens anyway.

23. Suppose Wegman's is the only grocery store in Rochester, and there is an admission fee to enter Wegman's. **True or False:** If the admission fee were outlawed, consumers would be better off and social gain would increase.

24. Snidely Whiplash owns all the houses in the Yukon Territory, where he charges the highest rent the citizens (who are all identical) are willing to pay. Snidely has just bought all the grocery stores in town. Should he charge a monopoly price for groceries? (*Hint:* Start by using a graph to illustrate the market for groceries. If Snidely charges monopoly prices at the grocery store, how much will he have to lower the rent on houses to prevent everyone from leaving town?)

25. All Oxbridge University students are identical, and they are all indifferent between attending Oxbridge and the next best alternative. Students eat at the student union.

    a. If Oxbridge rents space in the student union to several food providers (such as Subway and McDonald's) who then compete with each other, how much rent can Oxbridge collect? (Illustrate your answer with a graph, showing the quantity of food bought on the horizontal axis and the price of food on the vertical.)

    b. If Oxbridge rents all the space in the student union to a single food provider who charges monopoly prices, how much rent can Oxbridge collect?

    c. If prospective students are aware of the dining situation on campus, how would the decision to go with a monopoly food provider affect the amount of tuition the university can collect?

    d. In order to maximize its profits, should Oxbridge rent to a monopolist or to several competitors?

26. All Oxbridge University students are identical, and they are all indifferent between attending the Oxbridge and their next best alternative. The only place students can buy textbooks is at the Barnes and Noble bookstore on campus. The bookstore wants to start charging admission, but needs the university's permission to do so. Use a graph to illustrate the answers to the following questions:

    a. How much is the bookstore willing to pay the University for permission to charge admission?

**b.** If the bookstore starts charging admission, how much must the university cut tuition to prevent all the students from leaving?

**c.** Will the bookstore get the permission it's seeking? Why or why not?

27. In downtown Whoville, there are several department stores and several parking lots. The department stores face upward sloping marginal cost curves. Parking spaces are provided at zero marginal cost. To shop at the stores, you have to park your car. (There is no other way to get downtown.)

**a.** Suppose the department stores are competitive, and all the parking lots are owned by a single monopolist. Use a graph to illustrate the price of department store merchandise. In terms of your graph, what determines the price of a parking space?

**b.** Suppose the department stores are owned by a single monopolist and the parking lots are competitive. Now what determines the price of a parking space?

**c.** Which is better for consumers: competitive department stores and monopolized parking lots, or monopolized stores and competitive parking lots? Which yields a higher social gain?

28. Hughes Tool produces a patented drill bit (thus, it has a monopoly on the bit). Only Hughes Tool can resharpen the bit. Suppose it costs Hughes Tool exactly $100 to resharpen a drill bit.

**a.** **True or False:** If all of Hughes Tool's customers value the drill bit equally, then Hughes Tool should charge exactly $100 for a resharpening.

**b.** **True or False:** If Hughes Tool's customers differ significantly in how much they value the drill bit, then Hughes Tool should charge exactly $100 for a resharpening.

**c.** If you see Hughes Tool taking steps to prevent competitors from offering resharpening services, what can you conclude about the diversity of Hughes Tool's customers?

29. Suppose you are a monopoly seller of potatoes, facing a constant marginal cost of $10 per potato. Your customers are all identical, and they all have the following demand curve:

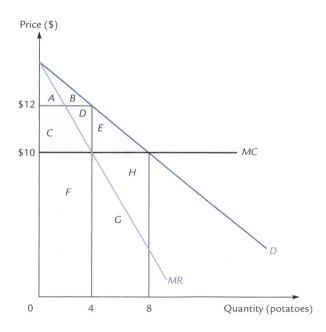

**a.** Suppose you announce a price per potato and allow consumers to buy as many potatoes as they like. What price do you charge? How much surplus do you earn per customer?

**b.** Suppose you package potatoes in bags of four and set the price per bag so that each consumer buys one bag. What price do you charge per bag and how much do you earn per customer?

**c.** Suppose you package potatoes in bags of four and set the price per bag so that each consumer buys two bags. What price do you charge per bag and how much do you earn per customer?

**d.** Suppose you package potatoes in bags of eight and set the price per bag so that each consumer buys one bag. What price do you charge per bag and how much do you earn per customer?

**e.** Which of the four strategies in parts (a) through (d) maximizes your profit?

**30.** You're the monopoly owner of a movie theater with two customers, Thelma and Louise. Thelma doesn't care at all about the movie; she just comes to buy popcorn. Louise doesn't like popcorn; she just comes to watch the movie. Thelma's demand curve for popcorn is as shown in the graph below. Louise is willing to pay up to $A + B + C$ to see the movie. It costs you 50¢ a bag to provide the popcorn. You're deciding whether to sell it for 50¢ a bag or for 40¢ a bag. Which of the illustrated areas in the graph would you want to measure to help you make your decision, and exactly how would you use that information?

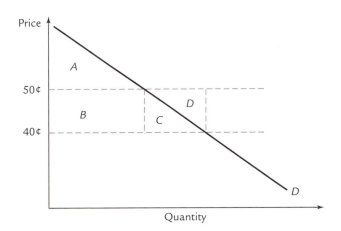

**31.** Suppose you are the owner of the only widget store in town. You purchase your widgets from the manufacturer at $50 apiece. Inside your store, you charge a single price for widgets; you can also charge an admission fee to enter the store. Your two customers, Adam and Eve, have the following demand curves:

Adam's demand for widgets                    Eve's demand for widgets

(The labels in the triangles stand for areas, measured in dollars.) Assume you are committed to keeping both of your customers. Is it best to price your widgets at $40, $50, or $60? Why?

**32.**   Suppose you are the monopoly owner of a movie theater. You can provide popcorn at a marginal cost of 50¢ per bag. It costs you nothing to allow people to enter the theater. You have two customers, Gene and Roger. Gene is willing to pay up to $20 to see the movie, and Roger is willing to pay up to $10. Gene never buys popcorn under any circumstances. Roger's demand for popcorn is the curve in the following graph:

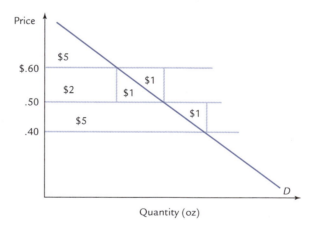

Quantity (oz)

**a.**   Suppose you charge 60¢ for popcorn. What's the highest admission price you can charge if you're determined to keep both customers?

**b.**   How does your answer to (a) change if you charge 50¢ or 40¢ for popcorn? If you want to maximize profits while keeping both customers, what price should you charge for popcorn?

**c.**   Could you do better if you were willing to charge an admission price that drives one of your customers away?

**d.**   How would your answers change if Gene is willing to pay not $20 to see the movie, but $4? What if he's willing to pay $9? $25?

# Market Power, Collusion, and Oligopoly

Market power is an elusive goal. It is limited everywhere by the threat of entry. Even a firm producing a unique product with no close substitutes might not be able to engage in monopoly pricing, because the profits that it would earn by doing so would lure entrants and destroy its market position.

But market power can be highly profitable to those who achieve it, and is therefore avidly pursued. In this chapter, we will look first at some of the strategies that firms employ in their quest for a monopoly position. These can include mergers, predatory pricing, and *fair trade* agreements. We will examine each strategy and each strategy's limits. We will also see that activities that appear to be attempts either to gain or to exploit monopoly power are not always what they seem.

Collusion among existing firms is one of the most straightforward and common methods of trying to monopolize a market. It is important enough that we devote an entire section to it, Section 11.2. Using tools from the theory of games, we will see why collusion is often doomed to fail.

We will then see that a collusive arrangement among firms that would ordinarily collapse under its own weight can at times be supported by various forms of regulation. This discussion occupies Section 11.3. Although regulation sometimes plays this role, it also plays a variety of others, and there are a great number of theories of the regulatory process. We will survey a few ideas from this large body of thought.

Finally, we will turn from the pursuit of market power to its exercise. We already have (from Chapter 10) a simple model of monopoly behavior, which ignores the firm's need to respond to other firms' actions. In Section 11.4, we will survey some theories of oligopoly that provide a starting point for thinking about industries with small numbers of firms, each enjoying some monopoly power but each affected by the others' behavior. Under this heading, we will consider some classical models of oligopoly and the contemporary theory of contestable markets. In Section 11.5, we will look at the related theory of monopolistic competition, which also tries to model firms that exercise some degree of monopoly power while simultaneously competing with other firms.

# 11.1 Acquiring Market Power

In this section, we will explore some methods that firms either use or are alleged to use in their attempts to acquire and exploit market power. We will explore the limits of these methods, and we will learn that they are not always what they seem.

## Mergers

**Horizontal integration**

A merger of firms that produce the same product.

**Vertical integration**

A merger between a firm that produces an input and a firm that uses that input.

The issue of monopoly power arises whenever two firms merge to form a larger firm. Mergers can be roughly classified into two types. Horizontal integration combines two or more producers of the same product. An example would be the combination of three computer manufacturers like Dell, Gateway, and IBM into a single company. Vertical integration combines firms one of which produces inputs for the other's production processes. An example would be the merger of a computer manufacturer (like Dell) with a chip manufacturer (like Intel).

## Horizontal Integration

There are essentially two different reasons why firms might want to merge horizontally. First, there may be economies of scale or other increased efficiencies associated with size so that a larger firm can produce output at a lower average cost. Second, there may be an opportunity for the larger firm to exercise some monopoly power. Of course, both motives may be present in a single merger.

From a welfare point of view, mergers are desirable insofar as they reduce costs, and they are undesirable insofar as they create monopoly power. Exhibit 11.1 illustrates the trade-off. We assume that the industry is initially competitive, with marginal cost curve $MC$. (The marginal cost curve is drawn horizontally in order to simplify the diagram; nothing of importance depends on this simplification.) If the firms in the industry merge, technical efficiencies will lower the marginal cost curve to $MC'$, but they will also enable the new, larger firm to exercise monopoly power, producing the monopoly quantity $Q'$, where $MC'$ crosses the marginal revenue curve $MR$.

The welfare consequences of the merger are ambiguous. There is a gain of $F + G$, representing the cost savings due to greater efficiency (the rectangle $F + G$ has area equal to $Q'$ times the cost savings per unit). There is also a loss of $E$, due to the reduction in output. Which of these is greater will vary from one individual case to another.

Dangerous
Curve

The analysis here is incomplete if it is possible for another firm to enter the market. Even if the new entrant has the relatively high marginal cost curve $MC$, it can undercut the price $P'$. Sufficiently many such new entrants—or even just the threat of new entrants—will drive the market price back down to $P$.

If $MC'$ is very much lower than $MC$, then the picture looks like Exhibit 11.2. In this case, the monopoly price $P'$ is actually lower than the competitive price $P$, and both consumers and producers gain from the merger.

**Exercise 11.1** Suppose that the merger does not reduce costs at all, so that $MC = MC'$. Draw the appropriate graph. In this case does the merger have an unambiguous effect on social welfare?

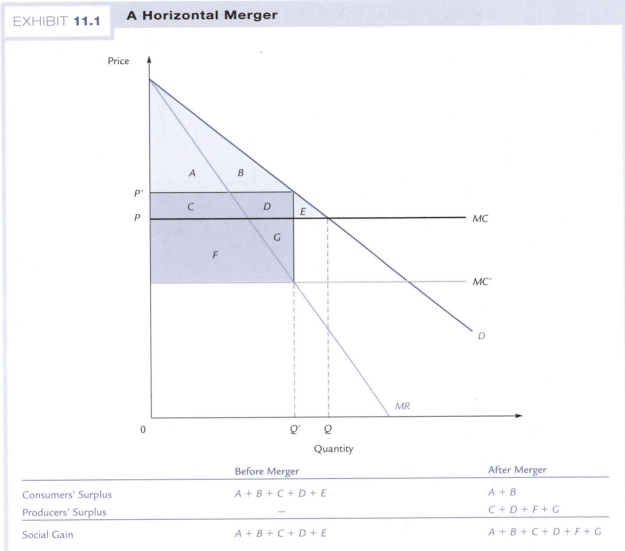

EXHIBIT **11.1**    **A Horizontal Merger**

|                     | Before Merger         | After Merger      |
|---------------------|-----------------------|-------------------|
| Consumers' Surplus  | A + B + C + D + E     | A + B             |
| Producers' Surplus  | —                     | C + D + F + G     |
| Social Gain         | A + B + C + D + E     | A + B + C + D + F + G |

Initially, the industry's marginal cost (= supply) curve is *MC*. If the industry is competitive, it produces the equilibrium output *Q* at the price *P*. Because the *MC* curve is horizontal, there is no producers' surplus.

Following a merger, marginal cost is reduced to *MC′*, but the newly created firm has monopoly power and so produces the quantity *Q′*, where *MC′* crosses the marginal revenue curve *MR*. The monopoly price is *P′*. The table above computes welfare before and after the merger.

## The Great American Merger Wave

In the years 1895–1904, a great wave of mergers swept through America's manufacturing industries. Many of the country's largest corporations—U.S. Steel, American Tobacco, Dupont, Eastman Kodak, General Electric, and dozens more—were formed at this time. The resulting megacorporations often controlled 70, 80, or even 90% of their markets, leading to the widespread assumption that the purpose of the mergers was to create monopoly power.

## EXHIBIT 11.2  A Horizontal Merger Leading to a Large Cost Reduction

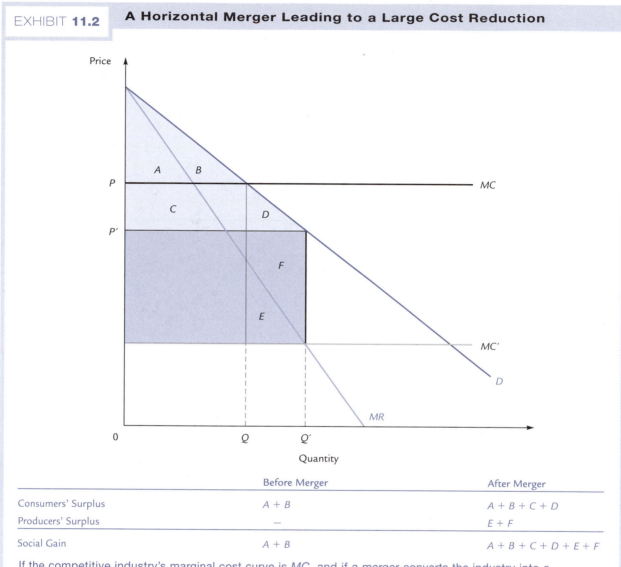

| | Before Merger | After Merger |
|---|---|---|
| Consumers' Surplus | $A + B$ | $A + B + C + D$ |
| Producers' Surplus | — | $E + F$ |
| Social Gain | $A + B$ | $A + B + C + D + E + F$ |

If the competitive industry's marginal cost curve is *MC,* and if a merger converts the industry into a monopoly with the much lower marginal cost curve *MC',* then price will fall from *P* to *P',* benefiting both consumers and producers.

But Professors Ajeyo Banerjee and Woodrow Eckard object to this assumption.[1] Here's why: Mergers that create monopoly power—and therefore raise prices—are good for every firm in the industry, whether or not they're part of the merger. If American Tobacco, with its 90% market share, was able to significantly raise prices, then small tobacco firms should have rejoiced, and their share prices should have risen. But that didn't happen. In general, firms that were left out of the mergers saw their share prices fall.

Banerjee and Eckard point out that this would all make sense if the mergers were designed not so much to create monopoly power as to lower production costs. In that

[1] A. Banerjee and E.W. Eckard, "Are Mega-Mergers Anti-Competitive? Evidence from the First Great Merger Wave," *Rand Journal of Economics* 29(4), Winter 1998, 803–827.

case, the firms that were left out would have found it difficult to compete with the more efficient megacorporations, which would explain why their stock prices fell.

## Antitrust Policies

The Sherman Act of 1890 and the Clayton Act of 1914 give the courts jurisdiction to prevent mergers that tend to reduce competition. There has been much controversy about exactly what criteria the courts should apply in determining whether a particular merger is illegal.

One viewpoint is that mergers should be prohibited only when they reduce economic efficiency. According to this viewpoint, the court should compare areas in Exhibit 11.1 before deciding whether or not to allow a particular merger. If a merger reduces costs by enough to make the graph look like Exhibit 11.2, then according to this viewpoint the merger should certainly be allowed.

In a series of decisions beginning with *Brown Shoe v. the United States* (1962), the Supreme Court under Chief Justice Earl Warren explicitly rejected this viewpoint. Instead, the Court placed particular emphasis on the welfare of small firms that are not involved in the merger. The Court held that the Sherman and Clayton acts should be interpreted so as to protect such firms by disallowing mergers that would make it difficult for them to compete. In these cases, the Court took the position that a merger could be illegal precisely *because* it would lead to a reduction in costs, lower prices, and increased economic efficiency. The reason is that smaller, less efficient firms would not be able to survive in the new environment, and the Court considered the interests of those firms to be protected by the law.

More recently, U.S. courts have largely retreated from this position and placed considerable emphasis on economic efficiency as a criterion for allowing mergers. Most European courts, however, continue to disallow mergers that create or strengthen dominant market positions, even when they are economically efficient. In the European Court of Justice, "Efficiencies are often seen as evidence of market power, rather than as benefits which may outweigh the anti-competitive consequences of mergers."[2]

## Vertical Integration

If there were only one computer manufacturer (say, Dell), you'd pay a monopoly price for your computer. If there were only one computer manufacturer *and* only one hard drive manufacturer (say, Seagate), you'd pay even more. That's because Seagate would charge Dell a monopoly price for hard drives, and Seagate's monopoly price would become part of Dell's marginal cost. When a monopolist's marginal cost curve rises, so does the price of his product.

Now suppose the two monopolies combine into a single company; say, for example, that the monopolist Dell acquires the monopolist Seagate. Suddenly, Dell isn't paying a monopoly price for hard drives anymore. That lowers Dell's marginal cost, which leads to a lower price for Dell's computers.

The moral of this fable is that vertical integration can eliminate monopoly power and benefit consumers. Exhibit 11.3 shows the argument in more detail. The graph represents the market for hard drives. Initially, Seagate charges Dell the price $P_M$, earning a producer's surplus of $C + D + F + G$ and leaving a consumer's surplus of

---

[2] P. Cayseele and R. Van den Bergh, "The Economics of Antitrust Laws," in: Bouckaert, B., and G. DeGeest (eds.), *Encyclopedia of Law and Economics*, Kluwer (2000).

EXHIBIT **11.3**    **Vertical Integration**

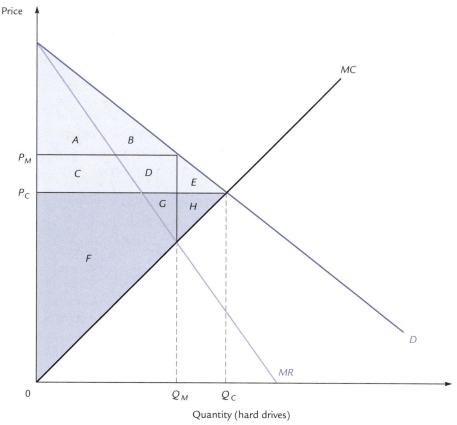

A monopoly hard drive manufacturer (Seagate) produces $Q_M$ hard drives for sale to a monopoly computer manufacturer (Dell). This maximizes producer's surplus at $C + D + F + G$ while restricting consumers' surplus to $A + B$.

If Dell acquires ownership of Seagate, it will earn both the producer's and the consumers' surpluses and will therefore want to maximize the sum of the two. This is accomplished by producing the quantity $Q_C$ of hard drives, creating a gain equal to the sum of all the lettered areas. Social gain is increased by $E + H$. More hard drives are produced, more computers are produced, and the price of computers goes down.

$A + B$ for Dell. (Note that although Dell is the *producer* in the market for computers, it is the *consumer* in the market for hard drives.)

But when Dell acquires Seagate, it is essentially in the position of selling hard drives to itself, which means that Dell collects both the producer's and consumer's surpluses. To maximize the sum of the surpluses, Dell increases production from the quantity $Q_M$ to $Q_C$, where the total surplus is $A + B + C + D + E + F + G + H$. More hard drives means more computers, and more computers means lower computer prices.

That shows that a vertical merger is attractive to consumers. Is it also attractive to Dell and Seagate? The answer is yes. Dell's total surplus after the merger is greater than the sum of the two companies' surpluses before the merger. Therefore, both companies' owners can come out ahead, provided Dell buys Seagate for an appropriate price.

**Exercise 11.2** In terms of the areas in Exhibit 11.3, what is an appropriate price for Dell's purchase of Seagate?

This example shows that when a monopolist integrates vertically with a monopolist, the net effect is to benefit everyone, including consumers. But there are other types of vertical integration. You could, for example, imagine a merger that combines a competitive computer manufacturer with a monopoly disk drive manufacturer, or a competitive disk drive manufacturer with a competitive computer manufacturer. Each case needs a separate analysis, and some cases are very complicated. In those cases, vertical integration can be either good or bad for consumers, depending on the specifics of market structure and the shapes of the demand and cost curves.

## Predatory Pricing

Predatory pricing occurs when a firm sets prices so low as to incur losses, forcing its rivals to do the same. If the firm can outlast the competition in the resulting "price war," it may hope to be the only survivor. Conceivably, a firm could engage in predatory pricing in some markets while continuing to charge normally in others. In this case, predatory pricing becomes a form of price discrimination.

Economists disagree about how widespread this practice really is. There are a number of reasons for skepticism. First, there is nothing to prevent the reemergence of rival firms as soon as the would-be monopolist raises its prices. Second, during the period of price warfare, all sides are losing money. The predator's losses, however, are greater: It is the predator who is attempting to expand market share and therefore selling greater quantities at the artificially low price. Indeed, if the other firms "lay low" by producing very little (or even nothing) for a while, they can force the predator to take losses that are enormous compared with their own. Finally, a firm being preyed upon, if it is capable of competing successfully in the long run, can usually borrow funds to get through the temporary period of price cutting. Thus, even a predator whose assets greatly outstrip its rivals' may not have any survival advantage over them.

The United States Supreme Court expressed its own skepticism of predatory pricing as a viable economic strategy when Zenith and other U.S. firms accused Matsushita and other Japanese firms of using predatory pricing to monopolize U.S. markets for consumer electronics. The court found it implausible that predatory pricing would be a profitable strategy, and concluded that the Japanese firms offered low prices because they were competing for business rather than implementing an "economically senseless conspiracy."

Despite all of these arguments, there are still reasons to think that predation might sometimes be profitable. The most significant of these is that predation can serve as a warning to future entrants. By driving one rival from the marketplace, the predator can prevent many additional rivals from entering in the first place. This can make predation a sensible strategy, even when the predator's losses from underpricing far exceed its gains from the first rival's elimination.

Even so, firms can sometimes protect themselves against predation. One recent case involved a company called Empire Gas, which sold liquid petroleum and competed against several smaller, more localized companies. By cutting prices below wholesale in just a few markets at a time, Empire tried to send a message about its willingness to punish competitors. But several competitors responded by offering

**Predatory pricing**

Setting an artificially low price so as to damage rival firms.

their customers long-term contracts at competitive prices. Even though Empire's prices were lower, many customers realized that the low prices were unlikely to last very long, and preferred to pay a bit more in exchange for the long-term assurance of a reasonable price. Eventually, the Court of Appeals ruled that Empire Gas surely did engage in predatory pricing, but no remedy was necessary because no harm had been done.

## Example: The Case Against Wal-Mart

In 1991, three pharmacies in Arkansas sued Wal-Mart for predatory pricing of prescription drugs. The three pharmacies maintained that Wal-Mart had deliberately set low prices to drive them out of business and establish a monopoly; Wal-Mart responded that it offered lower prices because it was more efficient than the other pharmacies. In essence, the plaintiffs were arguing that Wal-Mart priced below marginal cost, whereas Wal-Mart argued that both its prices and its marginal costs were low. A trial court agreed with the plaintiffs, but the Arkansas Supreme Court (in a 4–3 decision) overturned the trial court and ruled in Wal-Mart's favor.

Wal-Mart was helped at trial when one of the plaintiffs admitted that competition from Wal-Mart had provoked him to greater efficiency, which suggests that before Wal-Mart's arrival, prices had in fact been higher than necessary.

## Example: The Standard Oil Company

Historians have traditionally attributed much of the success of the Standard Oil Company to predatory price cutting. Founded in 1870 by John D. Rockefeller, Standard Oil was estimated to supply 75% of the oil sold in the United States by the 1890s. In 1911 Standard Oil (by now reorganized and called Standard Oil of New Jersey) was dissolved by order of the U.S. Supreme Court.

The role of predatory pricing in the Standard Oil case was reexamined by John McGee of the University of Washington in 1958.[3] In a widely quoted article, he argued that no historical evidence supports the assertion that predatory pricing played a major role in Rockefeller's success. Instead, McGee argued, this success could be attributed primarily to a successful policy of buying out rivals. The one-time cost of such buyouts was substantially less than the cost of predation.

Buyouts also have the advantage of allowing the would-be monopolist to acquire the rival firm's physical plant and equipment, which at least delays the rival's ability to reconstitute itself. A firm that stops producing in response to predatory price cutting still has its factories, ready to go back into production the instant prices are raised.

On the other hand, buyouts have the disadvantage of actually encouraging new entrants, who may be hoping to be bought out at a favorable price. And a firm that has been "bought" may soon reappear under a new name. It is said that more than a few nineteenth-century businessmen made lifetime careers out of being bought out by John D. Rockefeller.

---

[3] John McGee, "Predatory Price Cutting: The Standard Oil (N.J.) Case," *Journal of Law and Economics* 1 (1958): 137–169.

## The Robinson–Patman Act

Because of the potentially predatory nature of price discrimination, the Robinson–Patman Act of 1938 forbids price discrimination in cases where it tends to "create a monopoly, lessen competition, or injure competitors." This language is sufficiently imprecise as to invite controversy over exactly when price discrimination should be considered predatory. The most widely accepted standard (but by no means the only one) was offered in 1975 by Phillip Areeda and Donald Turner of the Harvard Law School.[4] They argue, among other things, that no price can be considered predatory unless it is below marginal cost. As long as the firm is pricing at or above marginal cost, those rivals who are more efficient (i.e., have even lower costs) should be able to survive. Only when the firm prices below marginal cost is there a risk of its driving out a more efficient rival.

The Supreme Court gave its interpretation of the Robinson–Patman Act in the 1967 case *Utah Pie v. Continental Baking Company*. Utah Pie was a small, local company with 18 employees marketing frozen pies in the Salt Lake City area. Continental Baking, Carnation, and Pet were large national producers of a wide variety of food products. Utah Pie alleged that these three giants price-discriminated in an injurious way by selling frozen pies at a lower price in Salt Lake City than they did elsewhere. The Supreme Court agreed.

All parties to the *Utah Pie* case were in agreement that the defendants charged lower prices in Utah Pie's marketing territory than they did outside it. However, this could have resulted from the fact that elasticity of demand for Continental pies was greater in areas where Utah Pie's products were sold. In other words, Continental's actions could have been a simple case of ordinary third-degree price discrimination.

According to the Areeda–Turner rule, the price discrimination could have been considered predatory only if the defendants had priced below marginal cost in the Salt Lake City area. No evidence was offered that they had done so. Thus, the Supreme Court's decision makes deviation from marginal cost an irrelevant criterion in deciding whether a pricing policy can be considered predatory. For this reason economists generally regard *Utah Pie* as a bad decision. By forbidding Continental et al. to undercut Utah Pie's prices, the Court is as likely to have created a local monopoly (in the hands of Utah Pie) as to have prevented one.

In fact, the Supreme Court essentially took the position that the mere fact that the price of pies decreased in Salt Lake City constituted a violation of the Robinson–Patman Act![5] This reinforced the Court's interpretation of the Sherman and Clayton acts, by reaffirming that benefits to consumers are not considered a defense against the charge of injury to other firms.

## Resale Price Maintenance

I (the author of your textbook) recently decided to buy a digital camcorder. So I drove to Best Buy, a major electronic retailing chain, where an extremely knowledgeable and helpful salesperson educated me about the available features and the pros and cons of each brand. After taking a half hour of his time, I knew which camera I wanted—a Panasonic. Best Buy's price was $900. I went home, found the identical camera on the World Wide Web for $600, and bought it online.

---

[4] P. Areeda and D. Turner, "Predatory Pricing and Related Practices Under Section 2 of the Sherman Act," *Harvard Law Review* 88 (1975): 689–733.

[5] For more on this point, see Bork, *The Antitrust Paradox,* pp. 386–387.

Obviously, this practice is a disaster for Best Buy. A little less obviously, it can be a disaster for Panasonic as well. If there are enough customers like me, Best Buy will stop offering its excellent service—which means that customers like me will be less likely to learn about the advantages of a Panasonic camera.

By supplying cameras to online discounters, Panasonic attracts additional customers (namely those who won't pay Best Buy prices) while risking the loss of Best Buy's promotional services. Apparently, they've decided that the benefits of dealing with discounters outweigh the costs. But not every firm in similar circumstances has reached the same conclusion. The Schwinn bicycle company used to require all sellers of Schwinn bicycles to charge a full retail price. If a seller was caught discounting, Schwinn would cut off that seller's supply. This practice—when a monopoly seller prohibits retailers from offering discounts—is called resale price maintenance or fair trade.

**Resale price maintenance or fair trade**

A practice by which the producer of a product sets a retail price and forbids any retailer to sell at a discount.

Resale price maintenance is sometimes misinterpreted as an attempt by the manufacturer to keep prices high. But the price consumers will pay for Schwinn bicycles is determined by the quantity of bicycles Schwinn chooses to produce. If Schwinn had a monopoly and wanted to raise prices, all it would have to do is restrict output. And conversely, unless Schwinn restricts output, no fair trade arrangement could have enabled it to sell its bicycles at a price higher than demanders were willing to pay.

It is most plausible, then, that Schwinn engaged in retail price maintenance in order to ensure that retailers would continue to offer a high level of service—displaying bicycles in showrooms and educating customers about their features. As with cameras, if some retailers offered cut-rate prices, customers would first go to the stores with the fancy showrooms and knowledgeable salesforces, ask their questions, make their decisions, and then buy from the discounters. Eventually, those retailers who offered quality service would find that there are no rewards in that activity, and so they would eliminate all of the costly forms of assistance that customers find valuable. Consumers could find themselves worse off, and so could Schwinn, as buyers would now have a greatly reduced incentive to purchase Schwinn bicycles.

Through resale price maintenance, Schwinn ensures that its dealers, who cannot compete with each other by offering lower prices, will instead compete with each other by attempting to offer higher-quality service. Thus, according to this theory, a practice that at first seems designed to establish monopoly power at the expense of consumers can actually be more plausibly explained as a practice designed to make the product more desirable by providing consumers with services that they value.

Exhibit 11.4 illustrates the theory. Suppose that $P_0$ is the wholesale price at which Schwinn sells its bicycles, and suppose, for simplicity, that retailers have no costs other than purchasing the bicycles from Schwinn. The retailers' marginal cost curve $MC$ is flat at $P_0$, and if the retail market is competitive, they sell $Q_0$ bicycles, where $MC$ meets the demand curve $D$. Now suppose that Schwinn sets a retail price of $P_1$ and requires all dealers to adhere to this price. Dealers will then compete for customers by providing additional services up to the point where the cost of providing these services is $P_1 - P_0$. This raises their marginal cost curve to $MC'$.

**Exercise 11.3** Explain why dealers provide services exactly up to the point where the cost of providing them is $P_1 - P_0$.

We assume that the dealer services add some quantity $V$ to the value of each bicycle; thus, the demand curve moves vertically upward a distance $V$ to $D'$. The new quantity sold is $Q_1$, where $MC'$ meets $D'$.

Notice that Schwinn would engage in this practice only if $Q_1$ is greater than $Q_0$; Schwinn wants to maximize the number of bicycles it can sell at a given wholesale

EXHIBIT **11.4**     **Resale Price Maintenance**

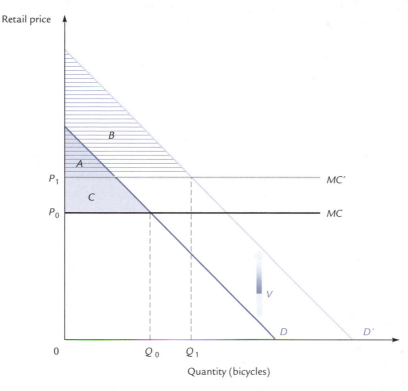

Suppose that Schwinn provides bicycles at a wholesale price of $P_0$ and that this is the only cost that retailers have. If the demand curve is $D$, then under competition the quantity sold is $Q_0$ and consumers' surplus is $A + C$.

If Schwinn maintains a retail price of $P_1$, dealers compete with each other by offering services that cost $P_1 - P_0$ per bicycle to provide. The value of these services to consumers is some amount $V$, so that the demand curve moves vertically upward a distance $V$ to $D'$. The new quantity sold is $Q_1$.

Because Schwinn chooses to engage in the practice, we can assume that $Q_1 > Q_0$. Elementary geometry now reveals that $V > P_1 - P_0$ (the value of the dealer services exceeds the cost of producing them) and $A + B > A + C$ (consumers' surplus is increased).

price. It is an easy exercise in geometry to check that if $Q_1 > Q_0$, then $V > P_1 - P_0$; that is, the value of the dealer services to consumers exceeds the cost of providing those services. This, in turn, by another easy exercise in geometry, implies that area $B$ is greater than area $C$, so that, for a given wholesale price $P_0$, the consumers' surplus with resale price maintenance $(A + B)$ is greater than the consumers' surplus without resale price maintenance $(A + C)$.

---

**Exercise 11.4** Perform the easy exercises in geometry.

---

Do not confuse the demand curves in Exhibit 11.4, which are the demand curves facing retailers, with the demand curve facing Schwinn. The demand curve facing Schwinn passes through the point $(P_0, Q_0)$ without resale price maintenance, and it moves out to pass through the point $(P_0, Q_1)$ when resale price maintenance is allowed.

Dangerous
Curve

Dangerous
Curve

The analysis (in Exhibit 11.4) is incomplete, because it takes the price $P_0$ as given. In fact, when resale price maintenance makes bicycles more attractive to consumers, the demand curve facing Schwinn moves out, leading Schwinn to set a new, higher price for bicycles. As a result, consumers keep only some of the increase in social welfare, and Schwinn gets the rest. Nevertheless, with the assumptions made here, it is possible to show that even after the price rises, consumers' surplus is still greater with resale price maintenance than without.

The theory that resale price maintenance exists to ensure a high level of service to customers is by no means the only one possible. A variety of other explanations have been offered. Indeed, in the same article where Professor Lester Telser first proposed the "service" argument, he went on to contend that it did *not* apply to resale price maintenance in the lightbulb industry, which was the special case that he was attempting to explain.[6] A recent study examined the evidence from a number of legal actions and found that the dealer service argument appears to correctly explain resale price maintenance approximately 65% of the time.[7]

The U.S. antitrust laws, as interpreted by the federal courts, severely limit the exercise of resale price maintenance. In May 1988, the Supreme Court issued a ruling that substantially relaxed these restrictions and made it easier for manufacturers to prevent retailers from offering discounts. In their decision, the justices called explicit attention to the role of resale price maintenance in maintaining high levels of dealer service. Later that week, the *New York Times* editorial page called for new legislation to overturn the effects of the ruling. The editorial called for giving manufacturers the right to "set high standards for service and refuse to supply retailers who don't meet them," while denying manufacturers the right to set prices.[8]

What the *Times* apparently failed to understand is that in the presence of competition among dealers, there is no difference between setting a standard for service and setting a retail price. Given a service standard, the price must rise until it just covers the cost of meeting the standard; given a price, the standard must rise until the cost of meeting it drives profits to zero. To allow manufacturers to set one but not the other is like allowing bathers to select the water level in the left half of the tub while disallowing them to select the water level in the right half. No matter how scrupulously you tried to obey such a law, you'd probably have trouble forcing yourself to forget that when you choose one level, you are automatically determining the other one.

### Example: Barnes and Noble versus Amazon

Barnes and Noble is a large chain bookstore that offers a comfortable atmosphere for browsing. You can sit in comfortable chairs, sip coffee, and listen to music while you contemplate your selections. These amenities are costly to provide, in some ways that are obvious and other ways that are not so obvious. Barnes and Noble rents large amounts of space to give its customers elbow room. It keeps the shelves well-stocked, which not only invites damage and theft but also requires a substantial financial investment and hence a forgone opportunity to earn interest.

---

[6] This point is reinforced in L. Telser, "Why Should Manufacturers Want Fair Trade II?" *Journal of Law and Economics* 33 (1990): 409–417.

[7] P. M. Ippolito, "Resale Price Maintenance: Economic Evidence from Litigation", *Journal of Law and Economics* (1988).

[8] "Let the Retail Price Be Right," *New York Times* editorial, May 6, 1988.

Amazon.com is a Web-based virtual bookstore that offers the convenience of shopping at home. Amazon has fewer expenses than Barnes and Noble: Rather than providing you with elbow room, Amazon invites you to keep your elbows on your desktop. Rather than keeping a large number of books in stock, Amazon orders many books from suppliers only after they have been requested by customers.

Amazon passes some of its cost savings on to the customer. Many popular hardcovers are about 20% cheaper at Amazon. This means you have two choices: Shop in comfort at Barnes and Noble, where you can look at the books before you buy them, or shop at Amazon and save a few dollars.

Unfortunately for Barnes and Noble—and for the people who like to shop there—there's also a third option: Browse at Barnes and Noble and then buy from Amazon. Consumers who behave this way raise Barnes and Noble's costs and therefore reduce the amount of space and comfortable chairs that Barnes and Noble is willing to provide.

Under these circumstances, it is plausible that book publishers would want to engage in retail price maintenance—essentially forbidding Amazon to offer discounts, so that the service at Barnes and Noble is not diminished. (Publishers care about the quality of service at Barnes and Noble because it entices people to buy books.)

However, the issue in book publishing is less clear-cut than in the case of bicycles or stereo equipment. A discount bike shop or a discount stereo store offers nothing special except discounts. By contrast, Amazon offers a service that many customers value highly: The opportunity to shop without leaving home.

Therefore, publishers probably have mixed emotions about Amazon. On the one hand, it threatens Barnes and Noble and so drives away those readers who will only buy books in comfortable surroundings; on the other hand, it brings in a different class of readers who might never have shopped at Barnes and Noble. Thus, it's not clear whether publishers should want to stifle Amazon's business practices.

# 11.2 Collusion and the Prisoner's Dilemma: An Introduction to Game Theory

Collusion takes place when the firms in an industry join together to set prices and outputs. The firms participating in such an arrangement are said to form a cartel. By restricting each firm's production, the cartel attempts to restrict industry output to the monopoly level, allowing all firms to charge a monopoly price. This maximizes the total producers' surplus of all firms in the industry. If necessary, the resulting profits can then be redistributed among firms so that each gets a bigger "piece of the pie" than it had under competition.

Collusion is an ancient phenomenon. In the tenth century B.C. the Queen of Sheba (near what is now Yemen) held a monopoly position in the shipment of spices, myrrh, and frankincense to the Mediterranean. When Solomon, the king of Israel, entered the same market, "she came to Jerusalem, with a very great train, with camels that bear spices, and very much gold, and precious stones," which could indicate how much she valued the prospect of an amicable agreement to divide the market.[9] More recently, Adam Smith observed:

**Collusion**

An agreement among firms to set prices and outputs.

**Cartel**

A group of firms engaged in collusion.

---

[9] 1 Kings 10:2.

*People of the same trade seldom meet together, even for merriment and diversion, but the conversation ends in a conspiracy against the public, or in some contrivance to raise prices.*[10]

A more contemporary example dates from the year 2000, when the world's two largest auction houses, Christie's and Sotheby's, paid hundreds of millions of dollars in fines after conspiring to fix the commissions they charged sellers. In yet another example, the Justice Department charged the eight Ivy League universities with illegally colluding to coordinate their financial aid offers. At an annual meeting called Overlap, the Ivy League schools (and fifteen others) negotiated agreements on both a general formula for determining aid offers and the specific amounts that would be offered to individual students. Because of the universities' agreement not to bid against each other, many students paid more for their educations than they would have under competition. The Justice Department argued that this made the Overlap group an illegal cartel.

According to the *Wall Street Journal*, the colleges defended their practices as a way of ensuring that students would not be influenced by financial considerations in choosing a college.[11] This defense was at least novel: If the major auto manufacturers had been caught colluding to fix high prices, they might not have thought to argue that they were performing a public service by ensuring that consumers would not be influenced by financial considerations in choosing a car. But the Justice Department was unimpressed, and the Ivy League schools, without admitting wrongdoing, agreed to cancel Overlap and not to collude in the future.

## Game Theory and the Prisoner's Dilemma

Cartels require cooperation. In order to understand the difficulties facing those who would cooperate, we will digress briefly into a topic from the theory of games.[12] The particular "game" we will analyze is called the *Prisoner's Dilemma*.

A crime has been committed and two suspects have been arrested. The suspects are taken to the police station and the district attorney meets with each one separately. To each she makes the following offer: "If you each confess, I'll send you both to jail for 5 years. If neither of you confesses, I can still get you on a lesser charge and send you to jail for 2 years each. If your buddy confesses and you don't, you'll get 10 years and he'll get 1. But if *you* are the only one to confess, you'll get off with 1 year while I put *him* away for 10. Now do you confess or don't you?" Each prisoner has to decide without conferring with the other.

Exhibit 11.5 will help you keep track of the district attorney's offer. Prisoner A, by choosing to confess or not confess, selects one of the columns in the table. Prisoner B selects one of the rows.

Let's evaluate the choices available to Prisoner A. What if B has confessed, thereby choosing the first row? Then A's choices are to confess and get 5 years, or to not confess and get 10 years. He should confess.

On the other hand, what if B has not confessed, thereby choosing the second row? Then A's choices are to confess and get 1 year, or to not confess and get 2 years. He should confess.

---

[10] Adam Smith, *The Wealth of Nations.*

[11] "U.S. Charges Eight Ivy League Universities and MIT with Fixing Financial Aid," *Wall Street Journal,* May 23, 1991.

[12] This theory was developed in the late 1940s by the mathematician John von Neumann and the economist Oscar Morgenstern. It has had a great deal of influence in economics and political science.

---

**EXHIBIT 11.5** — **The Prisoner's Dilemma**

|  |  | Action of Prisoner A | |
|---|---|---|---|
|  |  | Confess | Not Confess |
| Action of Prisoner B | Confess | 5 years each | A gets 10 years<br>B gets 1 year |
| | Not Confess | A gets 1 year<br>B gets 10 years | 2 years each |

Each prisoner must decide whether to confess or not to confess. Prisoner A reasons that there are two possibilities: Either B confesses, in which case A is better off confessing (so that he gets 5 years instead of 10), or B does not confess, in which case A is better off confessing (so that he gets 1 year instead of 2). Regardless of B's action, A should confess, and regardless of A's action, B should confess. As a result, they each go to jail for 5 years, whereas if neither had confessed they would only have gone to jail for 2 years.

---

Needless to say, Prisoner A confesses. Following the same logic, so does Prisoner B. They both end up with 5 years in jail, even though they would have both been better off if neither had confessed.

---

It is easy to misunderstand the point of this example. Students sometimes think that Prisoner A confesses because he is afraid that Prisoner B will confess. In fact, A confesses for a much deeper reason. He confesses because it is his best strategy *regardless* of what B does. Prisoner A would want to confess if he knew that B had confessed and would also want to confess if he knew that B had not confessed. The same is true for B.

Dangerous
Curve

---

## The Prisoner's Dilemma and the Invisible Hand

The Prisoner's Dilemma is an interesting case in which the invisible hand theorem is not true. When each party acts in his own self-interest, the outcome is not Pareto-optimal. If neither confessed, both would be better off. We saw in Chapter 8 that in competitive markets, by contrast, the equilibrium outcome is always Pareto-optimal. The fact that the invisible hand can fail in a simple example like the Prisoner's Dilemma makes its success in competitive markets all the more remarkable.

## Solving the Prisoner's Dilemma

How can the Prisoner's Dilemma be solved? Suppose that the prisoners of Exhibit 11.5 are members of a crime syndicate that can credibly threaten to impose severe penalties on anyone who confesses. Then the individual prisoners can be induced not to confess, and both will be better off. Contrary to what your intuition may tell you, they both benefit by being "victims" of coercion. (More precisely, each benefits from the coercion applied to the other, and this benefit exceeds the cost of the coercion applied to himself.)

Therefore, it is possible that people will prefer to have their options limited in situations that resemble the Prisoner's Dilemma. In China before World War II, goods were commonly transported on barges drawn by teams of about six men. If the barge reached its destination on time (often after a journey of several days), the men were rewarded handsomely. On such a team any given member has an incentive to shirk, in the sense of working less hard than is optimal from the team's point of view. This incentive exists regardless of whether he believes that the others are shirking. Thus, the situation is similar to the Prisoner's Dilemma, with the choices "Confess" and "Not Confess" replaced by "Shirk" and "Don't Shirk." As in the Prisoner's Dilemma, an outside enforcer commanding everyone not to shirk can make everyone better off. In recognition of this, it was apparently common for the bargemen themselves to hire a seventh man to whip them when they slacked off!

## The Repeated Prisoner's Dilemma

The Prisoner's Dilemma becomes a far richer problem when the two players expect to meet each other repeatedly in similar situations. Even though Prisoner A can always do better in the current game by confessing, he must also worry about whether his actions today will influence Prisoner B's actions tomorrow.

Suppose that A and B plan to play the Prisoner's Dilemma on three separate occasions: Monday, Tuesday, and Wednesday. You might think that each prisoner would have some incentive not to confess on Monday, so that he develops a reputation for reliability. Let us see whether this is true.

We begin by imagining the situation on Wednesday, which is the easiest day to think about. Because Wednesday is the last day, there are no future games to consider, and the game is just like an ordinary Prisoner's Dilemma. Regardless of what has gone before, each prisoner has the usual incentive to confess.

Now let us imagine the situation on Tuesday. Suppose that on Tuesday Prisoner A does not confess in order to convince Prisoner B that he won't confess on Wednesday. Will Prisoner B believe him? No, because Prisoner B realizes that once Wednesday arrives, Prisoner A will surely want to confess. Because he cannot convince Prisoner B of his goodwill anyway, Prisoner A confesses on Tuesday as well. By the same logic, so does Prisoner B.

Finally, how will the prisoners behave on Monday? Each one knows, by the logic of the preceding paragraph, that the other will confess on Tuesday. Thus, there is no credibility to be gained by not confessing on Monday. Both, therefore, confess on Monday as well.

The same reasoning applies to any repeated Prisoner's Dilemma with a definite ending date. By reasoning backward from that ending date, we see that there is never any incentive to establish a good reputation, because no such attempt can ever be credible. When there is no definite ending date, the analysis of the repeated Prisoner's Dilemma becomes a subtle and difficult problem.

## Tit-for-Tat

In 1984, Professor Robert Axelrod of the University of Michigan announced the results of a remarkable experiment.[13] Axelrod had invited various experts in the fields of psychology, economics, political science, mathematics, and sociology to submit strategies for the repeated Prisoner's Dilemma. Using a computer, he invented one imaginary prisoner with each strategy, and he had each prisoner play against each other prisoner in a 200-round repeated game. Each prisoner also played one 200-round game against a

---

[13] His results are reported in a fascinating book, *The Evolution of Cooperation* (New York: Basic Books, 1984).

carbon copy of himself, and one 200-round game against a prisoner who always played randomly. The jail sentences from Exhibit 11.5 were translated into points as follows:

| Sentence | Points |
| --- | --- |
| 1 year | 5 |
| 2 years | 3 |
| 5 years | 1 |
| 10 years | 0 |

One of the strategies submitted was called *Tit-for-Tat*. According to the Tit-for-Tat strategy, the prisoner does not confess in the first round. In future rounds he continues not confessing, except that if the opponent confesses, then the Tit-for-Tat player punishes him by confessing in the next round. In subsequent rounds, he returns to not confessing, confessing only once as punishment each time his opponent confesses.

Tit-for-Tat won the tournament decisively. Thereupon, Axelrod organized a new and much larger tournament with 62 entrants. In the second tournament the lengths of games were determined randomly, rather than making them all 200 rounds. Also, all participants in the second tournament were provided with detailed analysis of the outcome of the first tournament, so that they could use these lessons in designing their strategies. Once again, Tit-for-Tat, the simplest strategy submitted, was the decisive winner.

In a final experiment, Axelrod used his computer to simulate future repetitions of the tournament. He assumed that the strategies that did well would be more widely submitted as time went on. Thus, a strategy that did well in the first tournament, like Tit-for-Tat, was replicated many times in the second tournament, whereas strategies that did less well were replicated fewer times. This was intended to mimic evolutionary biology, where those animals that succeed in competition have more offspring in future generations. As the tournament was repeated, one could observe the evolution of various strategies. The chief result was that Tit-for-Tat never lost its dominance.

The success of Tit-for-Tat has a paradoxical flavor, in view of the fact that the backward reasoning of the preceding subsection suggests that there is no gain to acquiring a reputation for playing "reasonably" in a repeated Prisoner's Dilemma. The success of Tit-for-Tat seems to rely on just such reputational effects. Thus, we have a puzzle. Economists don't always have all the answers.

## The Prisoner's Dilemma and the Breakdown of Cartels

We now return to the topic of cartels. In a cartelized industry, price is set above marginal cost. In order to maintain this price, industry output must be held below the competitive level, and each firm is assigned a share of this production. Because price exceeds marginal cost, any given firm can increase its profits by selling a few more items at a slightly lower price. Of course, this increased output will tend to lower the price and to reduce industry-wide profits. For this reason, a monopolist would resist the temptation to increase output. However, a member of the cartel who "cheats" by increasing its output beyond its allotted share will reap all of the benefits from its action while bearing only some of the costs. It gets all of the additional revenue from the increment to output, whereas everybody shares the losses due to the fall in price.

It follows that a cartel member will be less mindful of the negative consequences of its actions than a single monopolist would be. It tends to cheat when it can get away

EXHIBIT **11.6**          **The Breakdown of Cartels**

|                       |            | **Action of Firm A** | |
|                       |            | Cheat | Not Cheat |
|-----------------------|------------|-------|-----------|
| **Action of Firm B**  | **Cheat**  | $5 profit each | A gets $3 profit<br>B gets $12 profit |
|                       | **Not Cheat** | A gets $12 profit<br>B gets $3 profit | $10 profit each |

Each member of the cartel must decide whether to cheat by producing more than the agreed-upon output. Cheating will increase the cheater's profits (because price is higher than marginal cost) and decrease the other firms' profits (by driving down the price of the product). It is in each firm's interest to cheat, whether it believes the other firm is cheating or not.

with it, and so does every other member of the cartel. Eventually, output increases all the way out to the competitive level.

The breakdown of cartels is perfectly analogous to the Prisoner's Dilemma. Imagine two firms, A and B, who have formed a cartel and must decide whether to abide by the agreement or to cheat. They are confronted by the options shown in Exhibit 11.6. Reasoning exactly as in the Prisoner's Dilemma, each firm chooses to cheat, and the cartel breaks down.

If a cartel is to succeed, it needs an enforcement mechanism. That is, it needs a way to monitor members' actions and a way to punish those who cheat. Because price-fixing agreements are illegal in the United States, the enforcement must be carried out in secret. (Indeed, since the *Madison Oil* case of 1940, the courts have held that even an attempt to fix prices is illegal under the Sherman Act, regardless of whether the attempt is successful.) Whenever you hear it asserted that a cartel has been successful, your first question should be: What is the enforcement mechanism?

### Example: The NCAA

The nation's colleges are suppliers of intercollegiate sports, and the television networks are demanders. In order to extract high prices from the networks, colleges want to limit the number of teams and the number of games they play each season. But the Prisoner's Dilemma makes this difficult: Each college wants to play additional games to earn additional revenue, regardless of how the other colleges are behaving.

To prevent such "cheating," most colleges have joined the National Collegiate Athletic Association (NCAA) and given it the right to regulate their sports programs. For a long time, the NCAA also negotiated directly with the television networks, but the Supreme Court ruled in 1984 that these negotiations were illegal and that individual colleges could negotiate separately with the networks.

You might think that colleges would benefit from their new negotiating power. The opposite is true. Now that they can negotiate separately, it has become harder to enforce the cartel agreement, as a result of which more games are played and revenues from television have fallen. However, the NCAA still wields considerable power and keeps revenues substantially higher than they would otherwise be.

## Example: The Dairy Compact

On its face, dairy farming is a highly competitive industry. However, dairy farmers in the eastern United States maintain artificially high milk prices through a cartel organization that sets and enforces minimum prices. Why is there a successful cartel in dairy farming and not, say, in wheat farming? The simple answer is that dairy farming is, through acts of Congress, exempt from antitrust laws that would make cartelization illegal. This allows the cartel to operate out in the open and to perform effectively.

The next question is: Why have dairy farmers won an exemption from the antitrust laws when wheat farmers have not? The author of your textbook does not know the answer to this question.

## Example: Concrete Pouring and Organized Crime

Throughout the 1980s, the concrete-pouring industry in New York City was dominated by a cartel of six firms called "The Concrete Club." Whenever a project was put out for bids, the Concrete Club chose one of its members to handle that project and agreed that no member of the Club would attempt to underbid that firm. As a result, the cost of a cubic yard of concrete rose to $85, the highest in the nation.

Without a strong enforcement mechanism, it would be very difficult for a cartel like the Concrete Club to succeed. Not only would its own members be tempted to cheat but competition from nonmembers would soon drive prices down to the competitive level.

In this case, the enforcement mechanism was provided by New York's organized crime families, who managed the cartel and imposed heavy penalties on cheaters. Competition from outside the cartel was eliminated by the families' control of the Concrete Workers Union, which prevented non-Club members from working on any project involving more than $2 million.[14]

## Example: The International Salt Case

To succeed, a cartel must know when its members are cheating. The International Salt Company may have discovered a creative solution to this monitoring problem. The company distributed a patented machine called the Lixator, which was used to dissolve rock salt. In some areas of the country, Lixators were sold outright; in others, they were leased subject to a requirement that the lessee agree to purchase all of its salt from International. In 1947 the Supreme Court ruled, in effect, that International Salt had attempted to create monopoly power in the market for salt. According to the analysis of two-part tariffs in Section 10.3, this explanation is unlikely to be correct. Instead, that analysis suggests that International was price discriminating by effectively charging heavier users more for a Lixator.

In 1985, John Peterman of the Federal Trade Commission reviewed the evidence and found that the economists' explanation was also suspect.[15] He discovered a clause in the

---

[14] The information in this section is taken partly from J. Cummings and E. Volkman, *Goombata* (Little Brown, 1990) and partly from P. Maas, *Underboss* (HarperCollins, 1997).

[15] John Peterman, "*The International Salt* Case," *Journal of Law and Economics* 22 (1985): 351–364.

Lixator rental contract that allowed any firm to buy its salt elsewhere if it could find it at a price lower than International's. Thus, International could not have charged more than the going market price for salt; if it had, it wouldn't have sold any.

What, then, could account for the structure of the Lixator contract? Here is one intriguing possibility. Suppose that salt suppliers were colluding. In that case, they would have needed a way to gather information on which suppliers were undercutting the agreement, so that the cheaters could be punished. The Lixator contract, with the clause that Peterman discovered, gave International's own customers an incentive to report low salt prices to International. In this way International could be continually informed of who the price cutters were and how much they were charging.

## The Government as Enforcer

When cartels have been successful, the outside enforcer has often been the government. The most candid example in U.S. history is the National Industrial Recovery Act of 1933, under the provisions of which government and industry leaders met together to plan output levels with the explicit purpose of keeping prices artificially high. The act was unanimously declared unconstitutional by the U.S. Supreme Court two years after its inception.

A more subtle channel through which government plays the role of enforcer is the apparatus of the various federal regulatory agencies. You may be surprised to learn that many industries welcome regulation. A firm that wants to be told how much to produce seems as unlikely as a bargeman who wants to be whipped. Yet, like the bargeman, the firm can find itself in a Prisoner's Dilemma where it benefits from having its actions restricted. In the next section we will explore some of the more common forms of regulatory activity.

## Monopolies as Enforcers

In Section 11.2, we saw that Wal-Mart has been accused of predatory pricing—charging artificially low prices for prescription drugs in order to drive competitors out of business.

If that was in fact Wal-Mart's intention, how would drug manufacturers like Merck and Pfizer respond? Two thoughtful economists[16] observe that a Wal-Mart monopoly, like any monopoly, would maintain high retail prices by restricting quantities, which is bad for the manufacturers. Therefore, the economists argue, the manufacturers would attempt to thwart Wal-Mart's predatory pricing through practices like resale price maintenance, requiring Wal-Mart to charge as much as its competitors. Ironically then, the laws against one "monopolistic" practice (namely resale price maintenance) make it harder for manufacturers to combat another monopolistic practice (namely price discrimination).

But alternative theories are possible. Suppose that Merck and Pfizer want to form a cartel. Because of Prisoner's Dilemma issues, they need an enforcer. Conceivably, a monopoly retailer could serve as that enforcer, by refusing to sell more than the agreed-upon quantities of any drug. Side payments among Wal-Mart, Merck, and Pfizer could then ensure that everyone shares in the profits from cartelization. Thus drug manufacturers might welcome monopoly power in the retail market.

---

[16] D. Boudreaux and A. Kleit, "How the Market Self-Polices Against Predatory Pricing," *Antitrust Reform Project* (June 1996).

It has been argued that the United Auto Workers (UAW), which has monopoly power in the market for labor, serves as a cartel enforcer for American auto makers; the idea is that the auto makers implicitly agree to produce restricted quantities of cars and the UAW enforces the cartel by refusing to provide additional labor to any manufacturer who attempts to exceed the agreed-upon quantities. If this theory is correct, car manufacturers should be glad that the UAW has monopoly power. How might you go about testing such a theory?

# 11.3 Regulation

In the United States, as in most industrialized countries, government regulation touches nearly every aspect of economic activity. Government agencies regulate hiring practices and working conditions, limit entry into professions as diverse as medicine and cosmetology, and dictate environmental standards that affect the design of everything from your car to your showerhead. Regulations are highly varied in their justifications, their effects, and the institutional arrangements through which they are enforced. Many different agencies are empowered to devise and enforce economic regulations. Some of these agencies function independently, while others are subsidiary to an executive department. Also, legislatures often pass specific statutes that are designed with regulatory intent.

Regulation has a wide variety of effects and purposes. Among these are the protection of consumers, the promotion of competition, and even the career interests of the regulators themselves. Another aspect of regulation is that it can sometimes serve to lessen competition in designated industries by introducing the government as the enforcer of a *de facto* cartel.

In the examples that follow, we will emphasize the *cartel enforcement* role of regulation, because that is the aspect of regulation that is relevant to the subject of this chapter. Do not allow this emphasis to mislead you into thinking that other aspects of regulation are less important or less interesting; they are only less germane to this discussion.

## Examples of Regulation

### Regulating Quantity

In the United States, the Interstate Commerce Commission (ICC) regulates railroads and trucking, and the Federal Aviation Administration (FAA) regulates airlines. No trucking company can operate without authority from the ICC and no airline can operate without authority from the FAA.

It has not always been easy to obtain that authority. For many years, the ICC routinely denied applications to enter the trucking industry and strictly limited the activities of existing firms by specifying the routes they were allowed to serve and the types of freight they were allowed to haul. These strict practices kept the price of trucking services high and were therefore vocally supported by trucking firms. The FAA was comparably strict about controlling entry by new airlines and the routes that existing airlines were allowed to serve.

Over the past two decades, with the encouragement of both parties in Congress, both the ICC and the FAA have significantly curtailed their regulatory activities. One result is that prices in both industries have fallen substantially—in the case of the airline industry, by about 50% over the past two decades.

But regulatory attempts to limit entry into other industries continue. Recently, the U.S. government has taken steps to limit entry into medical specialties, actually going so far as to pay $100 million to 42 New York hospitals in exchange for their *not* training doctors to become specialists. At around the same time, the University of California hospitals agreed to eliminate 452 residencies. The combined effect will be to raise the price of specialized medical care.

## Regulating Quality

Regulation often takes the form of minimum *quality* standards. By preventing goods below a prescribed minimum quality from reaching the marketplace, such regulations increase the market power of those suppliers whose output meets the prescribed standards. You might think that consumers always benefit when the average quality of goods increases, but a moment's reflection will convince you that this need not be the case. Few would prefer to live in a world in which every car had the quality (and the price tag) of a Rolls Royce. Many consumers choose goods of lower quality because they would rather devote more income to other things. The poor choose goods of lower quality more frequently, and they are therefore hurt disproportionately when low-quality goods disappear from the marketplace. A poor man who is permitted to purchase steak but not hamburger might have to eat potatoes instead of meat.

In 1989, there were two kinds of bread widely available in Egyptian retail markets. The lower-quality product sold for the equivalent of 0.8¢ U.S. per loaf, while the higher-quality product sold for 2¢. By the middle of 1990, the government forced the cheap bread to be withdrawn from the market. For many Egyptians, the results were disastrous. The *New York Times* reported the plight of a family of six, each of whom ate one loaf per meal.[17] Because they were forced to buy the more expensive bread, the family's food expenses increased by more than $10 per month—a quarter of their income. There is no sense in which this family can be said to have benefited from the new minimum quality standard.

But there are some markets, such as the market for drugs, where low-quality products can be harmful or even fatal. In those markets, many people will instinctively agree that minimum quality standards must be beneficial to consumers. Therefore it can be particularly instructive to investigate such markets to determine the actual effects of regulation.

In the United States, the sale of nonnarcotic drugs was largely unregulated until 1938. In that year, the Food and Drug Administration (FDA) first began requiring consumers to obtain a doctor's prescription before buying drugs. Have mandatory prescriptions improved consumers' health? Professor Sam Peltzman of the University of Chicago investigated this question in two ways: (1) by comparing American death rates before and after 1938; and (2) by comparing American death rates with death rates in other countries where prescriptions are still not mandatory. (Except for Argentina and Uruguay, most Latin American countries do not require prescriptions. Neither does Greece, and neither do many countries in Asia.) Peltzman concluded that, while the available evidence is too weak to support a firm conclusion, it appears that mandatory prescriptions do not save lives or lead to other improvements in health.[18]

In 1962, the U.S. Congress passed the Kefauver Amendments, which required drug manufacturers to prove that their products are safe and effective; the Kefauver

---

[17] "2 Cent Loaf Is Family Heartbreak in Egypt," *New York Times*, July 9, 1990.
[18] S. Peltzman, "The Health Effects of Mandatory Prescriptions," *Journal of Law and Economics* 30 (1987): 207–238.

Amendments are enforced by the FDA. To investigate the effect of this regulation, Professor Peltzman looked at the rate of new-product development in the drug industry both before and after 1962, and concluded that the Kefauver Amendments have cost more lives than they have saved.[19]

For nearly 40 years, the Kefauver Amendments have saved some lives by protecting consumers from harmful drugs. At the same time, they have cost other lives by delaying the appearance of useful drugs; people have died while drugs that could have saved them were still being tested. Because the cost of testing is a disincentive to innovate, the amendments have probably cost additional lives by reducing the number of new drugs that are developed in the first place. They have also raised the price of existing drugs by reducing the number of substitutes.

Peltzman estimated such costs and benefits by observing the behavior of pharmaceutical companies both before and after 1962. He found that the net effect was overwhelmingly negative. The amendments reduced the number of new drugs entering the marketplace from approximately 41 per year to approximately 16 per year, and they introduced an average delay of two years for a drug to reach the marketplace. In recent years, partly because of studies like Peltzman's and partly in response to the spread of AIDS, the FDA has relaxed its rules substantially, allowing new and important drugs to be fast-tracked into the marketplace.

The FDA regulates not only the quality of drugs but also of medical devices and food additives. A few years ago, the fast-track program was extended to apply to medical devices. In many areas, though, FDA approval continues to take a long time. It was not until December 1997, after many years of delay, that the FDA approved irradiation of meat products for controlling disease- causing microorganisms. The FDA concluded that irradiation is a safe and important tool to protect consumers from food-bornediseases, effectively acknowledging that for several years it had denied consumers access to a safe and effective means of protecting their health. Of course, if irradiation had turned out to be harmful, the years of delay might have been a great blessing to consumers.

Frequently, quality regulations take the form of professional licensing requirements. Your doctor, your lawyer, your cab driver, and your beautician all need licenses to practice. Such requirements can help to establish minimal standards of competence; they can also restrict the number of practitioners and thereby keep prices above the competitive level.

## Regulating Information

Another way in which entry to a market can be effectively curtailed is by restricting the ability of consumers to learn about new suppliers. Suppliers who cannot make their existence known are essentially excluded from the market. In practice, this is often accomplished through restrictions on advertising. Professional societies such as the American Medical Association and the American Bar Association have gone to extraordinary lengths to restrict advertising by their members.

Many reasons have been offered to support the idea that advertising raises prices. It is sometimes alleged that buyers must "pay for the advertising as well as the product." On the other hand, advertising saves the consumer the cost of having to search for information about available products. Indeed, a buyer who prefers not to pay for

---

[19] S. Peltzman, "An Evaluation of Consumer Protection Legislation: The 1962 Drug Amendments," *Journal of Political Economy* 81 (1973): 1049–1091.

advertising always has the option to incur the costs of seeking out a seller who does not advertise and to buy the product at a correspondingly lower price. When buyers do not do this, they reveal that they value the informational content of advertising at a price at least equal to whatever they are paying for it.

In fact, by providing information about a wide array of sellers, advertising can promote competition and might therefore actually *reduce* prices. In 1972, Lee Benham set out to investigate this question in the market for eyeglasses.[20] This market was particularly suitable for study since there is wide variation in advertising restrictions across states. He found that in states where advertising was prohibited, the price of eyeglasses was higher by 25 to 100%. This particularly persuasive empirical study has convinced many economists that the net effect of advertising is often (though surely not always) to lower prices.

## Regulating Prices

Instead of setting quality standards, the government sometimes sets minimum prices below which goods cannot be sold. This excludes the producers of low-quality goods from the marketplace, increasing the demand for those high-quality goods that are close substitutes.

By far the most important example is the federal minimum wage law. Although this law is often presented as protective of the unskilled, it is precisely they whom it excludes from the labor market. At a minimum wage of $5.15 per hour, someone who produces $3.00 worth of output per hour will not be hired to work. Overwhelming empirical evidence has convinced most economists that the minimum wage is a significant cause of unemployment, particularly among the unskilled.

Among the beneficiaries of the minimum wage law are the more highly skilled workers who remain employed and who can command higher wages in the absence of less-skilled competition. These more highly skilled workers tend to be represented by labor unions, which, not surprisingly, tend to support increases in the minimum wage.

Minimum wage laws also have other, less obvious effects. When the federal minimum wage was first proposed in the 1930s, it was heavily supported by the northern textile industry. The reason was that wages were lower in the South than in the North, due partly to a lower cost of living in the South. As a result, northern firms found it difficult to compete. By imposing a federally mandated minimum wage, northern producers hoped to eliminate the advantage held by their southern competition and indeed hoped to drive the South out of textile manufacturing altogether.

## Regulating Business Practices

Laws that prohibit transactions at certain times of the day or week tend to inhibit competition and raise prices. So-called blue laws in many states prohibit the sale of various goods on Sunday. This solves a Prisoner's Dilemma for suppliers. Any given supplier must choose between the options "Work on Sunday" and "Not Work on Sunday." Each will choose to work on Sunday whether its competitors are doing so or not; but each prefers to have nobody working Sunday than to have everybody working. Blue laws allow the supplier to watch football on Sunday afternoon without losing business to a rival. Of course, this boon to suppliers comes at the expense of consumers, for whom Sunday is a convenient shopping day.

---

[20] L. Benham, "The Effect of Advertising on the Price of Eyeglasses," *Journal of Law and Economics* 15 (1972): 337–352.

An interesting variant of the blue laws was recently in effect in the city of Chicago. Until quite recently, it was illegal to buy meat in Chicago after 6 P.M. and repeal was opposed by the butchers' union.

## The Economics of Polygamy

The laws against polygamy provide an instructive example of the effects of output restrictions. We will consider the effect of a law that forbids any man from marrying more than one woman.

We can view men as suppliers of "husbandships," which are purchased by women at a price.[21] This price has many subtle components, including all of the agreements, spoken and unspoken, that married couples enter into. Choices about where to live, how many children to have, who will do the dishes, and where to go on Saturday nights are all contained in the price of the marriage. When husbandships are scarce, men can require more concessions on such issues as conditions of their marriages. For example, if there were only one marriageable man and many marriageable women, the man would be in a position to insist that any woman he marries must agree to attend professional wrestling with him every weeknight (assuming that this is something he values). If one woman will not agree to this price, he can probably find another woman who will.

Thus, the price of a husbandship is higher when husbandships are scarce, and, similarly, the price of a husbandship is low when husbandships are abundant. If each man wanted to marry four women, the price of husbandships would be bid down (or, equivalently, the price of wifeships would be bid up) to the point where men would have to make considerable concessions in order to attract even one wife. It is in the interests of men as producers to restrict output so that this does not happen. Antipolygamy laws accomplish this. Thus, the analysis suggests that laws against polygamy, like other laws restricting output, benefit producers (in this case men) and hurt consumers (in this case women).

Sometimes students argue that no woman in the modern world would want to be part of a multiwife marriage and that therefore women could not possibly benefit from the legalization of polygamy. But this is incorrect, because even under polygamy those women who wanted to could demand as a condition of marriage that their husbands agree not to take any additional wives. And even if no man took more than one wife, the price of wives would still be higher.

For example, imagine a one-husband–one-wife family where an argument has begun over whose turn it is to do the dishes. If polygamy were legal, the wife could threaten to leave and go marry the couple next door unless the husband concedes that it is his turn. With polygamy outlawed, she does not have this option and might end up with dishpan hands.

Another reason why students are sometimes surprised by this conclusion is that they are aware of polygamous societies in which the status of women is not high. But, of course, the difference in polygamy laws is not the only important difference between those societies and our own. The fact that polygamy is legal in many places where women are otherwise oppressed does not constitute an argument that the oppression is caused by polygamy. Our analysis compares the status of women with and without legalized polygamy on the assumption that other social institutions are held constant.

---

[21] Because we are examining the market for husbands, men are the producers and women the consumers. It would be equally correct to treat the marriage market as a market for wives, in which women are the producers and men the consumers. Since we are investigating the effects of the law that restricts the supply of husbands, it is more convenient to think of "husbandships" rather than "wifeships" as the commodity being traded.

In view of our analysis, it is interesting that polygamy laws are often alleged to "protect" women. It has been observed that laws prohibiting any man from marrying more than one woman are perfectly analogous to laws preventing any firm from hiring more than one African-American.[22] Surely no one would be so audacious as to claim that the purpose of such a law was to protect African-Americans.

## What Can Regulators Regulate?

In any study of the effects of regulation, it is necessary to ask what regulators actually do. But regulators' own descriptions of their activities should not always be taken at face value.

Economists George Stigler and Claire Friedland examined the effects of regulation in the electric power industry.[23] They examined electric rates in the years, 1912–1937. During these years, some states regulated the price of electricity and others did not. Stigler and Friedland found that the presence of regulation had no observable effect on the actual price of electricity. The evidence suggested that the regulatory commission consistently ended up setting the price that the utilities would have chosen anyway.

Stigler applied a similar analysis to the regulation of the securities industry by the Securities and Exchange Commission (SEC).[24] The SEC requires issuers of securities (e.g., corporate stocks) to make public disclosures of relevant information. If you try to sell stock in a gold mine that has never produced any gold, the SEC will require that this fact be disclosed to potential buyers. Stigler examined the performance of newly issued stocks compared with the performance of the market as a whole before and after the formation of the SEC in 1934. He found that there was no change in the propensity of newly issued stocks to perform well. It appeared that the SEC made no real difference; there is no evidence that the mix of securities that was offered under regulation differed appreciably from the mix of securities that would have been offered in an unregulated market.

These and other studies have convinced a growing number of economists that an industry should not necessarily be considered regulated just because of the existence of an agency with the formal power to regulate it. In many cases, there may be political or other considerations that prevent the agency from ever taking any steps that actually have the effect of altering economic behavior. Whether or not an allegedly "regulated" industry is really regulated in any meaningful sense is an empirical question, one that must be decided on a case-by-case basis.

## Creative Response and Unexpected Consequences

**Creative response**

A response to a regulation that conforms to the letter of the law while undermining its spirit.

Although it can be in the interest of an industry to be regulated, it is almost always in the interest of an individual firm to avoid the effects of regulation when possible. This often leads firms to engage in **creative response,** behaving in ways that conform to the letter of the law while undermining its spirit. For this reason and others, regulations can have unexpected consequences—sometimes directly contrary to the intentions of the regulators.

---

[22] G. Becker, "A Theory of Marriage," *Journal of Political Economy* 81 (1973): 813–846.

[23] G. Stigler and C. Friedland, "What Can Regulators Regulate? The Case of Electricity," *Journal of Law and Economics* 82 (1974): S11–S26.

[24] G. Stigler, "Public Regulation of the Securities Market," *Journal of Business* 37 (1964).

Until a few years ago, parents traveling on airplanes were allowed to hold infants on their laps. More recently, parents have been required to buy a separate seat for the infant. This regulation, apparently motivated by a desire to make infants safer, has had exactly the opposite effect as many parents, unwilling to pay for the additional seats, have opted to travel by car instead of by airplane. Because the death rate per mile is about 70 times greater in a car, economists have estimated that the net effect of the regulation has been an increase in the number of infant deaths.

Another striking example concerns the use of pesticides. Certain pesticides are banned because of potential health hazards. But a side effect is to raise the cost of growing fruits and vegetables, thereby raising their price and lowering the quantity demanded. The prominent biologist Bruce Ames has pointed out that the fall in fruit and vegetable consumption is likely to be more damaging to health than the pesticides were.

Sometimes the unexpected consequences of regulation can be unexpectedly delightful. In renaissance Europe, regulations forbade unlicensed actors to speak on stage. According to some historians, the result was the advent of modern pantomime.

Here are some further examples from recent history, to demonstrate how creative responses can undermine the apparent intent of a regulation.

## Example: Affirmative Action Laws

Affirmative action laws provide an example where a creative response may have led to consequences directly contradictory to the intent of the original legislation. These laws and regulations arose from the observation that African-American workers were systematically paid less than white workers. They required employers to remedy this imbalance by paying higher wages to African-American workers.

However, wages are only part of the compensation that a worker receives. Typically, workers receive a variety of valuable fringe benefits as well. One of the most important fringe benefits, especially in entry-level positions, is on-the-job training. Such training enables employees to acquire basic skills that will raise their income later in life. Its value often represents a substantial portion of the employee's total compensation.

Since on-the-job training is largely unobservable to outsiders, employers can adjust its quantity without being found guilty of violating those laws that regulate workers' compensation. Thus, some employers were able to comply with the affirmative action regulations without actually changing the total value of the compensation that they offered to African-Americans. They simply paid a higher wage, satisfying the regulator, while compensating by offering less on-the-job training. Between the years 1966 and 1974 the *observable* wage differences between African-Americans and non-Hispanic caucasians were essentially eliminated, but they were partially replaced by *unobservable* differences. For African-American workers, this meant higher starting salaries, less on-the-job training, and lower future wages than before affirmative action.

The net effect of all this on the economic status of African-Americans could be either positive or negative. In one study Professor Edward Lazear found that the relative economic status of African-Americans (taking account of all their expected future earnings) was not improved by the affirmative action laws.[25] In fact, his evidence supported just the opposite conclusion—that during the period 1966–1972, the gap between African-American and white compensation, inclusive of the value of on-the-job training, actually widened.

[25] E. Lazear, "The Narrowing of Black-White Wage Differentials Is Illusory," *American Economic Review* 69 (1979): 553–564.

## Example: Reasonable Quantities of Sale Items

In the late 1970s, the Federal Trade Commission (FTC), which regulates (among other things) against false and deceptive advertising, discovered that one of its regulations led to responses that were counterproductive. The FTC periodically receives complaints about the unavailability of advertised specials. Consumers travel to stores that are advertising items at unusually low prices, only to find that those items are sold out shortly after the commencement of the sale. Understandably, these consumers are annoyed. The FTC responded to these complaints in the mid-1970s by issuing a series of regulations requiring stores to have on hand a "reasonable quantity" of any item that was advertised at a sale price.

To understand the effect of these regulations, it is necessary first to understand the reasons for sales. In many (though certainly not all) cases, a store will decide to discontinue stocking a certain item and will want to dispose quickly of its remaining stock. In such cases, ordering sufficient additional inventory to have a "reasonable quantity" on hand would contravene the very purpose of the sale. Therefore, one effect of the regulations was that sales of this type were discontinued. In view of this effect, fewer items were offered at sale prices. At the same time, it meant that when there *were* sales, the sale items were usually available.

Throughout the late 1970s, the FTC interviewed consumers about their feelings regarding the new rules. On the basis of these interviews, the FTC decided that the rules tended to benefit people with higher incomes at the expense of the poor. People with high incomes have a high value of time; they find it very costly to drive to a store only to discover that the item they are shopping for is out of stock. To them the cost of these fruitless shopping trips outweighs the benefit of having more sales to choose from. People with low incomes have a lower value of time and place greater value on being able to buy at sale prices. They prefer there to be more sales, even if the stores sometimes run out before they get there.

On the basis of this analysis, the FTC rescinded its rules on advertised specials.

## Positive Theories of Regulation

Throughout this section we have examined some of the consequences of certain existing regulations. However, we have made no attempt to address the question of why some industries are regulated and others are not. We have focused primarily on ways in which regulation might act to limit competition. But we have made no attempt to formulate a general principle concerning when regulations will limit competition and when they will serve some other function, such as promoting economic efficiency.

Many economists think that there is a need for a positive theory of regulation, to predict the circumstances under which various types of regulations arise and what their effects will be. Such a theory would have to explain why the trucking industry is more heavily regulated than the airline industry, why some occupations require professional licenses while others don't, and why electricity prices seem to have been unaffected by regulation. A complete theory would begin with an explicit account of what it is that regulators are trying to accomplish. For example, regulators might be motivated by a desire to redistribute wealth in certain ways, or by a desire to protect consumers from major disasters, or even by a desire to maximize their own power. From such assumptions, one could derive conclusions about when, where, and what types of regulations are most likely to occur.

A theory of this sort might also be used to explain why regulations are selectively enforced. For example, radar detectors are legal in 48 states, despite the fact that their only purpose is to facilitate breaking the law. Why are people permitted to purchase the opportunity to violate speed limits with a reduced probability of punishment? Various theories are consistent with this observation. If the goal of regulators is to increase economic efficiency, they might want to allow speeding by those whose time is sufficiently valuable. These would be primarily those who find it worthwhile to invest in a radar detector. An alternative theory is that regulators prefer not to antagonize the politically powerful and that those who are wealthy enough to want radar detectors are also powerful enough to keep the regulators at bay.

Which theory seems more sensible to you? Can you think of other examples that would tend to confirm or refute one of these theories? What alternative theories can you propose?

# 11.4 Oligopoly

An **oligopoly** is an industry in which the number of firms is sufficiently small that any one firm's actions can affect market conditions. Thus, in an oligopoly each firm has a certain degree of monopoly power. The behavior of such firms depends on many things, including whether they are threatened by potential entry. We will first consider markets in which entry is costless (and therefore an ever-present threat) and then markets in which the number of firms is fixed.

**Oligopoly**

An industry in which individual firms can influence market conditions.

## Contestable Markets

A market in which firms can enter and exit costlessly is called a **contestable market**.[26] A commonly cited example is the market for airplane service on a particular route, say, from Houston to Dallas. The owner of an airplane that is currently flying back and forth between Houston and San Antonio can easily move into the Houston-to-Dallas market if there is a profit opportunity, and can easily return to the Houston-to-San Antonio market at any time.

In a contestable market, even a single firm producing a unique product with no close substitutes might not be able to engage in monopoly pricing, because the profits that it would earn by doing so would lure entrants and destroy its market position. Exhibit 11.7 illustrates the position of a monopolist threatened by potential entry. Assuming all firms are identical, their entry price will be $P_0$.

**Contestable market**

A market in which firms can enter and exit costlessly.

---

**Exercise 11.5** Explain why firms would enter if the market price of output were $P_0$ but would not enter at any lower price.

---

It follows that the market price cannot be higher than $P_0$, since any higher price will attract entry. At this price the firm will produce the quantity $Q_0$. The market will demand $Q_1$, which may be several times $Q_0$. If, for example, $Q_1$ is twice $Q_0$, there will be room for a second firm to imitate exactly the actions of the first firm without exhausting market demand. If $Q_1$ is seven times $Q_0$, there will be room for seven firms

---

[26] The theory of contestable markets is surveyed by its founders in W. Baumol, S. Panzard, and R. Willig, *Contestable Markets and the Theory of Industry Structure* (San Diego: Harcourt Brace Jovanovich, 1982).

EXHIBIT **11.7**     **A Contestable Market**

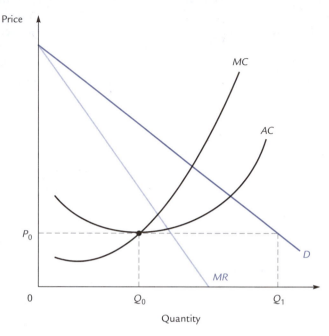

If the market is contestable, firms will enter at any price above $P_0$. Therefore, the market price cannot be higher than $P_0$, because any higher price would attract entry. At this price the firm supplies $Q_0$ units of output and the market demands $Q_1$. Thus, there is room in the industry for $Q_1/Q_0$ firms.

altogether. In general, the number of firms that actually enter will be equal to $Q_1/Q_0$, each producing $Q_0$ items at a price of $P_0$, which equals both average and marginal cost.[27] In other words, potential entry will force firms to behave as competitors, even if there are very few firms.

In a contestable market with identical firms whose average cost curves cross the industry demand curve in the region where they are upward sloping, price, average cost, and marginal cost are all equal.

## Contestable Markets and Natural Monopoly

There is also the possibility of natural monopoly in a contestable market. That is, the firm's average cost curve might still be downward sloping where it crosses industry demand. This is shown in Exhibit 11.8. In this case, a monopoly producer cannot operate at the "competitive" point $Q_0$, because its profits there would be negative. On the other hand, if it follows the usual monopoly pricing rule of setting marginal cost equal to marginal revenue (producing $Q_2$), it may earn positive profits and lure other firms into the industry. The threat of entry forces the producer to operate at the zero profits point $Q_1$.

---

[27] There is a slight problem related to the fact that $Q_1/Q_0$ may not be exactly equal to an integer, in which case we expect the number of firms to be either the integer just above or just below $Q_1/Q_0$.

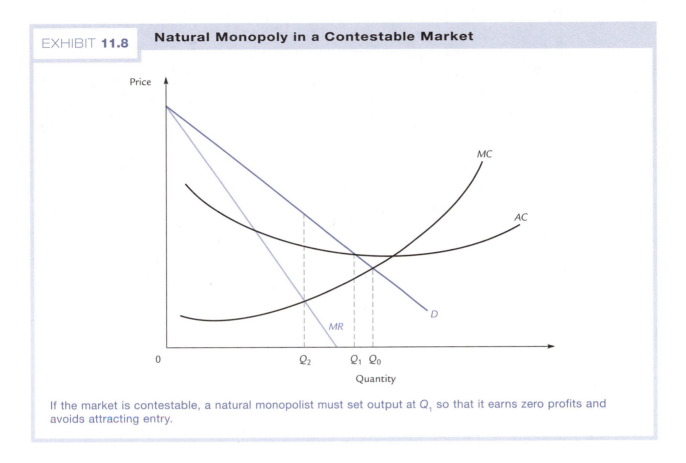

**EXHIBIT 11.8**

**Natural Monopoly in a Contestable Market**

If the market is contestable, a natural monopolist must set output at $Q_1$ so that it earns zero profits and avoids attracting entry.

## Oligopoly with a Fixed Number of Firms

When there is no threat of entry, the behavior of an oligopoly is more difficult to predict. One possibility is the formation of a cartel. As we have seen, the Prisoner's Dilemma guarantees that there are forces tending to undermine the success of cartels. On the other hand, cartels are really *repeated* Prisoner's Dilemmas, since firms produce output every day. We have also seen that the outcome of repeated Prisoner's Dilemmas is hard to predict.

When there is no collusion, each firm's actions depend on the actions that it expects the other firms to take. Therefore, the way in which firms form their expectations about each other's behavior is a crucial ingredient in modeling oligopoly. We will examine two different models that proceed from different assumptions about expectation formation. In one, the **Cournot model**,[28] firms take their rivals' output as given. In the other, the **Bertrand model**,[29] firms take their rivals' prices as given.

### The Cournot Model

To simplify the analysis, we will assume an industry with exactly two identical firms having the flat marginal cost curve shown in Exhibit 11.9. We will also assume a straight-line demand curve, so that marginal revenue has exactly twice the slope of

**Cournot model**

A model of oligopoly in which firms take their rivals' output as given.

**Bertrand model**

A model of oligopoly in which firms take their rivals' prices as given.

---

[28] For the nineteenth-century French mathematician Augustin Cournot.
[29] For the nineteenth-century French economist Joseph Bertrand.

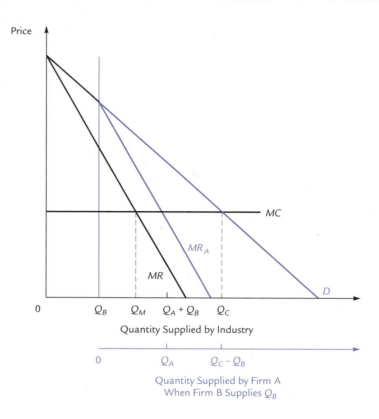

We assume that two identical firms have the flat marginal cost curve *MC* and face a market demand curve *D*. A competitive industry would produce the quantity $Q_C$. A monopolist would produce the quantity $Q_M = \frac{1}{2}Q_C$, where *MC* crosses the marginal revenue curve *MR*.

If Firm A assumes that Firm B will always produce quantity $Q_B$, then Firm A views itself as a monopolist in the market for the remaining quantity. The demand curve in that market is the colored part of the market demand curve, measured along the colored axis. The marginal revenue curve is the colored curve $MR_A$. Firm A produces the monopoly quantity $Q_A$, which is half the competitive quantity $(Q_C - Q_B)$. Combining this fact with the equation $Q_A = Q_B$ (which follows from the fact that the firms are identical), we compute that $Q_A = Q_B = \frac{1}{3}Q_C$. Thus, the industry output is $\frac{2}{3}Q_C$, less than the competitive output but more than the monopoly output.

demand. A monopoly would produce the quantity $Q_M$ and a competitive industry would produce the quantity $Q_C$. Because of what we have just said about the slopes of the curves, we must have:

$$Q_M = \frac{1}{2}\,Q_C$$

Now let us see what the two firms will produce. Suppose that Firm B produces the quantity $Q_B$ and Firm A makes the assumption that this quantity will never change. Then Firm A views itself as a monopolist in the market for the remaining quantity. That is, Firm A is a monopolist in a market where the zero quantity axis is the colored vertical line in Exhibit 11.9 and the demand curve is the color part of the industry demand curve. In such a market, the marginal revenue curve is the color curve $MR_A$ parallel to the industry marginal revenue curve *MR*. Firm A produces the quantity $Q_A$, where

$M_C = MR_A$. Since this is the monopoly quantity, it must lie halfway between Firm A's zero quantity axis at $Q_B$ and the competitive point $Q_C - Q_B$. That is,

$$Q_A = \frac{1}{2}(Q_C - Q_B)$$

We can also write one additional equation. Because it is assumed that Firms A and B are identical, it is reasonable to expect that they will produce equal quantities of output. This gives us the equation;

$$Q_A = Q_B$$

Putting the two equations together, we get:

$$Q_A = \frac{1}{2}(Q_C - Q_A)$$

which can be solved for $Q_A$, giving:

$$Q_A = \frac{1}{3}Q_C$$

In other words, each firm produces $^1/_3$ of the competitive quantity, so that between them they produce $^2/_3$ of the competitive quantity. This is more than the monopoly output, which is only $^1/_2$ of the competitive quantity.

## The Bertrand Model

The Bertrand model has the same flavor as the Cournot model. In the Cournot model, each firm assumes that its rivals will never change quantity. In the Bertrand model, each firm assumes that its rivals will never change price.

As long as price exceeds marginal cost, an oligopolist in the Bertrand model will always want to undercut its rivals by offering a slightly lower price. Since it assumes that its rivals will not meet this price cut, it follows that the oligopolist will be able to capture the entire market for itself. This is a profitable strategy. The tiniest of price cuts leads to a sizable increase in sales, and all of these sales are at a price that exceeds marginal cost.

Bertrand oligopolists will continue to undercut one another until price falls to marginal cost. Thus, according to Bertrand, price and output will be the same under oligopoly as they are under competition.

## Criticism of the Cournot and Bertrand Models

Many economists are uncomfortable with both the Cournot and the Bertrand models of oligopoly, because each model posits that firms make incorrect assumptions about their rivals' behavior. In the Cournot model, firms assume that their own choice of output will not affect their rivals' choices, despite the fact that they know that their rivals' choices are affecting their own. The same is true in the Bertrand model regarding prices instead of quantities.

This criticism highlights the major difficulty that economists face when they attempt to model oligopoly behavior. The assumptions that firms make about one another's behavior are crucial elements in the determination of their own behavior, and the economist must therefore presume to know something about those assumptions. If the assumptions turn out to be incorrect, firms should become aware of this fact over time, invalidating the model. In the real world we expect that oligopolists have at least reasonably accurate information about how their rivals behave, and we would like our models to reflect that fact. Unfortunately, satisfactory models with this property have proven difficult to construct. In much recent research, game theory has proved to be an increasingly effective tool.

# 11.5 Monopolistic Competition and Product Differentiation

**Product differentiation**

The production of a product that is unique but has many close substitutes.

One strategy for acquiring some degree of monopoly power in a market that is basically competitive is called **product differentiation.** As its name implies, this strategy involves producing a product that differs sufficiently from the output of other producers that some consumers will have a distinct preference for it. Crest and Colgate both produce toothpaste, but they do not produce identical products. The two products are close substitutes, and neither can be priced very differently from the other without a substantial loss of market share. At the same time, there are some consumers with a very strong preference for one or the other brand, so that each firm faces a demand curve that is at least slightly downward sloping.

Products with brand names are product differentiated simply by virtue of having different brand names. But other characteristics can differentiate them as well. The location at which a product is sold can differentiate it from others. A 7-Eleven two blocks from your house is not the same to you as a 7-Eleven a mile and a half away, although they are probably close substitutes.

**Monopolistic competition**

The theory of markets in which there are many similar but differentiated products.

## Monopolistic Competition

The theory of markets in which there are many similar but differentiated products is called the theory of **monopolistic competition.** The first panel of Exhibit 11.10 illustrates the conditions facing a monopolistically competitive firm. Suppose that the firm

---

EXHIBIT **11.10**    **Monopolistic Competition**

Panel A shows a short-run equilibrium in which the firm sells quantity Q at price P. Here price exceeds average cost, so the firm earns positive profits. In the long run, entry drives the demand curve facing this firm down to d' in panel B, where the firm is just able to earn zero profits by selling quantity Q' at price P'.

is currently charging price $P$ and selling quantity $Q$. The demand curve $d$ shows how much the firm can sell at any given price on the assumption that all other firms continue to charge the original price $P$.

---

**Exercise 11.6** Explain why you might expect the curve $d$ to be quite elastic compared with the demand curve facing an ordinary monopolist.

---

The quantity $Q$ is determined by the condition that $MC = mr$, where $MC$ is the firm's marginal cost curve and $mr$ is the marginal revenue curve associated with $d$. In panel A of the exhibit, the firm is earning positive profits, since the price $P$ exceeds average cost at quantity $Q$.

In the long run, these profits will attract entry by other firms selling similar products. As a result, the demand curve facing the firm will shift downward, to $d'$ in panel B of Exhibit 11.10. The firm produces quantity $Q'$ and charges price $P'$. At this point price and average cost are equal, so that profits are zero and there is no further entry.

---

At the long-run equilibrium quantity $Q'$, the demand curve must touch the average cost curve to give zero profits. You might wonder why we have drawn the curves tangent rather than crossing. The reason is that if the curves crossed, the firm could earn positive profits by producing a quantity slightly less than $Q'$. But we know that $Q'$, the zero-profits point, is also the point of maximum profits, since it is the point where $MC = mr$. Thus, it cannot be correct to draw the average cost curve actually crossing demand.

Dangerous
Curve

---

## Welfare Aspects of Monopolistic Competition

In Exhibit 11.10 we can see that price is set above marginal cost by a monopolistic competitor, so that the level of output is suboptimal. On the other hand, since we expect monopolistic competitors to face quite elastic demand curves, the deviation of output from the competitive level might not be too great.

A related issue is that a monopolistic competitor, as shown in Exhibit 11.10, does not produce at the minimum point of its average cost curve. Indeed, it cannot do so, since in long-run equilibrium it produces at a point of tangency between its average cost curve and its downward-sloping demand curve. It follows that if a monopolistically competitive industry were replaced by a competitive one, the same output could be produced at lower cost.

It is sometimes argued that monopolistically competitive firms tend to invest more in advertising and other methods of luring each other's customers than is socially optimal. Insofar as such practices simply shift customers from one firm to another without changing the nature of the products that are sold, their costs represent unnecessary social losses.

Balanced against all of this is the observation that monopolistically competitive industries do provide consumers with something that competitive industries do not, namely, differentiated products. Although Burger King and McDonald's are already similar, many people would be unhappy if one of them became exactly like the other.

How can we weigh the inefficiencies associated with monopolistic competition on the one hand against the benefits of product differentiation on the other? Although many economists have strong beliefs about the relative importance of these phenomena, there is not yet any general theory available that allows us to answer such a question in a definitive way.

| EXHIBIT 11.11 | Ice Cream Vendors on a Beach |
|---|---|

If the vendors start out in the locations shown, each will move toward the center in an attempt to gain more customers. The equilibrium is reached when they are located right next to each other and can move no farther.

## The Economics of Location

Depending on market conditions, firms may choose either to exaggerate or to minimize their differences. An amusing example involves two ice cream vendors on a beach. Suppose that the beach is a straight line one mile long and that bathers are distributed evenly along it. There are two ice cream vendors, indistinguishable except for location, and each bather will patronize the nearest vendor. Where will the vendors locate?

Exhibit 11.11 shows the initial positions of the vendors. Given these positions, vendor A will soon realize that she can have more customers if she moves to the right. As long as she stays to the left of vendor B, she will retain all of the customers to her own left and she can acquire more by moving a bit to the right. Similarly, vendor B has much to gain and nothing to lose by shifting to the left. The only possible equilibrium is for the two vendors to locate right next to each other, exactly at the half-mile mark!

**Exercise 11.7** What would happen if the vendors started out next to each other but somewhere other than at the halfway point?

Perhaps this example provides a metaphor for the behavior of the two major U.S. political parties. With voters distributed on a continuum from left to right, and voting for the party "closest" to themselves, the parties will behave just as the ice cream vendors do. Do you believe that this metaphor captures a significant feature of reality?

## Summary

This chapter surveys a number of examples and models in which firms exercise or attempt to exercise various degrees of monopoly power.

Horizontal mergers can both reduce production costs and create monopoly power, and therefore they have ambiguous welfare consequences. Vertical mergers can have the effect of reducing the exercise of monopoly power, since no monopolist would want to extract monopoly profits from one of its own subsidiaries.

In order to eliminate rivals, a firm might engage in the practice of predatory pricing, or it might attempt a strategy of buying out its rivals. Each of these strategies is severely limited. In the case of predatory pricing, there is the threat that rivals will resurface after prices are raised. In the case of buy outs, new rivals are attracted to the industry by the prospect of being bought out.

When the firms in an industry can collude, they increase producers' surplus and thus can improve each firm's welfare through a system of side payments. However, as in the Prisoner's Dilemma, each individual firm has an incentive to cheat. The reason is that a cartel sets price higher than marginal cost, so that each firm will want to sell more than it is supposed to under the cartel agreement. Therefore, cartels tend to break down unless there is a good enforcement mechanism.

In addition to its other purposes, government regulation can serve as an enforcement mechanism for a cartel. Regulations restrict output in many ways. Professional licensing, minimum quality standards, minimum prices, advertising restrictions, and blue laws can all serve to restrict output and keep prices high. However, there is some evidence that the power of regulators to alter market conditions is sometimes less than it seems.

In contestable markets, entry and exit are costless. Even when there is only one firm in a contestable market, that firm must earn zero profits because of the threat of entry.

The Cournot and Bertrand models apply to oligopolies with a fixed number of firms. In the Cournot model, firms take their rivals' output as given and end up producing more than the monopoly quantity but less than the competitive quantity. In the Bertrand model, firms take their rivals' prices as given and end up producing the competitive quantity.

Under monopolistic competition, firms produce differentiated products. Each firm's product is unique but is similar to those of other firms. Thus, each firm faces a downward-sloping but nevertheless quite elastic demand curve. In the long run, entry forces profits to zero, which implies that firms must *not* be operating at the point of minimum average cost. The negative welfare consequences of this must be balanced against the gains to consumers from having a wide variety of product options, but economists have developed no good general theory of the welfare consequences of monopolistic competition.

# Author Commentary   www.cengage.com/economics/landsburg

**AC1.** For more information on Barnes & Noble *v.* Amazon, read this article.

**AC2.** For more information on Microsoft *v.* Netscape, read this article.

**AC3.** Just as sellers can cartelize to keep prices up, so buyers can cartelize to keep prices down. Ordinarily, keeping prices down is an end in itself. However, the National Football League attempts to control players' salaries, not just for its own sake, but also to prevent a few teams from dominating the league. Does it work?

**AC4.** Regulators have an incentive to create the need for more regulators. For an application of the same principle to judges, read this article.

# Review Questions

**R1.** What is the distinction between a horizontal merger and a vertical merger?

**R2.** Under what circumstances is a horizontal merger welfare-improving?

**R3.** What are some of the advantages and disadvantages to a firm in engaging in predatory pricing? In a strategy of buying out rivals?

**R4.**  Explain why resale price maintenance might be expected to benefit consumers.

**R5.**  Why do both prisoners confess in the Prisoner's Dilemma? In what sense is the outcome not Pareto-optimal? How could both prisoners be made better off?

**R6.**  Explain the analogy between the Prisoner's Dilemma and the breakdown of cartels.

**R7.**  Why might the firms in an industry want to be regulated?

**R8.**  What determines the number of firms in a contestable market?

**R9.**  Explain carefully how output is determined in a Cournot oligopoly.

**R10.**  Explain carefully how price is determined in a Bertrand oligopoly.

**R11.**  What disturbing feature do the Bertrand and Cournot models have in common?

**R12.**  Explain carefully how price and output are determined under monopolistic competition.

**R13.**  Explain why, in a long-run monopolistically competitive equilibrium, average cost is never minimized.

# Numerical Exercises

**N1.**  Suppose that a monopoly steel producer produces steel at zero marginal costs and sells to a monopoly automaker at a price $P_{steel}$. The automaker has no costs other than the cost of steel, which is converted into cars at the rate of one ton of steel to one car. There is no other way to produce a car than to use a ton of steel. The demand for cars is given by $Q_{cars} = 100 - P_{cars}$.

    **a.**  For a given price of steel, what quantity of cars will the automaker produce in order to maximize profits? (*Hint:* The function $-Q_2 + kQ$, with $k$ constant, is maximized at $Q = k/2$.)

    **b.**  What is the equation for the automaker's demand curve for steel?

    **c.**  How much steel is produced? At what price? How many cars are produced? At what price?

    **d.**  If the steel producer acquires ownership of the automaker, how many cars are produced? At what price?

**N2.**  Suppose that Microsoft is the only producer of operating systems and Netscape is the only producer of Web browsers. Suppose also that nobody wants an operating system without a Web browser and nobody wants a Web browser without an operating system. Suppose that both firms produce at zero marginal cost and that the demand for a package consisting of an operating system and a browser is given by $Q = 100 - P$.

    **a.**  Suppose that Microsoft and Netscape take each others' prices as given. What is the price of an operating system? What is the price of a browser?

    **b.**  Suppose instead that Microsoft first announces a price for its operating system; then Netscape takes this price as given and sets a price for its browser. Now what is the price of an operating system? What is the price of a browser?

    **c.** Suppose that Microsoft merges with Netscape. Now what is the price for a package consisting of an operating system and a browser?

    **d.** Suppose instead that Microsoft sells consumers a package consisting of a operating system and a Netscape browser and pays Netscape a royalty for each package that it sells. What royalty does Netscape charge and what price do consumers pay for the package?

**N3.** Dr. Miles is a monopolist who sells a type of patent medicine through competitive retailers. The demand curve for this patent medicine is given by $Q = 100 - 2P$, where $P$ is the price and $Q$ is the number of bottles sold.

    **a.** If Dr. Miles has zero marginal cost, how many bottles of medicine will she sell and at what price? Calculate the consumers' surplus. Calculate Dr. Miles's producer's surplus.

    **b.** Now suppose that retailers are able to provide their customers with valuable services by explaining how the medicine is to be used, what ailments it is effective against, and so on. By incurring a cost of $C$ in time and effort per bottle sold, the retailer can provide services that consumers value at $V$ per bottle sold, where $V$ is given by $V = 5C - C^2$. What is the socially optimal amount of service per bottle for retailers to offer? What is the cost of this service?

    **c.** Now suppose that retailers who offer services do not sell any additional medicine, because customers accept the services and then shop elsewhere, buying from a cut-rate supplier who offers no services. To combat this, Dr. Miles institutes a fair trade agreement under which she will sell at a wholesale price of $P_0$ but retailers must charge a retail price of $P_1$. Retailers have no other costs. Explain why retailers will incur costs of service equal to $C = P_1 - P_0$. What is the socially optimal value for $C$?

    **d.** Taking $C$ as given, write the equation of the new demand curve that retailers face after Dr. Miles institutes fair trade. Write the equation of the new demand curve Dr. Miles faces. In view of her wanting to face the highest possible demand curve, what value will Dr. Miles choose for $C$?

    **e.** Using your answers to part (d), calculate the new price $P_0$ that Dr. Miles will charge, the new quantity sold, the new consumers' surplus, and the new producer's surplus.

**N4.** (This is a challenging problem which requires some calculus.) Only one road goes from Hereville to Thereville, and along that road you must cross two toll bridges. The number of travelers from Hereville to Thereville is given by $Q = 100 - P$ where $P$ is the price of travel; that is, $P$ is the sum of the two toll bridges.

    **a.** If one monopolist owns both bridges, how much does he charge to cross?

    **b.** If each bridge is owned by a separate monopolist, how much does each one charge?

    **c.** Is it better for the consumer if the bridges are owned by a single monopolist or by competing monopolists?

    **d.** Would you rather buy your computer operating system and your word processing software from a single monopolist or from competing monopolists? Why?

# Problem Set

1.  Consider a competitive industry where the demand and supply curves are straight lines of equal absolute value and the supply curve goes through the origin. If all of the firms in the industry merge into one, the new firm will be able to produce at zero marginal cost. On efficiency grounds, should the merger be allowed?

2.  Suppose that a monopoly supplier selling in two distinct markets wants to price discriminate. How might the monopolist benefit from a vertical merger?

3.  Candy makers sometimes print retail prices directly on the wrappers. Is this a form of resale price maintenance? If so, what are its benefits? If not, what is the reason for the practice?

4.  Suppose that a monopoly firm introduces a policy of resale price maintenance. Under the "special services" theory of resale price maintenance, would the firm's output increase or decrease? Conversely, suppose that the purpose of the resale price maintenance is to enforce a cartel among the dealers. Now would the firm's output increase or decrease?

5.  Many firms employ salespeople who are assigned exclusive territories. No salesperson may enter another's territory and attempt to sell the manufacturer's product there. Construct a theory to explain why firms adopt this practice. Does your theory suggest what kinds of products will be sold in this way and what kinds will not be?

6.  Suppose that bicycle dealers serve their customers by providing fancy showrooms and knowledgeable salesforces to answer questions, but that only a small number of customers value these services. Show that in this case, resale price maintenance can cause an increase in bicycle sales but a *decrease* in social welfare.[30]

7.  Suppose that airplane flights are provided at a constant marginal cost $P_C$. (That is, the marginal cost curve in the airline industry is flat at the price $P_C$.) If there were a single monopoly airline, it would sell tickets at the higher price $P_M$. Suppose that the government requires all airlines to charge the price $P_M$ and forbids new entry into the airline industry.

    a.  Show the consumers' surplus, the producers' surplus, and the deadweight loss.

    b.  Now suppose the airlines discover that they can make themselves more attractive to customers by offering costly "extras" ranging from in-flight movies to the scheduling of frequent flights that better accommodate travelers' schedules. By how much does the marginal cost curve rise and why?

    c.  In part (b), what happens to the demand for airline flights? Recalculate the consumers' and producers' surpluses.

    d.  In part (c), is it possible that the net social gain could be greater than it is under competition? (*Hint:* Which additional services would be offered under competition and which would not?)

8.  **True or False:** Resale price maintenance can be good for consumers because it means there will be more dealer services. Thus, if the marginal value of dealer services decreases rapidly, then the benefits of resale price maintenance are reduced.

---

[30] This is a hard problem. It is based on an analysis by W. S. Comanor in "Vertical Price Fixing, Vertical Market Restrictions, and the New Antitrust Policy," *Harvard Law Review* 98 (1985): 984–1002.

9. Offer some alternative theories to explain why manufacturers want fair trade. How might you go about testing your theories vis-á-vis the one outlined in the text? Do they have different implications about what sorts of products might be sold under these conditions, or about what industry structures are most conducive to fair trade?

10. Can you think of a reason why some manufacturers might want to set a *maximum* retail price for their products, and forbid sellers from charging more than the preset maximum?

11. The firms that sell personal computers have never banded together to form a cartel. **True or False:** We may infer from this that at least one firm would fail to benefit from a successful cartel.

12. In many industries workers are required to belong to a union and to pay union dues, even if they would prefer not to. **True or False:** Workers would be better off if each one could choose whether to belong to the union.

13. **True or False:** When all firms in an industry charge the same price, this is evidence of collusion.

14. In the example of Exhibit 11.1, suppose that the firms merge, but the market is contestable. What quantity does the merged firm produce, and at what price? Do any new firms actually enter?

15. Suppose that there are exactly $N$ identical firms in an industry, all with flat marginal cost curves. Industry demand is linear. How much does each firm produce, compared with the competitive quantity, under the Cournot assumption that each takes its rivals' outputs as given? How much does the industry produce? What happens to industry output as $N$ gets large? (*Hint:* Follow carefully the argument that is given in the text for the case $N = 2$.)

16. Consider an industry where there are two firms having identical flat marginal cost curves. Price and output in the industry are determined as follows: First Firm 1 announces how much it will produce, then Firm 2 decides how much to produce, then the industry's output is sold at a price read off the industry demand curve.

    a. Is the industry output greater or less than it would be under Cournot behavior?

    b. Which firm is better off: Firm 1 or Firm 2?

17. Suppose there are three ice cream vendors on the beach depicted in Exhibit 11.11. How will they locate themselves in equilibrium?

18. Suppose there are four ice cream vendors on the beach depicted in Exhibit 11.11. How will they locate themselves in equilibrium? What can you say if there are five vendors? What if there are more than five?

19. a. Suppose that two ice cream vendors are located on a circular beach that goes all the way around a lake. How will they locate themselves in equilibrium?

    b. Suppose instead that there are three ice cream vendors on the same circular beach. How will they locate themselves in equilibrium?

# CHAPTER 12

# The Theory of Games

If you had to be a pig, would you rather be a strong pig or a weak pig? Sometimes it pays to be weak.

The biologist John Maynard Smith reports an experiment where two pigs are kept in a box with a lever at one end and a food dispenser at the other.[1] When the lever is pushed, food appears at the dispenser.

If the weak pig pushes the lever, the strong pig waits by the dispenser and eats all the food. Even if the weak pig races to the dispenser and arrives before the food is gone, the strong pig pushes the weak pig away. The weak pig is smart enough to figure this out, so it never bothers pressing the lever in the first place.

On the other hand, if the strong pig pushes the lever, the weak pig waits by the dispenser and gets most of the food. But the strong pig can race to the dispenser and shove the weak pig aside before it has entirely finished eating and then help itself to the leftovers. This makes it worthwhile for the strong pig to push the lever.

The outcome is that the strong pig does all of the work, and the weak pig does most of the eating.

Strategic situations can yield surprising outcomes. The Prisoner's Dilemma of Chapter 11 provides one example; the pigs in a box provide another. In this chapter, we will study the **theory of games** (or **game theory** for short), which allows us to catalog many of those outcomes and to discuss both their positive and their normative aspects.

**Theory of games or game theory**

A system for studying strategic behavior.

## 12.1 Game Matrices

In this section, we will introduce game matrices and show how they can be used to systematically analyze strategic situations.

### Pigs in a Box

Consider the pigs from the introduction to this chapter. We represent the pigs' dilemma by a **game matrix** as in Exhibit 12.1. Across the top we list the possible strategies of the

**Game matrix**

A diagram showing one player's strategy choices across the top, the other player's along the left side, and the corresponding outcomes in the appropriate boxes.

---

[1] John Maynard Smith, *Evolution and the Theory of Games* (Cambridge, MA: Cambridge University Press, 1982).

**EXHIBIT 12.1**    **Pigs in a Box**

Strong Pig's Strategy

|  | Push lever | Wait by dispenser |
|---|---|---|
| **Push lever** | Strong pig gets 90 calories<br><br>Weak pig gets –10 calories | Strong pig gets 100 calories<br><br>Weak pig gets –10 calories |
| **Wait by dispenser** | Strong pig gets 15 calories<br><br>Weak pig gets 75 calories | Strong pig gets 0 calories<br><br>Weak pig gets 0 calories |

Weak Pig's Strategy

The dispenser gives 100 calories worth of food, and it requires 10 calories to push the lever. If both pigs arrive at the dispenser simultaneously, only the strong pig eats. But if the weak pig waits at the dispenser while the strong pig pushes the lever, he can eat ¾ of the food before the strong pig arrives. The game matrix shows the pigs' rewards for each combination of strategies.

The lower left-hand box is the only Nash equilibrium. Starting from any other box, at least one of the pigs would want to change his strategy.

strong pig, who can either push the lever or wait by the food dispenser. Along the left side we list the possible strategies of the weak pig, who has the same options.

In each of the four boxes of the matrix we show the consequences of the pigs' behavior. We assume that the food dispenser yields 100 calories worth of food and that pushing the lever burns 10 calories. We assume also that pigs care only about calories (which is presumably why they are called pigs).

If both pigs decide to push the lever, then they both run to the dispenser, where the strong pig shoves the weak pig aside and eats all of the food. The net gain is 90 calories for the strong pig (100 calories worth of food minus 10 calories burned pushing the lever) and *minus* 10 calories for the weak pig, who pushes the lever and runs but gets no food. The upper left-hand box in the exhibit shows this outcome.

If the strong pig waits by the dispenser while the weak pig pushes the lever, the strong pig gets all 100 calories worth of food and the weak pig loses 10 calories, as shown in the upper right-hand box.

If the strong pig pushes the lever while the weak pig waits by the dispenser, the weak pig is able to consume 75 calories before the strong pig arrives and takes the remaining 25, leaving him with a net gain of 15 after subtracting the 10 that he burns by pushing the lever. This is the outcome in the lower left-hand box.

And finally, if both pigs wait by the dispenser, then nobody gets to eat anything at all, as indicated in the lower right-hand box.

## Choosing Strategies

In the introduction to this chapter, we argued that the pigs will end up in the lower left-hand box, which is to say that the strong pig will push the lever while the weak pig waits by the dispenser and gets most of the food. Let us see how we can use the game matrix to reach this conclusion systematically.

When the strong pig selects a strategy, he decides which column of the matrix both pigs will occupy. When the weak pig selects a strategy, he decides on a row. There are four possible outcomes, represented by the four boxes of the game matrix. For each outcome, we can ask this question: If this *were* the outcome, would either pig want to change his mind? If one or both pigs *would* want to change their minds, then we can rule out that outcome as a possibility.

For example, suppose for the moment that we are in the upper left-hand box, where both pigs push the lever. If the strong pig changes his mind and waits by the dispenser, we move to the upper right-hand box, while if the weak pig changes his mind we move to the lower left-hand box. Would the strong pig want to change his mind? The answer is yes: By moving from the upper left to the upper right he gains 10 calories. *This is already enough to rule out the upper left-hand box.*

Would the weak pig want to change his mind? The answer is yes again: By moving from the upper left to the lower left he gains 10 calories (or more precisely, he avoids losing 10 calories). This by itself would *also* be enough to rule out the upper left. So the upper left is ruled out for each of two separate reasons: If that were the outcome, the strong pig would change his mind *and* the weak pig would change his mind.

Next suppose that we are in the upper right-hand box. Would the strong pig want to change his mind and move to the upper left? No; he prefers the upper right, gaining 100 calories instead of 90. Would the weak pig want to change his mind and move to the lower right? Yes; he can then avoid losing 10 calories. So we rule out the upper right on the grounds that the weak pig would change his mind.

What about the lower right? The weak pig would not want to change rows, but the strong pig *would* want to change columns. Because the strong pig wants to change his mind, this outcome can also be ruled out.

**Exercise 12.1** In the lower-right corner, how much would the weak pig lose by changing rows? How much would the strong pig gain by changing columns?

Finally, consider the lower left. Starting from here, the weak pig has the option to move up a box, reducing his calorie intake from 75 to −10; this option is not attractive. The strong pig has the option to move to the right, reducing his net calorie intake from 15 to 0; this is not attractive either. Neither pig changes his mind, and the pigs remain in the lower left-hand box.

Any outcome that survives this process of elimination is called a Nash equilibrium outcome. An outcome is a Nash equilibrium if neither player would want to deviate from it, taking his opponent's behavior as given. The phrase *taking his opponent's behavior as given* is an important one here. Starting in the lower left, the strong pig *would* want to deviate provided he thought that for some crazy reason the weak pig was going to deviate too and he could end up in the upper right. But as long as the strong pig assumes that the weak pig is going to stick to his strategy of waiting by the food dispenser, he has no desire to change his own strategy.

**Nash equilibrium**

An outcome from which neither player would want to deviate, taking the other player's behavior as given.

## The Prisoner's Dilemma Revisited

The Prisoner's Dilemma of Chapter 11 is already represented by a game matrix, which we reproduce in Exhibit 12.2. We argued in Chapter 11 that the prisoners land in the upper left-hand box. Let us confirm this conclusion using the techniques we've just developed.

Suppose the prisoners were in the upper right-hand box, with B confessing and A not confessing. If B switches strategies, we move down a row, increasing B's prison

**EXHIBIT 12.2**    **The Prisoner's Dilemma**

**Prisoner A's Strategy**

|  | Confess | Not confess |
|---|---|---|
| **Confess** | A gets 5 years<br>B gets 5 years | A gets 10 years<br>B gets 1 year |
| **Not confess** | A gets 1 year<br>B gets 10 years | A gets 2 years<br>B gets 2 years |

**Prisoner B's Strategy**

The prisoners face the same dilemma as in Chapter 11. The only Nash equilibrium is in the upper left-hand corner; this is also the only square that is not Pareto-optimal.

term; therefore B does *not* want to switch. But if A switches strategies, then we move a column to the left, where A's prison term falls from 10 years to 5; therefore A *does* want to switch. Because at least one of the prisoners wants to switch, the upper right-hand box is *not* a Nash equilibrium.

Dangerous Curve

It's worth noting that the pigs in a box were out to *maximize* their calorie intake, while the prisoners are out to *minimize* their jail sentences. In all of the other examples of this chapter, the goal will be to maximize outcomes (as the pigs do) rather than to minimize them (as the prisoners do).

**Exercise 12.2** Explain why the lower left-hand box and the lower right-hand box are not Nash equilibria. In each case, which prisoner wants to switch?

## Dominant Strategies

In Chapter 11, we pointed out that Prisoner A would want to confess *regardless* of his beliefs about Prisoner B's behavior. If Prisoner B is known to be confessing (placing us in the top row), then Prisoner A has a choice between getting a sentence of 5 years by confessing or getting a sentence of 10 years by not confessing. If Prisoner B is known to be not confessing (placing us in the bottom row), then Prisoner A has a choice between getting a sentence of 1 year by confessing or getting a sentence of 2 years by not confessing. Either way, Prisoner A prefers to confess.

**Dominant strategy**

A strategy that a player would want to follow regardless of the other player's behavior.

Confessing in the Prisoner's Dilemma is called a **dominant strategy** for Prisoner A, because he would want to follow that strategy regardless of what Prisoner B was up to. Confessing is also a dominant strategy for Prisoner B. When both prisoners follow their dominant strategies, we reach the Nash equilibrium outcome where both confess.

## Pigs in a Box Revisited

Sometimes a player has no dominant strategy. Let us return to the pigs of Exhibit 12.1. Should the strong pig push the lever or wait by the dispenser?

It depends on what he thinks the weak pig is doing. If the weak pig can be counted on to push the lever, then the strong pig should wait by the dispenser; but if the weak pig waits by the dispenser, then the strong pig should push the lever.

We can see this in the game matrix. If the weak pig pushes the lever we are in the first row. The strong pig can push (for a gain of 90) or wait (for a gain of 100); it is better to wait (that is, to choose the second column). But if the weak pig waits by the dispenser, we are in the second row. The strong pig can push (for a gain of 15) or wait (for a gain of 0); it is better to push (that is, to choose the first column).

Before the strong pig can choose his strategy, he'd like to know what the weak pig is going to do. This means that the strong pig has no dominant strategy. If he had a dominant strategy, he would not need to inquire about the weak pig's behavior before deciding on his own.

The weak pig, by contrast, *does* have a dominant strategy: He should wait by the dispenser regardless of how the strong pig behaves. If the strong pig pushes (choosing the first column), then the weak pig can push (for a gain of $-10$) or wait (for a gain of 75); it is better to wait (that is, to choose the second row). If the strong pig waits (choosing the second column), then the weak pig can push (for a gain of $-10$) or wait (for a gain of 0); it is still better to wait (that is, to choose the second row).

## Dominant Strategies versus Nash Equilibria

When both players have dominant strategies, as in the Prisoner's Dilemma, there is one and only one Nash equilibrium. In the Nash equilibrium, both players play their dominant strategies.

But Nash equilibria can exist even when one or both players have no dominant strategy. In the "pigs in a box" example of Exhibit 12.1, the strong pig has no dominant strategy, but the lower-left corner is still a Nash equilibrium.

To keep track of the differences in these concepts, continue to focus on the pigs. We know that it is a dominant strategy for the weak pig to wait by the dispenser; in terms of the game matrix this means that the weak pig will always choose the second row.

Now suppose that we are in the lower-left box (where the strong pig is pushing the lever) and consider the following two questions:

1. Would the strong pig want to change strategies, given that he knows the weak pig will choose the second row?

2. Might the strong pig want to change strategies if he wasn't sure what the weak pig will do?

The answer to question 1 is no. Once the second row is chosen, the strong pig certainly prefers the first column to the second. Neither the strong pig nor the weak pig wants to change, so the lower left is a Nash equilibrium.

The answer to question 2 is yes. If the strong pig thought that the weak pig had (foolishly) chosen the first row, then he would want to switch to the second column. His choice of columns depends on what he thinks the weak pig is doing, so he has no dominant strategy.

## The Battle of the Sexes

Exhibit 12.3 shows a game that is usually called the *Battle of the Sexes*.

Fred prefers to go to boxing matches and Ethel prefers to go to the opera, but they both like doing things together. If they go their separate ways, both are miserable. The

EXHIBIT **12.3**    **The Battle of the Sexes**

**Fred's Strategy**

|  | Boxing match | Opera |
|---|---|---|
| **Boxing match** | Fred gets 5 / Ethel gets 3 | Fred gets 0 / Ethel gets 0 |
| **Opera** | Fred gets 1 / Ethel gets 1 | Fred gets 3 / Ethel gets 5 |

**Ethel's Strategy**

Fred likes boxing and Ethel likes opera, but they both like to be together. The upper-left and lower-right corners are Nash equilibria.

game matrix puts numerical values on Fred and Ethel's happiness (which economists sometimes call *utility*). If Fred goes to the opera while Ethel goes to the boxing match, they each earn zero units of utility; if Fred goes to the boxing match while Ethel goes to the opera, they each earn 1 unit.

But if Fred and Ethel attend the boxing match together, then Fred earns 5 units of utility while Ethel earns 3 just by being with Fred; if they attend the opera together, then Ethel earns 5 units of utility and Fred earns 3 just by being with Ethel.

Does Fred have a dominant strategy in this game? If he thinks that Ethel is going to the boxing match, he prefers to be at the boxing match, while if he thinks that Ethel is going to the opera, he prefers to be at the opera. This means that he has no dominant strategy. Neither does Ethel.

What about Nash equilibria? Suppose that Fred and Ethel both go to the boxing match (the upper left-hand corner). Would Fred want to switch to the opera, knowing that Ethel is going to the boxing match? The answer is no. And would Ethel want to switch to the opera knowing that Fred is going to the boxing match? No again. So this outcome is a Nash equilibrium.

The lower right-hand corner (both going to the opera) is also a Nash equilibrium. But the two outcomes where Fred and Ethel go their separate ways are *not* Nash equilibria, because in either of these situations both Fred and Ethel would want to switch.

Dangerous
Curve

Suppose that Fred goes to the boxing match while Ethel goes to the opera (the lower left-hand box). Then, given Ethel's plans, Fred prefers to switch, and, given Fred's plans, Ethel prefers to switch. You might wonder whether Ethel would reason a little more deeply. "I know that as long as I am going to the opera, Fred will want to switch to the opera as well, so I think that I'll just head over to the opera and wait for him to follow along." It is true that Ethel might think this way, but such reasoning is not relevant to the question of whether this outcome is a Nash equilibrium. Given Fred's intention to attend the boxing match, Ethel does want to switch. This rules out the lower left-hand corner as a Nash equilibrium.

From the lower left-hand box (or from the upper right-hand box) both Fred and Ethel want to switch (each taking the other's behavior as given). This is more information than necessary to rule out these boxes as Nash equilibria; as long as at least one of Fred and Ethel wants to switch, the box is ruled out.

Dangerous
Curve

## The Copycat Game

Dot's brother Ditto is a copycat. If Dot watches television, Ditto wants to watch television, too. If Dot goes out to play in the yard, then so does Ditto.

Dot, on the other hand, always wants to be by herself. She's happy watching television as long as Ditto is out in the yard, and happy in the yard as long as Ditto is watching television.

The matrix in Exhibit 12.4 shows Dot and Ditto's game. As long as they are doing something together, Ditto gets 5 units of utility and Dot gets 0. As long as they are apart, Ditto gets 0 units of utility and Dot gets 5.

Are there any Nash equilibria in this game? Consider the upper left-hand corner. If Dot and Ditto are both watching television, Ditto sees no reason to switch columns—but Dot wants to switch rows by going out to the yard. So the upper left-hand corner is not a Nash equilibrium. Neither is any other corner.

**Exercise 12.3** Explain why the upper-right, lower-left, and lower-right corners are not Nash equilibria.

## Nash Equilibrium as a Solution Concept

A **solution concept** is a rule for predicting how games will turn out when they are played. Nash equilibrium is one of the most popular solution concepts; that is, economists like to posit that when people play games, they end up in Nash equilibria. There are, however, some reasons to be uncomfortable with Nash equilibrium as a solution concept.

**Solution concept**

A rule for predicting how games will turn out.

---

EXHIBIT **12.4**    **The Copycat Game**

|  |  | Dot's Strategy | |
|---|---|---|---|
|  |  | Watch television | Play in yard |
| **Ditto's Strategy** | Watch television | Dot gets 0 / Ditto gets 5 | Dot gets 5 / Ditto gets 0 |
|  | Play in yard | Dot gets 5 / Ditto gets 0 | Dot gets 0 / Ditto gets 5 |

Dot is happy as long as she is alone; Ditto is happy as long as he is with Dot. There is no Nash equilibrium in this game.

One problem is that some games, like the Battle of the Sexes, have more than one Nash equilibrium. There is no way to predict which Nash equilibrium is more likely.

Another problem is that some games, like the Copycat Game, have no Nash equilibrium at all. If Dot and Ditto start out watching television together, Dot will go out to the yard, whereupon Ditto will follow her out, whereupon Dot will come back in, whereupon Ditto will follow her in, whereupon. . . . There is nothing in the Nash equilibrium concept to tell us where this process will end.

## Example: The Price of Car Insurance

A 19-year-old male who drives a five-year-old Chevrolet Caprice will pay about $1,800 a year for car insurance if he lives in Columbus, Ohio. That same 19-year-old male will pay about $2,500 if he lives in Detroit, $4,000 if he lives in Philadelphia, and $5,000 if he lives in Los Angeles! What can account for such enormous differences in price?

In a provocatively titled essay,[2] two economists have drawn attention to the "game" where each driver decides whether to buy insurance. They argue that observed price differences can be attributed to multiple Nash equilibria in this game.

Suppose, for example, that very few drivers buy insurance. Then insured drivers, when they have accidents, will usually have to collect from their own insurance companies—the other party will typically be uninsured. Therefore insurance becomes very expensive, so few drivers want to buy it. In other words, uninsured motorists cause high insurance prices, and high insurance prices cause uninsured motorists. This is an example of a Nash equilibrium: Everyone behaves rationally, taking everyone else's behavior as given.

On the other hand, suppose that most drivers buy insurance. Then insurance becomes cheaper and therefore, most drivers want to buy it. Again, we have a Nash equilibrium.

When a game has more than one Nash equilibrium, it's difficult to predict which of the equilibria will actually occur. But once an equilibrium is reached, it tends to remain stable. So if, for any reason, Columbus fell into the "bad" equilibrium while Philadelphia fell into the "good" equilibrium, it's not surprising that these equilibria would maintain themselves over time.

## Example: Social Status

The average American earns almost $30,000 a year, according to official statistics, while the average citizen of Mali earns about $100. The latter figure is surely misleadingly low, but the fact remains that there are enormous differences in income across countries. No economist has succeeded in giving a complete account of those differences. Most partial explanations rely on differences in tastes (e.g., people with a strong preference for saving will be wealthier in the long run) and differences in available technology. But recently, a number of economists have pointed to the possibility of multiple equilibria.

---

[2] E. Smith and R. Wright, "Why is Automobile Insurance in Philadelphia So Damn Expensive?" *American Economic Review* 82 (1992), 756–772.

One intriguing story is that the relevant game is the mating game—the "game" in which people select marriage partners. To see how this can be relevant, let's imagine two stylized extremes.[3]

First, imagine a society where the richest people get the most desirable mates. In that society, people will be motivated to save, not just to acquire better mates for themselves, but also to acquire better mates for their children. And as long as all your neighbors play that strategy, you'll want to play it, too. In other words, we have a Nash equilibrium.

Now imagine a society where mates are allocated according to social status, which is inherited from your parents independent of wealth. In such a society, low-status people might try to attract high-status mates by acquiring a lot of wealth. But this strategy is discouraged if it dooms your children to even lower status. So *if* the "rules of the game" are that children of such "mixed marriages" have the lowest status of all, then there can be a Nash equilibrium in which people save very little.

Notice that even if the two societies are populated by identical people, their incomes will evolve very differently. A society that lands in either of the two equilibria will tend to remain there.

These highly stylized examples are far too simplistic to explain all the differences between the United States and Mali, but they do demonstrate that it's possible for multiple Nash equilibria to occur in this context and therefore that multiple equilibria might play an important role in understanding why some countries are so much wealthier than others.

## Mixed Strategies

The Copycat Game has no Nash equilibrium. How might we expect Dot and Ditto to select their strategies in this game?

If Ditto can predict Dot's behavior, he will simply mimic it; therefore, it is important for Dot to keep Ditto off guard. One way for her to do this is to flip a coin. On heads, she watches television and on tails she plays in the yard. Because her behavior is now totally unpredictable, Ditto can do no better than to flip his own coin and hope that it lands the same way Dot's does.

Notice that it is important to both Dot and Ditto that their coins be *fair coins,* with heads and tails equally probable. If Dot's coin is weighted so that she is more likely to watch television than to play outside, then Ditto will throw his coin away and watch television, giving him a better than even chance to win the game. And likewise, if Ditto's coin is weighted, then Dot has an opportunity to discard her own coin and follow a strategy that puts the odds on her side.

The Copycat Game is quite symmetric, in the sense that there is always a "winner" with 5 utilities and a "loser" with 0. In a game with less symmetry, Dot and Ditto might prefer to flip weighted coins, sacrificing some unpredictability in exchange for improving the chances of their preferred outcomes. We can view each possible weighting as an alternative strategy. (That is, "flip a fair coin" is one strategy; "flip a coin that comes up heads two-thirds of the time" is another; "flip a coin that comes up heads three-fourths

---

[3] The example to follow is based on H. Cole, G. Maulath, and A. Postlewaite, "Social Norms, Savings Behavior and Growth," *Journal of Political Economy* 100 (1992), 1092–1125.

**Mixed strategy**

A strategy that involves a random choice among pure strategies.

of the time" is still another.) We call these options mixed strategies, as opposed to the pure strategies illustrated in Exhibit 12.3. If mixed strategies are allowed, then it is possible to prove under quite general circumstances that a Nash equilibrium must exist.

**Pure strategy**

A single choice of row (or column) in the game matrix.

## Mixed Strategies in Sports

In the international tournaments organized by the World Rock Paper Scissors Society (yes, that's a real organization), nobody ever consistently plays "Rock." Instead, the best players are the least predictable players. In Nash equilibrium, everyone plays a mixed strategy—1/3 "Rock," 1/3 "Paper," and 1/3 "Scissors."

---

**Exercise 12.4** Explain why a strategy consisting of ½ "Rock," ¼ "Paper," and ¼ "Scissors" cannot be part of a Nash equilibrium.

---

Mixed strategies are common in more traditional sports as well. In baseball, pitchers want to be unpredictable—the pitcher who always throws a fastball will always face a batter who is prepared for a fastball. A football team that always passes will always face a defense that's prepared for a pass. In soccer, a kicker who always aims his penalty kicks in the same direction will always face a goalie who dives in that direction.

Recently, two economists[4] examined the strategies of championship tennis players. To keep it simple, they assumed that the server has just two options: Serve to the receiver's left or to the receiver's right. And the receiver has just two options: Prepare to receive the serve on the left or on the right. The payoffs depend on the particular strengths of particular players, so the associated game matrix depends on who's playing. The economists estimated the game matrices for various players, computed the Nash equilibrium mixed strategies, and examined the players' actual play. Their conclusion: The evidence is very strong that players do play just as the theory predicts.

## Pareto Optima

Nash equilibrium is a *positive* (as opposed to normative) concept; it is designed to predict what *will* happen as opposed to enabling us to discuss what *ought* to happen. In this section, we will discuss the normative side of game theory.

Look again at Fred and Ethel, who played the Battle of the Sexes Game in Exhibit 12.3; this game is reproduced in Exhibit 12.5. In Exhibit 12.5, each of the four outcomes has been labeled with a letter (from A through D) for easy reference.

Fred and Ethel disagree about the desirability of the various outcomes; for example, Fred thinks outcome A is better than outcome D, while Ethel thinks just the opposite. But there are certain things they both agree on. For example, both agree that outcome C (where Fred and Ethel each get 1) is better than outcome B (where they both get 0).

**Pareto improvement or Pareto-preferred**

A change to which nobody objects.

Because Fred and Ethel are unanimous in this judgment, we say that moving from B to C is a Pareto improvement, or that C is Pareto-preferred to B. In general, a change is a Pareto improvement if nobody objects to it.[5]

---

[4] Mark Walker and John Wooders, "Minimax Play at Wimbledon," *American Economic Review* 91 (2002): 1521–1538.

[5] In some books, the phrase *Pareto improvement* is reserved for a change to which nobody objects *and* at least one person prefers.

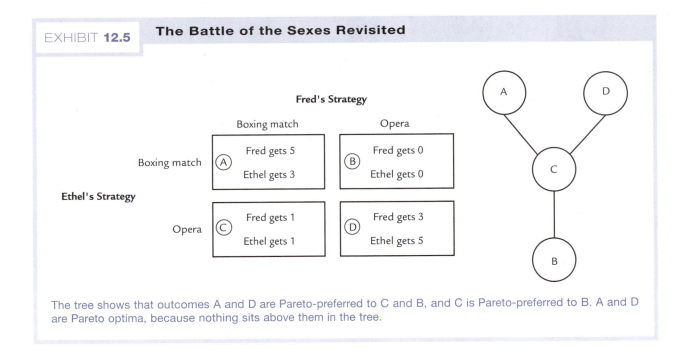

**EXHIBIT 12.5** **The Battle of the Sexes Revisited**

**Fred's Strategy**

|  | Boxing match | Opera |
|---|---|---|
| **Boxing match** (A) | Fred gets 5 / Ethel gets 3 | (B) Fred gets 0 / Ethel gets 0 |
| **Opera** (C) | Fred gets 1 / Ethel gets 1 | (D) Fred gets 3 / Ethel gets 5 |

**Ethel's Strategy**

The tree shows that outcomes A and D are Pareto-preferred to C and B, and C is Pareto-preferred to B. A and D are Pareto optima, because nothing sits above them in the tree.

Similarly, outcomes A and D are both Pareto improvements over B; nobody would object to a move from B to A or from B to D. A move from A to D is *not* a Pareto improvement, because Fred would object, and a move from D to A is not a Pareto improvement, because Ethel would object.

To the right of the game matrix in Exhibit 12.5, we have arranged the four outcomes in a "tree," where upward movements represent Pareto improvements. A, C, and D are all Pareto improvements over B, so A, C, and D all sit higher than B in the tree. Likewise, A and D both sit above C. But A sits neither above nor below D, because A is not a Pareto improvement over D and D is not a Pareto improvement over A.

We say that an outcome is **Pareto-optimal** if nothing sits above it in the tree. In this example, outcomes A and D are Pareto-optimal. From a normative point of view, we can think of outcomes that are *not* Pareto-optimal as "bad" outcomes. Outcome C, for example, is "bad" in the sense that both Fred and Ethel would prefer to climb higher in the tree, though they might disagree about whether it would be better to climb to A or to D.

Exhibit 12.6 revisits the pigs in a box from Exhibit 12.1. Here outcome B is Pareto-preferred to outcome A and outcome C is Pareto-preferred to outcome D, but there are no other instances of Pareto improvements. Thus, the "tree" breaks into two pieces, one of which shows B above A and one of which shows C above D. The Pareto-optimal outcomes are at the tops of the trees: B and C.

**Pareto-optimal**

An outcome that allows no possibility of a Pareto improvement.

**Exercise 12.5** Explain why B is not Pareto-preferred to C or D. Explain why C is not Pareto-preferred to A or B.

**Exercise 12.6** Build a tree for the Prisoner's Dilemma of Exhibit 12.2, keeping in mind that in this game, a shorter prison sentence is better than a long one. What are the Pareto optima in this game?

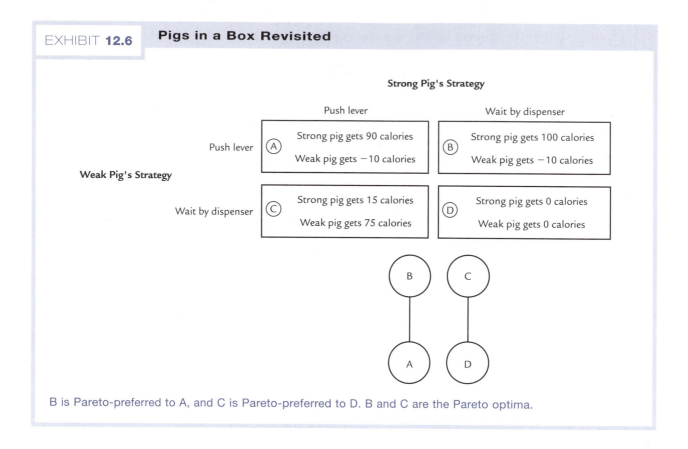

**EXHIBIT 12.6**   **Pigs in a Box Revisited**

B is Pareto-preferred to A, and C is Pareto-preferred to D. B and C are the Pareto optima.

## Pareto Optima versus Nash Equilibria

The pigs in Exhibit 12.1 have two Pareto optima (the lower left and upper right) but only one Nash equilibrium (the lower left). The Nash equilibrium happens to be one of the Pareto optima. But this is not always the case.

Consider the Prisoner's Dilemma of Exhibit 12.2. Here we have already seen that the only Nash equilibrium occurs in the upper left. This outcome is not Pareto-optimal, because a shift to the lower right would benefit both prisoners. In fact, the Nash equilibrium is the only outcome that is not Pareto-optimal.

**Exercise 12.7** Explain why the upper-right box in the Prisoner's Dilemma is Pareto-optimal.

**Exercise 12.8** Explain why the lower-left box in the Prisoner's Dilemma is Pareto-optimal.

In the Battle of the Sexes (Exhibit 12.3), both of the Nash equilibria (in the upper left and lower right) are Pareto-optimal. Starting in the upper left, any other square would be worse for Fred, and starting in the lower right, any other square would be worse for Ethel. Neither of the other two squares is Pareto-optimal.

**Exercise 12.9** Explain why neither of the other two squares is Pareto-optimal.

# 12.2 Sequential Games

You have probably played the game of "scissors, paper, rock." Each player chooses one of three strategies (scissors, paper, or rock) and then the winner is determined by these rules: Scissors "cut" paper, paper "covers" rock, and rock "smashes" scissors.

Usually both players are required to choose their strategies simultaneously. There is a good reason for this. If players took turns, the second player would always win. Once you know what your opponent is doing, it is easy to choose a strategy that will defeat him.

On the other hand, there are games where it pays to go first instead of second. Consider the Battle of the Sexes (Exhibit 12.3), where Fred and Ethel disagree about where to spend the evening but want above all to be together. If Fred moves first, by going to the boxing match and waiting for Ethel to follow along, then she is sure to do so, giving Fred his most preferred outcome. If Ethel moves first by going to the opera, Fred follows her and Ethel wins.

In the games of Section 12.1, we have always assumed that both players must choose their strategies simultaneously. In this section, we will assume instead that there is a first player, who chooses a column in the game matrix, and then a second player, who chooses a row. This will require a new way of thinking about the outcome. We will illustrate the new method with some examples.

## An Oligopoly Problem

Kodak and Fuji produce photographic film. Suppose that there are no other significant firms in this industry, so that Kodak and Fuji constitute an oligopoly. Industrywide profits depend on industrywide output according to the following table:

| Quantity (rolls of film per day) | Profits (dollars per day) |
| --- | --- |
| 100 | 32 |
| 125 | 35 |
| 150 | 30 |
| 175 | 21 |
| 200 | 10 |

Moreover, the profits are divided in proportion to the firms' output. Thus, if one firm produces 100 rolls of film while the other produces 75 rolls (a ratio of 4 to 3), then the $21 profit is divided in the same ratio ($12 for one firm and $9 for the other).

Exhibit 12.7 shows the game matrix, where each company can produce either 50, 75, or 100 rolls of film.

The outcome of this game depends very much on how the game is played. Suppose first that the companies are able to collude, maximizing their joint profits and splitting them afterward. Then they will produce 125 rolls of film, for the maximum possible profit of $35.

Suppose instead that each company takes its rival's output as given and chooses its own output accordingly. In the language of game theory, this means that the companies achieve a Nash equilibrium in Exhibit 12.7. In the language of Chapter 11, we called the same thing a *Cournot equilibrium*. A Cournot equilibrium is nothing but a Nash equilibrium in a game where each company chooses its quantity.

## EXHIBIT 12.7    An Oligopoly Problem

**Kodak's Strategy**

|  |  | 50 | 75 | 100 |
|---|---|---|---|---|
| **Fuji's Strategy** | 50 | Kodak gets 16<br><br>Fuji gets 16 | Kodak gets 21<br><br>Fuji gets 14 | Kodak gets 20<br><br>Fuji gets 10 |
|  | 75 | Kodak gets 14<br><br>Fuji gets 21 | Kodak gets 15<br><br>Fuji gets 15 | Kodak gets 12<br><br>Fuji gets 9 |
|  | 100 | Kodak gets 10<br><br>Fuji gets 20 | Kodak gets 9<br><br>Fuji gets 12 | Kodak gets 5<br><br>Fuji gets 5 |

The only Nash equilibrium is in the center square, where Kodak and Fuji each earn profits of $15. But if the game is played sequentially and Kodak moves first, then Kodak announces a policy of producing 100 rolls of film. Fuji's best response is to produce 50, leading to the upper right-hand square.

In Exhibit 12.7, the only Nash equilibrium is the center square. If each firm makes 75 rolls of film, neither wants to deviate. Kodak recognizes that dropping its output to 50 rolls would lower its profits from $15 to $14 and raising its output to 100 rolls would lower its profits from $15 to $12. Fuji recognizes the same thing.

**Exercise 12.10** Explain why no other square in Exhibit 12.7 is a Nash equilibrium.

But now let's change the rules of the game. Suppose that Kodak is able to announce its output before Fuji gets to make a move. Now what will Kodak do?

Kodak needs to think through the consequences of each possible strategy. Suppose that Kodak produces 50 rolls of film (committing itself to the first column). Fuji will then pick its favorite square in the first column, producing 75 rolls for a profit of $21 (beating $16 and $20 in the other squares). Kodak ends up with $14 profit.

Suppose instead that Kodak produces 75 rolls of film (committing itself to the second column). Fuji will then pick its favorite square in the second column, producing 75 rolls for a profit of $15 (beating $14 and $12 in the other squares). Kodak ends up with $15 profit.

Suppose instead that Kodak produces 100 rolls of film (committing itself to the third column). Fuji will then pick its favorite square in the third column, producing 50 rolls for a profit of $10 (beating $9 and $5). Kodak ends up with $20 profit.

Among these choices, Kodak likes the last one best. So Kodak announces that it will produce 100 rolls. Fuji responds by producing 50, and the game ends in the upper right-hand square, where Kodak earns twice what Fuji earns.

The outcome we have just described is called a **Stackelberg equilibrium.** A Stackelberg equilibrium occurs when one player commits to a strategy at the outset, accounting for the fact that the second player will choose an optimal response.

**Stackelberg equilibrium**

An equilibrium concept that arises when one player announces his strategy before the other.

## The Importance of Commitment

Suppose that Kodak announces it will produce 100 rolls of film and Fuji responds by producing 50 rolls as in the Stackelberg equilibrium of Exhibit 12.7. Once Fuji has agreed to produce only 50 rolls, Kodak wants to deviate. It is better for Kodak to produce 75 rolls for a profit of $21 than 100 rolls for a profit of $20.

So if Kodak moves first and Fuji moves second, then Kodak wants to change its move. If Kodak does change its move, and if Fuji foresees this, then Fuji goes ahead with plans to produce not 50 rolls of film but 75. (After all, Kodak will eventually place it in the middle column, where Fuji's optimal strategy is not 50 but 75.) The firms end up at the Nash equilibrium in the center instead of the Stackelberg equilibrium in the upper right. Kodak's profits fall from $20 to $15.

This means that Kodak is better off if it can commit itself to producing 100 rolls and assure Fuji that it is never going to back down from that commitment. This might surprise you. You might think that a firm is better off leaving itself some flexibility to deal with unforeseen contingencies. But that is not always so.

Consider the game of chicken, where two cretins drive their cars directly at each other until one of them loses by swerving. If you can absolutely guarantee that you will never swerve, you are a sure winner at this game. If you leave yourself the leeway to swerve in case your opponent is crazier than you are, then your opponent will have an incentive to *become* crazier than you are and you are liable to lose. The way to win the game of chicken is to disable your steering column and make sure your opponent is aware of it.

# Summary

Strategic situations can be represented by game matrices, showing the outcome that results from each combination of strategies that the players can choose.

A Nash equilibrium is an outcome from which neither player would deviate, taking the other's behavior as given. A game can have one Nash equilibrium, no Nash equilibrium, or many Nash equilibria.

A dominant strategy is a strategy that a player would want to adopt regardless of his beliefs about the other player's strategy choice. The Prisoner's Dilemma is an example of a game where both players have dominant strategies.

One outcome is a Pareto improvement over another if it makes at least one player better off without making any player worse off. An outcome is Pareto-optimal if it allows no Pareto improvements.

There can be Nash equilibria that are not Pareto-optimal, and there can be Pareto optima that are not Nash equilibria.

When games are played sequentially instead of simultaneously, the Nash equilibrium is no longer a natural solution concept. Instead, we use the Stackelberg equilibrium, where the first player calculates the second player's responses to each of his possible strategies and then chooses the strategy that will yield him the best outcome. In a sequential game, it can be advantageous to go first or advantageous to go second, depending on the particular game.

In some games it is important to be able to commit to following a strategy even if better options become available. By committing, you can sometimes convince your opponent to behave in ways that are advantageous to you.

# Author Commentary          www.cengage.com/economics/landsburg

**AC1.** For more information on multiple equilibria in the market for car insurance, see this article.

**AC2.** Read this article to learn about some slightly outdated applications of game theory to American politics.

**AC3.** This article is about the social status game.

# Problem Set

The problems in this problem set refer to the following game matrices. In each case, Jack chooses "left or right" and Jill chooses "up or down." The outcomes show how many buckets of water are rewarded.

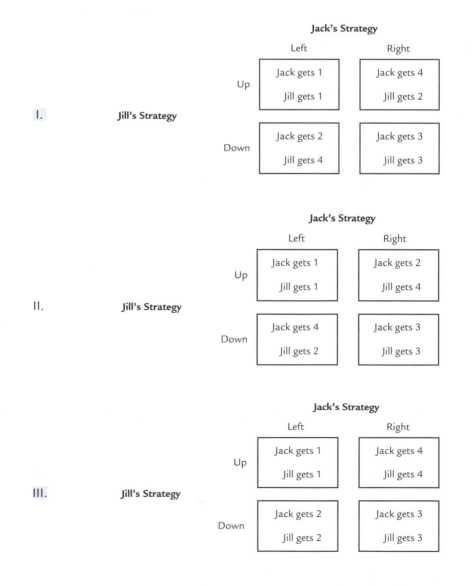

**I.**          **Jill's Strategy**

|  | **Jack's Strategy** | |
|---|---|---|
|  | **Left** | **Right** |
| **Up** | Jack gets 1 / Jill gets 1 | Jack gets 4 / Jill gets 2 |
| **Down** | Jack gets 2 / Jill gets 4 | Jack gets 3 / Jill gets 3 |

**II.**          **Jill's Strategy**

|  | **Jack's Strategy** | |
|---|---|---|
|  | **Left** | **Right** |
| **Up** | Jack gets 1 / Jill gets 1 | Jack gets 2 / Jill gets 4 |
| **Down** | Jack gets 4 / Jill gets 2 | Jack gets 3 / Jill gets 3 |

**III.**          **Jill's Strategy**

|  | **Jack's Strategy** | |
|---|---|---|
|  | **Left** | **Right** |
| **Up** | Jack gets 1 / Jill gets 1 | Jack gets 4 / Jill gets 4 |
| **Down** | Jack gets 2 / Jill gets 2 | Jack gets 3 / Jill gets 3 |

**IV.**

**Jill's Strategy**

**Jack's Strategy**

|  | Left | Right |
|---|---|---|
| Up | Jack gets 2 / Jill gets 2 | Jack gets 4 / Jill gets 1 |
| Down | Jack gets 1 / Jill gets 4 | Jack gets 3 / Jill gets 3 |

**V.**

**Jill's Strategy**

**Jack's Strategy**

|  | Left | Right |
|---|---|---|
| Up | Jack gets 1 / Jill gets 3 | Jack gets 3 / Jill gets 1 |
| Down | Jack gets 4 / Jill gets 2 | Jack gets 2 / Jill gets 4 |

**VI.**

**Jill's Strategy**

**Jack's Strategy**

|  | Left | Right |
|---|---|---|
| Up | Jack gets 2 / Jill gets 2 | Jack gets 1 / Jill gets 1 |
| Down | Jack gets 1 / Jill gets 1 | Jack gets 3 / Jill gets 3 |

**VII.**

**Jill's Strategy**

**Jack's Strategy**

|  | Left | Right |
|---|---|---|
| Up | Jack gets 2 / Jill gets 3 | Jack gets 1 / Jill gets 1 |
| Down | Jack gets 1 / Jill gets 1 | Jack gets 3 / Jill gets 2 |

**VIII.**

**Jill's Strategy**

**Jack's Strategy**

|  | Left | Right |
|---|---|---|
| Up | Jack gets 12 / Jill gets 8 | Jack gets 9 / Jill gets 8 |
| Down | Jack gets 15 / Jill gets 7 | Jack gets 14 / Jill gets 10 |

1. In each game above, identify all of the Nash equilibria.

2. In each game above, identify all of the Pareto optima.

3. In each game above, does Jack have a dominant strategy? Does Jill?

4. In each game above, what happens if Jack goes first?

5. In each game above, what happens if Jill goes first?

6. For each game above, create a reasonable story (like those that go with the exhibits in the text) that might lead to these numbers appearing in the matrix.

7. Create a "tree" showing which outcomes are Pareto-preferred to which in the Kodak–Fuji game of Exhibit 12.7.

8. Can you find examples of games (either among those that have appeared in the chapter or by creating them yourself) with the following characteristics?

   a. There are no Nash equilibria.

   b. There is exactly one Nash equilibrium, but it is not Pareto-optimal.

   c. There is more than one Nash equilibrium, but none of them is Pareto-optimal.

   d. There is more than one Nash equilibrium, and all of them are Pareto-optimal.

   e. There is more than one Nash equilibrium, and some are Pareto-optimal while others are not.

9. Can there be a game with no Pareto optimum?

10. Suppose that the games of Exhibits 12.1, 12.2, 12.3, and 12.4 were played as sequential games. In each case, suppose that the player who chooses a column goes first. What are the outcomes of these games? Now suppose that the player who chooses a row goes first. In which cases do the outcomes change?

11. **True or False:** In a sequential game where the second player has a dominant strategy, he will always adopt that strategy.

12. **True or False:** In a sequential game where the first player has a dominant strategy, he will always adopt that strategy.

# External Costs and Benefits

In previous chapters, we have analyzed the gains from trade that accrue to voluntary participants in transactions. However, many transactions involve involuntary participants as well. The neighbors who breathe the smoke from a polluting factory, the naturalist who deplores the "harvesting" of whales, the shoppers who enjoy the spectacle of department store Christmas displays—all are incurring costs or benefits from transactions in which they had no part. Such costs and benefits are said to be **external** and are collectively referred to as **externalities.** External costs (like the annoyance of breathing factory smoke) are called **negative externalities,** and external benefits (like the pleasure from seeing Christmas decorations) are called **positive externalities.**

In this chapter, we will see how externalities can be a source of economic inefficiency. We also will discuss what can be done about that problem.

## 13.1  The Problem of Pollution

Pollution is an important example of a negative externality. Cars, for example, cause pollution—both when they are being manufactured and when they are being driven. We will use this example to illustrate all of the key ideas concerning externalities.

### Private Costs, Social Costs, and Externalities

When car companies decide how many cars to produce, they consider such costs as labor, raw materials, and factory space. They typically do not, however, fully consider the costs their cars will impose on bystanders who are forced to breathe exhaust fumes. So when we talk about the cost of building a car, we need to distinguish between the **private cost**—the sum of all those costs the manufacturer accounts for—and the **social cost**—the sum of *all* costs, including both private costs and external costs.

Exhibit 13.1 shows the private and marginal costs of automobile production. The private marginal cost curve includes all the costs *felt by the manufacturers,* while the social marginal cost curve includes all the costs *felt by anyone,* including the manufacturers. Therefore, the social marginal cost curve lies *above* the private marginal cost curve; it includes everything the private curve includes and more besides.

**External costs and benefits, or externalities**

Costs and benefits imposed on others.

**Negative externalities**

External costs.

**Positive externalities**

External benefits.

**Private cost**

The sum of those costs of a decision that are borne by the decision maker.

**Social cost**

The sum of all of the costs of a decision, including the private costs and the costs imposed on others.

EXHIBIT 13.1          **Measuring Externalities**

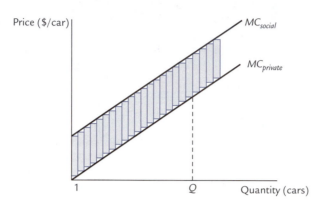

The private marginal cost curve accounts for all costs felt by manufacturers (labor, raw materials, factory space, etc.). The social marginal cost curve accounts for everything in the private marginal cost curve *plus* the external costs felt by people who suffer from pollution.

The first shaded rectangle has a height, and hence an area, equal to the external cost of producing the first car; the second has an area equal to the external cost of producing the second car, and so forth. If $Q$ cars are produced, the total external cost is equal to the area between the two marginal cost curves, out to quantity $Q$.

## Measuring the Externality

Look at the first rectangle in Exhibit 13.1. The top and bottom of that rectangle show the private and social marginal costs of producing a single car. The external cost of producing that car is equal to the social cost minus the private cost, which is illustrated by the *height* of the rectangle. Because the rectangle has width 1, we can equally well say that the external cost of producing the first car is equal to the *area* of the first rectangle.

The second rectangle has an area equal to the external cost of producing a second car, and so forth. If $Q$ cars are produced, the total externality is equal to the sum of the areas of the rectangles out to quantity $Q$; in other words:

The total externality is equal to the area between the two marginal cost curves, out to the quantity produced.

## Welfare Analysis

We can now incorporate externalities into our welfare analysis of the car market. Exhibit 13.2 illustrates that market, which we assume is competitive, so that the industry supply curve is equal to the industry's marginal cost curve. *Which* marginal cost curve? Answer: The one that reflects costs firms care about—the *private* marginal cost curve.

The equilbrium quantity of cars is $Q_E$. At this quantity, consumers earn $A + B$ in surplus and producers earn $C + D$. If there were no external costs, that would be the end of the analysis. But in this case we have to *subtract* the value of the damage done to pollution-sufferers, which (as we learned in Exhibit 13.1) is the area between the marginal cost curves, $B + D + E$. This leaves a social gain of $A + C - E$.

In the right-hand panel of Exhibit 13.2, we reach the same conclusion in a different way. How much does the first car contribute to social gain? Answer: The value of that car to a consumer (measured on the demand curve) minus the cost of producing

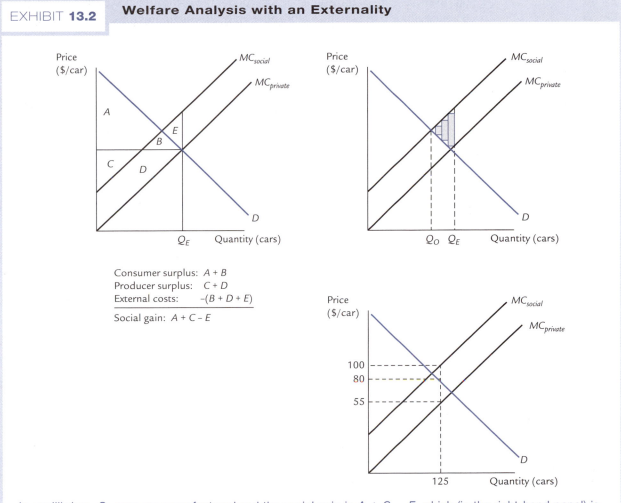

EXHIBIT **13.2**    **Welfare Analysis with an Externality**

Consumer surplus:  $A + B$
Producer surplus:   $C + D$
External costs:      $-(B + D + E)$
_____
Social gain:  $A + C - E$

In equilibrium, $Q_E$ cars are manufactured and the social gain is $A + C - E$, which (in the right-hand panel) is equal to the sum of the "good" (unshaded) rectangles minus the "bad" (shaded) rectangles. If the number of cars were reduced to $Q_O$, social gain would increase to $A + C$.

The bottom panel shows why the shaded rectangles contribute negatively to social gain. Car number 125 (where 125 is assumed to lie between $Q_O$ and $Q_E$) is worth $80 to the consumer, but creates $100 in costs ($55 in costs to the manufacturer plus $45 in costs to the pollution-breathers). Therefore, it contributes *minus* $(100 − 80) = $20 to social gain.

that car *including all costs, whether private or external.* In other words, it's the vertical distance between the demand curve and the social marginal cost curve, which is to say the area of the first unshaded rectangle. The second car contributes the area of the second unshaded rectangle, and so on until we reach car number $Q_O$. The next car after that is worth *less* to the consumer than the social cost of producing it; the difference is measured by the first shaded rectangle, which contributes *negatively* to social gain, as do all the other shaded rectangles. So social gain is equal to the sum of the unshaded rectangles minus the sum of the shaded rectangles—the same area that is labeled $A + C - E$ in the left-hand panel.

Several things are worth noting here. First, the mere fact that cars pollute does not mean that they are necessarily bad things. In Exhibit 13.2, the value of the first car is worth more than the associated cost, even when the cost of pollution is accounted for. That car adds to social gain, so its production is a good thing according to the efficiency criterion. Of course, if we'd drawn the picture differently, this might not have been the case.

---

**Exercise 13.1** How would the graph look if the first car contributed negatively to social gain?

---

Next, even though *some* cars contribute positively to social gain, it is definitely not true that *all* cars contribute positively to social gain. All cars after car number $Q_O$ contribute negatively. Suppose, for example, that car number 125 is one of those cars. Then you can see in the bottom panel of Exhibit 13.2 that this car is worth $80 to a consumer, but it costs $100 to produce. (That is, it costs the manufacturer $55 and the pollution-breathers an additional $45.) Therefore, this car contributes *minus* $20 to social gain, which is reflected by the first shaded rectangle, which has area 20.

## Government Policies

Is there a way to get a better outcome? A glance at the right-hand panel of Exhibit 13.2 reveals that the answer is yes. If manufacturers could somehow be induced to produce only $Q_O$ cars instead of $Q_E$, we would get all the "good" (unshaded) rectangles of social gain without having to accept any of the "bad" (shaded) rectangles. Social gain would increase to the total area of the good rectangles, which is to say area $A + C$ in the left-hand panel.[1]

How can we get manufacturers to produce fewer cars? There are at least two obvious possibilities. We could set a legal limit on the number of cars produced, or we could tax car production. Let's examine each method, beginning with the tax.

### Pigou Taxes

Suppose you want to get producers to build exactly $Q_O$ cars in Exhibit 13.2. How big an excise tax should you impose? Answer: Enough to make $Q_O$ the new equilibrium quantity. For this, you want the industry supply curve to rise from the level of the *private* marginal cost curve to the level of the *social* marginal cost curve. The tax per car, then, should be equal to the vertical distance between the two curves. But that distance is equal to the externality per car.

**Pigou tax or Pigovian tax**

*A tax equal to the amount of an externality.*

So the right excise tax is one that requires producers to pay a tax per car that is equal to the external cost per car. Such a tax is called a **Pigou tax.** An alternate form of Pigou tax requires consumers, rather than producers, to pay the amount of the externality. We will analyze a tax on producers, but a tax on consumers would have exactly the same effects.

The first panel of Exhibit 13.3 is identical to the panels in Exhibit 13.2 except that the areas have been carved up a bit more finely, and then even more so in the second panel of the exhibit. Without the Pigou tax, we can repeat the analysis of Exhibit 13.2 (though some of the names of the areas have changed). Consumers earn $A + B + E + F$; producers earn $C + D + G$; externalities (which count negative) amount to $D + E + F + G + H$; and social gain is $A + B + C - H$.

With the Pigou tax, the industry supply curve shifts vertically upward by the amount of the tax per car. But the tax per car is equal to the amount of the externality

---

[1] The invisible hand theorem tells us that competitive markets maximize social welfare. Exhibit 13.2 seems to present a counterexample. But in fact the reason why the equilibrium in Exhibit 13.2 is suboptimal is precisely that a market is lacking, namely, the market for air. When nobody owns the air, it can be neither bought nor sold. If companies had to purchase the air they pollute, that cost would be included in their private costs and the equilibrium quantity would be the optimal quantity $Q_O$.

| EXHIBIT 13.3 | A Pigou Tax |
|---|---|

|  | Without Tax | With Tax |
|---|---|---|
| Consumer surplus: | $A + B + E + F$ | $A$ |
| Producer surplus: | $C + D + G$ | $B + C$ |
| External costs: | $-(D + E + F + G + H)$ | $-(D + E)$ |
| Tax revenue |  | $D + E$ |
| Social gain | $A + B + C - H$ | $A + B + C$ |

|  | Without Tax | With Tax |
|---|---|---|
| Consumer surplus: | $A + B + E + F$ | $A$ |
| Producer surplus: | $C + D + G$ | $C_2 + D_2$ |
| External costs: | $-(D + E + F + G + H)$ | $-(D_1 + D_2 + E)$ |
| Tax revenue |  | $B + E + C_1 D_1$ |
| Social gain | $A + B + C - H$ | $A + B + C$ |

Both panels are identical except that the areas have been carved up a bit more finely on the right. Using either graph, we can compute social gain without a Pigou tax and social gain with a Pigou tax. As we predicted in Exhibit 13.2, the Pigou tax, by reducing quantity from $Q_E$ to $Q_O$, increases social gain by $H$.

per car, so the supply curve shifts up by the amount of that externality—which is exactly the vertical distance between the two marginal cost curves. The result, then, is that with a Pigou tax in place, the supply curve shifts upward until it sits directly on top of the *social* marginal cost curve. Indeed, we designed the Pigou tax with exactly this effect in mind![2] The equilibrium quantity is now reduced to $Q_O$. According to what we said in our discussion of Exhibit 13.2, social gain should rise to $A + B + C$. Let's make sure that this is what happens.

The two panels of Exhibit 13.3 illustrate the analysis in slightly different ways. The first panel is a little simpler, and the second panel is a little more familiar; you can choose whichever makes you comfortable. First, given the new equilibrium price and quantity, consumer surplus falls to $A$ in either panel. Next, producer surplus falls to $C_2 + D_2$ in the second panel (this is the familiar computation). In the first panel, we have represented the same surplus by the triangle $B + C$, which has exactly the same area as $C_2 + B_2$ (it's the same triangle shifted upward).[3] External costs, which are represented by the area between the two marginal cost curves out to the quantity produced, are reduced to $D + E$ in both panels.

Finally, we must not forget the tax revenue. Ordinarily we represent tax revenue by the rectangle $B + E + C_1 + D_1$ in the second panel. That's fine. But it's also fine to

[2] We are assuming for simplicity that the external cost is the same for each car, so that the vertical distance between the two marginal cost curves is the same wherever it is measured. Without this assumption, the picture would look more complicated, but the analysis would be fundamentally unchanged.

[3] This is the analogue for producer surplus of the "other way" to compute consumer surplus in Exhibit 8.13.

notice that *we have set the tax equal to the amount of the externality,* and that amount is $D + E$ in the first panel. Therefore, the tax revenue is also equal to $D + E$. So, we have learned that $D + E$ has the same area as $B + E + C_1 + D_1$. Either way, we get the expected $A + B + C$ for social gain.

## Why the Pigou Tax Works

Firms produce too many polluting cars for the same reason that people drop too much litter in the park: They don't have to live with the consequences of their actions. A Pigou tax forces the firm to live with the consequences of its actions by making sure it pays for those consequences. Without the tax, the firm does not care about pollution; with the tax, it does care, at least indirectly.

As a general rule, we tend to get good outcomes when decision makers have to live with the consequences of their choices. In such cases, we say that the decision makers have **internalized** those consequences. A Pigou tax forces car manufacturers to internalize the external cost of pollution.

**Internalize**

To treat an external cost as a private cost.

## Liability Rules as Pigou Taxes

Instead of implementing a Pigou tax, we could just as well institute a rule of law under which the polluter is **liable** for his actions. This means that the victims have the legal right to sue for damages. From the polluter's point of view, paying off lawsuits feels exactly like an excise tax. So, from an economic point of view, a liability rule is equivalent to a Pigou tax, with the revenue paid directly to the victims. (Of course, from a social gain point of view, paying the revenue directly to the victims is neither better nor worse than paying it to anyone else.)

**Liable**

Legally responsible to compensate another party for damage.

## Quantity Restrictions

As an alternative to the Pigou tax, the government could simply require firms to produce fewer cars. If the equilibrium quantity of cars is too high by, say, 30,000 (in other words, if the distance from $Q_O$ to $Q_E$ in Exhibit 13.2 is 30,000), then the government could order each of three firms to produce 10,000 fewer cars (and order other firms not to take up the slack).

This, however, is a very poor solution, because in order to implement it efficiently, we would need to know more than we could plausibly know about each firm's cost curves. Is it more efficient to have firms *A*, *B*, and *C* cut back by 10,000 cars each; or to have firm *A* cut back by 30,000 and the others not at all; or to have firm *A* cut back by 20,000, firm *B* by 9,000, and firm *C* by 1,000? The rectangles in Exhibit 13.2 are drawn on the assumption that cars are produced in the cheapest possible way. But if we make the wrong decisions about who should cut back, that assumption is violated and social gain can be substantially less than what is shown in the picture. (See the discussion surrounding Exhibit 9.3 for more on this point.)

A better idea is to issue exactly $Q_O$ car-building permits, require manufacturers to present a permit each time they produce a car, and allow the permits to be freely traded so they end up in the hands of the firms that can use them most efficiently. Such arrangements are sometimes called **cap-and-trade** systems.

**Cap-and-trade**

A system of tradable permits to produce goods that create externalities.

In practice, it is not just the car industry that creates pollution. We might also want to mandate the use of permits for other polluting industries, and allow permits to be traded across industries. This is exactly what happens under the various cap-and-trade systems that have been recently implemented in the United States and Europe. To keep things simple, we will assume that our cap-and-trade system is confined to the car industry, but a similar analysis would apply to real-world cap-and-trade arrangements.

## The Pigou Tax versus Cap-and-Trade

Which is better—a Pigou tax or a cap-and-trade system? Exhibit 13.4 compares and contrasts the two alternatives.

A Pigou tax causes the quantity of cars to fall to $Q_O$; so does a cap-and-trade system that limits the number of permits to $Q_O$. With a Pigou tax, the price of cars increases to the level marked "new price." After paying the tax, suppliers are left with the amount marked "new price to suppliers." With cap-and-trade, the price paid by demanders and the price received by suppliers are determined by the demand and supply curves at the quantity $Q_O$. As you can see from Exhibit 13.4, this makes both consumers and producers indifferent between the Pigou tax and the cap-and-trade system. The difference between the amount paid by demanders and the amount kept by suppliers is accounted for by the price of a permit; multiplying that price by the number ($Q_O$) of permits gives the area $B + E + C_1 + D_1$. The government can capture this area as revenue by selling the permits, just as it captures exactly the same area under a Pigou tax.

Conclusion: The quantity of cars, the price of cars, the amount kept by sellers, and the revenue to the government are all exactly the same under both systems.

This conclusion makes sense when you think about it. Both the Pigou tax and the cap-and-trade system restrict the quantity of cars to $Q_O$; in both cases, the cars are produced by the most efficient producers and end up in the hands of the consumers who value them most. In both cases, the price to consumers is bid up until consumers want exactly $Q_O$ cars, and in both cases the part of the price kept by producers is bid down until producers want to provide exactly $Q_O$ cars. So why should anyone care which system is implemented?

## The Real World

Our model suggests that there is no reason anyone should have a preference between a Pigou tax and a cap-and-trade system. However, there are a few possibly relevant considerations not accounted for by the model.

EXHIBIT **13.4** **A Pigou Tax versus Cap-and-Trade**

We contrast a cap-and-trade system that restricts quantity to $Q_O$, on the one hand, with a Pigou tax on the other. In either case, quantity is reduced to $Q_O$, consumers pay the new price marked on the diagram, producers keep the "new price to suppliers," and the government can capture area $B + E + C_1 + D_1$ as revenue.

First, ideally the Pigou tax is equal to the externality per car. In practice, there might be some uncertainty about this externality. For example, exactly how much damage, in dollar terms, does a Ford Taurus do to the atmosphere? Clearly some guesswork must be involved in any answer to this question. Therefore, the government might mistakenly set the Pigou tax either too high or too low. Ideally, the cap-and-trade system issues exactly $Q_O$ permits (in Exhibit 13.4). In practice, there might be some uncertainty about exactly where the demand and social marginal cost curves cross. Therefore, the government might mistakenly set the quantity of permits either too high or too low. So, in the real world, either system is likely to be implemented imperfectly.

In most cases, however, estimating the right cap-and-trade limit requires considerably more information than estimating the right Pigou tax, and therefore the cap-and-trade system is more prone to error. To get the right Pigou tax, you need to know the external costs. To get the right cap-and-trade limit, you need to know the social marginal cost curve, which includes both those external costs *and* the private costs—and then you need to know the demand curve as well. This is an argument in favor of the Pigou tax.

Second, the Pigou tax is largely "pay as you go." Cap-and-trade permits, depending on how the system is implemented, might have to be purchased well in advance of production—and hence long before revenues start to flow in. As long as firms can borrow against future revenues, this is no problem. But if, for example, small firms have more difficulty borrowing than big firms do, then cap-and-trade gives an advantage to big firms, even though they might be less efficient producers. This is another argument in favor of the Pigou tax.

Third, once you implement a Pigou tax, you can be quite sure that producers will start lobbying to have it repealed. But once you issue cap-and-trade permits, the political pressure could well go in the other direction: Firms that have bought permits will lobby to maintain the system (so as to maintain the value of their permits). So, as a political matter, cap-and-trade might be easier to maintain in the long run. This is an argument in favor of cap-and-trade.

Fourth, at the onset of a new cap-and-trade program, the government has a choice: They can sell permits, or they can give the permits away to existing firms. (Either way, the permits can be freely resold.) By selling permits, the government collects the same revenue that would be generated by a Pigou tax. By giving permits away, the government allows that revenue to end up in the hands of the firms that receive the free permits. There are arguments to be made in favor of either option.[4] Depending on where you stand on this issue, and depending on how you think the issue is likely to be resolved, you might consider this an argument either for or against cap-and-trade.

## 13.2 The Coase Theorem

**Transactions cost**

Any cost of negotiating or enforcing a contract.

The modern approach to externalities recognizes that although Pigou taxes can be effective policy instruments, there are some occasions when they are not needed and others when they are actually counterproductive. These points were driven home to economists by the lawyer and legal scholar Ronald Coase, who emphasized the importance of **transactions costs**.[5] A transactions cost is a cost of negotiating or enforcing a

---

[4] You can read some of these arguments at http://www.landsburg.com/mankiw.html.

[5] His analysis appears in R. H. Coase, "The Problem of Social Cost," *Journal of Law and Economics* 3 (1960): 1–4.

contact. If you hire someone to repair your roof, transactions costs might include the time spent locating an appropriate contractor, time or energy spent haggling over the price, the cost of hiring an inspector to make sure the job has been done correctly, and the potential costs of filing a lawsuit if the roofer fails to make repairs as promised. Anything that interferes with people's ability to engage in mutually beneficial bargaining is a transactions cost.

Coase's analysis of the externality problem led him to two conclusions:

1. In the absence of transactions costs, Pigou taxes are unnecessary.

2. In the presence of transactions costs, Pigou taxes can be counterproductive.

In this section, we will see how Coase was led to the first of these conclusions. In Section 13.3, we will see how he was led to the second.

## The Doctor and the Confectioner

In nineteenth-century England, a doctor named Sturges lived around the corner from a confectioner (i.e., a candy-maker) named Bridgman. Sturges saw patients in an office attached to his house, and Bridgman made candy in his basement. They had never been good friends, but they had certainly never been enemies.

That changed when Dr. Sturges decided to expand his office space by building an addition to his house. The day the addition was completed, Sturges discovered for the first time that Brigdman's machines were very loud—so loud, according to Sturges's later testimony, he could not hear his patients' hearts through his stethoscope.

Sturges and Bridgman ended up in court, where the judges ruled that Bridgman would have to stop using his machines. In their decision, the judges said that they were concerned about making sure that the land in the neighborhood would be put to its most valuable use; presumably they believed that an additional doctor was more socially valuable than an additional confectioner.

The judges, in other words, seem to have believed that their decision could affect the future course of Dr. Sturges's medical practice. But they were probably wrong. Let's think through what might actually have happened following the court decision.

### Example 1

Suppose for concreteness that Bridgman values his business at $100 and Sturges values his new office at $200. If the judges rule in Sturges's favor, Bridgman retires and Sturges goes on practicing medicine in his new quarters.

But what if the judges had ruled the other way, allowing Bridgman to make all the noise he wanted to? Would Sturges shut down his new office? Not at all. Instead, Sturges walks around the corner, knocks on Bridgman's door, and offers him $150 to turn the machines off. Bridgman accepts and considers himself $50 ahead. So Bridgman retires and Sturges goes on practicing medicine—*exactly as when the judges ruled for Sturges.*

Perhaps the payoff is something other than $150. Perhaps, if Bridgman is a hard bargainer, he can demand $190. Perhaps, if he's a soft touch, he'll settle for $110. But any payoff between $100 and $200 is beneficial for both parties, so there's plenty of room to reach an agreement.

The key point is this: *No matter how the judges rule,* Bridgman is going to stop making noise and Sturges is going to be able to use his new office. Economists sum up this observation by saying that the judges' decision "doesn't matter."

| EXHIBIT 13.5 | **The Doctor and the Confectioner** | |
|---|---|---|

| | Judges Rule for Sturges | Judges Rule for Bridgman |
|---|---|---|
| Example 1:<br>Bridgman's candy business worth $100; Sturges's medical practice worth $200 | Court orders Bridgman to quit. Society gets medical office, no candy. | Sturges bribes Bridgman $150 to quit. Society gets medical office, no candy. |
| Example 2:<br>Bridgman's candy business worth $200; Sturges's medical practice worth 100 | Bridgman bribes Sturges $150 to close office. Society gets candy, no medical office. | Bridgman makes noise; Sturges closes office. Society gets candy, no medical office. |

The two rows correspond to two different assumptions about the values of Bridgman's and Sturges's businesses. In each example, we ask what happens if the court rules for Sturges (ordering Bridgman to shut down his machines) and what happens if the court rules for Bridgman (allowing Bridgman to make all the noise he wants to). From a social point of view, the judges' decision never matters—in Example 1, society always gets Sturges's medical office but not Bridgman's candy; in Example 2, the reverse is always true.

Surely Sturges and Bridgman would take exception to the notion that the decision doesn't matter; indeed, it matters very much to Sturges and to Bridgman. Bridgman certainly prefers being paid off to being shut down by the court, and Sturges certainly prefers the opposite. But the judges' decision does not matter in the following limited sense: The decision has no effect on whether Bridgman stays in business, and it has no effect on how Sturges practices medicine. It has no effect on how much candy or medical care will be produced.

This example is summarized in the first row of Exhibit 13.5.

## Example 2

Now we reverse the numbers: Suppose Bridgman values his business at $200, and Sturges values his medical practice at $100. If the judges rule in Bridgman's favor (saying, in effect, "go ahead and make all the noise you want to"), then Bridgman stays in business and Sturges gives up his new office. If, instead, the judges rule in Sturges's favor and order Bridgman to shut down, here's what happens: Bridgman walks around the corner, knocks on Sturges's door, and says, "I'd like to keep right on running my machines. I'll give you $150 (or maybe $190 or $110) if you don't turn me in." Once again, Bridgman stays in business and Sturges gives up his new office.

In this example, as in Example 1, the judges' decision does not matter (except to Bridgman and to Sturges). This example is summarized in the second row of Exhibit 13.5.

## Alternative Solutions

In Examples 1 and 2, we have made the simplifying assumption that one of two things must happen: Either Bridgman shuts down completely or Sturges abandons his new office. But there may be some other solution. Perhaps Bridgman can acquire more modern machinery that is not as loud. Or maybe Sturges can move his office to the other side of his house. Or perhaps one or the other, or both together, can erect a sound barrier between their properties.

In the absence of transactions costs—that is, as long as Bridgman and Sturges can costlessly negotiate and enforce agreements—they can both come out ahead by finding the cheapest of all possible solutions and agreeing to a payoff or "bribe" that allows everyone to come out ahead. This is true no matter how the judges rule.

Sometimes the cheapest solution is for Bridgman to retire or for Sturges to close his office. Other times the cheapest solution is something more creative. If the judges order an unnecessarily expensive solution, Bridgman and Sturges can always agree to something cheaper, and split the savings between them. The judges cannot change the fact that one solution is cheaper than another, and therefore cannot affect the ultimate choice of solution.

## The Bottom Line

The bottom line is this: In both of our examples, and in any other example you might cook up (as long as there are no transactions costs), the parties involved—Bridgman and Sturges, in our examples—are effectively arguing about how to divide up the "pie" consisting of the joint profits from their two enterprises. The one thing they are sure to agree on is that the pie ought to be as big as possible. If only one business can continue to operate, both parties will want it to be the more profitable business; if more profit can be made by installing a sound barrier and keeping both businesses active, they both will agree on that—and then proceed to argue about how to divide that profit.

## The Coase Theorem

We can now state the **Coase theorem** in two equivalent forms. First:

*In the absence of transactions costs, social gain is always maximized.*

In other words, if Bridgman's business is worth more than Sturges's office, then Bridgman's business will survive; if Sturges's office is worth more than Bridgman's business, then Sturges's office will survive; if a sound barrier is worth erecting, the sound barrier will be erected. Sturges and Bridgman might argue for awhile about who gets the lion's share of social gain, but they will have no trouble agreeing that social gain should be as large as possible. When the pie is bigger, everyone can have a bigger piece.

An equivalent form of the Coase theorem is:

*In the absence of transaction costs, all externalities are internalized.*

Bridgman's noise creates an externality, but in the absence of transaction costs, he is certain to act as if he cares about that externality—either because the court orders him to act that way or because Sturges bribes him to.

We have already argued that the recipe for optimal outcomes is to internalize all externalities—that's why the Pigou tax works. That also is why the conclusions "all externalities are internalized" and "social gain is always maximized" are equivalent.

## Property Rights, Liability Rules, and the Coase Theorem

When Sturges disputes Bridgman's right to run his noisy machines, he is in effect claiming a **property right** to the noise-free air around his office. Surely if Sturges owns the air, he ought to be able to charge Bridgman for its use as a noise receptacle. When Bridgman claims that he is perfectly within his rights to run those machines, he is

**Coase theorem**

In the absence of transactions costs, all externalities are internalized; therefore, social gain is maximized.

**Property right**

The right to decide how some resource shall be used.

essentially claiming that the air belongs to *him*—and therefore he can use it as a noise receptacle if he wants to.

So what we initially saw as an externality problem can be recast as a dispute over a property right. If the court sides with Sturges and orders Bridgman to turn off his machines, the court is essentially granting the property right to Sturges. If the court allows Bridgman to make all the noise he likes, it is essentially granting the property right to Bridgman.

We have seen that the court's decision has no effect on either Sturges's medical practice or Bridgman's candy business. Therefore, the Coase theorem is often restated in this way:

*In the absence of transaction costs, the assignment of property rights does not matter.*

Here we must be careful in our interpretation of the phrase "does not matter." The assignment of property rights—that is, the decision of the court—matters considerably to both Sturges and Bridgman. Sturges would much rather win in court than pay Bridgman to shut down; Bridgman would much prefer the opposite. But the court decision has no effect on either man's economic activity, and hence no effect on social gain; this is what economists mean when they say that the court's decision "does not matter."

Ordering Bridgman to shut down amounts to awarding Sturges a property right. Alternatively, the court could allow Bridgman to continue making noise, but order him to reimburse Sturges for the damage. In other words, the court could establish a liability rule favoring Sturges. From an economic point of view, there is no difference between the property right and the liability rule.[6] Under either ruling, Bridgman has to shut down or pay up.

Likewise, allowing Bridgman to continue making noise amounts to awarding Bridgman a property right. This is entirely equivalent to establishing a liability rule that says Bridgman need not reimburse Sturges for any damage. Either way, Sturges still has the option of bribing Bridgman to turn off his machines.

Because the choice of a liability rule is equivalent to the choice of a property right, we can restate the Coase theorem this way:

*In the absence of transactions costs, the choice of liability rule does not matter.*

### Example: The Capitol Records Studio[7]

For over half a century, many of the biggest hits in popular music have been recorded at the Capitol Records Studio in Hollywood, California. The studio features an underground echo chamber whose unique sound is considered irreproducible.

But in 2008, the Los Angeles City Council gave the go-ahead for construction of a 16-story condominium project next door to the Capitol Studio—a project that Capitol says will make its studio unusable because of construction noise while the condos are being built and traffic noise once they are occupied.

As this is written, it is unclear whether Capitol will convince the City Council to overturn its decision, or whether the entire issue might end up being decided in a courtroom.

---

[6] Later in this chapter, we will see other examples in which property rights and liability rules might *not* be equivalent.

[7] This example is based on an Associated Press story by Solvej Schou that was called to my attention by Cyril Morong.

From an economic point of view, the good news is that it is impossible for any decision to be wrong. In fact, the decision doesn't matter.

More precisely, although the decision matters very much to the owners of Capitol and to the condo developers, it will nevertheless have no effect on how much music is produced at the Capitol Studio. If the studio is more valuable than the condo project, the studio will continue to operate; if the condo project is more valuable than the studio, then the studio will shut down. Or perhaps a third option will be found—some creative use of sound barriers, for example. Whether this third way is adopted will depend on whether it is cost-justified, without regard to what the City Council or a judge decides.

By issuing a building permit for the condo project, the City Council effectively granted the condo developers a property right that allows them to build on that land; by denying a building permit, the City Council would effectively transfer the property right to Capitol Studios. A court that denies Capitol the right to sue for damages would establish a liability rule in the condo developer's favor, which would amount in this case to the same thing as a property right for the developers; alternatively, a court that allowed Capitol the right to sue would be establishing the opposite liability rule and effectively granting the property right to Capitol.

In any event, side payments between Capitol and the condo developers are sure to lead to whatever outcome generates the most joint profit for the two enterprises. This case illustrates the Coase theorem in all its forms: No matter what decision is made, all externalities will be internalized, social gain will be maximized, and the assignment of property rights (or, equivalently, the choice of liability rule) will have no effect on the future of American popular music.

## The Coase Theorem in the Marketplace

The case of Bridgman and Sturges involves just two people. But in many real-world situations, externalities affect many people at once. Consider, for example, the polluting industry of Exhibit 13.6 (which is identical to the first panel of Exhibit 13.3). Suppose the vertical distance between the marginal cost curves is $200 per car. Then, as illustrated in the exhibit, a Pigou tax of $200 per car causes firms to cut back their collective quantity from $Q_E$ to $Q_O$ and increases social gain by the amount $H$.

However, in the absence of transaction costs, we get the same outcome even without a Pigou tax. Here's why: The neighbors of the auto makers will offer them up to $200 per car to cut their output back below $Q_E$. Therefore, every time the auto makers produce a car, they forgo a $200 bribe. That $200 bribe becomes part of the private cost of production, and therefore raises the private marginal cost curve by $200, just as a Pigou tax would.

As a result, firms cut back to $Q_E$ and we get exactly the same welfare analysis as in the case of a tax—with one additional twist. Because they cut back from $Q_O$ to $Q_E$, the firms collect a side payment of $(Q_O - Q_E) \times \$200$, which is equal to the area of the trapezoid $F + G + H$. This side payment, which comes out of the neighbors' pockets and goes into the factory owners', has no additional effect on social gain.

---

The neighbors are willing to pay *up to* $200 for each car that is not produced. If they are hard bargainers, they might be able to get away with smaller payments.

---

Dangerous
Curve

## EXHIBIT 13.6    The Coase Theorem in a Competitive Market

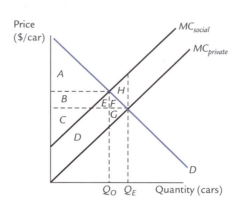

|  | Without Tax | With Tax |
|---|---|---|
| Consumers' surplus: | $A + B + E + F$ | $A$ |
| Producers' surplus: | $C + D + G$ | $B + C$ |
| External costs: | $-(D + E + F + G + H)$ | $-(D + E)$ |
| Tax revenue | — | $D + E$ |
| Social gain | $A + B + C + H$ | $A + B + C$ |

The picture is identical to the first panel of Exhibit 13.3. Each car produced creates an externality of $200, which is the vertical distance between the marginal cost curves. Ordinarily we would expect firms to produce $Q_E$ cars. A Pigou tax can reduce this quantity to $Q_O$ and increase social gain. But in the absence of transactions costs, we achieve the same outcome even without a Pigou tax, because the neighbors are willing to pay up to $200 per car to get the factory owners to reduce output.

Although it's important to understand the logic of the Coase theorem, you should also realize that in this case, the "no transactions cost" assumption is probably highly unrealistic. The logistical problem of organizing hundreds of homeowners to jointly bribe a factory owner is already a formidable transactions cost. In Section 13.3, we will see how our conclusions have to be modified in the presence of just such considerations.

### Example: Smoking Bans in Bars

In the past few years, several of the states have banned smoking in public restaurants, bars, and taverns. Supporters of the bans argue that smokers impose externalities on non-smokers, so that when smoking is permitted the outcome is suboptimal.

The Coase theorem suggests otherwise: Even in the absence of a smoking ban, non-smokers can always bribe smokers to put out their cigarettes. Such bribes will be success-ful exactly when they ought to be—that is, exactly when the costs of secondhand smoke exceed the benefits to smokers of their firsthand smoke.

Are such bribes feasible? If nonsmokers had to approach smokers in bars and offer them cash to extinguish their cigarettes, the Coase theorem would not apply, because of the obvious transactions costs (nobody wants to interrupt his dinner for an extended bar-gaining session involving everyone in the restaurant). But that's not the only form a bribe can take. Each bar has an owner who can charge higher prices to nonsmokers if he bans smokers from the bar. This leaves the owner with every incentive to *fully internalize the externality*—that is, he treats all external costs to nonsmokers as if they were costs to him personally. The owner bans smoking if the benefits of the ban exceed its costs, and otherwise not. That's because every cost and every benefit hits the owner's pocketbook through customers' willingness to pay, and therefore every cost and every benefit gets weighed in the owner's decision.

In general, when owners set prices, "bribes" easily take place in the form of higher or lower prices, so that transactions costs are typically low and the Coase theorem applies. If the owner chooses to allow smoking, that's because smoking is the efficient outcome. A law that overrides the owners' decision can only convert an efficient outcome to an inefficient one.

The situation would be quite different in, say, a public library where no admissions fees are charged. Here transactions costs are higher because we are back to the case where nonsmokers must negotiate with smokers directly. In this case, nobody would claim that the Coase theorem is applicable.

## The Pigou Tax Reconsidered

If transactions are costless, then the Coase theorem tells us that the Pigou tax is unnecessary. In fact, we can say more: If only *some* transactions are costless, it is possible for the Pigou tax to be positively harmful.

To see why, suppose in Exhibit 13.6 that sprocket producers and homeowners can transact costlessly. Then by offering side payments, homeowners will bid the $MC_P$ curve up to the level of the $MC_S$ curve. Now suppose that a Pigou tax is imposed, with the revenue collected by some third party. This will move the $MC_P$ curve up higher yet, so that it now lies *above* the $MC_S$ curve! The number of cars produced will be *less* than the optimal quantity $Q_O$.[8]

The problem here is that producers receive a double incentive to reduce their output. When the production of a car costs $200 worth of damage, the producer is both charged a $200 tax and made to forgo a $200 bribe, raising his costs by $400. This extra incentive causes him to continue cutting back on output even after the social optimum has been reached.

If *all* parties, including consumers and the recipients of tax revenue, can enter the negotiations, then the social optimum is achieved with or without a Pigou tax. It is always possible to arrange a system of side payments that will benefit everyone when the size of the social pie is maximized. However, the example here shows that when some but not all of the parties can negotiate, the Pigou tax can actually reduce social welfare.[9]

## Example: The Nature Conservancy

Environmental pollution is often cited as an example of an externality that cannot be bargained away because of high transactions costs. It is alleged that the large number of people affected suffices to negate any possibility of negotiating side payments. There is undoubtedly much truth in this assertion, but it is far from entirely true.

---

[8] The problem does not occur if the Pigou tax is paid to the homeowners rather than a third party. If the homeowners are reimbursed for the pollution, they are indifferent to how much pollution occurs and will therefore not offer bribes.

[9] This point seems to have first been clearly exposited by Ralph Turvey in "On Divergences Between Social Cost and Private Cost," *Economica* 30 (1963): 309–313.

In Arlington, Virginia, a charitable organization called the Nature Conservancy solicits funds from the public and uses those funds exactly in the way that Coase would predict. It purchases land in ecologically significant areas and maintains that land to preserve threatened species and places of special beauty. Its current holdings comprise 2.8 million acres in 4,100 locations. In making its purchases, the Conservancy bids against other potential users of the land, forcing those other potential users to take account of the land's ecological significance.

At the same time, because it pays market prices, the Conservancy must take account of the value of the land in its alternative (nonecological) uses. When a parcel of land has exceptional value in other uses, the price of the land is high and the Conservancy is less likely to acquire it. Thus, from a social point of view, the Conservancy's approach has a distinct advantage over, for example, legally mandating that landowners follow policies that are oriented toward conservation.

Unfortunately, even those who value conservation highly have an incentive to "free ride" on the efforts of groups like the Nature Conservancy, so that the actual level of contributions may inadequately reflect the true demand for conservation. Nevertheless, the organization has been extraordinarily successful. In 1997, it received private contributions of over $150 million. The Nature Conservancy's success is a striking reminder that seemingly insurmountable transactions costs can be at least partially overcome.

## External Benefits

Everything we have said about external costs has its analogue regarding external benefits. Suppose that Nabisco can produce a cookie at a (private) marginal cost of 5¢. At the same time, the factory produces a pleasant aroma worth 2¢ to motorists driving by. Then the cookie is produced at a social marginal cost of only 3¢; part of the private costs are returned to society via the external benefit from the aroma. In the presence of external benefits, the social marginal cost curve lies below the private marginal cost curve and too few cookies are produced.

Just as a Pigou tax internalizes external costs, so a "Pigou subsidy" equal to the benefits conferred on others can internalize external benefits, leading to an efficient level of output. However, the Coase Theorem applies in this case as well. In the absence of transactions costs, the recipients of the benefit will offer a bribe in exchange for greater production, and this bribe will operate just like a Pigou subsidy.

### Example: The Fable of the Bees

An interesting real-world example is what Professor Steven Cheung has called *The Fable of the Bees*.[10] In the literature of economics, the standard example of a positive externality is the interaction between apple growing and beekeeping. When these two activities are carried on in close physical proximity, one might expect each to confer benefits on the other. More apple trees mean more honey; more bees mean more cross-pollination and eventually more apples. Pigou would have argued (and his disciples did argue) that this situation must result in suboptimal levels of output in both activities. An apple grower

---

[10] S. Cheung, "The Fable of the Bees: An Economic Investigation," *Journal of Law and Economics* 16 (1973):11–34.

stops planting new trees as soon as the marginal cost of planting exceeds his private marginal benefit, failing to consider that further trees would benefit his neighbor. The beekeeper performs a similar unfortunate calculation. Both could be made better off by a system of taxes and subsidies that encouraged them to consider their neighbor's welfare as part of their own.

Cheung investigated the accuracy of this fable by interviewing apple growers and bee-keepers. He found that, contrary to the expectations of Pigou-style economists and exactly as Coase would have predicted, there is an elaborate system of contracts under which the two groups reimburse each other with "bribes" for increasing output to the socially opti-mal levels.[11] The evidence that such contracts exist is not hard to find; Cheung pointed out that one need only look in the Yellow Pages under nectar and pollination services. Nevertheless, a generation of economists had somehow managed to deny that such con-tracts were possible.

**Exercise 13.2** State an appropriate moral for *The Fable of the Bees*.

## Income Effects and the Coase Theorem

According to the Coase theorem, assignments of property rights do not matter from the point of view of economic efficiency. In the example of Exhibit 13.5 an even stron-ger statement can be made. Not only does a change in property rights have no effect on economic efficiency, it also has no effect on the amounts of medical care and candy that are produced. The "resource" consisting of the air around Bridgman's confection-ery and Sturges's office is allocated either to the production of candy (via its use as a "dumping ground" for Bridgman's noise) or to the production of medical care (via its use as a quiet, conducive environment in which Sturges can practice), depending on where it is most valuable and regardless of who has the property rights. We will refer to this outcome as the *strong Coase theorem*:

*Strong Coase Theorem:* In the absence of transactions costs, the assignment of property rights has no effect on the allocation of resources.

The strong Coase theorem is not universally true. Suppose that a law were passed requiring all classical music lovers to give half of their wealth to people who like rock and roll. Although this is just a change in property rights, the demand for classical records would fall, the demand for rock records would rise, and resources formerly allocated to producing classical music would be reallocated to the production of rock. However, although the allocation of resources has changed, it is still efficient (i.e., Pareto-optimal). Rock fans are happier, classical music lovers are less happy, but social welfare is still being maximized *given* the new wealth distribution. This is an example of what we will call the *weak Coase theorem*:

*Weak Coase Theorem:* In the absence of transactions costs, the assignment of prop-erty rights does not affect the *efficiency* of resource allocation (though it might cause resources to be diverted from one efficient allocation to another).

---

[11] He also discovered that, contrary to a widespread assertion in economic literature, apples produce almost no honey. Therefore, he extended his investigation to include many other plants.

The weak Coase theorem is always true. The strong Coase theorem is true whenever the reallocation of property rights does not change people's wealth enough to have significant effects on market demand curves. (In other words, the redistribution of income that results from the change in property rights should have negligible income effects.)

Notice that changes in the assets of *firms* do not affect the validity of the strong Coase theorem. Only changes in the assets of individuals are relevant, because individuals are the source of demand curves. For the strong Coase theorem to fail, there must be large changes in the wealth of enough individuals to make a significant difference in the relevant market.

In Exhibit 13.5 a shift in property rights from Sturges to Bridgman makes Bridgman richer. If Bridgman loves candy, this could raise the demand for candy and cause more candy production; if he loves medical care, it could bring about more medical care. (For that matter, if Bridgman loves carrots, it will raise carrot production.) The fact that Bridgman is a *producer* of candy is irrelevant to how demands will shift. In any event, Bridgman as a consumer is undoubtedly such an insignificant part of either market that no real change will come about.

## Example: The Reserve Clause in Baseball

Before 1972 all major league baseball players had contracts containing a *reserve clause.* The reserve clause forbade the player from attempting to sell his services to any other team. If the Chicago White Sox wanted to acquire a player from the New York Yankees, the White Sox had to buy that player's contract from the Yankees. They could not simply offer him a higher salary to try to lure him away.

In the 1970s, the reserve clause was substantially weakened, and now a number of players are *free agents* who can sell their services to the highest bidder. At the time, it was argued that the weakening of the reserve clause would enable the wealthiest teams to buy up all of the best players. Let us subject this assertion to some economic analysis.

The weakening of the reserve clause is a transfer of property rights. Player's services, which used to belong to the teams they played for, now belong to the players themselves. The Coase theorem suggests that such a transfer of property rights should not affect the allocation of players to teams.

Consider a player, Frank DeMeyer, who currently plays for the New York Yankees. Having DeMeyer on the team is worth $100,000 to the Yankees. This is because his presence increases the Yankees' revenue by $100,000. He would be worth only $75,000 to the Chicago White Sox.

Under the reserve clause, the Yankees will not sell DeMeyer for any amount less than $100,000, and the White Sox will not offer any amount more than $75,000. No exchange takes place, and DeMeyer continues to play for the Yankees.

On the other hand, suppose that DeMeyer becomes a free agent. Then the Yankees will offer him up to $100,000 to play for them. This is because he can produce an additional $100,000 in revenue for the Yankees and has nothing to do with whether the Yankees are rich or poor. The White Sox will offer DeMeyer up to $75,000. If DeMeyer maximizes his salary, he will play for the Yankees. Thus, free agency has no effect on where DeMeyer plays.

We have implicitly made the simplifying assumption that DeMeyer receives no salary under the reserve clause. If he receives $20,000 in salary, then the Yankees will value his contract at $80,000, not $100,000, and the White Sox will value his contract at $55,000. However, the conclusion that he continues to play for the Yankees does not change.

Dangerous
Curve

**Exercise 13.3** Assume that DeMeyer is worth $100,000 to the Yankees and $150,000 to the White Sox. For whom does he play under the reserve clause? For whom does he play under free agency?

Now let's throw in a complication. Suppose that DeMeyer hates living in New York, so much so that he would be willing to pay up to $50,000 to move to the White Sox. Under free agency, DeMeyer will move. The White Sox offer him $75,000 and the Yankees offer him $100,000. The additional $25,000 he can earn in New York is not enough to overcome his $50,000 preference for Chicago.

Under the reserve clause, DeMeyer will also move. The White Sox are willing to buy him from the Yankees for $75,000. In addition, DeMeyer himself is willing to "bribe" the Yankees up to $50,000 in exchange for their agreeing to sell him. Thus, the Yankees can collect a total of $125,000 for letting DeMeyer go. Because he is worth only $100,000 to the Yankees, DeMeyer ends up in Chicago.

This example illustrates the strong Coase theorem. The reallocation of property rights that results from free agency has no effect on where DeMeyer plays.

**Exercise 13.4** Suppose that DeMeyer is willing to pay only $10,000 to live in Chicago. Where does he play under free agency? Where does he play under the reserve clause?

Finally, let's throw in one additional complication. Suppose that DeMeyer's demand for living in Chicago depends upon his income. When he is a poor reserve player, he is willing to pay only $10,000 to live in Chicago, but when he is a rich free agent, he is willing to pay $50,000. Now under the reserve clause, the Yankees can collect a total of only $85,000 for DeMeyer ($75,000 from the White Sox plus a $10,000 bribe from DeMeyer himself) and will not sell. In this case, DeMeyer continues to play for the Yankees. Under free agency, the $25,000 difference in salary offers does not compensate DeMeyer for his $50,000 preference for Chicago, and so he plays for the White Sox.

The preceding paragraph shows how income effects enter the analysis. A change in property rights can affect the allocation of resources (the resource here being DeMeyer) only if it alters incomes in such a way as to change the demand for some resource (in this case DeMeyer's demand to live in Chicago). In such cases, the strong Coase theorem fails, but the weak Coase theorem is still true. Either allocation of resources is efficient, given DeMeyer's income.

How does free agency affect the allocation of players to teams? If players' preferences about where to live are unaffected by their incomes, then it does not affect the allocation. Otherwise, it increases the wealth of players and makes it more likely that they will choose the teams that they personally value playing for. This means that with the advent of free agency, it is the teams that are desirable to players, not the wealthy teams, that gain an advantage.

## 13.3 Transactions Costs

In the presence of transactions costs, it might not be possible to negotiate side payments leading to efficient outcomes. In that case, the analysis of Exhibit 13.3 suggests that a Pigou tax can improve social welfare—and indeed it often can.

However, as Ronald Coase first pointed out, there is more to the story. In this section, we will see how, in some situations, a Pigou tax can actually lead to a reduction in social gain.

### Trains, Sparks, and Crops

Railway engines create sparks, and these sparks sometimes set fire to crops planted near the tracks. A large number of farmers are affected, and transactions costs prevent deals from being struck between these farmers and the railroad. If the railroad company is not liable for the ensuing damage, it will not consider the effects of this damage in deciding how many trains to run. A liability rule requiring the railroad to indemnify the farmers (in other words, a Pigou tax with proceeds assigned to the farmers) would provide such an incentive. There would be less rail service but more wheat and corn, which appears to be a social improvement.

The Coase theorem says that if there were no transactions costs, this argument would be wrong because even without a Pigou tax, farmers would offer side payments to the railroad in exchange for running fewer trains. The railroad would be bribed into cutting back to the optimal level of rail service regardless of liability rules. But Coase made another, equally important point: When there *are* transactions costs, the conclusion that the railroads should be made liable may still be wrong, though for a different reason.

The flaw in the argument is that we do not know the cheapest way to prevent the fires. Suppose that farmers, at very little cost to themselves, can move their crops back a few feet from the railway bed, out of all danger from sparks. This would remove the externality and increase the social gain from the running of the railroad. However, if the railroad reimburses the farmers for all damage done, the farmers have no incentive to move their crops. Crops will be planted and burned, and fewer trains will be run because of the cost of reimbursement. If farmers were made to bear the losses from fires, they would move their crops, to society's benefit.

Exhibit 13.7 shows the picture, assuming a competitive railroad industry. Additional trains mean additional fire damage; the cost of that damage accounts for the difference between the private and social marginal cost curves. The first two columns of the chart reiterate the analysis we have seen before: When they are untaxed, the railroads run $Q_E$ trains and generate a social gain of $A + B + C - H$; when they face a Pigou tax, the railroads run $Q_O$ trains and generate a social gain of $A + B + C$.

But this analysis overlooks the possibility that farmers can avoid damage by moving their crops. The third column analyzes this possibility. If the crops are removed, there is no externality, and the social $MC$ curve disappears. We calculate consumer and producer surplus as in the first column. We must also subtract the cost of moving the crops, which we have denoted $X$. Note that *the value of $X$ is not represented anywhere on the graph*—it can't be, because this is a graph about the costs and benefits of railroad trains, not of moving crops. Therefore, without additional information, there is no way to know whether the social gain in the third column is greater or less than the social gain in the second.

Will the farmers actually move their crops? That depends. Notice first that if the Pigou tax is paid directly to the farmers (in the form of reimbursement for crop damage), then the farmers have absolutely no incentive to move. So a Pigou tax paid to the

EXHIBIT **13.7**    **Trains, Sparks, and Crops**

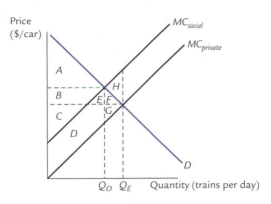

| | Without Tax | With Tax | Without Tax; crops moved |
|---|---|---|---|
| Consumers' surplus: | $A + B + E + F$ | $A$ | $A + B + E + F$ |
| Producers' surplus: | $C + D + G$ | $B + C$ | $C + D + G$ |
| External costs: | $-(D + E + F + G + H)$ | $-(D + E)$ | |
| Tax revenue | | $D + E$ | |
| coost of moving | | | $-X$ |
| Social gain | $A + B + C + H$ | $A + B + C$ | $A + B + C + D + E + F + G - X$ |

Railroad trains throw off sparks that start fires and destroy farmers' crops; the fire damage is an externality. If the railroads are untaxed, they run $Q_E$ trains and generate a social gain of $A + B + C - H$; if they face a Pigou tax, they run $Q_O$ trains and generate a social gain of $A + B + C$. This makes it appear that the Pigou tax is socially desirable.

However, the analysis overlooks the possibility that farmers could move their crops to a location where the sparks can't reach them. The third column displays the welfare analysis in that case. The cost of moving the crops, denoted $X$, appears nowhere in the graph. Without more information, we cannot know whether social gain is higher in the second column or in the third.

The potential problem with a Pigou tax is that it can discourage farmers from moving their crops, eliminating the possibility of reaching the outcome in the third column—an outcome that might or might not be the best possible.

farmers—or, equivalently, a liability rule that requires the railroad to reimburse farmers for damage—guarantees that the third column outcome will never be achieved.

What about a Pigou tax paid to the government? Such a Pigou tax does not completely eliminate the externality, but it does reduce it—from $D + E + F + G + H$ to $D + E$. Farmers will move crops only if the cost of moving is less than the cost of putting up with the externality. Therefore, if the cost of moving—what we have called $X$—falls between $D + E$ and $D + E + F + G + H$, the Pigou tax will cause farmers to switch from moving their crops to not moving their crops, again eliminating the possibility of the third column outcome.

So a Pigou tax might eliminate that third column option, and will certainly do so if the Pigou tax is paid to the farmers. The third column outcome might or might not be the most efficient solution. Therefore, a Pigou tax might or might not eliminate the most efficient solution.

Does it follow that there should be no Pigou tax, and that the railroad should not be liable for its actions? Not necessarily. Suppose that the railroad can cheaply install safety equipment that will prevent sparks from being thrown by the engines. If the railroad has no liability for fire damage, it will have no incentive to install this equipment. Once again, it is possible that the low-cost solution has been sacrificed.

Exhibit 13.7 simply does not contain the information necessary to determine how property rights should be allocated. (The property right in question is the right to the unencumbered use of the land adjacent to the tracks—either for agriculture or for spark disposal.) Whoever has the property right has no incentive to seek a solution to the problem. If farmers can move their crops very cheaply, then it is most efficient for the railroad to have the property right so that farmers will have the incentive to move their crops. If the railroad can install safety equipment very cheaply, then it is more efficient for the farmers to have the property right so that the railroad will have the appropriate incentive.

In cases such as this one, courts often concern themselves (or profess to concern themselves) with questions of economic efficiency. If a judge has efficiency foremost in his mind, then he must attempt to determine which party can solve the problem at the lowest possible cost and make that party bear the costs of the damage (i.e., the property right should be assigned to the other party). Unfortunately, this can be difficult. If the judge asks the railroad whether it can prevent spark damage at a relatively low cost (planning to make the railroad bear this cost if the answer is yes), the railroad has every incentive to conceal the truth by claiming that controlling the sparks would be prohibitively expensive. The farmers have the same incentive to exaggerate the cost of moving their crops.

When there is a great deal of uncertainty about the costs of various solutions, a judge may be well advised to assign property rights according to some secondary criterion and then to attempt to reduce transactions costs between the parties. If he can do so (say, by appointing a spokesman for the farmers and facilitating negotiation between this spokesman and the railroad company), then any mistake in the initial allocation of property rights will tend to be mitigated by the action of the Coase theorem.

## The Reciprocal Nature of the Problem

In Exhibit 13.7, the choice to run $Q_E$ trains when there are crops planted near the railroad tracks is not socially optimal. The market's failure to produce the optimal outcome is due to the divergence between private and social costs. A Pigou tax remedies this divergence by shifting the private marginal cost curve upward. Coase's observation is that the divergence can be remedied equally well by moving the social marginal cost curve downward (e.g., by having the farmers move their crops).

Why did economists in the Pigovian tradition fail to recognize the alternative remedy? Coarse argues that the error arises from the mistaken notion that the railroad is the "cause" of the fires and therefore must curtail its activities if the damage is to be reduced. In actuality, the railroad is no more the cause of the fires than the crops are. Although it is true that if there were no railroads, there would be no fires, it is equally true that if there were no crops, there would be no fires. Ultimately, the problem is caused by the fact that the railroad and the farmers are attempting to use the same land for two different purposes, and this is no more one party's fault than it is the other's. Either party might be in possession of the cheapest means of dealing with the problem.

Every case of externalities is similarly reciprocal in nature. The neighborhood residents denounce the owner of a polluting factory; the owner might respond that there would be no externality if it weren't for the existence of the neighbors. The factory owner can mitigate the problem through cutbacks in production or pollution-control equipment; the neighbors can contribute equally well to a solution by moving away.

Each of these options has a cost.[12] If the factory owner is allowed to pollute without penalty, he has no incentive to reduce pollution. If the neighbors are fully compensated by the factory for damage to their lungs and houses, they have no incentive to move away. Either liability rule might cause the elimination of the low-cost option; the "right" liability rule depends on the actual costs.

It is often argued that the pollution of a lake or river is an economic problem that must be solved, especially if the water would otherwise be available for recreation. If the pollution is curtailed and the lake is reclaimed, it makes equal sense to say that the boaters and fishermen are the source of a problem in that they cause a reduction in the output of a socially valuable product. Which is worth more, the additional product or the boating and fishing? There is no way to tell without examining actual costs and benefits.

Nonsmokers like to view cigarette smoke as a cost imposed on them unfairly by smokers. The problem, however, is a reciprocal one: It is caused by smokers and nonsmokers wanting to use the same air for two different purposes. Conceivably, it could be cheaper (i.e., less unpleasant) for the nonsmokers to wear gas masks than for the smokers to curtail their smoking.

Automobiles sometimes hit pedestrians, injuring or killing them. The problem is caused by cars and people being in the same place at the same time; it can be partially alleviated by more care on the part of drivers or by more care on the part of pedestrians. In the 1970s the state of California, seeking to give appropriate incentives to drivers, made them legally responsible for any injury they caused to pedestrians. As a result, pedestrians had a greatly reduced incentive to take precautions, and they do, in fact, take fewer precautions. Whether the net effect has been to reduce accidents is unclear.

## Sources of Transactions Costs

An understanding of the nature of transactions costs can be useful to one who is attempting to reduce them. The following series of examples illustrates some of the sources from which transactions costs are likely to arise.

### Example: Mining Safety and the Principal–Agent Problem

Coal mining is an inherently dangerous activity. Mining companies are able to reduce the frequency of injury to miners by the purchase of various types of safety equipment. If the companies are liable for injuries sustained on the job, they will have an obvious incentive to invest in such equipment until the marginal cost of one more unit of equipment is equal to the marginal benefit of that unit in terms of accident prevention. If, on the other hand, the companies bear no liability, you might at first think that they will have no incentive to make any investment in safety. The Coase theorem suggests that this conclusion is wrong: Miners (who will now have to bear the costs of their own injuries) will be willing to "bribe" the company to buy safety equipment in the optimal amount. The most convenient form of such a bribe is for the miners to accept a lower wage. This is, of course, equivalent to a direct payment from the miners to the mining company.

Now suppose that there is another way to improve mining safety, which involves precautions taken by the miners themselves in the course of their underground activity. If miners bear the costs of their own injuries, they will engage in an appropriate level of precautionary activity. Alternatively, suppose that miners are fully reimbursed for all injuries by the mining company. In this case there appears to be no incentive for miners to take

---

[12] Of course, the cost of moving does not consist only of the fees paid to the moving companies; it includes the value of the dissatisfaction generated by leaving one's friends and gathering places as well.

appropriate care. (If they are reimbursed but not fully, then they will take some care but less than the optimal amount.)

In the absence of transactions costs, however, the Coase theorem suggests that the company itself will offer to pay the miners a bonus in exchange for their agreement to behave cautiously. Both sides benefit, as the miners collect the bonus and there are fewer injuries whose cost the company must bear.

But, unfortunately, there is no way to guarantee that an individual miner will live up to his part of the bargain. There is nothing to stop a miner from collecting the bonus and then behaving recklessly underground, where there is no one to observe him, knowing that he will be compensated by the company for any injury he sustains.

The fact that the miner's behavior is *unobservable* constitutes a transactions cost that can prevent the enforcement of the optimal contract. If all liability is with the company, and if precautionary behavior by miners is totally unobservable, then there will be no precautionary activity, regardless of what the optimal level might be.

In our simplified model of the mining industry, the most efficient liability rule is one that relieves owners of all responsibility to compensate miners for injuries. This in no way affects the incentives of owners to provide safety equipment, because their workers can still bribe them into behaving optimally. It also has the advantage of giving workers appropriate incentives, which they would not otherwise have because of the transactions costs involved in observing their behavior.[13]

Whenever one party contracts to pay another to behave in a certain way, we call the first party a *principal* and the second an *agent*. If the mine owner attempts to pay the workers for behaving cautiously, then the owner is the principal and the workers are the agents. We say that a *principal–agent problem* arises when the principal cannot verify that the agent is abiding by the bargain, as in this example.[14]

In general, if A's behavior is observable and B's is not, then, in the absence of other transactions costs, it is efficient for B to bear the costs of damage resulting from interactions between A and B. This gives B the appropriate incentives; A has them already because of the Coase theorem.

## Example: AIDS and Blood Transfusions

The recipients of blood transfusions sometimes contract infectious diseases as a result. AIDS is the most significant example. Who should bear the costs of such illnesses, the patient or the doctor?

In the absence of transactions costs, the placement of liability would not matter. If doctors were liable, they would adopt appropriate standards of safety in order to avoid lawsuits; if patients were liable (as, in fact, they legally are), they would offer higher fees to doctors and elicit the same standard of safety.

Here we face a close analogy with mining accidents. The patient's behavior is perfectly observable: A simple test reveals whether he has contracted AIDS. The doctor's behavior, however, is not. Thus, there is a principal problem. If a patient pays extra for

---

[13] An interesting aspect of this choice of liability rule is that in the long run miners themselves will be indifferent to which rule is chosen (unlike Sturges and Bridgman, who cared very much). The reason is that entry and exit from the mining industry will eventually leave mining just as attractive (or just as unattractive) as the alternative occupations.

[14] Principal–agent problems were introduced in a different context in Chapter 9.

blood that is 99% certain to be AIDS-free and is instead given blood that is 95% certain to be AIDS-free, he is likely never to know the difference, whether or not he eventually becomes ill. If he does contract AIDS and suspects the doctor of cheating him, he will have great difficulty proving his suspicion. The inability to monitor doctors' compliance is a transactions cost that suggests that doctors should bear the liability for transfusion-induced illnesses.

We have been assuming that a transfusion patient is unlikely to contract AIDS in any other way. Without this assumption, our analysis must be modified. Suppose that doctors are fully liable when their patients develop AIDS. Then a recent transfusion recipient has reduced incentives to avoid other activities that may lead to the disease. If he contracts AIDS through riotous living, he can blame the doctor and be compensated. As a result, he may engage in such activities to a greater than optimal degree. The unobservability of the patient's behavior constitutes an argument for patient liability.

---

If doctors are liable to transfusion patients who contract AIDS, then some doctors will have to pay for patients who get the disease elsewhere. Although this might strike you as "unfair," the argument we have made does not concern this unfairness. It concerns only the inefficiency that arises if incentives are distorted so that the number of AIDS cases ends up being either more or less than optimal.

Dangerous
Curve

---

## Incomplete Property Rights

Transactions costs also arise when property rights are ill-defined or nonexistent. Not knowing who owns something makes it difficult to bargain over its use. If Jack owns a tree that is worth more to Jill than to him, he will sell it to Jill. If Jill owns the tree and values it more than Jack does, she will keep it. If the tree belongs to some third party, he will sell it to whoever values it the most. In any event, the tree ends up in the hands of whoever values it the most, regardless of who owns it initially—provided *someone* owns it initially.

Suppose, alternatively, that there are no property rights to trees and that a tree belongs to the person who takes it. The tree is worth $3 to Jack and $5 to Jill. Nevertheless, if Jack is first to spot the tree, he will claim it for his own. If Jack had a well-defined property right, he could agree to sell the tree to Jill; unfortunately, unless he uses the tree immediately, Jill will claim it for her own. Jack takes the tree for himself.

You might think that Jack could call Jill on the phone, warn her that he is about to claim the tree, and offer to leave it standing for her if she will pay him $4. Unfortunately, Jack has 13 identical cousins, all named Jack, each of whom is prepared to present Jill with the same threat. To save the tree for herself, she would have to pay $13 \times \$4 = \$52$, or $47 more than it is worth to her. She passes up this opportunity, and the tree goes to one of the Jacks, who values it less than Jill does.

The lack of property rights in trees can present other problems as well. In the absence of property rights, nobody will plant or nurture trees, even though the benefit from doing so may exceed the cost. Another difficulty arises if Jill values a tree most for its decorative beauty. A tree left standing is a tree left vulnerable to expropriation, so Jill uses the tree for firewood, reducing its value to her and creating a social loss.

## Liability Rules as Incomplete Property Rights

In Section 13.2 we treated liability rules and property rights as different ways to describe the same thing. In the examples considered there, this was an accurate depiction. In other instances, however, liability rules can better be viewed as *incomplete* property rights.

Consider again Bridgman the confectioner and Sturges the doctor. Bridgman makes noise damaging to Sturges's practice. If Bridgman is granted the right to make noise, we say either that he has a property right to the air or that there is a liability rule in his favor.

However, we must distinguish between two different legal situations. Is it *Bridgman* personally who is granted a right to the air, or is it *confectioners in general* who have this right? In the first case, any other confectioner who wants to make noise in the neighborhood must first purchase the right from Bridgman. And Bridgman will take Sturges's desires into account, because Sturges will offer to pay him *not* to sell the right to a confectioner.

But if all confectioners, just by being confectioners, acquire the right to make noise, and hence the opportunity to be bribed by Sturges, then some people in other industries might become confectioners just in order to collect these bribes. As a result, there will be overproduction of candy, because the bribes from Sturges constitute a subsidy and an artificial incentive to enter the candy industry. Similarly, there will be a suboptimal number of doctors, as each potential doctor recognizes that he will be subject to such extortion and takes this into account in his decision about whether to enter the profession.

The reason for the inefficiency here is that when the air belongs to confectioners generally, it does not really belong to anybody. Like the tree in the forest, it belongs to whoever takes it. If the efficient use of the air is to sell it to Sturges as a quiet zone, this outcome cannot be achieved, because after Sturges pays Bridgman to keep quiet, he will still have to contend with Bridgman's 13 identical cousins, all named Bridgman.

As long as the number of firms in each industry is fixed, a liability rule is the same as a property right. But if the number of practitioners in either industry can change, then the liability rule is likely to convey only a partial property right and hence can lead to inefficiency.[15]

## Free Riding

**Free riders**

People who benefit from the actions of others and therefore have reduced incentives to engage in those actions themselves.

Another important source of transactions costs is the problem of free riders. Suppose that a factory causes pollution that adversely affects the lives of 50 families. The families would like to take up a collection to bribe the owner of the factory so that he will reduce the scale of his operation. There are logistical difficulties involved in communicating with so many people at one time, but we shall suppose that these have been overcome. Each family would be willing to pay $100 to reduce pollution and is therefore asked to contribute $100 to the fund. However, each family reasons as follows: "We don't know whether the other families are contributing their share. If they are, the fundraising drive is bound to be successful even without our contribution. Everyone else will pay and we

---

[15] The importance of this distinction between property rights and liability rules was clarified by H. E. Frech III in "The Extended Coase Theorem and Long Run Equilibrium: The Nonequivalence of Liability Rules and Property Rights," *Economic Inquiry* 17 (1974): 254–268. There has been much confusion among both economists and legal scholars about this issue. Frech points out that in most of the examples that are used to illustrate the Coase theorem (such as the case of Bridgman and Sturges), there are fixed numbers of participants, so that liability rules and property rights are equivalent.

will share in the benefits; we can 'ride for free' while others pay the fare. Another possibility is that the other families aren't paying, in which case our $100 certainly won't be enough of a bribe to make a significant difference. Either way, let's not contribute."

You might recognize this reasoning; it is precisely that of the prisoners in the Prisoner's Dilemma. It is rational reasoning on the part of each individual family, but it prevents the socially optimal contract from being reached, and as such can be counted as a transactions cost. An alternative view is that this is just another example of ill-defined property rights: If property rights to the newly clean air were well established, those who have bought it could demand payment from other families who make use of it.

# 13.4 The Law and Economics

Historically, English and U.S. courts have often expressed a desire to adopt liability rules and systems of property rights that have the effect of fostering economic efficiency. The system of legal precedents that has evolved from centuries of court decisions is known as the **common law.** The common law promotes efficiency both when it directly creates incentives for problems to be solved in the least expensive way and when it acts to reduce transactions costs so that the parties to a dispute can reach low-cost solutions not directly observable by the court.

**Common law**

The system of legal precedents that has evolved from court decisions.

## The Law of Torts

The law of torts provides some interesting examples. A **tort** is an action that intentionally or unintentionally causes damage to another party. Once this damage has been done, there is generally no way to rectify it. If you hit a pedestrian with your car, causing him injury and 6 months' lost income, those costs become sunk at the moment of the accident. Regardless of whether the court orders you to pay for these damages, the damages still exist. The court can redistribute income, but it cannot change the size of the social pie. In this sense, it seems that the court's decision is irrelevant to social welfare.

However, this view fails to take account of how the court's decision affects the future behavior of others. While a ruling in favor of the pedestrian will not affect social welfare in the current case, it will send a signal to future drivers in similar situations that they are likely to be held liable as well, and it may affect their behavior in ways that have important social consequences.

**Tort**

Acts that injure others.

## Standards of Liability

The common law assigns liability according to different standards in different sorts of cases. One standard is the standard of **negligence.** Under this standard a defendant is held liable for the costs of an accident if those costs, multiplied by the probability of the accident occurring, exceed the cost at which he could have prevented the accident.[16] Suppose that your barbecue grill sets fire to your neighbor's garage, causing $1,000 worth of damage, and that the court determines that there was initially a 25% chance of

**Negligence**

A defendant's failure to take precautions whose cost is less than the damage caused by an accident multiplied by the probability that the accident will occur.

---

[16] The legal literature defines negligence in a variety of ways. At least to a rough approximation, the definitions are all equivalent (although to an economist not trained in the law, some of them seem vague to the point of incomprehensibility). The one we are adopting here was stated explicitly by Judge Learned Hand when he decided the case of *United States v. Carroll Towing Co.* 159 F.2d 169, 173 (2d Cir. 1947).

the fire's getting started. Then you are negligent (and hence liable under a negligence standard) if you could have taken safety precautions to prevent the fire at a cost to you of less than $250; you are not negligent if those same precautions would have cost more than $250. This standard encourages low-cost precautions while discouraging precautions whose cost exceeds their value.

There is a problem with the negligence standard, however. Suppose that you can prevent fires at a cost of $200, while your neighbor can fireproof his garage at a cost of $100. In this case a negligence standard will hold you liable for fire damage, leaving your neighbor no incentive to implement the true low-cost solution. For this reason, the negligence standard is often modified by allowing a defense of **contributory negligence,** under which the plaintiff (i.e., the accident victim) cannot collect for damages in cases where he himself could have prevented the accident at a cost less than the cost of the accident multiplied by the probability of occurrence.[17]

The contributory negligence standard can also lead to inefficient outcomes. Continue to assume a $1,000 fire that had a 25% chance of occurring. Suppose that you could prevent the accident at a cost of $100, while your neighbor could fireproof his garage for $200. Under contributory negligence, he cannot collect for damages, so you have no incentive to guard against starting fires, even though it would be efficient for you to do so.

There is another reason why a negligence standard, with or without the allowance of contributory negligence, can lead to an outcome that is socially undesirable. Suppose that your barbecuing has a 25% chance of causing a $1,000 fire, which cannot be prevented at any reasonable cost *so long as you continue to barbecue.* But suppose that the cheapest way to prevent the fire is for you to give up barbecuing altogether, which would cause you only $75 worth of regret. This $75 figure is known only to you and is completely unobservable to the court. Therefore, as long as you continue to take all other reasonable precautions, the court cannot find you negligent just for operating a barbecue, and you are left with no incentive to switch to indoor cooking.

The problem can be solved by scrapping negligence and instituting a standard of **strict liability,** according to which barbecue owners are liable for all fires involving barbecues, regardless of whether there is negligence. The good news about a strict liability standard is that if you expect to cause more damage than your barbecue is worth to you, you will give it up voluntarily. The bad news is that it leaves your neighbor with absolutely no incentive to take any precautions against a fire.

We can illustrate the relative merits of negligence and strict liability by considering the law that governs auto accidents. Suppose that only negligent drivers are held liable for the accidents they cause. Then pedestrians have appropriate incentives to be cautious; the pedestrian who darts recklessly into traffic will not be compensated for injuries and will therefore think twice before darting in the first place.

On the other hand, under a negligence standard, drivers make socially inappropriate calculations about whether to drive in the first place. Suppose that a trip to the grocery store gives you $1 worth of consumers' surplus and that, on average, such trips cause $2 worth of damage to others via accidents *that do not involve your own negligence.* Under a negligence standard, you are not liable for that damage and hence do not treat it as a private cost. You will choose to drive to the store even though it is socially inefficient. But under a standard of strict liability, you are liable for all accident damage and will therefore make the socially correct decision to forgo the trip.

**Contributory negligence**

A plaintiff's failure to take precautions whose cost is less than the damage caused by an accident multiplied by the probability that the accident will occur.

**Strict liability**

Liability that exists regardless of whether the defendant has been negligent.

---

[17] As with our definition of negligence, our definition of contributory negligence is one among several roughly equivalent definitions that appear in the legal literature.

In general, negligence can provide incentives for people to take appropriate precautions once an activity (like driving or crossing the street) is under way, whereas strict liability can provide incentives for people to make appropriate decisions about whether to undertake the activity in the first place.

## Example: Heartbreak Hotels

A defibrillator is a $2,000 device that can restart a heart following cardiac arrest. Given the low cost and high potential benefit, you might expect defibrillators to be common in highly trafficked areas, such as hotels. But according to *The Wall Street Journal,* fewer than 13% of hotels have defibrillators on hand.[18] Why? Because they worry they'll be sued for not using them properly.

This is a problem with the negligence standard. If hotels were held to a standard of strict liability for all deaths on their premises, regardless of the circumstances, then you can be sure that every hotel would keep an efficient number of defibrillators on hand.

That doesn't prove that strict liability would be desirable in this case—only that it has at least one advantage. Can you think of any offsetting disadvantages?

## Criminal Penalties and Punitive Damages

In 1989, the *Exxon Valdez* oil tanker went aground off Prince William Sound in Alaska, creating an oil spill of historic proportions. Exxon spent between $2 and $3 billion settling lawsuits and cleaning up the mess. However, government prosecutors argued that Exxon should pay *additional* penalties, in excess of the damage that the oil spill had actually caused. These penalties were effected by charging Exxon with a *criminal* act and assessing a $100 million fine. Exxon agreed not to contest this fine.

In 1991, Federal Judge Russel Holland overturned Exxon's agreement with the government, arguing that the criminal penalty should be far greater, so as to send a message that environmental spills will not be tolerated. What are the efficiency consequences of Judge Holland's ruling?

Let us suppose that an oil tanker traveling in the vicinity of Prince William Sound can be expected to cause, on average, $1 million worth of damage. (Most tankers cause almost no damage; an occasional tanker causes a great deal of damage; we assume that the average damage is $1 million.) In that case, it is efficient for Exxon to employ such tankers when and only when the resulting net benefits exceed $1 million. If Exxon is responsible for the full costs of oil spills, it has every incentive to make efficient choices.

But if an oil spill results in both full liability for the damage *and* a criminal penalty, then Exxon's private costs are driven *above* social costs and it will employ fewer tankers than are socially optimal. A more dramatic way to put this is that there will be *too few* oil spills. The optimal number of oil spills is likely not to be zero, given the costs of prevention (e.g., shipping much less oil). But the prospect of a sufficiently large criminal penalty could drive Exxon out of using tankers altogether, to the net detriment of society. Indeed, Judge Holland made his intentions clear on this matter when he suggested that the criminal penalty be increased so as to avoid sending the message that "spills are a cost of doing business that can be absorbed."[19]

---

[18] "Why Hotels Resist Having Defibrillators," *Wall Street Journal,* February 24, 2009.

[19] Judge Holland did go on to express skepticism about the wisdom of the law that he felt bound to enforce.

**Punitive damages**

Additional charges levied against one who commits a tort as punishment for his behavior.

Liability together with criminal penalties can raise private cost above social cost, with the result that too little of an activity is undertaken. A closely related institution that can similarly raise private cost above social cost is the assessment of **punitive damages,** under which someone who has committed a tort must pay to the victim a sum *greater* than the actual damage, as punishment for his actions. Punitive damages are most often assessed when a tort is judged to have been intentional or a result of grossly wanton misconduct.

Suppose that you are planning to build a dam in an area where there is some possibility that the dam will break and the resulting flood will damage the property of those living nearby. The larger the dam, the less likely it is to break. The courts have determined that it is negligent to build a dam under 15 feet high. Thus, if you build a 12-foot dam and it breaks, you are negligent and liable for the full damage to surrounding property.

Now suppose that you believe that a 12-foot dam can be expected to cause, on average, about $1 million worth of property damage via flooding. You also believe that by building a 12-foot dam instead of a 15-foot dam, you can save $2 million in building costs. Assuming that your estimates are correct, it is efficient for you to build the smaller dam, and under a negligence standard you will choose to do so. However, a negligence standard combined with large criminal penalties or punitive damages could deter you from making the efficient choice and induce you to build a 15-foot dam instead.

If judges knew as much about dams as people who build dams know about dams, there would be no problem: In this example, building an efficient 12-foot dam would not have been deemed negligent in the first place. Because judges sometimes make mistakes—and because they tend to have less information available to them than people who are actively involved in making economic decisions—it is desirable for dam builders to "override" judges' wisdom by accepting the penalties for negligence when they believe it is efficient to do so. Criminal penalties or punitive damages can deter the dam builder from making the best use of his specialized information and professional judgment.

In cases like this, punitive damages are rarely assessed, so that legal doctrine does encourage efficient behavior. Next we will learn about a positive theory of the common law that predicts that such outcomes are to be expected.

## A Positive Theory of the Common Law

Judge Richard Posner, of the Seventh Circuit Court of Appeals, argues that, as a matter of historical fact, the common law has tended to embody standards that encourage economic efficiency.[20] Posner presents this viewpoint as a *positive* (as opposed to normative) theory of the common law. That is, he argues that the positions of the courts can be predicted on the basis of the assumption that they are attempting to promote efficiency. Of course, he makes no attempt to argue that every court decision fits this mold, but he does make the case that the broad outlines of legal doctrine, and the directions in which those doctrines evolve over time, are consistent with this positive theory.

[20] You can read his arguments in "A Theory of Negligence," *Journal of Legal Studies* 1 (1972): 29, in his book *Economic Analysis of Law* (Little, Brown, 1972), and in *The Economic Structure of Tort Law* by William Landes and Richard Posner (Cambridge, MA: Harvard University Press, 1987). Many of the examples in this section are adapted from these sources.

Law students are frequently told that the key question in tort law is "Whose ox is being gored?" This is a shorthand way to say that the law cares who loses and who wins whenever there are losses and gains to be distributed. Posner's efficiency theory maintains to the contrary that the law's chief concern is only to minimize the number of gored oxen, without regard to who owns them. Or, if it is costly to prevent gorings, then the law is concerned with optimizing (not minimizing) their number; gorings should be prevented until the marginal benefit of preventing another is equal to the marginal cost of preventing it.

Posner and his disciples believe that the efficiency theory of the common law can be applied not only to the law of torts but to other areas of law such as the law of contracts and the law of property. We will consider just two of their many examples. One, the doctrine of *general average,* determines the distribution of losses from disasters at sea. The other, the doctrine of respondeat superior, determines an employer's liability for the conduct of his employees.

## Example: General Average

When ships encounter peril at sea, cargo sometimes has to be quickly thrown overboard. If you are unlucky enough to own that cargo, should you bear the loss alone, or should you be partially reimbursed by the other cargo owners and the owners of the ship? The legal principle of **general average** dictates that losses should be divided proportionately according to each person's share in the venture. If the ship itself is worth $25,000 and the cargo is worth $75,000, then the entire venture is worth $100,000 and the shipowner pays for 25% of the losses. If $3,000 worth of the cargo belongs to you, then you pay for 3% of the losses, regardless of whose belongings are jettisoned.

It is easy to see how this arrangement promotes efficiency. If the owner of the jettisoned cargo bore all of the loss, the captain would simply toss the heaviest items, or those most conveniently at hand, without regard to their value (as long as they didn't belong to him). General average gives him an incentive to be more prudent, insofar as he acts as an agent for the owner of the ship. The captain is unlikely to discard a passenger's $60,000 gold bar if he knows that it will cost his own shipping company $15,000.

Not only does general average give the captain an incentive to behave responsibly; in many instances it gives exactly the *right* incentive. When the captain tosses out your $10,000 jeweled paperweight, he increases the probability of the ship's survival. That increased probability has some dollar value $V$. The social benefit from tossing the paperweight is $V$, and the social cost is $10,000. If the captain has a 25% stake in the venture, then his private benefit from tossing the paperweight is $V / 4$ (because $1/4$ of everything that is saved belongs to him) and his private cost is $2,500 (because of the law of general average). His self-interested calculation (toss the paperweight if and only if $V / 4 > \$2,500$) leads to the same outcome as if all social costs and benefits were accounted for (toss the paperweight if and only if $V > \$10,000$).

## Example: Respondeat Superior

According to the legal doctrine of respondeat superior, employers are liable for torts committed by their employees. For example, if you get a job delivering pizza and you run down a pedestrian in the course of carrying out your duties, the pedestrian can successfully sue your employer. However, respondeat superior does not usually apply when the

**Respondeat superior**

The liability of an employer for torts committed by his employees.

**General average**

The rule of law that dictates the division of losses when cargo is jettisoned to prevent a disaster at sea.

victim is a fellow employee. If you run down one of your co-workers in the parking lot, he *cannot* successfully sue the employer. How do these rules help to promote economic efficiency?

The doctrine of respondeat superior creates an incentive for the employer to select employees whom he believes to be cautious and to oversee their activities. Although it might be more efficient for the burden of care to fall entirely on the employee, thus eliminating the costs of oversight, it is unfortunately the case that liability for accidents cannot deter an employee who has no money. Thus, in cases where the employer is much wealthier than the employee, respondeat superior at least ensures that someone will have an incentive to take appropriate safety precautions.

However, if respondeat superior applied to fellow workers as well, then workers would have no incentive to avoid the company of other workers whom they know to be habitually careless. Employees would be less likely to take extra precautions when the reckless drivers were working. They would also have no incentive to report the behavior of such employees to the employer. (Once the habitual carelessness has been reported, the employer does become liable.) The difference between the random pedestrian and the fellow employee is one of transactions costs. Because a pedestrian cannot be expected to know that a particular pizza truck driver is careless, he cannot negotiate with him to drive less recklessly. This high transactions cost makes it necessary to place liability in such a way as to create incentives to solve the problem, and respondeat superior can accomplish this. But fellow employees often have detailed information about each other's behavior, and this information may not be fully available to the employer. By eliminating the employer's liability in cases involving fellow employees, the law encourages workers to use this socially valuable information in an appropriate way.

## Normative Theories of the Common Law

Posner's positive theory of the common law asserts that the law seeks economic efficiency. A closely related normative theory asserts that the law *should* seek economic efficiency.

A number of authors have proposed changes in the existing system of tort law, often arguing that goals other than economic efficiency should be given greater weight. One of the most eloquent of these is Professor Richard Epstein of the University of Chicago School of Law.[21] Epstein argues that the negligence system should be largely replaced by a system of strict liability. He argues, contrary to Coase, that it is indeed *possible* to develop a consistent set of criteria according to which we can say who is the "cause" of an injury and, contrary to Posner, that it is *desirable* to make this determination and to assign liability accordingly.

**Good Samaritan rule**

A bystander has no duty to rescue a stranger in distress.

As an example, Epstein considers the Good Samaritan rule. According to this rule, a bystander has no duty to rescue a stranger in trouble, even when he can do so at low cost to himself. If you are walking along the beach carrying a life preserver and see a man drowning, the law does not require you to save him. This rule seems not to conform to the logic of efficiency, since the benefits of the rescue would clearly exceed the costs. Epstein offers this rule as evidence that the common law is not so concerned with efficiency as Posner believes it to be. From a normative point of view, he believes

---

[21] R. Epstein, "A Theory of Strict Liability," *Journal of Legal Studies* 2 (1973): 151 and *A Theory of Strict Liability: Toward a Reformulation of Tort Law* (San Francisco: Cato Institute, 1980).

that the rule is a good one, because the bystander is not the cause of the drowning. He argues both that the principles embodied in the Good Samaritan rule are applied more widely than many scholars believe and that it would be a good thing if they were applied more widely still.

## Optimal Systems of Law

An important role for the legal system is to maintain a system of well-defined property rights. We have seen that uncertainty about property rights can be an important source of inefficiency. For this reason courts are often well advised to adopt standards that are simple and well understood, even when more complicated rules appear to provide more appropriate incentives. The gain from clarity may suffice to justify a more straightforward legal standard.

Consider traffic lights, which constitute a method of allocating the property rights to an intersection. When you are stopped by a red light and there are obviously no cars coming in the opposite direction, property rights have been allocated inefficiently. You have an immediate use for the intersection, but the right has been granted to others who have no use for it. Nevertheless, the law does not allow you to enter the intersection. If it did, there would be ambiguity about when you could and could not take advantage of this exception, and that ambiguity could lead to an increase in the number of accidents. The law accepts inefficient outcomes in some cases in order to have the most efficient possible *system* of outcomes.

Another example is the "reasonable man" standard in tort law, where negligence is judged not by the actual costs of preventing a given accident, but by the typical costs of preventing similar accidents in similar circumstances. In individual cases this may lead to inefficient outcomes, but it has the salutary effect of making it easier to judge whether you or your neighbor is legally responsible for preventing his garage from catching fire. You may not be aware of his individual cost of fireproofing, but you are likely to be aware of the typical costs of fireproofing. The resulting clarification of property rights tends to ensure that at least *someone* will prevent fires, even if not always in the ideal way. Such approximations are often all that could be asked of the legal system by any reasonable man.

# Summary

An external cost is a cost imposed on others, such as the damage to neighboring homes (or homeowners) from a polluting factory. External costs represent a gap between private and social costs, and hence lead to inefficiency. The reason for the inefficiency is that producers make decisions based on their private costs, whereas efficient decisions should be based on social costs.

A Pigou tax, which charges producers an amount equal to the externality they cause, forces producers to internalize the externality (i.e., they act as if they care about the consequences of their choices), which can lead to an efficient outcome.

A liability rule that requires producers to reimburse the victims of their externalities is equivalent to a Pigou tax, with the proceeds of the tax paid to the victims.

In the absence of transactions costs, a Pigou tax is unnecessary. All affected parties will agree to maximize social gain and split the proceeds via side payments.

The argument in favor of Pigou taxes ignores the possibility that the "victims" of an externality might be able to alleviate the problem at a relatively low cost. In that case, a Pigou tax might erase the incentive for those victims to implement that solution. So, in some cases, a Pigou tax actually reduces efficiency.

Transactions costs arise when behavior is not observable, when property rights are incomplete, when free ridership problems occur, and in many other situations. In all of these cases, the allocation of property rights has important implications for economic efficiency via its effects on the incentive structure.

A court can attempt to promote efficiency by assigning rights so as to create appropriate incentives. Unfortunately, the court may be unaware of the costs of various alternatives and hence unable to determine what incentives are appropriate. An alternative approach is for the court to attempt to reduce transactions costs. If transactions costs are sufficiently low, the Coase theorem guarantees an efficient outcome regardless of how rights are assigned. In some cases, the court's decision itself can affect transactions costs. For example, the unobservability of someone's behavior becomes a transactions cost when he is awarded a right that leads others to attempt to bribe him. (Giving miners the right to be compensated for injuries is an example.)

Posner argues that the law of torts, with its emphasis on the negligence standard, has evolved to promote economic efficiency.

# Author Commentary     www.cengage.com/economics/landsburg

**AC1.** Read this article for an application of the Coase theorem to marriage contracts.

**AC2.** Should the law encourage people to install burglar alarms and other crime prevention devices?

**AC3.** See this article for an application of economic reasoning to criminal law.

# Review Questions

**R1.** What is a Pigou tax? Explain how it works.

**R2.** Under what circumstances and in what sense do assignments of property rights "not matter"?

**R3.** State the Coase theorem and explain what it means.

**R4.** Why might it be undesirable to make a railroad liable for the damage its trains cause to neighboring crops? Why might it be desirable? What sorts of information are necessary for determining the optimal liability rule?

**R5.** What is a principal–agent problem? Give some examples. How does the existence of a principal–agent problem affect the optimal choice of liability rule?

**R6.** How do incomplete property rights lead to inefficiency? In what way are many liability rules examples of this phenomenon?

**R7.** What is negligence? What is strict liability? What are some of the ways in which these standards can be conducive or nonconducive to economic efficiency?

# Problem Set

1. A competitive beekeeper sells honey at $5 per pound. In the course of producing a pound of honey, the bees pollinate apple trees in neighboring orchards, thereby saving the orchard owners $1 worth of effort.

   a. Draw a graph showing the beekeeper's social and marginal cost curves. (Remember that this is one competitive firm, not an entire industry!) What quantity does the beekeeper produce? Illustrate his producer's surplus, the gain to the orchard owners, and the total social gain.

   b. What policy could lead to a higher social gain? If the new policy is implemented, illustrate the gains and losses to all relevant groups.

   c. In the absence of transactions costs, in what sense does it not matter whether your policy is implemented, and why?

2. The City of Rochester is thinking of expanding its airport. The expansion will increase travelers' consumers' surplus by $100 and airlines' producers' surplus by $200, while costing taxpayers only $50. However, the expanded airport will be much noisier. Hearing the noise would impose a $10 cost on each of the airport's 30 neighbors. Can you tell whether the expansion would improve social welfare? Why or why not?

3. **True or False:** If universities were made liable to their students for the effects of assaults that occur on campus, the number of such assaults might go up.

4. **True or False:** If a new law requires married men to do at least half the housework, then a lot of men will have to do more housework than they do today.

5. Farmer Jones keeps rabbits; Farmer Smith grows lettuce on adjoining land. The rabbits like to visit Farmer Smith. **True or False:** Farmer Jones should reimburse Farmer Smith for the damage, since it is caused by the rabbits.

6. **True or False:** In the absence of transactions costs, every monopolist would act like a competitor.

7. Suppose that you are the judge in the lawsuit described in the following article. Under various assumptions, discuss the senses in which your decision "matters" and the senses in which it might not. Which of your assumptions seems most reasonable to you?

### Bee Trial Brings Up Sticky Mess

If you stay in this business long enough, sooner or later you deal with everything. This column, for example, is about insects depositing waste material—forgive the euphemism—on cars.

The issue comes up because in Macomb, Illinois, there is a lawsuit that charges that bees did $25,000 worth of damage to the paint on new cars by dropping their waste on them.

Anyway, the Macomb suit alleges that as much as 1.5 million bees were brought to a clover field across the road from a line of new car dealerships. The suit says the beekeeper and the landowner "should have known that said bees would rise up out of their hives and travel the short distance to the Mac Ford [or Kelly Pontiac] lot to deposit the fecal excrement upon said automobiles." Bee waste, it seems, contains acid that eats through automotive paint, right down to the bare metal, according to Bob Allen, a co-owner of Mac Ford.[22]

---

[22] *Chicago Tribune*, 1985.

Now suppose that the "victim" is not a car dealer but a large collection of motorists whose cars are attacked whenever they drive by the area. How would your answer change? What are some of the important factors that you would take into account in making your decision?

8. **True or False:** Monopolies lead to inefficient allocation of resources. Externalities lead to inefficient allocation of resources. Therefore, a firm that is both a monopoly *and* a source of negative externalities is an especially serious social problem.

9. Suppose that you are attempting to study for your economics final and are distracted by noise from your roommate's stereo. In some dormitories, there are rules allowing you to throw the stereo out the window under these circumstances. In other dormitories, roommates are allowed to play their stereos as much as they want to without punishment.

    a. In what sense does it not matter what the rules are in your particular dormitory? In what sense does it matter?

    b. Suppose that instead of just you and your roommate, there are many students making noise, and each of them disturbs many other students. In what sense do the rules now matter more than they used to?

    c. In case (b), what sorts of considerations would go into formulating the most efficient rule? Is it possible that the most efficient rule would lead to inefficient outcomes some of the time? Explain.

10. A factory is located next to a laundromat, and soot from the factory accumulates on the freshly washed clothes, significantly reducing demand for the laundromat's services. The owner of the laundromat asks the court to prevent the factory from emitting soot.

    a. Assuming that there are no transactions costs between the owners of the two business, which among the following are affected by the court's decision and which are not? (*i*) The number of goods produced at the factory. (*ii*) The prices at the laundromat. (*iii*) The wealth of the factory owner. (*iv*) The wealth of the laundromat owner. Explain *briefly*.

    b. Now suppose instead that transactions costs make it impossible for the owners of the two business to negotiate with each other. Assume that the court is interested in fostering efficiency. Give an example of a circumstance where it would be a mistake to rule *against* the laundromat. Give an example of a circumstance where it would be a mistake to rule *for* the laundromat.

11. The workers at a certain firm are exposed to radiation. This exposure can cause birth defects if the workers have children in future years. (If they don't have children, no health problems arise.) Some ex-workers have had children with birth defects and then sued the firm for large sums of money.

    a. Under what circumstances, and in what sense, does it not matter how the court rules in these lawsuits?

    b. Suppose that after an employee leaves the firm, all contracts between the employee and the firm become unenforceable. Now does it matter how the court rules?

    c. Suppose that the firm is considering a policy that requires all employees to be sterilized as a condition of employment. How does this possibility affect your analysis?

    d. Suppose that the firm is forbidden by law to adopt the policy described in part (c). How does this affect your analysis?

**12.** Suppose that Japanese cars and American cars are identical from the viewpoint of their owners, but that Japanese cars cause harmful pollution while American cars do not. Each American owner of a Japanese car imposes $1,000 worth of pollution costs on his neighbors. Suppose that the U.S. supply and demand curves for cars cross at a price of $10,000, but Americans can buy as many cars as they want to from Japan at $7,000 apiece.

    **a.** Draw a diagram to illustrate the social gain from the market for cars. Be sure to show gains and losses to all relevant groups of Americans.

    **b.** Now suppose that the government imposes a tariff of $1,000 on all Japanese cars sold in the United States. Once again illustrate the social gain, making sure to include all relevant groups of Americans.

    **c.** Does the tariff increase or decrease social welfare? By how much?

**13.** In the preceding problem, suppose that instead of imposing a $1,000 tariff on Japanese cars, the government imposes a sales tax of $1,000 on *all* cars sold in the United States whether foreign or domestic.

    **a.** Explain why U.S. producers must still receive $7,000 for every car they sell. How much must U.S. consumers now pay for a car?

    **b.** Illustrate the social gain, including gains to all relevant groups of Americans.

    **c.** Is the sales tax better or worse than the tariff of problem 3? Is it better or worse than doing nothing at all?

**14.** In problem 12, suppose that instead of imposing a tariff on Japanese cars, the government offers a $1,000 subsidy to each American who buys an American car. (To prevent abuse of the subsidy, U.S. consumers are not allowed to resell their cars abroad.) What price do U.S. producers receive for cars? What price do U.S. consumers pay? Does the subsidy increase social gain? By how much?

**15.** People who suffer from mange can purchase either of two cures: Mange-Away, which is made in the United States and sold by producers who have an upward-sloping supply curve, or Look-Ma-No-Mange, which is made in Mexico and available in any quantity at $5 per dose. The supply curve for Mange-Away crosses the (U.S.) demand curve for mange cures at a price of $8 per dose.

To the individual mange sufferer, Mange-Away and Look-Ma-No-Mange are interchangeable products. But although Mange-Away cures the disease, it also leaves the patient contagious to others. Look-Ma-No-Mange both cures the disease *and* renders the patient noncontagious; thus, every user of Look-Ma-No-Mange confers $1 worth of external benefits on his neighbors.

In order to encourage people to use more Mexican Look-Ma-No-Mange, the government has imposed a sales tax of $1 per dose on American Mange-Away.

    **a.** Before the tax is instituted, how much can U.S. producers charge for Mange-Away? After the tax is instituted, how much can U.S. producers charge for Mange-Away? Does the tax have any effect on the amount that U.S. consumers must pay for mange cures?

    **b.** Use a graph to show the quantities of Mange-Away and Look-Ma-No-Mange that Americans buy both before and after the tax is instituted.

    **c.** Use your graph to show how the tax on Mange-Away affects the welfare of all relevant groups of Americans, including the neighbors of potentially contagious mange sufferers and the recipients of tax revenue.

    **d.** Does the tax on Mange-Away create a net social loss or a net social gain? Of how much?

**16.** Widgets are provided by a single monopolist, whose production process pollutes the surrounding environment. The U.S. government is thinking about breaking the monopoly up into a large number of small firms, who would then form a competitive industry. The small firms would use exactly the same production process as the large firm; thus, a breakup would not affect either the private or the social marginal cost curve. Conditions in the industry are summarized by the following graph.

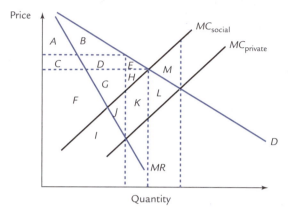

Suppose that you are called upon to advise the government as to whether breaking up the monopoly would improve social welfare. A magic oracle offers to reveal to you the exact numerical values of any *three* labeled areas in the graph. To help you give accurate advice, which three areas would you choose? Why?

**17.** A single competitive firm pollutes the air. There are no transactions costs between this firm and the neighbors who suffer from the pollution. In terms of the following diagram, what is the maximum amount that the neighbors would offer the firm in exchange for cutting its production back from $Q_E$ to $Q_O$? What is the minimum amount the firm would accept? How do you know that the deal is certain to go through?

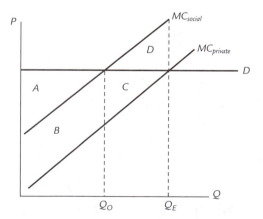

**18.** A competitive firm pollutes the air. The following graph shows the demand for the firm's product and the private and social marginal cost curves. The numbers in the graph represent areas.

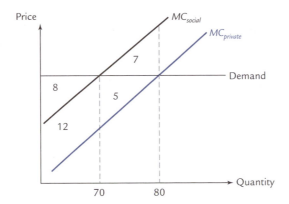

a. Suppose there are no transaction costs, that there is no legal penalty for polluting, and that it is impossible for the neighbors to move. What quantity does the firm produce? Give a concrete description of a deal that might be struck between the firm and the neighbors (including the exact amount of money that changes hands). What is the social gain from this transaction? (Your answer should be a *number*.)

b. Suppose transaction costs are so high that negotiation is impossible, and that it would cost the neighbors $6 to move. Under each of the following scenarios, determine whether or not the neighbors move, determine how much the firm produces, and compute the social gain. Which policy or policies are most efficient?

Policy I: The firm faces no penalty for pollution.

Policy II: The firm pays an excise tax equal to the amount of the externality it causes; all tax revenue is paid to people who live 3,000 miles away.

Policy III: The firm must reimburse the neighbors for all pollution damage.

c. Repeat part (b) on the assumption that it costs the neighbors $15 (instead of $6) to move.

d. Repeat part (b) on the assumption that it costs the neighbors $20 to move.

e. Repeat part (b) on the assumption that it costs the neighbors $25 to move.

19. Snidely Whiplash owns all the houses in the Yukon Territory, for which he charges the highest possible rent. He also owns the only electric company, which pollutes the territory's air. There is no way to negotiate with Snidely. It is costless for residents to leave the territory. The following graph shows the market for electricity:

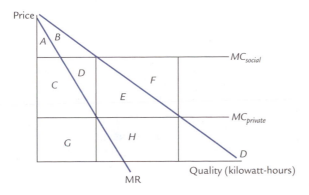

a. Snidely currently charges a monopoly price for electricity, but he is thinking of lowering the price to a competitive level. If he does so, how much does the price of housing change? Explain why. (*Hint:* Be sure to consider all the ways in which the electricity market affects the desirability of living in the Yukon Territory.)

b. Is it wise for Snidely to lower the price of electricity?

c. What is the combined deadweight loss due to Snidely's monopoly power and the pollution from the factory?

20. The widget industry is competitive. Widget factories pollute the neighborhoods where they are located. The following diagram shows the demand for widgets and the private and social marginal cost curves for the industry. There is no possibility of negotiation to reduce pollution. It would cost the neighbors $30 to move elsewhere.

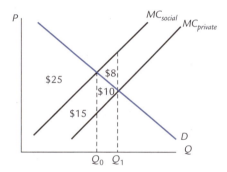

To maximize social gain, should the firm be subject to a Pigou tax? (*Note:* Assume all tax revenue goes to someone other than the neighbors.)

21. The widget industry is competitive and a source of localized air pollution (the pollution affects only people who live near widget factories). The following graph shows the demand for widgets and the private and social marginal cost curves.

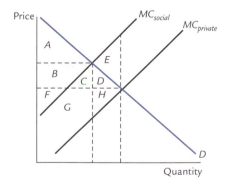

a. Suppose there has always been a Pigou tax, and that people have always lived near widget factories. One day the Pigou tax is eliminated, and all these neighbors move away. Fill in these blanks: The cost of moving must be greater than _____ but less than _____.

b. *Instead of the assumptions in part (a),* assume that there has never been a Pigou tax and that the factories still have neighbors. Assume also that if there *were* a Pigou tax, all of the revenue would be spent on entirely worthless projects. Which areas would you want to measure in order to determine whether a Pigou tax is an efficient policy?

**22.** Suppose that reckless driving imposes costs (in the form of medical bills) on both the drivers themselves and on pedestrians. Each mile of reckless driving costs drivers $1 and pedestrians $0.25. The marginal value to drivers of their reckless driving is indicated by the downward-sloping curve in the following figure:

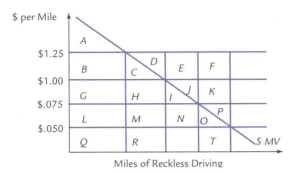

a. In terms of labeled areas on the graph, what is the social gain from reckless driving?

b. Suppose that you could require drivers to pay all the pedestrians' medical bills. According to the graph, how much would social gain increase?

c. Explain why, from the viewpoint of economic efficiency, requiring drivers to pay for pedestrians' medical bills might nevertheless be a mistake.

In the remainder of this problem, suppose that drivers can acquire air bags that reduce the cost (to them) of their reckless driving from $1 per mile to $0.50 per mile. The cost to pedestrians remains $0.25 per mile, regardless of whether drivers use air bags, and pedestrians pay their own medical bills.

d. Suppose you want to predict whether having air bags will increase or decrease drivers' medical costs. Which areas would you want to measure and compare?

e. Suppose you want to know whether air bags will increase or decrease the social gains from reckless driving. Which areas would you want to measure and compare?

f. Suppose you want to know how much drivers would be willing to pay for air bags. Which areas would you want to measure?

g. Suppose you are interested in maximizing social gain, so that you want drivers to buy air bags if and only if the social benefits of the air bags exceed their cost. You cannot tax reckless driving, but you can tax air bags. How much should you tax them?

**23.** **True or False:** If the courts enforce a negligence standard in determining liability for auto accidents, then people will take too many car trips.

**24.** A radical revision of accident law has been proposed. The proposal is that every individual who is within 1 mile of an auto accident when it occurs must pay a fine equal to the sum of all of the damages. No attempt will be made to determine who was responsible for the accident; everyone who was in the vicinity must pay the full amount. However, anyone who bears any personal costs as a result of the accident is permitted to deduct those costs from his fine. Evaluate the efficiency aspects of this proposal.

**25.** Betty hires Veronica to build an addition to Betty's house. They agree on a price and Veronica begins the job. After the work is partially completed, Betty changes her mind and decides that the addition is worth less than the price she has agreed to and announces that she will not pay for the job. Veronica then sues Betty for breach of contract.

Under these circumstances, a court can order Betty to pay either *reliance damages* or *expectation damages.* "Reliance damages" means a sum of money sufficient to make Veronica as well off as if she had never signed the contract. "Expectation damages" means a sum of money sufficient to make Veronica as well off as if the contract has been fulfilled.

Let A stand for the costs that Veronica has incurred so far, let $B$ stand for the total cost of building an addition, let $C$ stand for the amount Betty originally promised to pay, and let $D$ stand for the value that Betty places on having the job completed now that she has changed her mind about its worth.

a. How much will Betty have to pay Veronica under a rule of reliance damages? How much will Betty have to pay Veronica under a rule of expectation damages?

b. How much does Betty lose if she fulfills the contract?

c. Assuming that courts assess reliance damages, write down an inequality that expresses the condition under which Betty will break the contract. Do the same for expectation damages.

d. Write down an inequality that expresses the condition under which it is efficient for Betty to break the contract.

e. Which rule induces Betty to behave efficiently: reliance damages or expectation damages?

26. In the situation of the preceding problem, suppose that courts want to choose a standard (either reliance damages or expectation damages) that induces efficient behavior. Having worked the preceding problem, judges are aware that one of these standards results in contracts being broken when and only when it is efficient for them to be broken. (And, having worked the problem, they know *which* standard has this property.) Does it follow that this is the standard they should adopt?

# Common Property and Public Goods

In Chapter 13 we learned how incomplete property rights can lead to inefficiency. Here we will examine some important special cases. One is the theory of common property, which is property that has no owner. An example is a lake where any-body can fish and for which nobody has the authority to charge an admission fee. Another topic is the theory of public goods, which are goods that, once produced, are costlessly available for use by others. An example is a streetlight you install in front of your house, which illuminates your neighbor's properties for free.

Each of these theories is a topic in the theory of externalities. The user of a common property resource imposes a negative externality on other users, so that such property tends to be overused. The producer of a public good creates a posi-tive externality, so that such goods tend to be underproduced. We will explore the nature of these problems and will examine some potential solutions as well.

## 14.1 The Tragedy of the Commons

### The Springfield Aquarium

The small town of Springfield has a large city park that never gets crowded. Unfortunately, picnics in the park are pretty much the only recreational activity available in Springfield, and people have begun hankering to expand their options. Therefore, the town council wants to build an aquarium, financed by tax dollars and offering free admission. The aquarium will be small but excellent, and it is anticipated that it will always be crowded.

How much should the citizens of Springfield be willing to pay for their aquarium? That is, how much pleasure will the aquarium bring them? If Springfielders all have identical tastes, the remarkable answer is: Zero! If the aquarium costs so much as one penny to build, it is a bad idea.

How can this be true? To analyze the problem, we first measure the dollar value of a picnic in the park. Suppose that each picnic is worth $2. (Here is where we use the assumption that everyone's tastes are identical: We assume that the same $2 figure applies to everybody. Without this assumption, the analysis would be a bit more complicated.) Next we measure the dollar value of visiting the aquarium. Suppose that this value is $3.

Under these circumstances, aquarium visitors are happier than picnickers. The obvious consequence is that people start canceling their picnics and plan trips to the aquarium instead. As they do so, the aquarium becomes more crowded, and therefore less desirable. The value of a visit to the aquarium is now only $2.50.

You can probably foresee what comes next: Because the aquarium remains more desirable than the park, additional people skip the park and go to the aquarium. The crowds get even larger and the aquarium less desirable still. The process continues until an aquarium visit is worth only $2—neither more nor less than a picnic. But now the aquarium is worth nothing at all to the Springfielders. It makes them no more happy than a picnic, and picnics have always been available for free. Any resources spent to build the aquarium have been completely wasted.

Suppose that despite this argument, the aquarium gets built. Suppose also that two years later, a popular new television program about a school of Ninja Guppies inspires everyone in Springfield to learn more about fish. Does this increase the value of their aquarium? Unfortunately not. It certainly increases the value of *seeing the fish,* but it increases the size of the crowds as well. As before, the crowds must grow until an aquarium visit is no more fun than a picnic.

The aquarium is an example of **common property;** it has no owner and there are no restrictions on its use. Consequently, it is overused, to the point where it is of no value to anyone. All of the consumers' and producers' surpluses that the aquarium might have provided have vanished. Economists call this phenomenon the **dissipation of rents,** or, more poetically, the **tragedy of the commons.**

**Common property**

Property without a well-defined owner.

**Dissipation of rents or tragedy of the commons**

The elimination of social gains due to overuse of common property.

---

Dangerous
Curve

An important assumption has been slipped under the rug. We have assumed that the value of a picnic in the park is $2 for everyone. In particular, we have assumed that a picnic on Sunday is worth the same amount to people who are still cleaning ants out of Saturday's picnic basket as it is to people who have not picnicked in a year. If we assume instead that the value of a picnic depends on how much recent picnicking you've done, then the analysis becomes substantially more complicated, but dissipated rents remain the dominant theme.

---

## Admission Fees

What if the town decides to charge an aquarium admission fee of $1 per patron? The cost of a visit is now $3 (a forgone $2 picnic plus a $1 admission fee), and the size of the crowd readjusts downward so that the value of a visit is equal to the $3 cost. Aquarium-goers are still no happier than they were at the park.

Does this mean that the situation is no better than before? It does not mean that, and here is why: The revenue that the town collects is a social benefit that did not exist when the aquarium was free. All of that revenue is pure social gain, because it comes at nobody's expense: Those who pay the fee are fully compensated for it by the smaller crowds.

How can social gain be manufactured out of nothing at all? The answer is that each person who visits the aquarium imposes externalities on everyone whose elbows he jostles or whose view he obstructs. Because of these externalities, the free-admission equilibrium is inefficient. An admission fee acts as a Pigou tax that discourages overuse of the aquarium and increases the size of the social pie.

What is the best admission fee for the town to set? Because the only social gains in this situation are the revenues from the admission fee, the efficient fee is the one that maximizes those revenues. The socially optimal behavior for the town council is to behave like a profit-maximizing firm.

## A Graphical Analysis

Exhibit 14.1 shows the value of an aquarium visit as a function of the crowd size. The first two columns in the table show that if only 1 person is present, he values his visit at $10; if 2 are present, they value their visits at $9 each, and so forth. If 10 are present, they value their

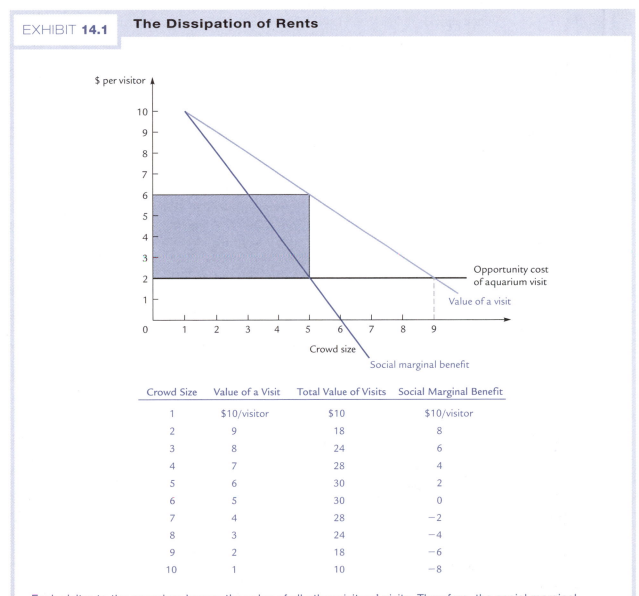

| EXHIBIT 14.1 | The Dissipation of Rents |
|---|---|

| Crowd Size | Value of a Visit | Total Value of Visits | Social Marginal Benefit |
|---|---|---|---|
| 1 | $10/visitor | $10 | $10/visitor |
| 2 | 9 | 18 | 8 |
| 3 | 8 | 24 | 6 |
| 4 | 7 | 28 | 4 |
| 5 | 6 | 30 | 2 |
| 6 | 5 | 30 | 0 |
| 7 | 4 | 28 | −2 |
| 8 | 3 | 24 | −4 |
| 9 | 2 | 18 | −6 |
| 10 | 1 | 10 | −8 |

Each visitor to the aquarium lowers the value of all other visitors' visits. Therefore, the social marginal benefit of adding a visitor is less than the value of his visit. If there is no admission fee, and the opportunity cost of a visit is $2, then 9 visitors enter, and there is no social gain. Rents are completely dissipated, and the aquarium is of no value to anybody.

If only 5 people come to the aquarium, each gains $4 (the $6 value of his visit minus his $2 opportunity cost). The social gain of $20, represented by the shaded area, is the largest possible. A $4 admission fee would ensure this optimal outcome.

visits at only $1 each. The numbers in the "value of a visit" column can also be thought of as the private marginal benefit that each new visitor gains from going to the aquarium.

The next column shows the total value of all aquarium visits. These numbers are constructed by multiplying the value of each visit times the size of the crowd. The final column shows the social marginal benefit due to each new visitor.

Notice that there is a discrepancy between private and social marginal benefits. For example, when the fourth visitor enters the aquarium, his private marginal benefit is $7 but the social marginal benefit is only $4. The $3 difference is accounted for by the externalities that his presence imposes on each of the first three visitors. The value of their visits is reduced by $1 apiece, from $8 to $7, for a total external cost of $3.

**Exercise 14.1** When the sixth visitor enters, what is the difference between his private marginal benefit and the social marginal benefit? What accounts for the difference?

The marginal cost of adding a visitor is a picnic forgone, or $2. We will assume that it costs the town nothing to let the visitor walk through the aquarium, so that this $2 is both the private marginal cost and the full social marginal cost. In the absence of an admission fee, the crowd grows until the private marginal benefit is equal to the $2 private marginal cost. The crowd size is 9 and there is no social gain.

The social optimum is achieved when the *social* marginal benefit is equal to the $2 marginal cost, at a crowd size of 5. At this crowd size, the difference between private marginal benefit and social marginal benefit (i.e., the externality) is $6 − $2 = $4. Therefore, the optimum can be achieved by imposing a Pigou tax—that is, an admission fee—of $4. This raises the private cost of a visit to $2 + $4 = $6, and the crowd stops growing when it reaches its optimal size of 5. The social gain is the sum of the admission fees, or 5 × $4 = $20, which is represented by the shaded area in the exhibit.

To check that we really have achieved a social optimum, we can compute what would happen if the admission fee were something different. If the fee is $8, then the private cost of a trip to the aquarium is $2 + $8 = $10 per person, and only 1 visitor attends. The town collects a total of $8 in fees. If the fee is $7, the private cost is $9 per person, and 2 visitors attend. The town collects $18. Continuing in this way, we can generate a table:

| Admission Fee | Crowd Size | Social Gain |
|---|---|---|
| $8 | 1 | $8 |
| 7 | 2 | 14 |
| 6 | 3 | 18 |
| 5 | 4 | 20 |
| 4 | 5 | 20 |
| 3 | 6 | 18 |
| 2 | 7 | 14 |
| 1 | 8 | 8 |
| 0 | 9 | 0 |

**Exercise 14.2** Check all of the entries in the table.

An examination of the table confirms that the $4 admission fee generates the largest possible social gain.

Throughout the analysis, we have treated crowding as something that *reduces the benefit* of visiting the aquarium. It would be equally correct to treat crowding as something that *increases the cost* of visiting the aquarium. Under the alternative analysis, the private and social marginal benefit curves would coincide, but the private and social marginal cost curves would diverge. For example, when the fifth person enters the aquarium, he lowers its value to the first four visitors by $1 each, so the social marginal cost of the fifth visitor is $6 ($2 private marginal cost plus $4 in externalities). The alternative analysis would result in a different graph, but the same numerical conclusions.

Dangerous
Curve

However, it is important not to double count. It is correct to count crowding as a reduction in benefit (as we have chosen to do in this text) or to count it as an increase in cost (as suggested in the preceding paragraph). It is *not* correct to treat it as both simultaneously.

## Property Rights

We have seen that if the Springfield aquarium were privately owned, all social gains would go to the owner in the form of entrance fees. To maximize these gains, the owner would set a $4 admission fee, ensuring the optimal crowd size of 5. Under private ownership, the socially efficient outcome is achieved automatically.

Indeed, any well-defined allocation of property rights leads to the socially efficient outcome. If it were feasible for visitors to demand compensation from others who jostled them or blocked their views, all of the externalities would be internalized and the crowd would adjust to its optimal size. In this scenario, property rights are allocated to some of the visitors rather than an aquarium owner. As always, it doesn't matter (for efficiency) who has the property rights as long as they are assigned and enforced.

But when there are no property rights at all—as when the town operates the aquarium and allows anyone to use it—we face the tragedy of the commons. In this example, rents are dissipated completely, and the aquarium might as well not exist.

## It Can Pay to Be Different

Consider again an aquarium with free admission. In our original analysis, we assumed that everyone values picnics at $2. Thus, we were implicitly assuming that everyone has identical tastes. Under this assumption, we discovered that the aquarium has no social value.

But now let us modify our assumption and suppose that tastes differ. Some Springfielders don't share their neighbors' enthusiasm for picnics; others are particularly keen on watching fish; still others are unusually serene about large crowds. Any of these people might have a positive preference for the aquarium over the park and can benefit from its presence. That benefit is a real social gain, and it means that the rents from the aquarium are not entirely dissipated.

Whether or not tastes differ, this much remains true: The marginal aquarium-goer is indifferent between the park and the aquarium. If he weren't, the crowd would grow and he wouldn't be marginal anymore. If everyone is identical to the fellow at the margin, then everyone shares his indifference and the aquarium is worthless. But if people are *not* all identical, the aquarium can yield positive social gains.

Unfortunately, even in this case the outcome is suboptimal. The crowd still grows until its marginal member has equated his private cost to his private benefit. That last entrant to the aquarium would be just as happy at the park, where he wouldn't be in other people's way. Moving him to the park would be a clear social improvement, but he has no incentive to move. An admission fee can provide the right incentive.

## A Graphical Analysis

Suppose that people differ in their enjoyment of picnics, so that some face higher opportunity costs than others when they visit the aquarium. Then the marginal cost of adding a visitor is upward sloping, as in Exhibit 14.2. The reason for the upward slope is that the first visitor is the one with the lowest opportunity cost, the second has a slightly higher opportunity cost, and so on.

Visitors arrive until the marginal visitor is just indifferent between entering the aquarium and going to the park; this occurs at a quantity $Q_C$. The visitors earn a total surplus of $F + G + H + I$. (This area can be divided into rectangles, each representing the excess of a visitor's benefit, which is always $P_C$, over his opportunity cost.) There would be more surplus if visitors stopped arriving when the marginal cost of entry equaled the marginal social benefit, at quantity $Q_O$. Here the surplus is $C + D + F + G + I$. This optimum can be achieved via an admission fee of $P_2 - P_1$.

---

**EXHIBIT 14.2**    **Gains from an Aquarium Whose Visitors Are Not Identical**

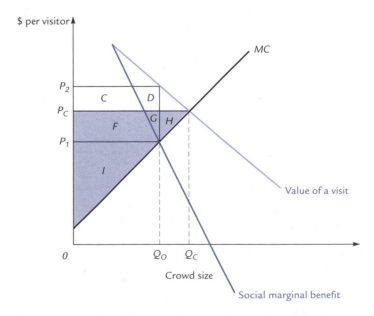

The $MC$ curve shows the cost of adding visitors to the aquarium. Visitors enter until the later entrant's visit has a value equal to his opportunity cost. This occurs at $Q_C$. Each visitor values his visit at $P_C$, and the total surplus is $F + G + H + I$. If it were possible to control entry, the optimal crowd size would be $Q_O$ and surplus would be $C + D + F + G + I$. An admission fee of $P_2 - P_1$ yields this optimal outcome, with $I$ going to visitors as surplus and $C + D + F + G$ going to the owner as revenue.

If the aquarium were run by a private competitor (competing with other aquariums), $P_2 - P_1$ is exactly the admission fee the owner would set. To discover this directly would require a little work, but we can jump to the conclusion because we know that competitive markets maximize social gains and that social gains are maximized by this admission fee. Under competition, then, the number of visitors is $Q_O$, the value of a visit is $P_2$, and the price of a visit is $P_2 - P_1$. Each visitor earns a surplus of $P_1$ minus his opportunity cost. The total surplus to visitors is area $I$. At the same time, the owner collects revenue equal to $C + D + F + G$. The social gain, consisting of visitors' surplus plus the owner's revenue, is $C + D + F + G + I$, the largest possible.

## Common Property

Common property is overused. At a common-property aquarium, the crowds grow too large. Rents are dissipated. This much we have seen. But there are still other problems associated with common property. One problem is that nobody has any incentive to maintain or improve that which is commonly owned. Imagine a large forest where many people come to cut trees. There might very well be nobody with the incentive to plant and tend new trees, because the planter has no well-defined property rights. Thus, we have two separate problems: First, if loggers impose externalities on each other, there will be too many loggers. Second, if planters have no rights to the fruit of their labors, there will be too few planters.

The most frequently cited example of a common-property resource is a lake stocked with fish. This example is cited so frequently, in fact, that economists sometimes refer to any commonly owned property as a fishery. Here the dissipation of rents and the lack of maintenance can be especially acute, because a fish caught today is a fish that does not reproduce tomorrow. As a result, the fish can be overharvested to the point of extinction. The whaling industry presents an important instance (whales are not fish, but whaling is a fishery). The imminent extinction of various species is a direct result of the fact that nobody owns the whales. In the timber industry, by contrast, trees are constantly replenished precisely because they are owned.

**Fishery**
Common property.

It is interesting to contrast the fate of elephants with the fate of cattle. Elephants are hunted for their ivory and, like whales, face possible extinction. It is sometimes claimed that the world's demand for ivory is the source of the problem. But the world's demand for meat far exceeds its demand for ivory, and nobody worries that cattle might become extinct. The key difference is that elephants are common property, and cattle are not.

## Optimal Activity Levels

Before we leave this subject, there is one further subtlety worth mentioning. There is a sense in which even an admission fee fails to completely alleviate the tragedy of the commons. The reason is this: Even though the admission fee can limit the number of entrants, it does nothing to limit people's activity after they have entered. Even at an aquarium where the crowd size is already optimal, there might be further social improvements if visitors could be induced to spend more time at the snack bar and less time standing in front of other visitors at the exhibits. To overcome this problem, the owner would have to be able to charge people separately for every activity that imposes externalities.

If you have ever been to Disneyland, you have directly observed this sort of inefficiency. There is a fee to enter the park, without which congestion would dissipate rents. But there are no fees for the individual rides, as a result of which people queue up for the popular rides without regard to the costs (in waiting time) that they are imposing on others.[1,2] The result can be waits of several hours, which would be alleviated by well-defined property rights.

Dangerous
Curve

This is not a complete analysis of the problem. The next question to ask is: If the pricing system at Disneyland is so inefficient, why don't they change it? The same question occurs for ski-lift tickets: Why do resorts sell tickets on a daily basis rather than a per-ride basis, when the former creates long lines that skiers would be willing to pay to avoid? These questions are difficult, but they have been addressed.

## Example-Splitting the Check

Suppose that you are eating dinner at a restaurant as part of a party of 10.[3] It comes time to decide whether to order dessert. You are surprised to discover that the dessert selections are very expensive, all priced at $10, whereas the most you would be willing to pay is $2. Of course, you choose to pass up dessert.

Now the waiter arrives at the table and announces that he forgot to keep separate checks and as a result will present one bill, which will be split 10 ways. Suddenly the dessert takes on the characteristics of common property: You can have it without paying the full cost. In fact, ordering a $10 dessert will raise everyone's bill, including your own, by only $1. You order dessert. This decision is individually optimal, regardless of what everyone else is doing.

Now, as it happens, everyone else at the table has the same preferences as you do and reasons in exactly the same way. Everyone orders dessert. You end up paying $10 (a $1 share of each of 10 desserts) and getting a dessert that you value at $2.

Perhaps this inefficient outcome should be referred to as the "tragedy of the compotes."

**Exercise 14.3** Find a better pun.

## Example-Bumblebees and Property Rights

Often, several species of bumblebees compete for nectar from the same flowers.[4] The nectar is a common-property resource, so each species has an incentive to extract more nectar than is optimal from the viewpoint of all the bees. A system of contracts limiting each species' harvesting would improve each species' welfare.

Evolution has provided an excellent substitute for such a system of contracts. In small locales only a few species of bees tend to be abundant, and these species tend to have tongues of widely varying lengths (typically, there are three species: one very

---

[1] As always, it doesn't matter who has these rights. If the park claimed them, it could set appropriate prices to discourage inefficient overuse of the rides. If the customers had well-defined, enforceable property rights, the people behind you in line could bribe you to leave, so that only those who valued the rides highly enough to justify the cost would remain.

[2] See R. Barro and P. Romer, "Ski-Lift Pricing, with Applications to Labor and Other Markets," *American Economic Review* 77 (1987): 875–890.

[3] This example is adapted from D. Weimer and A. Vining, *Policy Analysis: Concepts and Practice,* Chapter 3 (Englewood Cliffs, NJ: Prentice-Hall, 1989).

[4] This example is taken from the fascinating book *Bumblebee Economics* by Bernd Heinrich (Cambridge, MA: Harvard University Press, 1979).

short-tongued, one long-tongued, and one medium-tongued). These differences cause the bees to favor different flowers. Short-tongued bees cannot reach the nectar in flowers with deep corollas; on the other hand, a long tongue can be a clumsy liability on a short-corolla flower.

As a result, each species specializes in taking nectar from particular sorts of flowers. Tongue lengths allocate property rights, and the bees avoid dissipating rents from nectar, without which they could not survive.

# 14.2 Public Goods

A good is said to be a **public good** if one person's consumption increases the amount available to everybody. The most commonly cited example is national defense. An additional missile built to defend your house automatically defends your neighbor's houses as well. Police protection is another example, as are city parks, streetlights, and television programs (a program broadcast to your set is broadcast to other sets as well).

When called upon to make this definition more precise, economists define public goods in different ways. Some define a public good to be one that is **nonexcludable,** meaning that when one person consumes the good, there is no way to prevent others from consuming it as well. People define a public good to be one that is **nonrivalrous,** meaning that when one person consumes the good, it becomes possible to provide it to others at no additional cost. Yet other people define a public good to be one that is both nonrivalrous and nonexcludable simultaneously.

Common property, such as a fishery, is nonexcludable (anyone can use it) but not nonrivalrous (each fisherman reduces the number of fish available to others). Movie showings in uncrowded theaters are nonrivalrous (once the movie is being shown, it costs nothing to allow others to enter the theater) but not nonexcludable (theater owners can refuse admittance to anyone without a ticket). National defense, police protection, and uncrowded city parks are both nonexcludable and nonrivalrous.

## Some Market Failures

A **market failure** occurs when private markets fail to provide some good in socially efficient quantities. Nonexcludable and nonrivalrous goods are particularly susceptible to market failures, for reasons we shall now explore.

### Nonexcludability

In Section 14.1 we saw how nonexcludability (e.g., at an admission-free aquarium) can lead to inefficient crowding. Here we shall concentrate on a different form of inefficiency associated with nonexcludable goods: The market tends to undersupply them.

Suppose that it would cost $300 to install a streetlight that is worth $10 to each of 100 neighbors. The streetlight is socially desirable, but no individual is willing to pay for it. The neighborhood could take up a collection, asking everybody to contribute to a streetlight fund. If the fundraising drive is successful, the light gets built and everybody benefits. Nevertheless, people are not eager to contribute. Each reasons thus: "I'm not sure whether my neighbors are contributing generously, though I hope they are. But if they're

---

**Public good**

A good where one person's consumption increases the consumption available for others.

**Nonexcludable good**

A good that, if consumed by one person, is automatically available to others.

**Nonrivalrous good**

A good that, if consumed by one person, can be provided to others at no additional cost.

**Market failure**

An occasion on which private markets fail to provide some good in socially efficient quantities.

not, my contribution probably won't be enough to get the light built. And if they are, the light will get built without my contribution. Either way, I see no point in contributing."

This free riding is an example of the Prisoner's Dilemma that we met in Chapter 11. Although it is rational behavior for each individual separately, it leads to a socially sub-optimal outcome: The streetlight does not get built.

If streetlights were excludable, there would be no problem. The rule would simply be that if you don't contribute, you can't use the light. Unfortunately, there is no way to prevent people from making use of a streetlight once it is lit. This nonexcludability is the source of the free-riding problem.

## Nonrivalry

Computer software is expensive to develop but cheap to reproduce. Indeed, copies of sophisticated software can be reproduced at a marginal cost very close to zero. Thus, software is an example of a nonrivalrous good.

What is the efficient price for a software package once it has been produced? The answer is zero. At any higher price, some people who want the software will decide not to buy it. Because it would cost nothing to make the software available to everybody, it is inefficient to deny it to anybody.

The same is true of seats in an uncrowded movie theater. If the $5 admission fee keeps people away, there is a pure social loss. It would cost the theater owner nothing to allow people to sit in the unused seats.

Unfortunately, if nonrivalrous goods were really priced at zero, nobody would produce them. The software manufacturers and theater owners must set positive prices for their goods or there will be no goods to sell. These nonzero prices mean that nonrivalrous goods, if they are produced at all, are produced in inefficiently small quantities.

## The Provision of Public Goods

Because nonexcludable and nonrivalrous goods are supplied inadequately by the marketplace, they are often provided by the government. If it would cost $300 to build a streetlight that 100 neighbors value at $10 apiece, we have seen that the market can fail to provide the streetlight. A government, however, can assess a tax of $3 per neighbor and use the proceeds to build the light, yielding a clear gain in social welfare.

On the other hand, alternative mechanisms can sometimes accomplish the same job through the marketplace. In principle, an ambitious entrepreneur could buy all 100 houses in the neighborhood for their current market value, install the streetlight at a cost of $300, and then resell each house for $10 more than he paid for it—because we already know that a house near a streetlight is worth $10 more than a house that is in the dark at night.

For something as small as a streetlight, this kind of plan might be more trouble than it's worth—unless the entrepreneur already owns the houses. A builder who has just constructed a housing development will voluntarily install streetlights at his own expense if he thinks their value to potential buyers exceeds their cost. If the builder is a shrewd judge of preferences, he will provide such public goods in optimal quantities, without any need for the government to take action.

### Example-Clean Air

Cleantown and Grimyville are identical in every way except for air quality. The Grimyville Steel Plant accounts for the difference.

People moving in from out of state can rent apartments in either Cleantown or Grimyville. Why does anyone choose Grimyville? For one reason and one only: The rents are lower. In fact, the rents are just enough lower so that people are indifferent between the two towns. If people weren't indifferent, there would be migration between the two towns and rents would adjust until people *were* indifferent.

Grimyville Steel is capable of producing clean air by installing filters in its smoke-stacks. The reason it doesn't do so is that clean air is nonexcludable; there is no way to make the beneficiaries pay for it. This is just the sort of transactions cost that we often encountered in Chapter 13.

Because the market does not provide clean air in adequate quantities, the Grimyville City Council has ordered Grimyville Steel to clean up its act under penalty of law. The results have been remarkable: Grimyville's air is now indistinguishable from Cleantown's.

Of course, Grimyville's rents are also now indistinguishable from Cleantown's. So who benefits from the clean air legislation? Certainly not the apartment dwellers. Originally, they had a choice between living in Grimyville and Cleantown, and between the two they were indifferent. Now they have a choice between living in two copies of Cleantown. This makes them no worse off than before, but no better off either.[5]

The only beneficiaries of the clean air legislation are the landlords of Grimyville, who collect all of the benefits in the form of higher rents. It is therefore very easy to determine whether the clean air legislation is efficient: If rents rise by more than the cleanup costs, then there is a net social gain; if they rise by less, there is a net social loss.

Now the question is: Could the landlords of Grimyville have taken up a collection on their own to bribe Grimyville Steel and make it stop polluting, or to clean up the air in some other way? Surely there would be a free-rider problem here, but not so intractable a free-rider problem as if all the citizens of Grimyville had been beneficiaries. If there are only half a dozen landlords in town, it is conceivable that they could formulate and enforce an agreement that would obligate all of them to contribute to the antipollution fund.

When the benefits of a public good are concentrated among a small number of people, there is a better chance that the good can be provided by coordinated action among the beneficiaries. The point of this example is that a good that at first appears to benefit a very large class (here, all of the residents of Grimyville) may in fact benefit only a much smaller class (here, the Grimyville landlords). In fact, whenever a public good increases the desirability of living in a certain area, its benefits tend to be captured completely by an increase in land values. If the number of landlords is small, the public good can frequently be provided by private action.

## The Role of Government

When the benefits of a public good are widespread, private mechanisms can break down and the government plays a role as provider. Governments provide national defense and police services because such goods are nonexcludable. A private army or police force cannot charge for its services and protect only those who pay; an aggressor or criminal deterred is as much a benefit to those who don't contribute as to those who do.

---

[5] This analysis assumes that everyone's tastes are identical. Without this assumption the analysis is slightly subtler. This theme is taken up in the problems at the end of the chapter.

There is, however, a crucial difficulty. How can the government determine when it is optimal to purchase a public good? Suppose that some neighbors believe that the streetlight would be a net benefit to the neighborhood and others don't. One possibility is to conduct a vote on the matter. However, a disadvantage of voting is that it does not allow people to register the strengths of their preferences. If 19 people each value the light at $1 apiece and if one person would be willing to pay $40 to prevent its construction, an election will lead to an overwhelming victory for installing the light, even though installing it is socially undesirable.

Another possibility is for the government to ask people not just whether they want the light, but how much it is worth to them to either have it or not have it. This has the disadvantage that people will find it in their interest to exaggerate their preferences. If you want the light at all, you might as well claim that it is worth $1 million to you, just to increase the chance of its being built.

In order to create appropriate incentives, the government might say that your share of the tax burden for installing the streetlight will be proportional to its value to you. This makes it costly to exaggerate the value and discourages overstatements. Unfortunately, it encourages dishonesty of another sort. People will tend to understate their personal valuations so as to shift the tax burden to their neighbors. With everybody understating, there may be a false appearance of insufficient demand to justify installing the lamp.

In order for the government to provide public goods in appropriate quantities, it must find ways of gathering information that is initially available only to private individuals with no incentives to reveal it. One possible source of such information is the price of private goods that are similar in nature to the public good being contemplated. For example, suppose that the good under consideration is a dam that will make water available to surrounding farmland. If the farmers are currently purchasing water through a private mechanism, the price of that water is a good indication of its value to farmers.

The more common situation, however, is one in which no such easily observable good exists. The surprising fact is that in such a case it is often possible, by the clever structuring of incentives, to induce people to reveal their true demand for a public good.

Before describing such a mechanism, we present as puzzles two other situations in which there exist surprising mechanisms to elicit the revelation of privately held information. In each case try to figure out the scheme that works before looking at the answer later in this section.

*Puzzle No. 1:*  In Joseph Conrad's novel *Typhoon*, each of 200 men on a ship has stored several years' wages in his own personal strongbox. The ship encounters bad weather, the boxes are smashed, and all the coins are mixed together. The captain gathers up all the coins and wants to return them to the men, giving each the number of coins to which he is rightfully entitled. Each man knows how many coins were his, but nobody knows how many belong to anybody else. Obviously, each man, if asked, will exaggerate his fair share. How can the coins be returned to their owners?[6]

*Puzzle No. 2:*  Property taxes are levied in proportion to the value of people's homes. Ideally, each individual would be taxed a given fraction of the valuation that he personally places on his house. In practice, this is assumed to be equal to the market value of

---

[6] The analogy between this problem and the theory of public goods was suggested by Gene Mumy in "A Superior Solution to Captain MacWhirr's Problem," *Journal of Political Economy* 89 (1981). The solution he proposed was substantially more complicated (though identical in spirit) to the one that we will give.

similar houses. Because no two houses are alike, taxing agencies devote considerable resources to examining individual houses and assessing their values. Homeowners often protest these assessments, leading to costly disputes. How can the tax collector costlessly determine the true value of an individual house (keeping in mind that only the owner himself is initially in possession of this information)?

---

In interpreting Puzzle No. 2, keep in mind that the value a homeowner places on his home might be very different from its market value.

---

Dangerous
Curve

## Schemes for Eliciting Information

The town of Springfield is thinking of installing a streetlight, and the local newspaper has been lobbying for it very hard. Mayor June is interested to know just how much Ed the Editor really values a streetlight and doesn't trust him to tell the truth if he is asked outright. So the mayor has thought of a tricky plan.

Using his pocket calculator, the mayor has generated a random number $X$, which is recorded in a sealed envelope. He has walked into Ed's office and laid down some terms: "Ed, I want you to tell me how much you really value that streetlight. Whatever answer you give me I will call $E$. If my secret number $X$ is less than $E$, I will build the streetlight and I will raise your taxes by $X$ to pay for it. (The mayor has total control of the tax laws in Springfield.) But if $X$ is more than $E$, then I'm going to forget all about this streetlight thing and leave your taxes as they are."

Now Ed actually values the streetlight at $47. Because he'll have to pay $X$ in taxes to build it, Ed is thinking "If $X$ is less than $47, this streetlight is a good deal for me and I hope it gets built. But if $X$ is more than $47, I hope we can forget all about this streetlight thing."

If you compare the mayor's offer with Ed's silent calculation, you will discover something remarkable: If Ed tells the truth, so that $E = \$47$, then he is certain to get the outcome he prefers. Faced with the mayor's terms, Ed will choose to tell the truth and the mayor will learn the streetlight's true value.

## Reaching the Efficient Outcome

It is not only Ed's opinion that interests the mayor. What the mayor really wants to know is whether it would be efficient to build the streetlight. The light would cost $300 and it would benefit five people, one of whom is Ed. The problem is to simultaneously discover how much each of the five values the streetlight and to build it only if the sum of those values exceeds $300.

Here is the mayor's plan. Instead of walking into Ed's office with a secret number in his pocket, he asks each of the five (Al, Barb, Cassie, Dale, and Ed) to write down an assessment of the streetlight's value. The mayor plans to call these numbers $A, B, C, D,$ and $E$. He announces to Ed (in advance): "After the envelopes are opened I am going to compare your number $E$ with the number $X = 300 - A - B - C - D$. If $X$ is less than $E$, I will build the streetlight and charge you $X$. Otherwise, I will forget about the streetlight."

This is just like the mayor's earlier plan except that the unknown random number $X$ from the mayor's calculator is replaced by the unknown number $X = 300 - A - B - C - D$. Just as before, Ed is induced to tell the truth.

At the same time, the mayor tells Dale that he will decide whether to build the light by comparing Dale's number $D$ with the number $300 - A - B - C - E$. If $300 - A - B - C - E < D$, the mayor will build and charge Dale $300 - A - B - C - E$; otherwise, he will do nothing. Dale, like Ed, is induced to tell the truth.

The mayor makes similar announcements to Cassie, Barb, and Al. In Cassie's case he says he will make a decision by comparing $300 - A - B - D - E$ with $C$; this leads Cassie to tell the truth, and similarly for Barb and Al.

Now the mayor has made a lot of apparently contradictory promises, but fortunately the contradictions are only apparent. He has told Ed that he will build if and only if $300 - A - B - C - D < E$; he has told Dale that he will build if and only if $300 - A - B - C - E < D$, and so forth. A small amount of algebra reveals that each of these conditions is equivalent to the single condition $A + B + C + D + E > 300$. Therefore, all of the promises are equivalent and can be kept simultaneously.

And something even more wonderful is true: The streetlight gets built if and only if it is efficient. The inequality $A + B + C + D + E > 300$ says precisely that the light's benefits exceed its costs; and this is precisely the circumstance in which the light gets built.

Clarke tax

A tax designed to elicit information about the demand for public goods.

The mayor's tax plan is an example of a **Clarke tax.** The only problem with the Clarke tax is that if the light *does* get built, the mayor has made some promises about how much he will tax everybody, and there is no reason why the tax revenue should happen to just cover the $300 cost of the light: It could turn out to be either too high or too low. Thus, the mayor must be prepared either to turn a profit for the city treasury or to finance the light partly out of city coffers if that becomes necessary. If he is willing to do so, he can simultaneously elicit full information from everybody and guarantee an efficient outcome.

## Solutions to Puzzles

The mayor's cleverness solves a problem that initially appears insoluble. Here are some clever solutions to the puzzles from earlier in this chapter.

*Solution to Puzzle No. 1:* The captain can ask each man to write down the number of coins he started with. He announces that the numbers will be added up and that if the sum does not match exactly the total number of actual coins, all of the coins will be tossed overboard.

*Solution to Puzzle No. 2:* Ask each homeowner what his house is worth to him. The values will be made public, and each owner will be required to sell to anyone who offers him more than the stated value of his house. No truthful owner can be hurt by this scheme; he can only be forced to sell to someone he would be willing to sell to anyway.

# Summary

Commonly owned property is an important source of externalities. There is no way to limit use of the property in order to avoid problems of congestion. Also, there is no incentive to improve the property itself. If all users of the property are identical, then rents will be dissipated completely. This is because people continue to use the property until everyone is indifferent regarding its existence. An owner—any owner—will improve social welfare by setting entry fees that discourage overuse and also perhaps by improving the property.

If users of the property vary in their tastes or opportunity costs, then rents are partially, but not completely, dissipated in the absence of ownership.

Because public goods present incentives for free riding, they represent a type of externality. Because individuals will purchase less than the optimal quantity of public goods, public goods are often provided by the government. This makes it desirable for the government to be able to elicit information about how much people value public goods, which presents a problem in view of individuals' incentives to be untruthful. A number of clever schemes have been devised for eliciting truthful responses in a variety of circumstances.

## Review Questions

**R1.** What is the dissipation of rents? Under what circumstances are rents dissipated completely? Under what circumstances are they dissipated partially? Why?

**R2.** What is a nonrivalrous good? What is a nonexcludable good?

**R3.** Describe a mechanism that would induce each party to reveal how much he privately values a certain public good.

## Numerical Exercises

**N1.** Each potential user of the Phoenix River Bridge is willing to pay up to $299 per crossing, provided there are no other cars to slow him down. When there are more cars, willingness to pay goes down. Specifically, when there are $N$ cars per day on the bridge, each user is willing to pay up to ($300 − N^2$) to cross.

    **a.** In terms of $N$, what is the social gain from the existence of the bridge?

    **b.** If there is no bridge toll, how many people cross per day and what is the social gain?

    **c.** What is the optimal number of bridge crossings per day? (To answer this question, you will need either some calculus or some patience with trial and error.)

    **d.** If there is a bridge toll of $T$, how many people cross per day? (Answer in terms of $T$.)

    **e.** What is the optimal bridge toll? How much social gain results when this toll is set? Who gets the benefits?

**N2.** Let $A$ be the value of a visit to the aquarium and let $\eta$ be the elasticity of $A$ with respect to the number of visitors. (That is, $\eta$ is the elasticity of the lightly colored curve in Exhibit 13.1.) Show that the optimal admission fee is $A|\eta|$.

## Problem Set

**1.** A fisherman at Hardin Lake can catch 20 fish per day, provided he has the lake to himself. Two fishermen can catch 19 fish apiece per day, and three can catch 18 fish apiece per day. Other numbers are given by the table:

| Number of Fishermen | Fish per Day per Fisherman |
|:---:|:---:|
| 1 | 20 |
| 2 | 19 |
| 3 | 18 |
| 4 | 17 |
| 5 | 15 |
| 6 | 13 |
| 7 | 10 |
| 8 | 7 |

The opportunity cost of a day at the lake is 7 fish (i.e., the alternative activity is as valuable as 7 fish).

a.  How many fishermen come to the lake? How many fish do they catch? What is the social gain from the existence of the lake?

b.  What is the optimal number of fishermen at the lake? What is the social gain if this optimum is achieved?

c.  What entrance fee leads to the optimal outcome?

2.  Happy, Grumpy, Dopey, Sleepy, Sneezy, Doc, and Bashful are miners, who have nothing to do with their time but to go mining. There are no other miners in the vicinity. Each miner can dig in either of two mines. The number of gold nuggets that a miner can find in a day depends both on which mine he is working and how many other miners are present in that mine, as indicated by the following chart:

| Number of Miners | Nuggets per day in Mine A | Nuggets per day in Mine B |
|:---:|:---:|:---:|
| 1 | 20 | 30 |
| 2 | 18 | 27 |
| 3 | 16 | 24 |
| 4 | 14 | 21 |
| 5 | 12 | 18 |
| 6 | 10 | 15 |
| 7 | 8 | 12 |

a.  If entry to the mines is free, how many miners work in each mine?

b.  At the social optimum, how many miners would work in each mine?

c.  What system of entry fees to the mines could bring about that social optimum?

d.  Suppose that both mines are owned by a wicked queen who can set entry fees. What fees would she set?

3.  Two roads go from Hereville to Thereville. One road is very wide and can easily accommodate all the traffic that would ever want to use it, but it is in poor repair and unpleasant to drive on. The other road is in excellent repair and goes through the most scenic areas, but it has only one lane in each direction and easily becomes congested.

a.  Explain why, if there are sufficiently many drivers, both roads will be equally pleasant to drive on.

b.  How do the private marginal benefits compare for a driver entering the wide road and a driver entering the narrow road? How do the marginal social benefits compare?

    **c.** In view of your answer to part (b), could a social planner reallocate one car in order to make a welfare improvement?

    **d.** How much further reallocation would the planner want to make? How could the same thing be accomplished without a planner?

**4.** A race of dwarfs lived near a forest where apple trees grew wild. Any dwarf who wanted to could enter the forest and pick apples for himself and his family. One day a giant came, claimed the forest for himself, and began charging the dwarfs for the right to pick apples.

    **a.** Suppose that dwarfs can pick fewer apples when the forest is more crowded. Draw a graph with "Number of dwarfs in the forest" on the horizontal axis and "Apples per dwarf" on the vertical. Draw a curve representing the number of apples picked per dwarf and a curve representing each dwarf's marginal contribution to the apple harvest. Explain intuitively why the latter curve lies below the former.

    **b.** Suppose that all dwarfs have the same opportunity cost to enter the forest. Show on your graph how many dwarfs enter the forest before the giant arrives and how many enter after the giant arrives. Show the giant's revenue.

    **c.** Now drop the assumption that all dwarfs have the same opportunity cost, and assume that some dwarfs' time is more valuable than others'. On the graph you drew for part (a), add the upward-sloping curve that shows the marginal cost of adding dwarfs to the forest. Show the number of dwarfs that enter. Show the producers' surplus that the dwarfs earn as apple-pickers.

    **d.** Continuing to use your graph from part (c), show the optimal number of dwarfs in the forest. Show the entrance fee that achieves this optimal number. Explain why this is the entrance fee that a competitive giant would set.

    **e.** Can the dwarfs be made better off as a result of the giant's arrival and the entry fee? What about society as a whole (consisting of the dwarfs plus the giant)?

    **f.** (This is a difficult problem.) Assuming straight-line curves, and assuming that the giant sets a monopoly price to enter the forest, show that the monopolized forest is more socially efficient than the common-property forest if and only if the "marginal apple harvest" curve is steeper than the dwarfs' marginal cost curve.

**5.** **True or False:** A communally owned lake is more valuable in a town where everybody is an excellent fisherman than in a town where people vary widely in their fishing ability.

**6.** Suppose that the town of Springfield establishes an aquarium with free admission and that all residents of Springfield are identical. **True or False:** If the population of Springfield is sufficiently small, not all rents will be dissipated.

**7.** Rollo's Roller Rink is located in a town where everyone is identical. Rollo's is subject to crowding and becomes less pleasant when it is crowded. **True or False:** If Rollo is a monopolist, he will charge exactly the same price as he would under competition.

**8.** Which of the following are nonexcludable? Nonrivalrous? Both? Neither?

    **a.** Network TV programming

    **b.** Cable TV programming

    **c.** Textbooks

    **d.**    Statues in the park

    **e.**    Water fountains in the park

**9.**    A public radio station soliciting donations argued that its listeners would be irrational not to contribute. "Unless our fund drive is successful," they warned, "we will have to go off the air. Surely you get at least $20 worth of pleasure from listening to our station over the course of a year. Make your $20 pledge now to protect your own self-interest." Comment.

**10.**    Most of the people living on the north side of Boomtown are apartment dwellers who commute into the center of town every day to go to work. The city is considering building a new subway line between the north side and the center of town. **True or False:** Because the landlords all live on the south side of town, and the employers are all in the center of town, all of the benefits from the new subway will go to the working people on the north side of town.

**11.**    Cleantown and Grimyville are identical except for the inferior air quality in Grimyville. All potential residents have identical tastes. Apartments in Cleantown rent for $300 per month. The cost of breathing Grimyville air is $100 per month. The quantity of apartments in each town is fixed.

    **a.**    Explain why the demand curve for Grimyville apartments is flat at a price of $200 per month. Draw the supply and demand curves for Grimyville apartments and show the consumers' and producers' surpluses.

    **b.**    Suppose that the air in Grimyville is brought up to Cleantown standards. Show the effects of this change on your graph. Show the increase in social gain. Who benefits from the clean air?

**12.**    In the preceding problem, drop the assumption that everyone is identical. Some hate pollution more than others do. The one person in Grimyville who hates pollution the most considers the cost of breathing it to be $100 per month.

    **a.**    Explain why the demand curve for Grimyville apartments is downward sloping. At what price does it cross the supply curve? Draw the supply and demand curves for Grimyville apartments and show the consumers' and producers' surpluses.

    **b.**    Suppose that the air in Grimyville is brought up to Cleantown standards. Show the effects of this change on your graph. Show the increase in social gain. Who benefits from the clean air? Who loses from it?

**13.**    Suppose that you want to sell your car to one of several people and that you decide to auction it off. You are curious to know the highest price that each of the potential buyers would be willing to pay for the car. You ask each to submit a sealed bid, announcing that the car will go to the high bidder but that he will be charged the amount of the second-highest bid. Will the submitted bids be truthful? Why or why not?

**14.**    (This is a difficult problem.) A factory that emits noxious smoke is located near a small cluster of homes. It is up to you to decide whether the factory will have to install pollution-control equipment. A key variable in your decision is the extent of the cost imposed on the homeowners. How can you discover this cost?

# The Demand for Factors of Production

In the preceding 14 chapters, we have studied markets for consumption goods. In this and the next two chapters, we will study markets for factors of production (also called inputs). Factors of production, such as labor and capital, are supplied by individual households and demanded by firms, which use them to produce output for consumption. In this chapter, we will study the firm's demand for inputs.

Firms demand inputs only because they can be used to produce output. Therefore, the value of those inputs depends on conditions in the output market. For example, a farmer's demand for fertilizer depends on the price at which he can sell his crops. The need to take account of conditions in the output market means that the derivation of the firm's demand for factors will be more subtle than the derivation of the consumer's demand for consumption goods.

The firm's income is paid out to the various factors of production. Workers receive wages, the owners of capital receive rental payments for the use of their facilities, and so forth. In the last section of this chapter, we will use our understanding of the firm's factor demand curves to see what determines how the firm's income is distributed.

## 15.1 The Firm's Demand for Factors in the Short Run

In the short run, only one factor of production is variable, and we will assume that factor to be labor. Thus, we will study the demand for labor on the assumption that the firm uses some fixed quantity of capital.

### The Marginal Revenue Product of Labor

Recall from Chapter 6 that the total and marginal product of labor curves are typically shaped like those in the first two panels of Exhibit 15.1. We will also be interested in the **marginal revenue product of labor** $(MRP_L)$, defined as the additional revenue earned by the firm when one additional unit of labor is employed. The marginal revenue product of labor is measured in dollars per unit of labor, whereas the marginal product of labor is measured in units of output per unit of labor.

**Marginal revenue product of labor $(MRP_L)$**

The additional revenue that a firm earns when it employs one more unit of labor.

EXHIBIT **15.1**        The Total, Marginal, and Marginal Revenue Products of Labor

A

B

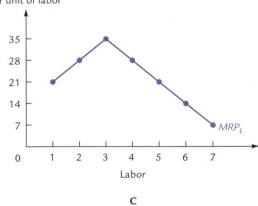

C

The total product and marginal product of labor ($MP_L$) curves are as in Exhibit 6.1. The marginal product of labor increases until diminishing marginal returns set in at $L = 3$, and it decreases thereafter. If the firm is competitive and sells its output at $7 per unit, then the marginal revenue product of labor ($MRP_L$) is given by

$$MRP_L = \$7 \times MP_L$$

Thus, the $MRP_L$ curve can be constructed from the $MP_L$ curve by simply changing the units on the vertical axis, as shown in panel C.

For a firm in a competitive industry, selling output at a going price $P_X$, the marginal revenue product of labor is given by:

$$MRP_L = P_X \cdot MP_L$$

Given the $MP_L$ curve from Exhibit 15.1 and given the price of output (say, $7 per unit), we can construct the $MRP_L$ curve simply by changing the units on the vertical axis. We have done so in panel C of the exhibit.

---

**Exercise 15.1** If the firm in question were a monopolist in the output market, how would the $MRP_L$ curve differ?

---

Suppose that the firm can hire labor at a going wage rate of $25 per unit of labor. How much labor will it hire? As long as additional units of labor yield marginal revenue products in excess of $25, it will continue hiring. As soon as the $MRP_L$ reaches $25, it will stop. Therefore, we see from Exhibit 15.1 that the firm will hire 4½ units of labor. In general, at any given wage rate, the firm will want to hire a quantity of labor read from the downward-sloping portion of the $MRP_L$ curve. We can summarize this by saying

The firm's short-run demand curve for labor coincides with the downward-sloping portion of the $MRP_L$ curve.

## The Algebra of Profit Maximization

The amount of labor needed to produce one more unit of output is $1/MP_L$. The cost of that labor is the price per unit of labor ($P_L$) times the quantity of labor ($1/MP_L$), or $P_L/MP_L$. Therefore, the marginal cost of producing another unit of output is given by:

$$MC = \frac{P_L}{MP_L}$$

When firms maximize profit, they set the price of output $P_X$ equal to marginal cost, or:

$$P_X = MC$$

Combining the two displayed equations, we find that profit maximization requires:

$$P_X = \frac{P_L}{MP_L}$$

or

$$P_L = P_X \cdot MP_L = MRP_L$$

This confirms that a profit-maximizing firm wants to operate where the wage rate of labor is equal to its marginal product; in other words, the firm's demand curve for labor coincides with the $MRP_L$ curve, as we have already determined.

These equations enable us to relate the firm's behavior in the labor and output markets. First suppose that the wage rate of labor $P_L$ goes up. The equation $MC = P_L/MP_L$ tells us that the firm's marginal cost curve must go up as well. With a higher marginal cost curve, the firm produces less output and so hires less labor. This confirms yet again that the demand curve for labor is downward sloping.

Exhibit 15.2 shows the picture. When the wage rate increases from $P_L$ to $P_L{}'$ in panel A, the marginal cost curve increases from $MC$ to $MC'$ in panel B. Output falls from $Q$ to $Q'$, and the amount of labor that the firm needs to hire falls from $L$ to $L'$ in panel C. This fall in the quantity of labor demanded could be read equally well directly off the demand for labor curve in panel A.

EXHIBIT **15.2**        **The Market for Labor and the Market for Output**

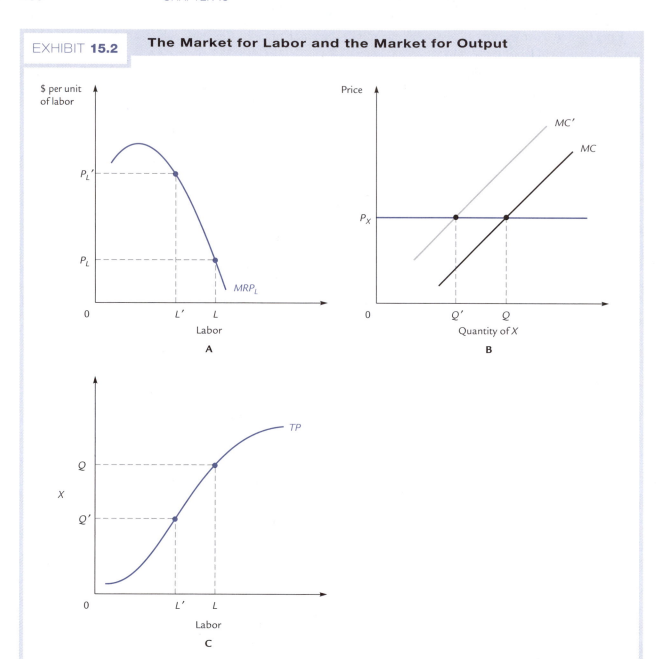

The marginal cost curve, *MC*, in panel B is derived from knowledge of the wage rate of labor, $P_L$, and the total product of labor curve, *TP*, in panel C. The derivation was given in Chapter 6. Thus, each graph contains some information that is also encoded in the other graphs.

To see the interrelations, notice that when the wage rate is $P_L$, panel A shows that the firm hires *L* units of labor, panel C shows that *L* units of labor will produce *Q* units of output, and panel B confirms that the firm's output is *Q*. If the wage rate rises to $P_L'$, the marginal cost curve rises to *MC'*. Now panel A shows that the firm hires *L'* units of labor, panel C shows that the firm produces *Q'* units of output, and panel B confirms this.

For an alternative exercise, imagine an increase in the price of output $P_X$ (with the wage rate of labor $P_L$ held fixed). Because $P_L = P_X \cdot \text{MP}_L$ it follows that $MP_L$ must go down, which requires that $L$ go up.

Exhibit 15.3 shows the picture. The increase in price from $P_X$ to $P_X{'}$ in panel B yields an increase in output from $Q$ to $Q'$. This requires more labor, as seen in panel C where the

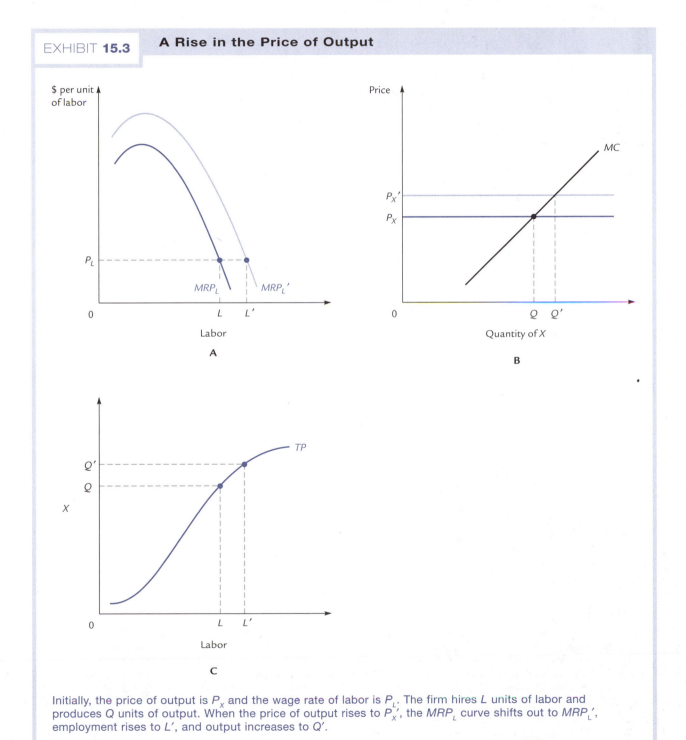

EXHIBIT **15.3**    **A Rise in the Price of Output**

Initially, the price of output is $P_X$ and the wage rate of labor is $P_L$. The firm hires $L$ units of labor and produces $Q$ units of output. When the price of output rises to $P_X{'}$, the $MRP_L$ curve shifts out to $MRP_L{'}$, employment rises to $L'$, and output increases to $Q'$.

quantity of labor must rise from $L$ to $L'$. Alternatively, we can argue that the increase in $P_X$ causes an outward shift in $MRP_L$ (because $MRP_L = P_X \cdot MP_L$), as seen in panel A. The quantity of labor demanded rises from $L$ to $L'$, just as we have already seen in panel A.

## The Effect of Plant Size

Our entire short-run analysis assumes a fixed plant size (that is, we assume that the firm does not vary its capital usage). It makes a difference what fixed plant size we assume. The marginal product of the 40th doctor in a major hospital equipped with the latest multimillion-dollar technology is different from the marginal product of the 40th doctor in a small practice with two offices and one examining room.

Suppose that the firm increases its capital usage. Then any number of workers will certainly be able to produce at least as much as before (they can always just continue what they were doing before, ignoring the new machinery) and will probably be able to produce more. Therefore, the total product curve can be expected to rise. This does not necessarily imply that the marginal product of labor will rise. In the two panels of Exhibit 15.4, we show two possibilities. In panel A the total product of labor rises while becoming steeper at each level of output. In this case, the marginal product of labor rises, and therefore so does the competitive firm's demand curve for labor. In panel B, the total product of labor rises while becoming shallower at each level of output. This leads to a fall in the marginal product of labor and so to a fall in the competitive firm's labor demand.

EXHIBIT **15.4**     **An Increase in Plant Size**

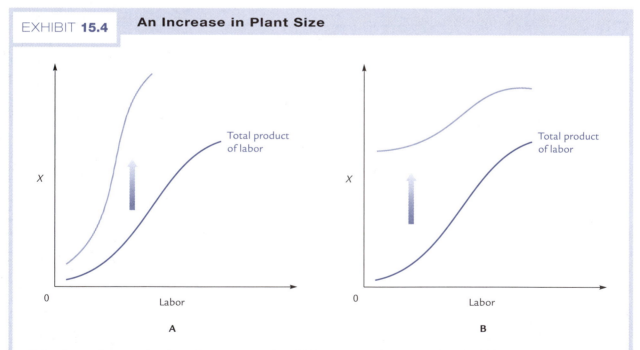

A                                                                    B

Following an increase in plant size, any quantity of labor can produce more than it did before. Thus, the total product curve shifts upward. Typically, it also becomes steeper, as in panel A, so that the marginal product of labor increases as well. In this case, we say that capital and labor are complements in production. But conceivably the total product could rise but become shallower, as in panel B. In this case, the marginal product of labor falls because of the increase in plant size; we say that capital and labor are substitutes in production.

In the first case, which is the typical one, we say that labor and capital are **complements in production.** When labor and capital are complements in production, increases in capital make workers more productive at the margin and lead to increases in the demand for labor. In the second case, we say that labor and capital are **substitutes in production.** When labor and capital are substitutes in production, an increase in capital leads to a fall in labor's marginal productivity and decreases the demand for labor. People who worry about "automation" reducing the demand for workers believe that capital and labor are substitutes in production. As an empirical matter, this case seems to be much rarer than it is often believed to be.

**Complements in production**

Two factors with the property that an increase in the employment of one raises the marginal product of the other.

A change in plant size is a long-run phenomenon. Thus, when we talk about the marginal product of labor before and after the capital adjustment, we are comparing one initial short-run situation with the new short-run situation that holds following a long-run adjustment.

Dangerous
Curve

## 15.2 The Firm's Demand for Factors in the Long Run

**Substitutes in production**

Two factors with the property that an increase in the employment of one lowers the marginal product of the other.

Next we will study the demand for labor in the long run, with both labor and capital treated as variables. (To study the demand for capital, simply interchange the words *capital* and *labor* throughout this section.)

### Constructing the Long-Run Labor Demand Curve

Now we will construct the firm's long-run labor demand curve. Throughout the discussion the following are held fixed:

*The technology available to the firm (that is, its isoquant diagram).*

*The rental rate on capital, which we denote by $P_K$.*

*The market price of output, which we denote by $P_X$.*

### Constructing a Point on the Curve

To find a point on the labor demand curve, we will take a particular wage rate, $P_L$, as given and see how much labor the firm chooses to employ.

The wage rate $P_L$ determines the slope of the firm's isocosts, which is $-P_L/P_K$. This allows us to draw in the family of isocosts and so to construct the expansion path as in panel A of Exhibit 15.5. In Section 6.3 we saw how the expansion path determines the firm's (long-run) total and marginal cost curves. The long-run marginal cost curve *(LRMC)* in panel B of Exhibit 15.5 is the one that arises from that process. The firm chooses a level of output, $Q_0$, so as to maximize its profits. It then looks to the $Q_0$-unit isoquant and finds the least-cost way of producing $Q_0$ units. That least-cost way is the basket labeled $A$ in panel A. The firm hires the basket of inputs represented by $A$. This basket includes $L_0$ units of labor. Therefore, a wage rate of $P_L$ leads to the firm's demanding $L_0$ units of labor. This entire process allows us to construct a single point on the firm's demand curve for labor, shown in panel C of the exhibit.

EXHIBIT **15.5**

**Constructing a Point on the Labor Demand Curve**

The graphs illustrate the construction of a single point on the firm's demand curve for labor, shown in panel C. The isoquant in panel A and the output price, $P_X$, shown in panel B are given and are independent of the wage rate. Now we assume a wage rate $P_L$. This enables us to draw the isocosts in the first panel, which have slope $-P_L P_K$. These in turn determine the expansion path, also shown in panel A. Using panel A, we can derive the firm's long-run marginal cost (=long-run supply) curve, *LRMC,* using the methods of Section 6.3. Panel B determines the firm's output, which is $Q_0$. We now return to panel A to see that when the firm produces the quantity $Q_0$, it chooses the basket of inputs A, and this basket contains $L_0$ units of labor. Finally, we conclude that the wage rate $P_L$ corresponds to the quantity of labor $L_0$, and we record this fact in panel C.

## The Demand for Inputs versus the Demand for Output

The construction of a firm's demand curve for a factor is similar in spirit to that of the consumer's demand curve for an output, but it is also more complicated. The key difference is that a consumer has a budget constraint. Given prices, we can determine that budget constraint and find the basket he consumes. A firm, by contrast, has no budget constraint. Instead, it has an infinite family of isocost lines, and it could choose to operate on any one of them. In order to find out what basket of inputs the firm chooses, we must refer to another market, the market for output (that is, we must use panel B in Exhibit 15.5).

**Derived demand**

Demand for an input, which depends on conditions in the output market.

The firm's demand curve for a factor of production is called **derived demand**, because it is partly derived from information external to the market for the factor itself.

## A Change in the Wage Rate

Continuing with the example of Exhibit 15.5, suppose that the price of labor rises, to $P_L'$. This causes all of the isocosts to become steeper, as in panel A of Exhibit 15.6, yielding a new expansion path shown in blue. The new expansion path leads to new (long-run) total and marginal cost curves. Suppose that the new marginal cost curve is the curve *LRMC'* in panel B of Exhibit 15.6. Then the firm reduces output to $Q_1$ and chooses an input basket where the $Q_1$-unit isoquant is tangent to an isocost. The new basket is the one labeled *B* in panel A of Exhibit 15.6. The quantity of labor demanded

**EXHIBIT 15.6**    **A Rise in the Wage Rate**

A rise in the wage rates raises the firm's long-run total cost curve, *TC,* to a new level, *TC'.* Usually, *TC'* is steeper than *TC,* as in panel A. In this case, the firm's long-run marginal cost curve moves upward and output decreases, as in panel B of Exhibit 15.6. However, it is possible that *TC'* could be shallower than *TC,* as in panel B. In this case, long-run marginal cost is reduced and output increases. When the latter case occurs, we say that labor is a regressive factor.

is $L_1$. This gives a second point on the firm's demand curve for labor, shown in panel C of the exhibit.

Continuing in this way, we can generate as many points as we want and can connect them to get the firm's labor demand curve.

## Substitution and Scale Effects

In Exhibit 15.6, when the price of labor rises from $P_L$ to $P_L'$, the firm moves from input basket *A* to input basket *B*. In particular, it reduces its employment of labor. This reduction comes about for two quite different reasons.

One reason is that labor is now more expensive relative to capital, so it pays to use less labor and more capital in producing any given quantity of output. In other words, the expansion path in panel A of the exhibit has shifted upward and to the left. (Instead of passing through *A*, it now passes through *B* and *C*.) This is called the **substitution effect** of the wage change.

The other reason is that the firm now faces higher costs and consequently produces less output, so that it wants less of every factor of production, including labor. We see this in panel B of the exhibit, where the higher marginal cost curve causes output to fall. This is called the **scale effect** of the wage change.

The substitution and scale effects of a change in the wage rate are closely analogous to the substitution and income effects that a consumer experiences in response to a change in the price of a consumption good.

**Substitution effect**

When the price of an input changes, that part of the effect on employment that results from the firm's substitution toward other inputs.

**Scale effect**

When the price of an input changes, that part of the effect on employment that results from changes in the firm's output.

## An Imaginary Experiment

In order to separate the substitution effect from the scale effect, we can conduct a hypothetical experiment. Suppose that the price of labor were to rise from $P_L$ to $P_L'$ but that the firm kept its output fixed at $Q_0$. (The experiment is hypothetical because the firm would *not*, in fact, keep its output fixed at $Q_0$.) In that case, where would the firm operate? It would want to be on its new expansion path but to remain on the $Q_0$-unit isoquant. That is, it would move to point $C$ in panel A of Exhibit 15.6. The movement from point $A$ to point $C$ is a pure substitution effect. The scale effect, which results from changes in the firm's output level, has been totally eliminated by assuming that the firm holds its output level constant.

Now, in fact, the firm does not hold its output level constant. Instead it moves to point $B$. The "move" from the hypothetical point $C$ to the firm's actual new basket $B$ is due entirely to the change in output from $Q_0$ to $Q_1$. It is the scale effect. To summarize:

The firm's movement from $A$ to $B$ can be thought of as a movement along the isoquant from $A$ to $C$ (called the *substitution effect*), followed by a movement along the expansion path from $C$ to $B$ (called the *scale effect*).

## Direction of the Substitution Effect

When the price of labor rises, the substitution effect is a movement along an isoquant to a tangency with a new, steeper isocost. It must be a movement to the left. This is because isoquants become steeper to the left and shallower to the right. In panel A of Exhibit 15.6 this means that point $C$ is to the left of point $A$ and this represents a basket with less labor.

The substitution effect of a rise in the wage always reduces the firm's employment of labor.

## Direction of the Scale Effect

An increase in the wage rate raises the firm's long-run total cost curve. However, this could happen in either of two ways. The long-run total cost curve could both rise and become steeper. In this case, because marginal cost is equal to the slope of total cost, and because that slope has increased, long-run marginal cost will rise. Alternatively, the long-run total cost curve could rise and become shallower, in which case long-run marginal cost will fall. The two possibilities are illustrated in Exhibit 15.7.

Panel A of Exhibit 15.7 is by far the more usual case. Here a rise in the wage leads to a rise in marginal cost, as was assumed in Exhibit 15.6. Thus, in Exhibit 15.6 output falls, from $Q_0$ to $Q_1$. Therefore, the scale effect is a movement along the expansion path to a lower isoquant and so must be a movement to the left. Recall that in Exhibit 15.6 the scale effect is the movement from point $C$ to point $B$. Because $B$ is to the left of $C$, the scale effect reduces the employment of labor, thereby reinforcing the substitution effect.

However, it is also possible that the rise in the wage rate could lead to an increase in total cost of the sort shown in panel B of Exhibit 15.7 and hence to a fall in the marginal cost curve. If so, we say that labor is a **regressive factor.** For example, the rise in wages might make it profitable for the firm to build a highly automated factory, allowing it to produce at very low marginal cost. This case is shown in Exhibit 15.8, where output rises from $Q_0$ to $Q_2$ in panel B. Because of the rise in output, the scale effect is a rightward move, from point $C$ to point $B'$ in panel A. That is, the scale effect causes the firm to employ more labor than it otherwise would.

**Regressive factor**

A factor with the property that an increase in its wage rate lowers the firm's long-run marginal cost curve.

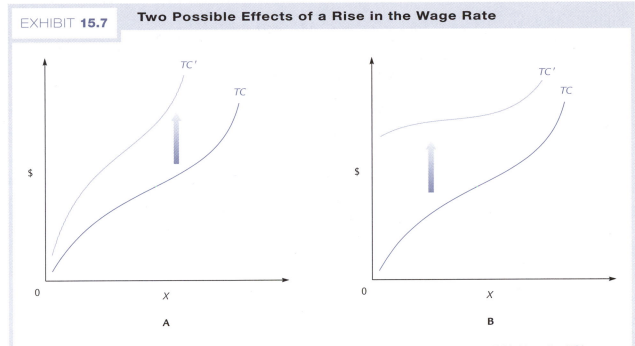

EXHIBIT **15.7**    **Two Possible Effects of a Rise in the Wage Rate**

A rise in the wage rates raises the firm's long-run total cost curve, *TC*, to a new level, *TC'*. Usually, *TC'* is steeper than *TC*, as in panel A. In this case, the firm's long-run marginal cost curve moves upward and output decreases, as in panel B of Exhibit 15.6. However, it is possible that *TC'* could be shallower than *TC*, as in panel B. In this case, long-run marginal cost is reduced and output increases. When the latter case occurs, we say that labor is a regressive factor.

## Combining the Substitution and Scale Effects

Exhibits 15.6 and 15.8 show two possibilities, corresponding to the two panels of Exhibit 15.7. In each case, the substitution effect, from point *A* to point *C*, is a movement to the left. In Exhibit 15.6, which is the usual case, the scale effect, from *C* to *B*, is a further movement to the left. Thus, we can conclude that *B* must lie to the left of *A*, which is to say that the quantity of labor demanded decreases in response to a rise in the wage rate. That is, in this case the demand curve for labor surely slopes down.

In Exhibit 15.8, where labor is a regressive factor, the substitution and scale effects work in opposite directions. The substitution effect reduces the quantity of labor demanded, whereas the scale effect increases it. That is, *C* is to the left of *A*, but *B'* is to the right of *C*. Where is *B'* with respect to *A*?

From what we can see in the diagram, there is no way to tell for sure whether *B'* is to the left or to the right of *A*. However, as a matter of mathematical fact, *B'* must lie to the left of *A*. That is, for a regressive factor the substitution effect must be greater than the scale effect. The proof of this is a bit subtle. If you are very talented mathematically, you will learn a lot from trying to discover it.

We can summarize by saying that in any case a rise in the wage rate leads to a fall in the quantity of labor demanded. Put another way:

The competitive firm's demand curve for labor (or any other factor of production) always slopes down.

In fact, the same statement is also true for a monopoly firm's demand curve for labor.

## EXHIBIT 15.8    A Rise in the Wage of a Regressive Factor

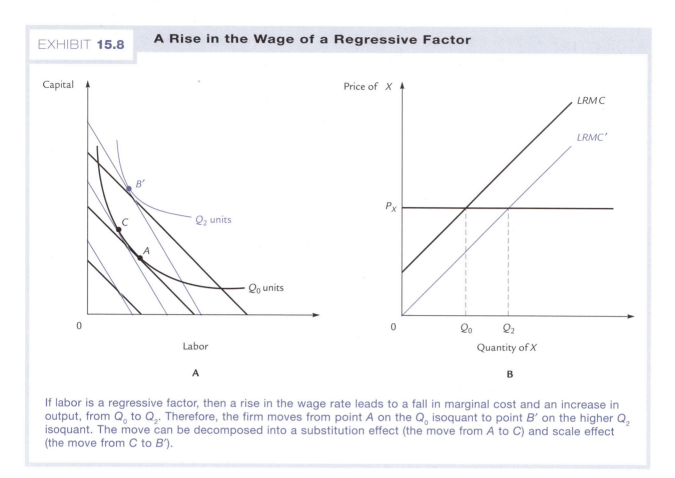

If labor is a regressive factor, then a rise in the wage rate leads to a fall in marginal cost and an increase in output, from $Q_0$ to $Q_2$. Therefore, the firm moves from point $A$ on the $Q_0$ isoquant to point $B'$ on the higher $Q_2$ isoquant. The move can be decomposed into a substitution effect (the move from $A$ to $C$) and scale effect (the move from $C$ to $B'$).

In the case of consumer goods, which we studied in Section 4.3, we had to admit the theoretical possibility of a Giffen good, for which the consumer's demand curve would slope up. However, there is not even a theoretical possibility of a Giffen *factor*. A firm's derived demand curves for factors of production must slope down.

## Relationships between the Short Run and the Long Run

We began this section by studying the case in which labor is the only variable input, and we argued that the firm's demand curve for labor is just the downward-sloping part of the $MRP_L$ curve. We then moved on to the more complicated case in which two factors are variable, and we derived the firm's demand curve for labor via the more complicated process depicted in Exhibit 15.6. What is the relationship between these two approaches to labor demand?

The answer is that in the long run the $MRP_L$ curve shifts because of adjustments in the employment of capital. For example, consider the effect of a rise in the wage when labor and capital are complements in production. Exhibit 15.9 shows the adjustment process. Initially, the wage rate of labor is $W_0$ and the rental rate on capital is $R_0$. At these prices, the firm hires $L_0$ units of labor (chosen from the $MRP_L$ curve) and $K_0$ units of capital (chosen from the $MRP_K$ curve).[1]

---

[1] Instead of using $P_K$ and $P_L$ for the prices of capital and labor, we are writing $R$ and $W$. The only reason for this is that we want to be able to use numerical subscripts, which look ugly when appended to $P_K$ and $P_L$.

## EXHIBIT 15.9 — Labor Demand in the Short Run and the Long Run

Initially, the wage rate of labor is $W_0$ and the rental rate on capital is $R_0$. The firm hires $L_0$ units of labor and $K_0$ units of capital.

Now the wage rate rises to $W_1$. In the short run, the firm reduces its employment of labor to $L_1$, read off the $MRP_L$ curve. Assuming that capital and labor are complements in production, this causes the $MRP_K$ curve to fall to the level of the middle curve in panel B. The firm reduces its capital employment to $K_1$.

The reduced capital employment lowers the $MRP_L$ curve to the level of the dashed curve in panel A, causing labor employment to fall to $L_2$. This lowers the $MRP_K$ still further, causing capital employment to fall to $K_2$, and the process repeats. Eventually, the $MRP_L$ curve settles at the new level $MRP_L'$. Here the firm hires $L_3$ units of labor. Thus, the long-run labor demand curve (in black) shows that a wage of $W_1$ corresponds to the quantity $L_3$ of labor employed.

When the wage rises to $W_1$, the firm's short-run response is to move along the $MRP_L$ curve and reduce the employment of labor to $L_1$. The reduction in labor reduces the marginal product of capital, so that the $MRP_K$ curve moves down to the middle curve in panel B. In the long run, the firm reduces its capital employment to $K_1$, causing the marginal product of labor to fall to the dashed curve in panel A. This causes employment to fall further, to $L_2$. This in turn leads to a further reduction in the marginal product of capital, which leads to even less capital employed, which reduces the marginal product of labor still further, and so on. After many iterations, the marginal product of labor settles down, as indicated in panel A, and the final level of employment is $L_3$.

In the long run, therefore, the firm hires $L_3$ units of labor when the wage is $W_1$. Thus, on the long-run labor demand curve, shown in black, the wage $W_0$ corresponds to $L_0$ and the wage $W_1$ corresponds to $L_3$.

**Dangerous Curve**

The adjustment process described here requires, in principle, an infinite number of steps. But because the firm can foresee the outcome of these infinitely many steps, it can simply move directly to the new level of employment without actually stopping at each step along the way.

# 15.3 The Industry's Demand Curve for Factors of Production

The industry's demand curve for factors of production can be approximated by adding the demand curves of the individual firms. However, this overlooks an important complication. When the wage rate goes up, in the usual case all firms' marginal cost curves move up. As a result, the industry supply curve shifts and the price of output rises. This in turn means that firms will not reduce output by as much as they would if price remained constant. The substitution effect is unchanged, but the scale effect is lessened. Firms reduce their employment of labor by less than Exhibit 15.6 predicts. On similar grounds, a fall in the wage leads to a smaller increase in employment than one would expect from our study of individual firms. The bottom line is that the industry's demand curve for a factor tends to be less elastic than the sum of the demand curves from the individual firms in the industry.

Finally, in any discussion of the demand for labor (or any input), it should be remembered that labor is demanded by many different industries. All the corresponding industry demand curves must be added together to get "the" demand curve for labor.

## Monopsony

Throughout this chapter we have assumed that firms take factor prices as given. This is equivalent to saying that for each factor the firm faces a supply curve that is horizontal at the market wage rate. However, there remains the possibility that a single firm could account for a substantial portion of the market for some factor. In this case, the quantity demanded by the firm affects that factor's wage rate. The firm faces an upward-sloping supply curve for that factor.

The most extreme example occurs if there is some factor of production that is demanded by only one firm. In that case, the firm in question is a "single buyer," just as a monopolist might be a "single seller." A single buyer is called a **monopsonist**. However, just as we use the word *monopolist* to describe any seller who faces a downward-sloping demand curve, so we shall use the word *monopsonist* to describe any buyer who faces an upward-sloping supply curve.

To a monopsony demander of labor, the cost of hiring an additional unit of labor exceeds the wage rate. The reason for this is that when the monopsonist hires an additional worker, there are two ways in which his costs increase: (1) he must pay the new worker's wage and (2) he bids up the wages of all workers. As a result, the monopsonist faces a **marginal labor cost (*MLC*)** curve that lies everywhere above the labor supply curve that he faces. He maximizes profits by choosing that quantity where the marginal revenue product of labor and the marginal cost of labor are equal; then he pays a wage read off the supply curve at that quantity. The process is illustrated in Exhibit 15.10.

**Monopsonist**

A buyer who faces an upward-sloping supply curve.

**Marginal labor cost (*MLC*)**

The cost of hiring an additional unit of labor.

EXHIBIT **15.10** **Monopsony**

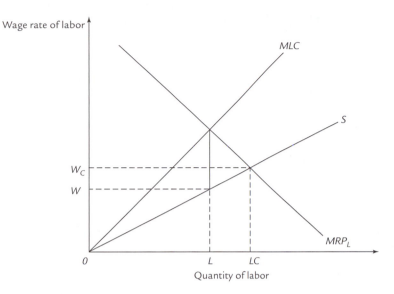

A monopsony demander of labor faces an upward-sloping labor supply curve (S) and a marginal labor cost (MLC) curve that lies everywhere above S. He hires L units of labor (where $MRP_L = MLC$) and pays the wage W that he reads off the supply curve at that quantity.

In an industry with many firms, the going price for labor would be $W_C$ and each firm would face a flat supply curve at this price. $L_C$ units of labor would be hired.

---

Do not confuse *MLC*, which is the cost of hiring one additional unit of labor, with *MC*, which is the cost of producing one additional unit of output.

---

Dangerous
Curve

The monopsonist hires fewer workers and pays a lower wage than would be the case if many firms competed to hire labor. Under competition there would be a going wage rate of $W_C$ in Exhibit 15.10, and employment would be $L_C$.

## How Widespread Is Monopsony?

In order for a firm to have monopsony power, it must constitute a substantial portion of the demand for some factor. Therefore, even a firm that is unique in its industry has no monopsony power, provided that there are firms in *other* industries competing with it for the use of factors.

For example, suppose that all of the major auto manufacturers were to merge into one giant firm. At first, this firm could well have monopsony power in the market for autoworkers, who would have no other employer competing to hire their valuable skills. However, if the giant auto firm were to exercise this monopsony power to keep wages low, some autoworkers would eventually decide to acquire other skills and to sell their services elsewhere—say, as shipbuilders. In the long run, the single automaker competes in the labor market with all of the firms in the shipbuilding industry and in countless other industries besides.

The same is true when a single employer dominates a certain geographic area. Although the employer may have some monopsony power in the short run, he may be unable to exercise that power without causing some of the area's residents to move elsewhere. Ultimately, he competes for the local workers with employers all over the world.

# 15.4 The Distribution of Income

Firms hire factors of production and combine them to create output. This output generates revenue, or income, for the firm. Each factor of production receives a portion of this revenue as its payment for participating in the firm's activity. (Economists persist in speaking of payments to factors of production, even though it would often be more accurate to speak of payments to the *owners* of the factors.) After all of these payments are made, any remaining revenue (positive or negative) accrues to the owners of the firm in the form of profit.

## Factor Shares and Rents

From the first part of this chapter, we know that when labor markets are competitive, the price of any factor is equal to its marginal revenue product, if a firm or an industry hires $L$ units of labor at a wage rate of $P_L \cdot L$. Therefore, we can say that labor's income is equal to $MRP_L \cdot L$.

If the supply curve of labor to this firm or industry is upward sloping, the suppliers of labor earn a producers' surplus, or rent, equal to area $B$ in Exhibit 15.11. Labor's income is the sum of areas $B$ and $C$, so that only a portion of this income can be considered rent.

Dangerous
Curve

Do not confuse the word *rent,* meaning producers' surplus, with the rental (i.e., wage) paid by the firm to hire a factor of production. The factor earns a producers' surplus equal to the payment it receives from the firm *minus* its opportunity costs. Only when the factor supply curve is perfectly vertical does the rental payment consist entirely of rent.

The area $A + B + C$ under the $MRP_L$ curve in Exhibit 15.11 is equal to the total revenue of the firm or of the industry. (The area can be broken into rectangles representing the revenue from the first unit of labor employed, the revenue from the second unit, and so on.) Because labor receives $B + C$, the remaining area $A$ must represent the sum of the payments to all other factors, plus any profits that are earned.

What is true of labor is also true of every other factor. Capital earns an income of $MRP_K \cdot K$, of which some portion is rent. There are also intangible factors like "entrepreneurial ability" that are typically supplied by the owners of the firm. Although such factors are not explicitly on the payroll, they should be viewed as implicitly receiving a wage equal to their marginal revenue product. If the owner supplies $E$ units of entrepreneurial ability, with a marginal revenue product of $MRP_E$, then we think of the firm as paying the owner an income of $MRP_E \cdot E$ in his capacity as a factor of production.

Inputs like entrepreneurial ability are often supplied quite inelastically. The owner of a shoe store has a great deal of knowledge about the specific workings of his own

EXHIBIT **15.11** **Labor's Share of Income**

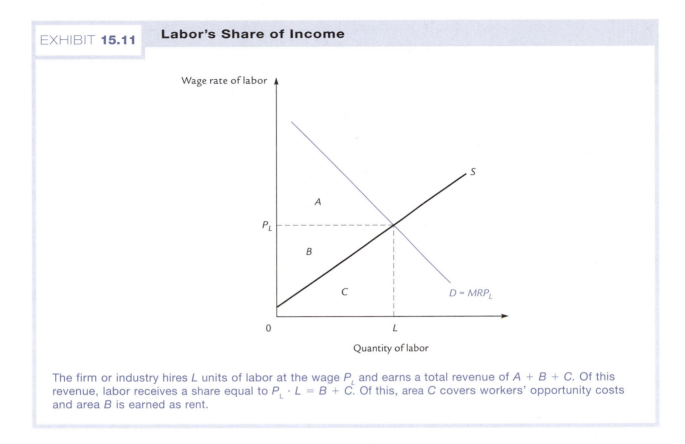

The firm or industry hires $L$ units of labor at the wage $P_L$ and earns a total revenue of $A + B + C$. Of this revenue, labor receives a share equal to $P_L \cdot L = B + C$. Of this, area $C$ covers workers' opportunity costs and area $B$ is earned as rent.

enterprise. Such knowledge is a factor of production that would be much less valuable in any alternative use. As a result, he might supply almost all of this knowledge to his own business, regardless of whether he earns a high or a low wage by doing so. Thus, the supply curve for the owner's entrepreneurial services is very inelastic, so that a large portion of the income earned by these services tends to be rent.

## Profit

The sum of the factor payments may be less than, equal to, or greater than the revenue of the firm. If the factor payments are less than the firm's revenue, then the difference is profit and accrues to the owner of the firm. If the factor payments exceed the firm's revenues, the firm takes a loss, sometimes called a *negative profit,* equal to the difference. This loss comes from the pocket of the firm's owner.

Notice that in our analysis the owner of the firm receives two very different kinds of payments. (They are different to the economist, although an accountant or a businessman would see no reason to distinguish them.) First, there is the income that he earns as the supplier of certain factors of production. Much of this income is usually a rent, or a producer's surplus. Second, there is the profit remaining after the firm has made all of its factor payments (including the ones to the owner).

As was discussed briefly in Chapter 7, many economists would prefer not to think of specialized skills, such as knowledge of the workings of a particular shoe store, as factors

Dangerous Curve

of production that are hired by the firm. They would prefer to think of the firm as earning positive profits due to the existence of these factors. The two analyses use different words but describe the same outcomes.

## Returns to Scale

In long-run equilibrium, it can be shown mathematically that when production is subject to decreasing returns to scale (that is, when average cost is increasing), factor shares add up to less than the firm's total revenue (so that the firm has a positive profit); when production is subject to constant returns to scale (that is, when average cost is flat), factor shares add up to the firm's revenue exactly (so that profit is zero); and when production is subject to increasing returns to scale (that is, when average cost is decreasing), factor shares add up to more than the firm's revenue (so that profit is negative).

In long-run competitive equilibrium, the firm operates at the minimum point of its average cost curve, where returns to scale are constant. Therefore, profits are zero, as we already know from Chapter 7.

However, Professor Paul Romer of the University of California at Berkeley argues that in many industries firms experience increasing returns to scale over the entire relevant range.[2] The reason is that many important inputs (unlike the labor and capital we have considered in this chapter) are *nonrivalrous:* Once produced, there is no limit to how much they can be used. A firm that produces one specialized software program to install on a manager's computer can allow other managers to install the same program at essentially no additional cost.

A firm that has one specialized software program but doubles all of its other inputs (number of computers, number of managers, number of factories, etc.) might be expected to double its output. If the firm really doubles *all* of its inputs by constructing a second specialized software program, then it should *more* than double its output. This is precisely the definition of increasing returns to scale.

If increasing returns are truly a common phenomenon, they present a major challenge to the standard competitive model of the firm. A competitive firm that experiences increasing returns must earn negative profits after all factors' shares are paid out. In such circumstances, we should not expect to see any competitive firms.

## Producers' Surplus

In earlier chapters, we talked about the producer's surplus earned by firms. It is often useful to think of producers' surplus in that way. However, in a more careful analysis, we recognize that at least part of the producers' surplus is actually earned by the factors that the firms employ.

In fact, in long-run competitive equilibrium, firms earn zero profits. This means that all of the producers' surplus that we have previously attributed to the firms is actually paid out to factors.

Exhibit 15.12 shows the relationship between the industry-wide markets for output, labor, and capital when each firm earns zero profits. The firms earn total revenue equal to $A + B$ in the output market, of which $A$ is producers' surplus. (The firms'

---

[2] P. Romer, "Are Nonconvexities Important for Understanding Growth?" *American Economic Review* 80 (1990): 97–107.

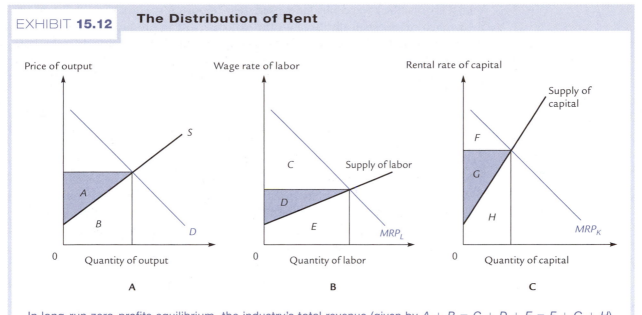

EXHIBIT **15.12**    **The Distribution of Rent**

In long-run zero-profits equilibrium, the industry's total revenue (given by $A + B = C + D + E = F + G + H$) is paid out to factors. Because labor's total wages are $D + E$ and the total rental payments to capital are $G + H$, we have $A + B = (D + E) + (G + H)$. Producers' surplus in the industry is equal to $A$, of which workers get $D$ and owners of capital get $G$. Therefore, $A = D + G$.

total revenue is also equal to $C + D + E$ in panel B and to $F + G + H$ in panel C.) This revenue is distributed to workers, who earn $D + E$ in panel B, and to the owners of capital, who earn $G + H$ in panel C. Because we assume that firms earn zero profits, these factor payments must exactly account for the firms' total revenue. That is, $(D + E) + (G + H) = A + B$.

The portion of total revenue that is producers' surplus is exactly $A$, of which $D$ is earned by workers and $G$ is earned by the owners of capital. Therefore, $A = D + G$. If profits were nonzero, then area $A$ would include those profits in addition to $D + G$.

---

Of course, when there are more than two factors of production, rents are divided among all of them, not just capital and labor.

---

Dangerous
Curve

## Who Benefits?

Factors that are supplied relatively inelastically (the most extreme case being a fixed factor) earn more rents than those supplied more elastically. As a result, the more nearly fixed factors have more to gain (or to lose) from changes in the demand for the output of the industry. If the demand for output rises, the derived demand for all inputs rises. This increases producers' surplus by more for those factors with inelastic supply curves than for other factors. By the same reasoning, these factors bear most of the loss when the demand for output falls.

For example, professional football games are produced with many inputs, including professional quarterbacks and footballs. The supply of quarterbacks is quite inelastic, because the particular skills of a quarterback have relatively few alternatives uses that are anywhere near as valuable. Therefore, quarterbacks earn substantial rents. (That is, their wage bills far exceed their opportunity costs.) Footballs are supplied much more elastically, because the skills needed to produce footballs are also useful in a variety of other industries. Therefore, suppliers of footballs earn comparatively little rent. Any change in the public's demand for football games will have a much greater effect on the fortunes of quarterbacks than it will on the fortunes of football manufacturers.

**Dangerous Curve**

What matters in this example is not the fact that quarterbacks' wages are high, but that their supply curve is inelastic. Suppose, for example, that all quarterbacks could equally well earn $500,000 a year as movie stars. Then, over a substantial range, the supply curve for quarterbacks would be flat (perfectly elastic) at $500,000 per year. In this case, the wage would be high, but there would be no producers' surplus. And, in fact, in this case quarterbacks would not be hurt if the public completely lost interest in football. Changes in the industry's fortunes are felt most by those factors that are inelastically supplied, not by those factors whose wage bills are high.

Some factors are fixed in the short run and variable in the long run. An increase in the price of output benefits these factors more in the short run than in the long run. For example, in the short run there are a fixed number of recording studios capable of producing compact discs. A rise in the price of compact discs will raise revenue in the recording industry, and in the short run this increased revenue will largely be paid as rent to the owners of the recording studios. In the long run, however, more recording studios can be built, and the owners of existing recording studios will not continue to reap this windfall benefit. Short-term rents due to inelastic short-run supply are sometimes called **quasi-rents.**

**Quasi-rents**

Producers' surplus earned in the short run by factors that are supplied inelastically in the short run.

Finally, we should note that the owners of the factors of production are the same individuals and households that are the consumers in the economy. In earlier chapters, we maintained a careful distinction between the consumers' surplus earned by individuals and the producers' surplus earned by firms. Now we see that the producers' surplus is actually earned by the same individuals who are earning the consumers' surplus. All gains from trade ultimately accrue to individuals. Who else is there to benefit?

## Summary

A factor's marginal revenue product is defined as the amount of additional revenue the firm can earn by employing one more unit of that factor. The equimarginal principle implies that the firm's demand curve for the factor will be identical with the downward-sloping portion of the factor's marginal revenue product curve.

An increase in employment of one factor will usually raise the marginal productivity of other factors; hence, it will raise the firm's demand curve for other factors. In this case, we say that the factors are complements in production. It is also possible that an increase in the employment of one factor will reduce the marginal productivity of other factors, in which case we say that the factors are substitutes in production.

In the long run, a change in the wage rate of labor will cause the firm to change its employment of both labor and capital. The firm's marginal cost curve will change, leading to a change in output as well.

In the hypothetical case in which the firm does *not* adjust output, the change in the wage rate leads to a movement along an isoquant, known as the *substitution effect.* The substitution effect is always in the expected direction: A rise in the wage rate reduces the quantity of labor demanded, and a fall in the wage rate increases the quantity demanded.

The scale effect of a wage change is that part of the change in employment that is due to the change in output. It is a movement along the new expansion path. The scale effect is usually in the same direction as the substitution effect, but it can go in the opposite direction, in which case we say that labor is a regressive factor. For a regressive factor, however, the substitution effect is always larger than the scale effect. Thus, even for a regressive factor the firm's labor demand curve must slope downward.

The firm's revenues are paid out to the factors of production, with each factor earning a wage equal to its marginal revenue product. Among these payments may be payments to the firm's owners for the use of specialized factors such as particular skills. After all these payments are made, whatever remains is the firm's profit. In long-run competitive equilibrium, profits are zero, so the factor payments exactly exhaust the firm's income.

Payments to factors minus the factors' opportunity costs are the factors' producers' surplus, or rent. The firm's producer's surplus (the area above the firm's supply curve up to the price and out to the quantity supplied) is the sum of all these factor rents plus the firm's profit, if any. Thus, the producers' surplus that we have attributed to firms in previous chapters is actually distributed as factor rents.

The more inelastically supplied the factor, the greater the percentage of its income that is rent. Thus, inelastically supplied factors benefit the most from the existence of the industry, and they stand to gain or lose the most when the industry's fortunes wax or wane.

## Review Questions

**R1.** What is the relationship between marginal product and marginal revenue product?

**R2.** Draw total and marginal product diagrams to show how a rise in the price of output affects the employment of labor.

**R3.** Draw total and marginal product diagrams to show how an increase in plant size affects the employment of labor.

**R4.** Explain how to construct a point on the firm's long-run demand curve for labor.

**R5.** Define the substitution and the scale effects of an increase in the wage rate. What can be said about their directions?

**R6.** Define monopsony. Does a monopsonist employ more or less labor than a firm that hires workers competitively? Why?

**R7.** In long-run competitive equilibrium, the firm's total revenue is equal to the sum of its factor payments. Why?

**R8.** What is the relationship between the producers' surplus measured above the firm's supply curve for output and the producers' surpluses measured above the factors' supply curves for their services?

**R9.** A factor that is supplied perfectly elastically to an industry has nothing to gain or lose from changes in the price of output. Explain why, first using graphs and then giving the verbal interpretation.

**R10.** A factor that is supplied perfectly inelastically to an industry earns rents equal to its entire wage bill. Thus, such a factor participates heavily in the industry's fortunes, be they good or bad. Explain why, first using graphs and then giving the verbal interpretation.

# Numerical Exercises

**N1.** Consider a firm that produces according to the production function:

$$Q = \sqrt{KL}$$

where $Q$ is the firm's output and $K$ and $L$ are the quantities of capital and labor that it employs. With this production function, the slope of an isoquant at the point $(L, K)$ is given by $-K/L$.

    **a.** Suppose that the going wage rate of labor is $W$ and the going rental rate on capital is $R$. What is the slope of an isocost? If the firm uses $K$ units of capital and $L$ of labor in long-run equilibrium, derive a formula for $K$ in terms of $L$, $W$, and $R$. Derive a formula for $L$ in terms of $K$, $W$, and $R$. (*Hint:* In long-run equilibrium, the firm operates at a point where the slope of an isocost and the slope of an isoquant are equal.)

    **b.** Using the production function and the result of part (a), write a formula for $L$ in terms of $Q$, $W$, and $R$, and a formula for $K$ in terms of $Q$, $W$, and $R$.

    **c.** Write a formula for the total cost of producing $Q$ units of output.

    **d.** Describe the firm's long-run marginal cost curve.

    **e.** In long-run equilibrium, what must the price of output be? Would you have had enough information to answer this question if your answer to part (d) had been different than it was?

    **f.** In terms of $Q$, how much does the firm pay out to labor and to capital? What is its total revenue? What is its profit?

**N2.** Consider a perfectly competitive industry with many identical firms, each producing according to the production function:

$$Q = \sqrt{KL}$$

Labor and capital are supplied to the industry according to the supply curves $L = W$ and $K = 4R$.

    **a.** Suppose that the industry produces $Q$ units of output, using $K$ units of capital and $L$ of labor. Write a formula for $L$ in terms of $Q$, $W$, and $R$ and for $K$ in terms of $Q$, $W$, and $R$.

    **b.** Write two equations expressing the conditions of equilibrium in the two factor markets. Use these equations to get a numerical value for $W/R$. (*Hint:* Divide one equation by the other.)

   **c.** Show that the industry's long-run total cost curve is given by:

$$Q = P$$

(*Hint:* Make use of your answers from N1.)

   **d.** Suppose that the demand curve for the industry's output is given by:

$$Q = 1/5{,}000 - P$$

What are the price and quantity of output? How much labor is hired, and at what wage? How much capital is rented, and at what rental rate?

   **e.** Under the conditions of part (d), calculate the producers' surplus in the output market. How much producers' surplus is earned by labor and how much by capital? How much profit is earned by firms? Is your answer consistent with your answer to Numerical Exercise N1(f)?

# Problem Set

**1.** **True or False:** A rise in the demand for apples has no effect on the productivity of apple-pickers and hence no effect on the demand for apple pickers.

**2.** **True or False:** If the demand curve for a product is vertical, then any rise in the wage rate could be passed on entirely from firms to customers, without any fall in production. Thus, a rise in the wage rate would not reduce employment, either in the short run or in the long run.

**3.** **True or False:** If labor and capital are complements in production, then the long-run labor demand curve is more elastic than the short-run labor demand curve.

**4.** **a.** Prepare graphs like those in Exhibit 15.9 to illustrate the relationships between short-run and long-run labor demand when capital and labor are substitutes in production.

   **b.** In this case, is the short-run labor demand curve more or less elastic than the long-run labor demand curve?

**5.** **a.** Use Exhibit 15.9 to show that when labor and capital are the only inputs and when they are complements in production, the long-run labor demand curve must slope downward.

   **b.** Use the graphs you prepared for Problem 4a to show that when labor and capital are the only inputs and when they are substitutes in production, the long-run labor demand curve must slope downward.

**6.** **True or False:** The industry demand curve, for a regressive factor is likely to be more elastic than the sum of the firms' demand curves.

**7.** **True or False:** The isocosts of a monopsonist in the labor market are not straight lines.

**8.** Use a graph to demonstrate the social welfare consequences of monopsony.

**9.** **True or False:** If there is monopsony in the labor market, a minimum wage law can lead to increased employment.

**10.** Suppose that labor and capital are both supplied perfectly inelastically to the U.S. economy.

    **a.** Show the producers' surplus earned by *capital* on a graph of the marginal product of *labor*. Explain where you make use of the fact that the supply of capital is perfectly inelastic.

    **b.** Suppose that General Motors moves one of its plants to South Korea, increasing the number of workers who can be combined with U.S. capital. Show the gains and losses to (1) U.S. workers, (2) U.S. owners of capital, and (3) South Korean workers.

    **c.** Does the plant's relocation help or hurt Americans as a whole?

**11.** **True or False:** If firms earn zero profits and if labor and capital are the only inputs, then a rise in wages must be bad for the owners of capital.

**12.** **True or False:** If firms earn zero profits and if labor and capital are the only inputs, then labor and capital must be complements in production. (*Hint:* Make use of your answer to the preceding problem.)

**13.** Suppose that there are exactly three factors of production: skilled labor, which is represented by unions; unskilled labor, which is not represented by unions; and capital. Currently, skilled labor earns $15 per hour and unskilled labor earns $5 per hour. Legislation has been proposed to establish a minimum wage of $10 per hour for all workers, and this legislation has been strongly endorsed by the unions.

Assuming that the unions act in the best interest of their members, can you determine whether skilled and unskilled labor are complements or substitutes in production? What about capital and unskilled labor? Can you predict how the owners of capital will feel about the legislation?

**14.** In order to promote economic expansion, the town of Hyde Park has declared certain areas of the city to be "no-tax zones." Businesses located in these areas are exempt from all city taxes. As a result, many new firms have started up, each of which rents offices and machinery and hires many workers.

In the long run, which of the following groups are likely to benefit from the existence of the no-tax zones: the owners of firms, the customers of the firms, landowners in the no-tax zones, the producers of machinery, the workers?

# CHAPTER 16

# The Market for Labor

There are two types of decision makers in the economy: individuals and firms. Individuals supply factors of production, such as labor, to firms and demand output in return. Firms demand factors of production, use them to produce output, and supply that output to individuals.

In Chapters 3 and 4, we studied the demand for output by individuals and in Chapters 5 through 7, we studied the supply of output by firms. In Chapter 15 we studied the demand for inputs by firms; now in this chapter and the next, we will complete the picture by studying the supply of inputs by individuals.

In a competitive economy all prices and quantities are determined by the intersections of supply and demand curves. We know that the firm's supply of output and demand for inputs depend on available technology (encoded in marginal product curves, isoquants, and the like) and that the individual's demand for output depends on his tastes (encoded in indifference curves). Now we will discover that the individual's supply of inputs also depends on his tastes. It follows that ultimately all prices and quantities are determined by just two things: the technology available to firms and the tastes of individuals.

We will begin in Section 16.1 by studying individual labor supply curves, and then in Section 16.2 we will study equilibrium in the labor market. Sections 16.3 and 16.4 survey two special topics related to labor markets: Why do some people earn more than others? and What are the extent, causes, and effects of discrimination in labor markets?

## 16.1 Individual Labor Supply

Individuals supply labor to the market at a price called the wage rate of labor. We will begin by deriving an individual's labor supply curve.

### Consumption versus Leisure

Each individual is endowed with 24 hours per day that he can allocate between labor and leisure. Labor consists of working in the marketplace for the going wage. **Leisure** consists of all other activities. Thus, leisure includes time spent on the beach, but it also includes time spent in productive activities such as going to school or looking for a better job.

**Leisure**

All activities other than labor.

**Consumption**

All goods other than leisure.

There are two goods relevant to the labor supply decision. One is leisure and the other is **consumption.** We use the word *consumption* to represent all the goods that can be purchased in the marketplace. Thus, *consumption* plays the same role that "all other goods" plays in the derivation of individual demand curves. Consumption stands for all goods other than leisure.

Consumption is often measured in dollars. We will find it more convenient to measure consumption in terms of the output good that the worker is producing. Thus, if he is a sausage maker, we will measure all consumption in terms of sausages.

It is often useful to pretend that there is only a single consumption good in the economy, so that all workers receive their wages in the form of this single good.

### Indifference Curves

We can draw indifference curves between leisure and consumption, and we will choose to draw them with the leisure axis running *from right to left.* This is pictured in panel A of Exhibit 16.1. Because it is not possible to have more than 24 hours of leisure per day, we have drawn a vertical barrier at the 24-hour mark. The number of hours that the individual devotes to labor is given by 24 minus the number of hours he devotes to leisure. This is indicated in the graph by the second row of labels on the horizontal axis.

EXHIBIT **16.1**     **Consumption versus Leisure**

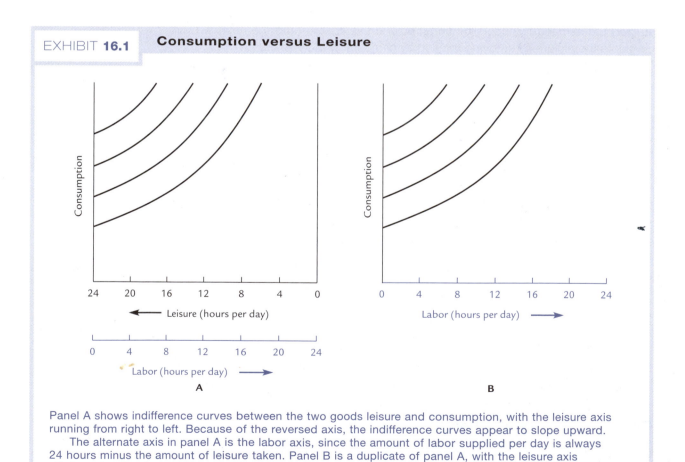

Panel A shows indifference curves between the two goods leisure and consumption, with the leisure axis running from right to left. Because of the reversed axis, the indifference curves appear to slope upward.

The alternate axis in panel A is the labor axis, since the amount of labor supplied per day is always 24 hours minus the amount of leisure taken. Panel B is a duplicate of panel A, with the leisure axis eliminated and only the labor axis shown.

In panel B of Exhibit 16.1 we have reproduced panel A without the right-hand vertical axis and with only the labor markings on the horizontal. This panel depicts the individual's indifference curves between labor and consumption. They are upward sloping, reflecting the fact that labor is considered undesirable. The slope of an indifference curve at any point is the amount of consumption needed to just compensate the worker for an additional hour of labor. It is the marginal value of leisure, measured in terms of consumption.

In Exhibit 3.16, where we studied the effects of a head tax and an income tax, we ran the leisure axis from left to right, rather than from right to left as we will in the present chapter. The choice of a direction for the axis is purely a matter of convenience and does not affect the substantive analysis in any way.

Dangerous Curve

**Exercise 16.1** Use the observation of the preceding sentence to explain why the indifference curves become steeper as you move up and to the right.

In Exhibit 16.2 we have added the budget constraint. When the individual does not work at all, he earns an income of $C_0$. This **nonlabor income** is a return to some asset owned by the individual, such as an apple tree, a portfolio of stocks, a small business, or a pension. The slope of the budget line is equal to the wage, which we call $W$.

**Nonlabor income**

Income from sources other than wages.

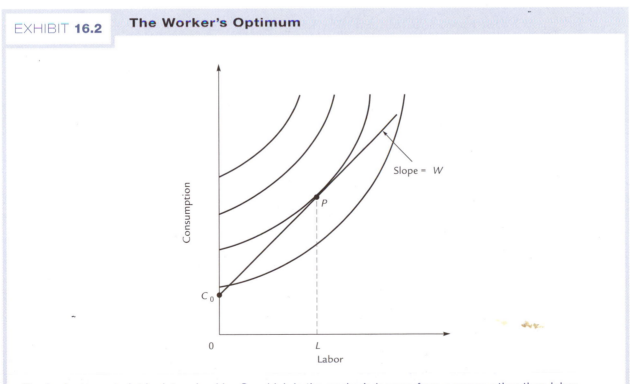

EXHIBIT **16.2**     **The Worker's Optimum**

The budget constraint is determined by $C_0$, which is the worker's income from sources other than labor, and the wage rate $W$, which gives the slope of the budget line. The optimum is at $P$, where the worker supplies $L$ units of labor. Here the wage rate (the slope of the budget line) is equal to the marginal value of leisure (the slope of the indifference curve).

If consumption is measured in sausages, then $W$ is measured in sausages per hour. Each additional hour of labor yields $W$ additional units of consumption.

The worker chooses his optimum point, which is at a tangency between an indifference curve and the budget line (point $P$ in the exhibit). At the wage $W$ the worker supplies $L$ units of labor. At point $P$ the wage rate (the slope of the budget line) is equal to the marginal value of leisure.

---

**Exercise 16.2** Justify the worker's choice on economic grounds: If the wage were either more or less than the marginal value of leisure, how could the worker improve his position?

---

## Changes in the Budget Line

The worker's budget line changes if either his nonlabor income $C_0$ or his wage rate $W$ changes. We will now study how the worker's optimum is affected by each of these possibilities.

### Changes in Income

Exhibit 16.3 shows the effect of an increase in the worker's nonlabor income from $C_0$ to $C_1$. The new optimum is at $P'$. If both consumption and leisure are normal (as opposed

| EXHIBIT **16.3** | **An Increase in Nonlabor Income** |
| --- | --- |

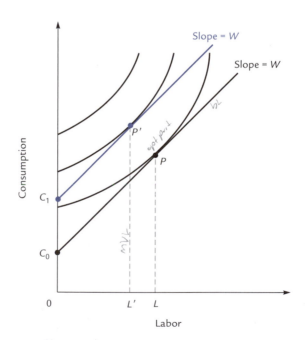

When nonlabor income increases from $C_0$ to $C_1$, the worker's budget line shifts upward parallel to itself. The new optimum is at point $P'$. If consumption and leisure are both normal (as opposed to inferior) goods, then $P'$ lies above and to the left of $P$. Thus, an increase in nonlabor income leads to increased consumption and less labor supplied. The quantity of labor that this worker supplies falls from $L$ to $L'$.

to inferior) goods, then the worker will choose more of each in response to his higher income; that is, $P'$ will be above and to the left of $P$. Although it is logically possible for $P'$ to be either below or to the right of $P$, we will assume that the income effects work in the expected directions, as in the exhibit. With this assumption:

An increase in nonlabor income leads to a fall in the quantity of labor supplied.

## An Increase in the Wage Rate

Suppose that the wage rises from $W$ to $W'$ while nonlabor income stays fixed. This has the effect of making the budget line steeper. Because there is no change in nonlabor income, the budget line swings through its intercept with the vertical axis. Exhibit 16.4 shows two possible outcomes. The optimum basket moves from $P$ to $Q$ in panel A of the exhibit or from $P$ to $R$ in panel B.

## Income and Substitution Effects

When the wage goes up, there is both a substitution effect and an income effect. The substitution effect is that an additional hour of leisure is now more expensive in terms of forgone consumption. To say the same thing another way, additional consumption is now less expensive in terms of forgone leisure. In consequence of the substitution effect, the worker chooses more consumption and less leisure. Because he chooses less leisure, he supplies more labor.

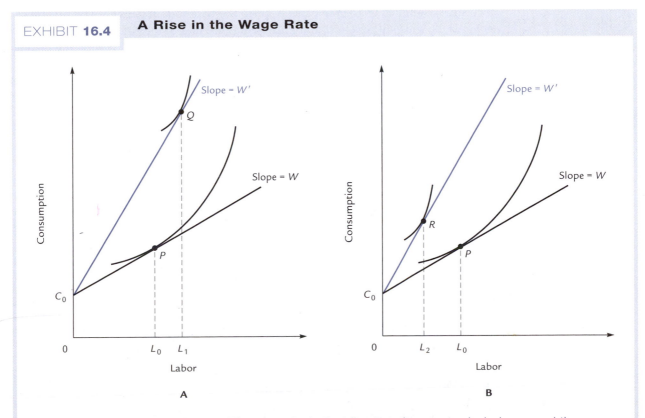

EXHIBIT 16.4    **A Rise in the Wage Rate**

An increase in the wage, from $W$ to $W'$, causes the budget line to swing counterclockwise around the intercept $C_0$. Depending on the slope of the indifference curves, the new optimum could be at a point like $Q$, where more labor than before is supplied, or at a point like $R$, where less labor is supplied.

The rise in the wage also has an income effect in that it makes suppliers of labor better off. As in Exhibit 16.3, we assume that both consumption and leisure are normal goods, so that the income effect leads the worker to choose more of both. Because the income effect leads the worker to choose more leisure, he supplies less labor.

Both the income and substitution effects lead to an increase in consumption (an upward movement in the consumer's optimum). These effects reinforce each other, and we can conclude that the new optimum ($Q$ or $R$ in the two panels of Exhibit 16.4) will be higher than the old optimum ($P$ in either panel).

Regarding leisure, the income and substitution effects are at cross-purposes. The higher wage elicits more labor via the substitution effect, but it also makes the worker richer, eliciting more leisure (hence less labor) via the income effect. Either effect can dominate, so that the new optimum can be either to the right of $P$ (as in panel A of Exhibit 16.4) or to the left of $P$ (as in panel B). The worker might supply either more or less labor when the wage rate increases.

## The Income and Substitution Effects via Geometry

We can use a graph to sort out the income and substitution effects. After the wage rises from $W$ to $W'$, we imagine a downward adjustment in the worker's nonlabor income that just compensates for the wage increase, leaving him on the same indifference curve as before. This gives a compensated budget line, shown in color in each of the panels in Exhibit 16.5. We now imagine the movement to the new optimum as taking place in two steps: from $P$ to $Q'$ to $Q$ in panel A or from $P$ to $R'$ to $R$ in panel B. The first movement is the substitution effect and must be upward and to the right (it is a movement along an indifference curve to a steeper point). The second movement is the income effect, as in Exhibit 16.3, which is a movement upward and to the left.

In panel A, the substitution effect is greater than the income effect, while in panel B the reverse is true. Thus, in panel A the wage increase leads to more labor supplied, and in panel B the wage increase leads to less labor supplied.

## Comparing the Two Effects

Which is larger, the income effect or the substitution effect? First, consider the situation when the wage is very low. In that case, the worker supplies very little labor (for example, if the wage is zero, there is no incentive to work at all!). Therefore, a change in the wage has little effect on the worker's income, so the income effect is negligible. It follows that at low wages, the substitution effect dominates the income effect, as in panel A of Exhibit 16.5. Therefore:

When the wage is very low to begin with, an increase in the wage leads to an increase in labor supplied.

When the wage rate is high, both the income and the substitution effects can be substantial. Therefore, at high wage rates there is no way to tell which effect will dominate.

## The Worker's Supply of Labor

### Deriving the Labor Supply Curve

From graphs like those in Exhibit 16.4, we can derive the labor supply curves of individuals. Exhibit 16.6 depicts the labor supply curves of the two individuals whose indifference curves appear in Exhibit 16.4. Both curves slope upward at low wages,

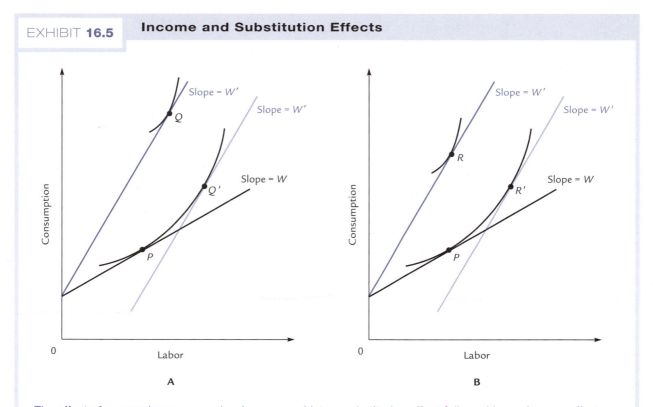

EXHIBIT **16.5**

**Income and Substitution Effects**

The effect of a wage increase can be decomposed into a substitution effect followed by an income effect. When the wage goes up, we pretend that the worker loses just enough nonlabor income to keep him on his original indifference curve. In either panel this yields the lightly colored budget line. The substitution effect is from $P$ to $Q'$ in panel A or from $P$ to $R'$ in panel B; it is a movement along the indifference curve and leads to more labor supplied.

The income effect is from $Q'$ to $Q$ in panel A or from $R'$ to $R$ in panel B. It leads to less labor supplied.

In panel A the substitution effect dominates the income effect, so that more labor is supplied after the wage increase. In panel B the opposite is true.

reflecting the dominance of the substitution effect over the income effect. The second curve "bends backward" at higher wages, to reflect the fact that for this individual the income effect eventually comes to dominate the substitution effect. An individual's labor supply curve might or might not be backward-bending.

## Using the Labor Supply Curve

Changes in wage rates correspond to movements along the labor supply curve, whereas changes in other things, such as nonlabor income, correspond to shifts of the curve.

Since the early days of the Industrial Revolution, wage rates have increased substantially and, at the same time, the quantity of labor supplied has decreased. The 60-hour workweeks that were common for unskilled laborers 100 years ago are uncommon today. This evidence is consistent with a backward-bending labor supply curve. However, there is an alternative explanation. Along with the increase in wages has come a substantial increase in nonlabor income. As you can see from Exhibit 16.3, an increase in nonlabor income leads to less labor supplied at any given wage; that is, it causes the labor supply curve to shift leftward. Thus, the fall in hours worked might be explained by an upward-sloping labor supply curve that has shifted leftward, as in Exhibit 16.7.

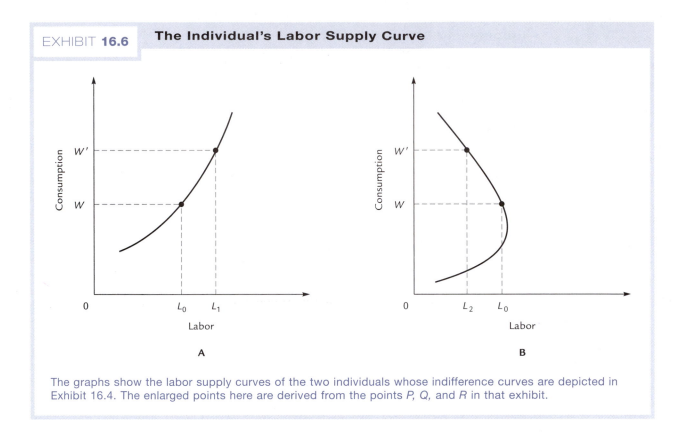

## EXHIBIT 16.6   The Individual's Labor Supply Curve

The graphs show the labor supply curves of the two individuals whose indifference curves are depicted in Exhibit 16.4. The enlarged points here are derived from the points *P*, *Q*, and *R* in that exhibit.

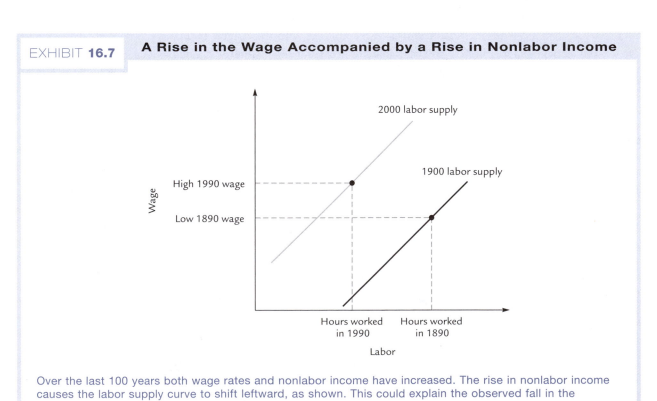

## EXHIBIT 16.7   A Rise in the Wage Accompanied by a Rise in Nonlabor Income

Over the last 100 years both wage rates and nonlabor income have increased. The rise in nonlabor income causes the labor supply curve to shift leftward, as shown. This could explain the observed fall in the quantity of labor supplied.

## International Differences in Labor Supply

The average American works 25 hours a week; the average Frenchman, 18; the average Italian, a bit more than 16 $\frac{1}{2}$. Even the hardest-working Europeans—the British who put in an average of 21 $\frac{1}{2}$ hours—work far less than their American cousins.

Several factors influence these averages. First, Europeans are more likely than Americans to be unemployed (and hence to work 0 hours a week). Next, even for the employed, workweeks are shorter in Europe; employed Americans put in about 3 hours more per week than employed Frenchmen. More importantly, Europeans take much longer and more frequent vacations. The average employed American takes less than 6 weeks of vacation per year; the average Frenchman takes 12. The world champion vacationers are the Swedes, who average 16 $\frac{1}{2}$ weeks of vacation per year.

Why do Americans choose to work so much? Or, if you prefer, why do Europeans choose to work so little?

The answer is unlikely to involve cultural differences, because all of this is quite recent. Just 30 years ago, Europeans worked slightly *more* than Americans. So the right question is not "Why is Europe different?" but rather "What changed?"

According to Nobel laureate Edward Prescott[1], the answer is tax policy. Thirty years ago, European and U.S. marginal tax rates were comparable—and so were European and U.S. labor supplies. Between the 1970s and the 1990s, the U.S. marginal rate stayed fixed at about 40%, while the French rate rose to 59% and the Italian rate to 64%. On a country-by-country basis, steeper marginal tax hikes are closely correlated with shrinking workweeks and expanding vacations.

Case closed? Not quite. The problem is that a 20-percentage-point increase in your marginal tax rate is essentially equivalent to a 20% pay cut. We have lots of data on how strongly people react to 20% pay cuts, and by and large those responses are nowhere near as dramatic as the changes we've seen in Europe. So although marginal tax rates do a good job of explaining *relative* changes (the countries with the biggest tax hikes have the biggest labor supply contractions), they do a poor job explaining *absolute* changes—that is, they can't explain why labor supplies across Europe have fallen so far.

One trio of economists[2] offers the following theory: When your own wages are cut by 20%, you'll take more vacations. But when your *friends'* wages are cut by 20%, you'll take even *more* vacations, because vacations are more fun when you have friends to share them with. So a 20% across-the-board tax hike, which affects both you and your friends, yields a more dramatic response than a 20% cut in your own wages.

## 16.2 Labor Market Equilibrium

We have now constructed a single individual's labor supply curve. Repeating this construction for each individual separately and then adding up, we can construct a market labor supply curve. At any given wage, we read each individual's quantity supplied from his own supply curve; then we add these quantities to get the quantity of labor supplied to the market.

There is also a market demand for labor, which we know from Chapter 15 coincides with the $MRP_L$ curve. Putting the supply and demand curves together, we can find

[1] E. Prescott, "Why Do Americans Work So Much More Than Europeans?," *Federal Reserve Bank of Minneapolis Quarterly Review* 28, July 2004.

[2] A. Alesina, E. Glaeser, and B. Sacerdote, "Work and Leisure in the U.S. and Europe: Why So Different?," *Harvard Institute of Economic Research Discussion Papers* 2068, April 2005.

the point of labor market equilibrium. Now we can use the machinery of supply and demand to analyze the effects of some simple changes.

To carry out the exercises of this section, we will assume that the labor supply curve is upward sloping.

## Changes in Nonlabor Income

Part A of Exhibit 16.8 illustrates what happens when a single worker experiences an increase in nonlabor income, such as an unexpected inheritance. The labor market (depicted in the left-hand panel) is in equilibrium at the wage $W$. The individual worker, who is a competitive supplier in the labor market, then faces a flat demand curve for his services at that wage. His initial supply curve is $s$ in the right-hand panel and he supplies $L$ units of labor.

When he learns about his inheritance, the worker feels wealthier and decides to work less, so his labor supply curve shifts back to $s'$. Because he represents an insignificant part of the market, the market curves in the left-hand panel do not move, and neither does the flat demand curve $d$. The worker now supplies $L'$ units of labor instead of $L$.

Part B of the same exhibit illustrates what happens when many workers experience a simultaneous increase in their nonlabor income. This could happen for a variety of reasons. Perhaps a lasting peace in the Middle East brings down the price of oil (which effectively increases the wealth of oil consumers); perhaps the same lasting peace leads to a reduction in U.S. military expenditures and a consequent reduction in taxes; perhaps (as happened in 1991) Rocky and Bullwinkle are released on videotape, yielding a widespread improvement in standards of living. Now the individual supply curve in the right-hand panel shifts back from $s$ to $s'$ as before. The new wrinkle is that the shift in supply occurs for every individual, not just one, and therefore, the market supply curve shifts back as well, from $S$ to $S'$ in the left-hand panel. The market wage rises from $W$ to $W'$. The total quantity of labor supplied to the market certainly falls, but a given worker, moving from the intersection of $s$ and $d$ to the intersection of $s'$ and $d'$, can either increase or decrease the quantity he supplies.

To sum up, a marketwide increase in nonlabor income can lead to either an increase or a decrease in any one individual's working hours, but the *average* or "representative" worker must decide to work less. We know this because the total quantity of labor supplied to the marketplace must fall.

## Changes in Productivity

Workers can be made more productive in many ways, including technological advances (like faster computers, which improve the productivity of office workers), improvements in the weather (which improves the productivity of agricultural workers), or unexpected disasters (which can improve the productivity of medical personnel).

Panel A of Exhibit 16.9 shows the effect of an increase in marginal productivity. The labor demand curve, which coincides with the $MRP_L$ curve, shifts rightward from $D$ to $D'$ in the left-hand panel. The market wage rises from $W$ to $W'$, and the flat demand curve for the services of an individual worker rises accordingly, from $d$ to $d'$ in the right-hand panel. Each individual worker supplies more labor than before.

That analysis holds workers' nonlabor income fixed. But when there is an economy-wide increase in productivity, such an analysis is likely to be incomplete, because workers' nonlabor income is likely to rise. Here's why: When workers become more productive, the value of capital increases. (For example, a factory employing highly

## EXHIBIT 16.8 — An Increase in Nonlabor Income

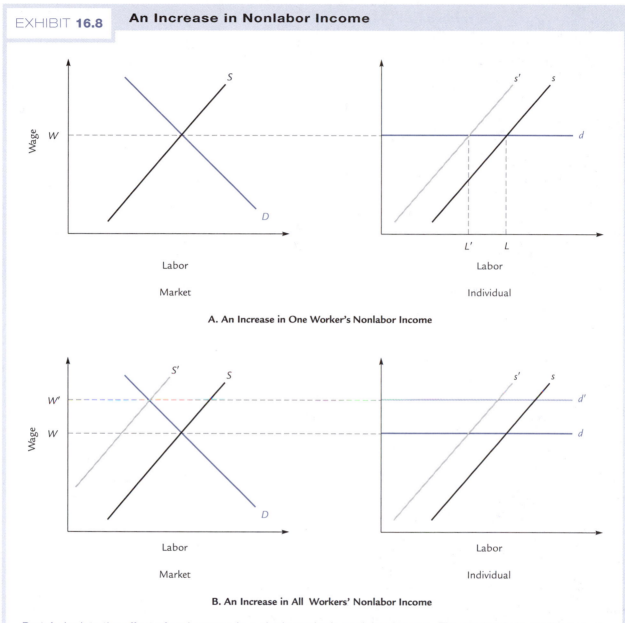

A. An Increase in One Worker's Nonlabor Income

B. An Increase in All Workers' Nonlabor Income

Part A depicts the effect of an increase in a single worker's nonlabor income. The market is in equilibrium at a wage of W. The worker faces a flat demand curve at that wage. When his income increases, the worker's supply curve shifts back from s to s′ and his quantity of labor supplied falls from L to L′.

Part B depicts the effect of a simultaneous increase in all workers' nonlabor income. The individual supply curve shifts back from s to s′ as before. Since *all* workers' supply curves shift, the market supply curve shifts back also, from S to S′. The wage rises from W to W′. The quantity of labor supplied to the market falls; the quantity supplied by a given individual can either rise or fall.

productive workers is worth more than a factory employing less productive workers.) Therefore, the owners of capital experience an increase in nonlabor income. But in many cases, the owners of capital include the workers themselves: Farmers own tractors; plumbers own plumbing tools; and many workers own stock in corporations that in turn own all sorts of capital equipment.

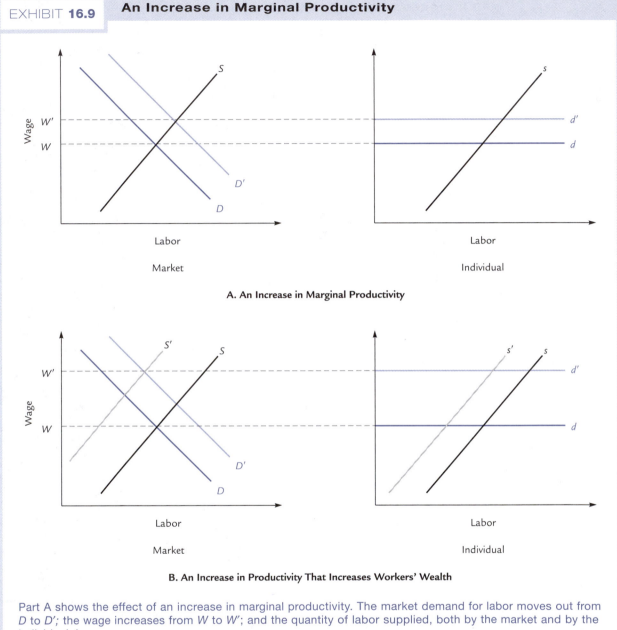

**EXHIBIT 16.9**    **An Increase in Marginal Productivity**

A. An Increase in Marginal Productivity

B. An Increase in Productivity That Increases Workers' Wealth

Part A shows the effect of an increase in marginal productivity. The market demand for labor moves out from D to D′; the wage increases from W to W′; and the quantity of labor supplied, both by the market and by the individual, increases.

    Part B shows the effect of an increase in marginal productivity that causes an increase in workers' non-labor income (by increasing the value of the capital that they own). Demand in the left-hand panel moves out as in part A. Supply in both panels moves back as in part B of Exhibit 16.8. The wage increases from W to W′, and the quantity of labor supplied, both by the market and by the individual, moves ambiguously.

Therefore, a general increase in productivity is likely to yield an increase in workers' nonlabor income. In that case, Panel A in Exhibit 16.9 must be replaced by panel B. Here the demand for labor shifts out, just as in panel A, but at the same time, the market and individual labor supply curves shift leftward, as in Exhibit 16.8. The wage rate increases, but the quantity of labor supplied, both by the entire market and by the individual, moves ambiguously.

## Temporary Changes in Productivity: Intertemporal Substitution

In March 1989, the *Exxon Valdez* oil tanker ran aground in Alaska, creating an oil spill of historic proportions. Clean-up operations were urgent, so the marginal productivity of Alaskan workers quickly jumped up.

According to panel A of Exhibit 16.9, there should have been increases in both the wage rate and the quantity of labor supplied by each worker. Both these predictions were borne out. Wages quickly rose (from about $9 an hour to about $10.60 an hour), and at the same time, the average workweek shot up from about 35 hours a week to about 49 hours a week.

What is surprising here is not that the average workweek increased, but that it increased so dramatically. In fact, Alaskan wages had been as high as $10.60 an hour just a few years earlier, but at that time average workweeks were just slightly more than 40 hours a week. To put this another way, the average worker's labor supply curve, which had recently passed through ($10.60, 40) now passed through ($10.60, 49). So the labor supply curve must have shifted far to the right in 1989. What could have caused that shift?

The answer is that the high productivity of Alaskan workers was *temporary*. When there is a temporary opportunity to earn high wages, workers often rush to take advantage of it, working extra hard during the brief window of opportunity and postponing leisure time. (For example, people who sell Christmas trees tend to work very hard in December and compensate by relaxing in January.) Such behavior is called intertemporal substitution.

Intertemporal substitution leads to a rightward shift in the labor supply curve, as shown in Exhibit 16.10. The labor demand curve in the left-hand panel shifts rightward as workers become more productive, just as in panel A of Exhibit 16.9. But now, because the opportunity to earn high wages is temporary rather than permanent, laborers rush to take advantage of this brief opportunity and their labor supply curves

**Intertemporal substitution**

Working additional hours during temporary periods of high productivity.

EXHIBIT **16.10**    **A Temporary Increase in Marginal Productivity**

When the marginal product of labor increases *temporarily,* individual labor supply curves shift rightward as workers rush to take advantage of the brief opportunity to earn high wages. As a result, employment rises by more than if the increase were permanent.

also shift rightward. The rightward shift in individual labor supply (in the right-hand panel) implies a rightward shift in the marketwide labor supply (in the left-hand panel).

Because the demand and supply curves both shift rightward in the left-hand panel of Exhibit 16.10, it appears that the equilibrium wage rate can either rise or fall. But a fall in the equilibrium wage rate would be inconsistent with the story we've been telling: The entire reason the supply curve shifts is so that workers can take advantage of temporarily high wages. This can happen only if wages *are* temporarily high; thus, the new (temporary) equilibrium must be higher than the old equilibrium to which the market will eventually return.

The conclusion is that, because of intertemporal substitution, a *temporary* increase in productivity has a much bigger effect on employment than a *permanent* increase in productivity. Therefore, intertemporal substitution might be an important factor in determining the severity of recessions (that is, temporary periods in which average income is low, and, typically, unemployment is high).

## 16.3  Differences in Wages

We have discussed the determination of "the" market wage. Yet it is a common observation that different people earn different wages. In this section, we will discuss some of the reasons for these differences.

### Human Capital

A firm that hires an employee is often hiring not just raw *labor*, but an entire package of productive skills. Some of those skills, like intelligence, may be innate, whereas others, like education and training, are the result of investments by the employee earlier in life. Such skills can productively be viewed as a form of capital, which we will call human capital.

**Human capital**

Productive skills.

We have seen in Section 15.4 that the revenues of the firm are divided among the productive inputs, with each earning its marginal product. A worker who brings both labor and human capital to an enterprise earns both the wage rate for his labor and the market rate of return for his skills. In practice, he usually receives the sum of these returns in a single paycheck, the size of which is described as his *wage*. Of course, workers with different amounts of human capital will earn differing returns.

The use of the word *capital* here is more than just a loose metaphor. As we will see in Chapter 17, capital consists of productive resources that have themselves been produced by forgoing consumption at earlier times. This description fits human capital perfectly. When you attend college, you forgo current consumption, both by making tuition payments that could be used for other things and by allocating time to your studies that could otherwise be spent earning income. The sum of these costs is an investment in human capital.

In the short run, human capital is a fixed factor (its supply curve is vertical). For this reason, payments to human capital are a form of rent. The difference between the earnings of a college graduate and those of an unskilled laborer constitutes the rent on human capital.

In the long run, people can vary their investments in human capital. As more investment takes place, the costs (like college tuition) are driven up and the rents to human capital are driven down. People will continue to invest until the marginal cost and marginal benefit from a unit of human capital are equal.

If all people can make equally productive use of an education, then everyone will be indifferent between becoming educated and not becoming educated. This is because the cost of an education will exactly offset the benefits. (If the benefits of going to college exceed the costs, additional people will enter college until this is no longer the case.) If, on the other hand, people are endowed with varying quantities of other skills (like intelligence or perseverance) that make education more productive, then those who have unusually large endowments of these other skills can benefit from education.

## Signaling

In Chapter 9, we discussed the phenomenon of *signaling*, whereby a college education can lead to higher wages even without contributing to productivity, provided that it helps employers identify people with intelligence and perseverance. Education can lead to higher wages either by adding to human capital or by performing a signaling function; in practice, both aspects are surely present.

## Education as Consumption

We have used education as an example of an investment in higher wages. We have suggested two ways in which this could happen. Perhaps education is a way to acquire human capital; perhaps it is a signal of certain innate skills; perhaps it is some combination of the two.

In fact, highly educated people do earn higher wages than do less highly educated people. However, there is yet another possible explanation for this. Rather than education causing high wages, perhaps high wages cause education.

Suppose that people actually enjoy going to college and view it as a consumption good. Then we expect people with greater wealth to consume more of this good. Just as richer people buy more Rolls Royces, so richer people buy more education. No one would suggest that because rich people drive Rolls Royces, buying a Rolls Royce will make you rich.

Undoubtedly, education is partly investment and partly consumption. To some extent, people purchase it to raise their incomes, and to some extent they purchase it because they enjoy it. Here is a question to ponder: What observable data would help you determine what percent of educational spending is pure consumption?

## Compensating Differentials

Another reason for differences in observed wage rates is that some jobs are more pleasant or less pleasant than others. When there is a large class of equally talented workers available to each of several occupations, these workers must be indifferent as to which occupation they choose.

**Exercise 16.3** Why must the workers be indifferent among occupations? If they were not indifferent, what would happen?

There are many reasons why one occupation might be inherently less pleasant than another. In some occupations the work itself is unpleasant, in others the people employed command less respect, and in still others there are greater degrees of risk. In order for workers to remain indifferent, the less pleasant occupations must pay more. We can view the wage in the less pleasant occupation as the sum of the market wage determined elsewhere plus an additional payment to compensate the worker for the unpleasant aspects of his job. This additional payment is known as a **compensating differential.**

Other occupations are unusually attractive. An employee in such an occupation earns less than one in a more typical job, the compensating differential being negative. For example, many positions offer workers the opportunity to invest in human capital at a cost much lower than the usual market rate. This comes about when an employee, in the course of performing his duties, acquires skills that he will later be able to sell in the marketplace. Such on-the-job training occurs at every level of skill. A postdoctoral instructor in physics at a top university is gaining valuable skills that will increase his marketability in later life, in exchange for which he accepts a wage that might be less than his marginal product. A clerk in a bookstore is observing and learning the business, gaining the skills necessary to be a manager or to open his own shop someday. Again, he pays for this opportunity through a lower wage.

Although on-the-job training is important at every level, it is particularly important at the very bottom of the career ladder, where the skills that are mastered (fundamentals such as knowing the importance of showing up for work on time and how to get along with co-workers) will be useful in any future occupation. In entry-level positions, on-the-job training is often a substantial portion of the employee's total compensation.

## Access to Capital

Wages would also differ if workers had access to capital of differing qualities. A secretary in New York City using the latest word processor might be more productive at the margin than a secretary using a manual typewriter in a locality with no electricity.

In making this argument, it is important not to confuse total productivity with marginal productivity. The lone secretary with the manual typewriter in a developing country can certainly be more productive *at the margin* than the 100,000th word-processing New Yorker. In fact, as long as people can move from country to country, wages will tend to become equal everywhere over time because of people leaving the low-wage countries to enter the high-wage countries. This equalization of wages implies an equalization of marginal products. Therefore, the access of different workers to different sorts of capital can explain wage differences in the long run only if there are barriers to the mobility of workers, such as immigration restrictions.

However, even immigration restrictions fail to explain wage differences across countries. If wages are lower in Mexico than in the United States, we at first expect Mexican workers to cross the border until wages are equalized. Then we are reminded that the immigration laws prevent this. But now we should expect U.S. firms to move their capital across the border into Mexico to take advantage of the low wages there. This will raise wages in Mexico and reduce wages in the United States, and the flow of capital across the border should continue until wages are equalized.

We do see some phenomena like this. In recent years, for example, many firms have relocated from the northern to the southern United States to take advantage of lower wage rates. But there has been nothing like the international movement of capital that one would expect on the basis of standard economic theory. Why not?[3]

[3] This riddle was posed by Robert E. Lucas, Jr., in a series of lectures titled "On the Mechanics of Economic Development," *Journal of Monetary Economics* 21 (1988). The answer we will propose is also taken from those lectures, although it is offered there as a clue to the solution of a much deeper riddle, namely: Why do different countries have different levels of economic development and different rates of growth?

An answer to this riddle might be found in the external effects of human capital accumulation.[4] When you invest in training or education, you increase not only your own productivity but that of your fellow workers through a variety of complicated interactions between you and them. Perhaps some of your new knowledge rubs off in conversations around the water cooler. Perhaps you are more likely to make suggestions or to have ideas that other workers can imitate or that will inspire them to formulate related new ideas of their own. These interactions need not be confined to your own workplace. To paraphrase Adam Smith, people of the same trade seldom meet together, even for merriment and diversion, without the conversation ending in a mutually beneficial exchange of ideas and methods or in some contrivance to increase efficiency.

Through such mechanisms, your accumulation of human capital can raise the productivity not only of your co-workers and of other workers in your industry but also of the physical capital with which you interact. In that case, those owners of physical capital who locate themselves in areas with large concentrations of highly trained people will reap a share of these external benefits. They might be willing to pay higher wages, or higher land rents, in exchange for such an opportunity. Consequently, the difference between land rents in, say, Manhattan and a more remote location might be a tolerably good measure of the value of those external benefits.

If human capital investment yields significant positive externalities, then there will be too little of it. People invest in human capital only up to the point where the marginal cost is equal to the marginal increase in their own productivity, without taking account of how their investment affects the productivity of others. This observation constitutes an efficiency-based argument for subsidizing investments in human capital, such as education. If, as we have argued, differences in land rents measure the value of human capital externalities, then the size of such rent differentials could be used in a calculation of the size of the optimal subsidy.

# 16.4 Discrimination

The average black person earns less than the average white person, and the average woman earns less than the average man. Parts of these differentials are easy to account for. The average African-American is about 6 $1/2$ years younger than the average white, and younger workers generally earn less than older workers do. A larger percentage of African-Americans live in the South, where wages are lower generally. Women are more likely than men to have studied sociology instead of engineering.

Economists disagree about whether such factors can account for all of the observed wage differentials. The alternative hypothesis is that the differentials are partly due to discrimination. The existence of discrimination is difficult to measure. One must ask not "Do African-Americans earn less than whites do?" but "Do African-Americans earn less than whites *with comparable market characteristics* [education, experience, age, etc.] do?"[5] The question is empirical but difficult to settle, because of the difficulty of measuring all of the relevant market characteristics.

---

[4] An alternative possible answer is that after adjusting for human capital differences, Mexican wages really *aren't* any lower than U.S. wages.

[5] The real question is "Do African-Americans earn less than do whites with the same marginal product?" In view of the difficulty of measuring marginal product directly, we hope to approximate it with a mix of observable market characteristics.

# Theories of Discrimination

If there is discrimination, employers engage in it at a cost. If African-Americans earn lower wages than equally productive whites, any employer who hires whites forgoes an opportunity to hire equally productive African-American labor at a lower wage.

In fact, a relatively small number of nondiscriminating employers could suffice to eliminate all wage differentials, even if the majority of employers discriminate. Suppose that 80% of employers are discriminatory and are unwilling to pay African-Americans more than half their marginal product. Suppose that the remaining 20% of employers are indifferent between hiring whites and hiring African-Americans and that these 20% are enough to employ all of the blacks in the economy. Then as long as African-Americans are paid less than their marginal product, the nondiscriminating firms will hire more of them. This will continue, bidding up the price of black labor, until African-Americans are earning their full marginal product, just as whites are.

It is sometimes alleged that employers discriminate not out of any genuine distaste for a particular group, but as a strategy to employ that group at a lower wage. Such a strategy would require the cooperation of thousands of employers and would be subject to exactly the same pressures that cause cartels to break down. Any individual employer could gain by cheating. In fact, such a strategy is far more implausible than a cartel, because a cartel requires cooperation only by the firms in a single industry, whereas the "fake discrimination" ploy requires the cooperation of all firms that hire labor.

One theory of discrimination says that while employers might be indifferent between hiring whites and African-Americans, they nevertheless discriminate because their white employees have a distaste for associating with African-Americans. Whenever a African-American is hired, the employer must increase the white workers' wages or they will leave the firm. Thus, because it is especially costly for employers to hire African-Americans, the demand for African-Americans is lower and they receive lower wages. If this theory is correct, employers should be able to benefit by hiring all-African-American workforces, paying the lower African-American wage without having to worry about the effect on white employees. Employers will adopt this strategy until African-American wages are bid up to the level of white wages. Thus, the theory predicts a heavily segregated workforce, with some all-white firms and some all-African-American firms, but no wage differentials.

Considerable sophistication is needed to find a theory consistent with sustained wage differentials in the face of profit maximization by even some employers. Since most theories predict a tendency toward complete segregation, it is necessary to postulate a force opposing that tendency in order to get realistic results. One possibility is that African-Americans and whites have different skills and that those skills are complementary in production. In this case, it would pay to combine African-American and white workers even if it required paying a premium to the whites. Another possibility is to develop a theory of the costs of changing personnel, so that an employer who would ultimately benefit from an all-African-American workforce will find it optimal to stretch the adjustment out over a long period of time.[6]

---

[6] See K. Arrow, "Some Models of Racial Discrimination in the Labor Market" in A. Pascal (ed.), *Racial Discrimination in Economic Life* (RAND Corporation, 1972), for a survey and detailed discussion of such theories. The first serious attempt by an economist to study questions related to discrimination was in G. Becker, *The Economics of Discrimination* (Chicago: University of Chicago Press, 1957).

## Wage Differences Due to Worker Preferences

Some apparent discrimination undoubtedly results from the preferences of the workers themselves. Here is an example of how this might come about.

When a worker seeks a job, he or she typically receives several offers at different salaries. Suppose that men and women typically receive the same range of offers, but that men on average are more inclined to accept their highest-paying offer, whereas women apply many other criteria in making their choice. In this case, statistics will show that women earn less than men do, even though men and women both receive exactly the same salary offers on average.

Why might men be more inclined than women to accept their highest-paying offers? One reason is that most married men are trained for more lucrative occupations than their wives are. Thus, if a married couple must live together in the same city, they usually maximize their total family income by moving to the city where the husband has the brightest prospects.

Imagine, for example, a couple in which the husband is a movie director and the wife a professor. The husband is offered a $100,000 job in California and a $50,000 job in Massachusetts. The wife is offered a $10,000 job in California and a $20,000 job in Massachusetts. In this case the couple maximizes its income by moving to California, where their combined salaries are $110,000 instead of $70,000. The wife will earn $10,000, whereas most male professors (who are not married to movie directors) will live in Massachusetts and earn $20,000.

Statistics will show that female professors generally earn less than their male counterparts do, while perhaps failing to show the reason why. The point of this example is not its empirical significance, which at any rate is unclear.[7] The point is that wage differentials can result from supply decisions (by workers) as well as from demand decisions (by employers) through subtle mechanisms that might not be apparent to the researcher. This is why questions about discrimination are so hard to settle.

## Human Capital Inheritance

If it is argued that African-Americans earn less than whites only because of inferior human capital, one must still attempt to account for this interracial difference in human capital. A common explanation is that human capital is largely inherited (we learn much from our parents' skills and attitudes) and that African-Americans have inherited less because of past discrimination. Of course, this is scant comfort to an African-American worker who is informed that he earns less than his white colleagues not because he is African-American, but because his parents were. Yet it surely does make a difference whether African-Americans and other groups are suffering only from past discrimination or from present discrimination as well. Although two diseases have the same symptoms, the prescribed medications could differ substantially.

Although past discrimination, via human capital inheritance, might play a role in determining the current incomes of African-Americans, it is at least reasonably certain that this is not true of women. African-American people tend to have mostly African-American ancestors, but women have only the same percentage of female ancestors that their brothers do.

---

[7] For some evidence, see R. Frank, "Why Women Earn Less: The Theory and Estimation of Differential Overqualification," *American Economic Review* 68 (1978): 360–373.

# Summary

Individuals supply labor to firms, which produce outputs that individuals demand. Labor supply, like output demand, depends on the tastes of individuals.

Thus, we need to study the individual's indifference curves between consumption and labor. We can begin by drawing his indifference curves between consumption and leisure, which are both goods, and then reversing the leisure axis.

The budget line is determined by nonlabor income (which gives the intercept) and the wage rate (which gives the slope). Once we have the indifference curves and the budget line, we can determine how much labor is supplied.

An increase in nonlabor income corresponds to a parallel shift of the budget line. We always assume that consumption and leisure are both normal goods, so that after a rise in nonlabor income, consumption increases and less labor is supplied.

A rise in an individual worker's wage rate has both an income effect and a substitution effect. The substitution effect, which is a movement to a steeper part of the original indifference curve, results in more labor supplied. The income effect, which is a movement to a higher indifference curve, results in less labor supplied. Either effect could dominate. When wages are low, however, income effects are small, so at least at low wages the substitution effect dominates. Thus, at low wages the individual's labor supply curve slopes upward, whereas at high wages it could either continue to slope upward or it could bend backward.

Combining the worker's labor supply curve with the firm's labor demand curve (and remembering that the labor demand curve is the $MRP_L$ curve), we can find the market equilibrium and study how it changes in response to changing market conditions. A rise in nonlabor income leads to a leftward shift in labor supply. A rise in marginal productivity leads to a rightward shift in labor demand. If the rise in marginal productivity increases the nonlabor income of workers (by increasing the value of the capital that they own) then it leads to a leftward shift in labor supply as well.

When wage changes are perceived to be temporary, intertemporal substitution takes place. That is, the labor supply curve shifts to reflect workers' response to their perception that the situation is temporary. If wages are perceived to be temporarily high, workers will reschedule their current vacation plans for later; if wages are perceived to be temporarily low, workers will reschedule their future vacation plans for today. Thus, it is possible that even small wage changes, if perceived to be temporary, could yield very large changes in employment. This is consistent with what we know of the history of recessions.

Different workers receive different wages for different reasons. Often, a portion of the worker's paycheck is not really a wage at all, but a return on human capital. Workers can benefit by having access to capital of differing qualities, including their colleagues' human capital, from which they receive external benefits. Some workers receive positive compensating differentials for work that is especially pleasant or negative ones for work that has special advantages.

There are substantial wage differences between African-Americans and whites and between men and women. Many factors, including discrimination, might be part of the explanation. Most of these factors, including differences in human capital, are very difficult to measure, making it hard to determine the significance of discrimination. Some wage differences result from the choices of workers themselves, as when married women choose to live in the cities where their husbands can earn the highest wage, rather than in the cities where they themselves can earn the highest wage. Economists do not know how important a role such phenomena play in determining wage differences.

# Review Questions

**R1.** Explain the income and substitution effects of a rise in an individual's wage. Which causes him to work less, and why?

**R2.** Under what circumstances can we be sure that the substitution effect will outweigh the income effect? What implications does this have for the shape of the individual's labor supply curve?

**R3.** What are the possible shapes for an individual's labor supply curve? Interpret them in terms of income and substitution effects.

**R4.** Draw a diagram with two panels depicting the supply and demand for labor both in the market as a whole and for an individual worker.

**R5.** In the preceding question, how is the supply curve affected by a change in nonlabor income? How is the demand curve affected by a change in productivity?

**R6.** Will employment fall more in response to a permanent fall in wages or in response to a temporary fall? Why?

**R7.** List some reasons why different people earn different wages.

**R8.** List some theories that might explain wage differences between African-Americans and whites. How might you go about testing some of these theories? What problems might you run into?

# Problem Set

**1.** **True or False:** If an individual suddenly found that he needed less sleep per night than previously, his consumption would go up.

**2.** Jack can work up to 8 hours a day at a wage rate of $W$ and as much more as he wants at the higher overtime rate of $W'$. He chooses to work 10 hours. Jill can work as many hours as she wants at a wage of $W''$. Jack and Jill have the same tastes, the same assets, and are equally happy. What can you conclude about the size of $W''$ compared with $W$ and $W'$? What can you conclude about the number of hours Jill works?

**3.** Suppose that all people have identical tastes and identical talents, but that those who attend college become more productive and hence earn higher wages. On the other hand, college students have to pay tuition.

**a.** Explain why college graduates and nongraduates must be equally happy. (*Hint:* What would happen to tuition if they weren't?) Use this observation and an indifference curve diagram to illustrate the equilibrium tuition cost.

**b.** **True or False:** Because college graduates earn higher wages, they might choose to work fewer hours than nongraduates.

4. Dick recently received a substantial inheritance from his aunt and immediately started working more hours at his job. If Dick's wage rate increases, can you predict what will happen to the number of hours that he works? Justify your answer.

5. Jane recently received a substantial inheritance from her aunt and immediately started working fewer hours at her job. If Jane's wage rate increases, can you predict what will happen to the number of hours that she works? Justify your answer.

6. Leisure is an inferior good for Horace.

**a.** Use indifference curves to show the income and substitution effects of an increase in Horace's wage rate.

**b.** Could Horace's labor supply curve be backward-bending? How do you know?

7. Hortense earns a wage of $10 per hour and chooses to work 35 hours per week. One day, her employer tells her that while he will continue to pay her $10 an hour for her first 35 hours each week, he will now pay her $15 per hour for any additional hours beyond the first 35.

**a.** Illustrate Hortense's situation with indifference curves.

**b.** **True or False:** Hortense might choose to continue working exactly 35 hours per week.

8. Car wash attendants currently earn $5 per hour and choose to work 50 hours per week. A law has just been passed requiring car washes to pay double wages for any hours in excess of 40 per week. The law does not, however, apply to any other occupations.

**a.** Explain why car wash attendants must remain on the same indifference curve. What must happen to their basic wage rate?

**b.** **True or False:** Car wash attendants will certainly now work more hours than they did previously.

9. **True or False:** A man who earns his entire income in wages will respond more sharply to a rise in the wage than will a man whose income is mostly from property.

10. **True or False:** Workers who like their jobs will be more productive at the margin than those who don't.

11. Suppose that an unexpected blight wipes out a large portion of this year's agricultural harvest. What happens to the wage rate, the amount of labor supplied to the marketplace, and the amount of labor supplied by any given individual?

12. Suppose that a tornado destroys a large number of major factories.

**a.** What is the effect on the demand for labor?

**b.** If the factories are owned by workers (say, through stock ownership), what is the effect on the supply of labor?

**c.** What is the effect on the wage rate, the amount of labor supplied to the marketplace, and the amount of labor supplied by any individual?

**13.** Suppose that an epidemic kills half the workers in an industry that produces goods for export. What is the effect on the wage rate, the amount of labor supplied to the marketplace, and the amount of labor supplied by any individual surviving worker?

**14.** In the preceding problem, suppose that instead of being produced for export, the good being manufactured is sold to the very workers who produce it. How does your answer change?

**15.** **True or False:** If the capital stock is fixed and if the level of output is fixed, then a rise in the marginal productivity of labor benefits the owners of capital.

**16.** How would the wage rate and the level of employment be affected by the invention of a costless pill that made it unnecessary for anyone to sleep?

**17.** Contrast the effects on employment, output, and wages of (a) a year of bad weather resulting in low agricultural productivity and (b) nuclear contamination that lowers agricultural productivity permanently.

**18.** Contrast the effects on employment, output, and wages of (a) an income tax that is expected to be in effect for 1 year and (b) an income tax that is expected to be permanent.

**19.** The current federal tax law allows deductions for the depreciation of physical capital. **True or False:** One effect of this deduction is to reduce the average level of education.

# CHAPTER 17

# Allocating Goods Over Time

Markets enable people to trade one kind of good for another. In some markets, you can trade an apple for some oranges. In others, you can trade an apple today for some apples tomorrow. In everyday language, the consumer who trades apples for oranges is a "seller" of apples and the consumer who trades apples today for apples tomorrow is a "lender" of apples. But there is no essential difference between the two transactions. In each case, the consumer is faced with a market price (for the lender, the relevant price is the interest rate) and must decide how much to buy or sell at that price. Therefore, many of the tools of consumer theory—most specifically the machinery of indifference curves—can also explain borrowing and lending.

In the first two sections of this chapter, we will emphasize the simple observation that an interest rate is nothing but a measure of relative price. In Section 17.2, we will see that this deceptively simple idea has some extraordinarily powerful applications.

Having come to understand the meaning of interest rates, we will turn to the question of how they are determined. We will answer this question in Section 17.3, using a simple supply and demand model. To simplify the discussion, we will assume that there is no technology available for converting current goods into future goods.

In Section 17.4, we will relax that assumption. This will enable us to study the market for capital and to increase our understanding of the determination of interest rates. However, one thing we will discover is that, despite the artificial assumptions of Section 17.3, many of its conclusions remain true in a far more general context.

## 17.1 Bonds and Interest Rates

When you trade an apple for some oranges, you are called a *seller* of apples, and the number of oranges that you receive is determined by the *relative price* at which you sell. When you trade an apple today for some apples tomorrow, you are called a *lender* of apples, and the number of apples that you receive tomorrow is determined by the *interest rate* at which you lend. Lending is a kind of selling, and an interest rate is a measure of relative price.

By the same token, *borrowing* an apple is precisely the same thing as buying an apple today and paying for it with apples tomorrow. Borrowing is a kind of buying.

In any trade, you are simultaneously a seller and a buyer. If you trade apples for oranges, you are both a seller of apples and a buyer of oranges. If you lend an apple today in exchange for some apples tomorrow, you are both a seller of apples today and a buyer of apples tomorrow. A borrower is both a buyer of apples today and a seller of apples tomorrow.

There is one important difference between buying oranges and buying tomorrow's apples. When you buy an orange, you get to hold it in your hand. When you buy an apple for delivery tomorrow, you hold only a promise. That promise might be strictly oral, it might be written down on a piece of paper, or it might be recorded on a computer disk. Another word for that promise is a **bond.** A bond is a promise to pay.

**Bond**

A promise to pay at some time in the future.

We have said that a lender simultaneously sells apples today and buys apples tomorrow. More precisely, he sells apples today and buys a *promise* of apples tomorrow; that is, he buys a bond.

A lender is the buyer of a bond.

By the same token, a borrower buys apples today in exchange for his promise to deliver apples tomorrow; he buys the current apples that the lender sells and sells the bond that the lender buys.

A borrower is the seller of a bond.

## Relative Prices, Interest Rates, and Present Values

Suppose that you lend an apple at an interest rate of 10% (= .10) per day. Tomorrow you receive 1.10 apples in return, so the relative price of an apple today in terms of apples tomorrow is 1.10.

More generally, if the interest rate is $r$ per day, then the relative price of an apple today in terms of an apple tomorrow is $1 + r$. So even though an interest rate is not exactly the same thing as a relative price, it is closely related to a relative price. To go from the interest rate to the relative price, just add 1; to go from the relative price to the interest rate, just subtract 1.

---

**Exercise 17.1** If 1 apple today can be traded for 2 apples tomorrow, what is the relative price of 1 apple today? What is the interest rate?

---

### Present Values

**Present value**

Relative price in terms of current consumption.

The **present value** of a future delivery is its relative price in terms of current goods. If the interest rate is 50% per day, or $r = .50$, then the relative price of an apple today is 1.5 apples tomorrow. Consequently, the relative price of an apple tomorrow in terms of apples today is $1/1.5 = 2/3$; we say that the present value of an apple tomorrow is equal to 2/3 apple today.

Because the relative price of today's apples in terms of tomorrow's is always given by $1 + r$, it follows that the relative price of tomorrow's apples in terms of today's is given by $1/(1 + r)$. If $r$ is 10% (= .10), this works out to about .91. An apple tomorrow is worth .91 apple today.

Another way to say this is that a bond promising 1 apple tomorrow can be purchased for a price of .91 apple today.

**The price of a bond is equal to the present value of what it promises to deliver.**

Thus, a bond that promises 1 apple tomorrow sells for a price of $1/(1+r)$ apples today. Notice that high values of $r$ correspond to low bond prices. If $r = .50$, then the bond sells for $2/3 = .67$ apple today (which grows to 1 apple tomorrow at the interest rate of 50%); whereas if $r = .10$, the bond sells for .91 apple today (which grows to 1 apple tomorrow at the interest rate of .10).

The **face value** of a bond is the number of future apples that it guarantees. A bond is said to sell at a **discount** equal to the difference between its face value and what it sells for today. Thus, if the interest rate is .50, a bond promising 1 apple tomorrow will sell for 2/3 apple today; the face value is 1 apple and the discount is 1/3 apple. If the interest rate is .10, a bond promising 10 apples tomorrow will sell for 9.1 apples today; the face value is 10 apples and the discount is .9 apple.

The **maturity date** of a bond is the date on which it promises a delivery. All of the bonds we have considered so far have maturity dates of "tomorrow."

**Exercise 17.2** If the interest rate is .25, what are the price, face value, and discount of a bond that promises 5 apples tomorrow?

**Face value**

The amount that a bond promises to pay.

**Discount**

The face value of a bond minus its current price.

**Maturity date**

The date on which a bond promises a delivery.

## Treasury Bills

When the U.S. government borrows, it does so by issuing bonds called Treasury bills. Treasury bills are issued with a fixed face value and maturity date and then auctioned to the highest bidder. Thus, the size of the discount (and consequently, the interest rate) is determined by the outcome of the auction.

For example, suppose that on January 1, 2005, the Treasury issues a bond reading, "We promise to pay $10,000 on January 1, 2006." The Treasury holds a regular weekly auction at which this bond will be offered for sale. Suppose that after much bidding you are able to purchase this bond for $9,500. This bond has sold at a $500 discount: you have lent $9,500 to the Treasury and will receive $10,000 back. Because you earn $500 in interest, the annual interest rate is $500/\$9,500 \approx 5.26\%$.

After you purchase the bond, you are entitled to resell it to anybody for whatever price you mutually agree upon. The government will make the final payment to whoever holds the bond on its maturity date. Thus, the value of the bond could vary quite a bit between the date of purchase and the date of maturity. For example, suppose that immediately after you purchase the bond, the market rate of interest rises to 12%. Then the value of the bond falls to $\$10,000 \times 1/(1+.12) \wedge \$8,928.57$.

Students sometimes want to know the direction of causality: Does a change in the interest rate cause the price of the bond to change, or does a change in the bond price cause the interest rate to change? The answer is that the interest rate and the bond price are two different descriptions of exactly the same thing, and therefore neither can be said to cause the other. The interest rate $r$ is *defined* by the condition that the price of current consumption in terms of future consumption is $1+r$. It is just a restatement of the definition to say that the price of future consumption in terms of current consumption (that is, the price of a bond) is $1/(1+r)$.

Dangerous Curve

## The More Distant Future

If we know the daily interest rate $r$, then we can compute the present value of an apple delivered 2 days from now. An apple delivered 2 days from now is worth $1 + r$ apples tomorrow, and each apple tomorrow is worth $1 + r$ apples today. Therefore, an apple delivered 2 days from now has a present value of

$$\frac{1}{(1 + r)} \times \frac{1}{(1 + r)} = \frac{1}{(1 + r)^2}$$

apples today. By the same reasoning, an apple delivered $n$ days in the future has a present value of $1 / (1 + r)n$ apples today.

---

**Exercise 17.3** If the daily interest rate is 50%, what is the present value of an apple delivered 2 days from now? Of an apple delivered 3 days from now?

---

**Exercise 17.4** Suppose that the daily interest rate is currently 10%, but that tomorrow it will rise to 20%. What is the present value of an apple delivered 2 days from now?

---

**Exercise 17.5** Suppose that the daily interest rate is 10%. What is the present value of an apple delivered yesterday?

---

## Coupon Bonds

We can also discuss the present value of a basket consisting of several apple deliveries on different dates. Suppose that on Monday Guildenstern promises that he will deliver to Rosencrantz 2 apples on Tuesday, 3 on Wednesday, and 1 on Friday. The present value of this multiple promise is the sum of the present values of the individual promises it comprises. That is, the present value is

$$\left(2 \times \frac{1}{(1 + r)}\right) + \left(3 \times \frac{1}{(1 + r)^2}\right) + 1 \times \left(\frac{1}{(1 + r)^4}\right)$$

apples today (today being Monday). With $r = 10\%$ ($= .10$), this works out to about 4.98 apples today.

**Coupon bond**

A bond that promises a series of payments on different dates.

Guildenstern's multiple promise is another example of a bond. A bond of this sort is sometimes called a **coupon bond.** The reason for the terminology is that Guildenstern might seal his promise by providing a set of "coupons," such as those in Exhibit 17.1.

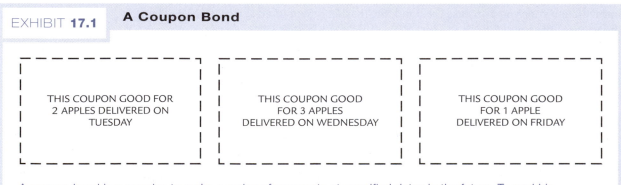

**EXHIBIT 17.1**    **A Coupon Bond**

| THIS COUPON GOOD FOR 2 APPLES DELIVERED ON TUESDAY | THIS COUPON GOOD FOR 3 APPLES DELIVERED ON WEDNESDAY | THIS COUPON GOOD FOR 1 APPLE DELIVERED ON FRIDAY |

A coupon bond is a promise to make a series of payments at specified dates in the future. To seal his promise, the seller of a coupon bond might issue a set of coupons such as those above.

## Perpetuities

A perpetuity is a promise to pay some fixed amount annually forever. A perpetuity is like a coupon bond with an infinite number of coupons.

Imagine a perpetuity that pays you $1 per year forever, starting one year hence. The present value of such a perpetuity in dollars is

$$\frac{1}{(1+r)} + \frac{1}{(1+r)^2} + \frac{1}{(1+r)^3} + \frac{1}{(1+r)^4} + \cdots$$

Perhaps you know how to sum such an infinite series. If not, don't panic. There is a sneaky way to compute the value of a perpetuity without using advanced mathematics.

If you place a dollar in the bank and leave it there forever, it will earn $r$ every year in interest, which you can withdraw and spend as you please. In other words, you can trade your dollar for a perpetuity of $r$ per year. Thus, a perpetuity of $r$ per year has a price—or present value—of exactly $1. It follows that a perpetuity of $1 per year must have a present value of exactly $1/r$ dollars. Our infinite series must sum to $1/r$.

For example, if the interest rate is 10%, then a perpetuity paying $1 per year has a present value of $1/.10 = $10. In other words, $10 today can be traded for $1 per year forever. And indeed it can: Deposit $10 in the bank forever and withdraw the interest each year. Or, if you prefer, you can make the opposite exchange: Trade a $1 annual perpetuity for $10 today by borrowing $10 and paying a $1 interest charge each year.

**Exercise 17.6** At an interest rate of 5%, what is the present value of a perpetuity that pays $1 per year forever?

## Bonds Denominated in Dollars

A bond that promises to pay 1 apple next year must sell for $1/(1+r)$ apples today, where $r$ is the annual interest rate. However, relatively few bonds promise to deliver apples. Far more often, they promise dollars. Such bonds are said to be *denominated* in dollars.

When bonds are denominated in dollars, there is a new complication to consider. We usually assume that an apple delivered in the future is identical to an apple delivered today in every respect except for the date of delivery. The same is *not* true of dollars. A dollar delivered in 1990 had far less purchasing power than one delivered in 1980 because of *inflation*: a general rise in the absolute price level, or, in other words, a fall in the value of the dollar.

Suppose that you deposit $1 in the bank today at 5% annual interest, so that next year your balance is $1.05. If there is simultaneously a 5% inflation rate, how much has your purchasing power really grown? The answer is that it has not grown at all. You will be able to buy no more apples with your $1.05 next year than you can with your $1 this year.

We distinguish between the nominal interest rate at which your *dollars* grow and the real interest rate at which your *purchasing power* grows. In the example just considered, you earned a nominal rate of 5% but a real rate of 0%. When a bond is denominated in dollars, the quoted interest rate is a nominal rate; when a bond is denominated in some real good, such as apples, the quoted interest rate is a real rate.

There is a simple equation relating the nominal interest rate $i$, the inflation rate $\pi$, and the real interest rate $r$. Your money grows at rate $i$, of which $\pi$ is necessary just to keep up with inflation. The real growth rate in your purchasing power is equal to the remainder

**Perpetuity**

A bond that promises to pay a fixed amount periodically forever.

**Nominal interest rate**

The relative price of current dollars in terms of future dollars, minus 1.

**Real interest rate**

The relative price of present consumption goods in terms of future consumption goods, minus 1.

$$r = i - \pi$$

or

$$i = r + \pi$$

---

**Exercise 17.7** Suppose that your bank account pays 8% interest on your money and that inflation is 5%. What nominal interest rate are you earning? What real interest rate are you earning?

---

In general, it is *real* interest rates that are of real interest in microeconomics, and whenever we speak of "the" interest rate we will mean the real interest rate. In times of zero inflation, the real and nominal interest rates will be the same.

## Default Risk

A bond is a promise to pay, and throughout this section we have assumed that promises are always kept. Those economists (perhaps a minority) who have been in love know better. The buyer of a bond that promises an apple tomorrow is buying not an apple tomorrow but a *chance* of receiving an apple tomorrow. When he thinks the chance is smaller, he will pay less for the bond. Thus, everything we have said about the pricing of bonds applies literally only to cases in which the lender feels quite certain that his bond will be redeemed. A less trustworthy borrower has to sell bonds at a greater discount in order to attract lenders. This is why different bonds carry different rates of interest.

The possibility that a borrower will fail to meet his obligations is known as a **default risk.** The higher the default risk, the higher will be the interest rate that the borrower has to pay in order to attract lenders. The additional interest that the borrower receives because of the default risk is called a **risk premium.** We will have more to say on the subject of risk and its effect on asset prices in Chapter 18.

**Default risk**

The possibility that the issuer of a bond will not meet obligations.

**Risk premium**

Additional interest, in excess of the market rate, that a bondholder receives to compensate him for default risk.

### Treasury Bills: A Risk-Free Asset?

It is widely believed that Treasury bills carry essentially no default risk and that the U.S. Treasury has never defaulted on its obligations. This is untrue. For example, the Treasury defaulted on bill #GS7-2-179-46-6606-1.

In order to purchase a Treasury bill at auction, the investor (that is, the buyer of the bond) must submit a payment equal to the full face value of the bond. Following the auction, the discount is supposed to be returned to the investor immediately. For example, suppose that you want to buy a Treasury bill that promises to pay $20,000 6 months from now. To do so, you submit a check for $20,000 before the auction is held. If the bill sells at auction for $19,000, your discount of $1,000 should be returned to you immediately following the auction.

One unfortunate investor followed this procedure. His discount, approximately $1,100, was not returned. Following a series of inquiries, the Treasury took the remarkable position that although the default was entirely due to its own clerical errors, there was a strong possibility that the errors were irreparable and that the discount would never be paid. It required nearly 9 months, considerable expense on the investor's part, and the intervention of several senators and congressmen before the Treasury met its obligation. Even then, the Treasury refused to pay interest for the 9 months in which it unlawfully held the funds.

The frequency of such occurrences is not known. This particular investor went on to write a textbook in price theory, yielding a bit more publicity than might ordinarily be expected. If there are many more such cases, and if they become well known, then the risk premium on Treasury bills will grow, so that the price of the bills will fall.

# 17.2 Applications

Suppose your company has the opportunity to undertake an investment project that requires $100 in expenditure today but will return revenues of $50 a year for 3 years, beginning 2 years from now. Is the project a good one?

Suppose that you buy a used car and the dealer offers you a choice of payment plans. You can make three annual payments of $400 each (beginning immediately) or you can pay nothing down and then two payments of $635 each (beginning 1 year from today). Which is better?

Present values give us a standard of comparison for different payment streams. If you are offered a choice between a new car and a Hawaiian vacation, and if you have easy access to resale markets, you should always take the one with the higher market value—even if it's not the one you really want. If the car is worth $10,000 and the vacation is worth $8,000, you can take the car, sell it, buy the vacation, and still have $2,000 left over. So it is with payment streams. After choosing the one with the highest present value, you can always make a sequence of market trades that converts your choice to any of the others and leaves you with extra money in your pocket.

If the market interest rate is 10%, then your company's investment project has a present value of $113.04 (this is the present value of three annual payments of $50, beginning in 2 years). Because the project only costs $100 to undertake, it is a good one. But if the interest rate is 15%, the project's present value is only $99.27, and not worth the $100 cost.

---

**Exercise 17.8** Using a calculator, verify the numbers in the preceding paragraph.

---

At an interest rate of 10%, three annual car payments of $400 each, beginning immediately, have a present value of $1,094.21, whereas two payments of $635 each beginning next year have a present value of $1,102.07. The first plan is better. But, if the interest rate is 15%, the first set of payments has a present value of $1,050.28 and the second set has a present value of only $1,032.33. In this case, you should choose the second plan.

---

**Exercise 17.9** Using a calculator, verify the numbers in the preceding paragraph.

---

Knowing how to calculate present values and recognizing that a present value is nothing but a relative price are the keys to understanding a wide variety of issues. In the remainder of this section we offer several examples.

## Valuing a Productive Asset

Suppose that you are thinking of buying a tree that will produce 10 apples per year forever. How much is the tree worth? The answer is the present value of a perpetuity of 10 apples per year. If the interest rate is 10%, the tree is worth 100 apples. In a competitive environment, the tree will sell for exactly that price (at any higher price there are no buyers and at any lower price there are no sellers).

The goods produced by a productive asset are called dividends. In this case, the dividends are the apples.

**Dividends**

Streams of benefits.

The value of a productive asset is equal to the present value of the stream of dividends that it produces.

## Corporate Stocks

Economists distinguish between productive assets such as apple trees and *financial assets* such as corporate stocks and bonds. A share of corporate stock (which is usually nothing but a piece of paper) produces nothing. Instead, it conveys the right to collect a share of the dividends from productive assets that the corporation owns. If General Enterprises owns productive assets yielding dividends worth $100 per year, and if you own 1% of General Enterprises' stock, then you are entitled to receive dividends of $1 per year.

Dividends can be paid in either of two forms. One possibility is that General Enterprises can take the $100 and convert it into cash for distribution among the shareholders. The other possibility is that General Enterprises can take the $100 that it earns and use it to purchase a new productive asset, such as an apple tree. Because the stockholders all share in ownership of the apple tree, the value of their stocks increases accordingly.

Accountants and stockbrokers distinguish between the two forms of distributing dividends. They call the cash payment a *dividend* and the apple tree purchase *growth*. To an economist, however, this is a distinction without a difference. It is easy enough for a shareholder to convert one to the other. If General Enterprises opts for growth (increasing the value of your shares by $1) and you would rather have the cash, you can simply sell $1 worth of your stock. If the company makes a cash payment and you'd rather have growth, you can simply take your cash payment and use it to buy more stock. Regardless of whether the company's income is initially distributed through cash payments or the purchase of new assets, the economist calls the benefit to the stockholder a *dividend*.

Using the economist's definition of a dividend, we can assert that

The value of a financial asset is equal to the present value of the stream of dividends that it provides.

One problem with this "law" is that in many cases nobody can confidently predict the stream of dividends that an asset will provide. A more careful statement would be that the value of a financial asset is equal to the present value of its *expected* stream of dividends, recognizing that there is some uncertainty surrounding any expectation. Even one more qualification is needed: Because shareholders do not like risk, greater uncertainty about performance tends to depress the value of a stock (just as default risk depresses the value of a bond).[1] Often, the present value of the expected stream of dividends is a good approximation to the stock's value; adding in an adjustment for risk makes the approximation better.

## Valuing Durable Commodities: Is Art a Good Investment?

Some assets, like apple trees, yield dividends in the form of physical commodities. Others yield dividends in the form of services. Typically, these assets are durable commodities such as sofas, cars, or houses.

---

[1] Even this needs to be qualified. We shall see in Chapter 18 that some risks can be "diversified away." It is only the undiversifiable part of the risk that requires compensation.

How much is a sofa worth? Suppose that the sofa lasts for 4 years before wearing out. During this time it yields a stream of benefits that you value at $100 per year. That is, $100 per year is the most you would be willing to pay to use the sofa. The present value of those services is the same as the present value of a coupon bond that pays $100 per year for 4 years. At 10% interest, this comes to about $349.[2] If you can buy the sofa for less than $349, you should grab the opportunity; if not, you are better off without it.

What is the market price of the sofa? The price is equal to the sofa's value to the marginal buyer. If the marginal buyer values the sofa's services at $100 a year, its price is $349. If he values its services at more or less than $100 a year, its price is more or less than $349.

The same principle applies to any durable commodity, such as a work of art. Paintings yield dividends because people like to look at them; the value of seeing the painting is the dividend. The price of a painting is the present value of those dividends.

Suppose you are given the opportunity to purchase a painting that you expect to hold for 4 years and then sell. During the 4 years that you hold the painting, it yields dividends that the market values at $100 per year. At the end of 4 years, you expect that the painting can be sold for $1,500. (This $1,500 is in turn a reflection of the dividends that the painting is expected to yield in the years after you sell it.) Assuming a 10% interest rate, the present value of this stream of payments is $1,373.21, and this will be the market value of the painting.

Now suppose that your personal pleasure from looking at this particular painting is only worth $50 per year. The stream of payments that you get if you buy it is $50 per year for 4 years and then a selling price of $1,500. The present value of this stream of payments is only $1,198.86. If you buy the painting, you will pay $1,373.21 for something that you value at $1,198.86. You shouldn't buy it.

What if for some reason the expected selling price 4 years from now rises from $1,500 to $2,500? Should this affect your decision? The market price of the painting rises to equal the present value of $100 per year for 4 years followed by a single payment of $2,500; your personal valuation rises to equal the present value of $50 per year for 4 years followed by a single payment of $2,500. The market price is $2,056.22 and your personal valuation is $1,881.88. You still shouldn't buy.

In general, any change in the expected future selling price adds the same amount to both the market price and your personal valuation and therefore makes the painting neither more nor less attractive to purchase than it was before.[3] If the dividends that you collect from looking at the painting exceed the market value of those dividends, then you will do well to buy the painting. Otherwise, you won't.

The bottom line, then, is that you should use the same rule when you shop for art that you use when you shop for clothes or food: Buy what you like. More precisely, buy those things that you value more than the market does.[4]

## Should You Pay with Cash or Credit?

Imagine that you've decided to spend $100 for a new suit of clothes. Several methods of finance are available. First, you can withdraw $100 from your bank account and pay for the purchases up front. Second, you can charge the purchases to your credit card and

---

[2] To simplify the calculation, we assume that each year's benefits are all collected at the beginning of the year.

[3] An exception would occur if you acquired access to information that was not publicly available, so that your personal expectation of the selling price changed while the market's remained constant.

[4] This is not to deny the possibility of remarkable luck, good or bad, that happens when the market's expectation of future prices turns out to be wrong. It says only that you cannot reasonably expect to come out ahead unless you value the dividends at more than their market price.

settle the debt a year from now. In this case, the credit card bill to be paid next year is $110, assuming a 10% interest rate.

There is also a third option—you can charge the $100 to your credit card with no intention of *ever* paying off the debt. Instead, you make a $10 interest payment to the finance company, every year forever.

Now the question is: Which payment scheme do you prefer? The answer is: Because they all have the same present value ($100 in each case), the options are all equally desirable. To verify this, let us assume that you start with $1,000 in the bank and compute your financial status 1 year from now under each of the three options.

If you pay for the clothes up front, your bank balance falls to $900, which earns $90 interest (continuing to assume a 10% interest rate) over the course of the year. One year from today your balance is $990.

If you charge to your credit card and pay next year, you leave $1,000 in the bank, which grows to $1,100 over the course of the year. You then withdraw $110 to pay the credit card bill, and your balance is again $990.

Finally, under the plan where you charge to your credit card and never pay the debt, your bank balance grows to $1,100, of which you withdraw $10 to make your first annual interest payment, leaving $1,090. Of this, there is $100 that you dare never withdraw, since the income that it yields is necessary to make your future credit card payments of $10 per year. This leaves you with a usable balance of $990, exactly as in the first two cases.

In other words, all three plans leave you equally wealthy, as we knew they must.

In this discussion we made the simplifying assumption that you pay the same interest rate on your credit card that you earn at the bank. Typically, these rates differ because you are a somewhat less reliable credit risk than your bank is. In that case, a complete analysis of the optimal financing plan would depend on the particulars of your other options and your opportunity costs. But the moral remains that any preference between cash and credit must be due to *differences* in interest rates. Just because you must pay interest on your credit card loans is not enough to make them undesirable.

## Government Debt

Instead of buying your own clothes, you might imagine hiring a purchasing agent to buy them for you. The agent has two decisions to make: How much should he spend on various sorts of clothes, and how (by spending your cash or by using your credit card) should he finance the purchases?

Regarding the first decision, your agent's choices might please or displease you very much. If he comes home with $5,000 worth of winter boots and you live in Florida, you might start looking for a new purchasing agent. Regarding the second decision, as we have just seen, the choice is largely a matter of indifference.

The government is like a purchasing agent. On your behalf, it purchases post offices, public radio programs, and strategic missiles. It decides how much to spend on all of these items, and then it decides how to finance them. Among the options, it can pay cash (which it gets by taxing you immediately), it can use "credit" to defer the payment (by borrowing money and taxing you in the future to pay the debt), or it can pay on credit and never pay off the debt (by borrowing money and taxing you annually to make the interest payments).

The parable of the clothes buyer suggests that while you might care very much about what the government spends your money on, and about how much it spends, you will be indifferent among the various methods of finance.

In fact, the argument is far *more* convincing in the case of the government than it is in the case of the clothes buyer. In the case of the clothes buyer, we assumed that the interest rate at which you borrow (the credit card rate) is equal to the interest rate at which you lend (the bank rate). We acknowledged that this equality was unlikely to hold in practice and that therefore the conclusion was only approximately true.

However, when the government borrows on your behalf, it does so by selling Treasury bills, and the interest rate that it pays is the Treasury bill rate. You can earn the same rate on your savings by the simple expedient of buying Treasury bills.

When the government borrows $1 to buy a paper clip, it is often alleged that taxpayers end up paying more than $1: A year down the line, they are taxed not only $1 to pay for the paper clip but also 10¢ to pay for interest on the loan. In exchange for that interest payment, goes the argument, the taxpayers receive nothing at all.

The argument is certainly wrong. Taxpayers *do* get something of value in exchange for their 10¢ interest payment. They get the right to pay for the paper clip one year hence instead of today, enabling them to keep $1 in the bank for one additional year and thereby earn 10¢ additional interest on their bank accounts. They spend 10¢ to get 10¢ and are made neither better nor worse off by the transaction.

---

Keep in mind that the purchase of the paper clip can certainly make taxpayers either more or less happy than they were before. It is only the choice between paying cash and incurring debt that is a matter of indifference.

---

Dangerous
Curve

This entire discussion goes to show that at a given prevailing interest rate, government debt is of no consequence to the taxpayer. However, it does not address another, more interesting question: Can government debt cause the prevailing interest rate to change? We will return to this question in Section 17.3.

## Planned Obsolescence

Larry's Light Bulb Company can produce light bulbs that burn for 1,000 hours or light bulbs that burn for 3,000 hours. The cost of production is the same in either case. Which kind of light bulb should Larry produce?

Many people think that Larry should produce the inferior light bulbs. They argue that if the average bulb is used 1,000 hours per year, the 3,000-hour bulbs will have to be replaced only once every 3 years, whereas the 1,000-hour bulbs will have to be replaced once every year, resulting in three times as many sales for Larry.

It is not hard to see that this reasoning cannot be correct if light bulbs are produced competitively. If Larry's competitors have access to the same technology that he does, he will be driven out of business as soon as somebody else decides to produce the better bulb.

However, this argument is actually beside the point. In fact, it is in Larry's interest to make the better bulbs regardless of whether he is a competitor, a monopolist, or anything in between.

To see the reason for this, notice that light bulbs are valuable only because they can be used to produce light. Suppose that customers use each light bulb to produce 1,000 hours of light per year and that they value an additional year's worth of light at $5. Then the price of a 1,000-hour light bulb will be $5. To compute the price of a 3,000-hour light bulb, think of the bulb as providing $5 worth of service this year, $5 worth next year, and $5 worth the year after that. The present value of this service is

$$\$5 + \frac{\$5}{(1 + r)} + \frac{\$5}{(1 + r)^2}$$

where $r$ is the yearly interest rate. When $r = .10$, a little arithmetic reveals that this expression is equal to $13.68, which is the price consumers will be willing to pay for a light bulb.

Larry has a choice between manufacturing a light bulb that he can sell for $5 and manufacturing a light bulb that he can sell for $13.68. Each costs him the same to produce. It isn't hard to see what choice he should make.

It is often alleged that firms, and particularly monopolies, engage in the practice of *planned obsolescence,* whereby goods are intentionally designed to wear out more quickly than necessary, without any justification in terms of costs of production. We have just seen that as long as customers are aware of differences in quality, there is never incentive for any firm to engage in this practice. A profit-maximizing firm will always make a longer-lived product, provided that the additional cost of manufacturing such a product is less than the present value of the additional stream of benefits that it provides. (Larry makes the better light bulb as long as its production cost exceeds the production cost of the cheaper bulb by less than $8.68.)

This decision rule for firms is economically efficient from a social point of view. The cost of providing longevity is weighed against its benefits. Because some of the benefits are delayed, they should be assessed at their present values.

Try the following experiment. Ask 25 of your friends what a camshaft is. Now have your friends ask their grandfathers. You will find that the percentage of correct answers is much higher among the grandfathers. Most of today's grandfathers learned what a camshaft was about 40 years ago when they had to have theirs repaired, often repeatedly. Most of today's college students will never have that experience. When car manufacturers learned how to make camshafts that lasted, they put their knowledge to work.

## Artists' Royalties

Prior to 1990, when artists sold their works, they relinquished any right to benefit from future increases in their value. Sydney J. Harris, formerly a syndicated columnist, argued repeatedly that artists should share in the benefits when their paintings appreciate. Specifically, he proposed that whenever a painting is resold, the artist should receive a percent of the increase in value since the last sale. We will evaluate the effect of this proposal from the artist's point of view.

When the artist first sells the painting, its price is equal to the present value of the stream of benefits that it will provide to future owners. At least this is the case if the stream of benefits can be foreseen. More realistically, we should allow for some uncertainty as to how the painting will be valued in the future. The price of the painting will be equal to the present value of the *expected* stream of benefits. We will study expectations and uncertainty more rigorously in Chapter 18.

Suppose an art lover buying an oil painting expects to derive $10 per year in pleasure from looking at the painting for each of this year and next year and then expects to be able to sell the painting for $50. (This $50 is his estimate of how the next buyer will value the future stream of benefits 2 years from now.) In that case, he will be willing to pay a price of

$$\$10 + \frac{\$10}{(1 + r)} + \frac{\$50}{(1 + r)^2}$$

where $r$ is the rate of interest.

Now suppose that the "Harris Plan" is enacted into law. The buyer is required to pay the artist 20% of the painting's resale price. In that case, the buyer can keep only $40 when he resells the painting, and its present value to him is reduced to

$$\$10 + \frac{\$10}{(1 + r)} + \frac{\$40}{(1 + r)^4}$$

This is a reduction of $\$10/(1 + r)^2$ from what the painting was worth before the Harris Plan was enacted. The current price of the painting will fall by $\$10/(1 + r)^2$, which is a loss to the artist.

On the other hand, when the painting is resold for $50 in 2 years, the artist will receive a royalty of 20%, or $10. The present value of that royalty is $\$10/(1 + r)^2$. From the artist's point of view, the benefits of the Harris Plan are equal to its costs. He is indifferent to whether it is enacted.

The foregoing supposes that the buyer is correct in his expectation that he can sell the painting in 2 years for $50. Suppose he turns out to be wrong. Suppose the artist's reputation blossoms, and the painting is sold for $100, on which the artist's royalty is $20. The present value of that royalty is $\$20/(1 + r)^2$. The Harris Plan has benefited this artist. The initial value of his painting fell by $\$10/(1 + r)^2$, but this is offset by a future royalty with twice that present value.

Another possibility is that the buyer has been too rosy in his expectations. Suppose that in 2 years the artist has been forgotten, and his painting sells for only $15. The royalty is $3, with a present value of $\$3/(1 + r)^2$. This is insufficient to offset the initial price reduction of $\$10/(1 + r)^2$. This artist is a loser under the Harris Plan.

Who gains and who loses? The average artist—the one whose career turns out about as expected—just breaks even. The artist whose career goes much better than expected is a winner, and the artist who is less successful than expected is a loser. Thus, the Harris Plan is a way to transfer income from unsuccessful artists to successful artists.

## Old Taxes Are Fair Taxes

One hundred fifty years ago, Coconino County imposed an annual tax of $10 per acre on all landowners. Landowners to this day grumble about the tax. The mayor has decided that the tax represents an unfair burden and has called for its repeal, to correct a historical injustice.

Although the tax might have been a great injustice, repealing the tax is unlikely to correct it. When the tax was imposed, the value of an acre of land plummeted by exactly $\$10/r$, the value of a perpetuity of $10 per year. Any land sold in the last 150 years has been sold at the new depressed value.

Exhibit 17.2 shows the market for land in Coconino County 150 years ago. After the tax was imposed, the demand curve fell by $\$10/r$ per acre. The price fell from $P$ to $P - \$10/r$. Producers' surplus fell from $C + D + E$ to just $E$. Consumers' surplus remained constant at $A + B$. Buyers of land lost nothing as a result of the tax; its burden fell completely on the sellers.

Any parcel of land in Coconino County that has been sold at any time in the last 150 years is now owned by somebody who was fully compensated for the infinite stream of future taxes through a reduced purchase price. If the tax is removed now, the current owners will receive a windfall, as the price of the land rises back to $P$ and its total value increases by $C + D$. The full burden of the tax is still being borne by the heirs of the original owners, now probably scattered and unidentifiable.

---

**EXHIBIT 17.2**   **Old Taxes Are Fair Taxes**

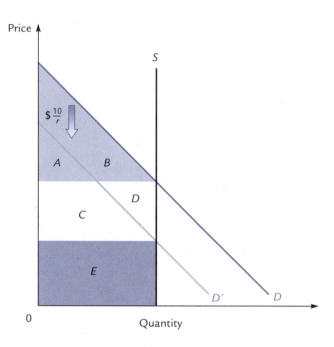

The graph shows the market for land in Coconino County 150 years ago, when an annual $10-per-acre tax on landholdings was first instituted. The demand curve fell by $10/r$ per acre, and because of the vertical supply curve, the price fell by $10/r$. The landowners of Coconino County suffered a loss in producers' surplus of C + D. The buyers of land lost nothing. The price of the land that they bought was reduced by enough to compensate them for the infinite stream of future taxation.

If the tax is repealed, everyone who has bought Coconino County land in the last 150 years will reap a windfall gain. Except in those cases where the land has never changed hands, the winners will be people who were never hurt by the tax in the first place.

---

## The Pricing of Exhaustible Resources

A resource is *exhaustible* if every unit consumed today implies that one less unit will be available in the future. Oil is often said to be an exhaustible resource. The coal available from a given mine is a good example.

When a resource is exhaustible, the forgone opportunity to use it in the future becomes a part of the cost of consuming it today. Suppose that coal sells competitively at a going price of $P_0$ today and is expected to sell at a price of $P_1$ tomorrow. Suppose also that the cost of digging out any particular nugget of coal is the same on each day. Then any nugget dug out and sold today entails a forgone opportunity to dig out and sell that same nugget tomorrow. The forgone profit on that nugget is $P_1 - MC$, where $MC$ is the marginal cost of physically removing the coal from the ground. The present value of that forgone opportunity is $(P_1 - MC)/(1 + r)$.

The full marginal cost of removing and selling a pound of coal is equal to the sum of the marginal cost of digging it out and the present value of the forgone opportunity to sell it tomorrow. This comes to

$$MC + \frac{P_1 - MC}{1 + r}$$

A competitive producer will choose a quantity where the current price is equal to this full marginal cost, or

$$P_0 = MC + \frac{P_1 - MC}{1 + r}$$

Now a little algebra shows that

$$P_1 = P_0 \cdot (1 + r) - r \cdot MC$$

This equation predicts the price of an exhaustible resource next year in terms of its price this year, the interest rate, and the marginal cost of production.

The equation is particularly simple and intuitive when marginal costs are negligible. In this case, we get

$$P_1 = P_0 \cdot (1 + r)$$

The price of the exhaustible resource grows at exactly the rate of interest.

There is a great deal of intuitive content to this result. If the price were growing faster than the rate of interest, coal in the ground would be a good investment and mine owners would increase the amount of coal left unmined. This would raise current prices and lower future prices, reducing the rate at which prices grow.

---

**Exercise 17.10** Explain how the rate of growth of prices would adjust if it were less than the rate of interest.

---

# 17.3 The Market for Current Consumption

Up until now, we have been taking market interest rates as given and examining how people react to them. The time has come to ask what determines interest rates.

The answer lies in our earlier observation (near the very beginning of Section 17.1) that the interest rate can be viewed as a measure of the relative price of current consumption in terms of future consumption. More precisely, if the daily interest rate is $r$, then the price of an apple today is $1 + r$ apples tomorrow. Knowing the interest rate is the same thing as knowing the relative price. Price is determined by demand and supply. Thus, we must examine the demand and supply for current consumption.

## The Consumer's Choice

When we want to study how people allocate their consumption between apples and oranges, we begin with an indifference curve diagram in which apples appear on the horizontal axis and oranges appear on the vertical. When we want to study how people allocate their consumption between apples today and apples tomorrow, we begin with an indifference curve diagram in which apples today appear on the horizontal axis and apples tomorrow appear on the vertical. The indifference curves of Ken the Consumer are shown in Exhibit 17.3.

We assume that Ken has an **endowment** of 6 apples today and 6 apples tomorrow. These are the apples that Ken starts with, prior to any trading. Perhaps they come from an apple tree in his backyard, or maybe he has a job that pays a wage of 6 apples per day. Point A represents Ken's endowment.

**Endowment**

The basket of goods that somebody starts with, before any trading.

EXHIBIT **17.3**    **The Consumer's Preferences**

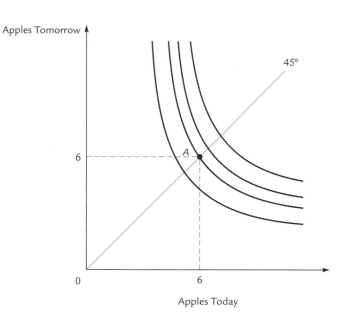

Apples Tomorrow

45°

6

A

0        6

Apples Today

Ken's preferences are represented by indifference curves. The endowment point *A* depicts his holdings before he does any trading. In this example, the endowment point is on the 45° line, which means that he is endowed with the same number of apples each day. Under these circumstances we expect that Ken values 1 additional apple today more than 1 additional apple tomorrow. Therefore, at a point like *A,* the absolute value of the slope of the indifference curve is greater than 1.

## Time Preference

As we know from consumer theory, the absolute slope of Ken's indifference curve represents the marginal value to Ken of an apple today, measured in terms of apples tomorrow. For a variety of reasons, we expect this slope to be greater than 1. That is, we think that 1 additional apple today is worth more to Ken than 1 additional apple tomorrow.

One reason for this expectation is our belief that people are naturally impatient and would prefer to eat now rather than later. Another reason is that Ken is unsure what the future will bring: Since he might be hit by a truck before tomorrow ever comes, he might never get to enjoy tomorrow's apple. Yet a third reason is that an apple once eaten yields a lifetime's worth of pleasant memories. An apple eaten today yields one more day of these pleasures than does an apple eaten tomorrow.

Without committing ourselves fully or exclusively to any of these combinations, we will assume that Ken prefers 1 more apple today to 1 more apple tomorrow, or, in other words, that the absolute slope of his indifference curve at point *A* is greater than 1.

If Ken had a different endowment, say with 100 apples today and 2 tomorrow, we might have a different expectation. In these circumstances, 1 additional apple today is not likely to be very valuable to Ken. Our belief that his indifference curve has absolute slope greater than 1 is predicated on the fact that his initial endowment contains equal numbers of apples on both days. Geometrically, this means that his initial endowment is on the 45° line. The 45° line is illustrated in Exhibit 17.3.

Our assumption, then, is this: At points on the 45° line, Ken's indifference curves have slopes that are greater than 1 in absolute value. Off the 45° line, this assumption need not hold.

## Opportunities

Suppose that Ken is given the opportunity to borrow or lend at a market interest rate of 10%. That is, he can buy and sell "apples today" at a relative price of 1.10 apples tomorrow. This means that he faces a budget line with absolute slope 1.10. We also know that his budget line must pass through his endowment point A, since he can achieve point A by simply not trading at all. The slope and a point are all we need to draw the budget line. It is illustrated in panel A of Exhibit 17.4.

If the interest rate were to change, Ken's budget line would rotate around point A, becoming steeper for a rise in the interest rate or flatter for a fall in the interest rate.

## The Consumer's Optimum

Ken chooses the point where his budget line is tangent to an indifference curve, which is point B in panel A of Exhibit 17.4. At this point he consumes 8 apples today and 3.8 tomorrow. Ken achieves this outcome by borrowing 2 apples to add to his endowment of 6 today; tomorrow he pays back the loan with 2.2 apples out of his endowment of 6 tomorrow.

Ken's neighbor Barb has the same endowment as Ken and the same budget line, but she has different preferences. Panel B of Exhibit 17.4 shows that Barb chooses point C, with 5 apples today and 7.1 tomorrow. She achieves this by lending 1 apple out of her endowment of 6 today and collecting 1.1 apples to add to her endowment of 6 tomorrow.

| EXHIBIT 17.4 | The Consumer's Choice |
| --- | --- |

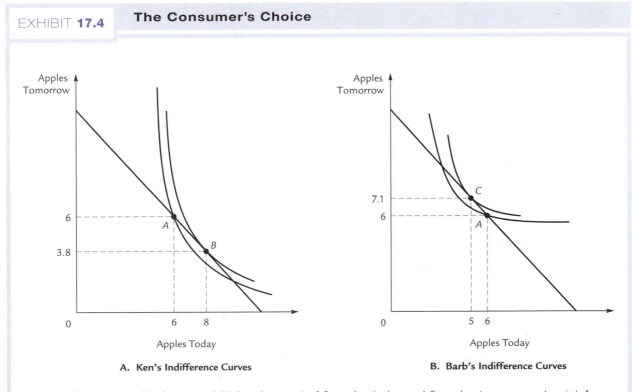

**A. Ken's Indifference Curves**          **B. Barb's Indifference Curves**

Ken and Barb start with the same initial endowment of 6 apples today and 6 apples tomorrow, at point A. They can each borrow and lend at a market interest rate of 10%, giving them identical budget lines of slope −1.10. Ken's preferences lead him to choose point B, which he achieves by borrowing 2 apples. Barb's preferences lead her to choose point C, which she achieves by lending 1 apple.

The two panels of Exhibit 17.4 illustrate that, depending on preferences, the consumer's optimum could occur on either side of the initial endowment, and therefore he might decide either to borrow or to lend. However, if the interest rate had been 0%, giving the budget lines a slope of −1, then we know that both Ken and Barb would have been borrowers, consuming more than 6 apples today. The reason is that both Ken and Barb have indifference curves whose slopes at point *A* exceed 1 in absolute value; this forces the tangency to occur below and to the right of *A*.

## The Demand for Current Consumption

We can use panel A of Exhibit 17.4 to generate a point on Ken's demand curve for current consumption. The exhibit tells us that when the interest rate is 10%, Ken demands 8 apples today. This information is recorded by point *B'* in panel B of Exhibit 17.5.

We can generate additional points in the same way. To see how much Ken would demand to borrow at an interest rate of 5%, first draw the corresponding budget line, which passes through his endowment point *A* with an absolute slope of 1.05. This

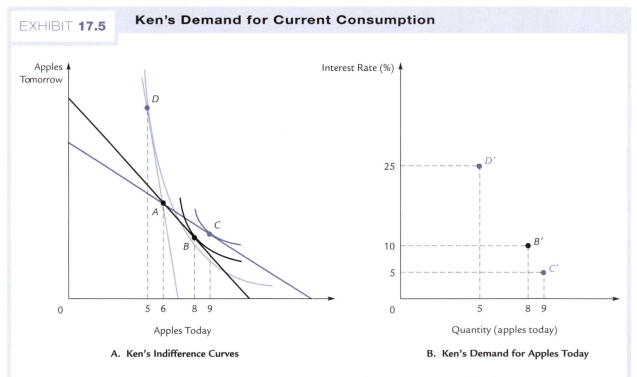

EXHIBIT **17.5**          **Ken's Demand for Current Consumption**

**A. Ken's Indifference Curves**

**B. Ken's Demand for Apples Today**

When the interest rate is 10%, Ken has the black budget line with slope −1.10, passing through his endowment point *A*. Ken chooses basket *B*, where he consumes 8 apples today, of which 6 come from his endowment and 2 must be borrowed. Point *B'* in panel B shows that when the interest rate is 10%, Ken eats 8 apples today.

When the interest rate is 5%, Ken's budget line pivots through point *A* to become the color line with slope −1.05. He chooses point *C*, eating 9 apples today (of which 3 are borrowed). This information is recorded by point *C'* in panel B.

At some interest rates, Ken chooses to be not a borrower but a lender. When the interest rate is 25%, he has the light-color budget line with slope −1.25 and chooses point *D*. He consumes only 5 apples, lending 1 apple out of his endowment of 6. This information is recorded by point *D'* in panel B.

line is drawn in color in panel A of Exhibit 17.5. (The drawing is not to scale!) Ken chooses point *C,* where he consumes 9 apples, of which 3 must be borrowed (since his endowment contains only 6). This information is recorded by point *C′* in panel B of the exhibit.

Generating a series of points in this manner and connecting them, we can derive Ken's entire demand curve for current consumption.

At some interest rates, Ken will not want to borrow at all, but to lend. Suppose that the interest rate rises to 25%. The corresponding budget line, shown in light color in panel A of Exhibit 17.5, passes through the endowment point *A* with absolute slope 1.25. The tangency is at point *D,* so that Ken wants to consume only 5 apples today, meaning that he seeks to lend an apple. Point *D′* in panel B records the information.

**Exercise 17.11** By examining panel B of Exhibit 17.4, generate a point on Barb's demand curve for current consumption.

At an interest rate of 10%, Ken is a borrower, whereas at an interest rate of 25%, he is a lender. In classifying people as borrowers or lenders, we refer always to their net borrowing or lending. If Ken borrows 3 apples and lends 1 apple, then he is a net borrower of 2 apples. If he borrows 2 and lends 6, he is a net lender of 4.

If Ken's endowment includes 6 apples today and he wants to eat 8 apples today, he must become a net borrower of 2 apples. Whether he accomplishes this by borrowing 2 and lending none or by borrowing 9 and lending 7 is of little consequence.

Dangerous
Curve

The vertical axis in panel B of Exhibit 17.5 is labeled with an interest rate, whereas the vertical axis for a demand curve should be labeled with a price. However, we know that interest rates can be converted to relative prices simply by adding 1. Therefore, it is legitimate to think of the interest rate axis as nothing but a relabeled price axis, and to think of the curve through *B′* and *C′* as a demand curve.

Dangerous
Curve

Having generated Ken's demand curves for current consumption, we can repeat the exercise for Barb and every other member of the economy. We can add all the demand curves to generate a market demand curve.

## The Supply of Current Consumption

In this section, we will assume that the supply of current consumption is fixed: A certain number of apples fall from apple trees and must be eaten immediately. There is (by assumption) no way to save an apple until tomorrow and no way to increase the number of apples in the harvest. Therefore, the supply curve for current apple consumption is *vertical.*

In Section 17.4, we will relax the assumption that the quantity of current consumption is fixed. However, the flavor of the conclusions we draw will not be changed. By working first with the simplest possible model, we will get a good feeling for the nature of equilibrium.

## Equilibrium

We can find the market demand curve for current consumption by adding individual demand curves, each of which is derived by the method of Exhibit 17.5. We have a

---

## EXHIBIT 17.6  Equilibrium

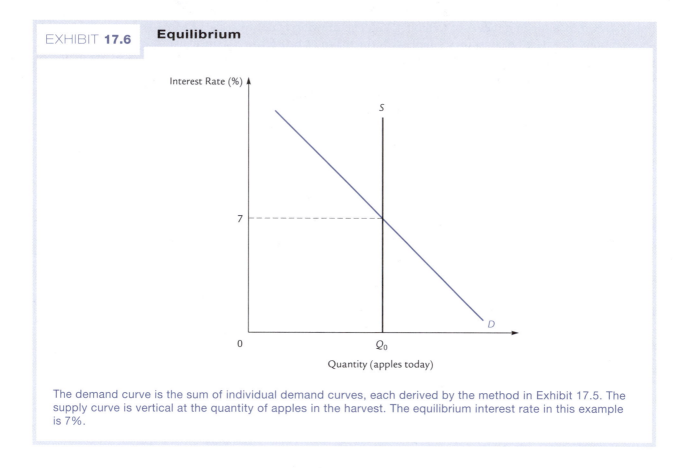

The demand curve is the sum of individual demand curves, each derived by the method in Exhibit 17.5. The supply curve is vertical at the quantity of apples in the harvest. The equilibrium interest rate in this example is 7%.

market supply curve that is vertical at the quantity of apples that happen to fall from the trees. Market equilibrium is determined by the intersection of the supply and demand curves. In Exhibit 17.6, the number of apples in the harvest is $Q_0$ and the equilibrium interest rate turns out to be 7%.

## Equilibrium and the Representative Agent

Equilibrium is determined by the intersection of supply and demand. Here we will pursue an alternative approach to the determination of equilibrium. Of course, both methods must lead to the same conclusion, but depending on circumstances one or the other can be easier to apply.

**Representative agent**

Someone whose tastes and assets are representative of the entire economy.

We reintroduce a fictional character who is called the **representative agent** and is a sort of "average" of all the people in the economy. Let us give our representative agent a name and call her Rebecca Representative.

Do you think Rebecca is a net borrower or a net lender? A bit of reflection reveals that she can be neither. Every dollar borrowed is a dollar lent, so the total of all borrowing in the economy must just equal the total of all lending. The average borrower borrows exactly the same amount that the average lender lends. Since Rebecca is an average of all the borrowers *and* all the lenders, she borrows exactly the same amount that she lends. That is, her net borrowing (or net lending) is exactly zero. Another way to say this is that Rebecca consumes exactly her endowment point.

**EXHIBIT 17.7    The Representative Agent**

Rebecca Representative's endowment point *E* happens to be on the 45° line. At that point her indifference curve has slope −1.07. Because the representative agent can be neither a borrower nor a lender, her budget line must be tangent to her indifference curve at the endowment point. Therefore, the budget line has slope −1.07 and the equilibrium interest rate is 7%.

Drawing Rebecca's indifference curves and endowment point as in Exhibit 17.7, we can deduce what her budget line must be. Since she chooses to consume her endowment, her budget line must be tangent to an indifference curve at that point. This tells us the slope of her budget line. In Exhibit 17.7, Rebecca's indifference curve happens to have slope −1.07 at the endowment point *E*. Therefore, the necessary budget line also has absolute slope 1.07. We can now infer that the equilibrium interest rate is 7%.

To compute the market interest rate, find the absolute slope of the representative agent's indifference curve at the endowment point, and subtract 1.

To understand this argument better, try thinking about what happens if the interest rate is less than 7%. Rebecca's budget line through point *E* is then flatter than in the exhibit, and her optimum lies to the southeast of *E*. Rebecca wants to be a net borrower, consuming more than her current endowment. Because she is the representative agent, this means that people on average want to consume more than their current endowments. The quantity of current consumption demanded exceeds the quantity supplied, so the interest rate must rise.

**Exercise 17.12** Explain what happens when the interest rate is greater than 7%.

We can calculate the equilibrium interest rate either by seeking the intersection of supply and demand or by calculating the slope of the representative agent's indifference curve at her endowment point. Because both procedures are correct, they must yield the same answer.

## Why Interest Rates Are Positive

In Exhibit 17.7, we assumed that Rebecca Representative's endowment point is on the 45° line. This is a reasonable assumption, tantamount to assuming that one day's apple harvest is no better or worse than another's. In that case, we know from earlier discussion that the slope of Rebecca's indifference curve at point $E$ must be greater than 1 in absolute value. It follows that the interest rate (which we get by taking the absolute value of the slope and subtracting 1) must be positive.

If Rebecca's endowment were elsewhere, this would not have to be the case. Suppose that Rebecca starts with 100 apples today and expects to receive only 1 apple tomorrow. (This is not just a statement about a single individual; since Rebecca is the representative agent it means that people *on average* expect their apple trees to produce far less tomorrow than they do today.) Then her endowment is far to the southeast in the indifference curve diagram, where the curves are very flat. The absolute slope of her indifference curve at the endowment point might then have a value of only .3, making the equilibrium interest rate $-.7 = -70\%$.

## Why Low Interest Rates Are Not Better Than High Ones

Politicians often talk about the urgency of bringing down interest rates, to make it easier for people to increase their current consumption of houses, cars, and other commodities. And lower interest rates are indeed a good thing for people who are net borrowers. On the other hand, it is equally clear that lower interest rates are a bad thing for people who are net lenders: If you are saving for your retirement by lending money to a bank, you will want the interest rate to be as high as possible.

When interest rates fall, helping borrowers and hurting lenders, does the good outweigh the bad? or vice versa? When you reflect on the fact that every dollar borrowed is a dollar lent, you will see that the good and the bad exactly cancel. Every penny that a borrower gains from lower interest rates is a penny that a lender loses. Put another way, the representative agent is neither a net borrower nor a net lender and therefore neither gains nor loses from a change in interest rates. Because the representative agent is the typical participant in the economy, people on average are neither helped nor hurt when interest rates change.

---

Dangerous
Curve

Because an interest rate is an equilibrium price, it cannot change without a reason: There must be either a change in supply or a change in demand. That change in supply or demand must, in turn, be caused by some outside disturbance. Typically, that disturbance has either good or bad effects in addition to its effect on interest rates. Therefore, interest rate changes tend to be *accompanied* by changes in welfare, but the changes in welfare are not caused by the changes in interest rates.

---

## Changes in Equilibrium

To calculate the effects of a change in market conditions, we can use either supply and demand curves or the method of the representative agent. We will carry out a few exercises illustrating both techniques.

### A Brighter Future

Suppose that a breakthrough in agricultural technology makes it clear that apple trees will become more productive in the future. Although each tree was initially expected to produce 6 apples per day every day, we now expect the trees to produce 6 apples today and 8 tomorrow. How will the equilibrium interest rate change?

To answer this question, we can consult either the market supply and demand curves or the representative agent's indifference curves. The two approaches are illustrated in the two panels of Exhibit 17.8.

When word gets out that apple harvests will improve in the future, people feel wealthier immediately. Assuming that current consumption is a normal good (as opposed to an inferior good), the demand curve shifts out. The outward shift in demand reflects the fact that when you hear that your future income will increase, you want to start spending part of it today. The supply of current apples is unchanged. Therefore, the market interest rate rises from $r$ to $r'$ in panel A of Exhibit 17.8.

Panel B derives the same outcome from Rebecca Representative's point of view. As soon as she hears the good news about tomorrow's apple harvest, Rebecca's endowment point shifts upward from point $A$ to point $B$. At the higher point $B$, we expect the indifference curve to be steeper. In fact, it is possible to show that the indifference curve at $B$ is steeper, provided that we maintain our assumption that current consumption is a normal good. (Verifying this assertion is a somewhat challenging exercise, recommended to the ambitious student.) Therefore, Rebecca's new budget line, tangent at $B$ instead of $A$, must be steeper. In fact, the slope of her original (black) budget line is $-(1 + r)$, while the slope of her new color budget line is $-(1 + r')$, where $r$ and $r'$ are the same equilibrium interest rates that we found in panel A. That the color line is steeper than the black one confirms that $r' > r$. When the future turns brighter, the interest rate increases.

EXHIBIT **17.8**    **An Increase in the Future Apple Supply**

An increase in the future apple supply moves the representative agent from point $A$ to point $B$ in panel B, increasing wealth and hence increasing the demand for all noninferior goods, including apples today. The demand curve shifts outward in panel A and the equilibrium interest rate rises from $r$ to $r'$.

The representative agent's budget line shifts from the black line (with absolute slope $1 + r$) to the color line (with absolute slope $1 + r'$). The fact that the color line is steeper confirms the observation that $r'$ is greater than $r$.

## A Brighter Present

Suppose that this year's apple harvest is unusually large (8 apples per tree instead of the expected 6) through some stroke of good luck that is not expected to persist.

Exhibit 17.9 illustrates. As in the preceding example, people feel wealthier and increase their demand for current consumption. At the same time, the supply of current consumption is increased because of the good apple harvest. It appears from the picture in panel A that the new interest rate $r''$ could be either below or above the old interest rate $r$. However, this is a case where an examination of the representative agent's indifference curves actually yields more information.

Turning to panel B, we see that Rebecca Representative's endowment moves rightward from point A to point C. At points farther to the right we expect that the indifference curves become flatter. (This can be proved if you start with the assumption that future consumption is not an inferior good.) Therefore, the color budget line with slope $-(1 + r'')$ is flatter than the black budget line with slope $-(1 + r)$. It follows that $r''$ is less than $r$. When the present turns brighter, the interest rate falls.

## A Permanent Productivity Increase

Suppose that apple trees, having always produced 6 apples per year, suddenly begin producing 8 apples per year on a permanent basis, beginning immediately. As in panel

**EXHIBIT 17.9**   **An Increase in the Current Apple Supply**

Panel A axes: Interest Rate (vertical), Quantity (apples today) (horizontal). Curves S, S', D, D', with $r$ and $r''$ marked. Label **A**.

Panel B axes: Apples Tomorrow (vertical), Apples Today (horizontal). Slope $= -(1+r)$, Slope $= -(1+r')$, points A and C. Label **B**.

Because people are wealthier when the current apple supply increases, demand increases as well. The supply and demand graph in panel A does not reveal whether the new equilibrium interest rate $r''$ is greater or less than the old interest rate $r$. However, we can make this determination on the basis of Rebecca Representative's indifference curves. Her endowment moves from point A to point C, so her budget line changes from the black line to the flatter color line. As the slope of the budget line determines the equilibrium interest rate, we conclude that the interest rate falls.

A of Exhibit 17.9, the demand and supply curves for current consumption both shift rightward and the diagram does not reveal whether the new interest rate is higher or lower than the old. An examination of the representative agent's situation does not relieve the ambiguity. In Exhibit 17.10, we see that Rebecca Representative's endowment point moves from (6, 6) to (8, 8), where there is no particular reason to believe that the indifference curve has become either shallower or steeper.

It is common, especially in macroeconomics, to make the additional assumption that at various points along the 45° line, the indifference curves all have the same slope. (Indifference curves with this property are called *homothetic* near the 45° line.) In this case, the black and the color budget lines in Exhibit 17.10 are parallel, and the change in productivity has no effect on the interest rate.

## Government Debt Revisited

When the government wants to spend money, it can either raise taxes immediately or it can borrow, in which case it issues an implicit promise to raise taxes in the future. We saw in Section 17.2 that as long as the market interest rate remains fixed, taxpayers are indifferent between the two methods of finance. Government *spending* can be either good or bad, but government *debt* is a matter of indifference.

In the discussion in Section 17.2, we left open the question of whether government debt can affect the interest rate itself. Here we will take up that question. We will see that in the simplest circumstances, the answer is "no." We will also see that in more complicated circumstances, the answer is "it depends." If that strikes you as

| EXHIBIT 17.10 | **A Permanent Productivity Increase** |

When apple trees become permanently more productive, effective immediately, Rebecca Representative's endowment point moves from *A* to *B* along the 45° line. The interest rate could either rise or fall. If Rebecca's indifference curves are homothetic, the slope of the indifference curves at *A* and at *B* are equal, and there is no change in the interest rate.

EXHIBIT **17.11**   **Taxation versus Borrowing**

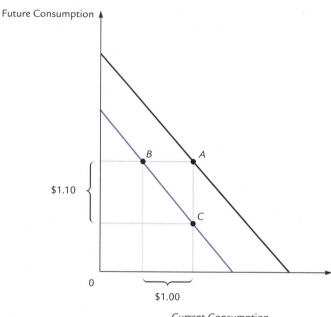

Terry Taxpayer starts with an endowment of *A,* faces an interest rate of 10%, and therefore has the black budget line with slope −1.10. If the government taxes him $1 to finance wasteful spending, his endowment falls to *B* and his budget line moves into the line shown in color. If the government borrows $1 to finance wasteful spending, Terry is taxed $1.10 in the future, so his endowment falls to *C* and his budget line is again the line shown in color. Because each plan leaves Terry with the same color budget line, each plan leads to the same demand for current consumption. Each plan also leads to the same supply of current consumption. Therefore, each plan leads to the same market interest rate.

depressingly ambiguous, don't despair. We will have a lot to say about what the answer depends *on,* and we will therefore come to understand the conditions necessary for government debt to matter.

Consider Terry Taxpayer, whose indifference curves are shown in Exhibit 17.11. Terry lives in a world where the market interest rate is 10%, so that his (black) budget line between current and future consumption has a slope of −1.10. His endowment point is marked *A.*

Terry's government has decided to spend $1 wastefully.[5] It can do so in either of two ways. One is to raise Terry's current taxes by $1, shifting his endowment point $1 to the left, to point *B.* The other is to borrow and raise Terry's future taxes by $1.10, shifting his endowment point down $1.10 to point *C.*

If the government raises current taxes, Terry's new budget line is the line with slope −1.10 through his new endowment point *B.* If it borrows, his new budget line is the line with slope −1.10 through his new endowment point *C.* But these are two descriptions of the same line; it is shown in color in the exhibit.

---

[5] We assume that the spending is wasteful to simplify the discussion of how Terry's endowment point shifts. If the spending is productive, a similar analysis yields identical conclusions.

Either plan—taxation or borrowing—causes Terry's current consumption demand to fall, because his budget line shifts in from the black to the colored. Because the color budget line is the same in either case, either plan leads Terry's demand to fall by the same amount.

What is true of Terry is true of all other taxpayers and hence of the market as a whole: *Government spending causes the demand for current consumption to fall. Demand falls by the same amount regardless of whether the spending is financed by taxation or by debt.*

Now let us turn our attention from demand to supply. When the government spends $1 to purchase and then wastes $1 worth of goods, the supply of current consumption falls by exactly $1 worth, regardless of where the government finds the $1.

Therefore, the two plans cause the supply of current consumption to fall by the same amount. We have already seen that both cause the demand for current consumption to fall by the same amount. We may conclude that they both lead to the same market interest rate. It doesn't matter whether the government taxes or borrows.

This result, sometimes summarized in the slogan "Deficits don't matter," is called the Ricardian Equivalence theorem.[6] The Ricardian Equivalence theorem is undoubtedly true as a matter of mathematical fact under the simple circumstances we have described here. A more interesting question is whether it is true in the world in which we live. Regarding this question, there is no consensus among economists. Some believe that there are important differences between our world and the world of Terry Taxpayer. We will now consider two of those differences.

One possible difference is that taxpayers in the real world, unlike Terry, might not be savvy enough to recognize that when the government borrows today, it must increase taxes tomorrow. Suppose that you start at point *A* in Exhibit 17.11 and the government borrows $1, implicitly promising to raise your future taxes. This shifts your endowment to point *C*. But if you fail to take notice that future taxes must rise, you will believe that your endowment is still at *A* and will therefore not change your current consumption demand. This contrasts with what happens under taxation, where your endowment point is shifted to *B*, you realize what is happening, and you reduce your current consumption demand accordingly. Under this scenario, borrowing has no effect on demand while taxation shifts demand downward; the interest rate is therefore higher under borrowing than it is under taxation.

According to this scenario, government debt fools people into thinking they are richer than they really are. That hypothesis is very much at odds with the spirit of microeconomics, in which the assumption of rationality plays a central role. As a result, many economists are quite uncomfortable with the notion that such misperceptions could be a significant factor in the determination of interest rates. However, there is insufficient empirical evidence to rule out the possibility.

The second possibly important difference between Terry's world and ours arises from default risk. Suppose, contrary to the picture in Exhibit 17.11, that Terry Taxpayer, because of his poor credit history, is unable to borrow at the market interest rate of 10%, but only at the higher rate of 25%. Then his budget line is not really the line shown in Exhibit 17.11, but something much steeper. Taxation shifts Terry's endowment to *B*, leaving him with a budget line through *B* that is steeper than the one in the exhibit and therefore passes below *C*. On the other hand, borrowing shifts Terry's endowment to *C* and leaves him with a steep budget line through *C*.

**Ricardian Equivalence theorem**

The statement that government borrowing has no effect on wealth, consequently no effect on the demand for current consumption, and consequently no effect on the interest rate.

---

[6] In honor of the nineteenth-century economist David Ricardo.

In this case, the "government borrowing" budget line through $C$ is higher than the "current taxation" budget line through $B$. Terry is richer when the government borrows for him at 10% than when he has to borrow for himself at 25%. Therefore, he demands more current consumption when the government borrows. Because government borrowing means higher current consumption demand, it also means a higher interest rate.

It is sometimes argued that default risk is especially important in view of the finiteness of life. People who would like to borrow and obligate their children to pay the debt are unable to do so, because there is no legal mechanism by which the children can be bound to fulfill their parents' obligations. The certainty of default on such debts makes the interest rate on them essentially infinite. Government borrowing reduces this rate from infinity to something on the order of 10%.

On the other hand, this is a significant consideration only if there are a significant number of people who would really like to live well at their children's expense. The commonly observed phenomenon of parents working hard in order to leave bequests to their children (or for that matter, in order to send them to college) is evidence to the contrary.

The current thinking of most economists is that Ricardian Equivalence must hold—government debt does not matter—unless either misperceptions or default risks are of serious consequence. There is great controversy over the question of whether these phenomena in fact *are* of serious consequence. However, these are very concrete questions that are amenable to empirical investigation, and one is entitled to hope that the controversies surrounding them will be resolved in the not-too-distant future.

# 17.4 Production and Investment

In Section 17.3, we treated the number of apples available today and tomorrow as fixed and unchangeable. Any individual was able to shift consumption from one period to another by borrowing or lending, but for the economy as a whole such transfers were impossible.

A more complete model should take account of opportunities for current goods to be converted into future goods on an economy-wide basis. There are many ways to do this. The simplest is *storage*. An apple placed in the refrigerator today becomes an apple available for consumption tomorrow. An economy equipped with refrigerators can choose to consume fewer apples today in exchange for additional apples tomorrow—not just for some individuals, but for the economy as a whole.

Even more important, there is the possibility of *production*. Grain can be either eaten today or planted to produce even more grain tomorrow. Much production involves the use of machinery and other capital equipment, which must itself be produced. To produce capital, people must forgo the opportunity to produce goods for current consumption. People can choose whether to spend their time picking apples or planting apple trees. In the first case, there are more apples today; in the second, more apples tomorrow.

In fact, understanding the decision to invest in producing capital is the key to this entire subject. We now turn to the market for capital.

## The Demand for Capital

Recall that the word *capital* in economics always refers to goods that are inputs to the physical production process. An apple tree, which is used in the production of apples, is an example of capital. In this section, we will measure the value of goods and the value of capital in terms of dollars. As always, those dollars are just stand-ins for physical goods.

## The Marginal Product of Capital

The *marginal product of capital (MPK)*, first introduced in Chapter 6, is the additional output available when one additional unit of capital is employed. There are many possible units in which to measure the *MPK*. We shall measure it as a percent of the cost of the capital. If it costs $10 to plant a tree that produces $1 worth of apples each year, we will say that the *MPK* is 10%. If it costs $200 to plant a tree that produces $50 worth of apples per year, we will say that the *MPK* is 25%.

Typically, the marginal product of capital decreases as more capital is added. Holding all other inputs fixed, the 100th apple tree adds less to the harvest than the 99th does, because the orchards become crowded, the water and nutrients must be shared, and the apple-pickers have only a limited amount of time. This observation is not new; we made it first in Chapter 6.

## The Marginal Product of Capital versus the Interest Rate

Suppose that the market interest rate is 10% and the marginal product of capital is 15%. Then there is an easy way to make a profit. Borrow $100 and use it to plant a tree that produces $15 worth of apples per year. Each year, harvest the fruit from your tree, make a $10 interest payment, and pocket the remaining $5.

This is a no-lose proposition, and everybody wants to undertake it. As they do, two things happen. First, because everybody wants to borrow and nobody wants to lend, there is upward pressure on the interest rate. Second, all the new apple trees drive down the marginal product of capital. The interest rate and the *MPK* move closer together, and the process continues until they are equal.

The same sort of thing happens if the numbers are initially reversed. Suppose that the market interest rate is 15% and the marginal product of capital is 10%. Now nobody is willing to borrow to plant apple trees. Of course, people might still want to borrow for other reasons, so the interest rate need not fall. However, as old apple trees die off, there is no incentive to replace them. Over time, the number of apple trees (that is, the quantity of capital) falls, and so the *MPK* rises. Eventually, the interest rate and the *MPK* are brought back to equality. This tells us the following:

In equilibrium, the quantity of capital adjusts until the interest rate is equal to the marginal product of capital.

There is another way to view this proposition. To a planter, the price of capital is measured by the interest rate, because meeting expenses means either borrowing or forgoing the opportunity to lend. We saw in Chapter 15 that the demand curve for a factor of production is equal to its marginal product curve. Exhibit 17.12 shows the *MPK* curve. If the rate of interest is 10%, then the quantity of capital demanded is $K_1$. The quantity of capital adjusts until the *MPK* is equal to the interest rate.

## The Supply of Current Consumption

Imagine a world with $10 worth of resources that can be devoted either to consumption or to the production of capital. If producers demand $2 worth of capital, then there is $8 left for current consumption. If they demand $7 worth of capital, then there is only

**The Demand for Capital**

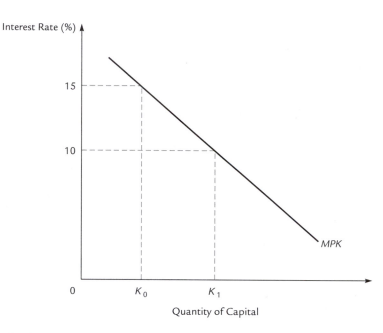

Suppose that the market interest rate is 10% but the marginal product of capital is 15% (so that the quantity of capital must be $K_0$). Then everybody wants to borrow to invest in capital. The quantity of capital increases and the marginal product of capital falls. This process continues until the quantity of capital reaches $K_1$, and the marginal product of capital is equal to the interest rate of 10%.

This argument shows that in equilibrium, the *MPK* must be equal to the interest rate. Put another way, the *MPK* curve is the demand curve for capital.

$3 left for current consumption. The more capital that is demanded, the less current consumption is supplied.

We know from Exhibit 17.12 that the demand for capital slopes downward as a function of the interest rate. It follows that the supply of capital slopes upward as a function of the interest rate. When the interest rate is low, much capital is demanded and few resources are available for current consumption. When the interest rate is high, little capital is demanded and many resources are available for current consumption.

## Equilibrium

In Exhibit 17.5, we derived the demand curve for current consumption, and in subsequent exhibits we made extensive use of this demand curve. There is no need to modify our theory of demand. However, throughout Section 17.3, we adopted a very naive theory of the supply for current consumption: We assumed that it was vertical. In an economy with production and capital investment, we now know that the supply curve can slope upward.

It turns out that this new observation does not necessitate any change in our earlier conclusions. We learned in Exhibit 17.8 that a brightening of the future causes

EXHIBIT **17.13**    **A Brighter Future**

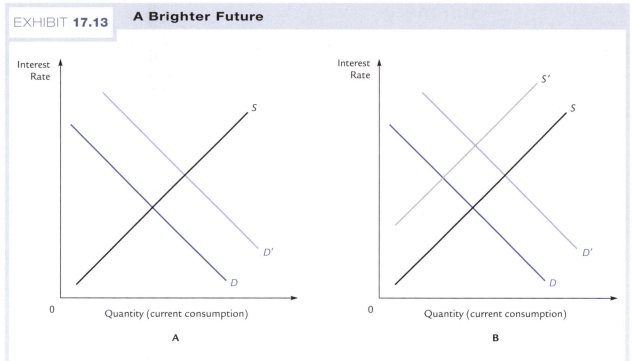

When the future looks brighter, the demand for current consumption increases. If the expected future windfall is unrelated to the productivity of capital, then there is no change in the supply of current consumption. If capital is expected to be more productive, the demand for capital increases, so the supply of current consumption falls.

In either case, the interest rate rises, though it rises by more in the second case. In the first case, current consumption increases, whereas in the second case current consumption moves ambiguously.

the interest rate to rise; we learned in Exhibit 17.9 that a current bumper crop causes the interest rate to fall. All of this remains true when the supply curve slopes upward, although the magnitudes of the shifts might be different.

By way of example, Exhibit 17.13 illustrates two scenarios in which something happens to make the future look brighter. In scenario A, it is discovered that people will be wealthier next year for some reason that has nothing to do with the productivity of capital. In scenario B, it is discovered that capital will be more productive than previously thought.

In either case, people are wealthier, so the demand curve for current consumption shifts out. In the first case, there is no change in the marginal product of capital, and so no change in the demand for capital, and so no change in the supply of current consumption. In the second case, the *MPK,* and consequently the demand for capital, goes up; when more resources are demanded for capital, fewer are supplied for current consumption. That is why the supply curve in panel B shifts back.

In each scenario, the interest rate rises (just as it did in Exhibit 17.8), though it rises by more in the second case. In the first case, current consumption increases, while in the second, current consumption moves ambiguously.

# Summary

The interest rate is a measure of the relative price of current consumption in terms of future consumption. More precisely, the relative price of current consumption is $1 + r$, where $r$ is the interest rate.

The relative price of future consumption in terms of current consumption is $1/(1 + r)$. This is also called the present value of a unit of future consumption. A bond that promises a unit of future consumption will sell today for the price $1/(1 + r)$.

Present values can be used to assign a value to any income stream and to compare the desirability of different income streams. The stream with the higher present value can always be traded for the stream with the lower present value, with something extra left over.

A consumer chooses between current and future consumption by seeking a tangency between his budget line and an indifference curve. The budget line has a slope of $-(1 + r)$ and passes through the consumer's endowment point. Using the machinery of indifference curves, we can derive the consumer's demand for current consumption. Adding up over all consumers, we can derive the market demand for current consumption.

The simplest assumption about the supply of current consumption is that it is fixed; that is, there is no way to convert current consumption to future consumption. In that case, the market supply curve for current consumption is vertical.

The equilibrium interest rate occurs at the intersection of supply with demand. The same equilibrium can be found from the condition that the representative agent must voluntarily consume his endowment. If the slope of his indifference curve at the endowment point is $-(1 + r)$, then $r$ must be the equilibrium interest rate.

In an economy where current consumption can be converted to capital, the quantity of capital always adjusts until the marginal product of capital is equal to the interest rate. When the interest rate is high, there is little capital demanded, so the quantity of current consumption supplied is high. When the interest rate is low, there is a lot of capital demanded, so the quantity of current consumption supplied is low. From these considerations, we derive an upward-sloping supply curve for current consumption. This can be combined with the demand curve for current consumption that was derived earlier to find the market equilibrium.

# Author Commentary    www.cengage.com/economics/landsburg

**AC1.**  See this article for more information on the effects of government debt.

**AC2.**  This article provides further discussion of the difficulty of righting past wrongs.

**AC3.**  Read this for more information on bequests.

# Review Questions

**R1.**    What is the relationship among (a) the present value of an apple delivered tomorrow, (b) the price of a bond having a face value of one apple and a maturity date of tomorrow, and (c) the rate of interest?

**R2.**  If you can either buy a house for $10,000 or rent the same house for $1,000 per year, should you buy or rent? In what way does your answer depend on the interest rate?

**R3.**  Is the buyer of a bond a borrower or a lender?

**R4.**  What is the present value of a perpetuity that pays $1 per year forever?

**R5.**  What determines the value of a productive asset?

**R6.**  What determines the value of a financial asset?

**R7.**  What determines the value of a durable commodity?

**R8.**  Explain why the purchaser of a new suit of clothes is indifferent between paying now and paying by credit card, provided that he can borrow and lend at the market interest rate.

**R9.**  Explain why the taxpayer is indifferent between higher current taxes and government borrowing.

**R10.** In general, will the price of an exhaustible resource grow at a rate higher or lower than the rate of interest? Why? Under what circumstances will it grow at exactly the rate of interest?

**R11.** Explain how to derive a point on the consumer's demand curve for current consumption.

**R12.** What assumptions lead to a vertical supply curve for current consumption?

**R13.** Explain how the equilibrium interest rate can be computed from an examination of the representative agent's indifference curves.

**R14.** Explain why the marginal product of capital must equal the interest rate in equilibrium.

**R15.** Explain why, when there are opportunities for capital investment, the supply curve for current consumption slopes upward.

# Problem Set

**1.**  **True or False:** When the interest rate falls, people want to borrow more and the additional borrowing tends to drive the interest rate back up.

**2.**  **True or False:** If the interest rate and the price of bonds both rise simultaneously, the quantity of borrowing could go either up or down.

**3.**  John bought a refrigerator and sold it 3 years later for exactly what he paid for it. **True or False:** It cost John nothing to have the use of the refrigerator for 3 years.

**4.**  Under the U.S. patent law, an inventor can be granted a patent that confers the exclusive right to produce and market his invention for 17 years. After that time, anybody can produce and market the invention. Assume that the annual profits that can be earned from the invention never change and that the interest rate is 10%. **True or False:** A 17-year patent is approximately 80% as valuable as a patent that lasts forever.

**5.** You have just been informed that you have 2 years to live and are considering a night of debauchery to take your mind off the news. The consequence of such behavior is eternal damnation, beginning on the date of your death. One year of fire and brimstone is equal in unpleasantness to the loss of $P. The interest rate is $r$.

  **a.** How pleasant would a night of sin have to be in order to be worth the cost?

  **b.** Which is more likely to deter you from sinning: a doubling of the torments of the underworld, or a halving of the interest rate?

**6.** Suppose that apartments in San Francisco typically sell for $300,000 and rent for $1,500 a month. The market interest rate is 10%. **True or False:** The market must be anticipating a rise in apartment rentals at some time in the future.

**7.** **True or False:** If a house in New York and a house in California are identical in every way except for the fact that the California house is susceptible to being destroyed by earthquakes, then the California homeowner must earn a greater rate of return than the New York homeowner to compensate him for the risk. Therefore, houses in California will increase in value more rapidly than houses in New York.

**8.** Textbook publishers typically issue new editions every 3 years, in order to keep copies of the old edition from circulating on the used-textbook market. Suppose that each student keeps his or her textbook for 1 year and values his possession of the textbook at $20 for that year. Suppose also that a new edition is no more intrinsically valuable than an old edition, but that the appearance of a new edition makes the old edition worthless. The market interest rate is 10%.

  **a.** If new editions cause old editions to become completely obsolete, what is the price of a new textbook?

  **b.** If the publisher issued just one edition of each book and credibly promised never to issue another one, what would be the price of a new textbook?

  **c.** If it is possible to issue a promise as in part (b), and if it is costly to bring out new editions, what is the publisher's optimal strategy?

  **d.** Suppose that publishers would like to issue a promise as in part (b), but that there is no way for them to legally bind themselves to keeping the promise. If students suspect publishers of dishonesty, what will be the price of a new textbook? Now what is the publisher's optimal strategy?

  **e.** **True or False:** Even though publishers voluntarily bring out new editions every 3 years, they might be better off if they were legally forbidden to do so.

**9.** **True or False:** The government's responsibility to bail out failed savings and loan institutions is monumentally expensive. But the longer it delays, the more expensive the bailout will be, since interest charges continue to build.

**10.** George F. Will, a humor columnist for the *Washington Post,* notes that interest payments on the federal debt in a recent year were equal to approximately one-half of all personal income tax receipts. He concludes that this represents "a transfer of wealth from labor to capital unprecedented in U.S. history. Tax revenues are being collected from average Americans and given to the buyers of U.S. government bonds—buyers in Beverly Hills, Lake Forest, Shaker Heights, and Grosse Point, and Tokyo and Riyadh."

Suppose it were the case that the *Washington Post* employed a columnist who viewed thinking as part of his job. What might such a columnist reply?

**11.** Explain exactly what is wrong with the following argument: If the government buys me a suit of clothes with borrowed money and never pays off the debt, then my grandchildren will be taxed to make interest payments even though they have never seen the clothes. Therefore, government borrowing allows me to live high on the hog at my grandchildren's expense.

**12.** **a.** Jeeter owes $1,000 on his student loan. The debt is growing at the market interest rate of 10%. Jeeter would like to pay off the loan now, but the bank will not allow him to do so until 5 years from now. What strategy can Jeeter follow that is equivalent to paying off the loan today?

**b.** Jeeter is also concerned about his share of the national debt, which he reckons to be $10,000. He wishes that the government would just tax him today and pay off the debt so that the accumulation of interest will not cause him to have to pay even more tomorrow. What would you suggest that Jeeter do?

**13.** Write a brief letter in response to the following column:[7]

**DEAR ANN LANDERS:** This is going to seem like a terrifically trivial problem compared to most you receive, but I've got to get it off my chest.

I'm sure almost every woman in America has gone through this slow burn. You spend two or three bucks for a pair of new pantyhose, and within a week, you have a big ugly runner and have to throw the pair away. Or, they're so stretchy they droop down around your knees and run within the week. Or, they're so NON-stretchy you can't get 'em up above your knees, and they still run within the week!

Why can't the hosiery manufacturers figure out how to make a nylon stocking that fits with a proper degree of stretch and doesn't fall to shreds in six days? Isn't nylon supposed to be one of the toughest substances made by man?

To put this into economic focus: Wanda Worker spends two bucks on nylons every week. That's over a hundred dollars a year, not to mention the aggravation and time spent running to the drugstore on a lunch hour to replace the pair that self-destructed on her way to work.

As I said, Ann, it seems terrifically trivial, but it's maddening. You have contacts all over. Will you please ask somebody who is big in hosiery manufacturing what gives—besides my stockings, that is.

Ladder Legs in Lima, Ohio

**Ann says:** You really hit a hot button! I contacted four of the leading hosiery manufacturers, and I have never heard so much double-talk, triple-talk and fancy ways of saying "no comment." All those contacted by my office asked that they not be identified—and would I please not name their companies. I am respecting their wishes.

But, of this you can be sure:

The hosiery industry has a mighty sweet thing going and has no intention of letting go. We have been ripped off, if you will pardon the pun, for lo, these many years, ladies. And they will continue to rip us off because the no-run nylons, which they know how to make, would put a serious crimp in their sales. In other words, we are at the mercy of a conspiracy of self-interest.

My advice is this: Shop around. Low-priced, good-fitting nylons are out there. (I wear them myself, and they look as good as the top-dollar variety. Sorry, I can't publish the brand name.) For daily wear, buy nylons with reinforced toe and heel. One final way to get a leg up: If you rip one stocking, cut it off and sew on the good stocking from another pair that similarly failed you.

**14.** In New York City, every taxicab driver must own a license (called a medallion) to drive a cab. The city has issued a fixed number of medallions, and they are traded on the open market. Because the number of medallions is small, the price of cab rides is higher than it otherwise would be. Suppose that the city decides to abolish the medallion program and allow free entry to the taxicab industry. **True or False:** The owners of medallions will be just as well off after the program is abolished as if it had never existed.

**15.** **True or False:** If a monopolist owned an exhaustible resource, he would control its availability so that the price rose faster than the rate of interest.

**16.** **True or False:** A net borrower is always made worse off by a rise in the rate of interest.

**17.** Herman has an income of $2 this year and will have an income of $3 next year. At the current rate of interest he chooses neither to borrow nor to lend. **True or False:** If the interest rate goes up, Herman will become a lender and be better off.

**18.** Contrast the effects on the interest rate of (a) a year of bad weather resulting in low agricultural productivity and (b) nuclear contamination that permanently lowers agricultural productivity.

**19.** Contrast the effects on current consumption and the interest rate of (a) a tax on production that is expected to be in effect for 1 year only and (b) a tax on production that is expected to be permanent. Assume in each case that the proceeds from the tax will be completely wasted.

**20.** Suppose that the interest rate is 12% and that the representative agent's tastes are such that the interest rate would have to rise to 20% to get him to voluntarily cut current consumption by $1,000. Suppose now that there is a war that destroys $1,000 worth of consumption goods for every agent in the economy. **True or False:** The interest rate must rise to 20% to restore equilibrium.

**21.** The discussion surrounding Exhibit 17.11 suggests that when the government spends $1 wastefully, it does not matter (for determining the equilibrium interest rate) whether the government gets the $1 by taxation or by borrowing. Draw a similar diagram to show that the same conclusion holds when the government spends $1 productively, say by using it to purchase $1 worth of goods for Terry Taxpayer.

**22.** Repeat problem 21 assuming that the government manages to spend the $1 *superproductively,* using it to provide Terry Taxpayer with goods that he values at $2.

**23.** **True or False:** When the government spends $1, the equilibrium interest rate is unaffected by whether the dollar is spent wastefully or productively.

**24.** Felix G. Rohatyn, a well-known financier, published a letter on the editorial page of the *New York Times* on July 1, 1990. He wrote:

> I was startled and dismayed by [an earlier *Times* editorial] supporting Government borrowing as the appropriate way to deal with the bailout of bankrupt savings and loan institutions. Borrowing may be politically expedient; it is, however, wrong, from both an economic and moral point of view. The straightforward, and least damaging, way to deal with this fiasco, is to pay off the $130 billion loss with a temporary three- to four-year surcharge on income taxes.

The economics are simple:

(1) Borrowing will turn a $130 billion loss into a $500 billion drain over 20 to 30 years. It will maintain pressure on the credit markets and lead to higher interest rates. It will add $10 billion to $15 billion annually in interest costs to the Federal budget deficit, when interest costs constitute, after defense, the largest Federal expenditure. It will require continued high inflows of foreign capital. It will squeeze out badly needed domestic programs.

(2) A three- to four-year temporary tax surcharge will eliminate $300 billion to $400 billion in interest costs and contribute to lower interest rates and capital costs. This will foster economic growth. The tax will not have negative economic impact because the bailout is basically a transfer program from taxpayers to depositors.

(3) A basic economic principle justifies borrowing only for assets with a useful life. Nothing is more remote from that definition than borrowing to finance losses that have already been incurred.

The moral issue is even simpler. Borrowing burdens the next generation with repayment of our foolishness and burdens lower-income Americans with the interest costs. The income tax puts the burden where it belongs: on the present generation and on higher-income Americans.

a. Find at least one elementary economic error per each paragraph.

b. Focus on the "basic economic principle" articulated under point 3. In an indifference curve diagram, show what happens if, after you have optimized, a tragedy destroys a substantial chunk of your current consumption. Is it better to reduce your consumption by that full amount in the current period? Or is it better to spread out the loss over the present and future by "borrowing to finance losses that have already been incurred"?

c. Suppose that the government does follow Mr. Rohatyn's advice and raises current taxes to meet the costs of the bailout in what is essentially the immediate present. How might individual taxpayers adjust their private borrowing and lending? Will the costs really be paid in the present, or will they be spread out over time despite the government policy? Explain why the Rohatyn plan might have no effect on any important economic variable.

d. Suppose that contrary to your argument in part (c), the Rohatyn plan does have a real effect, either because people are unable to borrow as much as they would like at the market interest rate or because they are insufficiently sophisticated to borrow their way through the higher tax years. In that case, does the Rohatyn plan make people better off or worse off?

25. **True or False:** When the interest rate goes up, investment becomes more desirable.

26. You are thinking of purchasing the house that you currently rent for $10,000 per year. What is the most you would pay for the house?

27. Suppose that scientists discover a new method of harnessing nuclear fusion as a practical energy source. At the moment, the method is still on the drawing boards, but it is clear that within 10 years this discovery will be the basis of a technological revolution. What happens to the interest rate?

28. Suppose that an increase in world tensions makes it more likely than before that there will soon be a nuclear war that destroys all life on earth. What happens to the interest rate?

29.    Suppose that an increase in world tensions makes it more likely than before that there will be a nuclear war within 10 years. Such a war would kill half the world's population and destroy 90% of the world's physical wealth. What happens to the interest rate?

30.    Consider an agricultural society in which seeds can either be planted immediately to produce food almost instantly or stored for planting next year to produce food then. Suppose that this society becomes convinced that the weather will improve dramatically next year. Show the effects on the amount of food produced this year and on the interest rate.

# Risk and Uncertainty

The future brings surprises. A rainstorm can change the price of wheat. A fire can destroy your house. The invention of the automobile can make you rich if you own rubber plantations or wipe you out if you manufacture buggy whips.

Your wealth tomorrow depends on the **state of the world.** Examples of alternative states of the world are "rain" versus "sunshine," "fire" versus "no fire," and "cars invented" versus "cars not invented."

**State of the world**

A potential set of conditions.

Markets abound for transferring wealth from one state of the world to another. By placing a bet that it will rain, you increase your wealth in the rainy state of the world while decreasing your wealth in the sunny state. (Of course, you will occupy only one of these states, but at the time you place the bet you don't know which it will be.) Purchasing fire insurance is a mechanism for increasing your wealth in the "fire" state at the expense of decreasing your wealth (by the amount of the insurance premium) in the "no fire" state. Organized markets in stocks and commodities afford numerous opportunities for transferring wealth between states of the world.

In this chapter, we will begin by studying the individual's choice about how much wealth to transfer from one state of the world to another and the determination of the equilibrium price at which he can do so. We will then examine some of the particular markets in which such transactions take place.

## 18.1 Attitudes Toward Risk

When there are two alternative states of the world, we can use diagrams like those in Exhibit 18.1 to represent your wealth in each of them. The horizontal axis measures your wealth in one state, and the vertical axis measures your wealth in the other. Suppose that your total wealth is $100 but that it will be reduced to $40 if there is a fire. In that case, your position is represented by point *A* in panel A of Exhibit 18.1.

Now suppose that for $20 you purchase an insurance contract that entitles you to collect $60 in the event of a fire. Then if there is no fire, your wealth is reduced to $80, whereas if the fire occurs your wealth is also $80 ($40 plus $60 insurance payment minus $20 to buy the insurance in the first place). Thus, your new position is represented by point *B*.

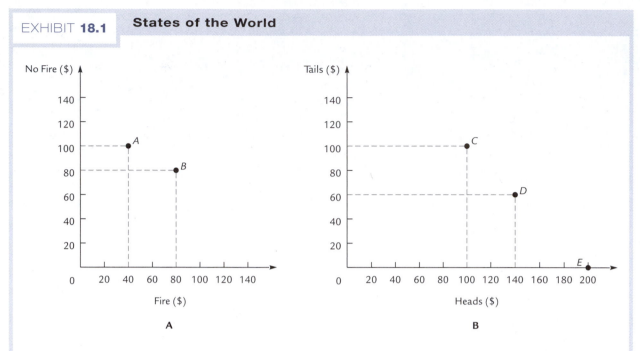

**EXHIBIT 18.1     States of the World**

In either panel the two axes represent your wealth in alternative states of the world. Panel A considers the states in which your house is destroyed by fire and in which it is not. Suppose that your wealth is initially $100 but that it will be reduced to $40 in the event of a fire. Then your position is represented by point *A*. Now suppose that for $20 you purchase an insurance contract that will return $60 in the event of a fire. Then your new position is represented by point *B*, where your wealth is $80 in either state of the world.

Panel B considers the two possible outcomes of a coin toss. If your initial wealth is $100 and if you do not bet on the outcome of the toss, then your position is represented by point *C*. If you wager $40 that the coin will come up heads, you move to point *D*.

For another example, suppose that you are a gambler, that you have total assets of $100, and that you have just bet $40 that a certain tossed coin will come up heads. The possible states of the world are "heads" and "tails." In case of heads, your wealth is $140; in case of tails it is $60. Your position is represented by point *D* in panel B of Exhibit 18.1. If you don't place the bet, your wealth is $100 regardless of whether the coin comes up heads or tails, and your position is represented by point *C*.

**Exercise 18.1** What bet would you have to place to move to basket *E* in Exhibit 18.1?

We can think of each of the points in Exhibit 18.1 as a *basket of outcomes,* and we can use indifference curves to represent an individual's preferences among these baskets. However, these baskets of outcomes differ in an important way from the baskets of consumer goods that we studied in Chapter 3. When you own a basket of apples and oranges, you can consume both apples and oranges. But when you own a basket of outcomes, you get only one of the outcomes. Once the state of the world has been determined, we do not need indifference curves to tell us which baskets are preferable to which others. After the coin comes up heads, everyone will agree that point *D* is better than point *C* in panel B of Exhibit 18.1. Or after it comes up tails, everyone will agree that *C* is better than *D*.

When we talk about preferences between baskets of outcomes, we are referring to the preferences of someone who does not know what the state of the world will be. Such preferences are called ex ante preferences, as distinguished from the ex post preferences of someone who has already learned the state of the world. If we say that Clarence prefers D to C, we mean that he would choose to bet $40 on heads rather than not bet at all, if he were asked *before* the coin was flipped.

## Characterizing Baskets

Before drawing budget constraints and indifference curves, we need to introduce two concepts that describe important characteristics of any basket of outcomes. One of these is the expected value of a basket; the other is its riskiness.

### Expected Values

The expected value of a basket is given by the formula

(Probability of state 1) $\times$ (Wealth in state 1) $+$ (Probability of state 2) $\times$ (Wealth in state 2)

For example, suppose that your basket of outcomes is represented by point $A$ in panel A of Exhibit 18.1 and that the probability of a fire is .25 (so that the probability of "no fire" is .75). Then the expected value of your wealth is

$$(.25 \times \$40) + (.75 \times \$100) = \$85$$

In panel B of Exhibit 18.1, if we assume that the coin is unbiased, meaning that it has probability .50 of coming up heads and probability .50 of coming up tails, then the expected value of basket $D$ is

$$(.50 \times \$140) + (.50 \times \$60) = \$100$$

---

**Exercise 18.2** If the coin is unbiased, what is the expected value of basket $C$? If the coin is weighted so that it comes up heads two-thirds of the time, what are the expected values of baskets $C$ and $D$? What if the coin is weighted so that it comes up tails two-thirds of the time?

---

If you repeat the same gamble a large number of times, the average outcome will be approximately equal to the expected value of the gamble. It is possible to formulate this statement more precisely and to prove it mathematically. The careful mathematical formulation is known as the law of large numbers.

Suppose that state 1 occurs with probability $P_1$ and state 2 occurs with probability $P_2$ (so that $P_1 + P_2 = 1$). Then along any line with slope $-P_1/P_2$, all baskets have the same expected value. A family of such "iso-expected value" lines is illustrated in Exhibit 18.2.

---

**Exercise 18.3** In panel B of Exhibit 18.1, what do the iso-expected value lines look like if the coin is unbiased? If the coin comes up heads two-thirds of the time? If it comes up tails two-thirds of the time? In each case, which point lies on the higher line, $C$ or $D$? Are your answers consistent with your calculations in Exercise 18.2?

---

**Ex ante**

Determined before the state of the world is known.

**Ex post**

Determined after the state of the world is known.

**Expected value**

The average value over all states of the world, with each state weighted by its probability.

**Law of large numbers**

When a gamble is repeated many times, the average outcome is the expected value.

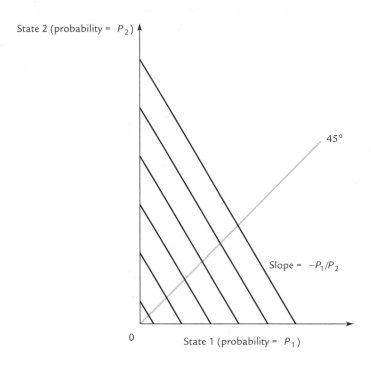

EXHIBIT **18.2**     **Baskets with the Same Expected Value**

State 2 (probability = $P_2$)

45°

Slope = $-P_1/P_2$

0     State 1 (probability = $P_1$)

If the probability of state 1 is $P_1$ and the probability of state 2 is $P_2$ (so that $P_1 + P_2 = 1$), then all of the baskets along a line of slope $-P_1/P_2$ have the same expected value. The graph shows a family of such lines.
    The baskets along the 45° line are risk-free, because a person holding such a basket will have the same wealth in either state of the world. Moving along an iso-expected value line away from the 45° line in either direction, the baskets become successively riskier.

## Riskiness

**Riskiness**

Variation in potential outcomes.

**Risk-free**

Having the same value in any state of the world.

Baskets differ not only in expected value but also in **riskiness.** Baskets on the 45° line (shown in Exhibit 18.2) are referred to as **risk-free,** because individuals who hold them know with certainty what their wealth will be regardless of the state of the world. Moving away from the 45° line along an iso-expected value line, the baskets become riskier, carrying more uncertainty about what the future will bring. In panel B of Exhibit 18.1, baskets *C* and *E* have the same expected value, but a person holding basket *C* knows for certain what his wealth will be, whereas a person with basket *E* could come away with either twice as much wealth or with nothing at all.

## Opportunities

Suppose that you enter a gambling parlor with $100 in your pocket. Bets are being taken on a coin flip. If you place no bets, your wealth is $100 in either state of the world. This is your endowment, and it is represented by point *C* in Exhibit 18.3. Suppose that you are invited to express your opinion about how the coin will turn up and to bet as much as you would like on the outcome. By betting $50 on tails, you can move yourself to point *X,* where your wealth is $150 if you win or $50 if you lose. Other bets can get you to any of the points on the black line shown in Exhibit 18.3. By placing bets, you can trade your endowment for any point along that line. In other words, it is your budget line.

EXHIBIT **18.3**    **Opportunities**

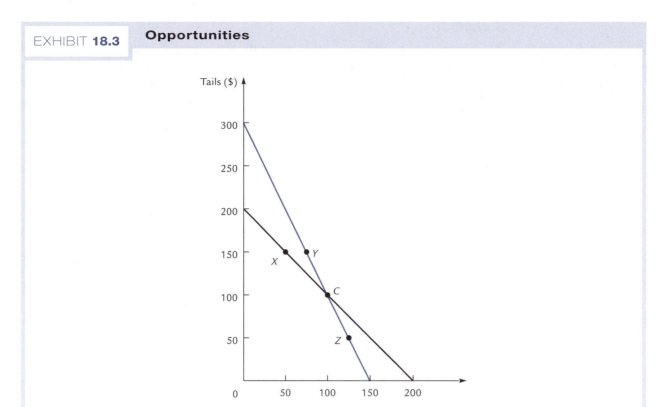

If you enter a gambling parlor with $100 in your pocket and choose not to bet on a coin toss, then your wealth will be $100 in either state of the world. Thus, you achieve point *C* without trading—point *C* is your endowment. By betting on either heads or tails at even odds, you can achieve any basket along the black budget line, such as *X*. If the odds are such that tails bettors receive 2 to 1 payoffs, you can achieve any point on the color budget line. The odds give the relative price of wealth in the tails state in terms of wealth in the heads state, and they therefore determine the slope of the budget line.

**Exercise 18.4** What would your budget line look like if you were permitted to bet only on heads?

The gambling parlor offers you the opportunity to trade dollars in the heads state of the world for dollars in the tails state at a relative price of 1. This price is reflected in the slope of the budget line, which is 1 in absolute value.

Other prices are also possible. Suppose that you are offered the opportunity to bet on tails and given *odds* of 2 to 1. This means that for every $1 you bet, you win $2 if tails comes up (but you still lose only $1 if the outcome is heads). Suppose that you are allowed to take either side of this bet: You can bet either on tails at odds of 2 to 1, or on heads, in which case you must grant odds of 2 to 1. You now have an opportunity to trade dollars between the heads state of the world and the tails state of the world. The relative price is 2 "tail-dollars" per "head-dollar." By betting $25 on tails, you can move from point *C* to point *Y* in Exhibit 18.3. In so doing, you are selling 25 head-dollars and receiving 50 tail-dollars in return. Alternatively, you could buy head-dollars and sell tail-dollars, moving to a point like *Z*. Your budget line is the color line in Exhibit 18.3, with an absolute slope of 2, reflecting the relative price of tail-dollars in terms of head-dollars.

## Fair Odds

**Fair odds**

Odds that reflect the true probabilities of various states of the world.

Odds are said to be **fair odds** if they reflect the actual probabilities of the two states of the world. An unbiased coin is equally likely to come up heads or tails, so the fair odds on the toss of such a coin are 1 to 1. A weighted coin might be twice as likely to come up heads as to come up tails, in which case the fair odds are 2 to 1 for those who bet on tails.

---

**Exercise 18.5** What are the fair odds on a bet that the roll of a die will turn up 1? What are the fair odds on a bet that it will turn up 4 or less? What are the fair odds on a bet that it will turn up an even number?

---

What is so fair about fair odds? The answer is that at fair odds the expected value of any bet is the same as the expected value of not betting at all. In other words, if two parties bet with each other repeatedly at fair odds, neither will come out very far ahead or very far behind in the long run. If a coin comes up heads twice as often as it comes up tails, and if the payoff for betting on heads is half the payoff for betting on tails, then each party's wins and losses will just cancel out.

When an individual is offered fair odds, any gamble has the same expected value as any other. Therefore,

When an individual is offered fair odds, his budget line coincides with an iso-expected value line.

## Preferences and the Consumer's Optimum

### The Frequent Gambler

A gambler who bets frequently with the goal of maximizing his winnings is concerned only with the expected values of his wagers. This is because any wager, when it is repeated sufficiently often, returns its expected value on average. In panel B of Exhibit 18.1, if the coin is unbiased, points *C, D,* and *E* all have the same expected value and hence are equally attractive to the frequent, repetitive gambler. If he holds basket *C* every day, he comes away with $100 every day. If he holds basket *E* every day, he comes away with $200 half the time and $0 the other half. Over time, this averages out to the same $100 per day that he can have with basket *C.*

The frequent gambler is indifferent between two baskets of equal expected value, regardless of the risk associated with each. We say that this is because he can **diversify** his risk by playing repeatedly so that he is guaranteed to win the expected value of any gamble in the long run.[1] When someone's preferences among baskets are determined solely on the basis of their expected values, we describe those preferences as **risk-neutral.** From the definition of risk neutrality, we can see this:

**Diversify**

To reduce risk.

**Risk-neutral**

Caring only about expected value.

The indifference curves of a risk-neutral individual are identical with the iso-expected value lines.

### Risk Neutrality

We have seen that the frequent gambler is risk-neutral. Conceivably, some infrequent gamblers might be risk-neutral as well.

---

[1] This assumes that he can always borrow enough to keep playing after he is wiped out by a run of bad luck—or by a single turn of bad luck after a large bet.

Consider a risk-neutral person who is given the opportunity to play at fair odds. Because he is risk-neutral, his indifference curves are the iso-expected value lines. Because the odds are fair, his budget line is the iso-expected value line through his endowment. The picture is as in panel A of Exhibit 18.4, where the gray iso-expected value lines are the indifference curves and the black budget line coincides with one of them. This individual is indifferent among all of the points on his budget line. Thus,

At fair odds, a risk-neutral individual is indifferent as to how much he bets.

Suppose that the risk-neutral person has an opportunity to play at other than fair odds. This rotates his budget line through his endowment, either clockwise, if the new odds favor betting on tails, or counterclockwise, if the new odds favor betting on heads. The first possibility is illustrated in panel B of Exhibit 18.4. As you can see, he now chooses a point on the vertical axis where his wealth becomes zero in the event that the coin turns up heads.

A risk-neutral individual faced with unfair odds will bet everything he owns on one or the other outcome.

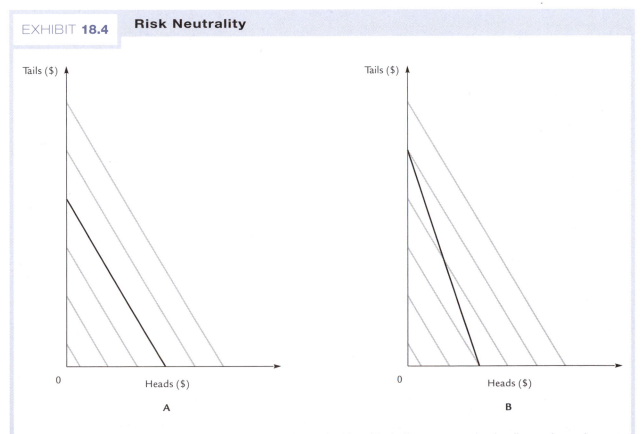

EXHIBIT **18.4**    **Risk Neutrality**

A risk-neutral individual has indifference curves that coincide with the iso-expected value lines, shown in gray in both panels. When he is offered fair odds, his budget line coincides with one of the indifference curves, as in panel A. In that case the individual is indifferent among all of the options available to him. When he is offered any odds other than fair odds, his budget line has a different slope than his indifference curves, like the black budget line in panel B. In that case, he will always choose a corner and bet everything he has on one outcome or the other.

**Dangerous Curve**

Unlike all of the indifference curves we have encountered previously, the indifference curves of this chapter depend on more than just tastes. They depend also on the probabilities associated with the two states of the world. If a fair coin is replaced by a biased coin, a gambler might change his mind about the desirability of various wagers, even though his underlying tastes have not changed.

## Risk Aversion

Now let us consider the preferences of someone who is not a frequent gambler. To such a person, the riskiness of his basket can be a significant consideration. He does not expect his gains and losses to cancel out in the long run.

**Risk-averse**

Always preferring the least risky among baskets with the same expected value.

Many people are **risk-averse**. This means that among baskets with the same expected value, they choose the one that is least risky. Consequently, when offered fair odds, they choose the basket that equalizes their incomes in both states of the world. Such baskets are located on the 45° line.

The two panels of Exhibit 18.5 show the indifference curves of typical risk-averse individuals facing fair odds. In panel A the individual has an initial wealth of $100 and

**EXHIBIT 18.5**   **Risk Aversion**

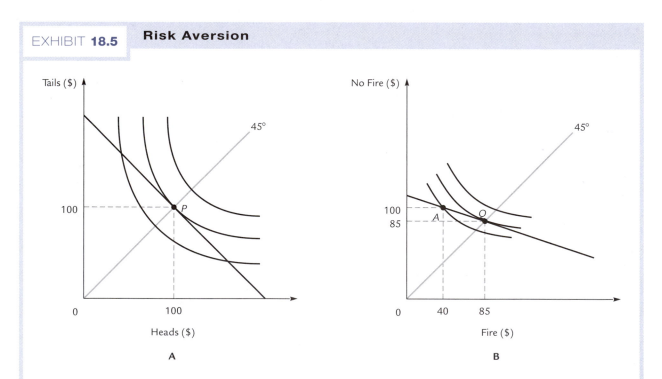

The two panels illustrate the indifference curves of individuals facing fair odds. In panel A the individual has initial wealth of $100 and is offered the opportunity to bet at even odds on the toss of a fair coin. His endowment is at point *P*, which is already on the 45° line. This is also his optimum, so he places no wager.

In panel B the individual has initial wealth of $100, which will be reduced to $40 in the event of a fire. His endowment is at point *A*. We assume that the probability of "no fire" is 3 times as great as the probability of "fire." Thus, the fair odds for an insurance policy are 3 to 1, and we assume that such a policy is available. This gives the illustrated budget line, which crosses the 45° line at (85, 85). Because he is risk-averse, his optimum is at *Q*. He achieves this point by purchasing $15 worth of insurance.

is offered the opportunity to bet on a coin toss at fair odds. His optimum point occurs right on the 45° line, at his endowment point *P*. He places no wager.

Panel B shows the situation of a risk-averse person whose wealth is $100, which is reduced to $40 if there is a fire. His endowment is at point *A*. We will assume that "fire" occurs with probability .25, so "no fire" occurs with probability .75.

Suppose that it is possible to buy fire insurance for $1. The insurance pays $4 in the event of fire, and the homeowner can buy as many units of this insurance as he wants to. Buying insurance is exactly like betting that there will be a fire. If there is no fire, he loses his $1. If there is a fire, there is a net gain of $3 (a $4 insurance payment minus the $1 cost of the insurance). Therefore, this particular insurance policy offers 3-to-1 odds when the homeowner bets that a fire will take place. These happen to be the fair odds, because the probability of "no fire" (.75) is 3 times the probability of "fire" (.25).

The homeowner's budget line has an absolute slope of 1/3, reflecting the odds of 3 to 1. Because the homeowner is assumed to be risk-averse, he always eliminates risk when he can bet at fair odds. That is, he chooses the point where his budget line crosses the 45° line, at point *Q* in panel B of Exhibit 18.5. At this point the homeowner is guaranteed that his wealth will be $85 regardless of whether or not the fire occurs. His indifference curves must be like those in the graph, with the optimum at *Q*.

---

**Exercise 18.6** Exactly how much insurance does the homeowner buy?

---

## Risk Preference

Another type of individual is risk-preferring. Given a choice between a "sure thing" and a lottery with the same expected value, he chooses the lottery. Such an individual has indifference curves as shown in Exhibit 18.6. They become tangent to the fair-odds budget lines at points along the 45° line, but this is because the individual considers any such point to be the *worst* he can do when trading at fair odds. You can see from Exhibit 18.6 that a risk-preferring person always chooses a lottery in which he risks sacrificing everything he owns in exchange for a chance at great wealth.

It is also possible for an individual to be risk-preferring in some situations and risk-averse in others. Consider an individual with the indifference curves and budget line shown in Exhibit 18.7. Starting from an endowment at point *A*, he indulges his risk preference by gambling to get to either point *B* or point *C*. At that point, risk aversion becomes dominant and he gambles no further.

**Risk-preferring**

Always preferring the most risky among baskets with the same expected value.

## Which Preferences Are Most Likely?

Attitudes toward risk typically vary with income. At very low levels of income, people are probably risk-preferring. To see the reason for this, suppose that $5 per year is the minimum income necessary for survival. In that case, an income of $3 per year is no more valuable than an income of zero. Somebody earning $3 per year would be willing to gamble, even at very unfavorable odds, for a chance to earn enough to stay alive.

Even at higher levels of income, we sometimes observe risk preference for similar reasons. If you are determined to purchase a particular sailboat for $20,000 and if your current assets total $19,000, you might be willing to take a very risky bet as long as it offered some chance to win $1,000.

EXHIBIT **18.6**          **Risk Preference**

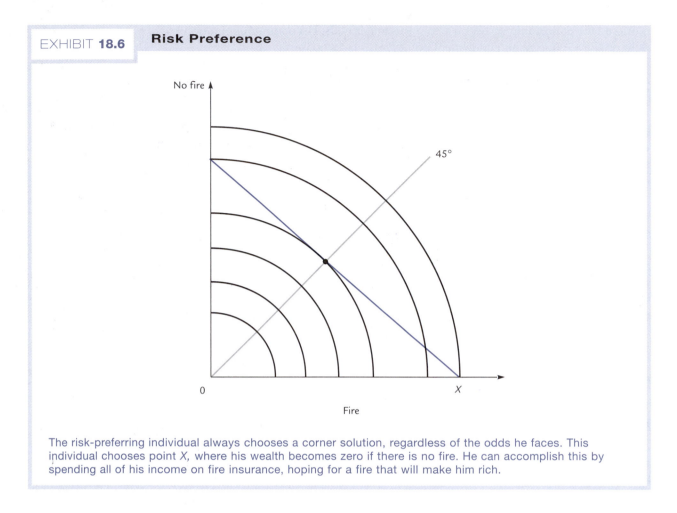

The risk-preferring individual always chooses a corner solution, regardless of the odds he faces. This individual chooses point *X*, where his wealth becomes zero if there is no fire. He can accomplish this by spending all of his income on fire insurance, hoping for a fire that will make him rich.

Nevertheless, most individuals exhibit some degree of risk aversion over most ranges of income. A person earning $20,000 per year is unlikely to be willing to trade a year's income for a 50-50 chance at $40,000, or even a 50-50 chance at $50,000. On the other hand, the same person might very well be willing to trade $20 for a 50-50 chance at $50, or $2 for a 50-50 chance at $5. When small amounts are involved, people tend to exhibit risk-neutral behavior. With large amounts at stake, however, risk aversion is the general rule.

Firms, as opposed to individuals, are more likely to exhibit risk neutrality. This is so for several reasons. First, many firms are frequent gamblers that participate in a large number of risky ventures and can expect their good and bad luck to cancel out over time. Second, unlike individuals, firms face no budget constraints. An individual who risks all his assets and loses is wiped out, whereas a firm that risks all its assets and loses can often borrow enough to continue operating. (Of course, the firm must convince lenders that it is showing good business sense in the long run.)

Those firms that are corporations have an additional reason for risk-neutral behavior. Corporate stockholders are able to diversify their risks by holding small amounts of stock in many different companies. Once diversified, they, like the frequent gambler, earn approximately the expected value of the return on their overall portfolios. For this reason, the stockholders are interested only in maximizing expected return, and they want the corporation to behave in a risk-neutral way.

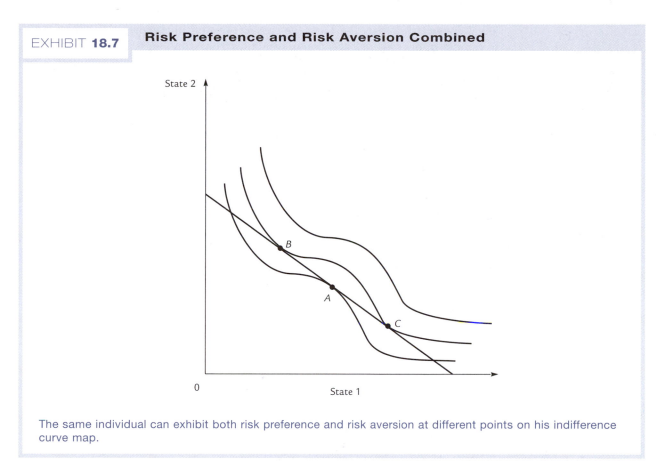

**EXHIBIT 18.7   Risk Preference and Risk Aversion Combined**

The same individual can exhibit both risk preference and risk aversion at different points on his indifference curve map.

## Gambling at Favorable Odds

Often we encounter opportunities to gamble at better than fair odds. Suppose that you own a restaurant and have the opportunity to run an advertising campaign that has a 50-50 chance of success. If the campaign succeeds, your profits (net of advertising costs) will increase by $2,000, whereas if it fails, you will lose $1,000. Because success and failure are equally likely, and because the gain from success exceeds the loss from failure, the odds are better than fair. If you run the campaign, you increase the expected value of your wealth. For another example, suppose that you have the opportunity to buy a ticket to a concert that you will enjoy with probability of .75. The ticket costs $1, and you receive $2 worth of pleasure if the concert turns out to be good. Thus, if the concert is bad, you lose $1, and if it is good, you gain $1 ($2 in enjoyment minus $1 for the ticket). Because the concert is more likely to be good than bad, the odds on this gamble are also favorable.

---

**Exercise 18.7** For each of the opportunities described in the preceding paragraph, what odds would be fair? What are the actual odds? What is the expected value of your winnings if you gamble?

---

We have already seen that a risk-neutral person always accepts any wager in which the odds are better than fair and that he wagers as much as he possibly can at such odds.

What does a risk-averter do? Does the prospect of a positive expected gain entice him to gamble, or does his risk aversion prevent him from gambling?

Consider an example. Suppose that you are risk-averse, have assets totaling $5, and have the opportunity to gamble at 3-to-1 odds on the toss of an unbiased coin. If you bet $1 on heads, then you either lose $1 (if tails comes up) or win $3 (if heads comes up).

Your budget line is then the black line in Exhibit 18.8. Your endowment is at point *A*, where you keep your $5 no matter how the coin turns up. We know that if you were offered the fair odds of 1 to 1, you would not bet at all, so the absolute slope of the indifference curve at *A* must be 1. It follows that the budget line cuts through the indifference curve, as shown in the exhibit.

By betting $1, you move from point *A* to point *B*, which is an improvement. Thus, if your only options are to bet $1 or to not bet at all, you choose to bet.

| EXHIBIT **18.8** | **Gambling at Favorable Odds** |
|---|---|

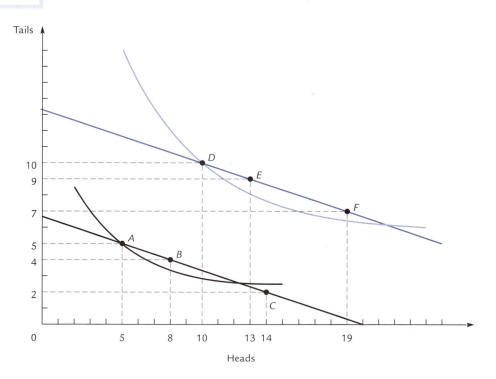

The indifference curves are those of a risk-averter facing the opportunity to bet on the toss of an unbiased coin. His initial wealth is $5, so point *A* is his endowment. Because he is risk-averse, the absolute slope of the indifference curve at *A* must reflect the fair odds of 1 to 1; in other words, it has an absolute slope of 1.

This individual is invited to bet on heads at the favorable odds of 3 to 1. By betting $1, he moves to point *B*, which he prefers to point *A*. If he bet $3, he would move to point *C*, which he likes less than point *A*. Thus, if he is allowed to place the small bet of $1, he will do so, but if he must place the large bet of $3, he will decline.

Suppose that this individual has an increase in wealth, to $10. Then his endowment moves to point *D*. From point *D* a $1 bet moves him to point *E* and a $3 bet moves him to point *F*. Either of these is an improvement over point *D*, and if offered either option, he will accept it. With greater initial wealth, he is willing to accept the $3 bet that he previously considered too large. However, he will continue to reject much larger bets.

Suppose, alternatively, that the house rules require you to bet either $3 or nothing at all. A $3 bet would move you to point *C,* which is less desirable than point *A.* Thus, in this case you would prefer not to bet.

Therefore, the exhibit demonstrates this principle:

A risk-averse person, offered the opportunity to place a sufficiently small bet at favorable odds, always accepts. If only offered the opportunity to place a very large bet at favorable odds, he always declines.

The largest bet that a risk-averter would be willing to make depends on his wealth. Suppose that instead of starting with $5, you started with $10. In that case, your endowment would be at point *D* in Exhibit 18.8. A $1 wager at the favorable odds of 3 to 1 brings you to point *E,* and a $3 wager brings you to point *F.* Either of these is preferable to point *D.* Thus, even if the house rules require the relatively large $3 wager, you still choose to bet.

The indifference curves of Exhibit 18.8 are typical. As a risk-averter acquires more wealth, he is willing to enter into larger wagers at favorable odds. However, there is always a limit to what size wager he will accept. Even with the initial wealth of $10, a person with the indifference curves of Exhibit 18.8 will not bet $5 on heads.

## Risk and Society

Societies, like corporations, must decide when to undertake risky projects. Just as risk-averse stockholders can prefer the corporations they own to behave risk-neutrally, so risk-averse citizens can prefer the societies they inhabit to behave risk-neutrally in some respects. In a society that undertakes a large number of independent investment projects, citizens will be best off in the long run if those projects are evaluated risk-neutrally. However, the individual entrepreneurs who actually decide how to allocate resources often have much personal wealth at stake, so risk aversion enters their decisions.

In some cases, however, entrepreneurial initiatives are intensely personal. In the 1950s Joseph Wilson (later the head of the Xerox Corporation) had a vision of the copying machine as a tool that would transform U.S. business. At the time few shared his vision. Entrepreneurial visions arise every day, and most do not succeed. Should such visions be pursued?

Suppose that Wilson had a 1 in 100 chance of succeeding in his project. Then from a social point of view, the project should be undertaken if the benefits from a success would be more than 100 times the losses from a failure. The frequency with which such projects arise in society justifies a risk-neutral calculation. But visions are the property of individuals, and individuals are risk-averse. From Wilson's point of view, a mere 100-to-1 payoff would not have sufficed. In order to induce him to risk a substantial fraction of his personal wealth for a 1% chance of success, Wilson might have required the prospect of a 500-fold multiplication of his wealth.

From a social point of view, risk-averse individuals underinvest in risky projects. The existence of corporations helps to solve this problem, because, as we have seen, the shareholders, with diversified portfolios, will encourage appropriate risk-taking. However, intensely personal visions cannot always be effectively pursued by large corporations. In such cases, only the prospect of great personal fortune will induce individuals to take great risks. A society that attempted to limit the amassing of great wealth might be a society without copying machines.

# 18.2 The Market for Insurance

Many markets have developed to facilitate transfers of risk from one party to another. In this and the next two sections, we will examine a few of these markets. We have already alluded to the insurance market in Section 18.1. Panel A of Exhibit 18.1 depicts the endowment of a homeowner facing the possibility of a fire. In Exhibit 18.5 we can see how the homeowner, when facing a given price, decides how much insurance to buy. But what determines the market price of insurance?

Insurance companies are highly diversified. If each individual house catches fire with probability .25, you must experience considerable uncertainty about whether yours will be one of those that burn. By contrast, a company that insures 1,000 houses can be sure that almost exactly 250 of them will burn. If there were no other considerations, an insurance company that offered fair odds would just break even. Any insurance company offering less than fair odds would earn profits, causing entry to the insurance industry and driving the odds down until they were fair. Thus, a $1 insurance policy must buy a $4 payoff in case of fire.[2]

There are, however, other considerations. For one thing, there are costs involved with running an insurance company—costs of maintaining an office, a sales force, an actuarial staff to estimate probabilities, assessors to estimate actual damages when they occur, and so forth. A firm offering fair odds could not cover these costs and would not survive. The odds must be tilted in the company's favor by enough so that these basic operating costs can be met.

However, more interesting and more important reasons exist as to why insurance is not offered at fair odds. In discussing them, we can safely ignore the relatively minor issue of operating costs.

## Imperfect Information

First, there are problems of information, such as *moral hazard* and *adverse selection,* which were discussed in Section 9.3. The moral hazard problem arises when people behave more recklessly because they are insured; this means that insurance companies must offer odds that are adjusted accordingly.

The adverse selection problem arises when fair odds are different for different people (as when some are more naturally susceptible to disease than others, which affects the fair odds for health insurance) and the insurance company is unable to tell who is who.

As in Section 9.3, assume that some people are "Healthies," with a 1 in 10 chance of becoming ill, while others are "Sicklies," with a 9 in 10 chance of becoming ill. If the insurance company could distinguish one group from the other, it would offer the appropriate odds to each group. If it can't tell the difference, then it can't simply offer odds that are appropriate for Healthies, because Sicklies will purchase the insurance and bankrupt the company.

The discussion in Section 9.3 suggested a solution: Offer two policies, one at "Healthy" odds and one at "Sickly" odds, but limit the quantity of Healthy insurance that any one person can buy. If the quantity is chosen correctly, each group will voluntarily purchase the right kind of insurance.

---

[2] With this policy you lose $1 when there is no fire and you gain $3 (the $4 payoff minus the $1 premium) if there is a fire. Therefore, the policy offers the fair odds of 3 to 1.

With the machinery of this chapter, we can show exactly how the limit is chosen. In panel A of Exhibit 18.9, Healthies and Sicklies both have endowment point A. The black budget line shows fair odds for Healthies and the color line shows fair odds for Sicklies. If Sicklies are offered insurance at fair odds, they choose point Q on the blue indifference curve. The point where the blue indifference curve crosses the black budget line is labeled R.

People who purchase insurance at Healthy fair odds move down along the black budget line from A. If purchases are limited so that nobody is allowed to move past R, then no Sickly ever chooses Healthy insurance. By purchasing Sickly insurance, the Sickly can achieve point Q, which is preferred to any point between A and R on the black budget line.

Healthies, on the other hand, who have a different family of indifference curves, might very well choose Healthy insurance. Panel B of Exhibit 18.9 shows that a Healthy would rather buy a limited quantity of Healthy insurance, achieving point R, than an unlimited quantity of Sickly insurance, which allows the Healthy to achieve point X.

Of course, if Sicklies voluntarily revealed their identities, the insurance company could offer each form of insurance in unlimited quantities to the appropriate group.

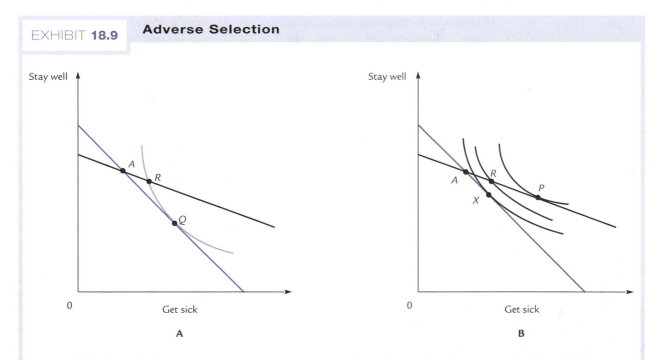

**EXHIBIT 18.9**   **Adverse Selection**

Healthies and Sicklies both have endowment point A. The black budget line represents fair odds for Healthies and the colored budget line represents fair odds for Sicklies. If Sicklies buy Sickly insurance, they choose the quantity to achieve point Q on the brown indifference curve in panel A. The point where that curve crosses the black budget line is labeled R.

The insurance company offers both types of insurance, but limits the quantity of Healthy insurance so that the purchaser cannot move past point R on the black budget line. Sicklies voluntarily choose Sickly insurance, because they prefer point Q to any point between A and R along the black line. Healthies, meanwhile, might have the black indifference curves shown in panel B and choose the limited Healthy insurance, because they prefer point R to anything they can achieve on the color budget line.

If Sicklies voluntarily identified themselves, the company could offer unlimited quantities of each type of insurance to the appropriate group. Sicklies would still achieve point Q, and Healthies would achieve point P.

Sicklies would still achieve point *Q*, and Healthies would be better off, achieving *P* instead of *X*. But, as discussed in Section 9.3, such voluntary revelation cannot be sustained in equilibrium.[3]

## Uninsurable Risks

**Uninsurable risk**

A risk that cannot be diversified.

Another reason why fair-odds insurance is not always available is that some risks are **uninsurable risks** because they cannot be diversified. This occurs when a large number of people are all adversely affected in the same state of the world.

Suppose that you and your friend must each carry a $10 bill through a bad neighborhood at different times. You can insure against robbery by agreeing that if either one is robbed, the other will ease the burden by paying $5 to the victim. But if you are traveling together, so that if one is robbed the other will also be robbed, then there is no advantage to such a contract and no way you can insure each other.

An insurance company brings together many people, its customers, who effectively insure each other against individual disasters. But a collective disaster cannot be insured against by everybody simultaneously. You cannot buy fair-odds insurance against a nuclear disaster. The insurance company is risk-neutral when it insures 1,000 people against a .25 chance of fire, because it knows that it will have to pay off in only 250 cases. It is no longer risk-neutral, and will not offer fair-odds insurance, when it insures 1,000 people against a .25 chance of a nuclear disaster, because there is a .25 chance that it will have to pay off in 1,000 cases.

# 18.3 Futures Markets

**Futures contract**

A contract to deliver a specified good at a specified future date for a specified price.

**Futures market**

The market for futures contracts.

**Spot market**

The market for goods for immediate delivery.

**Spot price**

Price in the spot market.

Suppose that you are a farmer, planting wheat in the spring to be harvested in the fall. You do not know whether the price of wheat will be $3 or $4 a bushel next fall, and you are therefore uncertain both about your future wealth and about the optimal amount of planting to do. If you are risk-averse, you will want to insure against the possibility of a low price.

In practice, this is often accomplished through the medium of a **futures contract.** A futures contract is an agreement to deliver a specified amount of something (in this case wheat) at some future date (in this case next fall) for a price agreed upon today. If the low price of $3 and the high price of $4 are equally likely, then a "fair-odds" delivery price is $3.50. By signing a contract to deliver at this price, you can reduce your risk without sacrificing expected value. At the same time, the buyer of the contract is able to insure against a high price, which is the unfavorable state of the world from the buyer's point of view.

The market for futures contracts is called the **futures market** for short. The market for wheat for immediate delivery is called the **spot market.** The **spot price** of wheat is the price of wheat in the spot market; in other words, it is simply what we would ordinarily call "the" price of wheat.

---

[3] The discussion of adverse selection is based on M. Rothschild and J. Stiglitz, "Equilibrium in Competitive Insurance Markets: An Essay in the Economics of Imperfect Information," *Quarterly Journal of Economics* 90 (1976):629–650. Rothschild and Stiglitz show that the solution in Exhibit 18.9 is the only possible equilibrium, although there might be no equilibrium at all.

## Speculation

Nonfarmers can also sell futures contracts. Suppose that in July wheat for September delivery is selling at $3.50 per bushel. You, however, believe that next September the spot price of wheat is likely to be only $3.25. In that case, you can sell a futures contract for $3.50, wait until September, and then buy a bushel of wheat for $3.25 to deliver in fulfillment of your contract. You will earn a profit of 25¢. On the other hand, if you are in error and the spot price next September turns out to be $3.75, then you will have to buy at that price and will end up with a net loss of 25¢.

Somebody who tries to outguess the market and earn profits by buying and selling futures contracts is called a speculator. Next we will see that when speculators are successful, they have the effect of improving economic efficiency.

Suppose that it is now February. A certain amount of grain is stored in grain elevators, and this is the only source of grain for this month and the next. The sellers (that is, the elevator owners) must decide how much to sell in February and how much to save for sale in March. Panel A of Exhibit 18.10 shows the February demand curve for grain. Panel B shows (in dark color) the expected March demand curve as foreseen by the sellers. Sellers choose to supply $Q_F$ bushels in February and save $Q_M$ bushels to supply in March. (If they are risk-averse, they sell futures contracts now, promising delivery of $Q_M$ bushels in March.) These quantities are chosen so that the equilibrium prices in the two months are equal. In Exhibit 18.10 the equilibrium price in each month is $P_0$.

To see why the equilibrium prices must be equal, let us see what would happen if the expected March spot price exceeded the current price. Sellers, sensing a profit, would save more grain for next month, reducing $Q_F$ and increasing $Q_M$. This would have the effect of raising the current price and reducing the March price and would continue until the two prices were equal.

**Exercise 18.8** Explain what happens if the current price exceeds the expected March spot price.

Actually, sellers equate the current price not to the March price, but to the present value of the March price. We are assuming that the interest rate is small enough so that, for practical purposes, a dollar delivered in March is worth as much as a dollar delivered in February. We are also ignoring storage costs, which, if significant, would make suppliers willing to provide grain at a lower price today than tomorrow. These assumptions simplify the analysis but do not affect the welfare conclusions.

Dangerous
Curve

**Speculator**

One who attempts to earn profits in the futures market by predicting future changes in supply or demand.

Now suppose that there arrives on the scene a speculator who believes that the market has made a mistake and that the March demand curve will be lower than everyone else expects. He believes that the March demand curve will be the light-colored demand curve shown in panel B of Exhibit 18.10. Anticipating a profit, he sells futures contracts, planning to fulfill them by buying cheap wheat on the spot market in March.

The speculator's advertised willingness to provide March wheat at less than the going price of $P_0$ drives down the expected price of March wheat and along with it the price of a March futures contract. With the discovery that March wheat is selling for less than $P_0$, grain suppliers sell more wheat today and save less for March, moving the vertical February supply curve to the right and the vertical March supply curve to the left. This process continues until the speculator no longer perceives any profit to

EXHIBIT **18.10** **Speculation**

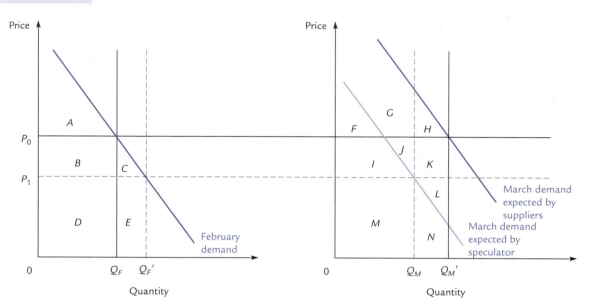

**A. Supply and Demand for February Grain**

**B. Supply and Demand for March Grain**

**Case 1: Speculator Right**

| Without Speculator: | With Speculator: |
|---|---|
| February welfare: $A + B + D$ | February welfare: $A + B + C + D + E$ |
| March welfare: $F + I + M + N$ | March welfare: $F + I + M$ |
| Total: $A + B + D + F + I + M + N$ | Total: $A + B + C + D + E + F + I + M$ |

Gain due to speculator: $C + E - N$

**Case 2: Speculator Wrong**

| Without Speculator: | With Speculator: |
|---|---|
| February welfare: $A + B + D$ | February welfare: $A + B + C + D + E$ |
| March welfare: $F + G + H + I + J + K + L + M + N$ | March: $F + G + I + J + M$ |
| Total: $A + B + D + F + G + H + I + J + K + L$ | Total: $A + B + C + D + E + F + G$ |
| $+ M + N$ | $+ I + J + M$ |

Loss due to speculator: $H + K + L + N - C - E$

The February demand curve for grain is shown in panel A. Suppliers expect the March demand curve to be the dark-color curve in panel B. Thus, they supply $Q_F$ bushels in February and $Q_M$ bushels in March, where these quantities are chosen to make the prices equal. The price in either month is $P_0$.

Now a speculator arrives on the scene, believing that the March demand curve will be the light-color curve in panel B. Thus, he offers to sell March futures contracts, driving down the price of March grain and leading suppliers to sell more in February and less in March. The quantities adjust to $Q_F{'}$ and $Q_M{'}$.

The table shows the welfare analysis, first when the speculator proves to be right and then when he proves to be wrong. In each case, we must use the appropriate March demand curve—the light-color one if the speculator is right and the dark-color one if he is wrong. If the speculator is right, his arrival increases welfare, and if the speculator is wrong, his arrival decreases welfare.

be earned by undercutting the price of March wheat, that is, until the quantities have moved to $Q_F'$ and $Q_M'$ and the price has fallen to $P_1$.

## Speculation and Welfare

The table in Exhibit 18.10 calculates the change in welfare due to the arrival of the speculator, first on the assumption that he is right about the March demand curve and then on the assumption that he is wrong. The marginal cost of providing grain that is already in storage has been taken to be zero, so social welfare is simply the area under the demand curve. To calculate March welfare, we must use the actual March demand curve, which is the light-color curve if the speculator is right and the dark-color curve if he is wrong.

To understand the gains and losses better, keep in mind that the distance from $Q_F$ to $Q_F'$ must equal the distance from $Q_M'$ to $Q_M$. (Either of these distances is the amount of additional grain sold in February instead of March.) From this it is easy to see that $N$ is less than $C + E$, so the speculator really increases social welfare when he is right. Similarly, $C + E$ is less than $H + K + L + N$, so the speculator really decreases social welfare when he is wrong.

Society gains when a speculator correctly alerts it to a coming drop in demand by bidding down the price of futures contracts. This information enables people to increase their current consumption, in recognition of the fact that grain will be less valuable at the margin tomorrow than it is today. Similarly, a speculator who correctly forecasts an increase in tomorrow's demand bids up the price of futures contracts, alerting people today that wheat will be more valuable tomorrow and ought to be conserved.

When the speculator guesses the future correctly, he earns profits and he increases social welfare. When he guesses incorrectly, both he and society lose. By and large, we expect successful speculators to increase the level of their speculative activity over time, and unsuccessful speculators to eventually drop out of the market. Therefore, it is a reasonable expectation that the majority of existing speculators serve a welfare-improving function.

# 18.4 Markets for Risky Assets

Many assets are valued not for their uses in consumption but for their potential to increase their owners' wealth. Corporate stocks are a prime example; real estate is another. The owner of a stock is often entitled to a stream of dividends of uncertain size. In addition, the value of the stock itself might rise or fall. Both the dividends and the changes in the stock price are referred to as **returns** to the owner of the stock. The expected present value of these returns is called the **expected return** to the stock owner.

A risk-neutral stockholder cares only about expected returns. A risk-averse stock-holder cares also about the certainty with which those returns will be realized. Such a stockholder is not indifferent between a stock that returns $5 next year for certain and one that returns either $0 or $10 next year with 50-50 probabilities, even though the expected returns are the same in each case.

The risk associated with a given stock can be described by a number called the **standard deviation** in its returns, abbreviated by σ (the Greek letter *sigma*). If you have taken a statistics course, you know a precise definition of the standard deviation. What you need to know here is that σ is a measure of the *spread* in possible outcomes. A stock that returns $5 with certainty has σ = $0. A stock that returns either $0 or $10 with

**Returns**

Gains to the holder of a financial asset, including dividends and increases in the asset's value.

**Expected return**

The expected value of returns.

**Standard deviation**

A precise measure of risk.

equal probability has σ = $5. A stock that returns either −$5 or $15 with equal probability has σ = $10.

We shall henceforth measure expected returns and standard deviations as percentages of current asset values. Thus, a stock that currently sells for $10 and is expected to return $5 (either by increasing in value or by paying dividends) has an expected return of 50%. If the $5 return is certain, then σ = 0%. If the return might be either −$5 or $15, then σ = 100%, because $10 is 100% of $10.

**Investors**

Buyers of risky assets.

People who buy financial assets in the hope of increasing their wealth are often referred to as investors. The language is unfortunate, because the purchase of existing stocks, bonds, and real estate does not constitute investment in the sense of Chapter 17. Economists generally reserve the word *investment* to describe the creation of new factors of production. Nevertheless, we will bow to popular usage and refer to the purchaser of stocks as an "investor."

## Portfolios

**Portfolios**

Combinations of risky assets.

An investor is interested not only in the characteristics of individual stocks, he is also interested in the characteristics of portfolios, or combinations of several stocks. In order to compare the characteristics of a portfolio with those of the stocks it comprises, let us consider some examples.

Exhibit 18.11 displays the characteristics of three stocks, each now selling for $10. The stocks are General Air-Conditioning (GAC), General Surfboards (GSB), and General Snowshoes (GSS). The value of each stock tomorrow depends on the state of the world. Either an ice age begins or it doesn't. Exhibit 18.11 shows what will happen to each stock in each state of the world. It also shows the expected return and the standard deviation for each stock, computed on the probability of an ice age is .50.

For each stock the expected return is the average of the returns in the two states of the world, and the standard deviation (σ) is equal to the absolute value of the difference between the expected return and either of the possible actual returns. For instance, the possible returns to General Surfboards are −40% and 120%. The average of these is 40%, which is the expected return. The possible returns of −40% and 120% differ from

---

| EXHIBIT **18.11** | **Expected Returns and Standard Deviations** |
|---|---|

| Stock | Current Value | Value If Ice Age Comes | Value If No Ice Age Comes | Expected Return | σ |
|---|---|---|---|---|---|
| General Air-Conditioning (GAC) | $10 | $5 (Return = −50%) | $25 (Return = 150%) | 50% | 100% |
| General Surfboards (GSB) | 10 | 6 (Return = −40%) | 22 (Return = 120%) | 40 | 80 |
| General Snowshoes (GSS) | 10 | 25 (Return = 150%) | 5 (Return = −50%) | 50 | 100 |

The table displays the characteristics of three hypothetical stocks. There is a 50% chance of an ice age beginning tomorrow, and each stock's value tomorrow depends on whether the ice age actually arrives. For each stock the expected return is the average of the two possible returns. For each stock the standard deviation is the absolute value of the difference between its return if the ice age arrives and its expected return.

the expected return of 40% by exactly 80% in absolute value, so for General Surfboards $\sigma = 80\%$.

We can now compute the returns and standard deviations on various portfolios. Consider first a portfolio consisting of one share each of GAC and GSB. Such a portfolio has a current value of $20 and could either go down to $11 (the sum of the values of the two stocks if the ice age arrives) or go up to $47 (the sum of the values if the ice age fails to arrive). These outcomes constitute returns of either −45% or +135%. The expected return is 45% and the standard deviation is 90%.

---

**Exercise 18.9** Verify the numbers in the preceding paragraph.

---

If you are rash enough to generalize on the basis of this single example, you might be tempted to conclude that the expected return and standard deviation of a portfolio are computed by taking the average expected return and the average standard deviation of the constituent stocks. If you succumbed to such a temptation, you would be right regarding the expected return, but wrong regarding the standard deviation.

Consider a portfolio consisting of one share each of GAC and GSS. The current value of such a portfolio is $20. In the event of an ice age, its value will be $5 + $25 = $30, and in the event of no ice age, its value will be $25 + $5 = $30. Such a portfolio earns a 50% return with certainty. Its standard deviation is zero.

A portfolio consisting of GAC and GSS is completely diversified. Whenever one of its constituent stocks goes up, the other goes down. As a result, all of the risk is eliminated and $\sigma$ is equal to zero. In general, the standard deviation of a portfolio is given by the average of the standard deviations of the individual stocks, *minus* a correction term for any diversification that takes place. Because of this correction term, we can say:

The standard deviation of a portfolio is *at most* equal to the average standard deviation of the individual stocks.

By contrast:

The expected return to a portfolio is *exactly* equal to the average expected return of the individual stocks.

We have seen an example of a completely undiversified portfolio (GAC and GSB) and of a completely diversified portfolio (GAC and GSS). It is also possible to construct a portfolio that is partially, but not completely, diversified. Consider the portfolio that combines one share of GSB with one share of GSS. This portfolio, initially worth $20, will either go up to $31 or go up to $27. The possible returns are 55% and 35%. The expected return is 45% (the average of the expected returns on the two stocks). The standard deviation is 10%, much less than the average of the standard deviations on the two stocks, but still not zero because the diversification is not complete.

## The Geometry of Portfolios

Any individual stock, and any portfolio, can be represented by a point in a diagram, as in Exhibit 18.12. The points labeled *GSB* and *GSS* represent the stocks General Surfboards and General Snowshoes from Exhibit 18.11.

It is possible for two different stocks to occupy the same position in the diagram. GAC is represented by the same point that represents General Snowshoes.

EXHIBIT **18.12** **The Geometry of Portfolios**

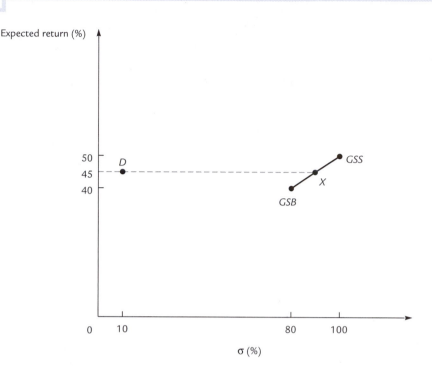

Every stock, and every portfolio, is represented by a point in the diagram. The points *GSS* and *GSB* represent General Snowshoes and General Surfboards, which are described in Exhibit 18.11.

The point *X*, which is midway between the stocks *GSS* and *GSB*, represents an asset with the average of their expected returns and the average of their standard deviations. The portfolio containing *GSS* and *GSB* has the average expected return but a smaller standard deviation. Thus, it is represented by a point directly to the left of *X*, namely, *D*.

There is a geometric construction of the portfolio that combines two given stocks. Consider the portfolio consisting of GSB and GSS. We begin by locating the midpoint of the line segment that connects the stocks. That point is labeled *X* in Exhibit 18.12. It represents a portfolio with the average of the two expected returns and the average of the two standard deviations. Because there is some diversification, the portfolio's standard deviation is less than the average of the two stocks' standard deviations. Thus, the portfolio is represented by a point some distance to the left of *X*. The size of the leftward shift depends on the amount of diversification. In this case we find that the combined portfolio is located at point *D*.

**Exercise 18.10** What point represents the portfolio consisting of GAC and GSS?

Two portfolios can be combined to make a new portfolio, using the same geometric prescription that is used to combine two stocks.

## The Efficient Set

In panel A of Exhibit 18.13 there are hypothetical dots representing all of the stocks that might be available at a given time. The shaded area represents all of the available portfolios. Any available stock must be in the shaded region, because one can always

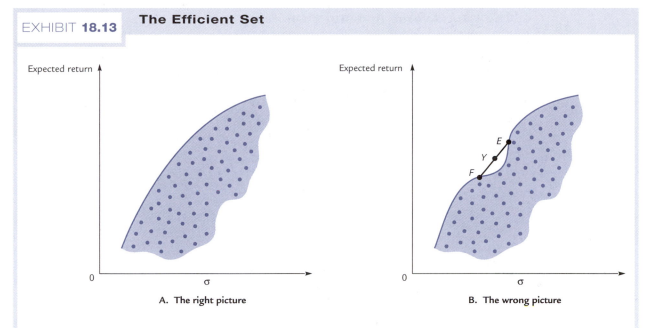

EXHIBIT **18.13**    **The Efficient Set**

The dots represent the stocks available in the marketplace, and the shaded region represents all of the portfolios that can be constructed from those stocks. The picture must look like panel A and cannot look like panel B. In panel B the portfolio that combines portfolios *E* and *F* must be located at *Y* or to the left of *Y*, where the picture shows no portfolios. Therefore, the picture is wrong.

In panel A, which is the correct picture, the northwest boundary of the shaded region is the efficient set. No risk-averse investor would choose a portfolio that is not in the efficient set.

hold a portfolio consisting of that stock alone. We have also darkened the northwest boundary of the shaded region.

It is no accident that the northwest boundary is shaped as it is. Panel B suggests another shape, which we shall argue is impossible. If the boundary were shaped as in panel B, then there would be portfolios represented by points *E* and *F*. Combining these portfolios yields a new portfolio, which must be represented either by point Y or by some point to its left. Some such point must therefore be in the shaded region, which is not true. Therefore, the shape depicted in panel B is impossible.

The northwest boundary of the shaded region in Exhibit 18.13 is called the **efficient set,** or the set of **efficient portfolios.** These are the only portfolios that a risk-averse individual would ever hold. The reason is that from any other point in the shaded region the investor can always move either upward (increasing expected returns) or to the left (decreasing risk) or both. Because both upward and leftward movements are desirable to the risk-averse investor, he would never remain at a point that was off the efficient set.

**Efficient set**

The northwest boundary of the set of all portfolios.

**Efficient portfolio**

A portfolio in the efficient set.

## The Investor's Choice

Because the risk-averse investor views expected return as a "good" and standard deviation as a "bad," his preferences among portfolios are represented by indifference curves such as those shown in Exhibit 18.14. He chooses among the portfolios in the efficient set (also shown) so as to be on the highest possible indifference curve (in this case "highest" means "most northwesterly"). That is, he will pick the portfolio where the efficient set is tangent to an indifference curve, as at point *P* in Exhibit 18.14.

## EXHIBIT 18.14 The Risk-Averse Investor's Choice

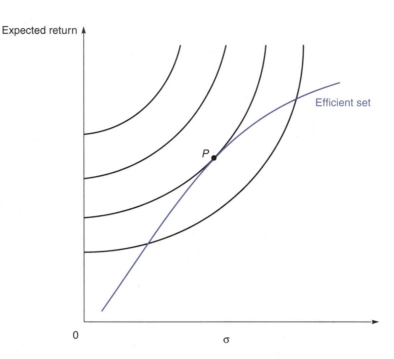

Expected return

Efficient set

P

0        σ

Because the risk-averse investor views expected return as good and standard deviation as bad, his indifference curves are shaped as shown. Of the portfolios in the efficient set, this investor selects the one on the "highest" (most northwesterly) indifference curve, which is at the tangency P.

Dangerous Curve

In practice, "choosing" portfolio P is not as easy as we have made it sound. Even though we know that some portfolio has the expected return and standard deviation associated with point P in Exhibit 18.14, actually constructing that portfolio—determining the particular combination of stocks from which it is built—can require considerable skill. For this reason, investors often find it in their interest to hire a professional *portfolio manager* to help them construct the portfolio they have chosen.

**Capital asset pricing model**

A model that assumes that investors care only about expected return and risk, where risk is measured by standard deviation.

In asserting that the investor will choose point P, we have assumed that expected return and standard deviation are the only characteristics of his portfolio that concern him. Conceivably, he could be concerned with other, more subtle, statistical features as well. Suppose that portfolio A could return −6%, −2%, 0%, 2%, or 6%, all with equal probability. Portfolio B could return −4% or 4%, each with equal probability. Both portfolios have the same expected return (0%) and the same standard deviation (4%). (If you know the precise definition of standard deviation, you should check this.) Therefore, both portfolios occupy the same position in the graph of Exhibit 18.14. Consequently, the theory embodied in that graph must assume that the investor is indifferent between these two portfolios.

The assumption that the investor cares only about expected return and standard deviation is the key assumption of the **capital asset pricing model,** which is often used to study markets for risky assets. A body of empirical evidence indicates that this assumption is not far wrong. We will continue to pursue its implications.

## Introduction of a Risk-Free Asset

Suppose now that in addition to all of the stocks shown in Exhibit 18.13, a risk-free asset is available. It is often asserted that U.S. Treasury bills constitute such an asset (but see the end of Section 17.1 for some contrary evidence). Whatever this risk-free asset might be, it is represented by a point on the vertical axis, like $R$ in Exhibit 18.15.

Let us see what happens when the risk-free asset is combined with a portfolio of stocks. Suppose that an investor holds half of his wealth in the form of stock portfolio $A$ and half in the form of the risk-free asset $R$. Then his overall portfolio is represented by the point $X$, midway between $A$ and $R$. (A risk-free asset cannot contribute to diversification, so the combined portfolio is represented by $X$ rather than some point to the left of $X$.) Similarly, if the investor holds three-fourths of his wealth in portfolio $A$ and one-fourth in the risk-free asset $R$, then his overall portfolio is represented by the point $Y$, three-fourths of the way along the line from $R$ to $A$.

In general, the investor can achieve any point along the line segment from $R$ to $A$ by combining portfolio $A$ with the risk-free asset. Similarly, he can achieve any point along the line segment from $R$ to $B$, or from $R$ to any other existing portfolio. The uppermost of these line segments, connecting $R$ with $M$, contains the most desirable combinations.

Under some circumstances, the investor can move past $M$ along the same line. This is possible when he can hold a *negative* amount of the risk-free asset $R$. For example, if

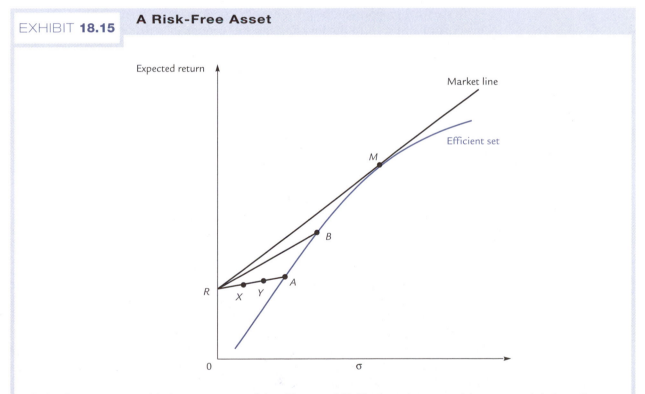

**EXHIBIT 18.15**    **A Risk-Free Asset**

Point $R$ represents a risk-free asset, possibly a Treasury bill. The investor can achieve any point along the illustrated line segments by combining $R$ with portfolios such as $A$, $B$, and $M$. For example, combining $R$ and $A$ in equal amounts yields point $X$. The line connecting $R$ and $M$ contains the most desirable possibilities; it is called the market line. If $R$ can be held in negative amounts (say by borrowing), then it is possible to move beyond point $M$ along the market line. No investor would ever want to be off the market line. Therefore, every investor wants to hold a portfolio consisting partly of $R$ and partly of a market portfolio $M$.

**Market line**

The line through a risk-free asset and tangent to the efficient set.

**Market portfolio**

The point of tangency between the market line and the efficient set.

$R$ is a Treasury bill and if the investor is able to borrow at the Treasury bill rate, then such borrowing is equivalent to holding a *negative quantity of Treasury bills.* (*Borrowing* equals *selling bonds* equals buying bonds in negative quantities.) Assuming that this is possible, the investor can achieve any point along the line passing through $R$ and $M$. This line is called the market line.

The market line is the line through $R$ that is just tangent to the efficient set. The market portfolio is the portfolio represented by the point where the market line touches the efficient set. In Exhibit 18.15 point $M$ represents the market portfolio.

There might be more than one market portfolio, since several portfolios can occupy the same position in the graph.

With the availability of the risk-free asset, an investor is no longer restricted to the old efficient set. He can reach any point on the market line by holding an appropriate combination of risk-free assets and shares of the market portfolio. These options are always preferable to points on the efficient set. For example, an investor holding portfolio $A$ in Exhibit 18.15 could move either directly upward to the market line, increasing his expected return, or directly leftward to the market line, decreasing his risk.

Investors choose only points on the market line. Points on the market line are obtained by combining the risk-free asset $R$ with the market portfolio $M$. Therefore,

A rational investor always holds a portfolio that combines the risk-free asset with the market portfolio in some proportions.

To see what proportions the investor will choose, we must examine his indifference curves. In Exhibit 18.16 the investor chooses proportions that enable him to reach point $Q$.

## Constructing a Market Portfolio

What happens if we create a giant portfolio consisting of all of the risky assets in the economy? Because every asset is held by somebody, this is the same thing as adding up all of the individual investors' portfolios. Because each investor holds a market portfolio at point $M$ in Exhibit 18.15, we are adding up many portfolios, all at point $M$. The result must be a portfolio at $M$, or a portfolio to the left of $M$ if there is further diversification. But we see from Exhibit 18.15 that there are no portfolios to the left of $M$. It follows that our giant portfolio is itself at point $M$. In other words,

A portfolio that consists of all of the risky assets in the economy, held in proportion to their existing quantities, must be a market portfolio.

The individual investor wants to hold a combination of two assets: the risk-free asset and a market portfolio. But how is he to construct a market portfolio? Actually, we have just described one: the portfolio consisting of all of the assets in the economy. An individual investor can hold a miniaturized copy of this portfolio by holding all of the risky assets in proportion to their existing quantities. By choosing an appropriate mix of this particular market portfolio and the risk-free asset, he can reach point $Q$ in Exhibit 18.16, which is his individual optimum.

Unfortunately, practical considerations prevent the investor from really holding all of the risky assets in proportion to their existing quantities. A shopping center in Dubuque, Iowa, might represent a .0001% share of the nation's economy. It is unrealistic to suggest that .0001% of an investor's portfolio should consist of shares in this shopping center. Typically, practical considerations make it necessary for an investor to approximate the market portfolio with a very small number of assets. To some extent

## EXHIBIT 18.16 — The Investor's Choice Revisited

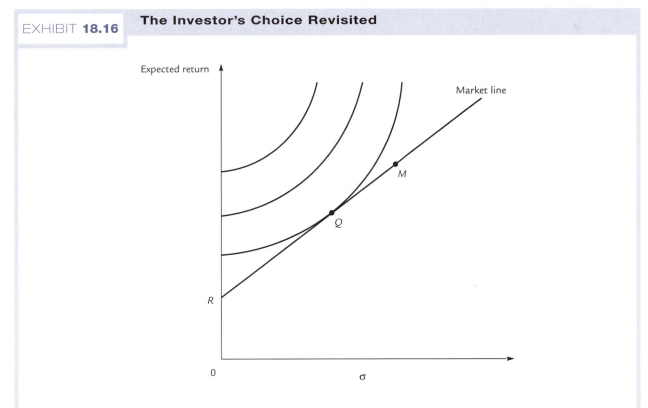

When there is a risk-free asset, the investor is no longer restricted to the old efficient set. He can now reach any point on the market line by combining the risk-free asset with the market portfolio in appropriate proportions. This investor chooses proportions that enable him to reach point Q.

The investor can never do better than to be on the market line. Thus, his portfolio of risky assets will always be the market portfolio. There is never any reason to hold any other portfolio of risky assets.

he can alleviate this problem by holding shares in mutual funds that in turn hold shares in a large and highly diversified collection of assets. Also, the services of a portfolio manager can be helpful.

# 18.5 Rational Expectations

In this section, we will examine how prices are set in a market where suppliers have to make decisions in the face of uncertain demand. We will discover that equilibrium prices depend very much on the way in which suppliers form their expectations. We will also discover an important reason why economists studying such markets are liable to make predictions that are drastically wrong.

## A Market with Uncertain Demand

Suppose that lettuce is sold in a central marketplace. Each day lettuce farmers must decide how much lettuce to load onto their trucks and bring to the market. If they knew what the price was going to be, this decision would be easy. They would simply bring lettuce until the marginal cost of supplying another head was equal to the price. Unfortunately, demand, and therefore price, fluctuates from day to day. The best that farmers can do is to form an *expectation* of the price. The amount they bring to market on a given day is given by an upward-sloping "supply curve," as shown in panel A of Exhibit 18.17. The difference between this curve and a true supply curve is that in this case the vertical axis measures not price, but expected price, which we denote by the symbol $P_E$.

When the farmers actually arrive at the marketplace, the supply curve for lettuce is vertical. The quantity of lettuce is equal to what the farmers have irrevocably decided to bring with them, and all of the lettuce must be sold or it will rot. The location of the vertical supply curve depends on the farmers' expectation of price at the time they start out in the morning. According to Exhibit 18.17, if the farmers expect a price of $1, the supply is 200 heads of lettuce; if they expect a price of $2, the supply is 400 heads, and so forth. Panel B of the exhibit shows the curve from panel A together with the various possible vertical supply curves, each labeled with the corresponding expected price.

Panel B of Exhibit 18.17 also shows the demand curve for lettuce on a particular day. The market price depends both on the location of this demand curve and on what expectation the farmers have when they start out. If the farmers expect a price of $2, they bring 400 heads of lettuce to market and the actual price is $4. If they expect a price of $4, they bring 800 heads and the actual price is $2. If they expect a price of $3, they bring 600 heads and the actual price is $3. Only in this last case does the farmers' expectation prove to be correct.

EXHIBIT **18.17**    **Expectations and Supply**

The curve in panel A shows how much lettuce the farmers bring to market at each expected price. It is like a supply curve, except that it depends on expected price rather than actual price. When the farmers arrive at the market, the supply curve is vertical. The position of the vertical supply curve depends on the farmers' expectation of the price. Panel B shows the supply curve from panel A superimposed on several possible vertical supply curves. The actual price depends on the expected price (which determines the vertical supply curve) and the actual demand.

**Exercise 18.11** What is the actual price of lettuce if the farmers expect a price of $1? If they expect a price of $5?

Each day demand is different. Suppose, for example, that the curves $D_1$ and $D_2$ in Exhibit 18.18 represent the lower and upper limits of demand. Some days demand is as low as $D_1$, some days it is as high as $D_2$, and on the average day it is given by the demand curve $D_{Average}$ between them. If farmers consistently expect a price of $1, they will find that the actual price is sometimes as low as $4, sometimes as high as $6, and about $5 on the average day. In other words, they will consistently find that their predictions are drastically wrong.

**Exercise 18.12** Explain how farmers' expectations are confounded if they consistently expect a price of $5.

Now, farmers are not omniscient; nobody expects them to make correct predictions all the time. But farmers are not foolish either, and when their predictions are consistently off in a systematic way, we expect them to revise those predictions. Farmers who expect a price of $1 will consistently find that they have underestimated, and therefore they will not persist in their belief.

EXHIBIT **18.18**  **Rational Expectations**

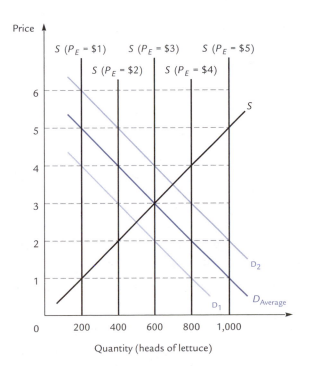

Demand fluctuates between $D_1$ and $D_2$; it is $D_{Average}$ on the average day. If farmers expect lettuce to sell at $1, they bring 200 heads of lettuce to market and the price on the average day is $5 (where $D_{Average}$, crosses the quantity 200). The farmers' expectation is systematically wrong.
    If, on the other hand, the farmers expect lettuce to sell at $3, they bring 600 heads of lettuce to market and the price on the average day is $3. Thus, the expectation of a $3 price is correct on average; we say that it is a rational expectation.

A similar argument can be made about any expected price except for an expected price of $3. If farmers expect a price of $3, then the price will be as low as $2 some days, as high as $4 other days, and $3 on average. Farmers will have no reason to revise their expectations either upward or downward. In this case we say that the farmers have **rational expectations.**

An expectation is rational when it does not lead to systematic, correctable errors in prediction. Nevertheless, a rational expectation is not always, nor even usually, a correct expectation. In our example the price might be $2 half of the time and $4 half of the time, in which case the rational expectation of $3 will *never* be correct.

Geometrically, the rational expectation occurs where the average day's demand curve crosses the farmers' upward-sloping supply curve.

**Rational expectations**

Expectations that, when held by market participants, lead to behavior that fulfills those expectations on average.

## Why Economists Make Wrong Predictions

Now let us embellish our model by making an assumption about why demand fluctuates. Suppose that the demand for lettuce is strictly determined by the income of the local lumberjacks. Exhibit 18.19 shows some possible demand curves. When the lumberjacks earn $100, the demand curve is $D_{100}$; when they earn $150, it is $D_{150}$, and so on. Let us also assume that on the average day lumberjacks earn $150.

If the farmers have rational expectations, they always expect a price of $3, which is correct on the average day. Thus, they always bring 600 heads of lettuce to market. The actual price on any given day is perfectly predictable on the basis of the lumberjacks' income. When the lumberjacks earn $100, the price of lettuce is $2; when the lumberjacks earn $150, the price is $3; and so on.

---

**Exercise 18.13** What is the price of lettuce when the lumberjacks' income is $200? When it is $250? When it is $300?

---

**Exercise 18.14** Suppose that the lumberjacks' income averaged $250. What would be the rational expectation of the price of lettuce? How many heads of lettuce would farmers bring to the market? What would be the actual price when the lumberjacks earned $100? When they earned $200? When they earned $300?

---

Suppose now that an econometrician comes to study this market. He is pleased to discover that he can predict the price of lettuce on the basis of the lumberjacks' income, as detailed in the preceding paragraph. He might even be so bold as to summarize his knowledge in an equation:

$$\text{Price of lettuce} = \frac{1}{50} \times \text{Lumberjack's income}$$

For example, because the lumberjacks earn $150 on average days, the price of lettuce is $1/50 \times \$150 = \$3$ on average days, which is correct.

One day a paper mill is built in the area. The owners of the mill announce that they will be purchasing a lot of lumber. As a result, the lumberjacks' income will now average $250 per day. What does the econometrician predict about the price of lettuce?

Drawing on past experience, the econometrician knows that lumberjack income of $250 implies a lettuce price of $5. Thus, he predicts that the price of lettuce will now be $5 on the average day.

EXHIBIT **18.19**    **Lumberjacks' Income and the Price of Lettuce**

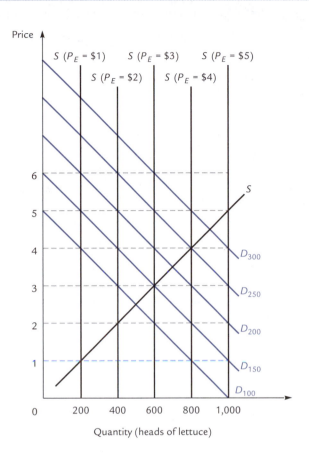

The demand curve for lettuce depends on the lumberjacks' income. When their income is $100, the demand curve is $D_{100}$; when their income is $150, the demand curve is $D_{150}$; and so on. Initially, the lumberjacks earn $150 on average. Thus, the rational expectation of the price is $3 (where $D_{150}$ crosses the upward-sloping supply curve), so farmers supply 600 heads of lettuce. When the lumberjacks really do earn $150, the rational expectation is fulfilled. On days when the lumberjacks earn $250, the price of lettuce is $5.

Now a paper mill arrives, raising the lumberjacks' income to $250 on average. The new rational expectation for the price is $4. Farmers bring 800 heads of lettuce to market. On an average day the lumberjacks earn $250 and the price of lettuce is $4.

An econometrician extrapolating from past experience would predict that on days when the lumberjacks earn $250, the price of lettuce is $5. Thus, he would predict that when the paper mill arrives, the price of lettuce will go up to $5 on average. But he is wrong, because past experience is no longer relevant. When farmers have rational expectations, the additional lettuce that they bring to market invalidates the old relationship between the lumberjacks' income and the price of lettuce.

But what actually happens? By examining Exhibit 18.19, you can see that the new rational-expectations price of lettuce is $4 (where supply crosses the new average demand curve $D_{250}$). Farmers now bring 800 heads of lettuce to market each day. When the lumberjacks earn $250, on the average day the price of lettuce is $4, not $5 as the econometrician predicted.

Where did the econometrician go wrong? All past experience supports his equation. It has always been true in the past that on days when the lumberjacks earn $250, the price of lettuce is \$5. What happened is that the arrival of the paper mill caused farmers to change their expectations and bring a different amount of lettuce to market. This, in turn, invalidated the econometrician's equation. The correct new equation is:

$$\text{Price of lettuce} = \left(\frac{1}{50} \times \text{Lumberjack's income}\right) - \$1$$

---

**Exercise 18.15** Suppose that a tree disease reduces the lumberjacks' average income to \$100. What is the new equation for the price of lettuce?

---

### Example - Tweedledum and Tweedledee

Tweedledum and Tweedledee have identical skills and have therefore always had identical incomes. In years when their skills are in demand, their incomes are both high, and at other times their incomes are both low. An econometrician, having carefully collected data, can confidently assert the truth of the equation

$$\text{Tweedledee's income} = \text{Tweedledum's income}$$

If he can observe Tweedledum's income, the econometrician can use his equation to predict Tweedledee's income, and he will always be right.

One day Tweedledee hired just such an econometrician to advise him on how to increase his income. The econometrician, having discovered the preceding equation, advised Tweedledee, "It's simple. Your income is always the same as Tweedledum's income, so if you want your income to rise, just give all of your money to Tweedledum." Tweedledee tried it, but it didn't work.

This simple example illustrates that even when equations predict very well, they can be entirely useless as guides to policy. The reason is that changes in policy can invalidate the equations.[4] The equality between Tweedledee's and Tweedledum's incomes existed for a *reason;* because their incomes were derived from selling identical skills in the marketplace. The econometrician's suggestion leads to behavior that eliminates this reason for equality, and as a result the equality itself disappears.

Similarly, we can imagine the econometrician of the preceding subsection advising farmers to try to attract a paper mill to the area, promising that the price of lettuce will rise to \$5. When it rises to only \$4, the farmers are disappointed, just like Tweedledee. Again the reason is that the policy change eliminates the reason underlying the validity of the very equation that was used to justify the policy change.

The example of Tweedledee and Tweedledum illustrates that this problem with policy evaluation can occur even in exceptionally simple examples. The lumberjacks/lettuce example illustrates that the problem is particularly likely to arise in the presence of rational expectations, because changes in policy lead to changes in those expectations and hence to changes in behavior.

Rational expectations play a central and exciting role in modern macroeconomics, although they are fundamentally a microeconomic concept.[5] Two important areas of research are the attempt to understand the ways in which econometricians can be led

---

[4] This point was made forcefully in R. E. Lucas, Jr., "Econometric Policy Evaluation: A Critique," in *The Phillips Curve and Labor Markets,* vol. 1 of *Carnegie-Rochester Conference Series on Public Policy,* Karl Brunner and Allan H. Meltzer, eds. (Amsterdam: North Holland, 1976), pp. 19–46.

[5] Rational expectations were introduced by the economist John Muth to study problems in agricultural economics.

astray in their predictions and the development of new econometric techniques that are appropriate for studying markets in which expectations are rational.

# Summary

In many cases an individual's wealth depends on the state of the world. It is possible to transfer income from one state of the world to another in a variety of ways. The gambler who bets that a tossed coin will turn up heads transfers income from the state of the world in which tails comes up to the state of the world in which heads comes up. The homeowner who buys fire insurance transfers income from the state of the world in which his house is undamaged to the state of the world in which his house burns down. The investor who buys a share of stock in a company that makes digital tapes transfers income from the state of the world in which digital tape technology is unsuccessful in the marketplace to the state of the world in which digital tapes completely replace compact discs.

There are thus many ways that an individual can distribute his income across states of the world. We can draw indifference curves to illustrate his preferences among these distributions. The indifference curves depend both on the consumer's tastes and on the probabilities of the various states of the world.

A risk-neutral individual is one who always chooses the lottery with the highest expected value, without regard to risk. We expect a frequent gambler to be risk-neutral, since his good and bad luck wash out over time. For someone who is risk-neutral, the indifference curves are straight lines whose absolute slope is the ratio of the probabilities of the states of the world. When he is offered the opportunity to gamble at fair odds, the risk-neutral person is indifferent among all of the opportunities on his budget line. When offered the opportunity to gamble at favorable odds, he will always bet everything he has.

In many situations we expect people to be risk-averse. Among baskets with the same expected value, a risk-averter always chooses the one with no risk, that is, the one on the 45° line. Thus, at points along the 45° line the risk-averter's indifference curves have an absolute slope that reflects the fair betting odds. When offered the opportunity to bet at favorable odds, the risk-averter always accepts a small wager, but never a large one. Usually, an increase in income will increase the size of the largest wager that the risk-averter will accept at given odds.

Many markets exist to facilitate the transfer of risk across individuals. One is the market for insurance. In a world of perfect information, much insurance would be offered at fair odds (except for a slight tilting in favor of the insurance company to allow it to cover its costs). However, there are important reasons why we do not observe this practice. Among these are moral hazard and adverse selection, which were introduced in Chapter 9. Another problem is that some risks are undiversifiable, hence uninsurable.

The futures market is another market for transferring risk. It enables farmers to reduce their risks by contracting now for the prices of future deliveries. It also creates the opportunity for speculation, which is welfare-improving when speculators are right and detrimental to welfare when speculators are wrong.

The stock market is yet another market for trading risky assets. In addition to individual stocks, investors can hold portfolios, created by combining various stocks in different proportions. The portfolio consisting of two stocks in equal proportions has the average expected return of the two but may have less than their average standard deviation (riskiness), because of diversification.

By combining the market portfolio (which consists of all of the risky assets in the economy held in proportion to their actual quantities) with a risk-free asset, the investor can create a portfolio that is superior to any other given portfolio in terms of risk and expected return. Thus, the only portfolio of risky assets that an investor would ever want to hold is the market portfolio. In practice, however, it is necessary to approximate this portfolio, which can require considerable expertise.

When there is uncertainty about the future, people may form rational expectations, which are expectations that are correct on the average day. If there is a change in circumstances, such as the arrival of a new industry or a change in some government policy, then the rational expectations may change, and consequently so may people's behavior. As a result, equations that have always predicted accurately in the past may prove drastically wrong following a policy change.

# Author Commentary     www.cengage.com/economics/landsburg

**AC1.** What is the best way to deter crime: with *harsher* punishments or with *more certain* punishments? The theory of risk aversion supplies the answer.

**AC2.** See this article for a challenge to the theory that attitudes toward risk vary with income.

**AC3.** This article also challenges risk theory.

**AC4.** For investors, the optimal portfolio is highly diversified. For charitable givers, exactly the opposite is true. For the reasons, see this article.

**AC5.** For another aspect of portfolio diversification, read this article.

# Review Questions

**R1.** Describe the indifference curves of (a) a person who is risk-neutral, (b) a person who is risk-averse, and (c) a person who is risk-preferring.

**R2.** Under what circumstances might a person be expected to be risk-neutral? Why is a firm more likely to be risk-neutral than an individual?

**R3.** Explain why the stockholders and the executives of a corporation might have different preferences with regard to the corporation's behavior toward risk. Describe some possible remedies and their pros and cons.

**R4.** What is moral hazard? Give some examples.

**R5.** What is adverse selection? Give some examples.

**R6.** Describe a possible equilibrium in an insurance market with adverse selection. In what sense is it suboptimal?

**R7.** What is an uninsurable risk? Give some examples.

**R8.** Explain what a futures contract is. How can a farmer or the owner of a grain elevator use futures contracts to eliminate risk?

**R9.** Explain what happens to the current and future supply of wheat when a speculator expects the price to fall. In what circumstances is this socially beneficial?

**R10.** What is the efficient set of portfolios? Explain why it is shaped as it is.

**R11.** Explain why the market portfolio is the only portfolio of risky assets that any investor would want to hold.

**R12.** What determines the daily equilibrium price in a market where demand fluctuates and suppliers have rational expectations?

**R13.** Explain how the arrival of a paper mill can cause a change in the relationship between lumberjacks' income and the price of lettuce.

# Problem Set

1. According to Dr. Johnson, "He is no wise man who will quit a certainty for an uncertainty." Comment.

2. **True or False:** If nothing is worth dying for, then going to war is irrational.

3. Whenever John is offered the opportunity to take either side of a bet in which the odds are even slightly unfair, he invariably does bet something. **True or False:** John is certainly not risk-averse.

4. Jill likes to bet on heads when the odds are fair, but will bet on tails only if offered very favorable odds. Draw her indifference curves.

5. **True or False:** A risk-preferring person will always bet, no matter how much the odds are against him.

6. Bookmakers organize betting on football games in the following way: First, they determine a "point spread" that one team is expected to beat with 50-50 probability. Then bettors are allowed to bet on whether the team will beat the spread. They may take either side of the bet and are offered slightly unfavorable odds either way. Show the budget line faced by the bettors. What will a risk-averse bettor do in these circumstances? What will a risk-preferring bettor do? Can you think of any reason why a risk averter might still bet?

7. **True or False:** If "sickly" people could insure against illness at the same rates available to healthy people, they would end up preferring illness to good health.

8. **True or False:** Speculators are less harmful to society than they at first appear, because they sometimes err in forecasting the future and their losses due to these errors compensate the rest of us for their gains when they are right.

9. Suppose that it is known for certain that the demand for wheat this year is identical to the demand for wheat next year. This year's wheat crop of 100 tons has just been harvested. Everybody believes that next year's wheat crop, which has already been planted, will also be 100 tons. Now a speculator arrives on the scene, convinced that next year's crop will be only 80 tons.

a. If wheat can be stored costlessly, what will the speculator do? What happens to this year's wheat supply and to next year's? (If it helps you, assume an interest rate of 0%.)

b. How long does the speculator continue this activity? What is this year's wheat supply when he is finished? What is next year's wheat supply when he is finished if he turns out to be right? What is it if he turns out to be wrong?

c. Use a graph to show the social gains with and without a speculator, on the assumption that the speculator is right. If he is right, does he improve social welfare?

d. Use a graph to show the social gains with and without a speculator, on the assumption that the speculator is wrong. If he is wrong, does he improve social welfare?

10. **True or False:** Nobody would ever hold a stock that was below the efficient set, since there is always an alternative with less risk or greater expected return.

11. Suppose that exactly half of all terrorists who take hostages kill their hostages. The government is considering a new policy under which all terrorist kidnappings will be met with massive military force intended to kill the kidnapper immediately. Unfortunately, it is estimated that in 90% of cases, the victim will die in the assault. **True or False:** Obviously, one drawback of this plan is that more hostages will die.

12. In New York State, the drinking age is 18. Studies show that 18-year-old drivers have a much higher crash rate than do 16- and 17-year-olds. The same studies indicate that if the drinking age were raised to 19, 30% of all crashes by 18-year-olds could be prevented, saving 25 to 35 lives per year. The *New York Times* has editorialized that the drinking age should be raised to 19, as 25 to 35 lives would be well worth saving. Assuming that all of the numbers in the studies are correct, comment on the *Times's* assertion that raising the drinking age would save 25 to 35 lives per year.

13. Suppose that in reality the number of cars demanded, $Q$, depends on the real interest rate, $r$, according to an equation of the form

$$Q = Ar + B$$

where A and B are constants. An econometrician believes that the number of cars demanded depends on the *nominal* interest rate, i, and uses data to estimate the coefficients C and D in the equation

$$Q = Ci + B$$

a. Express the estimated coefficients $C$ and $D$ in terms of the "true" coefficients $A$ and $B$ and the inflation rate, $\pi$.

b. Explain why this model will make good predictions as long as the inflation rate is constant.

c. Suppose that it is considered desirable to raise the demand for cars and that the government can affect $i$ by adopting policies that lead to a change in $\pi$. What will the econometrician advise?

d. When the new policy is adopted, what happens to $C$ and $D$? Explain why the recommended policy won't work.

# CHAPTER 19

# What Is Economics?

## 19.1 The Nature of Economic Analysis

Economics is one of several sciences that attempt to explain and predict human behavior. It is distinguished from the other behavioral sciences (psychology, anthropology, sociology, and political science) by its emphasis on rational decision making under conditions of scarcity. Economists generally assume that people have well-defined goals and preferences and that they allocate their limited resources so as to maximize their own well-being in accordance with those preferences.

### Stages of Economic Analysis

Much of economic analysis can be divided into three stages. First, we make explicit assumptions about people's goals and about the constraints on their behavior. This allows us to formulate an economic problem: Within the limits imposed by the constraints, what is the best way to achieve the goals? Second, we determine the solutions to these problems, and we see how the solutions vary in response to changes in the constraints. We assume that the individuals under study can also solve their economic problems and that they behave accordingly. We describe this by saying that the individuals *optimize*. Third, we examine the interactions among individuals: Each person's behavior affects each other person's constraints. In view of these interactions, we are often able to conclude that there is only one possible outcome in which all individuals are simultaneously optimizing. Such an outcome is called an *equilibrium*.

We shall now examine each of these stages in more detail.

### Formulating the Individual's Economic Problem

The first step in economic analysis is to make explicit assumptions about individuals' desires and the nature of the constraints that they face. For example, we assume that a consumer has indifference curves that are convex toward the origin and must select a market basket that is within his budget line. Or we assume that a competitive firm wants to maximize profits and must sell its output and purchase its inputs at fixed market prices. Or we assume that a worker views both leisure and consumption as desirable but can consume no more than he earns in the marketplace.

Each of the agents in these examples faces an economic problem: a choice among competing alternatives. The consumer can eat more eggs and drink less wine, or he can eat fewer eggs and drink more wine, but once he has allocated his entire income he cannot have more of both. The firm can reduce its costs by cutting back production, but it must accept a reduction in revenues as the consequence if it does. The worker can earn more income, or he can improve his suntan, but he must choose between the two.

The problem of an economic actor is to decide how to allocate scarce resources among competing ends. Such tradeoffs can always be expressed in terms of *costs,* which is another word for forgone opportunities. The cost of eating an egg is forgoing some amount of wine, the cost of increasing a firm's revenues is (at least partly) measured by the price of inputs, the cost of a day's wages is a forgone day at the beach. Therefore, we can say that the first step in economic analysis is to make explicit assumptions about both the desirability and the cost of various alternatives.

## Optimization

The second step in economic analysis is to solve the agent's economic problem. The solution can typically be expressed in terms of the crucial principle of *equimarginality:* If an activity is worth pursuing at all, then it should be pursued until the marginal cost is equal to the marginal benefit. The consumer should buy eggs until the marginal value of an additional egg is equal to the marginal value of the wine that he could trade it for. (This is another way of saying that he should move along his budget line until it is just tangent to an indifference curve.) The firm should produce until its marginal cost is equal to its marginal revenue. It should select an input combination that equates the marginal product of a dollar's worth of labor to the marginal product of a dollar's worth of capital. The worker should relax until the marginal cost in forgone wages is equal to the marginal benefit of relaxation—or, in other words, he should work until the marginal income from working is equal to the marginal cost in forgone leisure.

The economist assumes that people act according to the principle of equimarginality. This is often expressed by saying that the economist assumes that people are *rational.* Indeed, it has been said that a student becomes a true economist on the day when he fully understands and accepts the principle that people equate costs and benefits at the margin. In Section 19.2, we will address the question of whether the economist's assumption is a reasonable one. Here we will pursue its consequences.

In addition to solving the individual's optimization problem, the economist also asks how the solution would change if the constraints changed. For example, in modeling a consumer's behavior, the economist notes first that the consumer's optimum occurs at a point where the budget line is tangent to an indifference curve, but he is also interested in how this tangency moves when there is a shift in the budget line due to a change in prices or a change in income. Although the real-world consumer needs to choose only a single consumption basket, the economist imagines how the consumer would behave in a variety of hypothetical circumstances and predicts the basket that the consumer would choose in each situation. The consumer's demand curve is an example of the economist's solution to a family of optimization problems. The demand curve in Exhibit 4.8 shows that *if* the price of X is $6, the consumer's optimal basket will contain 2 units of X; *if* the price is $3, his optimal basket will contain 3 units; and so forth.

A competitive firm's supply curve constitutes another example of how the economist expresses his solutions to a family of optimization problems. The point corresponding to a price of P shows that quantity at which the firm can equate marginal cost with marginal revenue, given that it is constrained to sell at the market price of P. As the constraint (i.e., the price) varies, so does the solution to the problem (i.e., the corresponding quantity).

## Equilibrium

Solving the optimization problem tells the economist how people respond to various constraints. In order to predict their behavior, he must still determine what constraints are actually in force. The key here is that each individual's actions affect the options available to others. One of the constraints faced by a competitive firm is that it cannot sell its wares at a price higher than consumers will pay. That price is determined by the actions of other firms and of the consumers themselves, all of whom are solving their own optimization problems. Those optimization problems, in turn, involve constraints that are partly the result of the original firm's actions.

In Section 18.3, we saw the same thing in a slightly different context: Farmer Brown attempts to maximize profit under conditions of uncertainty; the constraints that he faces are the probabilities associated with various market prices; these constraints are themselves determined by the amount of wheat that other farmers bring to market, in other words, by the solutions to other farmers' optimization problems. And the entire process comes full circle, because the optimization problems faced by the other farmers include constraints that are partly the result of the actions of Farmer Brown.

In some sense the various optimization problems being solved by economic agents must have solutions that are compatible with each other. This requirement, known as an *equilibrium condition,* enables the economist to "solve" his model and make predictions about actual behavior. Consumers choose an optimal basket given the market prices that they face; firms supply a profit-maximizing mix of goods given those same market prices. In order for the quantity demanded by consumers to equal the quantity supplied by firms, prices cannot be arbitrary. In many circumstances there is only one equilibrium price that equates supply and demand.

Economists use many different equilibrium conditions. A *Nash equilibrium* is one in which each individual optimizes, taking the actions of other individuals as his constraints. The prisoners of Exhibit 11.6 achieve a Nash equilibrium when both confess. A *Walrasian equilibrium* is one in which each individual optimizes, taking market prices as given. The supply and demand diagrams of Chapter 1 illustrate Walrasian equilibria.

The third step in most economic analysis is the choice of an equilibrium condition and a study of the resulting equilibria: Do any exist? How many are there? How can they be computed? How will they change in response to changes in exogenous variables? (An *exogenous variable* is one that is taken to be determined outside the economic model under consideration. For example, the tastes of consumers and the technology available to firms are often treated as exogenous variables.[1])

## Other Aspects of Economic Analysis

The economic study of human behavior consists largely of analyzing problems in the way we have just described: First, specify agents' goals and the nature of their constraints; second, solve the corresponding optimization problems (usually employing the equimarginal principle); and third, impose an equilibrium condition to find out what particular constraints agents must be facing and to describe their behavior.

Not all economic analysis can be fit into this simple mold, however. For example, economists are often concerned with modeling the process by which an equilibrium

---

[1] The process of studying how equilibria change in response to changes in exogenous variables is known as *comparative statics.* When you solved problem 11 at the end of Chapter 1, you were performing an exercise in comparative statics.

is achieved. This is known as the study of *economic dynamics*. On the other hand, that process is often most productively viewed as the solution to another, more subtle problem of optimization and equilibrium.

Economics also provides tools for analyzing the desirability of outcomes according to various criteria. The efficiency criterion introduced in Chapter 8 is one of the most popular, but economists can and do consider many other criteria as well.

## The Value of Economic Analysis

In this book you have seen many examples of economic models. What do such models teach us? Some economic models are intended to reflect certain aspects of the world with sufficient accuracy to allow the economist to make precise numerical predictions. Such models are obviously of interest to anyone who must make decisions today that will be appropriate tomorrow. The shoemaker wants to know what the price of shoes will be next week; the policymaker wants to know how a tax on gasoline will affect the price of cars, or how a "comparable worth" law will affect the average size of firms.

Often, economic models are insufficient to make numerical predictions, but they do allow us to predict directions of change. Using the economic models in this book, you can predict that a tax on shoes will raise the price of shoes, reduce the quantity of shoes traded, and reduce economic efficiency. You can also predict a range for the possible price rise (at least zero and no more than the amount of the tax). A more precise model, incorporating more information about the supply and demand curves, would allow a more precise prediction, but even the rough prediction of the simple model is obviously of interest.

There is also a large class of economic models whose assumptions and conclusions are essentially untestable. Consider the Edgeworth box of Chapter 8. We used this box to describe the outcome of a situation in which exactly two people trade exactly two goods and are constrained to use the artificial medium of a price system in doing so. Outside of an experimental laboratory, no such situation would ever be observed.

Why, then, does the Edgeworth box interest us? The answer is that economists are often interested in understanding the outcomes of real-world situations involving bargaining. Many of these situations are far too difficult to model precisely or to think about in their entirety. But an economist who has studied a wide variety of bargaining models develops a strong "seat of the pants" intuition for what *sorts* of things are likely to affect the outcome. After years of studying abstract models—each one abstract in its own way—the economist develops a sense that certain factors matter in certain ways and others don't matter at all. This intuition is the most powerful tool an economist has for understanding the world, but he can only develop it by first understanding simplifications of the world such as the Edgeworth box.

For example, consider the proposition that the economic incidence of a tax is independent of its legal incidence. In Chapter 1, we proved this proposition under certain conditions—markets are competitive, all taxes are either sales or excise taxes, taxes are flat rate (5¢ per cup) as opposed to something more complicated, and so forth. Economists have examined the impact of taxation in a wide variety of models, each with its own special assumptions, and keep getting the same result: The legal incidence of taxation does not matter. Not only does the economist observe the pattern here but he begins to develop an intuition into *why* this result obtains in such a wide variety of circumstances. When the economist is asked to comment on the impact of a complicated taxation scheme in the real world, even though it might be the case that none of his models fits the situation exactly, he can predict with confidence that the legal incidence of the tax is irrelevant. He can do so because he understands why it is irrelevant in his models, and he can see that the same intuition is applicable in the case at hand.

Here is another, more general example: The economist's intuition always reminds him of the importance of incentives. Noneconomists are often skeptical that a rise in the price of gasoline will cause people to drive significantly less, that a tax on labor will reduce employment, or that rent controls will reduce the quantity and quality of housing. The economist knows these things to be true. His knowledge derives largely from his study of models of *other* markets, which have revealed the general principle that incentives matter.

In coming to understand the world by first understanding a potpourri of abstract models, the economist is no different from the physicist or any other scientist. Ask a physicist what will happen to your body if you slam on your brakes while going around a curve at 60 miles per hour. He will tell you, with sufficient accuracy to convince you not to do it. He will do so even if he has never written down or studied the physics of the particular situation you are describing. He is able to do so because he has studied the physics of a large number of models, each of which captures some important aspects of the situation, and has observed the common features of what these models predict. In the process he has developed a feel for the sorts of cause-and-effect relationships that are likely to hold. The kind of knowledge embodied in that "feel" is a large part of any successful science.

# 19.2  The Rationality Assumption

Models start with assumptions. Economic models start with the assumption of rational behavior, usually in the sense that actors accurately solve their optimization problems so as to maximize their well-being within the limits allowed by the constraints (that is, scarcities) with which they must contend. This assumption characterizes economic models. It is perfectly possible to study human behavior productively without assuming rationality, but then one isn't doing economics.

## The Role of Assumptions in Science

Students are sometimes uncomfortable with the assumption of universal rationality. Often they point out that the assumption is clearly false, and they are surprised that their economics professors don't seem particularly concerned about this. But the fact of the matter is that all assumptions made in all sciences are clearly false. Physicists, the most successful of scientists, routinely assume that the table is frictionless when called upon to model the motions of billiard balls. They assume that the billiard balls themselves are solid objects. They assume that objects fall in vacuums. They study the behavior of electric charges that are localized at mathematical points and that interact only with a small number of other charges, as if the rest of the universe did not exist.

All scientists make simplifying assumptions about the world, because the world itself is too complicated to study. All such assumptions are equally false, but not all such assumptions are equally valuable. Certain kinds of assumptions lead consistently to results that are interesting, nonobvious, and at some level testable and verifiable. Other kinds of assumptions do not. In any given problem it is important to make simplifying assumptions of the sort that have proved to be successful in the past. It is usually equally important that the model be *robust;* that is, the exact statements of the assumptions should not enter in a crucial way, so that slightly different assumptions would still lead to the same conclusion.

To a large extent, *learning to be an economist consists of learning to make the right simplifying assumptions.* Indeed, we could replace the word *economist* with *physicist* or *anthropologist* or more generally with *scientist,* and this statement would still be true. Unfortunately, no one has ever succeeded in expressing a set of rules for determining the difference between a good and a bad simplification. You undoubtedly discovered this to your frustration when you began working the problems in this book. Often, the problems require assumptions, and often your assumptions probably seemed as good to you as any others, but your teacher did not agree. If you were successful in the course, you gradually developed a sense for what is and what is not the right approach to a problem. If you go on in economics, you will continue to develop this sense, which is what will make you an economist.

## All We Really Need: No Unexploited Profit Opportunities

The rationality assumption in economics continues to disturb some students at a far more visceral level than the frictionless planes that other sciences assume. It seems plausible that a world without friction could resemble our own world in important ways, but students find it much more difficult to believe that the behavior of perfectly rational individuals could bear much resemblance to the behavior of the people they encounter in their everyday life. (This difficulty is particularly pronounced among students who live in dormitories!)

It is a misconception, however, to believe that a world in which most people are irrational would have to function very differently from a world in which everyone is rational. Imagine a world in which most people are irrational most of the time, but where enough people are rational enough of the time so that there are *no unexploited profit opportunities.* Such a world would function very similarly to one in which everyone is rational. Rather than give a general argument for this proposition, let us examine an illustrative example.

### The Law of One Price

Economists believe in the *law of one price,* which says that identical goods will sell for identical prices (here *identical* means identical in all relevant characteristics, including, for example, time of delivery). It is easy to believe that this law would hold in a world of perfectly rational individuals. But it also holds in a world with no unexploited profit opportunities. Why? Because if you value two identical goods at different prices, your neighbor can make money by selling you one and buying from you the other. In the course of doing this, he and others like him will cause the prices of the goods to change and will keep doing this until all of the profit opportunities have been exploited—that is, until the prices of the goods are equal.

### The Pricing of Call Options

You may think that the law of one price is a very trivial sort of example. Yet it can be applied to solve very nontrivial problems. One example is the pricing of *call options.*

A call option is a piece of paper entitling you to buy a share of some specified stock at some future date for some prespecified price. These pieces of paper are traded in organized markets called *options markets.* Exhibit 19.1 shows an example of a call option.

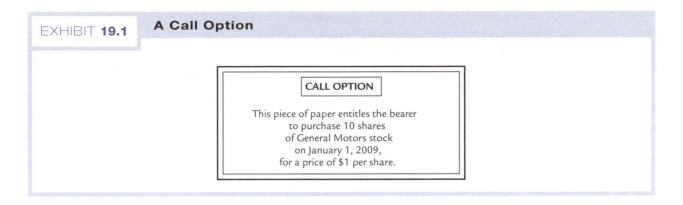

EXHIBIT **19.1**     **A Call Option**

> **CALL OPTION**
>
> This piece of paper entitles the bearer
> to purchase 10 shares
> of General Motors stock
> on January 1, 2009,
> for a price of $1 per share.

Suppose that it is now January 1, 2008, and General Motors stock is selling at $1.00 per share. Suppose also that on January 1, 2009, it will surely be selling for either $.50 per share or $1.50 per share. Suppose finally that the going rate of interest is 25%. How much should you pay for the call option?

The first thing to ask is what the option will be worth a year from today. If the stock goes up $1.50, then your option will enable you to purchase 10 shares (worth $15) for a price of $10; in other words, it will be worth $5. If the stock goes down to $.50, then you will choose not to exercise your option, so that it is worth zero. In Exhibit 19.2 we record the possibilities.

What is the call option worth today? You might suspect that this depends on the probability that the value of the stock will go up. You might think that if the stock is almost certain to go up, then the option is worth nearly $5, whereas if it is almost certain to go down, then the option is worth nearly zero. However, this is not correct.

To see why, and to price the call correctly, consider your friend Jeeter, who does not deal in options at all, but who adopts a strategy of borrowing $2 to buy 5 shares of stock. What will Jeeter's investment portfolio be worth a year from today? If the stock goes up, his 5 shares are worth $7.50, from which he must subtract $2.50 in order to repay his $2 debt with interest. In other words, his portfolio is worth $5. If the stock goes down, his 5 shares are worth $2.50, from which he must still subtract $2.50, so his portfolio is worth zero. In other words, *Jeeter's portfolio is identical to your call option* in the sense that it will have the same value as your option regardless of what happens to the price of the stock.

Now, by the law of one price, the call option must sell for the same amount of money that it would take to follow Jeeter's strategy. That strategy requires a net outlay

EXHIBIT **19.2**     **Values of a Call Option**

| Value of GM Stock on 1/1/09 | Value of Call Option on 1/1/09 |
|---|---|
| $1.50 | $5 |
| .50 | 0 |

We assume that on January 1, 2009, GM stock will surely sell for either $1.50 or $.50. The table shows the value of the call option from Exhibit 19.1. If the GM stock sells for $1.50, the option allows you to buy 10 shares at $1 apiece and to make a $5 profit. If the GM stock sells for $.50, the call option is worthless.

of $3 (he takes in $2 in borrowed funds and lays out $5 to buy the 5 shares of stock). Therefore, the call option also sells for $3.

We have just seen a highly streamlined example of the *Black–Scholes Option Pricing Model,* which is used to predict real-world option prices with remarkable accuracy.[2] The model not only assumes that all investors are rational, it also assumes that they are extraordinarily clever: Whenever an option is offered, all of the market participants conjure up imaginary friends with portfolios that are identical to the option in order to price it correctly. In fact, even more is assumed. In the full-blown model, prices change continuously and stocks can go up or down by arbitrary amounts (as opposed to our example, where we allowed only two possible future values). In this case, solving the model requires knowledge of a sophisticated area of mathematics called the "Ito calculus." Most professors of mathematics have never heard of the Ito calculus, but Black and Scholes assume that all investors are whizzes at it.

How can such an unrealistic model possibly make accurate predictions? (If your answer is that it can't, be reminded that it does.) The answer is that although the model appears to invoke universal rationality, its conclusions actually follow from the much weaker assumption that there are no unexploited profit opportunities. The few people in the market smart enough to exploit all of the profit opportunities cause prices to behave as if everyone were perfectly rational—and had a Ph.D. in mathematics besides. The same sort of phenomenon occurs in many economic models.

## 19.3 What Is an Economic Explanation?

Economists like to look for puzzling phenomena and see whether they can be explained on the basis of rational behavior. Explanations that have implications beyond the case at hand are especially desirable because they can be tested in other circumstances. Here are a few examples.

### Celebrity Endorsements

Why are there celebrity endorsements? Why is a stereo system advertised by radio personality Paul Harvey worth more than the same stereo system without a famous name attached to it?

One possible explanation is that buyers are either irrational or very foolish: They don't recognize that endorsements carry no information about product quality and are gulled into believing that because Paul Harvey is a famous and accomplished radio announcer, any stereo that he advertises is likely to be of high quality.

To an economist such an explanation is unsatisfactory. Economists insist on seeking explanations that are grounded in rational behavior. There are two reasons for this insistence. First, on the basis of his past experience, the economist is aware of the power and wide applicability of economic analysis, which presumes rationality. Second, by attempting to extend such analysis into realms where it first appears inapplicable, the economist tests the limits and the durability of his theories.

Imagine a physicist sitting in his garden who notices that a baseball lying on the grass has risen of its own accord and has begun to hover 3 feet off the ground. He could

---

[2] This model first appeared in F. Black and M. Scholes, "The Pricing of Options and Corporate Liabilities," *Journal of Political Economy* 81 (1973): 637–654.

"explain" this phenomenon by abandoning his former insistence on the universality of gravitation, or he could attempt to find an explanation that is consistent with all of his previous experience. His gut will lead him to the second course of action. Perhaps it will eventually turn out that the laws of gravitation *are* wrong, but it is most productive to begin with the assumption that there must be some less radical solution to the problem.

If physicists abandoned their theories so easily, physics could never progress. The first physicist to have observed a helium-filled balloon would have admitted that there was no gravity, and the true physics of the situation would not have been discovered. By attempting to fit unfamiliar phenomena into familiar patterns, we arrive at deeper understandings of both the patterns and the phenomena.

So the economist is unwilling to abandon rationality quite so easily. Another easy "solution" presents itself: Perhaps people have a *taste* for wearing celebrity-endorsed clothing. They don't expect higher quality from the endorsed products; they just like wearing products that have been endorsed.

This solution is marginally better than the first one, but only marginally. The objection is that it's just too easy. Any human action can be explained on the basis of someone's having had a taste for that action. If we allow ourselves this easy out, we will never seek for deeper explanations.

The physicist could explain the floating baseball by saying that all of the laws of gravitation are true but that this one baseball happens to contain a unique antigravity substance that is activated only at 2 P.M. on Tuesdays (or whatever time the physicist happens to be making his observation). We expect our physicists to work harder for their pay. We should expect the same of our economists.

Here is an *economic* explanation of celebrity endorsements: New firms enter the marketplace with different strategies. Some plan to make a quick killing by selling shoddy products and then getting out. Others plan to offer products of high quality, which is expensive for them at first, and to be successful by earning a good reputation that will pay off in future years. Firms of the second type would like to let you know that they are of the second type. One way for them to do so is to hire a celebrity at a very high price. This conveys the information that the firm plans to be around a long time—long enough to earn back its investment in celebrity advertising.

Whether or not this is the correct explanation, it is at least an economic one. It says that firms and individuals face certain constraints, one of which is the inability of firms to issue binding promises that they are not fly-by-nights and that they optimize within the limits that these constraints impose. They convey the information expensively, which is better than not conveying it at all.

The explanation also has testable implications, which is an extremely desirable feature. It suggests that firms whose reputations are already well established should invest less in celebrity endorsements than firms that are just starting up and that firms producing products whose quality is easily verified at the time of purchase should invest less in celebrity endorsements than those firms producing products whose quality is revealed only after a long period of use. Real-world observations can now be used to confirm or contest the theory.

## The Size of Shopping Carts

Celebrity endorsements are a puzzle, and economists love puzzles. Another puzzle that is very popular among some economists concerns the size of shopping carts. Shopping carts today are larger than they were 20 years ago. Why?

It has sometimes been suggested that the larger shopping carts constitute an attempt on the part of grocery store managers to induce shoppers to make more purchases. The idea is that shoppers are embarrassed to enter the checkout line with a half-full cart.

Not only does this fail as an economic explanation, it fails as any kind of explanation at all! In order to explain a new phenomenon, one must address the issue of why it arose when it did and not earlier. The "embarrassment" theory is a theory of why shopping carts should always be big, not one of why they should grow bigger.

Here is a menu of economic explanations, which might or might not be correct.

Over the past 20 years, large numbers of women have entered the marketplace, and relatively few households now have a member who engages in housework (including shopping) on a full-time basis. Therefore, people want to allocate less time to shopping and they accomplish this by reducing the number of trips to the store, while buying in larger quantities each time they go. Hence the need for larger shopping carts.

Or: Starting again with the observation that changes in family structure have led to people wanting to economize on their shopping trips, we observe that one response has been for supermarkets to carry a wider range of items. It is now possible to shop for groceries, pharmaceutical products, and even small appliances under one roof. This enables the shopper to spend less time running from store to store, but it also necessitates larger shopping carts.

Or: Large shopping carts, and the wide aisles that are necessary to accommodate them, have always been desirable luxury items. They are also expensive, because wide aisles mean that stores must occupy more land. As shoppers have become wealthier over the past few decades, they have become increasingly willing to pay higher prices in exchange for wider aisles and bigger carts.

Can you suggest other theories? Can you think of any evidence that would help you choose among the ones suggested here?

## Why Is There Mandatory Retirement?

In 1986 the U.S. Congress severely restricted the practice of mandatory retirement. The fact that it was necessary to pass legislation to curtail this practice is an indication of its popularity. What made mandatory retirement so popular?

Professor Edward Lazear raised this question in a 1979 article, in which he examined the inadequacies of various traditional explanations.[3] Most of those traditional explanations rely on the assertion that workers' productivity declines significantly after a certain age and that employers deal with this through mandatory retirement. However, this cannot be a complete explanation. Among workers of any given age, there is wide variability in productivity. Employers do not refuse to hire the less productive workers, they simply pay them lower wages. Thus, "low productivity" cannot be a full explanation of why employers want to eliminate older workers completely.

Lazear offers an alternative explanation of mandatory retirement. Suppose that a worker is employed by a given firm for his entire working life. In a competitive labor market, the worker must receive a stream of wages whose present value is equal to the present value of his lifetime marginal product. There are many ways in which he can receive this stream of wages. Under Plan A the worker might be paid $20,000 each year, whereas under Plan B he receives less than $20,000 in some years and more than

---

[3] E. Lazear, "Why Is There Mandatory Retirement?," *Journal of Political Economy* 87 (1979): 1261–1284.

$20,000 in other years. Both the firm and the worker will be indifferent between Plan A and Plan B provided the two streams of wages have the same present value.

Now suppose that the worker agrees to acquire special skills that involve working harder but make him worth $30,000 per year to the company. In exchange for this, the firm pays him a higher wage, and both parties benefit. However, there is a catch: There is no way for the worker to guarantee in advance that he will really perform as promised. If he is paid on Plan A and if his salary is raised from $20,000 per year to $29,000 per year, the firm must be concerned that he will work at the old level of effort for a year, collect the $29,000, and then skip town.

Suppose, alternatively, that the worker is paid under a form of Plan B in which he is paid much less than his marginal product when he is young and much more than his marginal product when he is old. Now the contract to acquire special skills is enforceable: The worker must actually perform before he is compensated. The firm has its guarantee, and both parties benefit because the mutually beneficial contract can now be enforced.

Only one problem remains. The worker agrees to be paid less than he is worth to the firm while he is young in exchange for being paid more than he is worth when he is old. The firm will agree to such an arrangement only if it has a definite ending date. Hence the need for mandatory retirement.

You are invited to consider this explanation of the prevalence of mandatory retirement in light of Lazear's criticisms of other explanations. To what extent does Lazear's explanation avoid those problems? To what new criticisms is it susceptible? Is it, on balance, an improvement over other theories? Can you advance a new theory that makes even more sense?

Notice that if Lazear's story, or anything like it, is true, then both employers and employees benefit from mandatory retirement. It is true that any employee approaching his retirement would prefer to be allowed to continue working. But it is also true that the same employee, at the beginning of his working life and taking into account his entire lifetime earnings, is better off when he can commit himself to accepting mandatory retirement than when he cannot. The abolition of mandatory retirement reduces the ability of workers to offer guarantees of performance, reduces the willingness of firms to pay for such guarantees, and thereby reduces both the lifetime productivity and the lifetime compensation of workers.

There is an important moral to be drawn here: In evaluating public policy toward a social institution, it is necessary first to ask why that institution arose. It is impossible to know whether mandatory retirement is a good or a bad thing—by *any* criterion—without knowing why it exists in the first place. Social practices do not arise in vacuums; they arise because somebody finds them useful. It is incumbent upon the critic of these practices to understand who finds them useful and why before discarding them.

## Why Rock Concerts Sell Out

Tickets for major entertainment events such as U2 concerts predictably sell out well in advance. Television news programs show footage of hopeful ticket buyers lined up for blocks and even camping out overnight so as not to lose their place in the ticket line. Clearly, if the promoters raised their prices they would still sell out. Why, then, do they not raise their prices?

A possible answer is that all of those overnight campers are good publicity for a rock group. A problem with this theory is that it seems like it would be equally good publicity to sell a lot of tickets at very high prices. If people think, "This group must be great; people camped out just to see them," would they not also think, "This group must be great; people paid hundreds just to see them"?

Another possible answer is that promoters are not interested in selling just concert tickets. They are also interested in selling T-shirts, CDs, and all of the other paraphernalia associated with rock groups. Typically, teenagers buy more of these paraphernalia than adults do. Also typically, teenagers are more willing to camp out overnight to buy a ticket than adults are. So by setting prices low and assuring long lines, the promoters also assure themselves of young audiences and lucrative T-shirt sales.

## 99¢ Pricing

We close with one more example of an attempt to offer an economic explanation of an apparently irrational phenomenon. Consider the following letter to Ann Landers:

> **DEAR ANN LANDERS:** I read your letter to E. A. in Riverside, the man who wanted to know why stores charge odd prices, such as 99 cents, $1.99, $29.99, etc. You answered: "It's a sales gimmick that's been around forever."
>
> I am a 10-year-old boy and I think I have a better answer.
>
> Around 1875, Melville Stone owned a newspaper named the Chicago Daily News. The price was a penny. Circulation was good, but after a while it began to drop off. He found that it was because pennies were in short supply. Mr. Stone persuaded Chicago merchants to sell their merchandise for a penny below the regular price. This put more pennies in circulation and it helped save the paper.
>
> My source is: "Why Didn't I Think of That?" by Webb Garrison.
>
> —N. C. Reader
>
> **DEAR N.C.:** When I receive a letter like this from a 10-year-old boy, it gives me fresh hope for the youth of this country. Thanks for writing.[4]

Ann's own explanation ("It's a sales gimmick . . ."), which is also the explanation given by most noneconomists, relies on irrational consumers and therefore doesn't conform to the rules of the economic game. Unfortunately, her correspondent's explanation is far worse, because it makes no sense from any point of view, economic or not. The child psychologist Jean Piaget has determined that most children begin to master the principle of conservation at about age 7. By the age of 8, they understand, for example, that when water is poured from a short, thick container into a tall, thin container, the quantity of water does not change. One might then expect a 10-year-old to recognize that when a penny changes hands, there are neither more nor fewer pennies in circulation than there were previously.

Here is a suggestion for an economic explanation of how the pricing scheme in question developed. Around the same time that Melville Stone was trying to boost the circulation of the *Chicago Daily News,* the cash register was invented. It was now much easier for store owners to prevent their employees from stealing, because the register kept records of each purchase. However, a sale is recorded only when the register is opened, which would be necessary only if it were required to make change. A clerk can quietly slip a $20 bill into his pocket if the price of the item is $20, but he must ring up the sale and open the register if he has to give a penny in change.

[4] Permission granted by Ann Landers and Creators Syndicate.

## Rationality Revisited

These examples illustrate one further point about the rationality assumption. To a large extent, the assumption of rationality is nothing more than a commitment to inquire sympathetically into people's motives. When we see people flocking to buy clothes endorsed by celebrities, or when we see concert promoters "underpricing" their tickets, we have a choice. Either we can remark—wistfully or cynically, according to our temperament—on the inadequacy of human nature, or we can ask, "How might such behavior be serving someone's purposes?" The first option offers the satisfaction of exempting oneself from the great mass of human folly. The second offers an opportunity to learn something.

Adopting the rationality assumption means pledging to treat all human behavior as worthy of respectful consideration. Rather than dismiss the buyers of stereos endorsed by Paul Harvey as victims of a herd mentality, or the concert promoter as a plodder who fails to see profit opportunities, we force ourselves to think deeply about what their true motives and strategies might be. In the process, we discover possibilities and develop insights that would never arise if we allowed ourselves to simply dismiss as "irrational" anything we failed to understand immediately. By disallowing the easy way out, we commit ourselves to careful and creative analysis of why people behave as they do, which is an excellent habit for any social scientist to cultivate.

## 19.4 The Scope of Economic Analysis

We began this chapter by saying that economics is the science that studies human behavior by positing rational action in the face of constraints. Traditionally, such reasoning was applied primarily to the trading of goods and services in the marketplace. However, in the last 30 years it has become clear that the economic way of thinking can be productively applied to a wide range of activities both in and out of the marketplace. Economists study love and marriage, the structure of families, medieval agriculture, religious activity, cannibalism, and evolution. By extending their methods into such areas, many of which are dominated by actors who are traditionally supposed to be engaged in nonrational behavior, economists have demonstrated the power of their approach. In this section, we will summarize a few of the most exciting nontraditional applications of economics.

### Laboratory Animals as Rational Agents

In a series of remarkable experiments, a group of researchers has demonstrated that laboratory animals respond to economic stimuli in the ways that economic theory would predict.[5]

#### Rats as Consumers

In one experiment rats were permitted to "purchase" root beer and collins mix by pressing levers that caused the liquids to be dispensed. The rats were given fixed incomes (e.g., 300 lever pushes per day) and prices (e.g., one lever push generates .05 ml of root

[5] J. H. Kagel, R. Battalio, H. Rachlin, L. Green, R. Basmann, and W. R. Klemm, "Experimental Studies of Consumer Demand Behavior Using Laboratory Animals," *Economic Inquiry* 13 (1975): 22–38; see also R. Battalio, L. Green, and J. H. Kagel, "Income-Leisure Tradeoffs of Animal Workers," *American Economic Review* 71 (1981): 621–632.

beer or .1 ml of collins mix). Their consumption patterns were noted. Then the rats' incomes and the prices they faced were varied, so that their behavior could be observed under a variety of budget constraints. The rats' behavior demonstrated downward-sloping demand curves and upward-sloping Engel curves, as an economist would expect.

Moreover, the rats' consumption patterns were internally consistent in the sense predicted by economic theory. For example, panel A of Exhibit 19.3 illustrates one rat's consumption point when given an income of 300 lever presses and facing prices of 1 press per .05 ml for both liquids. The rat chose point A. His income and prices were then adjusted to give him the color budget line shown in panel B. If the rat was a rational maximizer, with an indifference curve tangent to the first budget line at A, then his new optimum would have to occur at a point below A on the new budget line. In fact, he chose point B, confirming this prediction.

## Pigeons as Suppliers of Labor

In a later experiment, pigeons were required to earn their incomes (in this case, food) by pecking a response key. Their behavior was observed under variations in both wage rates (amount of food per peck) and nonlabor income (free food delivered at regular intervals). The pigeons demonstrated all of the expected substitution and income effects. In particular, when their nonlabor income was fixed, their labor supply curves were backward bending, as you would expect after having read Section 16.1 of this book.

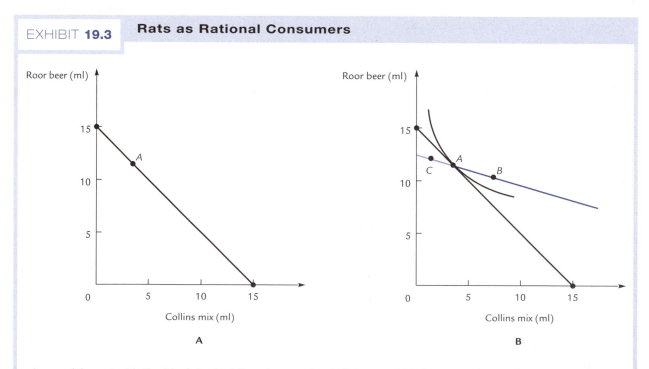

EXHIBIT **19.3**     **Rats as Rational Consumers**

In panel A a rat with the black budget line chose point A. Prices and his income were then adjusted so that he now had the color budget line in panel B. According to economic theory, the rat must now choose a point like B (on the darker part of the new line) rather than a point like C (on the lighter part). The reason is that if an indifference curve were tangent at C, it would have to cross the original indifference curve. In fact, the rat chose point B, confirming the economic prediction.

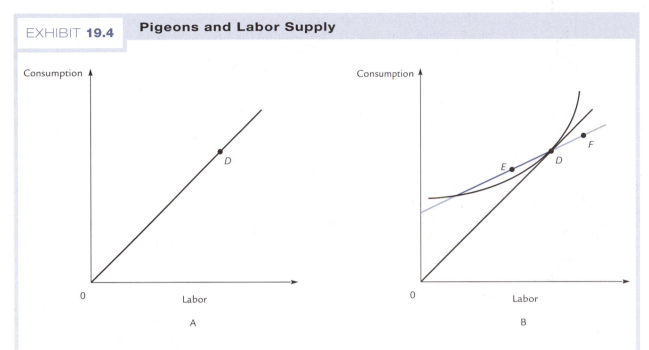

EXHIBIT **19.4**   **Pigeons and Labor Supply**

In panel A a pigeon with the black budget line chose point *D*. His wage and his nonlabor income were then adjusted so that he had the color budget line. According to economic theory, the pigeon must now choose a point like *E* (on the darker part of the new line) rather than a point like *F* (on the lighter part). The reason is that if an indifference curve were tangent at *F*, it would have to cross the original indifference curve. In fact, the pigeon chose point *E*, confirming the economic prediction.

In one version of the experiment, pigeons were initially presented with no nonlabor income, so that their budget line was as shown in panel A of Exhibit 19.4. They chose point *D*. Then their wages were lowered, while they were simultaneously given just enough nonlabor income to give them the color budget line shown in panel B. Assuming that the pigeons are rational maximizers, they must now choose a point on the darker portion of the color line, such as point *E*, and, in fact, they do so.

Often, noneconomists argue that economists are far too optimistic in their assumption that people have sufficient intelligence to respond appropriately to subtle changes in prices and income. The next time you find yourself in conversation with such a noneconomist, you can ask him whether he thinks that most human beings are as intelligent as rats and pigeons.

## Altruism and the Selfish Gene

There is a growing literature on the interface and analogies between economics and biology.[6] One area of mutual interest is the study of *altruism*. Economists have long been aware that people choose to give gifts to others, especially to their children and other close relatives. Perhaps you would not be in college if it weren't for this phenomenon. Such behavior can be explained by saying that people have a "taste" for it, but as we have noted before, economists are distinctly uncomfortable with this kind of glibness. So we must look deeper.

---

[6] See, for example, J. Hirshleifer, "Economics from a Biological Viewpoint," *Journal of Law and Economics* 20 (1977): 1–52; and G. Tullock, "Biological Externalities," *Journal of Theoretical Biology* 33 (1971): 565–576.

Recently, biologists have begun to explore the notion that altruism is a result of purely selfish (nonaltruistic) behavior on the part of the genetic material that is the true medium for natural selection. If you are carrying a certain gene, then there is a 50% chance that your child is carrying the same gene. The gene's survival probability is enhanced if you behave in a way that improves the survival prospects of your children. Now suppose that some particular gene has the effect of making you feel altruistic toward your children. Then that gene will gain an evolutionary advantage and tend to propagate.[7]

Economists have explored some of the consequences of altruistic behavior in the family. For example, suppose that the household is headed by an altruistic parent who gives bequests to the children in such a way as to equalize the children's "incomes," where these incomes include all of the things that are important to a child. If one child is more satisfied than the others, then the parent will tend to give more attention, presents, and so forth to the other children (and consequently less to the satisfied one) until the situation becomes more equal.

Now suppose that the family contains a "Rotten Kid" who is thinking of stealing his sister's marbles. Suppose also that the theft of the marbles would be economically inefficient, either because he values them less than she does or because some marbles are likely to be lost in the struggle over their ownership. The Rotten Kid might be deterred from stealing the marbles if he feared being found out and punished by the parent. But more remarkably, he will not steal the marbles even if the parent is totally unable to observe or discover the theft. The reason is that the reduction in his sister's level of satisfaction will cause the parent to divert resources to the sister and away from the Rotten Kid, even though the parent has no idea of the reason why the sister has seemed so unhappy lately. The economic inefficiency of the theft means that there will be a smaller social surplus to divide among the children, and an equal share of a smaller pie is not an improvement from the Rotten Kid's own point of view.

This "Rotten Kid theorem" is due to Professor Gary S. Becker, whose book on the economic analysis of family life is a highly recommended (but somewhat technically sophisticated) source of novel and clever economic argument.[8]

The analysis of altruism is by no means a frivolous pursuit. The extent to which parents care about their children's welfare is an important component in understanding savings behavior, responses to taxation, and responses to government debt. (For example, see the discussion of the Ricardian Equivalence theorem in Chapter 17.) Ultimately, the economic analysis of these important variables (which in turn are critical in the determination of the interest rate and the rate of inflation, among other things) must rest on an understanding of behavior in the household.

## The Economics of Scattering

In medieval Europe many small farmers held their land in scattered plots. This means that a typical farmer would own three or four small plots of land at considerable distances from each other. Historians and economists are puzzled by this phenomenon, which seems to entail unnecessary inefficiencies. (Here is an inefficiency you might not have thought of: With so many small plots, there are many more boundaries between neighbors, and consequently many more externalities. Farmers sometimes remove

---

[7] For a fascinating account of this fascinating approach to biology, see R. Dawkins, *The Selfish Gene* (New York: Oxford University Press, 1976). The book's proposed explanations of puzzles in animal behavior are very much in the spirit of economics.

[8] G. S. Becker, *A Treatise on the Family* (Cambridge, MA: Harvard University Press, 1981).

rocks from their own land near the boundary and toss them onto their neighbor's land. With scattering, almost all land is near a boundary, and a lot of energy gets spent tossing rocks back and forth.)

Many explanations have been offered for scattering. Professor Donald McCloskey has examined these explanations and found them wanting from the economist's viewpoint (he is also the source of the parenthetical observation in the preceding paragraph).[9] He has suggested an alternative. Farming communities are subject to localized disasters. Wind, rain, or fire can destroy all of the crops in one part of town while leaving those in other parts untouched. If there is no organized market for insurance, a rational farmer will be willing to accept the inefficiencies of scattering in exchange for the corresponding reduction in risk. With scattered plots, he will grow less in the average year, but he is much less likely to face a year in which all of his crops are destroyed.

It is sometimes argued that medieval and modern man differ so radically that the economic models developed in the nineteenth and twentieth centuries for understanding behavior in industrialized societies are not useful tools in the study of the distant past. McCloskey's work indicates the opposite: Peasants in the Middle Ages were willing to pay a price for a reduction in risk, just as economic theory would predict (see Chapter 18 of this book), and the price that they were willing to pay was a reasonable one, given the risks involved.

If economic theory applies to rats and pigeons, then surely we should expect it to apply to human beings in situations very different from our own. The scope of economic analysis is being extended every day. This is an exciting time to be studying economics.

## Author Commentary  www.cengage.com/economics/landsburg

**AC1.** Ancient rabbis seem to have solved a difficult economic problem by instinct.

**AC2.** For more information on shopping carts, read this article.

**AC3.** For another article on shopping carts, see this one.

## Problem Set

1. Reexamine problem 24 at the end of Chapter 3. What agents are involved in this problem? What are they maximizing and what are their constraints? When you work the problem, at what point are you solving an optimization problem? At what point are you computing an equilibrium?

2. Look back at various other problems in this book. Which are primarily concerned with optimization problems? Which with equilibria? Which with both?

3. Suppose that General Motors stock is currently selling for $\$S$ per share, that 1 year from today it will either have gone up to $\$U$ or down to $\$D,$ and that the

---

[9] D. McCloskey, "The Open Fields of England: Rent, Risk and the Rate of Interest, 1300–1815," in D. Galenson, ed., *Markets in History: Economic Studies of the Past* (Cambridge: Cambridge University Press, 1989). This article makes fascinating reading and applies many of the ideas you have learned in this course both to draw striking conclusions about the past and to refute alternative theories.

annual interest rate is *r*. You are offered a call option that will allow you to buy GM stock next year at a price of $C, where *C* is between *U* and *D*. In terms of *S, U, D, r,* and *C,* what is the value of this call option?

4. **True or False:** Television sets will be more expensive in an area with great reception and lots of channels than in an area served by only one channel, which comes in poorly.

5. Why do banks construct elaborate buildings with Greek columns? Does your explanation show why supermarkets don't do the same thing? Does it predict which banks are most likely to construct such buildings?

6. **True or False:** *Good Housekeeping* tests products and awards its Seal of Approval to those found to be of high quality. Manufacturers who have been judged worthy of the seal must still pay to display it. By being selective about how it awards the seal, the magazine has acquired a reputation for trustworthiness, which makes the seal a valuable commodity. Consider the proposition that Paul Harvey awards the use of his name in the same selective way that *Good Housekeeping* awards its seal and that his endorsement is valuable for that reason. Contrast this proposition with the explanation offered in the chapter. In what ways does one seem more reasonable than the other? What could you observe in the real world to test the truth of either proposition?

7. Evaluate the explanation of mandatory retirement given in the chapter.

8. Criticize the explanation of "99¢ pricing" given in the chapter. Can you think of an alternative economic explanation? What could you observe in the real world to help establish or refute the validity of the text's explanation?

9. Criticize the Rotten Kid theorem.

10. Suppose that McCloskey's theory of scattering is correct. What exogenous social developments would tend to reduce the preponderance of scattering? How would the amount of scattering be related to the interest rate?

11. Consider the following alternative theory of scattering: Every time a farmer dies, his land is divided among his children, creating several small plots. Whenever there is a marriage, the ownership of several of these plots becomes merged. What flaws are there in this theory? Is it consistent with rational behavior on the part of the peasants? Is it more or less plausible from that point of view than McCloskey's theory?

    In the remaining problems, construct theories to explain the phenomena described. Try to base your theories on rational behavior. In each case, describe some additional predictions of your theory, and present some ways that you could use real-world observations to test it.

12. Women spend more on medical care than men do.

13. Blockbuster movies generate long lines at the ticket counter, but theater owners don't raise prices for blockbusters.

14. Baseball tickets are priced in such a way that the box seats almost always sell out long before the bleachers do.

15. Ski resorts charge for lift tickets on a per-day rather than a per-ride basis, and there are often long lines at the lifts.

16. Firms lay off workers rather than reduce their salaries.

**17.** When workers go on strike, the firm loses profits and the workers lose wages. If the strike were called off, the two parties would have a bigger pie to divide between them. Nevertheless, there are strikes.

**18.** People prefer to bet on the sports teams they are rooting for than on the opposing teams.

**19.** Following an earthquake, sales of earthquake insurance go up.

**20.** Some items are sold in English auctions (where the item is offered for sale at a low price and buyers bid the price up until only one buyer is left). Others are sold in Dutch auctions (where the item is offered at a high price and the seller calls out successively lower prices until a buyer steps in).

Can you construct a theory that will predict which sort of auction will be used for which sort of item? Does your theory take into account the incentives that buyers have to attend the auction in the first place?

**21.** Many societies have strict taboos against baby selling.

**22.** People give each other gifts that they are not sure the recipient will like, even though they could as easily give cash instead. (Saying that a gift shows you took the time to shop is no answer, because cash shows you took the time to earn the money.)

**23.** People voluntarily leave tips in restaurants, even when they know they won't be returning.

**24.** People give to charitable organizations and to political causes.

**25.** Over half the electorate turns out to vote for presidential elections, even though the probability of any individual's changing the outcome is negligibly small.

**26.** Car manufacturers will sometimes offer a $500 rebate on a new car rather than take $500 off the sales price. This is so even though reducing the price would lower the sales tax and thus benefit the consumer by more than $500.

**27.** People in rural communities are often unhappy about the switch to daylight saving time, because they tend to wake up very early (say, at 5:30 A.M.) and under daylight saving time it is dark at that hour. A solution would be to continue waking up at the "old" 5:30 A.M. (which is renamed 6:30 A.M. under daylight saving time). But this solution is not implemented.

**28.** In the United States, a hotel room for two people usually costs less than twice as much as a hotel room for one person, whereas in England a room for two often costs exactly twice as much as a room for one.

**29.** *(This problem was suggested by Marvin Goodfriend.)* Governments are engaged in the business of redistributing income through the tax system. At the same time, private individuals are prohibited by law from redistributing income (via strong-arm tactics, breaking and entering, extortion, and the like). Thus, the government maintains and enforces a monopoly in the income redistribution market, and there is a general agreement, among both economists and noneconomists, that this is a good thing. But economists generally oppose government monopolies in other areas, such as the postal service. Are they being inconsistent?

# Calculus Supplement

This appendix briefly reviews the material of the textbook in the language of calculus. There are sections corresponding to most of the textbook chapters, and most have some brief exercises at the end.

## Chapter 1

**1. Demand and Supply.** Demand and supply are functions that convert prices to quantities. For a given price $P$, the demand and supply functions are defined by setting $D(P)$ = the quantity that demanders wish to buy at price $P$, and $S(P)$ = the quantity that suppliers wish to sell at price $P$.

When the price changes from $P_1$ to $P_2$, the quantity demanded changes from $D(P_1)$ to $D(P_2)$, but the function $D$ remains unchanged. A *change in demand* refers to a change in the function $D$ itself; similarly for supply.

Because the output from a demand or supply function represents a quantity, it is often denoted by the letter $Q$. Thus, if we are discussing demand we write

$$Q = D(P)$$

and if we are discussing supply we write

$$Q = S(P)$$

Of course, when we discuss supply and demand simultaneously, we cannot use the same symbol to denote the output from both functions. In that case, we usually write

$$Q_d = D(P)$$

$$Q_s = S(P)$$

to distinguish the quantity demanded $Q_d$ from the quantity supplied $Q_s$.

**2. Derivatives.** The fact that the demand curve slopes downward is expressed by the inequality

$$D'(P) < 0$$

or

$$\frac{dQ_d}{dP} < 0$$

The fact that the supply curve slopes upward is expressed by the inequality

$$S'(P) > 0$$

or

$$\frac{dQ_s}{dP} > 0$$

### 3. Equilibrium.
The equilibrium price is the price $P$ at which $D(P) = S(P)$, and the equilibrium quantity is this common value. The assumptions $D'(P) < 0$ and $S'(P) > 0$ ensure the uniqueness of the equilibrium.

### 4. Taxation.
Suppose that the demand for lettuce is given by the function $Qd = D_0(P)$. When a sales tax equal to $T$ per head of lettuce is imposed, the demander must pay $P + T$ to acquire a head of lettuce. Thus, the new demand function is given by the formula $D_1(P) = D_0(P + T)$. The graph of $D_1$ is identical to the graph of $D_0$ translated downward a distance $T$.

Similarly, an excise tax of $T$ per head of lettuce causes the supply function $S_0(P)$ to be replaced by the new function $S_1(P) = S_0(P + T)$. The graph of $S_1$ is identical to the graph of $S_0$ translated upward a distance $T$.

Continue to write $D_0$ and $S_0$ for the original demand and supply functions. A sales tax leads to the equilibrium price $P_{sales}$, where

$$D_1(P_{sales}) = S_0(P_{sales})$$

and an excise tax leads to the equilibrium price $P_{excise}$, where

$$D_0(P_{excise}) = S_1(P_{excise})$$

Substituting the expressions for $D_1$ and $S_1$ gives

$$D_0(P_{sales} + T) = S_0(P_{sales})$$

$$D_0(P_{excise}) = S_0(P_{excise} + T)$$

It is easy to check that if $P_{sales}$ satisfies the first equation, then $P_{excise} = P_{sales} + T$ satisfies the second equation. Moreover, there is only one solution to each equation because $D_0$ is decreasing and $S_0$ is increasing. It follows that we must have $P_{excise} = P_{sales} + T$.

Under a sales tax, demanders pay $P_{sales} + T = P_{excise}$ and suppliers get $P_{sales}$. Under an excise tax, demanders pay $P_{excise}$ and suppliers keep $P_{excise} - T = P_{sales}$. Therefore, the sales and excise taxes are equivalent.

## Exercises

1. Let $S(P)$ and $D(P)$ be the supply and demand functions for apples. Suppose that an excise tax of $T$ is imposed and the posttax equilibrium price for apples is $P$. Treating $P$ as a function of $T$, use the equation

$$D(P) = S(P - T)$$

and the chain rule to derive a formula for the derivative $dP/dT$.

$$Answer:\ \frac{dP}{dT} = \frac{S'(P - T)}{S'(P - T) - D'(P)}$$

2. In problem 1, let $P_{sellers}$ be the price that sellers actually receive for the items they sell. Use the result of problem 1 and the equation

$$P_{sellers} = P - T$$

to derive and simplify a formula for the derivative $dP_{sellers}/dT$.

$$\textit{Answer: } \frac{dP}{dT} = \frac{D'(P)}{S'(P - T) - D'(P)}$$

3. Let $S(P)$ and $D(P)$ be the supply and demand functions for apples. Suppose that a sales tax of $T$ is imposed and the posttax equilibrium price for apples is $P$. Treating $P$ as a function of $T$, use the equation

$$D(P + T) = S(P)$$

and the chain rule to derive a formula for the derivative $dP/dT$.

4. In problem 3, let $P_{buyers}$ be the price that buyers actually pay for the items they buy. Use the result of problem 3 and the equation

$$P_{buyers} = P + T$$

to derive and simplify a formula for the derivative $dP_{buyers}/dT$.

5. Explain how your solutions to problems 1 through 4 illustrate the proposition that the economic incidence of a tax is independent of its legal incidence.

# Chapter 3

## 1. Families of Indifference Curves.
A single indifference curve is defined by a single equation in $X$ and $Y$. A *family* of indifference curves must be defined by a *family* of equations. The easiest way to do this is to specify a function of two variables, $U(X, Y)$, and to consider the family of equations

$$U(X, Y) = C$$

where $C$ is any constant. Thus, for example, one indifference curve is given by $U(X, Y) = 1$, another by $U(X, Y) = 2$, and so forth.

When the indifference curves are described in this way, it is clear that they fill the plane (for every $(X, Y)$, $U(X, Y)$ has *some* value, and $(X, Y)$ is on the corresponding indifference curve) and that they never cross (for every $(X, Y)$ $U(X, Y)$ has only *one* value, and so $(X, Y)$ is on only one indifference curve). The other properties of indifference curves follow from some assumptions on $U$. A set of assumptions sufficient to guarantee the desired properties is

$$\frac{\partial U}{\partial X} > 0 \tag{1}$$

$$\frac{\partial U}{\partial Y} > 0 \tag{2}$$

$$\frac{\partial^2 U}{\partial X^2} < 0 \tag{3}$$

$$\frac{\partial^2 U}{\partial Y^2} < 0 \tag{4}$$

$$\frac{\partial^2 U}{\partial X^2} \cdot \frac{\partial^2 U}{\partial Y^2} - \left(\frac{\partial^2 U}{\partial X \, \partial Y}\right)^2 > 0 \tag{5}$$

## 2. Properties of Indifference Curves.

To see what our assumptions imply about the indifference curves, fix a constant $C$ and look at the indifference curve defined by $U(X, Y) = C$. This curve is also the graph of the function $Y = f(X)$, where $f$ is implicitly defined by the formula

$$U(X, f(X)) = C$$

The chain rule gives

$$\frac{\partial U}{\partial X}(X, f(X)) + \frac{\partial U}{\partial Y}(X, f(X)) \cdot \frac{df}{dX}(X) = \frac{dC}{dX} = 0$$

so that

$$\frac{df}{dX} = -\frac{\partial U/\partial X}{\partial U/\partial Y} < 0$$

(The final inequality follows from assumptions (1) and (2).) In other words, indifference curves slope downward.

By differentiating both sides of the formula

$$\frac{\partial U}{\partial X}(X, f(X)) + \frac{\partial U}{\partial Y}(X, f(X)) \cdot \frac{df}{dX}(X) = 0$$

we find that

$$\frac{\partial^2 U}{\partial X^2}(X, f(X)) + 2 \cdot \frac{\partial^2 U}{\partial X\, \partial Y}(X, f(X)) \cdot \frac{df}{dX}(X) + \frac{\partial^2 U}{\partial Y^2} \cdot \left(\frac{df}{dX}(X)\right)^2$$

$$= \frac{\partial U}{\partial Y}(X, f(X)) \cdot \frac{d^2 f}{dX^2}(X)$$

For a given value of $X$, the left side of this equation is equal to the value of the quadratic function

$$(t) = \frac{\partial^2 U}{\partial X^2}(X, f(X)) + 2 \cdot \frac{\partial^2 U}{\partial X\, \partial Y}(X, f(X)) \cdot t + \frac{\partial^2 U}{\partial Y^2}(X, f(X)) \cdot t^2$$

at the point $t = (df/dX)(X)$. Assumptions (3) and (5) imply that the quadratic function takes only negative values.* Thus, we know that $-(\partial U/\partial Y)(X, f(X))\, (\partial^2 f/\partial X^2)(X)$ is negative. Together with assumption 1 this allows us to conclude that $(d^2 f/dX^2)$ is everywhere positive. In other words, indifference curves are convex.

To summarize, we have shown that when the indifference curves are described by the formulas $U(X, Y) = C$, and when $U$ satisfies assumptions (1) through (5), we may conclude that indifference curves fill the plane, never cross, slope downward, and are convex.

## 3. The Marginal Rate of Substitution and the Consumer's Optimum.

According to the chain rule, the slope of the indifference curve at the point $(X, Y)$ is given by

$$-\frac{\partial U/\partial X}{\partial U/\partial Y}$$

---

* Assumption (3) implies that $Q(0) < 0$. Assumption (5) implies that $Q$ has no real roots. By the intermediate value theorem, a continuous function that takes one negative value and has no real roots must take only negative values.

evaluated at $(X, Y)$. The absolute value of this slope is the marginal rate of substitution between $X$ and $Y$.

The consumer's budget constraint is given by the equation

$$P_X \cdot X + P_Y \cdot Y = 1$$

where $P_X$, $P_Y$, and $I$ are constants. Its graph is the equation of the straight line through $(0, I/P_Y)$ and $(I/P_X, 0)$; the slope of this line is $-P_X/P_Y$.

In order to attain the highest possible indifference curve, the consumer maximizes $U(X, Y)$ subject to the budget constraint. There are two ways to solve this problem. One is to view it as a constrained maximization problem in the two variables $X$ and $Y$ so that the method of Lagrange multipliers applies. However, there is a much more elementary alternative. Using the budget constraint, we solve for $Y$ and get

$$Y = \frac{1}{P_Y} - \frac{P_X}{P_Y} \cdot X$$

Then we are reduced to solving a maximization problem in one variable; namely, maximize

$$U\left(X, \frac{1}{P_Y} - \frac{P_X}{P_Y} \cdot X\right)$$

The first-order condition is

$$\frac{\partial U}{\partial X} = \frac{P_X}{P_Y} \cdot \frac{\partial U}{\partial Y}$$

or

$$\frac{\partial U/\partial X}{\partial U/\partial Y} = \frac{P_X}{P_Y}$$

That is, the consumer selects the point on the budget constraint at which the marginal rate of substitution and the relative price of $X$ are equal. This has good intuitive content, as described in the textbook.

To verify that we have found a maximum, it is necessary to verify the second-order condition as well. Although it is geometrically obvious that we have indeed found a maximum (see, for example Exhibit 3.9 in the textbook), you might want to verify the second-order condition directly, using assumptions (1) through (5).

## Exercises

1. Suppose that your indifference curves between $X$ and $Y$ are given by the family of equations $U(X, Y) = C$, where $U(X, Y) = X^{1/2} \cdot Y^{1/2}$.

    a.  Does $U$ satisfy the conditions 1 through 5 of section 1?

    *Answer: Yes.*

    b.  Compute the slope of your indifference curve passing through the point $(X, Y)$ at that point, as a function of $X$ and $Y$.

    *Answer: Y/X.*

    c.  Show that your indifference curves are convex.

**d.** Suppose that the price of $X$ is \$1, the price of $Y$ is \$2, and your income is \$10. What basket of goods do you buy?

*Answer: X = 5, Y = 2½.*

**e.** Repeat part (d) if the price of $X$ goes up to \$5.

*Answer: X = 1, Y = 2½.*

**f.** Repeat part (d) if your income goes up to \$20.

**2.** Repeat problem 1 with the function $U$ replaced by $U(X, Y) = X^{1/4} \cdot Y^{1/4}$.

# Chapter 4

***1. The Engel Curve.*** We will continue to assume that the consumer's indifference curves are the curves $U(X, Y) = C$ for some fixed function $U$.

In order to see how the consumer reacts to changes in income, we hold the prices of $X$ and $Y$ fixed; that is, we treat $P_X$ and $P_Y$ as constants. We can always choose to measure $Y$ in units that make $P_Y = 1$ (for example, if $Y$ is Coca-Cola and it sells for 50¢ per can, then we will declare one "unit" of Coca-Cola to consist of two cans). This allows us to adopt the abbreviation $P = PX$; that is, $P$ is the relative price of $X$ in terms of $Y$.

At any given level of income $I$, the consumer decides what quantity of $X$ to purchase. We will denote this quantity by $E(I)$. $E(I)$ is chosen to maximize

$$U(E(I), I - PE(I))$$

That is, $E(I)$ satisfies the first-order condition

$$U_1(E(I), I - PE(I)) = PU_2(E(I), I - PE(I)) \tag{6}$$

where we have abbreviated

$$U_1 = \frac{\partial U}{\partial X} \qquad U_2 = \frac{\partial U}{\partial Y}$$

The function $E(I)$ implicitly defined by equation (6) is the consumer's Engel curve for $X$.

By differentiating equation (6) with respect to $I$, we can find the slope of the Engel curve. You should verify that

$$E'(I) = \frac{-U_{12} + PU_{22}}{U_{11} - 2PU_{12} - P^2 U_{22}} \tag{7}$$

As an example, suppose that there are constants $\alpha$ and $\beta$ such that

$$U(X, Y) = X^\alpha Y^\beta$$

Then you should be able to verify that the equation of the Engel curve is given by

$$E(I) = \frac{\alpha I}{(\alpha + \beta)P}$$

That is, in this case the consumer's Engel curve is a straight line through the origin with slope $\alpha/[(\alpha + \beta) \cdot P]$.

## 2. The Demand Curve.

The consumer's demand curve $D$ is derived in a similar way, by treating $I$ as a constant and noting that the consumer maximizes $U(X, I - PX)$ by setting $X = D(P)$, where $D(P)$ satisfies

$$U(D(P), I - PD(P)) = PU_2(D(P), I - PD(P)) \tag{8}$$

The function $D$ implicitly defined by equation (8) is the consumer's demand curve. For example, if the indifference curves are given by

$$U(X, Y) = X^\alpha Y^\beta$$

then the demand curve for $X$ is given by

$$D(P) = \frac{\alpha I}{(\alpha + \beta)P}$$

Although the right-hand expression looks exactly like the expression for the Engel curve, we are now treating $P$ as the independent variable and $I$ as a constant. Thus, the demand curve in this case is a hyperbola.

By differentiating equation (8) with respect to $P$, we can find the slope of the demand curve. You should verify that

$$D'(P) = \frac{U_{12}D(P) - PU_{22}D(P) + U_2}{U_{11} - 2PU_{12} + P^2U_{22}} \tag{9}$$

## 3. The Compensated Demand Curve.

We can also derive an expression for the compensated demand curve $Dc(X)$. Suppose the consumer starts out on the indifference curve $U(X, Y) = C$. In order to derive the compensated demand curve, we pretend that regardless of how the price $P$ changes, the consumer is constrained to remain on the same indifference curve. Thus, for any price $P$, the consumer selects quantities $X = Dc(P)$ and $Y = f(P)$ such that

$$U(D_c(P), f(P)) = C \tag{10}$$

Differentiating this with respect to $P$, we find that

$$f'(P) = \frac{U_1 D'_c}{U_2} = PD'_c \tag{11}$$

(The last equality results from the fact that the consumer still maximizes by setting $U_1 = PU_2$.)

From the fact that the consumer is maximizing subject to the price $P$, we have

$$U_1(D_c(P), f(P)) = PU_2(D_c(P), f(P)) \tag{12}$$

The function $D_c$ is defined implicitly by this together with equation (10). Differentiating equation (12) with respect to $P$ and substituting for $f'(P)$ as per equation (11), we get

$$D'_c = \frac{U_2}{U_{11} - 2PU_{12} + P^2U_{22}} \tag{13}$$

We have noted earlier that the denominator in this expression must be negative in consequence of equations (3) and (5), and the numerator is positive by equation (2). It follows that $D_c'(P)$ is unambiguously negative; the compensated demand curve must be downward-sloping.

### 4. Substitution and Income Effects.

There is an interesting consequence of equations (7), (9), and (13). Combining them, we find that for any given $P$ and $I$, we have

$$D'(P) = D'_c(P) - D(P)E'(I) \qquad (14)$$

(In interpreting this equation, keep in mind that the functions $D$ and $D_c$ depend on $I$ and that the function $E$ depends on $P$.) This says that when $P$ changes, the corresponding change in quantity demanded can be decomposed into two parts: first a movement along the compensated demand curve (the substitution effect) and then an additional movement whose size depends on the slope of the Engel curve (the income effect). If the Engel curve is upward sloping (that is, if $X$ is a normal good), then equation (14) shows that both components are negative—the income effect reinforces the substitution effect, so the demand curve must slope downward. If the Engel curve is downward sloping, then $D'(P)$ has one negative component and one positive component—the income effect works counter to the substitution effect. In this case, it is at least theoretically possible for the demand curve to slope upward—the case of a Giffen good.

### 5. Elasticities.

The income elasticity of demand for a commodity is

$$\frac{I}{Q} \cdot \frac{dQ}{dI}$$

where $dQ/dI$ is the derivative of the Engel curve, calculated in expression (7). An equivalent expression is

$$\frac{d(\log Q)}{d(\log I)}$$

Likewise, we define the price elasticity of demand to be

$$\frac{P}{Q} \cdot \frac{dQ}{dP}$$

where $dQ/dP$ is the derivative of the demand function calculated in expression (9). An equivalent expression is

$$\frac{d(\log Q)}{d(\log P)}$$

The compensated price elasticity of demand is

$$\frac{P}{Q_c} \cdot \frac{dQ_c}{dP}$$

where $dQ_c/dP$ is the derivative of the compensated demand function calculated in expression (13). An equivalent expression is

$$\frac{d(\log Q_c)}{d(\log P)}$$

### 6. The Slutsky Equation*

If we multiply equation (14) through by $P/D(P) = P/E(I)$, we get

$$\left( \begin{array}{c} \text{Elasticity of the} \\ \text{ordinary demand curve} \end{array} \right) = \left( \begin{array}{c} \text{Elasticity of the} \\ \text{compensated demand curve} \end{array} \right) + P \cdot E'(I)$$

---

* This is a topic not covered in the body of the textbook.

The last term on the right can be rewritten as

$$\frac{P \cdot E}{I} \cdot \left( \begin{array}{c} \text{Elasticity of the} \\ \text{Engel curve} \end{array} \right)$$

and $\dfrac{P \cdot E}{I}$ can be interpreted as the fraction of his income that the consumer spends on $X$. Thus, we have

$$\left( \begin{array}{c} \text{Elasticity of the} \\ \text{ordinary demand curve} \end{array} \right) = \left( \begin{array}{c} \text{Elasticity of the} \\ \text{compensated demand curve} \end{array} \right) - \left( \begin{array}{c} \text{Fraction of income} \\ \text{spent on } X \end{array} \right) \cdot \left( \begin{array}{c} \text{Elasticity of the} \\ \text{Engel curve} \end{array} \right)$$

The preceding equation is called the *Slutsky equation*. It shows, for example, that if the fraction of his income that the consumer spends on $X$ is small, then the elasticities of the ordinary and compensated demand curves are approximately equal.

## Exercises

1.  Suppose that indifference curves are given by the family of equations $U(X, Y) = X^{1/2} \cdot Y^{1/2} = C$, the price of $X$ is \$1, the price of $Y$ is \$2, and income is \$10. One day the price of $X$ goes up to \$2. What happens to consumption of $X$? How much of this change is due to the substitution effect and how much is due to the income effect?
    *Answer:* Consumption falls from 5 to 21/2. The fall from 5 to $\sqrt{7.5} \approx$ is the substitution effect and the remainder is the income effect.

2.  Repeat problem 1 with the function $U$ replaced by

$$V'(x) - C'(x) = C$$

# Chapter 5

***1. A Farmer's Problem.*** Consider a farmer who must decide how many acres of land to spray for insects. If he sprays $x$ acres, the value of the crops saved is given by the function $V(x)$. The rate at which $V$ grows as additional acres are sprayed is given by the derivative $V'(x)$, which we call the *marginal value* of the crops saved, or the *marginal benefit* from spraying. In general, the word *marginal* in economics refers to a first derivative.

When one acre is a small part of the total area under consideration, $V'(x)$ can be well approximated by the quantity $V(x) - V(x - 1)$. The latter expression is used as the definition of marginal value in the textbook, but the more precise definition is $V'(x)$.

Suppose that the cost of spraying $x$ acres is given by the function $C(x)$. The farmer's goal is to maximize the quantity $V(x) - C(x)$, which he accomplishes by setting

$$V'(x) - C'(x) = C$$

In other words, he sets

$$V'(x) = C'(x)$$

Or, in still other words, he chooses that quantity at which marginal benefit is equal to marginal cost.

If a constant is added to the function $C$, then that same constant is subtracted from the function $V - C$. The addition or subtraction of a constant cannot change the location of the maximum, and therefore the number of acres sprayed will not change. Put another way, the addition of the constant does not change the derivative $C'$ and hence the quantity at which $V' = C'$ does not change.

Of course, the function $C$ can change in many ways other than by the addition of a constant, and in general other such changes in $C$ will affect the farmer's actions.

### 2. Firms and Profit Maximization.

A firm seeks to maximize its profits, which are defined as revenues minus costs. The firm must select a quantity of output to produce. Let us denote the total revenue derived from producing and selling $Q$ units of output by $TR(Q)$ and the total cost of producing and selling $Q$ units of output by $TC(Q)$. Let $D(P)$ be the demand curve for the firm's product. Then since $D^{-1}(Q)$ is the maximum price at which the firm can sell $Q$ units of output, it follows that

$$TR(Q) = Q \cdot D^{-1}(Q)$$

The firm seeks to maximize

$$TR(Q) - TC(Q)$$

which it accomplishes by selecting the quantity $Q$, at which

$$TR'(Q) - TC'(Q) = 0$$

or

$$TR'(Q) = TC'(Q)$$

If the $TC$ function changes by the addition of a constant, then the derivative $TC'$ is unchanged and consequently so is the profit-maximizing quantity. Put another way, the addition of a constant to $TC$ simply subtracts a constant from the profit function $TR - TC$, and the subtraction of a constant cannot change the location of the maximum.

Other sorts of changes in $TC$ can change the optimal output level, as can changes in $TR$. Since we have already seen that $TR(Q) = Q \cdot D^{-1}(Q)$, it follows that any change in $TR$ must arise from a change in the demand function $D$.

## Exercises

1. A firm faces the demand function $D(P) = 100 - 2P$ and the total cost function $TC(Q) = Q^2$. How much does it produce and at what price?

   *Answer: $Q = 16\frac{2}{3}$, $P = 41\frac{2}{3}$.*

2. A firm faces the demand function $D(P) = P^{-1/2}$ and the total cost function $TC(Q) = Q^2$. How much does it produce and at what price?

## Chapter 6

### 1. Short-Run Costs.

In the short run, we take the firm's capital usage to be fixed at some quantity, so that total product $TP$ is a function only of labor $L$. The marginal product of labor is $MP(L) = TP'(L)$.

To find the short-run total cost of producing $Q$ units of output, note that it is necessary to employ $TP^{-1}(Q)$ units of labor so that the total cost of production is

$$P_K \cdot K_0 + P_L \cdot TP^{-1}(Q)$$

where $P_K$ and $P_L$ are the hire prices of capital and labor. Differentiating this total cost function, we find that the firm's short-run marginal cost curve is given by

$$MC(Q) = \frac{1}{MP_L(L)}$$

where $L$ is the quantity of labor used in the production of $Q$ units of output. We define the firm's *variable cost* ($VC$) to be $P_L \cdot L$, its *average cost* ($AC'$) to be $TC/Q$, and its *average variable cost* ($AVC$) to be $VC/Q$. To find the relations among these cost curves, note for example that

$$\frac{dAC}{dQ} = \frac{d(TC/Q)}{dQ}$$

$$= \frac{Q\dfrac{dTC}{dQ} - TC}{Q^2}$$

$$= \frac{MC}{Q} - \frac{AC}{Q}$$

From this we conclude that when $AC$ is minimized (so that $dAC/dQ$ is zero), we must have $MC/Q = AC/Q$, or equivalently, $MC = AC$. In other words, the bottom of the U-shaped average cost curve occurs where $MC$ crosses $AC$. A similar calculation holds with $AC$ replaced by $AVC$.

The same equation shows that when $MC$ is below $AC$, $dAC/dQ$ is negative, so that $AC$ is downward sloping, and when $MC$ is above $AC$, $dAC/dQ$ is positive, so that $AC$ is upward sloping.

### 2. Isoquants and the Production Function.

The technology available to a firm is specified by its *production function $f(L, K)$*, which tells how much output the firm can produce using $L$ units of labor and $K$ units of capital. We assume that the production function satisfies the analogues of properties (1) through (5), which were assumed for the utility function. The isoquants are then the graphs of the various curves $f(L, K) = C$, where $C$ is any constant.

Along the isoquant $f(L, K) = C$, $K$ is implicitly defined as a function $g(L)$. Using the chain rule to differentiate both sides of the formula

$$f(L, g(L)) = C$$

we find that the slope of the isoquant is

$$g'(L) = \frac{\partial f/\partial L}{\partial f/\partial K} \tag{15}$$

As we will see in the next paragraph, $\partial f/\partial L$ and $\partial f/\partial K$ can be interpreted as the marginal products of labor and of capital.

### 3. Long-Run Costs.

In the long run, both capital and labor can be varied. The firm seeks to maximize the output that it can produce at any given cost. For a given expenditure $E$, the firm can hire any basket of inputs $(L, K)$ such that

$$P_L \cdot L + P_K \cdot K = E$$

Let us rewrite this as

$$K = \frac{E}{P_K} - \frac{P_L \cdot L}{P_K}$$

Then the firm's problem is to maximize

$$f\left(L, \frac{E}{P_K} - \frac{P_L \cdot L}{P_K}\right)$$

Differentiating with respect to $L$, we find that the firm chooses those quantities $L$ of labor and $K = (E - P_L \cdot L)/P_K$ of capital at which

$$f_1(L, K) - \frac{P_L}{P_K} \cdot f_2(L, K) = 0$$

or equivalently

$$\frac{f_1(L, K)}{f_2(L, K)} = \frac{P_L}{P_K} \tag{16}$$

That is, the firm chooses an input mix at which the ratio of the marginal products is equal to the ratio of the input prices. Because the ratio of the marginal products is the absolute slope of the isoquant (that is, it is the marginal rate of technical substitution), and because the input price ratio is the absolute slope of the isocosts, it follows that the firm operates at a tangency between an isoquant and an isocost. There are many such tangencies, one for each level of expenditure. The curve formed by these tangencies is the *expansion path*. The expansion path is the graph of equation (16).

For an alternative viewpoint, we can envision the firm minimizing cost for any given level of output. Thus, if $K = g(L)$ is the equation of the isoquant corresponding to the given output, the firm's problem is to minimize

$$P_L \cdot L + P_K \cdot g(L)$$

Differentiating, we find that the firm operates where $g'(L) = -P_L/P_K$; in view of equation (15) this is the same condition as described by equation (16).

For a given quantity of output $Q$, let $L_0(Q)$ and $K_0(Q)$ be the quantities of inputs that the firm employs in order to produce $Q$ units at the lowest possible cost. Then the functions $L_0$ and $K_0$ are determined implicitly by the equations

$$\frac{f_1(L_0(Q), K_0(Q))}{f_2(L_0(Q), K_0(Q))} = \frac{P_L}{P_K}$$

$$f(L_0(Q), K_0(Q)) = Q$$

The first of these equations says that the firm is on its expansion path, and the second says that it produces quantity $Q$. Differentiating the second equation yields

$$f_1(L_0(Q), K_0(Q)) \cdot L'_0(Q) + f_2(L_0(Q), K_0(Q)) \cdot K'_0(Q) = 1$$

Combining this with first equation gives

$$f(L_0(Q), K_0(Q)) \cdot \left(L'_0(Q) + \frac{P_K}{P_L} \cdot K'_0(Q)\right) = 1 \tag{17}$$

The long-run total cost of producing $Q$ units of output is

$$LRTC(Q) = P_L \cdot L_0(Q) + P_K \cdot K_0(Q)$$

Thus, the long-run marginal cost is given by

$$LRMC(Q) = P_L \cdot L'_0(Q) + P_K \cdot K'_0(Q)$$

$$= P_L \cdot \left( L'_0(Q) + \frac{P_K}{P_L} \cdot K'_0(Q) \right)$$

$$= \frac{P_L}{f_1(L_0(Q), K_0(Q))} \tag{18}$$

(The last equality follows from equation (17).)

A similar calculation shows that we also have

$$LRMC(Q) = \frac{P_K}{f_2(L_0(Q), K_0(Q))}$$

Here is a slightly different way to view the long-run total cost curve: For each quantity of capital $K$, let $SRTC_K(Q)$ be the short-run total cost curve that results when the firm uses $K$ units of capital. In the long run, the firm chooses $K$ to minimize its costs, so

$$LRTC(Q) = \min_K SRTC_K(Q)$$

Thus, the long-run total cost curve lies below all of the short-run total cost curves.

## 4. Returns to Scale. For any given $L$ and $K$, define

$$\Gamma = \frac{L \cdot f_1(L, K) + K \cdot f_2(L, K)}{f(L, K)}$$

Then we say that the production function $f$ exhibits constant, decreasing, or increasing *returns to scale* at $(L, K)$ according to whether $\Gamma$ is equal to, less than, or greater than 1.

Suppose that both inputs are increased by the same proportion $h$, so that the new quantities of labor and capital are $(1 + h)L$ and $(1 + h)K$. Then for $h$ small we have

$$f((1 + h)L, (1 + h)K) = f(L + hL, K + hK)$$

$$= f(L, K) + hLf_1(L, K) + hKf_2(L, K)$$

$$= (1 + \Gamma \cdot h) \cdot f(L, K)$$

In other words, the proportional change in output is equal to, less than, or greater than the proportional change in the inputs depending on whether $f$ exhibits constant, decreasing, or increasing returns to scale. This is the definition given in the textbook.

A case of particular interest is that of a *homogeneous* production function. A homogeneous production function is defined to be one for which $\Gamma$ is a constant independent of $K$ and $L$. In this case, we say that $\Gamma$ is the *degree of homogeneity* of the function $f$, or that $f$ is *homogeneous of degree* $\Gamma$. As an immediate consequence of the definition in the textbook, a homogeneous function of degree 1 exhibits constant returns to scale, and a homogeneous function of degree less than (greater than) 1 exhibits decreasing (increasing) returns to scale.

### 5. Returns to Scale and the Long-Run Average Cost Curve.
We can relate the returns to scale to the slope of the long-run average cost curve. The slope of the long-run average cost curve is

$$\frac{dLRAC}{dQ} = \frac{d(LRTC/Q)}{dQ} = \frac{(dLRTC/dQ) \cdot Q - LRTC}{Q_2} = \frac{(LRMC - LRAC)}{Q}$$

Thus, long-run average cost is flat, increasing, or decreasing depending on whether $LRAC$ is equal to, less than, or greater than $LRMC$. To investigate this, we consider the ratio $LRAC/LRMC$. We have

$$\frac{LRAC(Q)}{LRMC(Q)} = \frac{(P_L \cdot L_0(Q) + P_K \cdot K_0(Q))}{f(L_0(Q), K_0(Q))} \Bigg| \frac{P_L}{f(L_0(Q), K_0(Q))} \qquad \textbf{(by (18))}$$

$$= \frac{L \cdot f_1(L_0(Q), K_0(Q)) + f_2(L_0(Q), K_0(Q))}{f(L_0(Q), K_0(Q))} \qquad \textbf{(by (16))}$$

Since the final term in the right-hand series of equations is none other than $\Gamma$, we see that

$$\text{When } \Gamma \text{ is} \begin{Bmatrix} \text{equal to} \\ \text{less than} \\ \text{greater than} \end{Bmatrix} 1, LRAC \text{ is} \begin{Bmatrix} \text{equal to} \\ \text{less than} \\ \text{greater than} \end{Bmatrix} LRMC \text{ and therefore} \begin{Bmatrix} \text{flat} \\ \text{increasing} \\ \text{decreasing} \end{Bmatrix}$$

In other words, constant returns to scale imply a flat $LRAC$, decreasing returns to scale imply an increasing $LRAC$, and increasing returns to scale imply a decreasing $LRAC$.

### 6. Relations between the Short Run and the Long Run.
Given the long-run production function $f(L, K)$, and given a fixed quantity of capital $K_0$, we derive the short-run production function

$$TP(L) = f(L, K_0)$$

Thus, the marginal product of labor is given by

$$MP(L) = TP'(L) = \frac{\partial f}{\partial L}(L, K_0)$$

Let $C(Q, K)$ be the cost of producing $Q$ units of output using $K$ units of capital (together with however much labor is necessary). Thus, for fixed $K$, $SKTC(Q) = C(Q, K)$ is the short-run total cost curve, and short-run marginal cost is given by

$$SRMC(Q) = \frac{\partial C}{\partial Q}(Q, K)$$

Now for any given $Q$ let $K_0(Q)$ be the quantity of capital that allows $Q$ units of output to be produced at the lowest cost. Then $LRTC(Q) = C(Q, K_0(Q))$ is the long-run total cost curve, and long-run marginal cost is given by

$$LRMC(Q) = \frac{\partial C}{\partial Q}(Q, K_0(Q)) + \frac{\partial C}{\partial K}(Q, K_0(Q)) \cdot K'_0(Q)$$

Since $K_0(Q)$ is determined by the first-order condition

$$\frac{\partial C}{\partial K}(Q, K_0(Q)) = 0$$

it follows that in long-run equilibrium (where $K = K_0(Q)$), we have

$$SRMC(Q) = LRMC(Q)$$

Interpreting marginal cost as the slope of total cost, this tells us that the short-run and long-run total cost curves are tangent where they touch. A similar argument applies to the short-run and long-run average cost curves.

## Exercises

1.  Suppose that a firm's production function is given by $f(L, K) = L^\alpha K^\beta$, where $\alpha$ and $\beta$ are positive constants and both $\alpha$ and $\beta$ are less than 1. When $K = 1$, write down the firm's (short-run) total product and marginal product of labor functions and its short-run marginal cost function, assuming that the wage rate of labor is 1. Repeat with $K = 2$. Does the firm experience diminishing marginal returns to labor?

    *Answer:* With $K = 1$, $TP_L = L^\alpha$, $MP_L = \alpha L^{\alpha-1}$, and $MC = \dfrac{1}{\alpha L^{\alpha-1}}$

2.  In problem 1, write down the equations for the 1-unit and 2-unit isoquant.

    *Answer:* The 1-unit isoquant is $L^\alpha K^\beta = 1$.

3.  When the price of labor is $W$ and the price of capital is $R$, what combination of inputs does the firm in problem 1 use to produce 1 unit of output? 2 units of output? $Q$ units of output?

    *Answer:* For 1 unit of output,

    $$L = \left(\frac{\alpha R}{\beta W}\right)^{\beta/\beta + \alpha} \text{ and } K = \left(\frac{\beta W}{\alpha R}\right)^{\alpha/\beta + \alpha}$$

4.  In problem 1, write down the equations for the firm's long-run total cost and marginal cost curves.

    *Answer:* $LRTC(Q) = (CR^\beta W^\alpha Q)^{1/\alpha + \beta}$ where $C = \left[\left(\frac{\alpha}{\beta}\right)^\beta + \left(\frac{\beta}{\alpha}\right)^\alpha\right]$

5.  In problem 1, suppose that $\alpha + \beta < 1$. Does the production function exhibit decreasing, constant, or increasing returns to scale? Repeat under the assumption that $\alpha + \beta = 1$ and then under the assumption that $\alpha + \beta > 1$.

6.  Repeat problems 1 through 5 with the production function replaced by

    $$f(L, K) = (L^\alpha + K^\alpha)^{\beta/\alpha}$$

# Chapter 7

### 1. The Competitive Firm.
A competitive firm is one that takes prices as given; that is, its own actions do not affect the market price of its product. For a competitive firm, total revenue is given by the simple formula $TR(Q) = P \cdot Q$, so that marginal revenue is the constant function $MR(Q) = P$.

For a competitive firm, the profit-maximizing rule $MC = MR$ simplifies to $MC = P$. That is, the firm produces that quantity $Q$ for which $MC(Q) = P$. The exception is that there are some circumstances in which the firm might choose to shut down. It is shown in the text that the firm shuts down precisely if $P < AVC$. Thus, the competitive firm's supply curve is completely specified by the equation

$$S(P) = \begin{cases} MC^{-1}(P) & \text{if } P \geq \min(AVC) \\ 0 & \text{if } P < \min(AVC) \end{cases}$$

This can be interpreted as a description of either the firm's short-run or long-run supply curve. To get the short-run cost curve, use the short-run marginal and average variable cost curves. To get the long-run cost curve, use the long-run marginal and average variable cost curves, keeping in mind that in the long run, average variable cost is just the same as average cost.*

## 2. The Competitive Industry in the Short Run.

In the short run, we take the number of firms in the industry as given. To a first approximation, the industry supply curve is the sum of the individual firms' supply curves. To derive the industry supply curve precisely, it is necessary to take account of the factor-price effect, as discussed in the textbook.

Suppose that there are $N$ firms in the industry, and that the $i^{th}$ firm has the total cost function $TC_i$. Let $Q$ be the total output of the entire industry. For each of the firms $2, \ldots, n$, let $Q_i$ be the output of firm $i$, so that firm 1 produces the quantity

$$Q_1 = Q - \sum_{i=2}^{n} Q_i$$

Then a planner who wanted to minimize the sum of all firms' costs in producing $Q$ units of output would choose the $Q_i$ to minimize the expression

$$TC_1\left(Q - \sum_{i=2}^{n} Q_i\right) + \sum_{i=2}^{n} TC_i(Q_i)$$

Differentiating with respect to $Q_i$, we see that this requires setting $MC_1(Q_1) = MC_i(Q_i)$ for each $i$; that is, $MC_i(Q_i)$ must be independent of $i$. This condition is satisfied automatically in competitive equilibrium, because the $i^{th}$ firm sets $MC_i(Q_i) = P$, and $P$ is independent of $i$. A competitive industry minimizes the total cost of producing a given quantity.

## 3. The Competitive Industry in the Long Run.

In the long run, we assume that there is free entry to the industry. The industry's long-run supply curve reflects this free entry. At any given price, we assume that sufficiently many firms enter to drive profits to zero, and the long-run supply curve shows the quantity that will be produced by that number of firms at the given price. The textbook discusses the various situations in which this could lead to a flat, increasing, or decreasing industry supply curve.

## Exercise

1. Work the Numerical Exercises at the end of Chapter 7 in the body of the textbook.

---

* It is standard to assume that there are no fixed costs in the long run, since in the long run all factors of production are variable. Thus, there are no fixed costs as long as the firm's only costs are factor payments. It is possible to imagine some costs—such as annual license fees—that are fixed even in the long run. In this case, the average variable cost curve differs from the average cost curve, and it is average cost, not average variable cost, that determines whether the firm will remain in the industry.

# Chapter 8

**1. *The Consumer's Surplus.*** Consider a consumer who has an income of $E and can purchase good $X$ in the marketplace at a going price of $P per unit. He will choose to purchase the quantity $x_0$ depicted in the following diagram:

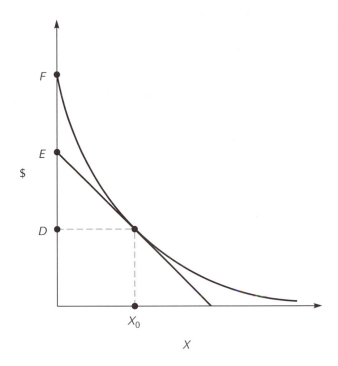

By enabling him to reach the illustrated indifference curve, the existence of the market has made the consumer as well off as if his income had increased to $F. We say that he has earned a *consumer's surplus* of $(F − E)$. The equation of the indifference curve can be put in the form $Y = f(X)$. Then the consumer's compensated demand curve is given by the function

$$D_c(P) = (f')^{-1}(-P)$$

The inverse function is

$$D_c^{-1}(X) = -f'(X)$$

The area under the demand curve is the integral of the *inverse* function, because $X$ is the variable on the horizontal axis. Therefore, the area under the compensated demand curve out to the quantity $x_0$ is given by

$$\int_0^{x_0} f'(X)dX = f(0) - f(x_0) = \$\,(F - D)$$

This is the total value to the consumer of $x_0$ units of $X$, in the sense that if all $x_0$ units were taken from the consumer and replaced by $(F − D)$, the consumer would remain on the same indifference curve.

When the consumer starts with $\$E$ and then trades for the optimal basket $O$, his total expenditure on good $X$ is $\$(E - D)$. When this is subtracted from the area under the demand curve, we find that the remaining area (that is, the area under the demand curve and out to the quantity $x_0$, down to the price $P$) is

$$\$(F - D) - \$(E - D) = \$(F - E)$$

which is precisely the consumer's surplus.[*]

## 2. The Producer's Surplus.

The producer's surplus is the excess of his revenue over his variable costs. Because

$$VC(Q) = \int_0^Q MC(x)dx$$

it follows that the producer's surplus is the area above the marginal cost curve, out to the quantity supplied and up to the market price, as discussed in the textbook.

## 3. The Invisible Hand.

Imagine a benevolent planner interested in the welfare of both consumers and producers. Suppose that the planner's goal is to maximize the total welfare gains earned in the market for $X$. That is, the planner wishes to maximize

$$TV(X) - TC(X)$$

where $TV$ represents total value to consumers and $TC$ represents total cost to producers. We have seen that when consumers purchase $x_0$ units of $X$, the total value of their purchases is

$$\int_0^{x_0} D_c(X)dX$$

Thus, the planner seeks to maximize

$$\int_0^{x_0} D_c(X)dX - TC(x_0)$$

Differentiating, we find that the optimum occurs where

$$D_c(x_0) = MC(x_0)$$

or, in other words, at the point where the demand and supply curves cross. This, of course, is none other than the point of equilibrium. The competitive equilibrium outcome is precisely the outcome sought by the planner.

## 4. General Equilibrium.

Consider the Edgeworth box economy described in the text. There are two individuals (Aline and Bob) and two goods (Food and Clothing). Suppose that Aline's indifference curves are given by the family of equations $U(X,Y) = C$ and that Bob's are given by the family of equations $V(X,Y) = C$, where $X$ is the quantity of food, $Y$ is the quantity of clothing, and $C$ varies over all possible constants.

We assume that the quantities of food and clothing are permanently fixed at $X_0$ and $Y_0$.

---

[*] When we computed the total value to the consumer of being able to purchase good $X$, we assumed that the consumer is on the illustrated indifference curve, which is to say that we assumed that the market for good $X$ actually does exist. Our measure of total value is the amount that the consumer would be willing to pay in order to prevent the market from disappearing. The resulting measure of consumer's surplus is called the *equivalent variation*. An alternative approach is to assume that the market for good $X$ does not exist and to ask how much the consumer would be willing to pay to have the market come into existence. In this case, we would assume that the consumer is on the indifference curve through point E and integrate the corresponding compensated demand curve. The measure of consumer's surplus that arises in this way is called the *compensating variation*.

We will write $X$ and $Y$ for the quantities of food and clothing owned by Aline, so that $X_0 - X$ and $Y_0 - Y$ are the quantities owned by Bob. An *allocation* is a specification of Aline's basket $(X, Y)$ (which then determines Bob's basket as well). An allocation $(X, Y)$ is *Pareto-optimal* if no other allocation could make both Aline and Bob better off; that is, $(X, Y)$ is Pareto optimal if there does not exist any allocation $(X', Y')$ such that $U(X', Y') > U(X, Y)$ and $V(X_0 - X', Y_0 + Y') > V(X_0 + X, Y_0 + Y)$.*

We can show that the allocation $(X, Y)$ is Pareto-optimal if and only if

$$\frac{\partial U/\partial X}{\partial U/\partial Y}(X, Y) = \frac{\partial V/\partial X}{\partial V/\partial Y}(X_0 - X, Y_0 - Y) \tag{19}$$

Suppose first that equation (19) fails to hold; we will conclude that $(X, Y)$ cannot be Pareto-optimal. We can assume that

$$\frac{\partial U/\partial X}{\partial U/\partial Y}(X, Y) > \frac{\partial V/\partial X}{\partial V/\partial Y}(X_0 - X, Y_0 - Y)$$

Let $b$ and $j$ be small positive numbers such that

$$\frac{\partial U/\partial X}{\partial U/\partial Y}(X, Y) > \frac{j}{h} > \frac{\partial V/\partial X}{\partial V/\partial Y}(X_0 - X, Y_0 - Y)$$

and consider the allocation $(X + h, Y - j)$. We have

$$U(X + h, Y - j) \approx U(X, Y) + h \cdot \frac{\partial U}{\partial X} - j \cdot \frac{\partial U}{\partial Y} > U(X, Y)$$

$$V(X_0 - X - h, Y_0 - Y + j) \approx V(X_0 - X, Y_0 - Y) - h \cdot \frac{\partial V}{\partial X} + j \cdot \frac{\partial V}{\partial Y} > V(X_0 - X, Y_0 - Y)$$

contradicting Pareto-optimality.

On the other hand, if equation (19) *does* hold, then it is possible to show that $(X, Y)$ must in fact be Pareto-optimal. Indeed, running the preceding argument backward shows that no allocation of the form $(X + h, Y - j)$ can be Pareto-preferred to $(X, Y)$ when $h$ and $j$ are small. To show the same thing when $h$ and $j$ are arbitrary requires a little work using the convexity of indifference curves. If you are ambitious, you might try to complete the proof.

In competitive equilibrium, both Aline and Bob choose baskets where their marginal rates of substitution between $X$ and $Y$ are equal to the relative price of $X$ in terms of $Y$. Because they both face the same relative price, it follows that their marginal rates of substitution are equal. But this is precisely the condition of equation (19). We conclude that a competitive equilibrium is Pareto-optimal. This is the theorem of the invisible hand.

## Exercise

1. Aline's indifference curves are given by the family of equations $X^{1/2} \cdot Y^{1/2} = C$ and Bob's by the family of equations $X^{1/4} \cdot Y^{3/4} = C$. Aline owns 2 $X$s and 5 $Y$s, while Bob owns 8 $X$s and 5 $Y$s. Characterize the Pareto-optimal outcomes (i.e., give the equation of the contract curve) and compute the competitive equilibrium.

   *Answer:* The equation of the contract curve is $3Y(10 - X) = X(10 - Y)$. In competitive equilibrium, Aline has $17/3$ $X$s and $85/28$ $Y$s.

---

* Other references use slightly different formulations involving ≥ signs as well as > signs, but if $U$ and $V$ are continuous, the formulations are equivalent.

# Chapter 10

**1. Monopoly Pricing.** The monopolist, like any producer, has a total revenue function $TR(Q) = Q \cdot P(Q)$, where $P(Q)$ is the maximum price at which demanders will purchase $Q$ items. That is, $P = D^{-1}$, where $D$ is the demand curve for the product. Differentiating, we find that the marginal revenue function is

$$MR(Q) = P(Q) + Q \cdot P'(Q)$$

Because $P'(Q)$ is negative, we conclude that for a monopolist, marginal revenue is always less than the price at which he sells his goods.

Note that $Q \cdot P'(Q) = P \cdot (1/|\eta|)$, where $\eta$ is the elasticity of the demand curve. Thus, we can write

$$MR = P \cdot \left(1 - \frac{1}{|\eta|}\right) \tag{20}$$

To maximize profits, the monopolist (like any producer) chooses the quantity at which $MC = MR$. Since $MR < P$, it follows that for a profit-maximizing monopolist, $MC < P$.

**2. Price Discrimination.** Consider a monopolist who sells in two markets. In market $A$, the inverse to the demand function is $P_A(Q)$ and in market $B$, the inverse to the demand function is $P_B(Q)$. By selling $Q_A$ items in market $A$ and $Q_B$ items in market $B$, the monopolist earns a total profit of

$$Q_A \cdot P_A(Q_A) + Q_B \cdot P_B(Q_B) - TC(Q_A + Q_B)$$

By differentiating separately with respect to $Q_A$ and $Q_B$, we find that the conditions for profit maximization are

$$MR_A(Q_A) = MC(Q_A + Q_B) = MR_B(Q_B)$$

where $MR_A$ and $MR_B$ are the marginal revenue functions in the two markets. Combining this observation with equation (20), we discover that

$$\frac{P_A}{P_B} = \frac{\left(1 - \dfrac{1}{|\eta_A|}\right)}{\left(1 - \dfrac{1}{|\eta_B|}\right)}$$

where $\eta_A$ and $\eta_B$ are the elasticities of demand in the two markets.

# Chapter 11

**1. Collusion.** Suppose that there are $N$ firms in an industry, and that the $i$th firm has marginal cost curve $MC_i$. The inverse demand curve for the industry's product is given by the function $P(Q)$. Under competition, firms take the market price as given, so they produce quantities $Q_i$ such that

$$MC_i(Q_i) = P\left(\sum_{i=1}^{N} Q_i\right)$$

This system of $N$ equations in $N$ unknowns determines the quantities $Q_i$.

Suppose alternatively that the firms collude in order to maximize industry profits. That is, the cartel seeks to maximize

$$\left(\sum_{j=1}^{N} Q_j\right) \cdot P\left(\sum_{j=1}^{N} Q_j\right) - \sum_{j=1}^{N} TC_i(Q_j)$$

The condition for this is that for each $i$,

$$MC_i(Q_i) = P\left(\sum_{j=1}^{N} Q_j\right) + \left(\sum_{j=1}^{N} Q_j\right) \cdot P'\left(\sum_{j=1}^{N} Q_j\right)$$

Note that the expression on the right is the industry's marginal revenue curve.

**2. *Cournot Oligopoly.*** Suppose that the $N$ firms in an industry are not able to collude. Then each maximizes its profits subject to the constraints placed upon it by the behavior of other firms. However, this formulation is imprecise and ambiguous. Exactly what aspects of other firms' behavior shall we assume that each firm takes as given? In the *Cournot model* of oligopoly, the assumption is that each firm takes its rivals' *quantities* as given. Thus, the $t^{th}$ firm attempts to maximize

$$Q_i \cdot P\left(Q_i + \sum_{ji} Q_j\right) - TC_i(Q_i)$$

treating each $Q_j (j \neq i)$ as a constant. This leads the firm to set

$$MC_1(Q_i) = P\left(Q_i + \sum_{ij} Q_j\right) + Q_i P'\left(Q_i + \sum_{ij} Q_j\right)$$

These $N$ equations in $N$ unknowns determine the quantities $Q_i$.

# Chapter 15

**1. *The Derived Demand for Factors of Production.*** In the short run, the firm's demand curve for a factor is the inverse function to that factor's marginal revenue product, as discussed in the text. To derive the demand for labor in the long run, we assume that the firm has the production function $f(L, K)$, and we take as given the price of capital, $P_K$, and the price of output, $P$.

At any given wage rate $P_L$, the firm chooses quantities $L$ of labor and $K$ of capital to maximize its profit

$$P \cdot f(L, K) - P_L \cdot L - P_K \cdot K$$

The first-order conditions for a maximum are

$$P \cdot \frac{\partial f}{\partial L}(L, K) = P_L$$

$$P \cdot \frac{\partial f}{\partial K}(L, K) = P_K$$

These two equations in the two unknowns $L$ and $K$ determine the firm's employment of labor and of capital. If $(L, K)$ is a solution to the system, then the quantity $L$ corresponds to the price $PL$ on the firm's long-run demand curve for labor.

Continuing to hold $P_K$ and $P$ fixed, let $L_0(P_L)$ and $K_0(P_L)$ be the profit-maximizing quantities of labor and capital when the wage rate of labor is $P_L$. Thus, the functions $L_0$ and $K_0$ are implicitly defined by the system

$$P \cdot \frac{\partial f}{\partial L}(L_0(P_L), K_0(P_L)) = P_L$$

$$P \cdot \frac{\partial f}{\partial K}(L_0(P_L), K_0(P_L)) = P_K$$

Differentiating with respect to the variable $P_L$, we get

$$P \cdot \frac{\partial^2 f}{\partial L^2}(L_0(P_L), K_0(P_L)) \cdot \frac{dL_0}{dP_L}(P_L) + \frac{\partial^2 f}{\partial L \partial K}(L_0(P_L), K_0(P_L)) \cdot \frac{dK_0}{dP_L}(P_L) = 1$$

$$P \cdot \frac{\partial^2 f}{\partial L \partial K}(L_0(P_L), K_0(P_L)) \cdot \frac{dL_0}{dP_L}(P_L) + \frac{\partial^2 f}{\partial K^2}(L_0(P_L), K_0(P_L)) \cdot \frac{dK_0}{dP_L}(P_L) = 0$$

Solving this system, we find that

$$\frac{dL_0}{dP_L}(P_L) = \frac{\partial^2 f / \partial K^2}{P \cdot \delta} \qquad (21)$$

$$\frac{dK_0}{dP_L}(P_L) = \frac{-\partial^2 f / \partial L \partial K}{P \cdot \delta} \qquad (22)$$

where

$$\delta = \left( \frac{\partial^2 f}{\partial K^2} \cdot \frac{\partial^2 f}{\partial L^2} - \left( \frac{\partial^2 f}{\partial L \partial K} \right)^2 \right)(L_0(P_L), K_0(P_L))$$

Because we assume that $f$ satisfies the analogues of equations (1) through (5), we know that $\partial^2 f / \partial K^2 < 0$ and that $\delta > 0$. It follows from this and equation (21) that $dL_0 / dP_L$ is everywhere negative. That is, the firm's demand curve for a factor of production must be everywhere downward sloping. This is in contrast to the consumer's demand curve for a consumption good, where the Giffen phenomenon is at least a theoretical possibility.

## 2. Changes in the Price of Another Factor.
In the preceding section we held the price of capital fixed and determined how the firm's employment of labor and of capital varied in response to a change in the wage rate of labor. In particular, we derived the equation for the firm's labor demand curve and showed that this curve must slope downward.

Equation (22) shows how the firm's employment of capital changes in response to a change in the wage rate of labor. Because $\delta$ is known to be positive, the sign of $dK_0 / dP_L$ depends only on the sign of the cross partial derivative $\partial^2 f / \partial L \partial K$. When the cross partial is positive, we say that capital and labor are *complements in production*, and when the cross partial is negative, we say that capital and labor are *substitutes in production*.

When labor and capital are complements in production, equation (22) shows that an increase in the wage rate of labor leads to a fall in the demand for capital (and similarly, an increase in the rental rate for capital leads to a fall in the demand for labor). When labor and capital are substitutes in production, the reverse is true.

Economists believe that labor and capital are more often complements than substitutes in production. For example, if labor and capital are the only two inputs and if the production function exhibits constant returns to scale, then we can show that labor and capital must be complements in production. To see this, write

$$f = \frac{\partial f}{\partial L} \cdot L + \frac{\partial f}{\partial K} \cdot K$$

and differentiate with respect to $L$ to get

$$\frac{\partial^2 f}{\partial L^2} \cdot L + \frac{\partial^2 f}{\partial K \partial L} \cdot K = 0$$

Because $\partial^2 f / \partial L^2$ is negative, the cross partial must be positive as needed.

### 3. Changes in the Price of Output.
Holding $P_L$ and $P_K$ fixed, we let the price $P$ of output vary and write $L_0(P)$ and $K_0(P)$ for the profit-maximizing levels of labor and capital employment. Beginning with the system

$$P \cdot \frac{\partial f}{\partial L}(L_0(P), K_0(P)) = P_L$$

$$P \cdot \frac{\partial f}{\partial K}(L_0(P), K_0(P)) = P_K$$

we differentiate with respect to $P$ and find

$$\frac{\partial^2 f}{\partial L^2} \cdot \frac{dL_0}{dP} + \frac{\partial^2 f}{\partial L \partial K} \cdot \frac{dK_0}{dP} = -\frac{\partial f}{\partial L}$$

$$\frac{\partial^2 f}{\partial L \partial K} \cdot \frac{dL_0}{dP} + \frac{\partial^2 f}{\partial K^2} \cdot \frac{dK_0}{dP} = -\frac{\partial f}{\partial K}$$

Solving for $dL_0/dP$ and $dK_0/dP$, we find that

$$\frac{dL_0}{dP} = \frac{1}{\delta} \cdot \left( -\frac{\partial^2 f}{\partial L^2} \cdot \frac{\partial f}{\partial L} + \frac{\partial^2 f}{\partial L \partial K} \cdot \frac{\partial f}{\partial K} \right)$$

$$\frac{dK_0}{dP} = \frac{1}{\delta} \cdot \left( -\frac{\partial^2 f}{\partial K^2} \cdot \frac{\partial f}{\partial K} + \frac{\partial^2 f}{\partial L \partial K} \cdot \frac{\partial f}{\partial L} \right)$$

This shows that when labor and capital are complements in production, an increase in the price of output leads to an increase in the demand for both labor and capital.

### 4. The Distribution of Income.
In equilibrium, the wage rate of labor is equal to its marginal revenue product $P \cdot \partial f / \partial L$, and the wage rate of capital is equal to its marginal revenue product $P \cdot \partial f / \partial K$. Thus, when labor and capital are the only inputs, the firm's total costs are

$$P \cdot \frac{\partial f}{\partial L}(L, K) \cdot L + P \cdot \frac{\partial f}{\partial K}(L, K) \cdot K$$

The total revenue of the firm is the price of output multiplied by the quantity of output, or

$$P \cdot f(L, K)$$

Finally, the profits of the firm are given by the difference between revenue and cost, or

$$P \cdot f(L, K) - P \cdot \frac{\partial f}{\partial L}(L, K) \cdot L + P \cdot \frac{\partial f}{\partial K}(L, K) \cdot K$$

From this expression we see immediately that a competitive firm earns zero profits if and only if it produces at a point where there are constant returns to scale. If returns to scale are decreasing, then the firm earns positive profits, and if returns to scale are increasing, then the firm earns negative profits.

In the long run, one can argue that all firms experience constant returns to scale provided that the production function really includes every factor of production. This is because of the principle that "what a firm does once, it can do twice" discussed in Chapter 6 of the textbook. It follows that when all payments to all factors are considered, the competitive firm earns zero profits in the long run.

## Exercise

1. A firm produces according to the production function $f(L, K) = L^{1/4} \cdot K^{1/4}$. Holding fixed the prices of output and of capital, derive the firm's short-run and long-run labor demand curves. How does the demand for labor vary with the price of capital? With the price of output?

    *Answer:* Fixing the price of output at 1 and the price of capital at $P_K$, short-run labor demand is

    $$\left[\frac{K}{256P_L^4}\right]^{1/3}$$

    and long-run labor demand is

    $$\frac{1}{16P_K^{1/2}P_L^{3/2}}$$

# Chapter 16

***1. The Supply of Labor.***  To model the supply of labor, we assume that the worker's indifference curves between consumption and labor are given by the family of equations

$$V(L, Y) = \text{constant}$$

where $L$ is labor and $Y$ is consumption. Given a wage rate $P_L$, the worker who works $L$ hours earns $P_L \cdot L$ units of consumption; thus, he chooses $L$ so as to maximize

$$V(L, C_0 + P_L \cdot L)$$

where $C_0$ is 1the worker's nonlabor income.

The first-order condition for a maximum is

$$\frac{-V_1(L, C_0 + P_L \cdot L)}{V_2(L, C_0 + P_L \cdot L)} = P_L$$

Thus, the labor supply function $S$ is implicitly defined by the equation

$$\frac{-V_1(S(P_L), C_0 + P_L \cdot S(P_L))}{V_2(S(P_L), C_0 + P_L \cdot S(P_L))} = P_L \tag{23}$$

Let $L_0$ be the total time available to the worker. For example, if we are deriving the supply of labor per day, then $L_0 = 24$ hours. Set $U(X, Y) = V(L_0 - L, Y)$ so that $X$ can be thought of as leisure. We assume that $U$ satisfies properties (1) through (5).

This guarantees that the first-order condition really is sufficient for the existence of a maximum.

The wage rate $P_L$ can be viewed as the price of leisure, and the effect of a change in the wage rate can be decomposed into income and substitution effects, working with the function $U$ just as in Chapter 4. Note that when leisure is a normal good, the income effect leads the worker to consume more leisure, which is the same thing as supplying *less* labor.

**2. The Representative Agent.** Suppose that there is a fixed amount of capital in society and that labor $L$ produces output $Y$ according to the total product function

$$Y = TP(L)$$

In an economy consisting of a single individual, that individual would choose the quantity of his labor input by maximizing the function

$$V(L, TP(L))$$

The first-order condition is

$$\frac{-V_1(L, TP(L))}{V_2(L, TP(L))} = TP'(L) \tag{24}$$

Given a wage $P_1$, each worker supplies a quantity of labor determined by equation (23). Each employer demands a quantity $D(P_1)$ of labor determined by the condition

$$TP'(D(P_L)) = P_L$$

For the representative agent, the quantity of labor demanded must coincide with the quantity supplied. Call this common quantity $L_0$. Then the representative agent employs $L_0$ units of labor, produces $Y_0 = TP(L_0)$ units of output, pays a wage bill of $P_t \cdot L_0$, and earns a nonlabor income $C_0$ equal to the difference between what he produces and his wage bill; that is

$$C_0 = TP(L_0) - P_L \cdot L_0 \tag{25}$$

In equilibrium, $L_0$ is also the quantity of labor supplied by the representative agent; that is, $S(P_L) = L_0$. Combining this with equation (23) and (25) and comparing with equation (24), we find that in a competitive economy, the representative agent supplies exactly the same amount of labor that he would choose to supply if he lived in isolation.

# Chapter 17

**1. A Two-Period Model.** The simplest way to model the allocation of goods over time is to imagine an individual who lives for two periods. We then treat consumption in period one and consumption in period two as different goods and apply all of the consumer theory that we have developed.

Let $C_0$ and $C_1$ denote "consumption today" and "consumption tomorrow." Then the consumer's indifference curves are given by the family of equations

$$U(C_0, C_1) = constant$$

for some function $U$ satisfying properties (1) through (5). We often assume that $U$ is of the special form

$$U(C_0, C_1) = V(C_0) + \beta \cdot V(C_1)$$

where $\beta$ is a constant satisfying $0 < \beta < 1$ and $V$ is a function of one variable satisfying

$$V'(C) > 0$$

$$V''(C) < 0$$

Suppose that the consumer is endowed with $E_0$ units of consumption today and $E_1$ units of consumption tomorrow. Then if the price of consumption today in terms of consumption tomorrow is $1/(1 + r)$, the present value of the consumer's wealth is

$$E = E_0 + \frac{1}{1 + r} \cdot E_1$$

and his goal is to maximize $V(C_0) + \beta \cdot V(C_1)$ subject to the constraint

$$C_0 + \frac{1}{1 + r} \cdot C_1 = E$$

The first-order condition is

$$\frac{V'(C_0)}{V'(C_1)} = \beta \cdot (1 + r)$$

The representative agent must consume his endowment, so for him we have $C_0 = E_0$ and $C_1 = E_1$. If in addition $E_0 = E_1$, then it follows that in equilibrium we must have

$$\beta = \frac{1}{1 + r}$$

# Answers to All the Exercises

## Chapter 1

**1.1** Demand for coffee rises. It depends on the related good.

**1.2** It would probably rise.

**1.3** The demand curve would shift downward a vertical distance 5¢. The demand curve would shift upward a vertical distance 10¢.

**1.4** The demand curve would shift downward, but not parallel to itself, because the amount of the tax per item varies with the quantity purchased.

**1.5** It would fall. It would fall because an increase in the price of leather belts would probably lead to an increase in the price of leather.

**1.6** At a price of 40¢ per cup, suppliers get to keep 30¢ per cup and so supply 300 cups (read off the second line of Table A). And so forth.

**1.7** Panel A. Price rises and quantity rises.

**1.8** The sales tax causes very little change in price if either the demand curve is quite steep or the supply curve is quite flat. Price drops by nearly the whole 5¢ if either the demand curve is quite flat or the supply curve is quite steep.

**1.9** Because the vertical distance from $S$ to $S'$ is 5¢ and the vertical distance from $E$ to $H$ is less than this.

**1.10** You should shift the supply curve up a vertical distance 2¢ and the demand curve down a vertical distance 3¢. The new price to suppliers is 2¢ less than the new market price and the new price to demanders is 3¢ more than the new market price. If you have drawn your picture correctly, you will find that the new price to suppliers is on the old supply curve, the new price to demanders is on the old demand curve, and the distance between the two is 5¢. Because this can happen at only one place, the effect must be the same as that of the pure 5¢ sales and excise taxes.

## Chapter 2

**2.1** The relative price of bread is the reciprocal of the relative price of wine. When a number increases, its reciprocal decreases.

---

Examples include VCD-player, CD-ROM player, mobile telephones, beepers, and video cameras. Garten, Jeffrey E., Opening the Doors for Business in China

**2.2**    For the carpenter to rewire takes 20 hours, during which time he could perform 20/18 = 10/9 paneling jobs.

# Chapter 3

**3.1**    B: 4 eggs, 7 root beers. C: 1 egg, 2 root beers. D: 4 eggs, 2 root beers.

**3.2**    Basket A, which has more of everything.

**3.3**    When you give Jeremy an egg, your stock of eggs is reduced from 7 to 6; when he gives you 4 root beers in exchange, your stock of root beers is increased from 2 to 6.

**3.4**    Imagine sacrificing 1 root beer in exchange for some eggs in such a way that the trade leaves you just as happy as you started out. This will bring you to a point on the indifference curve with vertical coordinate 1. The corresponding horizontal coordinate shows how many eggs you have at the end of the exchange; the excess of this quantity over the 7 eggs you started with shows the marginal value (to you) of a root beer.

**3.5**    If Jack sacrifices 1 egg for 6 root beers, he moves from point *C* to point *D*, staying on the same indifference curve. If Jill sacrifices 1 egg for 1 root beer, she moves from point *C* to point *E*, staying on the same indifference curve.

**3.6**    The consumer values additional root beers highly relative to additional eggs when he has few root beers and lots of eggs. Therefore, the indifference curve should be shallower toward the southeast, confirming our belief that indifference curves are convex.

**3.7**    Because it is on a higher indifference curve. The budget line would have to be flatter, intersecting the *x*-axis on a higher indifference curve than where it intersects the *y*-axis.

# Chapter 4

**4.1**    The new budget line is shifted southwest from the original line, and parallel to the original.

**4.2**    No. No. For *Y* to be inferior, point *B* would have to be located vertically below point *A*.

**4.3**    With an income of $12, the consumer chooses point *C* in panel *A*, and therefore consumes 12 eggs.

**4.5**    The budget line pivots inward around its x-intercept. If *Y* is not Giffen, the new optimum is vertically below the original. If *Y* is Giffen, the new optimum is vertically above the original.

**4.6** When the price of *X* is $6, the consumer chooses point *C* in Exhibit 4.8A and therefore consumes 2 eggs.

**4.7**

The movement from *A* to *D* represents the substitution effect, and the movement from *D* to *E* represents the income effect.

**4.8** It means that when income rises, quantity of *X* falls; in other words, *X* is an inferior good.

**4.9** For salt, a 10% price increase is associated with a 1% quantity decrease, so price elasticity = –1%/10% = .1. For tomatoes, price elasticity = –46%/10% = 4.6.

**4.10** 4.1%. 7.3%. 1.4%.

# Chapter 5

**5.1** The numbers decrease in this case because the farmer sprays the most productive acres first and less productive acres later. The total benefit of spraying 3 acres is the sum of the marginal benefits on the first, second, and third acres.

**5.2** The farmer still sprays 4 acres, because the marginal benefit and marginal cost columns remain unchanged.

**5.3** Yes. Now the marginal cost numbers are all $1/acre instead of $3/acre. The farmer now sprays 6 acres.

**5.4** $8 per dress. $3 per dress.

# Chapter 6

**6.5**  In the first row, $3 per dress = $15 per worker/5 units per worker, and so forth.

**6.7**  For given quantities $L$ and $K$ of labor and capital, the isoquant through $(L, K)$ shows the maximum quantity of output that can be produced with this basket of inputs. Because there is only one such maximum quantity, there can be only one isoquant through a given point. Because there is always some quantity that can be produced with $(L, K)$, there is always an isoquant through any given point.

**6.8**  At $E$, the isocost is steeper than the isoquant, so $MRTS_{LK} < P_t/P_K$. If the firm hires one less unit of labor and $MRTS_{LK}$ additional units of capital, it can stay on the isoquant, decrease its labor costs by $P_L$, and increase its capital costs by only $MRTS_{LK} \cdot P_K$, which is less than the decrease in labor costs. Total costs are decreased by this move, so it is a wise one for the firm. Having moved to the northwest, the firm continues moving in this direction until it reaches the point of tangency, $C$.

**6.9**  $145. $60. $77.50.

**6.10**  A 1% increase in output requires more than a 1% increase in all inputs. Therefore, average cost increases when output increases.

**6.11**  $115. $137.50. $165.

**6.12**  The medium plant is best; the large plant is second best. In the long run the firm chooses the medium plant. At $Q_2$, the $SRAC_2$ curve is tangent to the $LRAC$ curve.

# Chapter 7

**7.1**  Firm A produces 4, firm B produces 6, firm C produces 7, and the industry produces 17.

**7.2**

**7.3**

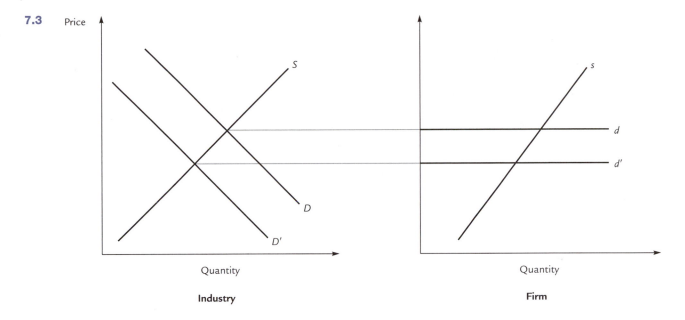

**7.4** $11.

**7.5** The demand curve rises, and all effects are opposite to those shown in Exhibit 7.22.

# Chapter 8

**8.1** The entries are $8, $14, $17, $17, $15, $10. The largest of these, 17, occurs at a quantity of 4.

**8.2** 5.

**8.3** Consumers lose $C + D + E$. Producers lose $F + G + H$. Tax recipients gain $C + D + F + G$. Yes.

**8.4** Refer to the graph at the top of the next page.

|  | Before Taxation | With Excise Tax |
|---|---|---|
| Consumer Surplus | $A + B + C + D$ | $A$ |
| Producer Surplus | $E + F + G + H + I$ | $H + I$ |
| Tax Revenue | — | $B + C + E + F$ |
| Social Gain | $A + B + C + D + E + F + H + I$ | $A + B + C + D + E + F + H + I$ |
| Deadweight Loss | $+ G$ | $D + G$ |

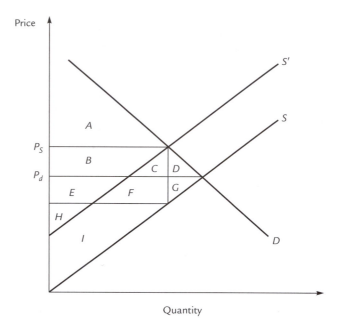

(Warning: these lettered areas are not the same as those in Exhibit 8.8.)

**8.7**   These calculations would be just like those of Exhibit 8.8. There are no gains or losses to the Japanese producers because their supply curve is flat.

**8.8**   In terms of Exhibit 8.17, take from the consumers $G + \frac{1}{2}H + I + \frac{1}{2}J$. Give the producers $G + \frac{1}{2}H$ and give the tax recipients $I + \frac{1}{2}J$. (This is only one of many possible solutions.)

**8.9**   In this drawing, the autarkic relative price is the slope of the budget line through $E$. The budget line through $F$ results when the world price of tomatoes is slightly lower, and the budget line through $G$ results when the world price is lower still. As the world price deviates more from the autarkic price, Robinson moves to higher indifference curves and becomes better off.

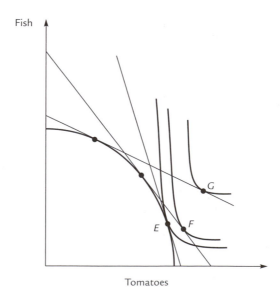

# Chapter 9

**9.1**  Total value = $54. Total cost = $35. Social gain = $19.

**9.2**  Total value = $46. Total cost = $35. Social gain = $11.

**9.3**  Give Curly's second egg to Moe. Simultaneously, take from Moe any amount of money between $3 and $11 and give it to Curly.

**9.4**  $8.

**9.5**  White rectangles are gains and shaded ones are losses.

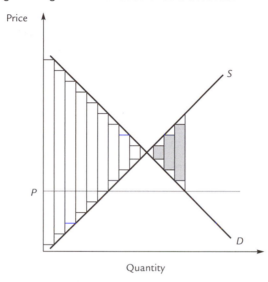

**9.7**  Under a limited draft, $B + C$ represents the amount by which each soldier's wages are reduced from equilibrium, times the number of soldiers. Thus, it is wealth transferred from soldiers to consumers.

**9.8**  In terms of Exhibit 9.7, the confiscation of rents adds $A$ to the pockets of those who confiscate and subtracts $A$ from Jennifer's producer surplus (leaving him with zero).

**9.9**  From $100 to $120. From $50 to $60.

**9.10**  The plumber today receives $100 to fix a leak. $100 will buy 20 movie tickets at $5 apiece. Overnight, all prices double, but the plumber thinks they have tripled. Tomorrow, he is offered $200 to fix the leak. Although $200 will still buy 20 movie tickets (now at $10 apiece), the plumber thinks that it will buy only 13.33 movie tickets (which he now believes sell at $15 apiece). Thus, he thinks he is being offered fewer movie tickets per plumbing repair than he is really being offered. This mistake leads him to supply less plumbing service.

# Chapter 10

**10.1**  $7 – $3 = $4. Yes.

**10.3**  The shaded area is additional deadweight loss due to the excise tax.

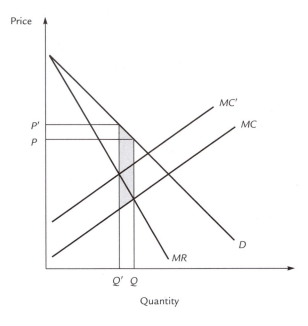

**10.4**    The shaded areas are deadweight loss.

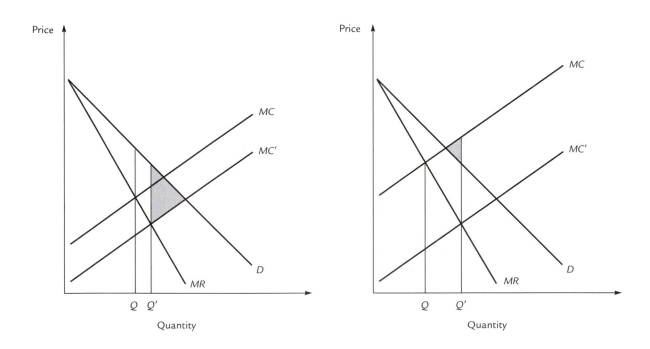

**10.5**    There are no waiting lines because the monopolist's price and quantity are given by a point on the demand curve. Thus, the quantity demanded is equal to the quantity supplied.

**10.6**

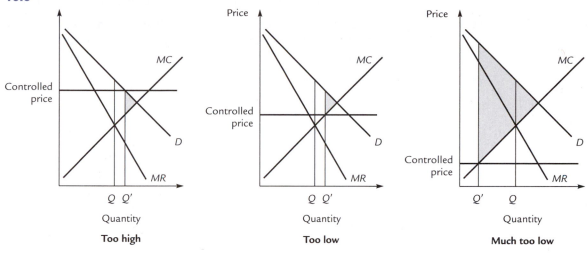

**Too high**  **Too low**  **Much too low**

**10.7** Lobbying uses up resources. Bribery merely transfers resources from one individual to another.

**10.8** If marginal revenue in the adult market is greater than in the children's market, he can sell one more haircut to an adult and one less to a child, increasing his revenue without affecting his cost. Similarly if adults and children are reversed. Thus, Benjamin is never satisfied if the two *MR*s are different. He also wants *MR* = *MC* just like any firm.

# Chapter 11

**11.1** Social welfare is unambiguously reduced by the merger, from $A + B + C + D + E$ to $A + B + C + D$.

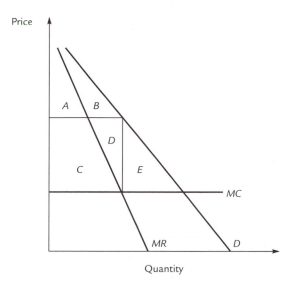

**11.2**    An appropriate price is any amount greater than $A + B$ but less than $A + B + E + H$.

**11.3**    If they produce anything less in the way of services, then they earn positive profits, leading them to compete with each other for additional customers by increasing the service level.

**11.4**    To see that $V > P_1 - P_0$, examine the vertical line at $Q_1$ in Exhibit 11.4. The portion of this line that stretches from MC′ to $D$ has length $V$, which is clearly greater than $P_1 - P_0$. To see that $A + B > A + C$, note that the two triangles are similar, so it suffices to check that the base of $A + B$ is longer than the base of $A + C$. That is, we must check that $Q_1 > Q_0$, which is given.

**11.5**    At price $P_0$, firms produce quantity $Q_0$. At this quantity, average cost is also $P_0$, so firms earn zero profits.

**11.6**    Because the other sellers in the marketplace provide close substitutes for the given seller's product.

**11.7**    The one closer to an endpoint would jump around the other one.

# Chapter 12

**12.1**    10 calories, 15 calories.

**12.2**    In the lower left, B wants to switch. In the lower right, both want to switch.

**12.3**    In the upper right, Ditto wants to switch. In the lower left, Ditto wants to switch. In the lower right, Dot wants to switch.

**12.4**    Because if you play this strategy, a wise opponent will always play "paper", beating you twice as often as you beat him. But if your opponent plays "paper" consistently, you'll want to play "scissors" consistently; that is, you'll deviate from the proposed strategy.

**12.5**    Because the weak pig prefers both $C$ and $D$ to $B$. Because the strong pig prefers both $A$ and $B$ to $C$.

**12.6**    The upper left, upper right, and lower left are Pareto optima.

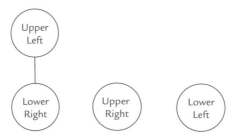

**12.7**    Because any shift away would hurt B.

**12.8**    Because any shift away would hurt A.

**12.9**    In each case, a move to either of the Pareto optima benefits both Fred and Ethel.

**12.10**   In each case, at least one firm can do better by changing its strategy.

# Chapter 13

**13.1** The demand curve would lie entirely above the social marginal cost curve.

**13.3** The White Sox. The White Sox.

**13.4** New York. New York.

# Chapter 14

**14.1** The difference is $5 – $0 = $5. The $5 benefit to the sixth visitor is completely off-set by the costs of $1 apiece that he imposes on each of the first 5 visitors.

# Chapter 15

**15.1** As labor input increases, so does output, and therefore the output price falls. The effect is to steepen the $MRP_t$ curve.

# Chapter 16

**16.1** As you move up and to the right you trade away leisure for consumption, so the marginal value of leisure increases.

**16.2** If the wage were greater than the marginal value of leisure, the worker could gain by working more. If the wage were less than the marginal value of leisure, he could gain by working less.

**16.3** If occupation A were more attractive than occupation B, then workers in occupation B would switch over to occupation A, raising wages in occupation B and lowering them in occupation A. This would continue until the two occupations were equally attractive.

# Chapter 17

**17.1** 2 apples tomorrow per apple today. 100%.

**17.2** The price is 4 apples. The face value is 5 apples. The discount is 1 apple.

**17.3** .44 apples today. .30 apples today.

**17.4** .76 apples today.

**17.5** 1.10 apples today.

**17.6** $20.

**17.7**   8%. 3%.

**17.11**  At an interest rate of 10%, Barb demands 5 units of current consumption.

**17.12**  Rebecca's budget line is steeper than in the exhibit and her optimum lies to the northwest of point *E*. She wants to be a net lender, consuming less than her current endowment. Therefore, people on average want to lend and this places downward pressure on the interest rate.

# Chapter 18

**18.1**   Bet $100 on heads.

**18.2**   The expected value of basket C is always $100, regardless of whether the coin is biased. If the coin comes up heads 2/3 of the time, the expected value of basket D is $113.33. If the coin comes up tails 2/3 of the time, the expected value of basket D is $86.67.

**18.3**   For an unbiased coin, the iso-expected value lines have slope –1 and *C* and *D* lie on the same line. For a coin that comes up heads 2/3 of the time, the iso-expected value lines are steeper and *D* is on a higher line than *C*. For a coin that comes up tails 2/3 of the time, the lines are shallower and *C* is on a higher line than *D*.

**18.4**   It would be that portion of the black line in Exhibit 18.3 that lies to the right of point C.

**18.5**   5 to 1 ½ to 1.1 to 1.

**18.6**   $15 worth.

**18.7**   For the advertising campaign fair odds are 1/2 to 1. The actual odds are 1 to 1. The expected winnings are $500. For the concert, fair odds are 1 to 1 and actual odds are 3 to 1. The expected winnings are 50¢.

**18.8**   Owners sell more today and less in March, driving down the current price and driving up the March spot price until the two are equal.

**18.10**  Expected return is 50%; $\sigma = 0$. Thus, the point is to the left of *GSS* and on the vertical axis.

**18.11**  $5. $1.

**18.12**  The actual price is sometimes as high as $2, sometimes as low as $0, and $1 on the average day.

**18.13**  $4. $5. $6.

**18.14**  $4. 800 heads. $1. $3. $5.

**18.15**  Price of lettuce = (1/50) × (Lumberjacks' income) + 50¢.

# Answers to Problem Sets

This appendix contains answers, hints, and discussions for many of the end-of-chapter problems throughout the book. In some cases, you will find complete answers with reasons. In others, you will find answers without reasons; it is still your job to provide the reasons. In still others, you will find hints but no answers. In a few cases, you will find complete answers together with additional related discussion that goes beyond what is necessary to answer the problem correctly.

## Chapter 1

1. False, in the sense of "not necessarily true." This new device will lead to an increase in the quantity demanded of those activities that are capable of leading to unwanted pregnancies; therefore the number of unwanted pregnancies could either rise or fall.

   Students sometimes object that there are people who won't use birth control no matter how safe, cheap, effective or easy it is. That's likely to be true, but irrelevant. Given the long list of advantages of this device, it's a save bet that *some* people will use it, which suffices to affect the number of pregnancies.

4. False. The demand curve for apartments shifts downward; therefore the price falls.

8. *Hint:* What happens to the demand curve for meat? What happens to the equilibrium quantity of meat supplied?

12a. 50¢, $2.50, 4 pounds.

14a. Supply shifts left, so price rises and quantity falls.

14d. As farm workers move to the city to earn the higher wages, the supply of corn falls. Price rises and quantity falls. Sometimes students argue that wealthier industrial workers will demand more corn and therefore the demand curve shifts out as well. This is a commendable insight, but it overlooks the fact that those higher wages are paid by employers, who might now *reduce* their demand for corn, offsetting the additional demand by the workers. Therefore, unless we know more about why wages went up, we need not expect the market demand curve to shift.

16. When the supply curve shifts up by the amount T of the tax, the new equilibrium point is exactly a distance T above the old equilibrium point. The market price rises by the full amount of the tax.

   Students commonly reach the correct answer *true* while offering a reason that is quite mistaken. Their (incorrect) argument is this: A vertical demand curve indicates that demanders will pay any price at all for lettuce; therefore, suppliers are able to pass the tax on completely without losing any sales. The argument is incorrect because it overlooks the fact that suppliers compete with each other. Any given supplier will indeed lose sales if he fails to match the going market price.

Indeed, to see that the argument cannot possibly be correct, ask yourself why suppliers don't raise their prices *before* the tax increase. If suppliers charge $1 originally and $1.25 after the imposition of a 25¢ tax, why don't they charge $1.25 (or more) even *before* the tax is imposed? The reason is that price is determined not by individual suppliers, but by the intersection of supply and demand.

**23a.**   Possibly true.

**23b.**   Certainly false.

**28.**   The price of a shower rises by more than $50 but less than $200, leaving both buyers and sellers worse off.

# Chapter 2

**2.**   You may conclude that he is confused. If the relative price of widgets in terms of gadgets has risen, then the relative price of gadgets in terms of widgets must have fallen.

**9.**   False, in the sense of "not necessarily true." The statement of the problem omits the key information that Mary is a highly skilled neurosurgeon, whereas George can do nothing except type. Mary's greater typing speed does not imply that she has a comparative advantage at typing.

Some students argue that *if* you are an employer who only wants to hire a typist, and *if* George and Mary are available at the same wage rate, then yes, it makes more sense to hire Mary as a typist than to hire George. But even this strained interpretation does not lead to the alleged conclusion. If you can really hire Mary at typist's wages, then you should set her to performing brain surgery, collect her fees as revenue to your firm, and use a small part of that revenue to hire George to do the typing.

**10.**   False. Suppose that the going wage for child labor on farms is $5 per hour. Then the farmer without children must pay $5 to employ someone else's children; the farmer *with* children must forgo $5 per hour (which he could earn by renting his children out to neighboring farmers) to employ his own children. Both face the same cost of $5 per hour.

Some students argue that the farmer with children incurs the costs of feeding, housing, and education. However, it is *not* correct to count these among the costs of putting the children to work, because they must be paid whether the children work or not.

Other students argue that the farmer with children is wealthier at the end of the year because he makes no cash payments to hire labor. Whether or not this is true, it is irrelevant to the question. The question does not ask which farmer is wealthier, it asks only which farmer has higher costs of harvesting. The answer is that both have the same costs.

**15.**   It goes wrong exactly where it says that in each case there are the same costs for producing, shipping, and marketing the clothes. If a professional middleman can perform some of these tasks more cheaply than Anderson-Little can, then Brand X might be able to pay the middleman more than enough to cover his costs and still deliver the clothes more cheaply than Anderson-Little.

# Chapter 3

1.  False. A change in price is a change in opportunities, not a change in tastes.

2.

3.

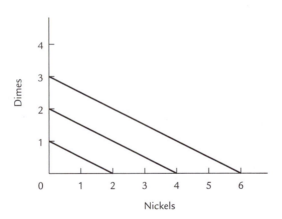

7.  Huey prefers both (1, 3) and (2, 2) to (3, 1).

9.  In 2011, you are happier, eat more pizza, and drink less beer.

12. It's better to lose the $6.

16. You should be able to draw a single family of indifference curves consistent with both Amelia's and Bernard's choices. It is possible that Amelia and Bernard share this family of indifference curves; in other words, it is possible (though not certain) that they have identical tastes.

    Assuming that Amelia and Bernard *do* have identical tastes, can you determine which of them is happier?

19. Of course not. The information given concerns opportunities, not tastes.

21. The program makes him worse off.

23d. It was a mistake for Pullman to institute the tax.

# Chapter 4

**1a.** Fewer.

**b.** No.

**5a.** C, D, E.

**b.** B.

**c.** C, D.

**8e.** True.

**8f.** True.

**12.** Probably up.

**13.** False; in fact, shoes *must* be inferior.

**15b.** True.

**19.** She is happier in May and eggs must be inferior.

**25.** Income elasticity is 1; price elasticity is –1.

**26.** It means that when your income goes up, your consumption of the luxury good increases by more than your income does. If your income increases by 1%, your consumption of luxury goods increases by more than 1%. But you cannot increase your consumption of *all* goods by more than 1% without violating the budget constraint. Therefore, not all goods can be luxuries.

In fact, this can be made more precise. When your income increases by 1%, your expenditures must increase by exactly 1% "on average" over all goods.

Thus, the average income elasticity over all goods must be 1. In the averaging process, goods must be weighted by the percent of your income that you spend on them. Suppose that you consume only X and Y. Write $k_x$ for the fraction of your income that you spend on X, $k_y$ for the fraction of your income that you spend on $Y_1$, $\eta_x$ for your income elasticity of demand for X, and $\eta_y$ for your income elasticity of demand for Y. Then we must have

$$k_X\eta_X + k_Y\eta_Y = 1$$

If you want to prove this formula, start with the expressions

$$k_X = P_X X / I$$
$$k_Y = P_Y Y / I$$
$$P_X DX + P_Y DY = DI$$

(First explain what each of these expressions means and why it is true.) Then insert the expressions for $k_X$, $k_Y$, $\eta_X$, and $\eta_Y$ into the final formula and simplify.

**30f.** Somebody whose income is derived entirely from wages feels a greater income effect from a change in the wage rate. Because the income effect works opposite to the substitution effect, such a person will respond less to a wage change than will somebody who has a lot of nonlabor income. Therefore, the person whose income is entirely from wages can be expected to have the steeper labor supply curve.

# Chapter 5

**2.** True.

**3.** (i) has no effect; (ii) does have an effect. Make sure you can explain why.

**6.** True. (Be sure you can explain why!)

**11.** The firm produces four items at $14 apiece.

**13.** If the area consists entirely of stores, then Wilma is correct. Rents are fixed costs that do not affect prices. The reason that rents are high is that stores are willing to pay a lot for this location, where prices are high. But if many of the buildings in the area are used for office space, or anything other than stores, then Fred might be right. The high rents (caused perhaps by a high demand for office space in this location) have driven some stores out of the area, raising the demand for the products of those that remain, and consequently increasing prices.

# Chapter 6

**1.**

**4.** The first two rows look like this:

| Quantity | VC | TC | AC | AVC |
|---|---|---|---|---|
| 1 | $12 | $42 | $42 | $12 |
| 2 | $20 | $50 | $25 | $10 |

**11.**

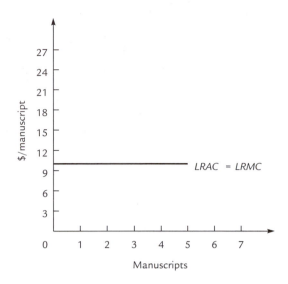

# Chapter 7

**1a.** No change.

**c.** Price falls; quantity falls.

**e.** No effect.

**g.** Price rises; quantity rises.

**i.** No effect.

**k.** Price falls; quantity falls.

**m.** No change.

**3.** False.

**10a.** Price falls; quantity falls.

**c.** Price and quantity unchanged.

**e.** No effect.

**g.** No effect.

**i.** Price rises; quantity rises.

**k.** Gus leaves the industry.

**m.** Gus leaves the industry.

**13a.** Short Run. (There is no change at all in the long run.)

**b.** Long Run.

**c.** Short Run.

**d.** Short Run.

**26.** The marginal cost of providing a gallon of gasoline has risen by 50¢; thus the supply curves for both the firm and the industry shift vertically upward by 50¢ per gallon. In the constant-cost case, price rises by 50¢ per gallon; in the increasing-cost case it rises by less (in the long run).

# Chapter 8

**2a.**   From buying the widgets.

**2b.**   A gadget.

**3.**    By the Pareto criterion, (c) is better than (e) and no other comparisons can be made. By the efficiency criterion, (a), (b), (c), and (d) are all equally good, and all are better than (e).

**6.**    One solution is to give consumers $F + G + \frac{1}{3}E$ and give producers $C + D + \frac{1}{3}E$, taking the necessary resources from the taxpayers.

**7.**    False. The line lengths adjust so that the value of waiting time is $9 in both countries.

**12.**   True. To see why, ask what happens to the "price to demanders" in the wheat market; then note that this price is part of the marginal cost of producing bread.

**20.**   The triangle on the left reflects the fact that people purchase foreign cars that could have been produced more cheaply at home. The triangle on the right reflects the fact that people now buy fewer cars. Can you explain why?

**21.**   The shaded area is deadweight loss:

**23.**   The shaded area is deadweight loss:

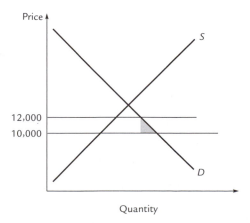

**34.**   True because the supply of robbers is horizontal.

# Chapter 9

2. None of the council members has the expertise to determine the extent of the risk from the chemical plant; none has the expertise (or the information) to determine the extent of the benefits. It is reasonable to expect that the company owners and their insurers (who are experts at assessing risks) have access to more information than the council has. Under the councilman's proposal, they have the incentive to make use of that information. If the chemical company agrees to bear all of the costs of reimbursement, we may infer that it expects to earn enough from the plant to more than cover those costs. Similarly, if the insurance company is willing to bear the risk in exchange for a price that the chemical company is willing to pay, we may infer that it expects the amount of damage to the townspeople to be less than the gains to the chemical company.

   The councilman's suggestion creates an incentive for those with easiest access to the relevant information to analyze that information and act on it in a socially desirable way.

5b. $12.

10. Consumers could be made worse off if the pizzas are distributed to those who value them relatively little.

15. *Hint:* Suppose that all 3 of the applicants with incomes more than $70,000 have revealed their incomes. Your income is exactly $70,000. What will you do?

# Chapter 10

2. False, because of the phrase "unlike competitors." Anybody can charge any price he wants to for anything. However, there is only one profit-maximizing price to charge, and it is foolish to deviate from this price, whether you are a monopolist, a competitor, or anything in between.

4. It drops a vertical distance $1.

10. The social loss from monopoly is $2.

13. True.

15. The firm sells 7 sweaters, 4 to men and 3 to women.

18. This appears to be price discrimination in favor of U.S. tourists, which would require that U.S. tourists have a greater elasticity of demand for meals at these restaurants than the natives do. But this would appear to be the exact opposite of the truth: Tourists, if they are to eat at all, must eat at restaurants, whereas natives have the option of eating at home. Also, tourists are less likely than natives are to know about alternative, out-of-the-way places to eat.

   This suggests looking for an explanation that does not involve price discrimination. That is, we must ask why these restaurants find it less expensive to serve tourists than to serve natives. One wild guess is that tourists, for some reason, are better tippers, so that they actually pay more (inclusive of tip) for their meals than the natives pay. Of course, this keeps the staff happy and enables the management to pay lower wages; hence, serving tourists helps to keep their costs down.

We repeat that this explanation is a wild guess. If you have a better one, please send it to the author in care of South-Western.

**32a.** $15.

**b.** At 60¢, profit (including admission fees) is $35. At 50¢, profit is $36. At 40¢, profit is $34.

# Chapter 11

**2.** Conceivably a vertical merger could be used to prevent resales. Suppose that a monopoly steel manufacturer wants to sell cheaply to automakers and expensively to construction firms. The steel firm worries that automakers can buy cheaply and resell to construction firms. But if the steel firm acquires an automaker as a subsidiary, it can sell cheaply to the automaker while ordering it not to engage in resales.

**4.** It would increase in the first case and decrease in the second.

**9.** One frequently cited alternative theory is that the manufacturer is acting as an enforcer for a cartel among the dealers. Under what circumstances do you find this theory either more or less plausible than the theory that is elaborated in the textbook?

**12.** False, because of the Prisoner's Dilemma. Each worker can rationally calculate that his own voluntary contribution is unlikely to be critical in determining the success of the union; therefore, he chooses not to join. It is important to notice that workers will elect not to join regardless of whether or not they believe that others are joining. It is possible that all workers could benefit from an outside enforcer who requires them to unionize.

**15.** The industry output is equal to $N/(N + 1)$ times the output of a competitive industry. When $N$ is large, the Cournot industry's output and the competitive industry's output are approximately equal.

**16.** The industry output is 3/4 of what it would be under competition, which is greater than what it would be under Cournot behavior. The first firm produces twice as much as the second firm and is better off than the second firm.

# Chapter 12

**1.** I. (Right, Down).

**1.** III. (Right, Up).

**1.** V. None.

**1.** VII. (Left, Up) and (Right, Down).

**2.** I. (Right, Up), (Left, Down), and (Right, Down).

**2.** III. (Right, Up).

**2.** V. (Left, Down) and (Right, Down).

2. VII. (Left, Up) and (Right, Down).

3. I. Yes, Yes.

3. III. Yes, No.

3. V. No. No.

3. VII. No. No.

4. I. (Right, Down).

4. III. (Right, Up).

4. V. (Right, Down).

4. VII. (Right, Down).

# Chapter 13

4. False. According to the Coase theorem, couples will negotiate so that housework is performed by the efficient provider.

   In existing marriages, there might be an income effect whereby husbands, feeling power because of the new law, will choose less leisure and more housework. But in new marriages, there is no income effect because men can opt out of marriage entirely.

   Therefore, existing marriages, maybe. In new marriages, false.

7. Assume first that there are no transactions costs between the beekeeper and the car dealer. In that case, your decision does not matter in the sense that it has no effect on the number of bees that are kept, the procedures used to contain the bees, the number of cars sold, the investment in tents by the car dealer, whether the car dealer will move away, and so forth. It matters in the sense that the beekeeper prefers one decision and the car dealer another.

   Alternatively, if there *are* transactions costs, then all of the things that were left unaffected in the preceding paragraph can indeed be affected. A ruling for the car dealer could induce the beekeeper to rein in his bees (say with better netting) or to scale back his operation, while a ruling for the beekeeper could induce the car dealer to erect a tent or to move.

   Because there are only two parties and they are in close proximity, the assumption of *no* transactions costs seems the more reasonable.

   If a large collection of motorists is involved, the transactions costs can become considerable. It is difficult for the motorists to collectively negotiate with the beekeeper, particularly if different motorists are affected on different days. Many motorists might not even recognize the source of the problem.

   In this case, some factors relevant to the decision are: How much would it cost the beekeeper to prevent his bees from flying over the roadway, either by containing them or moving elsewhere? What alternatives are available to motorists? Can they easily take a different route or would it be very costly to do so? How much damage do the bees actually do to the cars, and how much does it cost motorists to cope with this damage, either by having it repaired or by deciding to tolerate it?

**22g.**   The Optimal tax is $N+O+P$.

**25e.**   Expectation damages induce Betty to behave efficiently.

**26.**   It does *not* follow that expectation damages are the appropriate standard. Although expectation damages lead to efficient breaches of contract, they might not lead to an efficient number of contracts being signed in the first place. A full analysis of the problem must account for the fact that the number of contracts signed will vary depending on the legal standard that is in force. Such a full analysis is provided by David Friedman in "An Economic Analysis of Alternative Damage Rules for Breach of Contract," *Journal of Law and Economics* 23 (1989). Friedman establishes that either expectation or reliance damages could be more efficient, depending on circumstances.

# Chapter 14

**1c.**   The optimal outcome can be achieved with an entrance fee of 8 or 10 fish per day.

**2d.**   She will charge 16 nuggets a day at Mine A and 21 nuggets a day at Mine B.

**10.**   *Hint:* What happens to rental rates on the north side of town?

# Chapter 15

**4b.**   The short-run labor demand curve is less elastic than the long-run labor demand curve.

**7.**   True. The reason why isocosts are straight lines is that their equations are given by $P_K \cdot K + P_L \cdot L = C$ where $P_K$, $P_L$, and $C$ are constants. For a monopolist in the labor market, $P_L$ is not constant: It varies with his employment of labor. Thus, the isocosts are not straight lines.

**11.**   *Hint:* Graph the $MP_L$ curve. Assume that the wage rate of labor rises from $W$ to $W'$. Use your graph to illustrate the revenue earned by capital both before and after the wage change. Which is bigger?

**12.**   *Hint:* Graph the $MP_K$ curve. Assume that labor and capital are substitutes in production. Show how $MP_K$ shifts in response to a rise in the wage rate of labor. Use your graph to illustrate the revenue earned by capital both before and after the wage change. Which is bigger? Is your answer consistent with your answer to problem 10? If not, what is the source of the discrepancy?

**13.**   Apparently the union believes that a reduction in the quantity of unskilled labor (as would result from a minimum wage) would increase the demand for the skilled labor that its members supply. Thus, skilled and unskilled labor must be substitutes in production.

To investigate the relationship with capital, begin by dividing inputs into "unskilled labor" and "all other inputs," where the latter includes both skilled labor and capital. When there are zero profits and only two inputs, those inputs must be complements in production (this was shown in problem 10).

This means that a reduction in unskilled labor must reduce the demand for "all other inputs." Therefore, following a reduction in unskilled labor, the demand for either skilled labor or capital must fall. Because we have already agreed that the demand for skilled labor rises, it follows that the demand for capital falls. In other words, unskilled labor and capital are complements in production.

It follows that the owners of capital will oppose the minimum wage.

# Chapter 16

2. Jack's budget line has a "kink" at 8 hours and is tangent to an indifference curve at 10 hours. Jill's budget line intersects the consumption axis at the same point as Jack's and is tangent to the same indifference curve. Drawing the picture, you will find that Jane's budget line must be steeper than the initial portion of Jack's but less steep than the later portion; in other words, $W''$ is between $W$ and $W'$. The same picture should reveal that Jane works fewer than 10 hours.

4. *Hint:* Is leisure a normal or an inferior good for Dick?

9. *Hint:* Which of these men feels a greater income effect when his wage rate changes?

10. False. If workers come to enjoy their jobs, the supply curve of labor shifts out, the quantity supplied increases, and therefore the marginal product of labor decreases. So workers who enjoy their jobs more are *less* productive at the margin than those who enjoy them less.

11. The wage rate falls, less labor is supplied to the marketplace, and a given individual might supply either more or less labor than before.

13. The wage rate rises, less labor is supplied to the marketplace, and a given (surviving) individual supplies more labor than before.

17. One important difference arises from intertemporal substitution. In the circumstance of part (a), there is strong incentive to take one's vacation this year instead of next, whereas that incentive is missing from part (b). You should take account of this difference in determining the effects on wages and the quantity of labor supplied.

19. True, because education is a form of investment. Because the tax break applies to other forms of investment but not to education, investors tend to substitute toward those other forms of investment.

# Chapter 17

5b. The halving of the interest rate is the greater deterrent.

12a. Jeeter can purchase a bond for $1,000 at a 10% interest rate and pretend that he has spent the $1,000 to pay off his loan. Five years from today, he simply hands the bond over to the bank. Because the bond and the debt grow at the same rate, the bond covers the debt exactly.

18. The interest rate is higher in the circumstance of (a).

**21.**

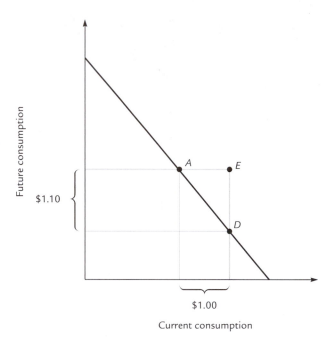

Terry starts with an endowment of A, faces an interest rate of 10%, and therefore has the pictured budget line with slope −1.10. If the government taxes him $1 and then provides him with $1 worth of current consumption, his endowment point remains A (nothing has really changed). If the government borrows $1 to provide Terry with $1 worth of current consumption, it then taxes him $1.10 in the future to repay the debt. Terry's endowment point shifts to D (with $1 more in present consumption and $1.10 less in future consumption). Because Terry's new endowment point is on his original budget line, his optimum consumption basket does not change. Each plan leads to the same demand for current consumption and so to the same equilibrium interest rate.

**24.**    Here are a few observations:

First, Mr. Rohatyn asserts that borrowing will convert a $130 billion loss into a $500 billion drain over 20 or 30 years. In other words, he treats a dollar paid 20 years from now as equal in value to a dollar paid today. If he is really committed to such reasoning, Mr. Rohatyn should be happy to offer you a loan of $200 billion today in exchange for a payback of $300 billion in 20 years. Try writing to him and see if he agrees.

Second, he asserts that one should not borrow to finance losses that have already occurred, and elevates this dictum to "a basic economic principle." On the contrary, people generally prefer to spread out their consumption evenly over their lifetimes rather than having some years of feast and some of famine. (This is why we tend to think of the Great Depression as a bad thing.) It follows that a one-shot unexpected large expense is precisely the sort of thing that ought to be financed by borrowing. Your indifference curve analysis in part (b) should confirm this assertion.

Third, he is wrong in thinking that a short-term tax surcharge would necessarily limit the costs of the bailout to the immediate future. Precisely because people like to smooth out their consumption, they would borrow more (or, equivalently, save less) in the present to get through the temporary period of high taxes. The result would be the same as if the government had done the borrowing.

But not quite. For a variety of reasons, individuals must usually borrow at higher rates than the government does. Therefore, Mr. Rohatyn's proposal comes down to this: Let people attempt to borrow for themselves at high interest rates, rather than let the government borrow for them at lower rates.

Finally, some economists would argue that people are insufficiently sophisticated to borrow their way through the higher tax years (that is, some would argue that people fail to move to the optimum point in the indifference curve diagram). If those economists are right, then Mr. Rohatyn is even further off the mark, because these taxpayers in their naivete will fail to smooth out their consumption streams unless the government leads the way by borrowing for them.

**26.**    $66,666.66

**27.**    The interest rate rises.

# Chapter 18

**1.**    The desirability of the trade depends on the possible outcomes of the uncertainty and it depends on the odds. Had the doctor himself been offered the opportunity to trade a certain shilling for a mere 99% chance at a million pounds, he might have reconsidered his position. Indeed, to forgo suicide is to sacrifice the certainty of death for the uncertainties of life, but most of us make this "unwise" choice.

**2.**    False. Even something that is not worth the certainty of death can still be worth some *chance* of death. If this were false, nobody would ever drive a car.

**12.**    Much depends on whether higher crash rates are attributable to age or to lack of driving experience. The *Times* assumes that 18-year-old first-time drivers will crash at the same rate as 18-year-olds with 2 years' experience, which seems debatable.

# Chapter 19

**3.**    $\dfrac{U-C}{D-U} \cdot \left[ \dfrac{D}{1+r} - S \right]$

# Glossary

## A

**Absolute price** The number of dollars that can be exchanged for a specified quantity of a given good.

**Accounting profit** Total revenue minus those costs that an accountant would consider.

**Adverse selection** The problem that arises when people know more about their own risk characteristics than others do.

**Autarkic relative price** The relative price that would prevail if there were no trade with foreigners.

**Average cost,** or **average total cost (AC)** Total cost divided by the quantity of output.

**Average product of labor (APL)** Total product divided by the number of workers.

**Average variable cost (AVC)** Variable cost divided by the quantity of output.

## B

**Bertrand model** A model of oligopoly in which firms take their rivals' prices as given.

**Bond** A promise to pay at some time in the future.

**Break-even price** The price at which a seller earns zero profit.

**Budget line** The set of all baskets that the consumer can afford, given prices and his or her income.

## C

**Cap-and-trade** A system of tradable permits to produce goods that create externalities.

**Capital** Physical assets used as factors of production.

**Capital asset pricing model** A model that assumes that investors care only about expected return and risk, where risk is measured by standard deviation.

**Cartel** A group of firms engaged in collusion.

**Clarke tax** A tax designed to elicit information about the demand for public goods.

**Coase theorem** In the absence of transactions costs, all externalities are internalized; therefore, social gain is maximized.

**Collusion** An agreement among firms to set prices and outputs.

**Common law** The system of legal precedents that has evolved from court decisions.

**Common property** Property without a well-defined owner.

**Comparative advantage** The ability to perform a given task at a lower cost.

**Compensated demand curve** A curve showing, for each price, what the quantity demanded would be if the consumer were income-compensated for all price changes.

**Compensating differential** A wage adjustment that comes about in equilibrium to compensate for a particularly pleasant or unpleasant aspect of a job.

**Competitive equilibrium** A point that everyone will choose to trade to, for some appropriate market prices.

**Competitive industry** An industry in which all firms are competitive.

**Complements** Goods for which the cross elasticity of demand is negative.

**Complements in production** Two factors with the property that an increase in the employment of one raises the marginal product of the other.

**Composite-good convention** The lumping together of all goods but one into a single portmanteau good.

**Consequentialist moral theories** Moral theories that assert that the correctness of an act can be judged by its consequences.

**Constant-cost industry** A competitive industry in which all firms have identical cost curves, which do not change as the industry expands or contracts.

**Constant returns to scale** A condition where increasing all input levels by the same proportion leads to a proportionate increase in output.

**Consumer's surplus** The consumer's gain from trade; the amount by which the value of his purchases exceeds what he actually pays for them.

**Consumption** All goods other than leisure.

**Consumption goods** (or **outputs**) Goods that individuals want to consume.

**Contestable market** A market in which firms can enter and exit costlessly.

**Contract curve** The set of Pareto-optimal points.

**Contributory negligence** A plaintiff's failure to take precautions whose cost is less than the damage caused by an accident multiplied by the probability that the accident will occur.

**Convex** Bowed in toward the origin, like the curves in panel A of Exhibit 3.6.

**Corner solution** An optimum occurring on one of the axes when there is no tangency between the budget line and an indifference curve.

**Cost** A forgone opportunity.

**Cost-benefit analysis**  Analysis of the costs and benefits of various public policies.

**Coupon bond**  A bond that promises a series of payments on different dates.

**Cournot model**  A model of oligopoly in which firms take their rivals' output as given.

**Creative response**  A response to a regulation that conforms to the letter of the law while undermining its spirit.

**Cross elasticity of demand**  The percent change in consumption that results from a 1% increase in the price of a related good.

# D

**Deadweight loss**  A reduction in social gain.

**Decreasing-cost industry**  A competitive industry where the break-even price for new entrants falls as the industry expands.

**Decreasing returns to scale**  A condition where increasing all input levels by the same proportion leads to a less than proportionate increase in output.

**Default risk**  The possibility that the issuer of a bond will not meet his obligations.

**Demand**  A family of numbers that lists the quantity demanded corresponding to each possible price.

**Demand curve**  A graph illustrating demand, with prices on the vertical axis and quantities demanded on the horizontal axis.

**Derived demand**  Demand for an input, which depends on conditions in the output market.

**Diminishing marginal returns to labor**  The circumstance in which each unit of labor has a smaller marginal product than the last.

**Discount**  The face value of a bond minus its current price.

**Dissipation of rents** or **tragedy of the commons**  The elimination of social gains due to overuse of common property.

**Diversify**  To reduce risk.

**Dividends**  Streams of benefits.

**Dominant strategy**  A strategy that a player would want to follow regardless of the other player's behavior.

# E

**Econometrics**  A family of statistical techniques used by economists.

**Economic incidence**  The division of a tax burden according to who actually pays the tax.

**Economic profit**  Total revenue minus all costs, including the opportunity cost of being in another industry.

**Economies of scope**  Efficiencies resulting from producing multiple products at a single firm.

**Edgeworth box**  A certain diagrammatic representation of an economy with two individuals, two goods, and no production.

**Effective price ceiling**  A price ceiling set below the equilibrium price.

**Efficiency criterion**  A normative criterion according to which your votes are weighted according to your willingness to pay for your preferred outcome.

**Efficiency wage**  A wage higher than market equilibrium, which employers pay in order to make workers want to keep their jobs.

**Efficient market**  A market in which prices fully reflect all available information.

**Efficient portfolio**  A portfolio in the efficient set.

**Efficient set**  The northwest boundary of the set of all portfolios.

**Elasticity of supply**  The percent change in quantity supplied resulting from a 1% increase in price.

**Endowment**  The basket of goods that somebody starts with, before any trading.

**Endowment point**  The point representing the initial holdings of an individual in an Edgeworth box.

**Engel curve**  A curve showing, for fixed prices, the relationship between income and the quantity of a good consumed.

**Entry price**  The minimum price that would cause a firm to enter a given industry.

**Envy-free allocation**  An outcome in which nobody would prefer to trade baskets with anybody else.

**Equilibrium point**  The point where the supply and demand curves intersect.

**Equimarginal principle**  The principle that an activity should be pursued to the point where marginal cost equals marginal benefit.

**Ex ante**  Determined before the state of the world is known.

**Ex post**  Determined after the state of the world is known.

**Excise tax**  In this book, a tax that is paid directly by suppliers to the government.

**Exit**  A firm's decision to leave the industry entirely. Firms that exit no longer incur any costs.

**Expansion path**  The set of tangencies between isoquants and isocosts.

**Expected return**  The expected value of returns.

**Expected value**  The average value over all states of the world, with each state weighted by its probability.

**External costs and benefits,** or **externalities**  Costs and benefits imposed on others.

# F

**Face value**  The amount that a bond promises to pay.

**Factor-price effect**  The effect that an expansion of industry output has on the price of a factor of production, thereby raising marginal costs in the industry.

**Factors of production**  (or **inputs**) Goods that are used to produce outputs.

**Fair odds**  Odds that reflect the true probabilities of various states of the world.

**Fall in demand**  A decision by demanders to buy a smaller quantity at each given price.

**Fall in supply**  A decrease in the quantities that suppliers will provide at each given price.

**Firm**  An entity that produces and sells goods, with the goal of maximizing its profits.

**First-degree price discrimination**  Charging each customer the most that he would be willing to pay for each item that he buys.

**First stage of production**  Production with relatively few workers, so that each additional worker increases the productivity of his colleagues. Therefore, the average product of labor is increasing and the marginal product exceeds the average product.

**Fishery**  Common property.

**Fixed costs**  Cost that don't vary with the quantity of output.

**Fixed factor of production**  One that the firm must employ in a given quantity.

**Free riders**  People who benefit from the actions of others and therefore have reduced incentives to engage in those actions themselves.

**Free riding**  Reaping benefits from the actions of others and consequently refusing to bear the full costs of those actions.

**Futures contract**  A contract to deliver a specified good at a specified future date for a specified price.

**Futures market**  The market for futures contracts.

# G

**Game matrix**  A diagram showing one player's strategy choices across the top, the other player's along the left side, and the corresponding outcomes in the appropriate boxes.

**General average**  The rule of law that dictates the division of losses when cargo is jettisoned to prevent a disaster at sea.

**General equilibrium analysis**  A way of modeling the economy so as to take account of all markets at once and of all the interactions among them.

**Giffen good**  A good that violates the law of demand, so that when the price goes up, the quantity demanded goes up.

**Good Samaritan rule**  A bystander has no duty to rescue a stranger in distress.

**Goods**  Items of which the consumer would prefer to have more rather than less.

# H

**Horizontal integration**  A merger of firms that produce the same product.

**Human capital**  Productive skills.

# I

**Income effect**  When the price of a good changes, that part of the effect on quantity demanded that results from the change in real income.

**Income elasticity of demand**  The percent change in consumption that results from a 1% increase in income.

**Increasing-cost industry**  A competitive industry where the break-even price for new entrants increases as the industry expands.

**Increasing marginal cost**  The condition where each additional unit of an activity is more expensive than the last.

**Increasing returns to scale**  A condition where increasing all input levels by the same proportion leads to a more than proportionate increase in output.

**Indifference curve**  A collection of baskets, all of which the consumer considers equally desirable.

**Inferior good**  A good that you consume less of when your income rises.

**Inflation**  An ongoing rise in the average level of absolute prices.

**Internalize**  To treat an external cost as a private cost.

**Intertemporal substitution**  Working additional hours during temporary periods of high productivity.

**Investors**  Buyers of risky assets.

**Isocost**  The set of all baskets of inputs that can be employed at a given cost.

# L

**Labor theory of value**  The assertion that the value of an object is determined by the amount of labor involved in its production.

**Laspeyres price index**  A price index based on the basket consumed in the earlier period.

**Law of demand**  The observation that when the price of a good goes up, people will buy less of that good.

**Law of large numbers**  When a gamble is repeated many times, the average outcome is the expected value.

**Law of supply**  The observation that when the price of a good goes up, the quantity supplied goes up.

**Legal incidence**  The division of a tax burden according to who is required under the law to pay the tax.

**Leisure**  All activities other than labor.

**Lerner Index**  The excess of price over marginal cost, expressed as a fraction of the price.

**Liable**  Legally responsible to compensate another party for damage.

**Long run**  A period of time over which all factors are variable.

**Long-run average cost**  Long-run total cost divided by quantity.

**Long-run marginal cost**  That part of long-run total cost attributable to the last unit produced.

**Long-run supply curve**  A curve that shows what quantity the firm will supply in the long run in response to any given price.

**Long-run total cost**  The cost of producing a given amount of output when the firm is able to operate on its expansion path.

# M

**Marginal benefit**  The additional benefit gained from the last unit of an activity.

**Marginal cost**  The additional cost associated with the last unit of an activity.

**Marginal labor cost ($MLC$)**  The cost of hiring an additional unit of labor.

**Marginal product of labor (MPL)**  The increase in total product due to hiring one additional worker (assuming that capital is held fixed).

**Marginal rate of substitution,**  or MRS, between X and Y  The value of a consumer's last unit of $X$, measured by the number of additional units of $Y$ that would just compensate for its loss.

**Marginal rate of technical substitution of labor for capital ($MRTS_{LK}$)**  The amount of capital that can be substituted for one unit of labor, holding output constant.

**Marginal revenue**  The additional revenue earned from the last item produced and sold.

**Marginal revenue product of labor ($MRP_L$)**  The additional revenue that a firm earns when it employs one more unit of labor.

**Marginal tax rate**  The amount of income tax you pay on the last dollar that you earn.

**Marginal utility of $X$ ($MU_X$)**  The amount of additional utility derived from an additional unit of $X$ when the quantity of $Y$ is held constant.

**Marginal value**  The maximum amount a consumer would be willing to pay to acquire one additional item.

**Marginal value of $X$ in terms of $Y$**  The number of $Y$s for which the consumer would be just willing to trade one $X$.

**Market failure**  An occasion on which private markets fail to provide some good in socially efficient quantities.

**Market line**  The line through a risk-free asset and tangent to the efficient set.

**Market portfolio**  The point of tangency between the market line and the efficient set.

**Market power** or **monopoly power**  The ability of a firm to affect market prices through its actions. A firm has monopoly power if and only if it faces a downward-sloping demand curve.

**Maturity date**  The date on which a bond promises a delivery.

**Mixed strategy**  A strategy that involves a random choice among pure strategies.

**Monopolistic competition**  The theory of markets in which there are many similar but differentiated products.

**Monopsonist**  A buyer who faces an upward-sloping supply curve.

**Moral hazard**  The incentive for an individual to take more risks when insured.

**More efficient**  Able to perform a given task at lower cost; having a comparative advantage.

# N

**Nash equilibrium**  An outcome from which neither player would want to deviate, taking the other player's behavior as given.

**Natural monopoly**  An industry in which each firm's average cost curve is decreasing at the point where it crosses market demand.

**Negative externalities**  External costs.

**Negligence**  A defendant's failure to take precautions whose cost is less than the damage caused by an accident multiplied by the probability that the accident will occur.

**Nominal**  Measured in terms of money.

**Nominal interest rate**  The relative price of current dollars in terms of future dollars, minus 1.

**Nonexcludable good**  A good that, if consumed by one person, is automatically available to others.

**Nonlabor income**  Income from sources other than wages.

**Nonrivalrous good** A good that, if consumed by one person, can be provided to others at no additional cost.

**Normal good** A good that you consume more of when your income rises.

**Normative criterion** A general method for choosing among alternative social policies.

**Normative question** A question about what *ought* to be.

# O

**Oligopoly** An industry in which individual firms can influence market conditions.

**Open economy** An economy that trades with outsiders at prices determined in world markets.

**Optimum (plural: optima)** The most preferred of the baskets on the budget line.

**Ordinary good** A good that obeys the law of demand: When the price goes up, the quantity demanded goes down.

# P

**Paasche price index** A price index based on the basket consumed in the later period.

**Pareto criterion** A normative criterion according to which one policy is better than another when it is preferred unanimously.

**Pareto improvement** or **Pareto-preferred outcome** A change to which nobody objects.

**Pareto-optimal outcome** An outcome that allows no possibility of a Pareto improvement.

**Perfectly competitive firm** One that can sell any quantity it wants to at some going market price.

**Perpetuity** A bond that promises to pay a fixed amount periodically forever.

**Pigou tax** or **Pigovian tax** A tax equal to the amount of an externality.

**Point of diminishing marginal returns** The point after which the marginal product curve begins to decrease.

**Portfolios** Combinations of risky assets.

**Positive externalities** External benefits.

**Positive question** A question about what *is* or *will be*.

**Potential Pareto criterion** A normative criterion according to which any proposal that can be unanimously defeated— even by a candidate not under consideration—should be rejected.

**Predatory pricing** Setting an artificially low price so as to damage rival firms.

**Present value** Relative price in terms of current consumption.

**Price ceiling** A maximum price at which a product can be legally sold.

**Price discrimination** Charging different prices for identical items.

**Price elasticity of demand** The percent change in consumption that results from a 1% increase in price.

**Price index** A measure of the cost of living, based on changes in the cost of some basket of goods.

**Price level** The price of goods in terms of money.

**Price to demanders** Price plus sales tax.

**Price to suppliers** Price minus excise tax.

**Principal–agent problem** The inability of the principal to verify the behavior of the agent.

**Private cost** The sum of those costs of a decision that are borne by the decision maker.

**Producer's surplus** The producer's gain from trade; the amount by which his revenue exceeds his variable production costs.

**Product differentiation** The production of a product that is unique but has many close substitutes.

**Production function** The rule for determining how much output can be produced with a given basket of inputs.

**Production possibility curve** The curve displaying all baskets that can be produced.

**Profit** The amount by which revenue exceeds costs.

**Property right** The right to decide how some resource shall be used.

**Public good** A good where one person's consumption increases the consumption available for others.

**Punitive damages** Additional charges levied against one who commits a tort as punishment for his behavior.

**Pure strategy** A single choice of row (or column) in the game matrix.

# Q

**Quantity demanded** The amount of a good that a given individual or group of individuals will choose to consume at a given price.

**Quantity supplied** The amount of a good that suppliers will provide at a given price.

**Quasi-rents** Producers' surplus earned in the short run by factors that are supplied inelastically in the short run.

# R

**Rational expectations** Expectations that, when held by market participants, lead to behavior that fulfills those expectations on average.

**Real interest rate**  The relative price of present consumption goods in terms of future consumption goods, minus 1.

**Region of mutual advantage**  The set of points that are considered at least as good as the initial endowment.

**Regressive factor**  A factor with the property that an increase in its wage rate lowers the firm's long-run marginal cost curve.

**Relative price**  The quantity of some other good that can be exchanged for a specified quantity of a given good.

**Rent**  Payments to a factor of production in excess of the minimum payments necessary to call it into existence. In other words, the producer's surplus earned by the factor.

**Rental rate**  The price of hiring capital.

**Representative agent**  Someone whose tastes and assets are representative of the entire economy.

**Resale price maintenance** or **fair trade**  A practice by which the producer of a product sets a retail price and forbids any retailer to sell at a discount.

**Respondeat superior**  The liability of an employer for torts committed by his employees.

**Returns**  Gains to the holder of a financial asset, including dividends and increases in the asset's value.

**Revenue**  The proceeds collected by a firm when it sells its products.

**Ricardian Equivalence theorem**  The statement that government borrowing has no effect on wealth, consequently no effect on the demand for current consumption, and consequently no effect on the interest rate.

**Rise in demand**  A decision by demanders to buy a larger quantity at each given price.

**Rise in supply**  An increase in the quantities that suppliers will provide at each given price.

**Risk-averse**  Always preferring the least risky among baskets with the same expected value.

**Risk-free**  Having the same value in any state of the world.

**Risk-neutral**  Caring only about expected value.

**Risk-preferring**  Always preferring the most risky among baskets with the same expected value.

**Risk premium**  Additional interest, in excess of the market rate, that a bondholder receives to compensate him for default risk.

**Riskiness**  Variation in potential outcomes.

# S

**Sales tax**  In this book, a tax that is paid directly by consumers to the government. Other texts use this phrase in different ways.

**Satisfied**  Able to behave as one wants to, taking market prices as given.

**Scale effect**  When the price of an input changes, that part of the effect on employment that results from changes in the firm's output.

**Second-degree price discrimination**  Charging the same customer different prices for identical items.

**Short run**  A period of time over which some factors are fixed.

**Short-run production function**  The function that associates to each quantity of labor its total product.

**Short-run supply curve**  A curve that shows what quantity the firm will supply in the short run in response to any given price.

**Shutdown**  A firm's decision to stop producing output. Firms that shut down continue to incur fixed costs.

**Shutdown price**  The output price below which the firm could no longer cover its average variable costs and would therefore shut down.

**Signal**  An activity that does not directly produce anything socially productive but that conveys information about one's talents, so that it is privately rewarding.

**Signaling equilibrium**  A Nash equilibrium in which signals are employed.

**Social cost**  The sum of all of the costs of a decision, including the private costs and the costs imposed on others.

**Social gain** or **welfare gain**  The sum of the gains from trade to all participants.

**Solution concept**  A rule for predicting how games will turn out.

**Speculative bubble**  A situation in which expectations of rising prices cause prices to rise.

**Speculator**  One who attempts to earn profits in the futures market by predicting future changes in supply or demand.

**Spot market**  The market for goods for immediate delivery.

**Spot price**  Price in the spot market.

**Stackelberg equilibrium**  An equilibrium concept that arises when one player announces his strategy before the other.

**Standard deviation**  A precise measure of risk.

**State of the world**  A potential set of conditions.

**Stock option**  The right to buy a share of stock at some future date at a price specified in advance.

**Strict liability**  Liability that exists regardless of whether the defendant has been negligent.

**Substitutes**  Goods for which the cross elasticity of demand is positive.

**Substitutes in production**  Two factors with the property that an increase in the employment of one lowers the marginal product of the other.

**Substitution effect**  When the price of an input changes, that part of the effect on employment that results from the firm's substitution toward other inputs.

**Sunk cost** A cost that can no longer be avoided.

**Supply** A family of numbers giving the quantities supplied at each possible price.

# T

**Technologically inefficient** A production process that uses more inputs than necessary to produce a given output.

**Theory of games** or **game theory** A system for studying strategic behavior.

**Third-degree price discrimination** Charging different prices in different markets.

**Tort** Acts that injure others.

**Total cost** The sum of fixed costs and variable costs.

**Total product (TP)** The quantity of output produced by the firm in a given amount of time. Total product depends on the quantity of labor the firm hires.

**Total revenue** The same thing as "revenue." It can be computed by the formula Revenue = Price × Quantity.

**Total value** The maximum amount a consumer would be willing to pay to acquire a given quantity of items.

**Tournament** Competition to dominate an industry by being slightly better than one's rivals.

**Transactions cost** Any cost of negotiating or enforcing a contract.

**Two-part tariff** An entry fee that allows you to purchase goods or services.

# U

**Uninsurable risk** A risk that cannot be diversified.

**Unit isoquant** The set of all technically efficient ways to produce one unit of output.

**Utilitarianism** The belief that utility, or happiness, can be meaningfully measured and that it is desirable to maximize the sum of everyone's utility.

**Utility** A measure of pleasure or satisfaction.

# V

**Value** The maximum amount that a consumer would be willing to pay for an item.

**Variable costs** Costs that vary with the quantity of output.

**Variable factor of production** One that the firm can employ in varying quantities.

**Versioning** Offering an inferior product to facilitate price discrimination.

**Vertical integration** A merger between a firm that produces an input and a firm that uses that input.

# W

**Wage rate** The price of hiring labor.

**World relative price** The relative price that prevails in the presence of trade with foreigners.

# Index